I am a lot more understanding when I am at work, and at home too. I accept things easier because I understand them better and I have more patience and tolerance. For example, in dealing with information overload, I seem to be able to do the same good job yet with a better attitude—one of understanding, patience, and tolerance. This is a huge thing. I can't change my organization, but I can be a better player in the game. I feel I now have the confidence and the know-how to change things that directly affect me and those I work with.

Everything is not always black and white. *There may be reasons behind why things happen that I don't understand, and I need to have all the facts before I start making decisions. I can still help people every day with the same work ethic, but now I feel better equipped to deal with my surroundings and issues that come up. It is a very good feeling. I am calmer and I tend to look at the bigger picture and not get worked up in the moment. I have a confidence and determination now that I didn't feel before, probably because I take my textbook to work with me and have no issues about opening it up and using it if I need to.*

Debbie Lundrigan, Organizational Behaviour student
using McShane, *Canadian Organizational Behaviour*
British Columbia Institute of Technology

Canadian Organizational Behaviour

Seventh Edition

STEVEN L. McSHANE

University of Western Australia

SANDRA L. STEEN

University of Regina

McGraw-Hill Ryerson

Toronto   Montréal   Boston   Burr Ridge, IL   Dubuque, IA   Madison, WI   New York
San Francisco   St. Louis   Bangkok   Bogotá   Caracas   Kuala Lumpur   Lisbon   London
Madrid   Mexico City   Milan   New Delhi   Santiago   Seoul   Singapore   Sydney   Taipei

McGraw-Hill Ryerson

Canadian Organizational Behaviour
Seventh Edition

ISBN-13: 978-0-07-097989-5
ISBN-10: 0-07-097989-8

3 4 5 6 7 8 9 10   WCD   0 9

Printed and bound in the United States of America.

Vice President and Editor-in-Chief: Joanna Cotton
Senior Sponsoring Editor: Kim Brewster
Senior Marketing Manager: Joy Armitage Taylor
Managing Editor, Development: Kelly Dickson
Developmental Editors: Tracey Haggert, Lori McLellan, Leslie Mutic
Permissions Editors: Tracy Leonard, Alison Derry
Senior Editorial Associate: Christine Lomas
Supervising Editor: Joanne Limebeer
Copy Editor: Erin Moore
Senior Production Coordinator: Paula Brown
Cover Design: Michelle Losier, Fine Lines
Cover Image: © Guido Daniele. Used with permission.
Interior Design: Michelle Losier, Fine Lines
Page Layout: Bookman Typesetting Co. Inc.
Printer: Worldcolor

Library and Archives Canada Cataloguing in Publication Data

McShane, Steven L. (Steven Lattimore)
    Canadian organizational behaviour / Steven L. McShane, Sandra Steen. — 7th ed.

Includes bibliographical references and indexes.
ISBN 978-0-07-097989-5

    1. Organizational behavior—Canada—Textbooks.   2. Organizational behavior—Canada—Case studies.
3. Teams in the workplace—Textbooks.   4. Corporate culture—Textbooks.   I. Steen, Sandra   II. Title.

HD58.7.M32 2008   658.3   C2008-905251-X

Dedicated with love and devotion to Donna,
and to our wonderful daughters,
Bryton and Madison—S.L.M.

For Aaron, Matt, and Jess—S.L.S.

ABOUT THE AUTHORS

STEVEN L. McSHANE

Steven L. McShane is Professor of Management in the Business School at the University of Western Australia (UWA). He is also an Honourary Professor at Universiti Tunku Abdul Rahman (UTAR) in Malaysia. Steve previously taught in the business faculties at Simon Fraser University and Queen's University in Canada. He is a past president of the Administrative Sciences Association of Canada.

Steve earned his PhD from Michigan State University, a Master of Industrial Relations from the University of Toronto, and an undergraduate degree from Queen's University in Kingston. He receives high teaching ratings from students in Perth, Australia, Singapore, Manila, and other cities where UWA offers its programs. Steve is also a popular visiting speaker, having given more than three dozen talks over the past three years to faculty and students at universities in Canada, the United States, and several countries in Asia.

Along with writing *Canadian Organizational Behaviour*, Steve is co-author with Professor Mary Anne Von Glinow (Florida International University) of *Organizational Behavior: Emerging Realities for the Workplace Revolution*, Fourth Edition (2008), McGraw-Hill's highly successful American version of this text, as well as their brief edition, *Organizational Behavior: Essentials*, Second Edition (2009). Steve is also co-author with Professor Tony Travaglione (Curtin University) of *Organisational Behaviour on the Pacific Rim*, Second Edition (2008), which has become the best-selling OB book in Australia and New Zealand. Steve is also co-author of Indian, Chinese, and Taiwanese editions of his OB book. In addition, Steve is co-author with Professor Charles Hill (University of Washington) of a new *Principles of Management* book (2008). Steve has published several dozen articles and conference papers on workplace values, training transfer, organizational learning, exit-voice-loyalty, employee socialization, wrongful dismissal, media bias in business magazines, and other diverse issues.

Along with teaching and writing, Steve enjoys spending his leisure time swimming, body board surfing, canoeing, skiing, and travelling with his wife and two daughters.

SANDRA L. STEEN

Sandra Steen is a faculty member of the Paul J. Hill School of Business and the Kenneth Levene Graduate School of Business at the University of Regina. Sandra has an integrated education and background in both Organizational Behaviour and Human Resource Management. She has more than 25 years of leading, managing, teaching, and consulting across a wide range of organizations in the private, public, and not-for-profit sectors. Her knowledge base combines both theory gained from an MBA focusing on human resource management and organizational behaviour from the University of Regina as well as from practitioner and consultant perspectives. Sandra teaches in the undergraduate, MBA, and Executive MBA programs at the University of Regina. Sandra holds the designation of Certified Human Resources Professional (CHRP) and she is a member of the Saskatchewan Association of Human Resource Professionals. Recent accomplishments include recognition as "Inspiring Teacher Award—Business Administration" and the publication of *Fundamentals of Human Resource Management*, Canadian edition by McGraw-Hill Ryerson. In her leisure time, Sandra enjoys spending time at the lake with her husband Aaron, and their children, Matt and Jess.

BRIEF CONTENTS

CONTENTS

PART THREE

Team Processes

CHAPTER ELEVEN

Conflict and Negotiation in the Workplace   257

CHAPTER TWELVE

Leadership in Organizational Settings   283

PART FOUR

Organizational Processes

CHAPTER THIRTEEN
Organizational Structure   307

CHAPTER FOURTEEN
Organizational Culture   333

CHAPTER FIFTEEN
Organizational Change   353

PREFACE

Welcome to the evolving world of organizational behaviour! Social networks and virtual teams are replacing committee meetings. Knowledge is replacing infrastructure. Values and self-leadership are replacing command-and-control management. Companies are looking for employees with emotional intelligence and team competencies, not just technical smarts. Diversity and globalization have become challenges as well as competitive opportunities for organizations. Co-workers aren't down the hall; they're at the other end of an Internet connection located somewhere else on the planet.

Canadian Organizational Behaviour, Seventh Edition is written in the context of these emerging workplace realities. This edition explains how emotions guide employee motivation, attitudes, and decisions; how values have become important for guiding workplace behaviour; how self-concept influences employee motivation, team cohesion, leadership, and behaviour; and how appreciative inquiry has become an important strategy for changing organizations. This book also presents the new reality that organizational behaviour is not just for managers; it is relevant and useful to anyone who works in and around organizations.

CANADIAN AND GLOBAL ORIENTATION

Canadian Organizational Behaviour, Seventh Edition is written by Canadians for Canadians. It includes several Canadian cases, is anchored by Canadian and global scholarship, and is filled with Canadian examples of organizational behaviour in practice.

For example, you will read about practising virtual work at Telus; generating positive workplace emotions at Tri-Fit Inc. in Oakville, Ont.; Glen Cooke's visionary leadership at Cooke Aquaculture Inc. in Atlantic Canada; fostering creativity at GenoLogics in Victoria, B.C.; maintaining an organic organizational structure at Montreal-based creative agency TAXI Canada; and motivating performance at Spruceland Millworks in Alberta.

Along with its Canadian focus, *Canadian Organizational Behaviour,* Seventh Edition introduces globalization in the opening chapter and highlights global issues throughout the book. To further emphasize the emerging reality of globalization, every chapter includes global examples that illustrate OB concepts. Some of these appear in *GLOBAL Connections* features, but most are embedded in the text or found in captioned photos. For example, you will read how Royal/Dutch Shell uses a game to find team players in Europe, Asia, and North America; how Pretoria Portland Cement relied on empowerment practices to become one of South Africa's best employers; how Shanghai-based creative agency Nitro remains flexible as it expands to Europe and North America; and how executives at Axa SA, the giant French insurance company, are minimizing discrimination through anonymous resumes.

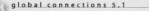

global connections 5.1

Never Enough Motivation through Recognition

David Gachiru lives by a motto that motivates employees with much more than money: "If an employee's work calls for a thumbs-up, I will appreciate him or her as many times as possible." Translating this advice into practice is a daily event for the general manager of Sarova Panafric Hotel in Nairobi, Kenya. In addition to thanking staff personally and through emails, Gachiru holds bi-monthly meetings where top performing employees are congratulated and receive paid holidays with their family. Employee achievements are also celebrated in the hotel's newsletter, which is distributed to guests as well as to employees.

Sarova Panafric Hotel and other firms are returning to good old-fashioned praise and recognition to regularly motivate staff. Good thing, because recent surveys in several countries identify lack of praise, recognition, or appreciation as a major reason why employees are demotivated, unsatisfied, or decide to find work elsewhere. For instance, based on 1,000 exit interviews, the Small Firms Association (SMA) recently reported that lack of recognition was a top reason why Irish employees quit their jobs. "Increasingly people need to feel that their contribution is valued," suggests SMA director Patricia Callan. "If people do not feel important, they are not motivated to stay."

The challenge of recognition is to "catch" employees doing extraordinary work or showing organizational citizenship. To this end, many companies have turned to peer recognition, in which co-workers show their appreciation and document this praise so the company can offer financial rewards. An example is ScotiaBank's award-winning Applause program, in which employees use a special website to identify peers or teams who have

Panafric Hotel in Nairobi, Kenya, motivates its employees through plenty of praise and recognition. *Photo courtesy of Sarova, Panafric Hotel in Nairobi, Kenya*

demonstrated the five Applause Principles: integrity, respect, commitment, insight, and spirit. The name of the submitter as well as the name of individuals being recognized are entered into monthly sweepstakes. In a recent year, ScotiaBank staff submitted more than 500,000 peer recognition certificates.

The Ritz Carlton Hotel in Kuala Lumpur applies a similar peer recognition process using First Class Cards. A Ritz Carlton Kuala Lumpur manager explains that "congratulatory messages or words of appreciation are written down by any member of the team to another and even as far as from the hotel and corporate senior leaders. This serves as a motivational aspect of the work environment."[17]

LINKING THEORY WITH REALITY

Every chapter of *Canadian Organizational Behaviour*, Seventh Edition is filled with examples to make OB knowledge more meaningful and reflect the relevance and excitement of this field. These stories about real people and organizations translate academic theories into relevant knowledge. For example, you will read why Edmonton-based Bioware Corp. chose a matrix organizational structure to support its growing electronic games business; why Outback Steakhouse relies on happy employees to maintain high standards of customer service; how Invesco's acquisition of Trimark led to conflicting values and eventual departure of several Trimark investment experts; and how Fairmont Hotels has built a brand focused on values and cross-cultural competence. Organizations small and large, public and private were selected to illustrate key concepts.

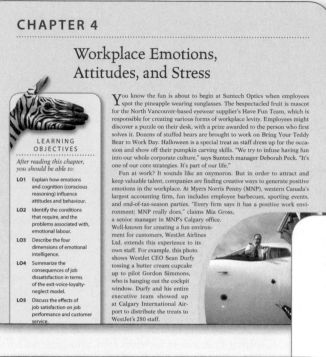

CHAPTER 4

Workplace Emotions, Attitudes, and Stress

LEARNING OBJECTIVES

After reading this chapter, you should be able to:

LO1 Explain how emotions and cognition (conscious reasoning) influence attitudes and behaviour.

LO2 Identify the conditions that require, and the problems associated with, emotional labour.

LO3 Describe the four dimensions of emotional intelligence.

LO4 Summarize the consequences of job dissatisfaction in terms of the exit-voice-loyalty-neglect model.

LO5 Discuss the effects of job satisfaction on job performance and customer service.

You know the fun is about to begin at Suntech Optics when employees spot the pineapple wearing sunglasses. The bespectacled fruit is mascot for the North Vancouver-based eyewear supplier's Have Fun Team, which is responsible for creating various forms of workplace levity. Employees might discover a puzzle on their desk, with a prize awarded to the person who first solves it. Dozens of stuffed bears are brought to work on Bring Your Teddy Bear to Work Day. Halloween is a special treat as staff dress up for the occasion and show off their pumpkin carving skills. "We try to infuse having fun into our whole corporate culture," says Suntech manager Deborah Peck. "It's one of our core strategies. It's part of our life."

Fun at work? It sounds like an oxymoron. But in order to attract and keep valuable talent, companies are finding creative ways to generate positive emotions in the workplace. At Myers Norris Penny (MNP), western Canada's largest accounting firm, fun includes employee barbecues, sporting events, and end-of-tax-season parties. "Every firm says it has a positive work environment; MNP really does," claims Mia Gross, a senior manager in MNP's Calgary office. Well-known for creating a fun environment for customers, WestJet Airlines Ltd. extends this experience to its own staff. For example, this photo shows WestJet CEO Sean Durfy tossing a butter cream cupcake up to pilot Gordon Simmons, who is hanging out the cockpit window. Durfy and his entire executive team showed up at Calgary International Airport to distribute the treats to WestJet's 280 staff.

Blackberry Addiction

Nick Salaysay (shown in this photo) admits that his work routinely gets mixed in with his personal time. "I have a BlackBerry, so I check my email a lot when I'm supposed to be on vacation," says the Calgary lawyer. Salaysay also acknowledges that having work spill over into his time off "really annoys my girlfriend." Amy Schulman is another dedicated Black-Berry user. The New York City lawyer recalls that "the BlackBerry was at first a significant intrusion on family life," but she can't resist how the device helps her to process several hundred emails each day. As a consolation, Schulman says she usually avoids looking at her emails while dining with her family "and I try not to look at it in movie theatres." Although Nick Salaysay and Amy Schulman are comfortable using their BlackBerrys during family time, research indicates that the increased workload and work preoccupation caused by these devices can result in the additional stress of relationship and marital problems. One law report recently warned that employers who issue Blackberrys could also incur liability of stress-related illnesses as the devices keep employees on an "electronic leash."[16] *Photo by Mikael Kjellstrom; article "Hard-working Canadians Find it Tough to Disconnect" by Theresa Taylor, May 18, 2008, Calgary Herald. Reprinted with permission of The Calgary Herald.*

Waving the Red Flag in Open-Office Communication

eBay Canada has an open-concept office to encourage communication and camaraderie, but the noise can be distracting. "Our employees sometimes bid on items on eBay and when it gets down to the final seconds of an auction, tension mounts and the bidder often shouts out in excitement," says eBay Canada spokeswoman, Alexandra Brown. Fortunately, eBay staff found a solution that seems to work. When employees need quiet time they drape colourful bandanas across the top of their desks, on desk lamps, or around their heads, which communicates to others "QUIET PLEASE!" To reduce some of the distractions and stress associated with open-space offices, everyone also turns off the audio alert signal for incoming email messages and uses wireless headsets rather than hands-free handsets. When employees need privacy to do undisturbed work, they can book and bring their laptops into meeting rooms that have intranet and Internet access.[16] © National Post/Peter Redman

These real-life stories appear in many forms. Every chapter of *Canadian Organizational Behaviour*, Seventh Edition is filled with photo captions and in-text anecdotes about work life. Specific individuals are also featured to provide meaningful connections for instructors and students. For example, you will read about how one recent graduate chose the job offer that provided the best fit with his values, how an emergency nurse deals with the emotions that come with the job; and how an entrepreneurial business student is providing leadership in the business community.

Case studies in each chapter and video case studies in each part related to various topics in this book also connect OB theories to emerging workplace realities. These stories represent a wide range of industries—from natural resources to government—and from small businesses to the largest global organizations.

ORGANIZATIONAL BEHAVIOUR KNOWLEDGE FOR EVERYONE

connections 6.1

When Rewards Go Wrong

There is an old saying that "what gets rewarded, gets done." But what companies reward isn't always what they had intended for employees to do. Here are a few dramatic examples:[27]

- Stock options are supposed to motivate executives to improve corporate performance. Instead, they seem to motivate some leaders to inflate share values through dodgy accounting practices. Recent research estimates that for every 25 percent increase in stock options awarded to executives, the risk of fraud rises by 68 percent. The companies with the largest corporate frauds in recent years have, on average, eight times as many options as similar companies that did not experience fraud.

- Integrated steel companies often rewarded managers for increased labour efficiency. The lower the labour hours required to produce a tonne of steel, the larger the manager's bonus. Unfortunately, steel firms usually didn't count the work of outside contractors in the formula, so the reward system motivated managers to hire expensive contractors in the

production process. By employing more contractors, the cost of production actually increased, not decreased.

- Toyota rewards its dealerships based on customer satisfaction surveys, not just car sales. What Toyota discovered, however, is that this motivates dealers to increase satisfaction scores, not customer satisfaction. One Toyota dealership received high ratings because it offered free detailing to every customer who returned a "Very Satisfied" survey. The dealership even had a special copy of the survey showing clients which boxes to check off. This increased customer ratings, but not customer satisfaction.

- Donnelly Mirrors (now part of Canada's Magna International empire) introduced a gainsharing plan that motivated employees to reduce labour but not material costs. Employees at the automobile parts manufacturer knew they worked faster with sharp grinding wheels, so they replaced the expensive diamond wheels more often. This action reduced labour costs, thereby giving employees the gainsharing bonus. However, the labour savings were easily offset by much higher costs for diamond grinding wheels.

Another distinctive feature of *Canadian Organizational Behaviour,* Seventh Edition is that it is written for everyone in organizations, not just "managers." The philosophy of this book is that everyone who works in and around organizations needs to understand and make use of organizational behaviour knowledge. The contemporary reality is that people throughout the organization—systems analysts, production employees, accounting professionals—are assuming more responsibilities as companies remove layers of management and give the rest of us more autonomy over our work. This book helps everyone to make sense of organizational behaviour, and provides the conceptual tools to work more effectively in the workplace.

CONTEMPORARY THEORY FOUNDATION

Canadian Organizational Behaviour, Seventh Edition has a solid foundation of contemporary and classic research and writing. You can see this in the references. Each chapter is based on dozens of articles, books, and other sources. The most recent literature receives thorough coverage, resulting in what we believe is the most up-to-date organizational behaviour textbook available. These references also reveal that we reach out to marketing, information management, human resource management, and

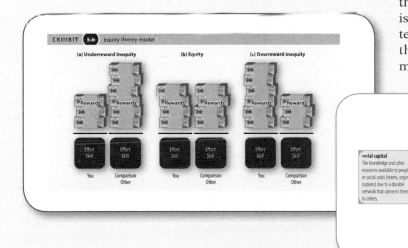

EXHIBIT 5.6 Equity theory model

(a) Underreward Inequity   (b) Equity   (c) Overreward Inequity

social capital
The knowledge and other resources available to people or social units (teams, organizations) due to a durable network that connects them to others.

SOCIAL NETWORKING AND POWER

"It's not what you know, but who you know that counts!" This often heard statement reflects the fact that employees get ahead not just by developing their competencies, but by *networking*—cultivating social relationships with others to accomplish one's goals. Networking increases a person's power in three ways. First, networks represent a critical component of **social capital**—the knowledge and other resources available to people or social units (teams, organizations) due to a durable network that connects them to others. Networks consist of people who trust each other, which increases the flow of knowledge among those within the network. The more you network, the more likely you will receive valuable information that increases your expert power in the organization.[23]

Second, people tend to identify more with partners within their own networks, which increases referent power among people within each network. This network-based referent power may lead to more favourable decisions by others in the network. Finally, effective networkers are better known by others in the organization, so their talents are more readily recognized. This power increases when networkers place themselves in strategic positions in the network, thereby gaining centrality.[24] For example, an individual might be regarded as the main person who distributes information in the network or who keeps the network connected through informal gatherings.

other disciplines for new ideas. At the same time, this textbook is written for students, not the scholars whose work is cited. So while this book provides new knowledge and its practical implications, you won't find detailed summaries of specific research studies. Also, this textbook rarely names researchers and their university affiliations. It focuses on organizational behaviour knowledge rather than "who's-who" in the field.

Canadian Organizational Behaviour is the first textbook to discuss workplace emotions, social identity theory, four-drive theory, appreciative inquiry, affective events theory (but without the jargon), somatic marker theory (also without the jargon), virtual teams, future search events, Schwartz's values model, resilience, employee engagement, learning orientation, workaholism, and several other groundbreaking topics. This edition continues this leadership by introducing the latest knowledge on social networking communication, exceptions to media richness theory, and the importance of self-concept in organizational behaviour.

ACTIVE LEARNING AND CRITICAL THINKING SUPPORT

KEY TERMS

bounded rationality, p. 158
creativity, p. 166
decision making, p. 154
divergent thinking, p. 167
employee involvement, p. 164

escalation of commitment, p. 162
implicit favourite, p. 159
intuition, p. 160
postdecisional justification, p. 162
prospect theory, p. 163

rational choice paradigm, p. 154
satisficing, p. 159
scenario planning, p. 161
subjective expected utility, p. 154

CRITICAL THINKING QUESTIONS

1. A management consultant is hired by a manufacturing firm to determine the best site for its next production facility. The consultant has had several meetings with the company's senior executives regarding the factors to consider when making the recommendation. Discuss the decision-making problems that might prevent the consultant from choosing the best site location.

2. You have been asked to personally recommend a new travel agency to handle all airfare, accommodation, and related travel needs for your organization of 500

staff. One of your colleagues, who is responsible for the company's economic planning, suggests that the best travel agent could be selected mathematically by inputting the relevant factors for each agency and the weight (importance) of each factor. What decision-making approach is your colleague recommending? Is this recommendation a good idea in this situation? Why or why not?

3. Intuition is both an emotional experience and an unconscious analytic process. One problem, however, is that

We teach organizational behaviour, so we understand how important it is to use a textbook that offers deep support for active learning and critical thinking. The fact that business school accreditation associations also emphasize the importance of the learning experience further reinforces our attention on classroom activities. *Canadian Organizational Behaviour,* Seventh Edition includes more than two dozen case studies in various forms and levels of complexity. It offers three dozen self-assessments, most of which have received construct validation. This book is also a rich resource for in-class activities, some of which are not available in other organizational behaviour textbooks, such as Test Your Knowledge of Personality, Where in the World Are We?, and the Cross-Cultural Communication Game.

CONTINUOUS DEVELOPMENT

Canadian Organizational Behaviour is *not* a "Canadianized" adaptation of an American book. Although Steve also co-authors *Organizational Behaviour* in the United States and internationally (now in its successful fourth edition) and *Organisational Behaviour on the Pacific Rim,* Second Edition (now the bestselling OB book in that region), all three books update each other in a virtuous cycle of continuous development. *Canadian Organizational Behaviour,* Seventh Edition updates information from the current American and Pacific Rim editions, which will be incorporated into the next editions of these kindred publications.

This is apparently the only business textbook anywhere that practises continuous development because it is the only book where the lead author actively writes in all three regions. This global approach to textbook development ensures that *Canadian Organizational Behaviour* offers Canadians the latest organizational behaviour knowledge, issues, and examples at the time of publication. The next section highlights the results of this continuous development process.

CHANGES TO THE SEVENTH EDITION

surface-level diversity
Observable demographic and other overt differences in people, such as their race, ethnicity, gender, age, and physical capabilities.

deep-level diversity
Differences in the psychological characteristics of employees, including personalities, beliefs, values, and attitudes.

Canadian Organizational Behaviour, Seventh Edition has benefited from reviews by over forty organizational behaviour scholars and teachers in several countries over the past three years, including two rounds of feedback from many Canadian OB experts. The most significant structural change is that we have reduced the book to 15 chapters so it more closely parallels the number of weeks in a typical OB course. This edition also continues to update current knowledge in every chapter and provides fresh examples to illustrate theories and concepts. The most notable improvements to this edition are described below:

- *Chapter 1: Introduction to the Field of Organizational Behaviour*—This chapter has been substantially revised and updated. It introduces four perspectives of organizational effectiveness (the ultimate dependent variable in OB), so students now have an excellent macro-OB foundation for topics throughout this book. This theme also provides better organization for open systems, organizational learning, high performance work practices, and values and ethics. The five types of individual behaviour are also described in this chapter as a natural micro-OB flow from the organizational effectiveness discussion. The topic of workforce diversity now distinguishes surface from deep-level diversity.

- *Chapter 2: Individual Behaviour, Personality, and Values*—This edition provides important new knowledge about self-concept, including its main components (self-enhancement, self-verification, self-evaluation, and social identity) and their relevance for organizational behaviour. This edition also has a rewritten and expanded discussion of personality in line with the topic's increasing importance in OB.

- *Chapter 3: Perception and Learning in Organizations*—This edition updates the section on selective attention, organization, and interpretation based on the rapidly developing research on this topic. The chapter adds discussion about false-consensus effect as well as the implicit association test. It also re-organizes into one section the discussion about practices that minimize perceptual problems.

- *Chapter 4: Workplace Emotions, Attitudes, and Stress*—This chapter now incorporates the topic of stress, which is closely related to workplace emotions. It continues to present a clearer explanation of the dual (cognitive and emotional) processes of attitudes and provides a fuller understanding about the dimensions of emotional intelligence. This chapter also discusses "shock events" in job satisfaction.

- *Chapter 5: Foundations of Employee Motivation*—The previous edition was apparently the first OB book to discuss employee engagement. This edition moves the topic to this chapter, so employee engagement is more closely connected to employee motivation as well as the MARS model. The chapter also distinguishes drives from needs and explains how drives and emotions are the prime movers of human motivation. It also describes Maslow's contribution to the field of human motivation as well as positive organizational behaviour. *Canadian Organizational Behaviour* was the first OB textbook to introduce four-drive theory, and this edition further refines the description of that model and its practical implications.

- *Chapter 6: Applied Performance Practices*—This edition adds emerging information about the situational and personal influences on self-leadership. It also updates information about reward practices and the effectiveness of those practices.

- *Chapter 7: Decision Making and Creativity*—This edition revises and updates the discussion of problems with problem identification, the section on the influence of emotions on making choices, and the section on characteristics of creative people.

- *Chapter 8: Team Dynamics*—This edition combines the two chapters on teams found in previous editions. It summarizes types of teams and more fully discusses the potential benefits and problems with teams. This edition also introduces new information on the characteristics of effective team members and revises the writing on self-directed teams and virtual teams.

- *Chapter 9: Communicating in Teams and Organizations*—The previous edition was apparently the first OB textbook to discuss the role of blogs and wikis in organizations. This edition continues this leadership with new information about social networking communication. This chapter includes other innovations, including the topic of multi-communicating, the role of social acceptance in communication channel preference, conditions that offset the effects of media richness, and factors influencing the effectiveness of encoding and decoding messages.

- *Chapter 10: Power and Influence in the Workplace*—This chapter has relatively minor updates, including a separate discussion of the consequences of power.

- *Chapter 11: Conflict and Negotiation in the Workplace*—This edition offers a more detailed look at the contingencies of conflict handling. It also revises and updates the evolution of thinking on whether conflict is good or bad. This description includes the emerging model of constructive versus relationship conflict and the ways to allow the former while suppressing the latter.

- *Chapter 12: Leadership in Organizational Settings*—In this edition, the competency perspective of leadership has been rewritten to incorporate new information about personality, self-concept, practical intelligence, and other specific competencies. The topic of implicit leadership has also been revised to incorporate the distinction

employee engagement
The employee's emotional and cognitive motivation, self-efficacy to perform the job, a clear understanding of his or her role in the organization's vision, and a belief that he or she has the resources to perform their job done.

wikis
Collaborative Web spaces in which anyone in a group can write, edit, or remove material from the website.

implicit leadership theory
A theory stating that people evaluate a leader's effectiveness in terms of how well that person fits preconceived beliefs about the features and behaviours of effective leaders (leadership prototypes), and that they tend to inflate the influence of leaders on organizational events.

attraction-selection-attrition (ASA) theory
States that organizations have a natural tendency to attract, select, and retain people with values and personality characteristics that are consistent with the organization's character, resulting in a more homogeneous organization and a stronger culture.

between leadership prototypes and the romance of leadership. The topic of shared leadership has also been expanded.

- *Chapter 13: Organizational Structure*—This edition has minor updates, including revised writing on span of control and tall/flat structures. It also describes the liability of newness in the section on organic structures.
- *Chapter 14: Organizational Culture*—This edition describes attraction-selection-attrition theory as well as the Organizational Culture Profile model. The section on organizational culture and performance as well as the section on changing/strengthening organizational culture have been substantially rewritten.
- *Chapter 15: Organizational Change*—In this edition, the topic of resistance to change is further updated regarding the three functions of resistance. The topics of urgency for change and future search conferences also received minor updates.

SUPPORTING THE OB LEARNING EXPERIENCE

The changes described above refer only to the text material. *Canadian Organizational Behaviour,* Seventh Edition also has improved technology supplements, cases, videos, team exercises, and self-assessments.

CASE STUDY 4.1

Conestoga-Rovers and Associates

At first glance, the thick, hardcover books featured prominently in the reception area of Conestoga-Rovers and Associates in Waterloo, Ontario, have the appearance of dry legal volumes. Then you notice the word "Yearbook" inscribed in large, gold letters across their covers; a peek inside reveals a vividly photographed encapsulation of the company's unspoken, but well understood, work hard–play hard mantra. Within their pages, hundreds of photographs capture smiling, laughing, and often zanily dressed Conestoga-Rovers employees engaged in any number of social events, clubs, and activities that play an integral role in the company's culture.

There are plenty of events to choose from. Hardly a weekend goes by when a group of employees is not engaged in some social event, be it jet-boating on the Niagara River, taking a bus trip to a Buffalo Bills football game, celebrating Roverfest (a massive annual bash for employees and their families), or indulging in a death-by-chocolate night.

Conestoga-Rovers and Associates has forged an exemplary reputation for its expertise in the fields of engineering, the environment, construction, and information technology.

CHAPTER CASES AND ADDITIONAL CASES

Every chapter includes at least one short case that challenges students to diagnose issues and apply ideas from that chapter. One dozen additional cases appear at the end of the book. Several cases are new to this book and are written by Canadian instructors. Others, such as Arctic Mining Consultants, are classics that have withstood the test of time.

ADDITIONAL CASES

Case 1:	**A Mir Kiss?**
Case 2:	**Arctic Mining Consultants**
Case 3:	**Big Screen's Big Failure**
Case 4:	**Bridging the Two Worlds—The Organizational Dilemma**
Case 5:	**Fran Hayden Joins Dairy Engineering**
Case 6:	**High Noon at Alpha Mills**
Case 7:	**Keeping Suzanne Chalmers**
Case 8:	**Nirvana Art Gallery**
Case 9:	**Northwest Canadian Forest Products Limited**
Case 10:	**Perfect Pizzeria**
Case 11:	**Rhonda Clark: Taking Charge at the Smith Foundation**
Case 12:	**Treetop Forest Products**

PART TWO VIDEO CASE STUDIES

Case 1   Workplace Bias

Wal-Mart is known for its low prices, but many former and current female employees claim the company also has discriminatory low pay and promotional opportunities for women. This video program presents the views of several women who have joined in one of the largest class action sex discrimination lawsuits in history. They claim that qualified women at Wal-Mart receive fewer promotions than their male counterparts. Others say they were fired for launching a sexual harassment complaint. The program describes statistics showing that male district managers earn significantly more than their female counterparts.

Discussion Questions
1. Use your knowledge of social identity theory, stereotyping, and prejudice to explain how sex discrimination might exist at Wal-Mart and in other large retail organizations. Be sure to note any evidence described in this program to support your explanation.
2. If you were a senior manager at Wal-Mart and believed that some of these complaints are due to stereotyping and other biases among middle managers, what interventions would you recommend to correct these biases?

VIDEO CASES

Canadian Organizational Behaviour, Seventh Edition provides a full complement of video cases to liven up the classroom experience. Many are from the Canadian Broadcasting Corporation, such as workplace loyalty, work/life balance, drum room team building, and workplace change at Wendy's Restaurants of Canada. Other excellent video programs look at stress in Japan, workplace emotions at Pike Place Fish Market, charismatic CEOs, and business ethics at Wal-Mart.

TEAM EXERCISES AND SELF-ASSESSMENTS

Experiential exercises and self-assessments represent an important part of the active learning process. *Canadian Organizational Behaviour,* Seventh Edition facilitates that process by offering team/class exercises in every chapter. Many of these learning activities are not available in other organizational behaviour textbooks, such as Test Your Knowledge of Personality (Chapter 2), the Cross-Cultural Communication Game (Chapter 9), and Contingencies of Conflict Handling (Chapter 11).

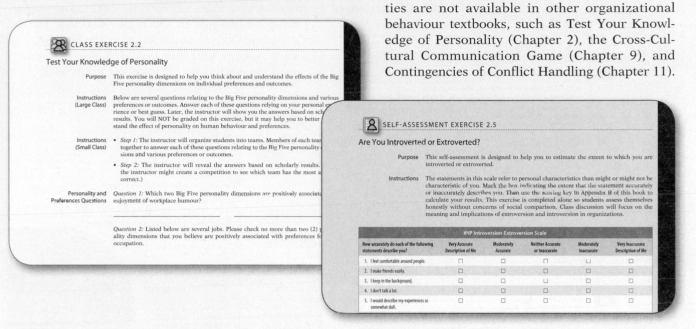

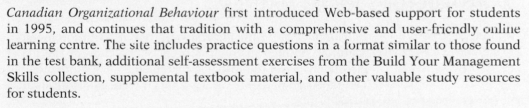

This edition also has three dozen self-assessments in the book. Self-assessments personalize the meaning of several organizational behaviour concepts, such as extroversion/introversion, self-leadership, empathy, stress, creative disposition, and tolerance of change. Additional and self-scoring, interactive self-assessments with detailed feedback can be found on the Student Online Learning Centre.

STUDENT ONLINE LEARNING CENTRE (*www.mcgrawhill.ca/olc/mcshane*)

Canadian Organizational Behaviour first introduced Web-based support for students in 1995, and continues that tradition with a comprehensive and user-friendly online learning centre. The site includes practice questions in a format similar to those found in the test bank, additional self-assessment exercises from the Build Your Management Skills collection, supplemental textbook material, and other valuable study resources for students.

*i*STUDY OB (*www.istudyob.ca*)

Available 24/7: Instant feedback so you can study when you want, how you want, and where you want: www.istudyob.ca. This online *i*Study space was developed and written by Claude Dupuis, Athabasca University, to help you master the concepts and achieve better grades with all of the learning tools you've come to expect (e.g., multiple-choice and true/false quizzes) plus flashcards, videos, and added quizzes, including chapter-by-chapter diagnostic assessments that point you to the concepts you need to focus on to improve your grades. Pick and choose from all of these features to develop your own personalized study plan. *i*Study offers the best, most convenient way to interact, learn, and succeed.

*i*StudyOB can be purchased through the Online Learning Centre (www.mcgrawhill.ca/olc/mcshane) or through the *i*StudyOB web site: www.istudyob.ca

Instructors: Please contact your *i*Learning Sales Specialist for more information on how to make *i*StudyOB part of your student's success.

INDEXES, MARGIN NOTES, AND GLOSSARY

While minimizing unnecessary jargon, *Canadian Organizational Behaviour* assists the learning process by highlighting key terms in bold and providing brief definitions in the margin. These definitions are also presented in an alphabetical glossary at the end of the text. We have also developed a comprehensive index of content, names, and organizations described in this book. Also look for the Learning Objectives presented at the beginning of each chapter, and then linked to chapter content by numbered icons. An excellent study tool!

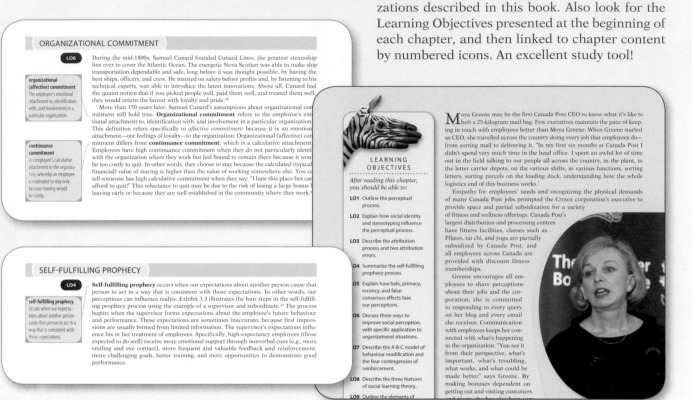

INSTRUCTOR SUPPORT MATERIALS

Canadian Organizational Behaviour, Seventh Edition includes a variety of supplemental materials to help instructors prepare and present the material in this textbook more effectively. All of the Instructor supplements described below can be found on the text's Online Learning Centre at www.mcgrawhill.ca/olc/mcshane.

INSTRUCTOR'S RESOURCE GUIDE

This is one of the few textbooks where the authors (McShane and Steen, with contributions from Claude Dupuis, Athabasca University) write the *Instructor's Resource Guide*. This ensures that the instructor materials represent the textbook's content and support instructor needs. Each chapter includes the learning objectives, glossary of key terms, a chapter synopsis, complete lecture outline with thumbnail images of corresponding PowerPoint® slides, and solutions to the end-of-chapter discussion questions. It also includes teaching notes for the chapter case(s), team exercises, and self-assessments. The *Instructor's Resource Guide* also includes complete teaching notes for the additional cases.

COMPUTERIZED TEST BANK

The Test Bank, thoroughly revised and updated for this edition by Claude Dupuis of Athabasca University, includes more than 2,700 multiple choice, true/false, and essay questions. Each question identifies the relevant page reference and difficulty level. Available for Macintosh or Windows users, the computerized test bank using EZ Test—

a flexible and easy-to-use electronic testing program—allows instructors to create tests from book-specific items. EZ Test accommodates a wide range of question types and allows instructors to add their own questions. Test items are also available in Word format (Rich Text format). For secure online testing, exams created in EZ Test can be exported to WebCT, Blackboard, and EZ Test Online. EZ Test comes with a Quick Start Guide, and once the program is installed, users have access to a User's Manual and Flash tutorials. Additional help is available online at www.mhhe.com/eztest.

POWERPOINT PRESENTATIONS

Canadian Organizational Behaviour was apparently the first OB textbook (in 1995) to introduce a complete set of PowerPoint® Presentation files. This resource is now more sophisticated than ever and created by the text authors for maximum alignment with the text content. Each PowerPoint® file has more than 18 professional-quality slides relating to the chapter, all of which display one or more photographs from the textbook.

VIDEO PROGRAM

The accompanying video program is available to instructors on DVD, VHS, or through video streaming on the Online Learning Centre. Teaching notes can be found in the Instructor's Resource Guide.

INSTRUCTOR ONLINE LEARNING CENTRE (*www.mcgrawhill.ca/olc/mcshane*)

Along with the Student OLC (see above), *Canadian Organizational Behaviour* includes a password-protected website for instructors including downloadable supplements, an Image Bank, Video and Case Teaching Notes, CURRENTS newsletter, and more valuable teaching resources.

INTEGRATOR

Keyed to the chapters and Learning Objectives, the Integrator ties together all the elements in your resource package, guiding you to where you'll find corresponding coverage in the supplement material. Link to the Integrator from the Online Learning Centre, at www.mcgrawhill.ca/olc/mcshane.

MANAGER'S HOT SEAT ONLINE (*www.mhhe.com/mhs*)

The Manager's Hot Seat Online is an interactive Web site in which students watch 15 real managers use their years of experience to solve important management and organizational behaviour issues. Students assume the role of the manager as they watch the video and answer multiple-choice questions that pop up during the segment, inviting them to make decisions on the spot. Students learn from the manager's mistakes and successes, and then prepare a report in which they evaluate the manager's approach and defend their reasoning. Ask your local *i*Learning Sales Specialist how you can obtain access to the Manager's Hot Seat Online for your course.

GROUP AND VIDEO RESOURCE MANUAL: AN INSTRUCTOR'S GUIDE TO AN ACTIVE CLASSROOM (*www.mhhe.com/mobmanual*)

This manual, created for instructors, contains everything needed to successfully integrate activities into the classroom. Instructor notes to accompany the Build Your Management Skills exercises (Self-Assessments and Test Your Knowledge quizzes), Group Exercises, and Manager's Hot Seat videos are located in this one manual, along with PowerPoint slides to use in class. Group exercises include everything you would need to use the exercise in class—handouts, figures, etc. The manual is organized into 25 topics such as ethics, decision-making, change, and leadership, for easy inclusion into your lecture. It also includes a matrix that organizes and hot-links each resource by topic. Students can access all of the exercises and self-assessments on the text's Online Learning Centre.

*i*LEARNING SERVICES

McGraw-Hill Ryerson offers a unique *i*Services package designed for Canadian faculty. Our mission is to equip higher education providers with superior tools and resources required for excellence in teaching. For additional information about these tools as well as our National Teaching and Learning Conference Series, visit www.mcgrawhill.ca/highereducation/iservices.

ACKNOWLEDGMENTS

Have you ever worked on a high-performance team where everything just seems to "click"? We have—on this Seventh Edition of *Canadian Organizational Behaviour*! Sure, we spend plenty of time alone writing and researching for this book, and of course there are challenges along the way. But it never ceases to amaze how teamwork *really does* make a difference. Several people provided valued expertise to smooth out the rough spots of writing, search out the most challenging photos, create a fantastic design, develop the various forms of student and instructor support, and pull together these many pieces into a comprehensive textbook. This teamwork is even more amazing when you consider that most of these team members live throughout Canada and Steve spends most of his time on the other side of the world.

Senior sponsoring editor Kim Brewster led the way with unwavering enthusiasm and foresight, while deflecting any challenges. She also deserves an award for identifying the fantastic cover art! Developmental editors Tracey Haggert, Lori McLellan and Leslie Mutic demonstrated amazing skills at coordinating the volumes of emails and files that produced this edition as well as the supplements package. The keen copy editing skills of Erin Moore made *Canadian Organizational Behaviour*, Seventh Edition incredibly error-free. Joanne Limebeer, our supervising editor, was another true professional as she guided the project through a tight production schedule. Thanks also to Tracy Leonard for locating the many photos that we had identified for this book, to Alison Derry for managing the photos and permission process, and to Michelle Losier for producing a refreshing elegant design. Thanks to you all. This has been an exceptional team effort!

As was mentioned earlier, over forty instructors around the world reviewed parts or all of *Canadian Organizational Behaviour*, Seventh Edition or related editions in the United States, Pacific Rim, and elsewhere over the past three years. Their compliments were energizing, and their suggestions significantly improved the final product. The following people from Canadian colleges and universities are among those who provided the most recent feedback for improvements specifically for *Canadian Organizational Behaviour*, Seventh Edition, and many participated in our cross-Canada focus groups. Thank you to all for your participation in the development and your enthusiasm for excellence.

Marcelle Allen, *Seneca College of Applied Arts and Technology*
Kathryn Arnold, *Grant MacEwan College*
Stan Arnold, *Humber Institute of Technology & Advanced Learning*
Vishwanath Baba, *McMaster University*
Gordon Barnard, *Durham College*
Kelly Beechey, *Northern Alberta Institute of Technology*
Ingrid Brand, *Durham College*
George Broderick, *Kwantlen Polytechnic University*
Jim Bryson, *Georgian College*
Don Caplan, *Royal Roads University*
Rudy Chernecki, *Durham College*
Debby Cleveland, *British Columbia Institute of Technology*
Robert Dabous, *Cambrian College*
Shawna DePlonty, *Sault College of Applied Arts and Technology*

Victoria Digby, *Fanshawe College*
Claude Dupuis, *Athabasca University*
Kelly Dye, *Acadia University*
Douglas Fletcher, *Kwantlen Polytechnic University*
Bill Fricker, *Northern Alberta Institute of Technology*
Ginger Grant, *Simon Fraser University*
Laura Guerrero, *King's University College*
Judith Hunter, *Sheridan College Institute of Technology and Advanced Learning*
Scott Jeffrey, *University of Waterloo*
Diane Jurkowsky, *York University*
Lisa Keeping, *Wilfrid Laurier University*
Elizabeth Kelley, *Dalhousie University*
Sue Kieswetter, *Conestoga College Institute of Technology and Advanced Learning*
Joan Kinsey, *Seneca College of Applied Arts and Technology*
Nelson Lacroix, *Niagara College*
Laurent Lapierre, *University of Ottawa*
Stephen Lynch, *University of Guelph*
Patsy Marshall, *University of Guelph*
Louis Masson, *Southern Alberta Institute of Technology*
Lesley McCannell, *Kwantlen Polytechnic University*
Bonnie Milne, *British Columbia Institute of Technology*
Don Miskiman, *Vancouver Island University*
Leila Rahemtulla, *British Columbia Institute of Technology*
Carolin Rekar Munro, *Durham College*
Shirley Rose, *Mount Royal College*
Stephen Rose, *University of Ontario Institute of Technology*
Carol Ann Samhaber, *Algonquin College*
Laura Jean Taplin, *Humber Institute of Technology & Advanced Learning*
Paul Tu, *University of Calgary*
Claire Ward, *University of Victoria*
Debra Warren, *Centennial College of Applied Arts and Technology*
Ken Yandeau, *Conestoga College Institute of Technology and Advanced Learning*

We would also like to extend sincere thanks to the exceptional efforts of Claude Dupuis, Athabasca University, who championed and wrote iStudy, revised the test bank, and assisted Steve and Sandra with the instructor's resource guide. Claude's enthusiasm and expertise in organizational behaviour teaching really comes through in his work on this project. We would also like to extend my sincerest thanks to the many instructors in Canada and abroad who contributed cases and exercises to this edition of *Canadian Organizational Behaviour*.

Steve would also like to extend special thanks to his students in Perth, Manila, and Singapore for sharing their learning experiences and assisting with the development of the three organizational behaviour textbooks in Canada, the United States, and the Pacific Rim, as well as their adaptations or translations in India, China, and Taiwan. Steve is also very grateful to his colleagues at the University of Western Australia for their support during challenging times. But more than anything else, Steve is forever indebted to his wife Donna McClement and to their wonderful daughters, Bryton and Madison. Their love and support give special meaning to Steve's life.

Sandra would like to extend appreciation to her students and colleagues at the University of Regina for sharing their passion for learning and teaching.

CHAPTER 1

Introduction to the Field of Organizational Behaviour

LEARNING OBJECTIVES

After reading this chapter, you should be able to:

LO1 Define organizational behaviour and organizations, and discuss the importance of this field of inquiry.

LO2 Diagram an organization from an open systems perspective.

LO3 Define intellectual capital and describe the organizational learning perspective of organizational effectiveness.

LO4 Diagnose the extent to which an organization or one of its work units applies high-performance work practices.

LO5 Explain how the stakeholder perspective emphasizes the importance of values, ethics, and corporate social responsibility.

LO6 Summarize the five types of individual behaviour in organizations.

LO7 Debate the organizational opportunities and challenges of globalization, workforce diversity, and virtual work.

LO8 Discuss how employment relationships are changing, and explain why these changes are occurring.

LO9 Discuss the anchors on which organizational behaviour knowledge is based.

The PCL family of companies is Canada's largest construction organization, 8th largest in the United States, and one of the best-managed companies in North America. It is listed on *Fortune* magazine's 100 Best Companies to Work for in America, *Report on Business Magazine*'s 50 Best Employers, and Mediacorp's Top 100 Employers in Canada. And in spite of cyclical swings of the construction business, PCL has been profitable every year for the past three decades. What makes the Edmonton-based contracting organization so successful? One factor is that PCL diversifies its work geographically and across industries to minimize effects of the boom-bust construction market. Another factor is that PCL's leaders diligently apply several organizational behaviour principles and practices.

PCL founder Ernie Poole introduced "Poole's Rules" in 1948—several bits of business advice that include the company's core values of integrity, loyalty, and fairness in all dealings. These values are apparent in PCL's employment practices. Whereas short-term work arrangements are commonplace in the construction industry, PCL maintains long-term employment by investing heavily in employee training and career development. Even with massive projects from Alberta's oil sands to Toronto's Pearson International Airport, PCL seeks out small jobs for employee development. "These $80,000 to $100,000 jobs help young staff cut their teeth, and develop relationships with clients for the future," explains PCL president and chief executive officer Ross Grieve.

In 1977, the Poole family sold PCL to its employees. This employee ownership arrangement (approximately 80 percent of PCL staff hold shares) reinforces the company's egalitarian no-nonsense corporate culture and generates high levels of employee engagement. Senior management discusses financial and operational matters to staff through 'fireside chats' held twice a year, but open communication is also a daily routine. "It's very much an open-door environment," says Dennis Wiens, PCL's director of human resource services.

Several organizational behaviour practices have helped the Edmonton-based PCL family of companies become an employer of choice, a leader in the construction industry, and a valued community member. *Photo and logo copyright © PCL Construction Ltd.*

Paul Douglas, president and chief operating officer of PCL's buildings and civil operations in Canada describes a time when he was setting up PCL's Ottawa operation and was quietly approached by an administrative assistant about some staff practices that she felt did not support the company's goals. She indicated she probably should not be bothering someone at this senior level in the company "but as an owner and an employee, she said she felt an obligation," says Douglas. "That's when I said, 'Wow, that's the difference right there.' Employees feel empowered."[1]

Values, motivation, employee development, communication, employee engagement, empowerment. These are some of the organizational behaviour concepts behind the success of PCL and other companies. They are also some of the topics featured in this book. Our main objective is to help you understand behaviour in organizations and to work more effectively in organizational settings. We begin in this chapter by introducing you to the field of organizational behaviour and explaining why it is important to your career and to organizations. Next, this chapter describes the "ultimate dependent variable" in this field by presenting the four main perspectives of organizational effectiveness. This is followed by an overview of the five types of individual behaviours that are most often studied as dependent variables in organizational behaviour. This chapter also introduces three challenges facing organizations—globalization, increasing workforce diversity, and emerging employment relationships—and highlights the anchors that guide organizational behaviour knowledge development.

THE FIELD OF ORGANIZATIONAL BEHAVIOUR

LO1

organizational behaviour (OB)
The study of what people think, feel, and do in and around organizations.

organizations
Groups of people who work interdependently toward some purpose.

Organizational behaviour (OB) is the study of what people think, feel, and do in and around organizations. OB researchers systematically study individual, team (including interpersonal), and organizational-level characteristics that influence behaviour within work settings.[2] **Organizations** are groups of people who work interdependently toward some purpose.[3] Organizations are not buildings or government registered entities. Rather, they consist of people who interact with each other to achieve a common purpose. Employees have structured patterns of interaction, meaning that they expect each other to complete certain tasks in a coordinated way—in an *organized* way. Organizations also have a collective sense of purpose, whether it is constructing airport terminals or producing animated films. "A company is one of humanity's most amazing inventions," says Steven Jobs, CEO of Pixar Animation Studios and Apple, Inc. "It's totally abstract. Sure, you have to build something with bricks and mortar to put the people in, but basically a company is this abstract construct we've invented, and it's incredibly powerful."[4]

OB emerged as a distinct field around the 1940s, although people have been studying organizations for centuries.[5] For example, the Greek philosopher Plato wrote about the essence of leadership. Around the same time, the Chinese philosopher Confucius extolled the virtues of ethics and leadership. In 1776, Adam Smith advocated a new form of organizational structure based on the division of labour. One hundred years later, German sociologist Max Weber wrote about rational organizations, work ethic, and charismatic leadership. Soon after, Frederick Winslow Taylor introduced the systematic use of goal setting and rewards to motivate employees. In the 1920s, Elton Mayo and his colleagues discovered the importance of formal and informal group dynamics in the workplace, resulting in a dramatic shift towards the "human relations" school of thought. A decade later, Chester Barnard, a business executive who is frequently identified as one of the founders of contemporary organizational behaviour thought, brought insightful views regarding individual behaviour, motivation, communication, leadership and authority, and team dynamics in organizational settings. OB has been around for a long time; it just wasn't organized into a unified discipline until after World War II.

WHY STUDY ORGANIZATIONAL BEHAVIOUR?

Organizational behaviour instructors face a challenge: On the one hand, students just beginning their careers tend to focus their attention on courses related to specific jobs, such as accounting and marketing.[6] OB doesn't have a specific career path—there is no "vice-president of OB"—so instructors have some difficulty conveying the importance of OB to these students. On the other hand, students with several years of work experience place OB courses near the top of their list of important courses. They have directly observed that OB *does make a difference* to their career success. Each one of us has an inherent need to understand and predict the world in which we live.[7] Since much of our time is spent working in or around organizations, OB theories help you to make sense of the workplace. OB theories also give you the opportunity to question and rebuild your personal mental models that have developed through observation and experience.

But the main reason why people with work experience value OB is that almost everyone needs to work with other people to get things done, and OB provides the knowledge and tools to work with and through others. Influencing your boss, building a high-performance team, motivating co-workers (or yourself!), handling workplace conflicts, and changing employee behaviour are just a few of the areas of knowledge and skills offered in organizational behaviour. No matter what career path you choose, you'll find that OB concepts play an important role in performing your job and working more effectively within organizations. This practical side of organizational behaviour is, according to some experts, a critical feature of the best OB theories.[8]

Organizational Behaviour is for Everyone Our explanation about why organizational behaviour is important for your career success does not assume that you are, or intend to be, a manager. In fact, this book pioneered the notion that OB knowledge is for everyone. Whether you are a geologist, financial analyst, customer service representative, or chief executive officer, you need to understand and apply the many organizational behaviour topics that are discussed in this book. Yes, organizations will continue to have managers, but their roles have changed and more importantly, the rest of us are increasingly expected to manage ourselves in the workplace. In the words of one forward-thinking OB writer many years ago: Everyone is a manager.[9]

OB and the Bottom Line So far, our answer to the question "Why study OB?" has focused on how OB knowledge benefits you as an individual. But organizational behaviour knowledge is just as important for the organization's financial health. This was apparent in the opening story about the PCL family of companies, which has benefited from several OB concepts and practices. According to one estimate, firms that apply performance-based rewards, employee communication, work/life balance, and other OB practices have three times the level of financial success as companies where these practices are absent. Another study concluded that companies that earn "the best place to work" awards have significantly higher financial and long-term stock market performance. Essentially, these firms leverage the power of OB practices, which translate into more favourable employee attitudes, decisions, and performance. The benefits of OB are well known to Warren Buffett and other financial gurus; they consider the organization's leadership and quality of employees as two of the best predictors of the firm's financial potential.[10]

PERSPECTIVES OF ORGANIZATIONAL EFFECTIVENESS

Almost all organizational behaviour theories have the implicit or explicit objective of making organizations more effective.[11] In fact, organizational effectiveness is considered the "ultimate dependent variable" in organizational behaviour.[12] The first challenge, however, is to define organizational effectiveness. Experts agree that this topic is burdened with too many labels—organizational performance, success, goodness, health, competitiveness, excellence, etc.—with no consensus on the meaning of each label.

organizational effectiveness
A broad concept represented by several perspectives, including the organization's fit with the external environment, internal subsystems configuration for high-performance, emphasis on organizational learning, and ability to satisfy the needs of key stakeholders.

Long ago, organizational effectiveness was defined as the extent to which an organization achieved its stated goals.[13] According to this view, PCL is effective because it completes construction projects on time and on budget. The goal attainment view is no longer accepted, however, because a company can be considered effective simply by establishing easily achievable goals. Also, some goals—such as social responsibility to the community—are so abstract that it would be very difficult to know whether the organization has achieved them. A third flaw with the goal attainment definition is that a company's stated objectives might threaten its long-term survival. For example, some corporate leaders have been "incentivized" to maximize short-term profits, but they did so by dramatically reducing research and development or new investment, which put the company at a competitive disadvantage in the long run.

How is **organizational effectiveness** defined today? The answer is that there are several perspectives of effectiveness, so this concept is defined in terms of *all of these perspectives*.[14] Organizations are considered effective when they have a good fit with their external environment, when their internal subsystems are configured for a high-performance workplace, when they are learning organizations, and when they satisfy the needs of key stakeholders. Let's now look at the four perspectives embedded in this definition of organizational effectiveness.

L02

OPEN SYSTEMS PERSPECTIVE

open systems
A perspective that organizations take their sustenance from the environment and, in turn, affect that environment through their output.

The **open systems** perspective of organizational effectiveness is one of the earliest and deeply entrenched ways of thinking about organizations. In fact, the other major organizational effectiveness perspectives might be considered detailed extensions of the open systems model.[15] As depicted in Exhibit 1.1, the open systems perspective views organizations as complex organisms that "live" within an external environment. The word "open" describes this permeable relationship, whereas "closed systems" can exist without dependence on an external environment.

As open systems, organizations depend on the external environment for resources, including raw materials, employees, financial resources, information, and equipment. PCL Constructors Ltd. and other companies could not survive without employees, building materials, knowledge, and so forth. Inside the organization are numerous subsystems, such as processes (communication and reward systems), task activities (production, marketing), and social dynamics (informal groups, power relationships). With the aid of technology (such as equipment, work methods, and information), these subsystems transform inputs into various outputs. Some outputs (e.g., products and services) may be valued by the external environment, whereas other outputs (e.g., employee layoffs, pollution) have adverse effects. The organization receives feedback from the external environment regarding the value of its outputs and the availability of future inputs.

According to the open systems perspective, successful organizations monitor their environments and are able to maintain a close "fit" with those changing conditions.[16] One way they do this is by finding new opportunities to secure essential inputs. For instance, McDonald's Restaurants has developed innovative ways to maintain an adequate supply of people. Years ago, the company was among the first to recruit retirees as employees. Recently, McDonald's UK introduced the Family Contract, an employment arrangement that allows members of the employee's family (spouses, grandparents, and children over the age of 16) to swap shifts without notifying management.[17] Successful organizations also redesign outputs so they remain compatible with needs in the external environment. Food manufacturers have changed their ingredients to satisfy more health-conscious consumers. Grocery stores have added more ethnically diverse foods to reflect the increasing ethnic diversity of shoppers.

Internal Subsystems Effectiveness   The open systems perspective considers more than an organization's fit with the external environment. It also examines how well it operates internally, that is, how well the company transforms inputs into outputs.

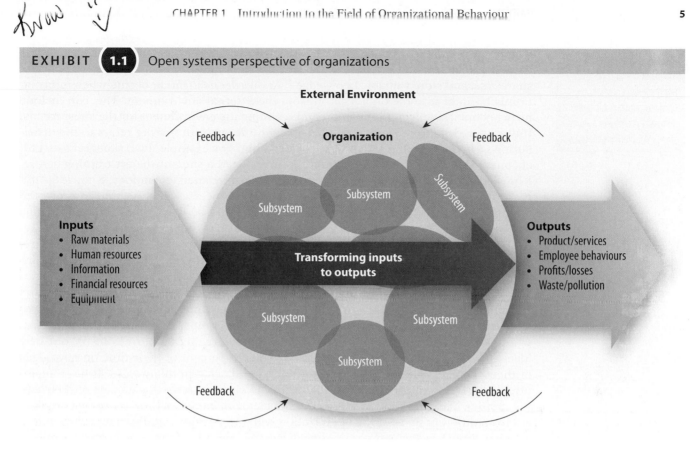

EXHIBIT 1.1   Open systems perspective of organizations

External Environment

Feedback

Organization

Feedback

Inputs
- Raw materials
- Human resources
- Information
- Financial resources
- Equipment

Transforming inputs to outputs

Subsystem

Outputs
- Product/services
- Employee behaviours
- Profits/losses
- Waste/pollution

Feedback

Feedback

---

organizational efficiency
The amount of outputs relative to inputs in the organization's transformation process.

The most common indicator of this internal transformation process is **organizational efficiency** (also called *productivity*), which is the amount of outputs relative to inputs.[18] Companies that produce more goods or services with less labour, materials, and energy are more efficient. The most efficient companies are not necessarily the most effective, however. Organizations often need more *adaptive* and *innovative* transformation processes, not just more efficient ones. For example, German engineering conglomerate Siemens AG has an effective transformation process because its subsystems are innovative and responsive, not necessarily the most efficient. "Whether I have additional costs or not doesn't matter as much as the speed to market and the quality of the design," says a Siemens executive. "We're not talking about a pure cost game."[19]

Organizational subsystems are dependent on each other to varying degrees, but this coordination is usually far from ideal.[20] Information gets lost, ideas are not shared, materials are hoarded, communication messages are misinterpreted, resources and rewards are distributed unfairly, and so forth. These coordination challenges are amplified as organizations grow, such as when employees are clustered into several departments and when departments are clustered into several organizational divisions. That's why even the best-laid plans are paved with unintended consequences. A slight change in work practices in one subsystem may ripple through the organization and affect other subsystems. For example, a new accounting procedure in the financial subsystem may motivate sales staff to alter their selling tactics or administrative staff to avoid completing certain types of documentation.

LO3

ORGANIZATIONAL LEARNING PERSPECTIVE

The open systems perspective has traditionally focused on physical resources that enter the organization and are processed into physical goods (outputs). This was representative of the industrial economy but not the "new economy," where the most valued input is knowledge. Knowledge is the driver of competitive advantage, however, in the

organizational learning
A perspective that organizational effectiveness depends on the organization's capacity to acquire, share, use, and store valuable knowledge.

organizational learning perspective (also called *knowledge management*). Through this lens, organizational effectiveness depends on the organization's capacity to acquire, share, use, and store valuable knowledge.[21] *Knowledge acquisition* occurs when information is brought into the organization from the external environment. This can include hiring people, acquiring companies, and scanning the environment for the latest trends. It also includes the process of creative insight.[22] *Knowledge sharing* refers to the distribution of knowledge throughout the organization. For example, PCL Constructors Ltd. encourages daily communication and has introduced a state-of-the-art training centre. Knowledge sharing also occurs through computer-mediated technology. *Knowledge use* is the application of knowledge to organizational processes in ways that improve the organization's effectiveness. Essentially, any new work activity is a form of knowledge use because this innovation requires knowledge to break out of past routines and practices. *Storage* refers to ways that companies retain valuable knowledge. For instance, they document best practices, record experiments (including those that didn't work out), and keep samples of past products.

To understand these processes, consider how Google engages in organizational learning. The company that brought us the ubiquitous Internet search engine acquires knowledge by hiring the best talent, buying entire companies (such as Keyhole, Inc, whose knowledge created Google Earth), and encouraging employees to try out new ideas. In fact, employees are expected to devote 20 percent of their time on new ideas of their choosing. Google encourages knowledge sharing in many ways. It has a team-oriented project culture that encourages staff to share information as part of their job. It's campus-like environment (called the Googleplex), increases the chance that employees from different parts of the organization will mingle and casually share information, whether dining at the company's subsidized gourmet restaurant or playing a game of volleyball in the sports area. Knowledge sharing also occurs through sophisticated information technologies. Along with knowledge acquisition and sharing, Google encourages knowledge use by giving employees the freedom to apply their newfound knowledge and encouraging them to experiment with that knowledge. "Google is truly a learning organization," says Google's chief financial officer George Reyes.[23]

Intellectual Capital: The Stock of Organizational Knowledge   Knowledge acquisition, sharing, and use represents the flow of knowledge. The organizational learning perspective also considers the company's stock of knowledge, called its **intellectual capital**.[24] The most obvious form of intellectual capital is *human capital*—the knowledge, skills, and abilities that employees carry around in their heads. This is an important part of a company's stock of knowledge, and a huge risk in companies where knowledge is the main competitive advantage. When key people leave, they take with them some of the knowledge that makes the company effective. But even if everyone left the organization, intellectual capital would still remain in the form of *structural capital*. This includes the knowledge captured and retained in an organization's systems and structures, such as documentation of work procedures and physical layout of the production line. Structural capital even includes the organization's finished products because knowledge can be extracted by taking them apart to discover how they work and are constructed (i.e., reverse engineering). Finally, intellectual capital includes *relationship capital*, which is the value derived from an organization's relationships with customers, suppliers, and others who provide added mutual value for the organization.

intellectual capital
Company's stock of knowledge, including human capital, structural capital, and relationship capital.

Organizational Memory and Unlearning   Corporate leaders need to recognize that they are the keepers of an **organizational memory**.[25] This unusual metaphor refers to the storage and preservation of intellectual capital. It includes information that employees possess as well as knowledge embedded in the organization's systems and structures. It includes documents, objects, and anything else that provides meaningful information about how the organization should operate.

organizational memory
The storage and preservation of intellectual capital.

How do organizations retain intellectual capital? One way is by keeping good employees. "Our assets walk up and down the stairs every day," says Ian Wilkinson, founder

OPG Captures the Power of Knowledge

The lights might not go out, but Ontario Power Generation (OPG) could face an expensive and somewhat risky period of corporate amnesia. Over the next five years, the Crown corporation that manages Ontario's electricity supply is about to lose one-quarter of its 11,000 employees due to retirement, many of them senior engineers and managers with valuable knowledge locked inside their heads. "Somebody with intellectual capital walking out the door could cause a team of 20 or 30 people to spend several weeks trying to re-study a particular piece of technology to come up with a solution," says John Murphy, OPG's executive vice-president of human resources. Fortunately, OPG is minimizing the amount of corporate memory loss by introducing several practices that capture knowledge. It introduced an online knowledge portal to document and store information. Younger employees are being groomed now for future leadership roles, and some are encouraged to develop skills for two or more future jobs so the Crown corporation can fill sudden knowledge gaps.[26] *Courtesy of Ontario Power Generation*

of Radical Entertainment in Vancouver. "If we keep smart, motivated people, we can do everything."[27] Radical Entertainment and other progressive companies are keeping smart, motivated staff by adapting their employment practices to become more compatible with emerging workforce expectations, including work/life balance, egalitarian hierarchy, and a workspace that generates more fun. A second organizational memory strategy is to systematically transfer knowledge to other employees. This occurs when new recruits apprentice with skilled employees, thereby acquiring knowledge that is not documented. A third strategy is to transfer knowledge into structural capital. This includes bringing out hidden knowledge, organizing it, and putting it in a form that can be available to others (e.g., video recording an expert performing a task).

The organizational learning perspective states not only that effective organizations learn; they also unlearn routines and patterns of behaviour that are no longer appropriate.[28] Unlearning removes knowledge that no longer adds value and, in fact, may undermine the organization's effectiveness. Some forms of unlearning involve replacing dysfunctional policies, procedures, and routines. Other forms of unlearning erase attitudes, beliefs, and assumptions. For instance, employees rethink how they should interact with customers and which is the "best way" to perform a task.

HIGH PERFORMANCE WORK PRACTICES (HPWP) PERSPECTIVE

Although the open systems perspective states that successful companies are good at transforming inputs to outputs, it does not offer specific advice about which bundle of subsystems are the most important. Consequently, an entire field of research has blossomed around the objective of identifying internal systems and structures that are associated with successful companies. This research has had various labels over the years, but it is now mostly categorized as the study of **high performance work practices (HPWP)**.[29]

The HPWP perspective begins with the idea that *human capital*—the knowledge, skills, and abilities that employees possess—is an important source of competitive advantage for organizations.[30] Human capital helps the organization realize opportunities or minimize threats in the external environment. Furthermore, human capital is neither widely available nor easily duplicated. For instance, a new company cannot quickly acquire a workforce with the same capabilities as an established company. Nor can technology replace the capabilities that employees bring to the workplace. In short, human capital is valuable, rare, difficult to imitate, and nonsubstitutable.[31] Therefore, organizations excel by finding ways to leverage the potential of their workforce.

> **high performance work practices (HPWP)**
> A perspective that effective organizations incorporate several workplace practices that leverage the potential of human capital.

Researchers have investigated numerous organizational practices in various combinations, but a few common activities stand out as high-performance work practices.[32] Two of the most widely mentioned high-performance work practices are employee involvement and job autonomy. As we will learn in several chapters of this book, both activities tend to strengthen employee motivation as well as improve decision making, organizational responsiveness, and commitment to change. HPWP writers often relate employee involvement and job autonomy in the form of high-performance work teams, which will be discussed in Chapter 8.

Another key variable in the HPWP model is employee competence. Specifically, organizations are more effective when they invest in employee skills and knowledge development, and when they carefully select job applicants with strong skills and performance potential (see Chapter 2). Finally, high-performance organizations link performance and skill development to various forms of financial and nonfinancial rewards valued by employees. We will discuss reward systems in Chapter 6 as one of several practices to improve employee performance.

The HPWP perspective is currently popular among scholars and practitioners, but it also has its share of critics. One concern is that many studies try to find out which practices predict organizational performance without theoretically understanding *why* those practices should have this effect.[33] It is important to know the causal connection between work practices and organizational effectiveness in order to be confident that the practice will be valuable in the future and in other situations. A second concern with the HPWP perspective is that it may satisfy shareholder and customer needs at the expense of employee well-being.[34] Some experts point out that HPWPs increase work stress and that management is reluctant to delegate power or share the financial benefits of productivity improvements. If high-performance work practices improve organizational performance at a cost to employee well-being, then this perspective (along with the open systems and organizational learning perspectives) have not yet painted the entire organizational effectiveness picture. The remaining gaps are mostly filled by the stakeholder perspective of organizational effectiveness.

LO5

STAKEHOLDER PERSPECTIVE

The three organizational effectiveness perspectives described so far mainly focus on processes and resources, yet they only minimally recognize the importance of relations with **stakeholders**. Stakeholders include individuals, organizations, or other entities that affect, or are affected by, the organization's objectives and actions. They include anyone with a stake in the company, such as employees, shareholders, suppliers, labour unions, government, communities, consumer and environmental interest groups, and so on. The essence of the stakeholder perspective is that companies must take into account how their actions affect others, which requires them to understand, manage, and satisfy the interests of their stakeholders.[35] The stakeholder perspective personalizes the open systems perspective; it identifies specific people and social entities in the external and internal environment. It also recognizes that stakeholder relations are dynamic; they can be negotiated and managed, not just taken as a fixed condition.[36]

stakeholders
Individuals, organizations, or other entities who affect, or are affected by, the organization's objectives and actions.

Consider the troubles that Wal-Mart has faced in recent years.[37] For decades, the world's largest retailer provided customers with the lowest possible prices and, through high volume, generated healthy financial returns to shareholders. Yet by emphasizing the needs of customers and shareholders, the company faced increasing hostility from other groups in society. Some interest groups complained that Wal-Mart was destroying North America's manufacturing base and promoting unethical business practices (such as child labour) in countries where it purchased goods. Other groups pointed out that Wal-Mart had a poor record of environmental and social responsibility. Still other groups lobbied to keep Wal-Mart out of their communities because the giant retailer typically built in outlying areas where land is cheap, thereby fading the vibrancy of the community's downtown area. These stakeholder pressure points existed for some time, but Wal-Mart mostly ignored them until they became a serious threat. In fact, Wal-Mart recently created the position "senior director of stakeholder engagement" to ensure that it pays more attention to the fuller set of stakeholders, and to proactively manage those relationships.

Understanding, managing, and satisfying the interests of stakeholders is more challenging than it sounds because stakeholders have conflicting interests and organizations don't have the resources to satisfy every stakeholder to the fullest. Therefore, organizational leaders need to decide how much priority to give each group. One commonly cited factor is to favour stakeholders with the most power.[38] This makes sense when one considers that the most powerful stakeholders hold the greatest threat and opportunity to the company's survival. Yet stakeholder power should not be the only criterion for determining organizational strategy and resource allocation. Ignoring less powerful stakeholders might motivate them to become more powerful. It might also aggravate more powerful stakeholders if ignoring weaker interests violates the norms and standards of society.

Values, Ethics, and Corporate Social Responsibility   This brings us to one of the key strengths of the stakeholder perspective; it incorporates values, ethics, and corporate social responsibility into the organizational effectiveness equation.[39] To manage the interests of diverse stakeholders, the stakeholder perspective states that leaders ultimately need to rely on their personal and organizational values for guidance. **Values** are relatively stable, evaluative beliefs that guide our preferences for outcomes or courses of action in a variety of situations.[40] Values help us to know what is right or wrong, or good or bad, in the world. Chapter 2 describes how values are an important part of our self-concept and, as such, motivate our actions. Although values exist within individuals, groups of people often hold similar values, so we tend to ascribe these *shared values* to the team, department, organization, profession, or entire society. Chapter 14 discusses the importance and dynamics of an organization's shared values.

> **values**
> Relatively stable, evaluative beliefs that guide a person's preferences for outcomes or courses of action in a variety of situations.

Driven by Values in the Public Service of Canada

The Canadian government has actively promoted ethical conduct and values-based decision making for several decades. In 1999, it established the Office of Values and Ethics to further strengthen values-driven leadership in the Canadian public service. The federal public service is now launching the next step in its values-driven approach by carefully examining the values and competencies required of leaders at all levels. The four clusters of overlapping values core to the public service are: democratic values, ethical values, professional values, and people values. These values guide the behaviours expected of public service leaders. Ultimately, the Canadian government hopes this values-based approach will replace the existing control system based on hierarchy and compliance.[41] © *Jean Levac/Ottawa Citizen. Republished by permission.*

Values have become a popular topic in corporate boardrooms because leaders are discovering that the command-and-control approach that guided decisions and behaviour in the past is less acceptable to employees and less effective in complex environments compared to the values-driven organization approach. Bank of Montreal (BMO) is a case in point. A few years ago, BMO's top executives reflected on the financial institution's history and had deep conversations to identify the values upon which BMO was built. Out of this dialogue emerged four value statements that were distributed to employees and built into a revised reward system. Why did BMO go to such trouble to identify and communicate their shared values? "[BMO's values] provide a stable base for guiding employee decisions and actions in an otherwise rapidly changing workplace," explains a BMO executive who attended these meetings. "Simply put, *values matter* and employees care that the organizations they work for and represent are ethical and walk the talk of their values."[42]

By incorporating values into organizational effectiveness, the stakeholder perspective also provides the strongest case for ethics and corporate social responsibility. In fact, the stakeholder perspective emerged out of earlier writing on ethics and corporate social responsibility. **Ethics** refers to the study of moral principles or values that determine whether actions are right or wrong and outcomes are good or bad. We rely on our ethical values to determine 'the right thing to do.' Ethical behaviour is driven by the moral principles we use to make decisions. These moral principles represent fundamental values. Chapter 2 will provide more detail about ethical principles and related influences on moral reasoning.

ethics
The study of moral principles or values that determine whether actions are right or wrong and outcomes are good or bad.

corporate social responsibility (CSR)
Organizational activities intended to benefit society and the environment beyond the firm's immediate financial interests or legal obligations.

Corporate social responsibility (CSR) consists of organizational activities intended to benefit society and the environment beyond the firm's immediate financial interests or legal obligations.[43] It is the view that companies have a contract with society, in which they must serve stakeholders beyond shareholders and customers. In some situations, the interests of the firm's shareholders should be secondary to other stakeholders.[44] As part of CSR, many companies have adopted the triple bottom line philosophy. This means that they try to support or "earn positive returns" in the economic, social, and environmental spheres of sustainability. Firms that adopt the triple bottom line aim to survive and be profitable in the marketplace (economic), but they also intend to maintain or improve conditions for society (social) as well as the physical environment.[45]

Triple Bottom Line

The idea that organizations are more effective when they cater to a wide variety of stakeholders has its share of critics. More than 30 years ago, economist Milton Friedman pronounced that "there is one and only one social responsibility of business—to use its resources and engage in activities designed to increase its profits." Although few writers take this extreme view today, some continue to argue that companies must place shareholder interests above all others. Most Canadians disagree. In fact, 93 percent of Canadians believe that CSR should be as important to companies as profit and shareholder value. Another survey reported that 78 percent of Canadians would leave their current job for a more environmentally friendly employer. "Our company's position on corporate social responsibility and the environment is a significant part of what job candidates find attractive about HBC," acknowledges a senior executive at Hudson's Bay Co.[46] In short, leaders may put their organization at risk if they pay attention only to shareholders and ignore the broader corporate social responsibility.[47]

TYPES OF INDIVIDUAL BEHAVIOUR

LO6

The four perspectives described over the past few pages—open systems, organizational learning, high-performance work practices, and stakeholders—provide a multi-dimensional view of what makes companies effective. Within these models, however, are numerous behaviours that employees need to perform that enable companies to interact with their environments, acquire, share, and use knowledge to the best advantage, process inputs to outputs efficiently and responsively, and meet the needs of various stakeholders. While organizational effectiveness is the ultimate dependent variable, these behaviours are the individual-level dependent variables found in most OB research. Exhibit 1.2 highlights the five types of behaviour discussed most often in the organizational behaviour literature: task performance, organizational citizenship, counterproductive work behaviours, joining and staying with the organization, and work attendance.

TASK PERFORMANCE

Task performance refers to goal-directed behaviours under the individual's control that support organizational objectives. Task performance behaviours transform raw materials into goods and services or support and maintain the technical activities.[48] For example, foreign exchange traders at TD Waterhouse make decisions and take actions to exchange currencies. Employees in most jobs have more than one performance dimension. Foreign exchange traders must be able to identify profitable trades, work cooperatively with clients and co-workers in a stressful environment, assist in training new staff, and work on special telecommunications equipment without error. Some of these performance dimensions are more important than others, but only by considering all of them can we fully evaluate an employee's contribution to the organization.

ORGANIZATIONAL CITIZENSHIP

Companies could not effectively compete, transform resources, or serve the needs of their stakeholders if employees performed only their formal job duties. They also need to engage in **organizational citizenship behaviours (OCBs)**—various forms of cooperation and helpfulness to others that support the organization's social and psychological context.[49] In other words, companies require contextual performance (i.e., OCBs) along with task performance.

organizational citizenship behaviours (OCBs)
Various forms of cooperation and helpfulness to others that support the organization's social and psychological context.

EXHIBIT   1.2   Types of work-related behaviour

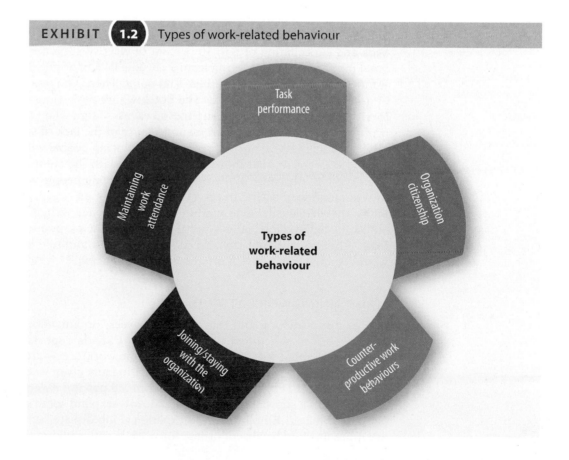

Organizational citizenship behaviours take many forms. Some are directed toward individuals, such as assisting co-workers with their work problems, adjusting your work schedule to accommodate co-workers, showing genuine courtesy toward co-workers, and sharing your work resources (supplies, technology, staff) with co-workers. Other OCBs represent cooperation and helpfulness toward the organization in general. These include supporting the company's public image, taking discretionary action to help the organization avoid potential problems, offering ideas beyond those required for your own job, attending voluntary functions that support the organization, and keeping up with new developments in the organization.[50]

COUNTERPRODUCTIVE WORK BEHAVIOURS

> **counterproductive work behaviours (CWBs)**
> Voluntary behaviours that have the potential to directly or indirectly harm the organization.

Organizational behaviour is interested in all workplace behaviours, including those on the "dark side," collectively known as **counterproductive work behaviours (CWBs).** CWBs are voluntary behaviours that have the potential to directly or indirectly harm the organization. These CWBs can be organized into five categories: abuse of others (e.g., insults and nasty comments), threats (threatening harm), work avoidance (e.g., tardiness), work sabotage (doing work incorrectly), and overt acts (theft). CWBs are not minor concerns. One recent study found that units of a fast-food restaurant chain with higher CWBs had a significantly worse performance, whereas organizational citizenship had a relatively minor benefit.[51]

JOINING AND STAYING WITH THE ORGANIZATION

Task performance, organizational citizenship, and the lack of counterproductive work behaviours are obviously important, but if qualified people don't join and stay with the organization, none of these performance-related behaviours would occur. Attracting and retaining talented people is particularly important as worries about skills shortages heat up. For instance, 70 percent of companies in the trucking industry have recently refused or delayed shipments due to a shortage of skilled drivers. A severe shortage of nurses in the Edmonton health system has resulted in closure of dozens of hospital beds and cancellation of 5 to 10 percent of elective surgeries every day. The Canadian hotel industry is also suffering from a chronic lack of applicants. "I don't even run help-wanted ads anymore because there's no point. There's no one to hire," says the manager of a 120-room hotel in Alberta. The hotel, which pays thousands of dollars to bring in foreign help, sometimes lights up the 'no vacancy' sign when there are empty rooms and is offering a smaller restaurant menu because of the lack of staff.[52]

Companies survive and thrive not just by hiring people with talent or potential; they also need to ensure that these employees stay with the company. Companies with high turnover suffer because of the high cost of replacing people who leave. More important, as was mentioned earlier in this chapter, much of an organization's intellectual capital is the knowledge carried around in employees' heads. When people leave, some of this vital knowledge is lost, often resulting in inefficiencies, poorer customer service, and so forth. This threat is not trivial: between one-third and one-half of employees say they would change companies if offered a comparable job.[53]

MAINTAINING WORK ATTENDANCE

Along with attracting and retaining employees, organizations need everyone to show up for work at scheduled times. Statistics Canada reports that more than 750,000 employees—about 5.4 percent of the full-time workforce—are absent from work due to illness or personal reasons at some time during any given week. This rate is higher than most other OECD countries and is up from 3.8 percent a decade ago.[54] Situational factors—such as a snowstorm or car breakdown—explain some work absences. Motivation is another factor. Employees who experience job dissatisfaction or work-related stress are more likely to be absent or late for work because taking time off is a way to temporarily withdraw from stressful or dissatisfying conditions. Absenteeism is also higher in organizations with generous sick leave because this benefit limits the negative financial impact of taking time away from work. Studies have found that absenteeism is also higher in teams with strong absence norms, meaning that team members tolerate and even expect co-workers to take time off.[55]

CONTEMPORARY CHALLENGES FOR ORGANIZATIONS

LO7

An underlying theme of the earlier discussion on organizational effectiveness was that organizations are deeply affected by the external environment. Consequently, they need to anticipate and adjust to environment changes in order to maintain a good fit with their environment. This external environment is continuously changing, but some changes for the past decade and in the decade to come are more profound than others. These changes will require corporate leaders and all other employees to adjust to the new realities. In this section, we highlight three of the major challenges facing organizations: globalization, increasing workforce diversity, and emerging employment relationships.

GLOBALIZATION

You might not have heard of Fonterra, but chances are that you have purchased or eaten one of its products recently. The New Zealand-based company is the world's largest dairy exporting business and the world's lowest-cost dairy ingredients producer. It operates in 140 countries, employs 20,000 people, and represents 40 percent of the global dairy trade. In many countries, it forms joint partnerships, such as with the Dairy Farmers of America, SanCor in Argentina, and Arla in Europe. Fonterra's current position on the world stage is quite different from a decade ago when three New Zealand dairy companies joined forces. They realized that globalization was shaking up the industry and that they needed to form a global enterprise to survive. The merged company was so globally focused from the outset that it was temporarily called GlobalCo until the name Fonterra was chosen. Fonterra's adjustment to a global operation was not easy. Executives were replaced as the company needed to adopt a different mindset. "A lot of people in the [pre-merger companies] were very New Zealand-centric and culturally did not understand the global challenges of the teams offshore and the different operating companies," acknowledges a Fonterra executive.[56]

Fonterra is a rich example of the globalization of business over the past few decades. **Globalization** refers to economic, social, and cultural connectivity with people in other parts of the world. Fonterra and other organizations globalize when they actively participate in other countries and cultures. Although businesses have traded goods across borders for centuries, the degree of globalization today is unprecedented because information technology and transportation systems allow a much more intense level of connectivity and interdependence around the planet.[57]

Globalization offers numerous benefits to organizations in terms of larger markets, lower costs, and greater access to knowledge and innovation. At the same time, there is considerable debate about whether globalization benefits developing nations, and whether it is primarily responsible for increasing work intensification, as well as reducing job security and work/life balance in developed countries.[58] Globalization is now well entrenched, so the real issue in organizational behaviour is how corporate leaders and employees alike can lead and work effectively in this emerging reality[59] OB researchers are turning their attention to this topic. In Project GLOBE, dozens of experts are studying leadership and organizational practices around the globe.[60]

globalization
Economic, social, and cultural connectivity with people in other parts of the world.

INCREASING WORKFORCE DIVERSITY

Walk into the offices of ProMation Engineering Ltd. and you might think you have entered a United Nations building. The Toronto-based company that produces sophisticated robotics for the automotive and nuclear industries employs 77 people who hail from Canada, Poland, India, China, Romania, Ukraine, Colombia, Peru, Serbia, Afghanistan, Angola, Belarus, Bosnia, Czech Republic, Croatia, England, Germany, Hong Kong, Hungary, Iran, Ireland, Italy, Jamaica, Macedonia, and the Philippines. "We take the best of all the people and try to find one common base for all of us in one small shop," says Promation's CEO Mark Zimny. He adds that the challenges of diversity require some patience but "the results are fantastic."[61]

ProMation is a reflection of Canada as a multicultural society that embraces diversity. Indeed, if Canada has a global "brand" image, it is as a country that has pioneered and leveraged the benefits of multiculturalism. When describing multiculturalism, we are primarily referring to **surface-level diversity**—the observable demographic and other overt differences in people, such as their race, ethnicity, gender, age, and physical capabilities. Surface-level diversity has changed considerably in Canada over the past few decades. The percentage of Canadian residents identified as members of a visible minority jumped from less than 5 percent in 1981 to more than 13 percent in 2001 and will exceed 20 percent of the population by 2017. This increasing cultural diversity is most apparent in Toronto and Vancouver where nearly 40 percent of residents are currently in a visible minority group, rising to more than 50 percent by 2017.[62]

Diversity also includes differences in the psychological characteristics of employees, including personalities, beliefs, values, and attitudes.[63] We can't directly see this **deep-level diversity**, but it is evident in a person's decisions, statements, and actions. One illustration of deep-level diversity is the different attitudes and expectations held by employees across generational cohorts.[64] *Baby boomers*—people born between 1946 and 1964—seem to expect and desire more job security, and are more intent on improving their economic and social status. In contrast, *Generation-X* employees—those born between 1965 and 1979—expect less job security and are motivated more by workplace flexibility, the opportunity to learn (particularly new technology), and working in an egalitarian and "fun" organization. Meanwhile, some observers suggest that *Generation-Y* employees (those born after 1979) are noticeably self-confident, optimistic, multitasking, and more independent than even Gen-X co-workers. These statements certainly don't apply to everyone in each cohort, but they do reflect the dynamics of deep-level diversity and shifting values and expectations across generations.

Consequences of Diversity   Diversity presents both opportunities and challenges in organizations.[65] In some circumstances and to some degree, diversity can become a competitive advantage by improving decision making and team performance on complex tasks. Studies suggest that teams with some forms of diversity (particularly occupational diversity) make better decisions on complex problems than do teams whose members have similar backgrounds. One study also found that companies with the highest representation of women on their top management teams experienced significantly better financial performance than firms with the lowest representation of women. Furthermore, many businesses report that having a diverse workforce has improved customer service and creativity. For instance, PepsiCo estimates that one-eighth of revenue growth is directly attributable to new products inspired by diversity efforts.[66]

Based on this evidence, the popular refrain is that workforce diversity is a sound business proposition. Unfortunately, it's not that simple. There is growing evidence that most forms of diversity offer both advantages and disadvantages.[67] Teams with diverse employees usually take longer to perform effectively. Diversity brings numerous communication problems as well as "faultlines" in informal group dynamics. Diversity is also a source of conflict, which can lead to lack of information sharing and, in extreme cases, morale problems and higher turnover. But whether or not workforce diversity is a business advantage, companies need to make it a priority because surface-level diversity is a moral and legal imperative. Ethically, companies that offer an inclusive workplace are, in essence, making fair and just decisions regarding employment, promotions, rewards, and so on. Fairness is a well-established influence on employee loyalty and satisfaction. Our main point here, though, is that workforce diversity is the new reality,

---

surface-level diversity
Observable demographic and other overt differences in people, such as their race, ethnicity, gender, age, and physical capabilities.

deep-level diversity
Differences in the psychological characteristics of employees, including personalities, beliefs, values, and attitudes.

and that organizations need to adjust to this reality both to survive and to experience its potential benefits for organizational success.

LO8

EMERGING EMPLOYMENT RELATIONSHIPS

Combine globalization with emerging workforce diversity, and add in new information technology. The resulting concoction has created incredible changes in employment relationships. A few decades ago, most (although not all) employees in Canada, the United States, and similar cultures would finish their workday after eight or nine hours and could separate their personal time from the work day. There were no BlackBerrys and no Internet connections to keep staff tethered to work on a 24/7 schedule. Even business travel was more of an exception due to its high cost. Most competitors were located in the same country, so they had similar work practices and labour costs. Today, work hours are longer (although arguably less than 100 years ago), employees experience more work-related stress, and there is growing evidence that family and personal relations are suffering. Little wonder that one of the emerging issues in this new century is for more **work/life balance**—minimizing conflict between work and nonwork demands.[68]

Another employment relationship trend is **virtual work**, whereby employees use information technology to perform their jobs away from the traditional physical workplace. The most common form of virtual work, called *telecommuting* or *teleworking*, involves working at home rather than commuting to the office. Virtual work also includes employees connected to the office while on the road or at clients' offices. For example, almost one-third of IBM's Canadian workforce have exchanged their assigned work stations for virtual work arrangements, including working from home or at the company's mobility centres.[69]

Some research suggests that virtual work, particularly telecommuting, potentially reduces employee stress by offering better work/life balance and dramatically reducing time lost through commuting to the office. Nortel Networks reports that 71 percent of its U.K. staff feels more empowered through virtual work arrangements. AT&T estimates that its telecommuters reduce pollution and are about 10 percent more productive than before they started working from home. IBM's virtual work program annually saves the company $20 million in Canada and $400 million a year globally, mostly in real estate costs.[70] Against these potential benefits, virtual workers face a number of real or potential challenges. Family relations may suffer rather than improve if employees lack sufficient space and resources for a home office. Some virtual workers complain of social isolation and reduced promotion opportunities. Virtual work is clearly better suited to people who are self-motivated, organized, can work effectively with contempo-

work/life balance
The degree to which a person minimizes conflict between work and nonwork demands.

virtual work
Work performed away from the traditional physical workplace using information technology.

Welcome to My Office!

Meridith Forsythe kick-starts her work day at sunrise in order to stay on top of her jam-packed schedule. The TELUS customer service agent has reports to complete and a team meeting to attend, and her goal is to exceed her customer service objectives. It is a good thing she has a very short commute. As a participant in TELUS' At Home Agent project, Meridith works out of her home in Barrie, Ontario. Since 2005, TELUS has provided hundreds of frontline agents with all the technical requirements they need to do their job from home."[71] © *Jim Craigmyle/Corbis*

rary information technologies, and have sufficient fulfillment of social needs elsewhere in their life. They also work better in organizations that evaluate employees by their performance outcomes rather than 'face time.'[72]

ANCHORS OF ORGANIZATIONAL BEHAVIOUR KNOWLEDGE

LO9

Globalization, increasing workforce diversity, and emerging employment relationships are just a few of the trends that challenge organizations and make OB knowledge more relevant than ever before. To understand these and other topics, the field of organizational behaviour relies on a set of basic beliefs or knowledge structures (see Exhibit 1.3). These conceptual anchors represent the principles on which OB knowledge is developed and refined.

THE MULTIDISCIPLINARY ANCHOR

Organizational behaviour is anchored around the idea that the field should develop from knowledge in other disciplines, not just from its own isolated research base. For instance, psychological research has aided our understanding of individual and interpersonal behaviour. Sociologists have contributed to our knowledge of team dynamics, organizational socialization, organizational power, and other aspects of the social system. OB knowledge has also benefited from knowledge in emerging fields such as communications, marketing, and information systems. Some OB experts have recently argued that the field suffers from a "trade deficit"—importing far more knowledge from other disciplines than is exported to other disciplines. While this is a possible concern, organizational behaviour has thrived through its diversity of knowledge from other fields of study.[73]

THE SYSTEMATIC RESEARCH ANCHOR

A critical feature of OB knowledge is that it should be based on systematic research, which typically involves forming research questions, systematically collecting data, and testing hypotheses against those data (see Appendix A). The result is evidence-based management, which involves making decisions and taking actions based on this research evidence. This makes perfect sense, does it? Yet OB scholars are often amazed

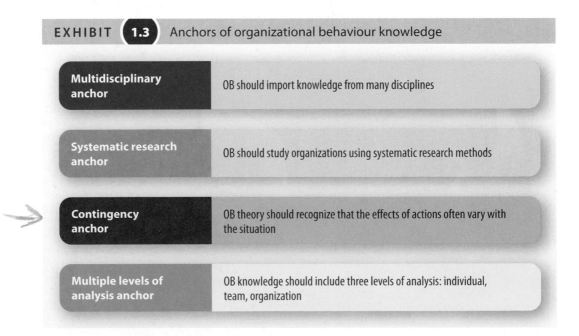

EXHIBIT 1.3 Anchors of organizational behaviour knowledge

Multidisciplinary anchor	OB should import knowledge from many disciplines
Systematic research anchor	OB should study organizations using systematic research methods
Contingency anchor	OB theory should recognize that the effects of actions often vary with the situation
Multiple levels of analysis anchor	OB knowledge should include three levels of analysis: individual, team, organization

at how often corporate leaders embrace fads, consulting models, and their own pet beliefs without bothering to find out if they actually work![74]

There are many reasons why people have difficulty applying evidence-based management. Leaders and other decision makers are bombarded with so many ideas from newspapers, books, consultant reports, and other sources that it is a challenge to figure out which ones are based on good evidence. Another problem is that good OB research is necessarily generic; it is rarely described in the context of a specific problem in a specific organization. Managers therefore have the difficult task of figuring out which theories are relevant to their unique situation. A third problem is that many consultants and popular book writers are rewarded for marketing their concepts and theories, not for testing to see if they actually work. Indeed, some management concepts have become popular—they are even found in some OB textbooks!—because of heavy marketing, not because of any evidence that they are valid. Finally, as we will learn in Chapter 3, people form perceptions and beliefs quickly and tend to ignore evidence that their beliefs are inaccurate.

THE CONTINGENCY ANCHOR

People and their work environments are complex, and the field of organizational behaviour recognizes this by stating that a particular action may have different consequences in different situations. In other words, no single solution is best in all circumstances.[75] Of course, it would be so much simpler if we could rely on 'one best way' theories, in which a particular concept or practice has the same results in every situation. OB experts do search for simpler theories, but they also remain skeptical about 'sure fire' recommendations, an exception is somewhere around the corner. Thus, when faced with a particular problem or opportunity, we need to understand and diagnose the situation and select the strategy most appropriate *under those conditions*.[76]

THE MULTIPLE LEVELS OF ANALYSIS ANCHOR

This textbook divides organizational behaviour topics into three levels of analysis: individual, team, and organization. The individual level includes the characteristics and behaviours of employees as well as the thought processes that are attributed to them, such as motivation, perceptions, personalities, attitudes, and values. The team level of analysis looks at the way people interact. This includes team dynamics, decisions, power, organizational politics, conflict, and leadership. At the organizational level, we focus on how people structure their working relationships and on how organizations interact with their environments.

Although an OB topic is typically pegged into one level of analysis, it usually relates to multiple levels.[77] For instance, communication is located in this book as a team (interpersonal) process, but we also recognize that it includes individual and organizational processes. Therefore, you should try to think about each OB topic at the individual, team, and organizational levels, not just at one of these levels.

CHAPTER SUMMARY

Organizational behaviour is the study of what people think, feel, and do in and around organizations. Organizations are groups of people who work interdependently toward some purpose. Although OB doesn't have a specific career path, it offers knowledge and skills that are vitally important to anyone who works in organizations. OB knowledge also has a significant effect on the success of organizations. This book takes the view that OB is for everyone, not just managers.

Organizational effectiveness is a multi-dimensional concept represented by four perspectives: open systems, organizational learning, high-performance work practices, and stakeholders. The open systems perspective says that organizations need to adapt to their external environment and configure their internal subsystems to maximize efficiency and responsiveness. For the most part, the other perspectives of organizational effectiveness are detailed extensions of the open systems model. The organizational learning perspective states that organizational effectiveness depends on the organization's capacity to acquire, share, use, and store valuable knowledge. Intellectual capital is knowledge that resides in an organization, including its human capital, structural capital, and relationship capital. Effective organizations also "unlearn," meaning that they remove knowledge that no longer adds value.

The high performance work practices (HPWP) perspective states that effective organizations leverage the human capital potential of their employees. Specific HPWPs have been identified, and experts in this field suggest that they need to be bundled together for maximum benefit. The stakeholder perspective states that effective organizations take into account how their actions affect others, which requires them to understand, manage, and satisfy the interests of their stakeholders. This perspective incorporates values, ethics, and corporate social responsibility into the organizational effectiveness equation.

The five main types of workplace behaviour are task performance, organizational citizenship, counterproductive work behaviours, joining and staying with the organization, and work attendance. These represent the individual-level dependent variables found in most OB research.

Three environmental shifts that are challenging organizations include globalization, increasing workforce diversity, and emerging employment relationships. Globalization refers to economic, social, and cultural connectivity with people in other parts of the world. Workforce diversity includes both surface-level and deep-level diversity. Two emerging employment relationship changes are demands for work/life balance and virtual work.

Several conceptual anchors represent the principles on which OB knowledge is developed and refined. These anchors include beliefs that OB knowledge should be multidisciplinary and based on systematic research, that organizational events usually have contingencies, and that organizational behaviour can be viewed from three levels of analysis (individual, team, and organization).

KEY TERMS

corporate social responsibility (CSR), p. 10

counterproductive work behaviours, (CWBs), p. 12

deep-level diversity, p. 14

ethics, p. 10

globalization, p. 13

high performance work practices (HPWP), p. 7

intellectual capital, p. 6

open systems, p. 4

organizational behaviour (OB), p. 2

organizational citizenship behaviours (OCBs), p. 11

organizational effectiveness, p. 4

organizational efficiency, p. 5

organizational learning, p. 6

organizational memory, p. 6

organizations, p. 2

stakeholders, p. 8

surface-level diversity, p. 14

values, p. 9

virtual work, p. 15

work/life balance, p. 15

CRITICAL THINKING QUESTIONS

1. A friend suggests that organizational behaviour courses are useful only to people who will enter management careers. Discuss the accuracy of your friend's statement.

2. A number of years ago, employees in a city water distribution department were put into teams and encouraged to find ways to improve efficiency. The teams boldly crossed departmental boundaries and areas of management discretion in search of problems. Employees working in other parts of the city began to complain about these intrusions. Moreover, when some team ideas were implemented, the city managers discovered that a dollar saved in the water distribution unit may have cost the organization two dollars in higher costs elsewhere. Use the open systems perspective to explain what happened here.

3. After hearing a seminar on organizational learning, a mining company executive argues that this perspective ignores the fact that mining companies could not rely on knowledge alone to stay in business. They also need physical capital (such as digging and ore processing equipment) and land (where the minerals are located). In fact, these two may be more important than what employees carry around in their heads. Evaluate the mining executive's comments.

4. A common refrain among executives is "People are our most important asset." Relate this statement to any two of the four perspectives of organizational effectiveness presented in this chapter. Does this statement apply better to some perspectives than to others? Why or why not?

5. Corporate social responsibility is one of the hottest issues in corporate boardrooms these days, partly because it is becoming increasingly important to employees and other stakeholders. In your opinion, why have stakeholders given CSR more attention recently? Does abiding by CSR standards potentially cause companies to have conflicting objectives with some stakeholders in some situations?

6. Look through the list of chapters in this textbook and discuss how globalization could influence each organizational behaviour topic.

7. "Organizational theories should follow the contingency approach." Comment on the accuracy of this statement.

8. What does "evidence-based management" mean? Describe situations where you have heard about companies practising evidence-based management, as well as situations where companies have relied on fads that lacked sufficient evidence of their worth.

CASE STUDY 1.1

Pixar Magic

One of Robert Iger's first tasks as Walt Disney Co.'s new CEO was to acquire Pixar Animation Studios and put its leaders in charge of Disney's own animation unit, Walt Disney Animation Studios. The studio that brought us *Mickey Mouse* and *The Lion King* had become moribund over the past decade, eclipsed by the successes of Pixar and other competitors. Iger didn't spend $7.4 billion to acquire Pixar's library of award-winning feature films. Disney already had lucrative distribution rights to Pixar's first five films, including any sequels to those films. What Iger wanted from Pixar was far more valuable—the organizational behaviour practices that helped Pixar generate a continuous string of blockbuster films, from *Toy Story* to *Ratatouille*.

For the past two decades, Pixar has relied on several principles that built it into a powerhouse in the film industry. Pixar's first principle is that successful companies consist of people with diverse and valued skill sets who effectively coordinate and collaborate with each other. "From the very beginning, we recognized we had to get the best people, technically, from the computer science world, and from the artistic filmmaking animation world, and get them working together," explains John Lasseter, chief creative officer at Pixar (and now Disney). "That, right there, is probably the secret to Pixar."

Pixar's second principle is to strengthen this coordination/collaboration model through long-term employment, rather than short-term project-based contracts that dominate other studios. "The problem with the Hollywood model is that it's generally the day you wrap production that you realize you've finally figured out how to work together," says Randy Nelson, head of Pixar University. "We've made the leap from an idea-centred business to a people-centred business."

Pixar's third principle, which is related to the first two, is teamwork. Pixar's campus in Emeryville, Calif. was specifically designed to cluster people into teams. At the same time, to encourage cross-fertilization of ideas, the building also creates chance encounters with people from other projects. "You run into people constantly," says Lasseter from a second floor balcony as he waves to a co-worker in the atrium below. "It worked from the minute we arrived. We just blossomed here!"

Compared to most other companies of similar size (Pixar employs around 1,000 employees) and stature, Pixar has an egalitarian no-nonsense culture where people are encouraged to speak honestly about the quality of the work in progress. Quality is a particularly important word around Pixar, representing the company's first priority when making films. This unique culture is supported by the leadership of John Lasseter as well as Edwin Catmull, Pixar's co-founder and president of both Pixar and Disney Animation Studios. "Ed, more than anyone else, provided that leadership to create this very unique Pixar culture," says Pixar CEO Steven Jobs.

Discussion Questions

1. Identify the organizational behaviour topics that Pixar Animation Studios relies on to build its success.

2. What perspective of organizational effectiveness seems to best explain the success of Pixar Animation Studios?

3. Do you think Pixar's leaders will be able to transform Disney Animation Studios? Why or why not?

Sources: G. Whipp, "Swimming Against the Tide," *Daily News of Los Angeles*, May 30, 2003, p. U6; "The Pixar Principle," *The Age (Melbourne, AU)*, May 28, 2006; D. F. Locke, J. Ressner, and R. Corliss, "When Woody Met Mickey," *Time*, February 6, 2006, p. 46; W. C. Taylor and P. LaBarre, "How Pixar Adds a New School of Thought to Disney," *New York Times*, January 29, 2006; N. Wingfield and M. Marr, "A Techie's Task," *Wall Street Journal*, January 30, 2006, p. B7; R. Grover, "How Bob Iger Unchained Disney," *BusinessWeek*, February 5, 2007, p. 74.

TEAM EXERCISE 1.2

Human Checkers

Purpose   This exercise is designed to help students understand the importance and application of organizational behaviour concepts.

Materials   None, but the instructor has more information about the team's task.

Instructions

- *Step 1*: Form teams with eight students. If possible, each team should have a private location where team members can plan and practise the required task without being observed or heard by other teams.

- *Step 2*: All teams will receive special instructions in class about the team's assigned task. All teams have the same task and will have the same amount of time to plan and practise the task. At the end of this planning and practice, each team will be timed while completing the task in class. The team that completes the task in the least time wins.

- *Step 3*: No special materials are required or allowed (see rules below) for this exercise. Although the task is not described here, students should learn the following rules for planning and implementing the task:

  Rule #1:   You cannot use any written form of communication or any props to assist in the planning or implementation of this task.

  Rule #2:   You may speak to other students in your team at any time during the planning and implementation of this task.

  Rule #3:   When performing the task, you can only move forward, not backward. (You are not allowed to turn around.)

  Rule #4:   When performing the task, you can move forward to the next space, but only if it is vacant. In Exhibit 1, the individual (black dot) can move directly into an empty space (white dot).

  Rule #5:   When performing the task, you can move forward two spaces, if that space is vacant. In other words, you can move around a person who is one space in front of you to the next space if that space is vacant. (In Exhibit 2, two people occupy the black dots and the white dot is an empty space. A person can move around the person in front to the empty space.)

Exhibit 1   **Exhibit 2**

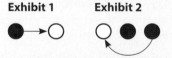

- *Step 4*: When all teams have completed their task, the class will discuss the implications of this exercise for organizational behaviour.

Discussion Questions

1. Identify organizational behaviour concepts that the team applied to complete this task.

2. What personal theories of people and work teams were applied to complete this task?

3. What organizational behaviour problems occurred and what actions were (or should have been) taken to solve them?

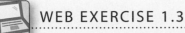 WEB EXERCISE 1.3

Diagnosing Organizational Stakeholders

Purpose   This exercise is designed to help you understand how stakeholders influence organizations as part of the open systems anchor.

Materials   Students need to select a company and, prior to class, retrieve and analyze publicly available information over the past year or two about that company. This may include annual reports, which are usually found on the websites of publicly traded companies. Where possible, students should also scan full-text newspaper and magazine databases for articles published over the previous year about the company.

Instructions   The instructor may have students work alone or in groups for this activity. Students will select a company and will investigate the relevance and influence of various stakeholder groups on the organization. Stakeholders will be identified from annual reports, newspaper articles, website statements, and other available sources. Stakeholders should be rank ordered in terms of their perceived importance to the organization.

  Students should be prepared to present or discuss their organization's rank ordering of stakeholders, including evidence for this rank ordering.

Discussion Questions   1. What are the main reasons why certain stakeholders are more important than others for this organization?

2. Based on your knowledge of the organization's environmental situation, is this rank order of stakeholders in the organization's best interest, or should specific other stakeholders be given higher priority?

3. What societal groups, if any, are not mentioned as stakeholders by the organization? Does this lack of reference to these unmentioned groups make sense?

www.mcgrawhill.ca/olc/mcshane

SELF-ASSESSMENT EXERCISE 1.4

It All Makes Sense?

Purpose   This exercise is designed to help you understand how organizational behaviour knowledge can help you to understand life in organizations.

Instructions   (Note: This activity may be done as a self-assessment or as a team activity.) Read each of the statements below and circle whether each statement is true or false, in your opinion. The class will consider the answers to each question and discuss the implications for studying organizational behaviour.

Due to the nature of this activity, the instructor will provide the answers to these questions. There is no scoring key in Appendix B.

1.	True	False	A happy worker is a productive worker.
2.	True	False	Decision makers tend to continue supporting a course of action even though information suggests that the decision is ineffective.
3.	True	False	Organizations are more effective when they prevent conflict among employees.
4.	True	False	It is better to negotiate alone than as a team.
5.	True	False	Companies are more successful with strong corporate cultures.
6.	True	False	Employees perform better without stress.
7.	True	False	The best way to change people and organizations is by pinpointing the source of their current problems.
8.	True	False	Female leaders involve employees in decisions to a greater degree than do male leaders.
9.	True	False	The best decisions are made without emotion.
10.	True	False	If employees feel they are paid unfairly, then nothing other than changing their pay will reduce their feelings of injustice.

Online Learning Centre   Go to the Online Learning Centre at www.mcgrawhill.ca/olc/mcshane to complete the following interactive self-assessment.

SELF-ASSESSMENT EXERCISE 1.5

Is Telework for You?

Some employees adapt better than others to telework (also called telecommuting) and other forms of virtual work. This self-assessment measures personal characteristics that seem to relate to telecommuting, and therefore provides a rough indication of how well you would adapt to telework. The instrument asks you to indicate how much you agree or disagree with each of the statements provided. You need to be honest with yourself to obtain a reasonable estimate of your telework disposition. Please keep in mind that this scale only considers your personal characteristics. Other factors, such as support from the organization, family, and technology must also be taken into account.

PART ONE VIDEO CASE STUDIES

Case 1   Johnson & Johnson: (a) Creating a Global Learning Organization: The Credo; (b) Management Fundamentals Training at Johnson & Johnson

Johnson & Johnson (J&J) is a family-oriented health care and personal products company with about 330 operating units and more than 150,000 employees around the world. The company is well known for "the Credo," a set of values statements introduced in 1938 to help J&J's executives and employees make better decisions. The Credo helps J&J staff to continuously be aware of and serve the needs of its core stakeholders. It also serves as the glue that holds the company's geographically and industrially diverse operating units together. This program introduces Johnson & Johnson's Credo and shows how the company instills those values in its managers.

Discussion Questions

1. Why does Johnson & Johnson place so much importance on the Credo?
2. How does Johnson & Johnson ensure that managers understand and apply the Credo in their daily decisions and actions?

Case 2   Good Business Deeds

You might not expect to see British American Tobacco, McDonald's, and Microsoft at a meeting on corporate social responsibility, but in their own way these firms are taking steps to become better employers and citizens in the community. This video program describes how these and other firms are embracing values and corporate social responsibility. It particularly highlights a few firms that serve as role models in this regard. One of these is Greyston Bakery, a multimillion dollar gourmet operation that takes people who need help and turns them into contributing members of the organization and society. Another is Eileen Fisher Company, which promotes good labour practices both at home and overseas, and helps customers meet their needs. In each case, the company's values are aligned more closely with employee values than at your typical organization.

Discussion Questions

1. Employees at Greyston Bakery, Eileen Fisher Company, Feed the Children, Green@ Work, and other organizations described in this video program seem to have a strong congruence of their personal values with the organization's values. What are the apparent benefits of this values congruence?
2. Discuss the implications of corporate social responsibility in terms of organizational effectiveness.

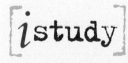

iInteract iLearn iSucceed

iStudy Available 24/7 with instant feedback so you can study when you want, how you want, and where you want. Visit www.istudyob.ca to register—take practice quizzes, run interactive scenarios, practice concepts, and much more. Also visit the Student Online Learning Centre for additional study tools.

Individual Behaviour, Personality, and Values

Yasmeen Youssef's self-confidence was a bit shaky when she and her husband moved from Egypt to Canada a few years ago. "I was worried no one would take a chance on me, would believe in me," she recalls. But any self-doubts slowly disappeared after taking an entry-level job with Fairmont Hotels & Resorts corporate offices in Toronto. "Everything changed when I started working at Fairmont," says Youssef, who is now on Fairmont's human resources team and recently trained new staff in Cairo. "I can't believe the amount of value, care, respect everyone has extended to me."

As North America's largest luxury hotel operator, Fairmont discovered long ago that one of the secret ingredients to employee performance and well-being is supporting the individual's self-concept. "People want to feel valued and they stay where they feel valued," says Carolyn Clark, Fairmont's senior vice-president of human resources. Clark also points out that Fairmont is able to nurture this talent by selecting the best, which means hiring people with the right values and personality for superb customer service. "We believed that we could train the technical skills—that's the easy part," Clark explained a few years ago. "What we can't train is the service orientation. We just can't put people in the training program and say they are going to come out smiling if that is not inherent in them."

Along with hiring people with the right values and personality and nurturing their self-concept, Fairmont is developing staff to work effectively in a multi-cultural world. Sean Billing is a case in point. The University of Western Ontario economics graduate had been working as Fairmont's director of rooms in Chicago when he casually asked his boss whether the hotel chain could use his skills and knowledge elsewhere. Soon after, Billing was offered a position in Kenya, bringing Fairmont's new properties in the African country up to world-class standards through training and technology without losing the distinctive Kenyan character. Billing jumped at the opportunity, but also recognized the challenge of instilling Fairmont's deep values of customer service, environmentalism, and empowerment in another culture. "It's a little bit of hotel culture shock . . . things are quite different here," he says.[1]

Fairmont Hotels has excelled as North America's largest luxury hotel operator by hiring people such as Yasmeen Youssef (shown here) with the right values and personality, and then nurturing their self-concept and cross-cultural competencies.
© National Post/Nathan Denette

What makes Fairmont Hotels & Resorts a successful company? There is no single explanation, but this opening vignette reveals that the Toronto-based company applies many of the theories and practices discussed in this chapter. It hires people with the right personality traits and values, trains them well, and nurtures their self-concept. Fairmont has become such a global enterprise that it also develops cross-cultural competencies in many staff.

This chapter concentrates our attention on the role of the individual in organizations. We begin by presenting the MARS model, which outlines the four direct drivers of individual behaviour and results. Next, we introduce the most stable aspect of individuals—personality—including where our personality comes from, various personality traits, and how personality relates to organizational behaviour. Our attention then turns to the individual's self-concept, including self-enhancement, self-verification, self-evaluation, and social identity. The latter part of this chapter examines another relatively stable characteristic of individuals: their personal values. We look at type of values, issues of values congruence in organizations, cross-cultural values, and ethical values and practices.

MARS MODEL OF INDIVIDUAL BEHAVIOUR AND PERFORMANCE

LO1

For most of the past century, experts in psychology, sociology, and more recently organizational behaviour have investigated the direct predictors of individual behaviour and performance.[2] One of the earliest formulas was *"performance = person × situation,"* where *person* includes individual characteristics, and *situation* represents external influences on the individual's behaviour. Another frequently mentioned formula is *"performance = ability × motivation."* Sometimes known as the "skill and will" model, this formula highlights two specific characteristics within the person that influence individual performance. Ability, motivation, and situation are by far the most commonly mentioned direct predictors of individual behaviour and performance, but in the 1960s researchers identified role perceptions as a fourth key factor.[3]

Exhibit 2.1 illustrates these four variables that directly influence voluntary individual behaviour and performance: motivation, ability, role perceptions, and situational factors. These four predictors are easily remembered by the acronym "MARS."[4] All four are important, so behaviour and performance would be low when any one of them is low. For example, enthusiastic salespeople (motivation) who understand their job duties (role perceptions) and have sufficient resources (situational factors) will not perform their jobs as well if they lack sufficient knowledge and sales skill (ability). Let's look at each of these four factors in more detail.

EMPLOYEE MOTIVATION

motivation
The forces within a person that affect his or her direction, intensity, and persistence of voluntary behaviour.

Motivation represents the forces within a person that affect his or her direction, intensity, and persistence of voluntary behaviour.[5] *Direction* refers to the path along which people engage their effort. This sense of direction of effort reflects the fact that people have choices about where they put their effort. In other words, motivation is goal-directed, not random. People are motivated to arrive at work on time, make a high quality product, or aim for many other targets. The second element of motivation, called *intensity*, is the amount of effort allocated to the goal. Intensity is all about how much you push yourself to complete the task. For example, two employees might be motivated to finish their project a few hours early (direction), but only one of them puts forth enough effort (intensity) to achieve this goal.

Finally, motivation involves varying levels of *persistence*, that is, continuing the effort for a certain amount of time. Employees sustain their effort until they reach their goal or give up beforehand. To help remember these three elements of motivation, consider the metaphor of driving a car in which the thrust of the engine is your effort. Direction refers to where you steer the car, intensity is how much you put your foot down on the gas pedal, and persistence is for how long you drive towards that destination.

EXHIBIT 2.1   MARS model of individual behaviour and results

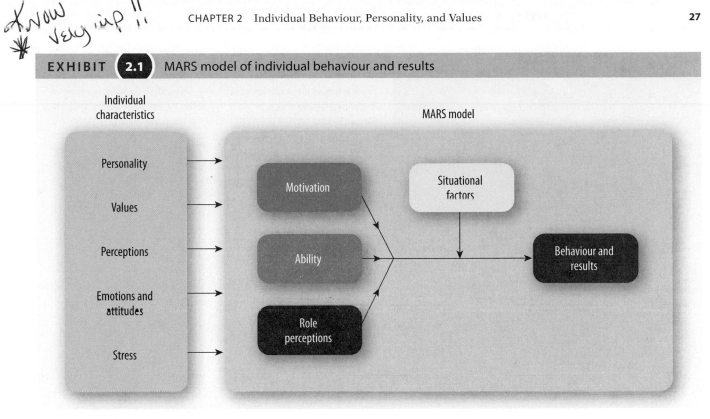

ABILITY

ability
The natural aptitudes and learned capabilities required to successfully complete a task.

Employee abilities also make a difference in behaviour and task performance. **Ability** includes both the natural aptitudes and learned capabilities required to successfully complete a task. *Aptitudes* are the natural talents that help employees learn specific tasks more quickly and perform them better. For example, some people have a higher natural ability than others to manipulate small objects with their fingers (called finger dexterity). There are many different physical and mental aptitudes, and our ability to acquire skills is affected by these aptitudes. *Learned capabilities* refer to the skills and knowledge that you have actually acquired. These include the physical and mental skills you possess as well as the knowledge you acquire and store for later use.

competencies
Skills, knowledge, aptitudes, and other personal characteristics that lead to superior performance.

Skills, knowledge, aptitudes, and other personal characteristics that lead to superior performance are bunched together into the concept of **competencies.** The challenge is to match a person's competencies with what each job requires. One strategy is to select applicants whose existing competencies best fit the required tasks. This includes comparing each applicant's competencies with the requirements of the job or work unit. A second approach is to provide training so employees develop required skills and knowledge. Recent evidence suggests that training has a strong influence on organizational performance.[6] The third way to match people with job requirements is to redesign the job so employees are given tasks only within their capabilities.

ROLE PERCEPTIONS

role perceptions
The accuracy of how people understand their job duties (roles) assigned to them or expected of them.

Motivation and ability are important influences on individual behaviour and performance, but employees also require accurate **role perceptions** to perform their job well. Role perceptions refer to how accurately people understand the job duties (roles) assigned to them or otherwise expected of them. Unfortunately, many employees do not have clear role perceptions. According to one large-scale survey, most Canadian employees understand their organization's business goals, but only 39 percent know what to do in their own jobs to achieve those business goals.[7]

There are three components of role perceptions. First, employees have accurate role perceptions when they understand the specific tasks assigned to them, meaning that they know the specific duties or consequences for which they are accountable. This

Training the Toyota Way

Poised to become the world's largest automaker, Toyota Motor Company is ramping up its training programs around the world to maintain the company's quality standards. Toyota's training methods make extensive use of visual and cognitive aptitudes that require considerable practice and coaching. For example, trainees learn how to spot defects on metal sheet panels where most of us would see none. They also develop visual gap measuring, such as determining how well the edge of the engine hood lines up with the adjacent part of the front grill. This photo shows Toyota production employee Ray Howley (right) from South Africa learning from master trainer Kazuo Hyodo how to tighten bolts so they are snug without being too tight.[8] *AP Images/The Canadian Press (Shizuo Kambayashi)*

may seem obvious, but Canadian employees have been fired (wrongfully) for failing to perform tasks that they didn't even know were part of their job duties! Second, people have accurate role perceptions when they understand the priority of their various tasks and performance expectations. This would include the quantity versus quality dilemma, such as how many customers to serve in an hour (quantity) versus how well you should serve each customer (quality). It also refers to properly allocating time and resources to various tasks, such as how much time a manager should spend coaching employees in a typical week. The third component of role perceptions is understanding the preferred behaviours to accomplish the assigned tasks. This refers to situations where more than one method could be followed to perform the work. Employees with clear role perceptions know which of these methods is preferred by the organization.

SITUATIONAL FACTORS

Employee behaviour and performance also depends on how well the situation supports their task goals. Situational factors include conditions beyond the employee's immediate control that constrain or facilitate behaviour and performance.[9] Some situational characteristics—such as consumer preferences and economic conditions—originate from the external environment and, consequently, are beyond the employee's and organization's control. However, other situational factors—such as time, people, budget, and physical work facilities—are controlled by people within the organization. Therefore, corporate leaders need to carefully arrange these conditions so employees can achieve their performance potential.

Motivation, ability, role perceptions, and situational factors affect all voluntary workplace behaviours and their performance outcomes. In the remainder of this chapter, we introduce the most stable characteristics of individuals that influence their motivation, ability, and role perceptions.

PERSONALITY IN ORGANIZATIONS

Brigitte Catellier's final hurdle to become vice-president of legal affairs at Astral Media Inc. wasn't what she anticipated. For seven hours, Catellier sat through eight aptitude, preferences, and personality tests, some of which asked unusual questions such as whether she would prefer to be an astronaut or an acrobat. "I was told very directly there are two candidates and you are both doing the same tests," says Catellier, who was later offered the job at the Montreal-based media giant. Astral decided a few years ago to include psychological tests in the hiring process, including instruments that measure several personality traits. "This helps us not make mistakes—and we *have* made mistakes from time to time in the past," says Astral's vice-president of human resources, referring to people hired whose personality didn't fit the company or job requirements.[10]

Personality is an important individual characteristic, which explains why Astral Media and many other companies are keen to understand the personality traits of job applicants and employees. **Personality** refers to the relatively enduring pattern of thoughts, emotions, and behaviours that characterize a person, along with the psychological processes behind those characteristics[11] It is, in essence, the bundle of characteristics that make us similar to or different from other people. We estimate an individual's personality in terms of what he or she says and does, and infer the person's internal states—including thoughts and emotions—from these observable behaviours.

> **personality**
> The relatively enduring pattern of thoughts, emotions, and behaviours that characterize a person, along with the psychological processes behind those characteristics.

A basic premise of personality theory is that people have inherent characteristics or traits that can be identified by the consistency or stability of their behaviour across time and situations.[12] For example, you probably have some friends who are more talkative than others. You might know some people who like to take chances and others who avoid taking risks. This consistency is an essential requirement for personality theory because it attributes a person's behaviour to something within them—their personality—rather than to purely environmental influences.

Of course, people do not act the same way in all situations; in fact, such consistency would be considered abnormal because it suggests insensitivity to social norms, reward systems, and other external conditions.[13] People vary their behaviour to suit the situation, even if it is at odds with their personality. For example, talkative people remain relatively quiet in a library where "no talking" rules are explicit and strictly enforced. People typically exhibit a wide range of behaviours, yet out of that variety are discernable patterns that we refer to as personality traits. Furthermore, these stable traits predict behaviour far into the future. For example, studies report that an individual's personality in childhood predicts various behaviours and outcomes in adulthood, including educational attainment, employment success, marital relationships, illegal activities, and health-risk behaviours.[14]

PERSONALITY DETERMINANTS: NATURE VERSUS NURTURE

What determines an individual's personality? Most experts now agree that personality is shaped by both nature and nurture, although the relative importance of each continues to be debated and studied. "Nature" refers to our genetic or hereditary origins—the genes that we inherit from our parents. Studies of identical twins, particularly those separated at birth, reveal that heredity has a very large effect on personality; up to 50 percent of variation in behaviour and 30 percent of temperament preferences can be attributed to a person's genetic characteristics.[15] In other words, genetic code not only determines our eye colour, skin tone, and physical shape; it also has a significant effect on our attitudes, decisions, and behaviour.

Some similarities of twins raised apart are surreal. Consider Jim Springer and Jim Lewis, twins who were separated when only four weeks old and didn't meet each other until age 39. In spite of being raised in different families and communities in Ohio, the "Jim twins" held similar jobs, smoked the same type of cigarettes, drove the same make and colour of car, spent their vacations on the same Florida beach, had the same woodworking hobby, gave their first sons almost identical names, and had been married twice. Both their first and second wives also had the same first names![16]

Although personality is heavily influenced by heredity, it is also affected to some degree by "nurture"—the person's socialization, life experiences, and other forms of interaction with the environment. Studies have found that the stability of an individual's personality increases up to at least age 30 and possibly to age 50, indicating that some personality development and change occurs when people are young.[17] The main explanation why personality becomes more stable over time is that people form clearer and more rigid self-concepts as they get older. The executive function—the part of the brain that manages goal-directed behaviour—tries to keep our behaviour consistent with our self-concept.[18] As self-concept becomes clearer and more stable with age, behaviour and personality therefore also become more stable. We will discuss self-concept in more detail later in this chapter. The main point here is that personality is not completely determined by heredity; life experiences, particularly early in life, also shape each individual's personality traits.

LO3

FIVE-FACTOR MODEL OF PERSONALITY

five-factor model (FFM)
The five abstract dimensions representing most personality traits: conscientiousness, emotional stability, openness to experience, agreeableness, and extroversion.

One of the most important elements of personality theory is that people possess specific personality traits. Traits are broad concepts that help us to label and understand individual differences. Traits such as sociable, depressed, cautious, and talkative represent clusters of thoughts, feelings, and behaviours that allow us to identify, differentiate, and understand people.[19] The most widely respected model of personality traits is the **five-factor model**. Several decades ago, personality experts identified more than 17,000 words in *Roget's Thesaurus* and *Webster's Dictionary* that describe an individual's personality. These words were aggregated into 171 clusters, then further reduced to five abstract personality dimensions. Using more sophisticated techniques, recent investigations identified the same five personality dimensions.[20] These "Big Five" dimensions, represented by the handy acronym CANOE, are outlined in Exhibit 2.2 and described below:

conscientiousness
A personality dimension describing people who are careful, dependable, and self-disciplined.

- *Conscientiousness*—**Conscientiousness** refers to people who are careful, dependable, and self-disciplined. Some scholars argue that this dimension also includes the will to achieve. People with low conscientiousness tend to be careless, less thorough, more disorganized, and irresponsible.

- *Agreeableness*—This includes the traits of being courteous, good-natured, empathic, and caring. Some scholars prefer the label of "friendly compliance" for this dimension, with its opposite being "hostile noncompliance." People with low agreeableness tend to be uncooperative, short-tempered, and irritable.

neuroticism
A personality dimension describing people with high levels of anxiety, hostility, depression, and self-consciousness.

- *Neuroticism*—**Neuroticism** characterizes people with high levels of anxiety, hostility, depression, and self-consciousness. In contrast, people with low neuroticism (high emotional stability) are poised, secure, and calm.

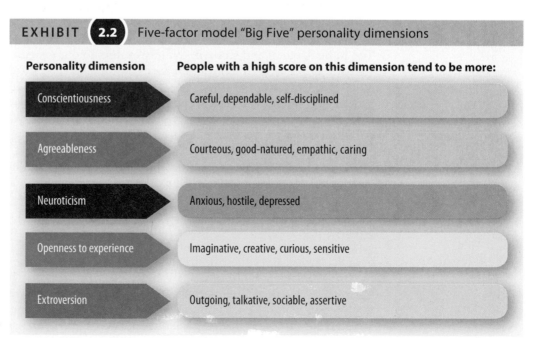

EXHIBIT 2.2   Five-factor model "Big Five" personality dimensions

Personality dimension	People with a high score on this dimension tend to be more:
Conscientiousness	Careful, dependable, self-disciplined
Agreeableness	Courteous, good-natured, empathic, caring
Neuroticism	Anxious, hostile, depressed
Openness to experience	Imaginative, creative, curious, sensitive
Extroversion	Outgoing, talkative, sociable, assertive

- *Openness to experience*—This dimension is the most complex and has the least agreement among scholars. It generally refers to the extent to which people are imaginative, creative, curious, and aesthetically sensitive. Those who score low on this dimension tend to be more resistant to change, less open to new ideas, and more conventional and fixed in their ways.

> **extroversion**
> A personality dimension describing people who are outgoing, talkative, sociable, and assertive.

- *Extroversion*—**Extroversion** characterizes people who are outgoing, talkative, sociable, and assertive. The opposite is introversion, which refers to those who are quiet, shy, and cautious. Extroverts get their energy from the outer world (people and things around them), whereas introverts get their energy from the internal world, such as personal reflection on concepts and ideas. Introverts do not necessarily lack social skills. Rather, they are more inclined to direct their interests to ideas than to social events. Introverts feel quite comfortable being alone, whereas extroverts do not.

These five personality dimensions are not independent of each other. Conscientiousness, agreeableness, and low neuroticism (high emotional stability) represent a common underlying characteristic broadly described as "getting along"; people with these traits are aware of and more likely to abide by rules and norms of society. The other two dimensions share the common underlying factor called "getting ahead"; people with high scores on extroversion and openness to experience exhibit more behaviours aimed at achieving goals, managing their environment, and advancing themselves in teams.[21]

Five Factor Personality Dimensions and Organizational Behaviour   Studies report fairly strong associations between personality and a variety of workplace behaviours and outcomes, even when employee ability and other factors are taken into account. Conscientiousness and emotional stability (low neuroticism) stand out as the personality traits that best predict individual performance in almost every job group.[22] Both are motivational components of personality because they energize a willingness to fulfill work obligations within established rules (conscientiousness) and to allocate resources to accomplish those tasks (emotional stability). Various studies have reported that conscientious employees set higher personal goals for themselves, are more motivated, and have higher performance expectations than do employees with low levels of conscientiousness. They also tend to have higher levels of organizational citizenship and work better in organizations that give employees more freedom than in traditional "command and control" workplaces.[23]

The other three personality dimensions predict more specific types of employee behaviour and performance. Extroversion is associated with performance in sales and management jobs, where employees must interact with and influence people. Agreeableness is associated with performance in jobs where employees are expected to be cooperative and helpful, such as working in teams, customer relations, and other conflict-handling situations. People high on the openness to experience personality dimension tend to be more creative and adaptable to change. Finally, personality influences employee well-being in various ways. Studies report that personality influences a person's emotional reactions to their job, how well they cope with stress, and what type of career paths make them happiest.[24]

JUNGIAN PERSONALITY THEORY AND MYERS-BRIGGS TYPE INDICATOR

> **Myers-Briggs Type Indicator (MBTI)**
> A personality test that measures each of the traits in Jung's model.

Although the five-factor model of personality is the most respected and supported in research, it is not the most popular in practice. That distinction goes to Jungian personality theory, which is measured through the **Myers-Briggs Type Indicator (MBTI).** Nearly a century ago, Swiss psychiatrist Carl Jung proposed that personality is primarily represented by the individual's preferences regarding perceiving and judging information.[25] Jung explained that perceiving, which refers to how people prefer to gather information or perceive the world around them, occurs through two competing orientations: *sensing* (S) and *intuition* (N). Sensing involves perceiving information directly through the five senses; it relies on an organized structure to acquire factual and preferably quantitative details. Intuition, on the other hand, relies more on insight and subjective experience to see relationships among variables. Sensing types focus on the here and now, whereas intuitive types focus more on the future possibilities.

Jung also proposed that judging—how people process information or make decisions based on what they have perceived—consists of two competing processes: *thinking* (T) versus *feeling* (F). People with a thinking orientation rely on rational cause-effect logic and systematic data collection to make decisions. Those with a strong feeling orientation, on the other hand, rely on their emotional responses to the options presented, as well as to how those choices affect others. Along with the four core processes of sensing, intuition, thinking, and feeling, Jung noted that people also differ in their degrees of extroversion-introversion, which was introduced earlier as one of the Big Five personality traits.

In addition to the personality traits originally identified by Jung, the MBTI measures Jung's broader categories of *perceiving* and *judging*. People with a perceiving orientation are open, curious, flexible, prefer to adapt spontaneously to events as they unfold, and prefer to keep their options open. Judging types prefer order and structure, and want to resolve problems quickly.

Effectiveness of the MBTI   The MBTI is one of the most widely used personality tests in work settings as well as in career counselling and executive coaching.[26] Still, evidence regarding the effectiveness of the MBTI and Jung's psychological types is mixed.[27] On the one hand, MBTI does a reasonably good job of measuring Jung's psychological types and seems to improve self-awareness for career development and mutual understanding. On the other hand, it poorly predicts job performance and is generally not recommended for employment selection or promotion decisions. Furthermore, MBTI overlaps with the five-factor personality model, yet does so less satisfactorily than existing measures of the Big Five personality dimensions.[28]

SELF-CONCEPT: THE "I" IN ORGANIZATIONAL BEHAVIOUR

LO4

self-concept
An individual's self-beliefs and self-evaluations.

To more fully understand individual behaviour in organizations, we need to realize that people develop, nurture, and act in ways that maintain and enhance their self-concept. **Self-concept** refers to an individual's self-beliefs and self-evaluations. It is the "Who am I?" and "How do I feel about myself?" that people ask themselves and that guide their decisions and actions. Self-concept has not received much attention in organizational behaviour research, but scholars in psychology, social psychology, and other disciplines have discovered that it is a critically important concept for understanding individual perceptions, attitudes, decisions, and behaviour. Indeed, as the opening vignette to this chapter illustrated, managers at Fairmont Hotels & Resorts have known for years that nurturing an employee's self-concept can be a powerful way to strengthen his or her motivation and well-being.

People do not have a single unitary self-concept.[29] Rather, they think of themselves in several ways in various situations. For example, you might think of yourself as a creative employee, a health-conscious vegetarian, and an aggressive skier. A person's self-concept has higher complexity when it consists of many categories. Along with complexity, self-concept varies in the degree of its consistency. People have high consistency when similar personality traits and values are required across all aspects of self-concept. Low consistency occurs when some aspects of self require personal characteristics that conflict with the characteristics required for other aspects of self. A third structural feature of self-concept is clarity; that is, the degree to which a person's self-conceptions are clearly and confidently described, internally consistent, and stable across time. A clear self-concept necessarily requires a consistent self-concept. Generally, people develop a clearer self-concept as they get older.

These three structural dimensions of self-concept—complexity, consistency, and clarity—influence our adaptability and well-being. People function better when their self-concept has many elements (high complexity) that are compatible with each other (high consistency) and relatively clear. In contrast, people are more rigid and inflexible, and therefore less adaptable, when they view themselves in terms of only a few similar characteristics (low complexity). People also have poorer psychological adjustment when their self-concept is less clear and includes conflicting elements.

SELF-ENHANCEMENT AND SELF-VERIFICATION

A key ingredient in a person's self-concept is their desire to feel valued. We are inherently motivated to promote and protect a self-view of being competent, attractive, lucky, ethical, valued, and so forth.[30] This *self-enhancement* is observed in many ways. People tend to rate themselves above average, selectively recall positive feedback while forgetting negative feedback, attribute their successes to personal motivation or ability while blaming the situation for their mistakes, and believe that they have a better than average probability of success. We don't see ourselves as above average in all circumstances, but this bias is apparent for conditions that are common rather than rare and that are important to us.[31]

Self-enhancement has both positive and negative consequences in organizational settings. On the positive side, research has found that individuals have better personal adjustment and experience better mental and physical health when they view their self-concept in a positive light. On the negative side, self-enhancement can result in bad decisions. For example, studies report that self-enhancement causes managers to overestimate the probability of success in investment decisions, such as acquiring another company.[32] Generally, though, successful companies, such as Fairmont Hotels & Resorts, strive to help employees feel valued and an integral member of the organization. As GLOBAL Connections 2.1 describes, this practice is so important at Johnson & Johnson, Inc., that the health and personal care products company makes it part of their credo.

Self-verification Along with self-enhancement, people are motivated to verify and maintain their existing self-concept.[33] *Self-verification* stabilizes our self-concept which, in turn, provides an important anchor to guide our thoughts and actions. Self-verification differs from self-enhancement because people will usually prefer feedback that is consistent with their self-concept even when that feedback is unflattering. Self-verification has several implications for organizational behaviour.[34] First, it affects the perceptual process because employees are more likely to remember information that is consistent with their self-concept. Second, the more confident employees are in their self-concept, the less they will accept feedback—positive or negative—that is at odds with their self-concept. Finally, employees are motivated to interact with others who affirm their self-concept, which affects how well they get along with their boss and with co-workers in teams.

SELF-EVALUATION

Almost everyone strives to have a positive self-concept, but some people have a more positive evaluation of themselves than do others. This self-evaluation is mostly defined in terms of three concepts: self-esteem, self-efficacy, and locus of control.[35]

Self-esteem *Self-esteem* is a fundamental component of self-concept because it represents a global self-evaluation; that is, the extent to which people like, respect, and are satisfied with themselves. People with a high self-esteem are less influenced by others, tend to be persistent in spite of failure, and think more rationally. Self-esteem regarding specific aspects of self (e.g., a good student, a good driver, a good parent) predicts specific thoughts and behaviours, whereas a person's overall self-esteem predicts only large bundles of thoughts and behaviours.[36]

self-efficacy
A person's belief that he or she has the ability, motivation, correct role perceptions, and favourable situation to complete a task successfully.

Self-efficacy **Self-efficacy** refers to a person's belief that he or she has the ability, motivation, correct role perceptions, and favourable situation to complete a task

global connections 2.1

Feeling Valued Adds Value at Johnson & Johnson

Every Saturday, Vikas Shirodkar takes his daughter to dance lessons and pops into his office at Johnson & Johnson's (J&J) Indian headquarters in Mumbai, which is located next door to the dance class. Doing work at the office saves Shirodkar the trouble of driving home and back again to pick up his daughter after class. After three weeks, Shirodkar received a call from J&J's managing director, Narendra Ambwani, asking if he was overburdened and needed additional staff. Shirodkar was surprised by the question, until Ambwani explained that he noticed the executive's name on the register every Saturday and was concerned about his workload.

The managing director's call was a defining moment for Shirodkar because it reflected J&J's value system in which every employee "must be considered as an individual" and that the company "must respect their dignity and recognize their merit." The credo recognizes employees, customers, communities, and the environment, as well as shareholders. In India, where job-hopping has become the norm, the average J&J employee has more than 15 years of service. Asked about J&J's success at attracting and retaining talent, India managing director Narendra Ambwani answers: "We make them feel the company belongs to them."

J&J also supports each employee's self-concept in day-to-day coaching. For example, J&J's North American Pharmaceutical Research & Development division

Johnson & Johnson is one of the world's most respected employers because it recognizes the value of supporting each employee's self-concept. "We make them feel the company belongs to them," says Narendra Ambwani, the company's managing director in India (shown here). © *India Today Group. Reprinted with permission.*

discovered that a key ingredient to employee motivation and well-being is for managers to ensure that employees feel valued as contributors to the company's success. The European operations of J&J's Global Pharmaceutical Supply Group also introduced a new career program that takes into account their self-concept by matching their personal values with corresponding job preferences.[37]

---

successfully.[38] People with high self-efficacy have a "can do" attitude. They believe they possess the energy (motivation), resources (situational factors), understanding of the correct course of action (role perceptions), and competencies (ability) to perform the task. In other words, self-efficacy is an individual's perception regarding the MARS model in a specific situation. Although originally defined in terms of specific tasks, self-efficacy is also a general trait related to self-concept.[39] General self-efficacy is a perception of one's competence to perform across a variety of situations. The higher the person's general self-efficacy, the higher is their overall self-evaluation.

Locus of Control   A third concept related to a person's self-evaluation is **locus of control**, which is defined as a person's general belief about the amount of control he or she has over personal life events. Individuals who think that events in their life are due mainly to external events, people, or fate/luck have an external locus of control. Those who feel that they can influence their own destiny have an internal locus of control. Locus of control is a generalized belief, so people with an external locus can feel in control in familiar situations (such as performing common tasks). However, their underlying locus of control would be apparent in new situations in which control over events is uncertain.

People with a higher internal locus of control have a more positive self-evaluation. They also tend to perform better in most employment situations, are more successful in their careers, earn more money, and are better suited for leadership positions. Internals are also more satisfied with their jobs, cope better in stressful situations, and are more motivated by performance-based reward systems.[40]

> **locus of control**
> A person's general belief about the amount of control he or she has over personal life events.

LO5

THE SOCIAL SELF

A person's self concept can be organized into two fairly distinct categories: personal identity characteristics and social identity characteristics.[41] *Personal identity* consists of characteristics that make us unique and distinct from people in the social groups to which we have a connection. For instance, an unusual achievement that distinguishes you from other people typically becomes a personal identity characteristic. Personal identity refers to something about you as an individual without reference to a larger group. At the same time, human beings are social animals; they have an inherent drive to be associated with others and to be recognized as part of social communities. This drive to belong is reflected in self-concept by the fact that everyone defines themselves to some degree by their association with others.[42]

social identity theory
A theory that explains self-concept in terms of the person's unique characteristics (personal identity) and membership in various social groups (social identity).

This social element of self-concept is described in **social identity theory**. According to social identity theory, people define themselves in terms of the groups to which they belong or have an emotional attachment. For instance, someone might have a social identity as a Canadian, a graduate of the University of Manitoba, and an employee at Great West Life Assurance Co. (see Exhibit 2.3). Social identity is a complex combination of many memberships arranged in a hierarchy of importance. One factor determining this importance is how obvious our membership is in the group. We tend to define ourselves by our gender, race, age, and other observable characteristics because other people easily identify our membership in those groups. It is difficult to ignore your gender in a class where most other students are the opposite gender, for example. In that context, gender tends to become a stronger defining feature of your social identity than in social settings where there are many people of the same gender.

Along with our demographic characteristics, group status is typically an important influence on our social identity. We identify with groups that have high status or respect because this aids the self-enhancement of our self-concept. Medical doctors usually define themselves in terms of their profession because of its high status, whereas people in low-status jobs tend to define themselves in terms of non-job groups. Some people define themselves in terms of where they work because their employer has a favourable reputation in the community. For instance, as GLOBAL Connections 2.1 stated, Johnson & Johnson employees are so proud of and involved in the company that they "feel the company belongs to them." In contrast, people in some other companies never mention where they work because of poor relations with employees and poor reputation in the community.[43]

EXHIBIT 2.3 Social identity theory example

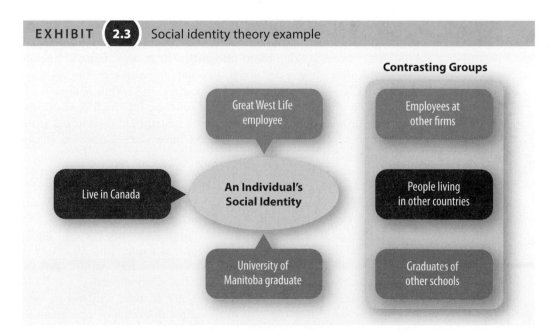

SELF-CONCEPT AND ORGANIZATIONAL BEHAVIOUR

We began this section by stating that self-concept is an important concept for understanding individual perceptions, attitudes, decisions, and behaviour. It influences the individual's motivation and well-being. Some aspects of self-concept, such as self-efficacy and locus of control, are related to job performance. Self-concept also affects how people select and interpret information, as well as their biases in judgments (such as probability of success). And as we shall learn in future chapters, the social identity component of self-concept influences team dynamics, organizational commitment, and other OB concepts.

VALUES IN THE WORKPLACE

LO6

A person's self-concept consists of more than their personality traits and social identities; it is also heavily shaped by their hierarchy of personal values.[44] *Values* are stable, evaluative beliefs that guide our preferences for outcomes or courses of action in a variety of situations. They are perceptions about what is good or bad, right or wrong. Values tell us what we "ought" to do. They serve as a moral compass that directs our motivation and, potentially, our decisions and actions. Values partly define who we are as individuals and as members of groups with similar values.

People arrange values into a hierarchy of preferences, called a *value system*. Some individuals value new challenges more than they value conformity. Others value generosity more than frugality. Each person's unique value system is developed and reinforced through socialization from parents, religious institutions, friends, personal experiences, and the society in which he or she lives. As such, a person's hierarchy of values is stable and long lasting. For example, one study found that value systems of a sample of adolescents were remarkably similar 20 years later as adults.[45]

Notice that our description of values has focused on individuals, whereas executives often describe values as though they belong to the organization. In reality, values exist only within individuals, which we call *personal values*. However, groups of people might hold the same or similar values, so we tend to ascribe these *shared values* to the team, department, organization, profession, or entire society. The values shared by people throughout an organization (*organizational values*) will receive fuller discussion in Chapter 14 because they are a key part of corporate culture. The values shared across a society (*cultural values*) will receive attention later in this chapter.

TYPES OF VALUES

Values come in many forms, and experts on this topic have devoted considerable attention to organizing them into coherent groups. Several decades ago, social psychologist Milton Rokeach developed two lists of values, distinguishing means (instrumental values) from end goals (terminal values). Although Rokeach's lists are still mentioned in some organizational behaviour sources, it is no longer considered an acceptable representation of personal values. The instrumental-terminal values distinction was neither accurate nor useful, and experts have since identified values that are not reported in Rokeach's lists.

Today, by far the most respected and widely studied set of values is the model developed and tested by social psychologist Shalom Schwartz and his colleagues.[46] Schwartz's list of 57 values builds on Rokeach's earlier work but does not distinguish instrumental from terminal values. Instead, through painstaking empirical research, Schwartz reported that human values are organized into the circular model (circumplex) shown in Exhibit 2.4.[47] The model organizes values into 10 broad categories, each representing several specific values. For example, conformity consists of four values: politeness, honouring parents, self-discipline, and obedience.

These 10 categories of values are further reduced to two bipolar dimensions. One dimension has the opposing values domains of openness to change versus conserva-

Know !!

EXHIBIT   2.4   Schwartz's values circumplex

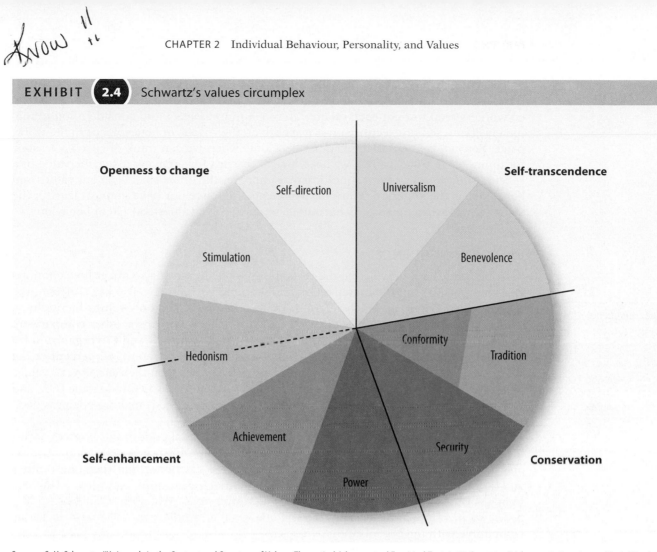

Sources: S. H. Schwartz, "Universals in the Content and Structure of Values: Theoretical Advances and Empirical Tests in 20 Countries," *Advances in Experimental Social Psychology*, 25 (1992), pp. 1–65; S. H. Schwartz and G. Sagie, "Value Consensus and Importance: A Cross-national Study," *Journal of Cross Cultural Psychology*, 31 (July 2000), pp. 465–97.

tion. *Openness to change* refers to the extent to which a person is motivated to pursue innovative ways. It includes the value domains of self-direction (creativity, independent thought) and stimulation (excitement and challenge). *Conservation* is the extent to which a person is motivated to preserve the status quo. This dimension includes the values clusters of conformity (adherence to social norms and expectations), security (safety and stability), and tradition (moderation and preservation of the status quo).

The other bipolar dimension in Schwartz's model has the opposing values domains of self-enhancement versus self-transcendence. *Self-enhancement*—how much a person is motivated by self-interest—includes the values categories of achievement (pursuit of personal success) and power (dominance over others). The opposite of self-enhancement is *self-transcendence*, which refers to the motivation to promote the welfare of others and nature. Self-transcendence includes the values of benevolence (concern for others in one's life) and universalism (concern for the welfare of all people and nature).

VALUES AND INDIVIDUAL BEHAVIOUR

Personal values guide our decisions and actions to some extent, but this connection isn't always as strong as some would like to believe. Habitual behaviour tends to be consistent with our values, but our everyday conscious decisions and actions apply our values much less consistently. The main reason for the "disconnect" between personal values and individual behaviour is that values are abstract concepts that sound good in theory but are less easily followed in practice.

Three conditions strengthen the linkage between person values and behaviour.[48] First, we are more likely to apply values when we are reminded of them. For example, co-workers tend to treat each other with much more respect and consideration immediately after a senior executive gives a speech on the virtues of benevolence in the workplace. Second, we tend to apply our values only when we can think of specific reasons for doing so. In other words, we need logical reasons for applying a specific value in a specific situation. The third condition that improves the linkage between our values and behaviour is the situation. Work environments influence our behaviour, at least in the short term, so they necessarily encourage or discourage values-consistent behaviour.

VALUES CONGRUENCE

Personal values not only define the person's self-concept; they also affect how comfortable that person is in the organization and working with others. The key concept here is **values congruence**, which refers to the extent that a person's values hierarchy is similar to the values hierarchy of the organization, a co-worker, or other comparison. *Person-organization values incongruence*—where the employee's and the organization's dominant values differ—seems to be common. In one recent report, 65 percent of the 1,508 Canadian employees surveyed said there is a gap between their employer's values and their own personal values. A major survey of MBA students in Canada, the U.S., and U.K. revealed that half of them anticipate (or have experienced) making business decisions that conflict with their personal values.[49]

Person-organization values incongruence has a number of undesirable consequences, including higher stress and turnover as well as lower organizational citizenship, loyalty, and job satisfaction. "We've found that the higher the disconnect between one's values and those of the organization, the higher the potential for burnout," says Jayne Hayden, manager of the Career Resource Centre at the University of Waterloo. Values are guideposts, so incongruence also reduces the chance that employees will make decisions compatible with the organization's values.[50]

Does this mean that the most successful organizations perfectly align employee values with the organization's values? Not at all! While a comfortable degree of values congruence is necessary for the reasons just noted, organizations also benefit from some level of values incongruence. Employees with diverse values offer different perspectives, which potentially leads to better decision making. Also, too much congruence can create a "corporate cult" that potentially undermines creativity, organizational flexibility, and business ethics.

> **values congruence**
> The extent to which a person's values hierarchy is similar to the values hierarchy of another entity.

In Search of Congruent Values

Chad Hunt received two appealing job offers after graduating from university, one from a manufacturer of injection molding equipment and the other from an automobile manufacturer. The car company offered a higher salary, but Hunt was also weighing these firms on another important factor. "I'm part of a generation that grew up knowing we had to reduce, reuse, and recycle. So, it's important for me to work for a company that's also environmentally conscious," he says. Environmentalism is such an important part of Hunt's value system that he chose the offer from Husky Injection Molding Systems Ltd., of Bolton, Ontario, north of Toronto. Husky's environmental initiatives include an active recycling program, pesticide-free landscaping, and a head office that uses natural lighting. For Chad Hunt, the difference in starting salaries paled against the issue of values congruence. "It's not even an option," he explains. "I need to work for a company that shares my values, and that includes caring about our impact on the environment."[51] *Courtesy of Husky Injection Molding Systems*

A second type of values congruence refers to how closely the values apparent in our actions (enacted values) are consistent with what we say we believe in (espoused values). This *espoused-enacted values congruence* is especially important for people in leadership positions because any obvious gap between espoused and enacted values undermines their perceived integrity, a critical feature of effective leaders. One global survey reported recently that 55 percent of employees believe senior management behaves consistently with the company's core values.[52]

A third type of values congruence refers to the compatibility of an organization's dominant values with the prevailing values of the community or society in which it conducts business.[53] This creates a delicate balancing act, because companies depend on shared values to maintain consistent standards and behaviours, yet need to operate within the values of different cultures around the world. Let's look more closely at how values vary across cultures.

VALUES ACROSS CULTURES

Fairmont Hotels & Resorts operates world class hotels in several countries, and is rapidly expanding its operations into the Middle East, Africa, and other regions. As the opening story to this chapter described, Fairmont actively develops cross-cultural competencies in its staff through work experience and formal training. Sean Billing and other Fairmont staff soon realize that they need to be sensitive to the fact that cultural differences exist and, although often subtle, can influence decisions, behaviour, and interpersonal relations.

individualism

A cross-cultural value describing the degree to which people in a culture emphasize independence and personal uniqueness.

INDIVIDUALISM AND COLLECTIVISM

Many values have been studied in the context of cross-cultural differences, but the two most commonly mentioned are individualism and collectivism. **Individualism** is the extent to which we value independence and personal uniqueness. Highly individualist people value personal freedom, self-sufficiency, control over their own lives, and appreciation of the unique qualities that distinguish them from others. As shown in Exhibit 2.5, Canadians and Italians generally exhibit high individualism, whereas Taiwanese tend to have low individualism. **Collectivism** is the extent to which we value our duty to groups to which we belong, and to group harmony. Highly collectivist people define themselves by their group membership and value harmonious relationships within those groups.[54] Canadians generally have low collectivism whereas Italians and Taiwanese have relatively high collectivism.

collectivism

A cross-cultural value describing the degree to which people in a culture emphasize duty to groups to which people belong, and to group harmony.

Contrary to popular belief, individualism is not the opposite of collectivism. In fact, an analysis of previous studies reports that the two concepts are unrelated.[55] Some cultures that highly value duty to one's group do not necessarily give a low priority to personal freedom and self-sufficiency. The distinction between individualism and collectivism makes sense when we realize that people across all cultures define themselves in terms of both their uniqueness (personal identity) and relationship to others (social identity). Some cultures emphasize more of one than the other, but both have a place in a person's values and self-concept.

POWER DISTANCE

power distance

A cross-cultural value describing the degree to which people in a culture accept unequal distribution of power in a society.

A third frequently mentioned cross-cultural value is **power distance**. Power distance refers to the extent that people accept unequal distribution of power in a society.[56] Those with high power distance accept and value unequal power. They value obedience to authority and are comfortable receiving commands from their superiors without consultation or debate, and prefer to resolve differences through formal procedures rather than directly. In contrast, people with low power distance expect relatively equal power sharing. They view the relationship with their boss as one of interdependence, not

EXHIBIT 2.5   Five cross-cultural values in selected countries

Country	Individualism	Collectivism	Power Distance	Uncertainty Avoidance	Achievement Orientation
Canada	High	Low	Medium low	Medium low	Medium
Denmark	Medium	Medium low	Low	Low	Low
India	Medium high	Medium	High	Medium low	Medium high
Italy	High	High	Medium	High	High
Japan	Medium high	Low	Medium	High	High
Taiwan	Low	High	Medium	High	Medium

Sources: Individualism and collectivism results are from the meta-analysis reported in D. Oyserman, H. M. Coon, and M. Kemmelmeier, "Rethinking Individualism and Collectivism: Evaluation of Theoretical Assumptions and Meta-Analyses," *Psychological Bulletin*, 128 (2002), pp. 3–72. The other results are from G. Hofstede, *Culture's Consequences*, 2nd ed. (Thousand Oaks, CA: Sage Publications, 2001).

dependence; that is, they believe their boss is also dependent on them, so they expect power sharing and consultation before decisions affecting them are made. People in India tend to have high power distance, whereas people in Denmark generally have low power distance.

To understand the effect of power distance, consider the experience of an engineer from Southeast Asia who immigrated to Canada. In his home country, the engineer generated data analysis reports and submitted them to his supervisor without recommendations. His boss would look at the factual information and make a decision. Including recommendations in those reports would have shown disrespect for the supervisor's higher position, which may have resulted in dismissal. But when the engineer moved to Canada, he was expected to propose recommendations along with the technical data. Excluding recommendations from an engineering report in Canada would be evidence of incompetence, which may result in dismissal. To remain employed, the engineer had to overcome a huge shift in expectations and power distance values.[57]

OTHER CROSS-CULTURAL VALUES

Cross-cultural researchers have investigated many other values, but the only other two that we will mention are uncertainty avoidance and achievement-nurturing orientation. **Uncertainty avoidance** is the degree to which people tolerate ambiguity (low uncertainty avoidance) or feel threatened by ambiguity and uncertainty (high uncertainty avoidance). Employees with high uncertainty avoidance value structured situations where rules of conduct and decision making are clearly documented. They usually prefer direct rather than indirect or ambiguous communications. Uncertainty avoidance tends to be high in Italy and Taiwan and very high in Japan. It is generally low in Denmark.

Achievement-nurturing orientation reflects a competitive versus cooperative view of relations with other people.[58] People with a high achievement orientation value assertiveness, competitiveness, and materialism. They appreciate people who are tough and favour the acquisition of money and material goods. In contrast, people in nurturing-oriented cultures emphasize relationships and the well-being of others. They focus on human interaction and caring rather than competition and personal success. People in Sweden, Norway, and Denmark score very low on achievement orientation (i.e., they have a high nurturing orientation). In contrast, very high achievement orientation scores have been reported in Japan and Hungary, with fairly high scores in the United States and Italy.

uncertainty avoidance
A cross-cultural value describing the degree to which people in a culture tolerate ambiguity (low uncertainty avoidance) or feel threatened by ambiguity and uncertainty (high uncertainty avoidance).

achievement-nurturing orientation
A cross-cultural value describing the degree to which people in a culture emphasize competitive versus cooperative relations with other people.

You're the CEO? So What!

As a senior manager in Asia, Stephen Roberts rarely received questions or critiques from staff about his proposals or ideas. "I spent nine years in Asia and managing in Asia was a relatively easy process because no one pushed back," he recalls. The high power distance in those countries motivated staff to defer to Roberts' judgment. In contrast, Roberts experienced very low power distance when he transferred to Australia. Even though he was now a chief executive officer at Citibank, his ideas were quickly, and sometimes brutally, questioned. "I remember arriving in Australia and I was asked to present to an executive committee of our equities team, and it felt like a medical examination," recalls Roberts, who was born and raised in Australia. "I walked out battered and bruised. So to be pushed, challenged all the time, is more Australian than most other [cultures]."[59] © Stephen Roberts

Before leaving this topic, we need to point out two concerns about cross-cultural values.[60] One concern is that country scores on power distance, uncertainty avoidance, and achievement-nurturing orientation are based on a survey of IBM employees worldwide more than a quarter century ago. More than 100,000 IBM staff in dozens of countries completed that survey, but these IBM employees might not represent the general population. There is also evidence that values have changed quite a bit in some countries since then. A second concern is the assumption that everyone in a society has similar cultural values. This may be true in a few countries, but multiculturalism—where several micro cultures co-exist in the same country—is becoming the more common trend. By attributing specific values to an entire society, we are engaging in a form of stereotyping that limits our ability to understand the more complex reality of that society. To illustrate the limitations of attributing one set of values to an entire society, let's look briefly at the diversity of values within Canada and the United States.

DIVERSITY OF CANADIAN CULTURAL VALUES

Read some cross-cultural studies and you would think that Canada is a homogenous country where people hold identical or very similar values. Of course, anyone who lives here knows otherwise. But even the average Canadian may be surprised at how much cultural diversity exists, even when excluding the incredible variety of new Canadians who grew up elsewhere in the world.[61] Consider Canada's historical diversity of two cultural clusters—Anglophones and Francophones. At one time, Francophones were more religious, traditional, and deferent to authority, compared with Anglophones. Now, the opposite is almost true. Francophones have lower scores than Anglophones on respect for patriarchal authority (i.e., the father should be the head of the household), and they tend to have more tolerant or morally permissive opinions regarding marriage, sexual activity, and nonmarried parenthood.[62] There is some evidence that Anglophone and Francophone values are converging, but these two sub-cultures within Canada are still easily identifiable as a form of deep-level diversity.[63]

Canada's cultural diversity is further evident in the values of First Nations people and their organizations. Organizations with First Nations founders and leaders tend to have a strong collectivist value, low power distance, low uncertainty avoidance, and a relatively nurturing rather than achievement orientation. These values are evident from consensus-oriented decision making (low power distance), focus more on the group than individuals (high collectivism), fewer rules and procedures (low uncertainty avoidance), and emphasis on the holistic well-being of employees and community (nurturing more than achievement orientation).[64]

Canadian versus American Values   Canadians increasingly shop at American stores and have close associations with friends and co-workers in the United States. Yet, the values held by people in these two countries are more divergent today than a few decades ago. "Canadians may like Americans, speak the same language, and consume more of their fast food and popular culture, but we embrace a different hierarchy of values," writes social policy researcher Michael Adams.[65] Another Canadian cultural expert is even more emphatic: the 49th parallel border is more than just an imaginary geographic division; it is a symbol of the widening ideological divide in North America.[66]

Canadians have significantly higher tolerance or moral permissiveness than do Americans. Canadians are also more willing to allow collective rights over individual rights and are less accepting of large wealth differences within society.[67] Another striking difference is that Canadians are more likely to question the authority of government and other institutions, whereas Americans have a relatively high deference to authority. Canadians are almost half as likely as Americans to be associated with a religious institution and are less likely to believe that these institutions should influence public policy. They are also more than twice as likely as Americans to believe that organizations work better without a single leader. Perhaps the most significant difference is in the value of patriarchal authority. In the early 1980s, more than 40 percent of Canadians and Americans believed that the father should be the master of the home. Today, only 18 percent of Canadians hold this view, compared to almost 50 percent of Americans.[68]

Although there is strong evidence that Canadian and American values differ, we also need to take into account diversity of values within each country. With this reality in mind, one major study reported that the United States and Canada seem to consist of four cultural groups: the Southern U.S., Northern U.S., Anglophone (English-speaking) Canada, and Francophone (French-speaking) Canada. The Southern U.S. is largely inhabited by people with the most conservative, hawkish, and deeply religious values of the four groups. Francophone Canadians, the second cluster, hold the most tolerant or morally permissive values. This leaves Anglophone Canadians and Americans residing in the northern U.S. Research suggests that these two groups have very similar cultural values.[69]

ETHICAL VALUES AND BEHAVIOUR

When employees are asked to list the most important characteristic they look for in a leader, the top factor isn't intelligence, courage, or even being inspirational. Although these characteristics are important, the most important factor in most surveys is honesty/ethics.[70] *Ethics* refers to the study of moral principles or values that determine whether actions are right or wrong and outcomes are good or bad. People rely on their ethical values to determine "the right thing to do." Canada is recognized around the world for its high ethical standards—it ranks ninth lowest on the global corruption index, for example—yet it has its share of scandals involving unethical corporate behaviour. A small sample of alleged wrongdoing (many of these cases are still in court or being investigated) include misappropriating pension funds for human resource projects at the RCMP, misuse of company funds at Hollinger, and accounting fraud at Nortel and Livent.[71]

THREE ETHICAL PRINCIPLES

To better understand business ethics, we need to consider three distinct types of ethical principles: utilitarianism, individual rights, and distributive justice.[72] While you might prefer one principle more than the others based on your personal values, all three should be actively considered to put important ethical issues to the test.

- *Utilitarianism*—This principle advises us to seek the greatest good for the greatest number of people. In other words, we should choose the option providing the highest degree of satisfaction to those affected. This is sometimes known as a consequential principle because it focuses on the consequences of our actions, not on how we achieve those consequences. One problem with utilitarianism is that it is almost impossible to evaluate the benefits or costs of many decisions, particularly when many stakeholders have wide-ranging needs and values. Another problem is that even if an action achieves the greatest good for the greatest number, the action itself might seem unethical.

- *Individual rights*—This principle reflects the belief that everyone has entitlements that let them act in a certain way. Some of the most widely cited rights are freedom of movement, physical security, freedom of speech, fair trial, and freedom from torture. The individual rights principle includes more than legal rights; it also includes human rights that everyone is granted as a moral norm of society. One problem with individual rights is that certain individual rights may conflict with others. The shareholders' right to be informed about corporate activities may ultimately conflict with an executive's right to privacy, for example.

- *Distributive justice*—This principle suggests that people who are similar to each other should receive similar benefits and burdens; those who are dissimilar should receive different benefits and burdens in proportion to their dissimilarity. For example, we expect that two employees who contribute equally in their work should receive similar rewards, whereas those who make a lesser contribution should receive less. A variation of the distributive justice principle says that inequalities are acceptable where they benefit the least well off in society. Thus, employees in risky jobs should be paid more if this benefits others who are less well off. One problem with the distributive justice principle is that it is difficult to agree on who is "similar" and what factors are "relevant."

LO8

MORAL INTENSITY, ETHICAL SENSITIVITY, AND SITUATIONAL INFLUENCES

moral intensity
The degree to which an issue demands the application of ethical principles.

Along with ethical principles, we need to consider the moral intensity of the issue, the individual's ethical sensitivity, and situational factors. **Moral intensity** is the degree to which an issue demands the application of ethical principles. Decisions with high moral intensity are more important, so the decision maker needs to more carefully apply ethical principles to resolve it. Several factors influence the moral intensity of an issue, including those listed in Exhibit 2.6. Keep in mind that this list represents the factors people tend to think about; some of them might not be considered morally acceptable when formally making ethical decisions.[73]

ethical sensitivity
A personal characteristic that enables people to recognize the presence and determine the relative importance of an ethical issue.

Even if an issue has high moral intensity, some employees might not recognize its ethical importance because they have low **ethical sensitivity**. Ethical sensitivity is a personal characteristic that enables people to recognize the presence and determine the relative importance of an ethical issue.[74] Ethically sensitive people are not necessarily more ethical. Rather, they can more accurately estimate the moral intensity of the issue. The third important factor explaining why good people do bad things is the situation in which the unethical conduct occurs. Employees say they regularly experience pressure from top management that motivates them to lie to customers, breach regulations, or otherwise act unethically.[75] Situational factors do not justify unethical conduct. Rather, we need to recognize these factors so that organizations can reduce their influence in the future.

EXHIBIT 2.6   Factors influencing perceived moral intensity

Moral Intensity Factor	Moral Intensity Question	Moral Intensity is Higher When...
Magnitude of consequences	How much harm or benefit will occur to others as a result of this action?	...the harm or benefit is larger
Social consensus	How many other people agree that this action is ethically good or bad?	...many people agree
Probability of effect	(a) What is the chance that this action will actually occur?	...the probability is higher
	(b) What is the chance that this action will actually cause good or bad consequences?	
Temporal immediacy	How long after the action will the consequences occur?	...the time delay is shorter
Proximity	How socially, culturally, psychologically, and/or physically close to me are the people affected by this decision?	...those affected are close rather than distant
Concentration of effect	(a) How many people are affected by this action?	...many people are affected
	(b) Are the people affected by this action easily identifiable as a group?	...easily identifiable as a group

NOTE: These are factors people tend to ask themselves when determining the moral intensity of an issue. Whether some of these questions should be relevant is itself an ethical question.

Source: Based on information in T. J. Jones, "Ethical Decision Making by Individuals in Organizations: An Issue Contingent Model." *Academy of Management Review* 16 (1991), pp. 366–395.

SUPPORTING ETHICAL BEHAVIOUR

Most large and medium-size organizations in Canada and several other countries have developed and communicate ethical codes of conduct. These statements establish the organization's ethical standards and signal to employees that the company takes ethical conduct seriously. However, written ethics codes alone won't prevent wrongdoing in the workplace.[76] To supplement ethics codes, many firms provide ethics training. Some firms, such as Toronto-based Rogers Cable Communications Inc., also rely on an anonymous "star hotline" as well as a Weblink that employees can use to raise ethical issues or concerns about ethical conduct. Rogers employees can even call back to find out what actions have been taken to resolve the ethical issue.[77]

These additional measures seem to support ethical conduct to some extent, but the most powerful foundation is a set of shared values that reinforce ethical conduct. "If you don't have a culture of ethical decision making to begin with, all the controls and compliance regulations you care to deploy won't necessarily prevent ethical misconduct," warns Devin Brougham, director of British communications giant Vodafone. This culture is supported by the ethical conduct and vigilance of corporate leaders. By acting with the highest standards of moral conduct, leaders not only gain support and trust from followers; they role model the ethical standards that employees are more likely to follow.[78]

CHAPTER SUMMARY

Individual behaviour is influenced by motivation, ability, role perceptions, and situational factors (MARS). Motivation consists of internal forces that affect the direction, intensity, and persistence of a person's voluntary choice of behaviour. Ability includes both the natural aptitudes and learned capabilities required to successfully complete a task. Role perceptions are a person's beliefs about what behaviours are appropriate or necessary in a particular situation. Situational factors are environmental conditions that constrain or facilitate employee behaviour and performance.

Personality refers to the relatively enduring pattern of thoughts, emotions, and behaviours that characterize a person, along with the psychological processes behind those characteristics. Most experts now agree that personality is shaped by both nature and nurture. Most personality traits are represented within the five-factor model, which includes conscientiousness, agreeableness, neuroticism, openness to experience, and extroversion. Conscientiousness and emotional stability (low neuroticism) stand out as the personality traits that best predict individual performance in almost every job group. The other three personality dimensions predict more specific types of employee behaviour and performance. Another set of traits, measured by the Myers-Briggs Type Indicator, represents how people prefer to perceive and judge information.

Self-concept refers to an individual's self-beliefs and self-evaluations. It has three structural dimensions: complexity, consistency, and clarity. People are inherently motivated to promote and protect their self-concept (called self-enhancement). At the same time, people are motivated to verify and maintain their existing self-concept (called self-verification).

Self-evaluation, an important aspect of self-concept, consists of self-esteem, self-efficacy, and locus of control. Self-esteem is the extent to which people like, respect, and are satisfied with themselves. Self-efficacy refers to a person's belief that he or she has the ability, motivation, correct role perceptions, and favourable situation to complete a task successfully; general self-efficacy is a perception of one's competence to perform across a variety of situations. Locus of control is defined as a person's general belief about the amount of control he or she has over personal life events. Self-concept consists of both personality identity and social identity. Social identity theory explains how people define themselves in terms of the groups to which they belong or have an emotional attachment.

Values are stable, evaluative beliefs that guide our preferences for outcomes or courses of action in a variety of situations. People arrange values into a hierarchy of preferences, called a value system. Values have been organized into a circle with 10 clusters. Values congruence refers to the similarity of value systems between two entities.

Five values that differ across cultures are individualism, collectivism, power distance, uncertainty avoidance, and achievement-nurturing orientation. Values differ within Canada and between Canada and the United States. Three values that guide ethical conduct are utilitarianism, individual rights, and distributive justice.

Three factors that influence ethical conduct are the extent that an issue demands ethical principles (moral intensity), the person's ethical sensitivity to the presence and importance of an ethical dilemma, and situational factors that cause people to deviate from their moral values. Companies improve ethical conduct through a code of ethics, ethics training, ethics hot lines, and the conduct of corporate leaders.

KEY TERMS

ability, p. 27
achievement-nurturing orientation, p. 40
collectivism, p. 39
competencies, p. 27
conscientiousness, p. 30
ethical sensitivity, p. 43
extroversion, p. 31

five-factor model (FFM), p. 30
individualism, p. 39
locus of control, p. 34
moral intensity, p. 43
motivation, p. 26
Myers-Briggs Type Indicator (MBTI), p. 31
neuroticism, p. 30

personality, p. 29
power distance, p. 39
role perceptions, p. 27
self-concept, p. 32
self-efficacy, p. 33
social identity theory, p. 35
uncertainty avoidance, p. 40
values congruence, p. 38

CRITICAL THINKING QUESTIONS

1. An insurance company has high levels of absenteeism among the office staff. The head of office administration argues that employees are misusing the company's sick leave benefits. However, some of the mostly female staff members have explained that family responsibilities interfere with work. Using the MARS model, as well as your knowledge of absenteeism behaviour, discuss some of the possible reasons for absenteeism here and how it might be reduced.

2. As the district manager responsible for six stores in a large electronics retail chain, you have had difficulty with the performance of some sales staff. Although they are initially motivated and generally have good interpersonal skills, many have difficulty with the complex knowledge of the diverse range of store products, ranging from computers to high fidelity sound systems. Describe three strategies you might apply to improve the match between the competencies of new sales staff and the job requirements.

3. Research has found that heredity has a strong influence on an individual's personality. What are the implications of this in organizational settings?

4. Suppose that you give all candidates applying for a management trainee position a personality test that measures the five dimensions in the five-factor model. Which personality traits would you consider to be the most important for this type of job? Explain your answer.

5. An important aspect of self-concept is the idea that almost everyone engages in self-enhancement. What problems tend to occur in organizations as a result of this self-enhancement phenomenon? What can organizational leaders do to make use of a person's inherent drive for self-enhancement?

6. This chapter discussed the concept of values congruence in the context of an employee's personal values with the organization's values. But values congruence also relates to the juxtaposition of other pairs of value

systems. Explain how values congruence is relevant with respect to organizational versus professional values.

7. People in a particular South American country have high power distance and high collectivism. What does this mean, and what are the implications of this infor-

mation when you (a senior executive) visit employees working for your company in that country?

8. "All decisions are ethical decisions." Comment on this statement, particularly by referring to the concepts of moral intensity and ethical sensitivity.

CASE STUDY 2.1

Pushing Paper Can Be Fun

A large city government was putting on a number of seminars for managers of various departments throughout the city. At one of these sessions, the topic discussed was motivation—how we can get public servants motivated to do a good job. The plight of a police captain became the central focus of the discussion:

I've got a real problem with my officers. They come on the force as young, inexperienced rookies, and we send them out on the street, either in cars or on a beat. They seem to like the contact they have with the public, the action involved in crime prevention, and the apprehension of criminals. They also like helping people out at fires, accidents, and other emergencies.

The problem occurs when they get back to the station. They hate to do the paperwork, and because they dislike it, the job is frequently put off or done inadequately. This lack of attention hurts us later on when we get to court. We need clear, factual reports. They must be highly detailed and unambiguous. As soon as one part of a report is shown to be inadequate or incorrect, the rest of the report is suspect. Poor reporting probably causes us to lose more cases than any other factor.

I just don't know how to motivate them to do a better job. We're in a budget crunch and I have absolutely no financial rewards at my disposal. In fact, we'll probably have to lay some people off in the near future. It's hard for me to make the job interesting and challenging because it isn't—it's boring, routine paperwork, and there isn't much you can do about it.

Finally, I can't say to them that their promotions will hinge on the excellence of their paperwork. First of all, they know it's not true. If their performance is adequate, most are more likely to get promoted just by staying on the force a certain number of years than for some specific outstanding act. Second, they were trained to do the job they do out in the streets, not to fill out forms. All through their career it is the arrests and interventions that get noticed.

Some people have suggested a number of things, like using conviction records as a performance criterion. However, we know that's not fair—too many other things are involved. Bad paperwork increases the chance that you lose in court, but good paperwork doesn't necessarily mean you'll win. We tried setting up team competitions based upon the excellence of the reports, but the officers caught on to that pretty quickly. No one was getting any type of reward for winning the competition, and they figured why should they bust a gut when there was no payoff.

I just don't know what to do.

Discussion Questions

1. What performance problems is the captain trying to correct?

2. Use the **MARS** model of individual behaviour and performance to diagnose the possible causes of the unacceptable behaviour.

3. Has the captain considered all possible solutions to the problem? If not, what else might be done?

Source: T. R. Mitchell and J. R. Larson, Jr., *People in Organizations*, 3rd ed. (New York: McGraw-Hill, 1987), p. 184. Used with permission.

www.mcgrawhill.ca/olc/mcshane

CLASS EXERCISE 2.2

Test Your Knowledge of Personality

Purpose This exercise is designed to help you think about and understand the effects of the Big Five personality dimensions on individual preferences and outcomes.

Instructions (Large Class) Below are several questions relating to the Big Five personality dimensions and various preferences or outcomes. Answer each of these questions relying on your personal experience or best guess. Later, the instructor will show you the answers based on scholarly results. You will NOT be graded on this exercise, but it may help you to better understand the effect of personality on human behaviour and preferences.

Instructions (Small Class)
- *Step 1:* The instructor will organize students into teams. Members of each team work together to answer each of these questions relating to the Big Five personality dimensions and various preferences or outcomes.

- *Step 2:* The instructor will reveal the answers based on scholarly results. (Note: the instructor might create a competition to see which team has the most answers correct.)

Personality and Preferences Questions *Question 1:* Which two Big Five personality dimensions are positively associated with enjoyment of workplace humour?

_____   _____

Question 2: Listed below are several jobs. Please check no more than two (2) personality dimensions that you believe are positively associated with preferences for each occupation.

Personality Dimension	Extroversion	Conscientiousness	Agreeableness	Neuroticism	Openness to experience
Budget analyst	☐	☐	☐	☐	☐
Corporate executive	☐	☐	☐	☐	☐
Engineer	☐	☐	☐	☐	☐
Journalist	☐	☐	☐	☐	☐
Life insurance agent	☐	☐	☐	☐	☐
Nurse	☐	☐	☐	☐	☐
Physician	☐	☐	☐	☐	☐
Production supervisor	☐	☐	☐	☐	☐
Public relations director	☐	☐	☐	☐	☐
Research analyst	☐	☐	☐	☐	☐
School teacher	☐	☐	☐	☐	☐
Sculptor	☐	☐	☐	☐	☐

Question 3: Rank order (1 = highest; 5 = lowest) the Big Five personality dimensions in terms of how much you think they predict a person's degree of life satisfaction. (Note: personality dimensions are ranked by their absolute effect, so ignore the negative or positive direction of association.)

_____ Extroversion

_____ Conscientiousness

_____ Agreeableness

_____ Neuroticism

_____ Openness to experience

TEAM EXERCISE 2.3

Comparing Cultural Values

Purpose

This exercise is designed to help you determine the extent that students hold similar assumptions about the values that dominate in other countries.

Instructions (Small Class)

The names in the left column represent labels that a major consulting project identified with business people in a particular country, based on its national culture and values. These names appear in alphabetical order. In the right column are the names of countries, also in alphabetical order, corresponding to the labels in the left column.

- *Step 1:* Working alone, connect the labels with the countries by relying on your perceptions of these countries. Each label is associated with only one country, so each label will be connected to only one country, and vice versa. Draw a line to connect the pairs, or put the label number beside the country name.

- *Step 2*: The instructor will form teams of four or five members. Members of each team will compare their results and try to reach consensus on a common set of connecting pairs.

- *Step 3*: Teams or the instructor will post the results for all to see the extent that students hold common opinions about business people in other cultures. Class discussion can then consider the reasons why the results are so similar or different, as well as the implications of these results for working in a global work environment.

Instructions (Large Class)

- *Step 1:* Working alone, connect the labels with the countries by relying on your perceptions of these countries. Each label is associated with only one country, so each label will be connected to only one country, and vice versa. Draw a line to connect the pairs, or put the label number beside the country name.

- *Step 2:* Asking for a show of hands, the instructor will find out which country is identified by most students with each label. The instructor will then post the correct answer.

Values Labels and Country Names	
Country Label (alphabetical)	**Country Name (alphabetical)**
1. Affable Humanists	Australia
2. Ancient Modernizers	Brazil
3. Commercial Catalysts	Canada
4. Conceptual Strategists	China
5. Efficient Manufacturers	France
6. Ethical Statesmen	Germany
7. Informal Egalitarians	India
8. Modernizing Traditionalists	Netherlands
9. Optimistic Entrepreneurs	New Zealand
10. Quality Perfectionists	Singapore
11. Rugged Individualists	Taiwan
12. Serving Merchants	United Kingdom
13. Tolerant Traders	United States

Source: Based on R. Rosen, P. Digh, M. Singer, and C. Phillips, *Global Literacies* (New York: Simon & Schuster, 2000).

 TEAM EXERCISE 2.4

Ethics Dilemma Vignettes

Purpose   This exercise is designed to make you aware of the ethical dilemmas people face in various business situations, as well as the competing principles and values that operate in these situations.

Instructions   The instructor will form teams of four or five students. Team members will read each
(Small Class)   case below and discuss the extent to which the company's action in each case was ethical. Teams should be prepared to justify their evaluation using ethics principles and perceived moral intensity of each incident.

Instructions   Working alone, students read each case below and determine the extent to which the
(Large Class)   company's action in each case was ethical. The instructor will use a show of hands to determine the extent to which students believe each case represents an ethical dilemma (high or low moral intensity), and the extent to which the main people or company in each incident acted ethically.

Case One

An employee who worked in Toronto for a major food retailer wrote a Weblog (blog) and, in one of his writings, complained that his boss wouldn't let him go home when he felt sick and that his district manager refused to promote him because of his dreadlocks. His blog named the employer, but the employee didn't use his real name. Although all blogs are on the Internet, the employee claims that his was low profile and that it didn't show up when doing a Google search of his name or the company. Still, the employer somehow discovered the blog, figured out the employee's real name, and fired him for "speaking ill-will of the company in a public domain."

Case Two

Computer printer manufacturers usually sell printers at a low margin over cost and generate much more income from subsequent sales of the high-margin ink cartridges required for each printer. One global printer manufacturer now designs its printers so they only work with ink cartridges made in the same region. Ink cartridges purchased in North America will not work for the same printer model sold in Europe, for example. This "region coding" of ink cartridges does not improve performance. Rather, this action prevents consumers and grey marketers from buying the product at a lower price in another region. The company says this action allows it to maintain stable prices within a region rather than continually changing prices due to currency fluctuations.

Case Three

For the past few years, the design department of a small (40-employee) company has been using a particular software program, but the three employees who use the software have been complaining for more than a year that the software is out of date and is slowing down their performance. The department agreed to switch to a competing software program, costing several thousand dollars. However, the next version won't be released for six months and buying the current version will not allow much discount toward the next version. The company has put in advanced orders for the next version. Meanwhile, one employee was able to get a copy of the current version of the software from a friend in the industry. The company has allowed the three employees to use this current version of the software even though they did not pay for it.

Case Four

Judy Price is a popular talk show radio personality and opinionated commentator on the morning phone-in show of a Toronto radio station. Ms. Price is married to John Tremble, a lawyer who was recently elected for the first time to the parliament of Ontario. He also became Minister of the Environment and Conservation in the newly formed government that defeated the previous government. The radio station's board of directors is very concerned that the station's perceived objectivity will be compromised if Ms. Price remains on air as a commentator and talk show host while her husband holds such a public position in the province. For example, the radio station manager believes that Ms. Price gave minimal attention to the Environment Ministry's slow response to a leakage of toxic chemicals a week ago at a large manufacturing company. Ms. Price denied that her views are biased and that the incident didn't merit as much attention as other issues on that particular day. To ease the board's concerns, the station manager has transferred Ms. Price from a talk show host and commentator to the hourly news reporting position, where most script is edited by others. Although technically a lower position, Ms. Price's total salary package remains the same. Ms. Price is now seeking professional advice to determine whether the radio station's action represents a form of discrimination on the basis of marital status.

SELF-ASSESSMENT EXERCISE 2.5

Are You Introverted or Extroverted?

Purpose This self-assessment is designed to help you to estimate the extent to which you are introverted or extroverted.

Instructions The statements in this scale refer to personal characteristics than might or might not be characteristic of you. Mark the box indicating the extent that the statement accurately or inaccurately describes you. Then use the scoring key in Appendix B of this book to calculate your results. This exercise is completed alone so students assess themselves honestly without concerns of social comparison. Class discussion will focus on the meaning and implications of extroversion and introversion in organizations.

IPIP Introversion-Extroversion Scale					
How accurately do each of the following statements describe you?	Very Accurate Description of Me	Moderately Accurate	Neither Accurate or Inaccurate	Moderately Inaccurate	Very Inaccurate Description of Me
1. I feel comfortable around people.	☐	☐	☐	☐	☐
2. I make friends easily.	☐	☐	☐	☐	☐
3. I keep in the background.	☐	☐	☐	☐	☐
4. I don't talk a lot.	☐	☐	☐	☐	☐
5. I would describe my experiences as somewhat dull.	☐	☐	☐	☐	☐
6. I know how to captivate people.	☐	☐	☐	☐	☐
7. I don't like to draw attention to myself.	☐	☐	☐	☐	☐
8. I am the life of the party.	☐	☐	☐	☐	☐
9. I am skilled in handling social situations.	☐	☐	☐	☐	☐
10. I have little to say.	☐	☐	☐	☐	☐

Source: Adapted from instruments described and/or presented in: L. R. Goldberg, J. A. Johnson, H. W. Eber, R. Hogan, M. C. Ashton, C. R. Cloninger, & H. C. Gough (2006), "The International Personality Item Pool and the Future of Public-Domain Personality Measures," *Journal of Research in Personality*, 40, pp. 84–96.

Online LearningCentre Go to the Online Learning Centre at www.mcgrawhill.ca/olc/mcshane to complete the following interactive self-assessments.

SELF-ASSESSMENT EXERCISE 2.6

What are Your Dominant Values?

Values have taken centre stage in organizational behaviour. Increasingly, OB experts are realizing that our personal values influence our motivation, decisions, and attitudes. This self-assessment is designed to help you to estimate your personal values and value system. The instrument consists of several words and phrases, and you are asked to indicate whether each word or phrase is highly opposed or highly similar to your personal values, or some point in between these two extremes. As with all self-assessments, you need to be honest with yourself when completing this activity in order to get the most accurate results.

SELF-ASSESSMENT EXERCISE 2.7

How Much Do You Value Individualism and Collectivism?

Two of the most important concepts in cross-cultural organizational behaviour are individualism and collectivism. This self-assessment measures your levels of individualism and collectivism with one of the most widely adopted measures. This scale consists of several statements, and you are asked to indicate how well each statement describes you. You need to be honest with yourself to receive a reasonable estimate of your level of individualism and collectivism.

SELF-ASSESSMENT EXERCISE 2.8

Estimating Your Locus of Control

This self-assessment is designed to help you to estimate the extent to which you have an internal or external locus of control personality. The instrument asks you to indicate the degree to which you agree or disagree with each of the statements provided. As with all self-assessments, you need to be honest with yourself when completing this activity in order to get the most accurate results. The results show your relative position in the internal-external locus continuum and the general meaning of this score.

SELF-ASSESSMENT EXERCISE 2.9

Identifying Your General Self-Efficacy

Self-efficacy refers to a person's belief that he or she has the ability, motivation, and resources to complete a task successfully. Self-efficacy is usually conceptualized as a situation-specific belief. You may believe that you can perform a certain task in one situation, but are less confident with that task in another situation. However, there is also evidence that people develop a more general self-efficacy. This exercise helps you to estimate your general self-efficacy. Read each of the statements in this self-assessment and select the response that best fits your personal belief. This self-assessment is completed alone so that students rate themselves honestly without concerns of social comparison. However, class discussion will focus on the meaning and importance of self-efficacy in the workplace.

iStudy—Available 24/7 with instant feedback so you can study when you want, how you want, and where you want. Visit www.istudyob.ca to register—take practice quizzes, run interactive scenarios, practice concepts, and much more. Also visit the Student Online Learning Centre for additional study tools.

www.mcgrawhill.ca/olc/mcshane

CHAPTER 3

Perception and Learning in Organizations

After reading this chapter, you should be able to:

LO1 Outline the perceptual process.

LO2 Explain how social identity and stereotyping influence the perceptual process.

LO3 Describe the attribution process and two attribution errors.

LO4 Summarize the self-fulfilling prophecy process.

LO5 Explain how halo, primacy, recency, and false-consensus effects bias our perceptions.

LO6 Discuss three ways to improve social perception, with specific application to organizational situations.

LO7 Describe the A-B-C model of behaviour modification and the four contingencies of reinforcement.

LO8 Describe the three features of social learning theory.

LO9 Outline the elements of organizational learning and ways to improve each element.

Moya Greene may be the first Canada Post CEO to know what it's like to heft a 25-kilogram mail bag. Few executives maintain the pace of keeping in touch with employees better than Moya Greene. When Greene started as CEO, she travelled across the country doing every job that employees do—from sorting mail to delivering it. "In my first six months at Canada Post I didn't spend very much time in the head office. I spent an awful lot of time out in the field talking to our people all across the country, in the plant, in the letter carrier depots, on the various shifts, in various functions, sorting letters, sorting parcels on the loading dock, understanding how the whole logistics end of this business works."

Empathy for employees' needs and recognizing the physical demands of many Canada Post jobs prompted the Crown corporation's executive to provide space and partial subsidization for a variety of fitness and wellness offerings. Canada Post's largest distribution and processing centres have fitness facilities, classes such as Pilates, tai chi, and yoga are partially subsidized by Canada Post, and all employees across Canada are provided with discount fitness memberships.

Greene encourages all employees to share perceptions about their jobs and the corporation; she is committed to responding to every query on her blog and every email she receives. Communication with employees keeps her connected with what's happening in the organization. "You see it from their perspective, what's important, what's troubling, what works, and what could be made better" says Greene. By making bonuses dependent on getting out and visiting customers and plants she has also been very influential in encouraging managers to walk in employees' and customers' shoes.[1]

Canada Post CEO, Moya Greene keeps her perceptions in focus by staying close to employees. Listening to and learning about what is important to employees has helped Canada Post be recognized for the second consecutive year as one of Canada's Top 100 Employers.
The Canadian Press (Bayne Stanley)

perception
The process of receiving information about and making sense of the world around us.

Working in front-line jobs and keeping in close contact with staff and customers is a powerful way for executives and head office employees to improve their perceptions. **Perception** is the process of receiving information about and making sense of the world around us. It entails deciding which information to notice, how to categorize this information, and how to interpret it within the framework of our existing knowledge. This chapter begins by describing the perceptual process, that is, the dynamics of selecting, organizing, and interpreting external stimuli. Next, we examine the perceptual processes of social identity and stereotyping, attribution, and self-fulfilling prophecy, including biases created within these processes. Four other perceptual biases—halo, primacy, recency, and false consensus—are also briefly introduced. We then identify three potentially effective ways to improve perceptions. The latter part of this chapter looks at three perspectives of learning: behaviour modification, social learning theory, and experiential learning, followed by the key elements in organizational learning.

THE PERCEPTUAL PROCESS

LO1

Information from the world around us is filtered through an imperfect perceptual process. This imperfect process, which is illustrated in Exhibit 3.1, begins when environmental stimuli are received through our senses. Most stimuli that bombard our senses are screened out; the rest are organized and interpreted. The process of attending to some information received by our senses and ignoring other information is called **selective attention.** Selective attention is influenced by characteristics of the person or object being perceived, particularly its size, intensity, motion, repetition, and novelty. For example, a small flashing red light on a nurses' station console is immediately noticed because it is bright (intensity), flashing (motion), a rare event (novelty), and has symbolic meaning that a patient's vital signs are failing. Notice that selective attention is also influenced by the context in which the target is perceived. Our selective attention process is triggered by things or people who might be out of context, such as hearing someone with a foreign accent in a setting where most people have Canadian accents.

selective attention
The process of attending to some information received by our senses and ignoring other information.

Characteristics of the perceiver play an important role in selection attention, much of it without the perceiver's awareness.[2] When information is received through the senses, our brain quickly and nonconsciously assesses whether it is relevant or irrelevant to us, then attaches emotional markers (worry, happiness, boredom) to that information.

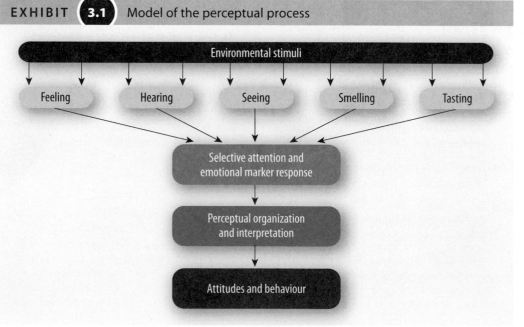

EXHIBIT 3.1 Model of the perceptual process

Environmental stimuli

Feeling · Hearing · Seeing · Smelling · Tasting

Selective attention and emotional marker response

Perceptual organization and interpretation

Attitudes and behaviour

These emotional markers help us to store information in memory; they also reproduce these emotions when subsequently thinking about this information.[3]

The automatic selection of incoming information is far from perfect, however. As was mentioned in Chapter 2, we have a natural and usually nonconscious tendency to seek out information that supports our self-concept or puts us in a favourable light, and to ignore or undervalue information that is contrary to our self-concept. This *confirmation bias* also screens out information that is contrary to our values and assumptions.[4] Several studies have found that people fail to perceive (or soon forget) statements and events that undermine political parties that they support. One recent study examined how people perceived and accepted stories during the first weeks of the Iraq war that were subsequently retracted (acknowledged by the media as false stories). The study found that most of the Germans and Australians surveyed dismissed the retracted events, whereas a significantly large percentage of Americans continued to believe these false stories, even though many of them recalled that the stories had been retracted by the media. In essence, people in the American sample were reluctant to reject and forget about information that supported their beliefs about the Iraq war.[5]

Finally, selective attention is influenced by our assumptions and conscious anticipation of future events. An email from a co-worker is more likely to get noticed among the daily bombardment of messages when you expect to receive that email (particularly when it is important to you). Unfortunately, expectations and assumptions also cause us to screen out potentially important information. If we form an opinion or theory about something—such as a consumer trend or an employee's potential—then we tend to select information that is consistent with the theory and ignore contrary information. Police detectives, forensic experts, and others whose job is to diagnose problems or opportunities try to avoid these selective attention traps by keeping an open mind, absorbing as much information as possible, and avoiding theories too early in the investigation.

Detectives Avoid Tunnel Vision with Art Appreciation

Good detective work involves more than forming a good theory about the crime. It also involves *not* forming a theory too early in the investigation. "We have to be extremely careful not to have tunnel vision and not to come up with a theory and start to go down that road," advises RCMP spokesperson Corporal Dale Carr, referring to investigation of a recent mass murder in Surrey, British Columbia. Keith Findley, co-director of the Wisconsin Innocence Project, warns that becoming preoccupied with a single theory causes police to "focus on a suspect, select and filter the evidence that will build a case for conviction, while ignoring or suppressing evidence that points away from guilt." To minimize this selective attention problem, officers in the New York Police Department are attending art classes, where they learn to be more mindful and take multiple perspectives of all information. "[The class] reminded me to stop and take in the whole scene and not just have tunnel vision," says NYPD captain David Grossi, adding that the class helped him to discover evidence outside the area he normally would have investigated.[6] *The Canadian Press (Jeff Roberson)*

PERCEPTUAL ORGANIZATION AND INTERPRETATION

categorical thinking
Organizing people and objects into preconceived categories that are stored in our long-term memory.

People make sense of information even before they become aware of it. This sense making partly includes **categorical thinking**—the mostly nonconscious process of organizing people and objects into preconceived categories that are stored in our long-term memory.[7] Categorical thinking relies on a variety of automatic perceptual grouping principles. Things are often grouped together based on their similarity or proximity to others. If you notice that a group of similar-looking people includes several professors, for instance, then you will likely assume that the others in that group are also professors. Another form of perceptual grouping is based on the need for cognitive closure, such as filling in missing information about what happened at a meeting that you didn't attend (e.g., who was there, where it was held). A third form of grouping occurs when we think we see trends in otherwise ambiguous information. Several research studies have found that people have a natural tendency to see patterns that really are random events, such as presumed winning streaks among sports stars or in gambling.[8]

Making sense also involves interpreting incoming information, and this happens just as quickly as the brain selects and organizes that information. We mentioned that emotional markers are tagged to incoming stimuli, which are essentially quick judgments about whether that information is good or bad for us. To give you an idea about how quickly and systematically this nonconscious perceptual interpretation process occurs, consider the following study:[9] Eight observers were shown video clips of university instructors teaching an undergraduate class, then rated the instructors on several personal characteristics (optimistic, likeable, anxious, active, etc.). The observers did not know the instructors, and they completed their ratings independently, yet their scores were remarkably similar on most characteristics. Equally important, these ratings were very similar to the ratings completed by students who attended the entire class.

These results may be interesting, but they become extraordinary when you realize that the observers formed their perceptions based on as little as *six seconds* of video—three segments of two seconds each selected randomly across the one-hour class! Furthermore, the video didn't have any sound. In other words, people form similar perceptions and judgments based on very thin slices of information. Other studies have reported similar findings for observations of high school teachers, courtroom judges, and physicians. Collectively, these "thin slices" studies reveal that selective attention as well as perceptual organization and interpretation operate very quickly and to a large extent without our awareness.

mental models
Visual or relational images in our mind representing the external world.

Mental Models   To achieve our goals with some degree of predictability and sanity, we need road maps of the environments in which we live. These road maps, called **mental models**, are internal representations of the external world.[10] They consist of visual or relational images in our mind, such as what the classroom looks like or conceptually what happens when you submit an assignment late. We rely on mental models to make sense of our environment through perceptual grouping; they fill in the missing pieces, including the causal connection among events. For example, you have a mental model about attending a class lecture or seminar, including assumptions or expectations about where students arrange themselves in the room, how they ask and answer questions, and so forth. We can create a mental image of a class in progress.

We rely on mental models to make sense of our environment through perceptual grouping; they fill in the missing pieces, including the causal connection among events. Yet, mental models may also blind us from seeing that world in different ways. For example, accounting professionals tend to see corporate problems in terms of accounting solutions, whereas marketing professionals see the same problems from a marketing perspective. Mental models also block our recognition of new opportunities. How do we change mental models? It's a tough challenge. After all, we developed models from several years of experience and reinforcement. The most important way to minimize the perceptual problems with mental models is to constantly question them. We need to ask ourselves about the assumptions we make. Working with people from diverse backgrounds is another way to break out of existing mental models. Colleagues from different cultures and areas of expertise tend to have different mental models, so working with them makes your assumptions more obvious.

SOCIAL IDENTITY AND STEREOTYPING

LO2

In the previous chapter, we learned that social identity is an important component of a person's self-concept. We define ourselves to a large extent by the groups to which we belong or have an emotional attachment. Along with shaping our self-concept, social identity theory explains the dynamics of *social perception*—how we perceive others.[11] This social perception is influenced by three activities in the process of forming and maintaining our social identity: categorization, homogenization, and differentiation.

- *Categorization*—Social identity is a comparative process, and that comparison begins by categorizing people into distinct groups. By viewing someone (including yourself) as an Albertan, for example, you remove that person's individuality and, instead, see him or her as prototypical representative of the group called Albertans. This categorization then allows you to distinguish Albertans from people who live in, say, Nova Scotia and elsewhere.

- *Homogenization*—To simplify the comparison process, we tend to think that people within each group are very similar to each other. For instance, we think Albertans collectively have similar attitudes and characteristics, whereas Nova Scotians collectively have their own set of characteristics. Of course, every individual is unique, but we tend to lose sight of this fact when thinking about our social identity and how we compare to people in other social groups.

- *Differentiation*—Social identity fulfills our inherent need to have a distinct and positive self-concept. To achieve this, we do more than categorize people and homogenize them; we also differentiate groups by assigning more favourable characteristics to people in our groups than to people in other groups. This differentiation is often subtle, but it can escalate into a "good guy-bad guy" contrast when groups are in conflict with each other.[12]

STEREOTYPING IN ORGANIZATIONS

stereotyping
The process of assigning traits to people based on their membership in a social category.

Stereotyping is an extension of social identity theory and a product of our natural process of organizing information through categorical thinking.[13] Stereotyping has three elements. First, we develop social categories and assign traits that are difficult to observe. For instance, students might form a stereotype that professors are both intelligent and absentminded. Personal experiences shape stereotypes to some extent, but they are mainly provided to us through cultural upbringing and media images (e.g., movie characters). Second, we assign people to one or more social categories based on easily observable information about them, such as their gender, appearance, or physical location. Third, people who seem to belong to the stereotyped group are assigned non-observable traits associated with the group. For example, if we learn that someone is a professor, we implicitly tend to assume the person is also intelligent and absentminded.

One reason why people engage in stereotyping is that, as a form of categorical thinking, it is a natural and mostly nonconscious "energy saving" process to simplify our understanding of the world. It is easier to remember features of a stereotype than the constellation of characteristics unique to everyone we meet.[14] A second reason is that we have an innate need to understand and anticipate how others will behave. We don't have much information when first meeting someone, so we rely heavily on stereotypes to fill in the missing pieces. People with a strong need for this cognitive closure have a higher tendency to rely on stereotypes. A third reason is that stereotyping enhances our self-concept. As was mentioned earlier, the social identity process includes differentiation such that we give more favourable views of members of our own groups than of people in other groups. When out-group members threaten our self-concept, we are particularly motivated (often without our awareness), to assign negative stereotypes to them.[15]

Problems with Stereotyping   Stereotypes are not completely fictional, but neither do they accurately describe every person in that social category. For instance, the widespread "bean counter" stereotype of accountants views people in this profession as "single-mindedly preoccupied with precision and form, methodical and conservative, and a boring joyless character."[16] Although this may be true of some accountants, it is certainly not characteristic of all—or even most—people in this profession.

Another problem with stereotyping is that it lays the foundation for discriminatory attitudes and behaviour. One recent study reported that 41 percent of Canadians say they have experienced discrimination in employment within the past five years, with age and race discrimination being the most common. Similarly, Statistics Canada reports that the majority of visible minorities in Canada say they feel or experience discrimination in the workplace.[17] Most of this perceptual bias occurs as *unintentional (systemic) discrimination*, whereby decision makers rely on stereotypes to establish notions of the "ideal" person in specific roles. A person who doesn't fit the ideal tends to receive a less favourable evaluation. This subtle discrimination often shows up in age discrimination claims, such as the recent case in which Ryanair's recruitment advertising said it was looking for "young dynamic" employees. Recruiters at the Irish discount airline probably didn't intentionally discriminate against older people, but the tribunal concluded that systemic discrimination did occur because none of the job applicants was over 40 years old.[18]

The more serious form of stereotype bias is *intentional discrimination* or *prejudice*, in which people hold unfounded negative attitudes toward people belonging to a particular stereotyped group.[19] Overt prejudice seems to be less common today than a few decades ago, but it still exists. Quebec's Human Rights Tribunal was recently shocked to discover that one of Canada's largest vegetable farms prevented black employees from eating in the regular cafeteria. Instead, they were relegated to a "blacks only" eating area that lacked heat, running water, proper toilets, and refrigeration.[20] As GLOBAL Connections 3.1 describes, France is also coming to terms with both intentional and unintentional discrimination against nonwhite job applicants.

If stereotyping is such a problem, shouldn't we try to avoid this process altogether? Unfortunately, it's not that simple. Most experts agree that categorical thinking (including stereotyping) is an automatic and nonconscious process. Intensive training can minimize stereotype activation to some extent, but for the most part the process is hardwired in our brain cells.[21] Also remember that stereotyping helps us in several valuable (although fallible) ways described earlier: minimizing mental effort, filling in missing information, and supporting our social identity. The good news is that while it is very difficult to prevent the *activation* of stereotypes, we can minimize the *application* of stereotypic information. Later in this chapter, we will identify ways to minimize stereotyping and other perceptual biases.

ATTRIBUTION THEORY

LO3

attribution process
The perceptual process of deciding whether an observed behaviour or event is caused largely by internal or external factors.

The **attribution process** involves deciding whether an observed behaviour or event is caused mainly by the person (internal factors) or the environment (external factors).[22] Internal factors include the person's ability or motivation, whereas external factors include lack of resources, other people, or just luck. If a co-worker doesn't show up for an important meeting, for instance, we infer either internal attributions (the co-worker is forgetful, lacks motivation, etc.) or external attributions (traffic, a family emergency, or other circumstances prevented the co-worker from attending).

People rely on the three attribution rules shown in Exhibit 3.2 on page 60 to determine whether someone's behaviour mainly has an internal or external attribution. Internal attributions are made when the observed individual behaved this way in the

global connections 3.1

"Your Name Says Everything in France": France's Employment Discrimination Problem

Hamid Senni wears a shirt and tie whenever he strolls along the Champs Elysées in Paris. The reason for this formality? "If I'm in jeans, people think I'm a shoplifter," he says. What makes this misperception even worse is that Senni, the son of Moroccan immigrants, was born and raised in France. And in spite of his education and fluent language skills, Senni was told more than once that he would never find a job in France. Incensed by the daily discrimination he experienced in his own country, Senni moved to Sweden and now lives in London, where he advises companies on ethnic diversity. "Going abroad was like an exorcism," he says bluntly. "In the U.K., diversity is seen as an opportunity. In France it's still seen as a problem."

Senni's perception of racial and ethnic discrimination in France is supported by a recent study conducted jointly by the French government and the International Labour Organization (ILO). Researchers submitted two nearly identical job applications to 2,440 help-wanted ads. The main difference was that the candidate in one application had a French-sounding name whereas the individual in the other application had a North African or Sub-Saharan African name. Almost 80 percent of employers preferred the applicant with the French-sounding name. Furthermore, when applicants personally visited human resource staff, those who had foreign names seldom received job interviews; instead, they were often told that the job had been filled or that the company would not be hiring after all. The report concluded that "almost 90 percent of overall discrimination occurred before the employer had even bothered to interview both test candidates."

One young black resident near Paris who calls himself Billy Fabrice, knows about the undercurrents of racial discrimination. "Your name says everything in France," says Fabrice. "If you are called Diallo or Amir, that's all they want to know. If you are called Jean-Pierre, you show up for a job and they take you." Some employers specifically ask hiring agencies for applicants who are "BBR." This acronym for the colours of

"In the U.K., diversity is seen as an opportunity. In France, it's still seen as a problem," says Hamid Senni (shown here), who left his home country of France due to its discriminatory employment practices. *Jonathan Player/IHT/Redux*

the French flag (bleu, blanc, rouge) is apparently a well-known employment code to hire only white French people. In one recent court case, prosecutors claimed that Garnier, a division of L'Oreal, tried to hire mostly white staff for in-store promotions. Garnier sent its temporary recruitment agency a fax specifying that those hired should be within a specific age range (18 to 22), clothing size, and be "BBR." Initially, 38 percent of candidates sent by the recruitment agency were nonwhite. After the fax was sent, this dropped to less than 5 percent.

While many French employers, including Garnier, deny prejudice or even systemic discrimination against nonwhite applicants, others are taking steps to make the hiring process more colour blind. Axa SA, the giant French insurance company, introduced anonymous resumes, in which job applicants provide their qualifications but not their names, addresses, gender, or age. Serge Simon, a 20-something French resident with Haitian origins, is hopeful. "I think that with an anonymous resume, a person will be hired for what they are—for their qualifications and not for the colour of their skin," he believes.[23]

past (high consistency), behaves like this toward other people or in different situations (low distinctiveness), and other people do not behave this way in similar situations (low consensus). On the other hand, an external attribution is made when there is low consistency, high distinctiveness, and high consensus.

To illustrate how these three attribution rules operate, suppose that an employee is making poor-quality products one day on a particular machine. We would probably conclude that there is something wrong with the machine (an external attribution) if the employee has made good-quality products on this machine in the past (low consistency), the employee makes good-quality products on other machines (high distinctiveness), and other employees have recently had quality problems on this machine (high consensus). We would make an internal attribution, on the other hand, if the employee

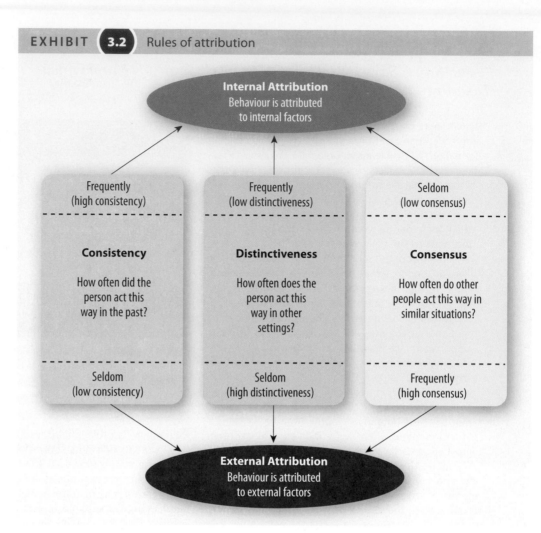

EXHIBIT 3.2   Rules of attribution

Internal Attribution
Behaviour is attributed to internal factors

Frequently
(high consistency)

Consistency

How often did the person act this way in the past?

Seldom
(low consistency)

Frequently
(low distinctiveness)

Distinctiveness

How often does the person act this way in other settings?

Seldom
(high distinctiveness)

Seldom
(low consensus)

Consensus

How often do other people act this way in similar situations?

Frequently
(high consensus)

External Attribution
Behaviour is attributed to external factors

usually makes poor-quality products on this machine (high consistency), other employees produce good-quality products on this machine (low consensus), and the employee also makes poor-quality products on other machines (low distinctiveness).[24]

Attribution is an essential perceptual process because it forms cause-effect relationships which, in turn, affect how we respond to others' behaviour and how we act in the future. How we react to a co-worker's poor performance depends on our internal or external attribution of that performance. Students who make internal attributions about their poor performance are more likely to drop out of their programs, for instance.[25]

ATTRIBUTION ERRORS

fundamental attribution error
The tendency to see the person rather than the situation as the main cause of that person's behaviour.

People are far from perfect when making attributions. One bias, called **fundamental attribution error**, refers to our tendency to see the person rather than the situation as the main cause of that person's behaviour.[26] If an employee is late for work, observers are more likely to conclude that the person is lazy than to realize that external factors may have caused this behaviour. Fundamental attribution error occurs because observers can't easily see the external factors that constrain the person's behaviour. We didn't see the traffic jam that caused the person to be late, for instance. Research suggests that fundamental attribution error is more common in Western countries than in Asian cultures, where people are taught from an early age to pay attention to the context in interpersonal relations and to see everything connected in a holistic way.[27]

self-serving bias
The tendency to attribute our favourable outcomes to internal factors and our failures to external factors.

Another attribution error, known as **self-serving bias**, is the tendency to attribute our favourable outcomes to internal factors and our failures to external factors. Simply put, we take credit for our successes and blame others or the situation for our mistakes. Self-serving bias is one of several related biases that maintain a positive self-concept, particularly engaging in self-enhancement to maintain a positive self-evaluation. It is evident in many aspects of work life. In annual reports, for example, executives mainly refer to their personal qualities as reasons for the company's successes and to external factors as reasons for the company's failures.[28]

SELF-FULFILLING PROPHECY

LO4

self-fulfilling prophecy
Occurs when our expectations about another person cause that person to act in a way that is consistent with those expectations.

Self-fulfilling prophecy occurs when our expectations about another person cause that person to act in a way that is consistent with those expectations. In other words, our perceptions can influence reality. Exhibit 3.3 illustrates the four steps in the self-fulfilling prophecy process using the example of a supervisor and subordinate.[29] The process begins when the supervisor forms expectations about the employee's future behaviour and performance. These expectations are sometimes inaccurate, because first impressions are usually formed from limited information. The supervisor's expectations influence his or her treatment of employees. Specifically, high-expectancy employees (those expected to do well) receive more emotional support through nonverbal cues (e.g., more smiling and eye contact), more frequent and valuable feedback and reinforcement, more challenging goals, better training, and more opportunities to demonstrate good performance.

The third step in self-fulfilling prophecy includes two effects of the supervisor's behaviours on the employee. First, through better training and more practise opportunities, a high-expectancy employee learns more skills and knowledge than a low-expectancy employee. Second, the employee becomes more self-confident, which results in higher motivation and willingness to set more challenging goals.[30] In the final step, high-expectancy employees have higher motivation and better skills, resulting in better performance, while the opposite is true of low-expectancy employees.

There are plenty of examples of self-fulfilling prophecies in work and school settings.[31] Research has found that women perform less well on math tests after being informed that men tend to perform better on them. Women perform better on these tests when they are not exposed to this negative self-fulfilling prophecy. Similarly, people over 65 receive lower results on memory tests after hearing that mental ability

EXHIBIT **3.3** The self-fulfilling prophecy cycle

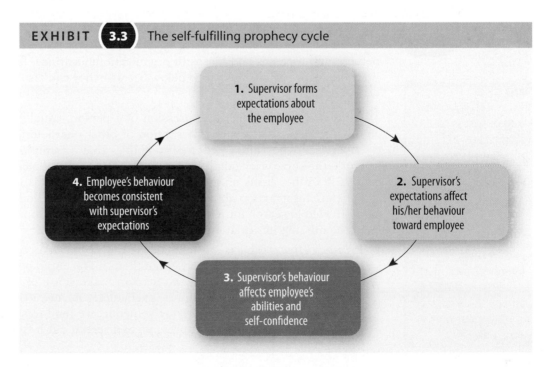

declines with age. Another study reported that the performance of Israeli Defence Force trainees was influenced by their instructor's expectations regarding the trainee's potential in the program. Self-fulfilling prophecy was at work here because the instructors' expectations were based on a list provided by researchers showing which recruits had high and low potential, even though the researchers had actually listed these trainees randomly.

CONTINGENCIES OF SELF-FULFILLING PROPHECY

Self-fulfilling prophecies are more powerful under some conditions than others. The self-fulfilling prophecy effect is stronger at the beginning of the relationship, such as when employees are first hired. It is also stronger when several people (rather than just one person) hold the same perception of the individual. In other words, we might be able to ignore one person's doubts about our potential, but not the collective doubts of several people. The self-fulfilling prophecy effect is also stronger among people with a history of low achievement. High achievers can draw upon their past successes to offset low expectations, whereas low achievers do not have these past successes to support their self-confidence. Fortunately, the opposite is also true: low achievers respond more favourably than high achievers to positive self-fulfilling prophecy. Low achievers don't receive this positive encouragement very often, so it probably has a strong effect on their motivation to excel.[32]

The main lesson from the self-fulfilling prophecy literature is that leaders need to develop and maintain a positive, yet realistic, expectation toward all employees. This recommendation is consistent with the emerging philosophy of *positive organizational behaviour*, which suggests that focusing on the positive rather than negative aspects of life will improve organizational success and individual well-being. Communicating hope and optimism is so important that it is identified as one of the critical success factors for physicians and surgeons. Unfortunately, training programs that make leaders aware of the power of positive expectations seem to have minimal effect. Instead, generating positive expectations and hope depend on a corporate culture of support and learning. Hiring supervisors who are inherently optimistic toward their staff is another way of increasing the incidence of positive self-fulfilling prophecies.

OTHER PERCEPTUAL ERRORS

LO5

Self-fulfilling prophecy, attribution, and stereotyping are among the most common perceptual processes and biases in organizational settings, but there are many others. Four others are briefly described below because they can also bias our perception of the world around us.

halo effect
A perceptual error whereby our general impression of a person, usually based on one prominent characteristic, colours our perception of other characteristics of that person.

- *Halo effect*—Our general impression of a person, usually based on one prominent characteristic, distorts our perception of other characteristics of that person.[33] If a supervisor who values punctuality notices that an employee is sometimes late for work, the supervisor might form a negative image of the employee and evaluate that person's other traits unfavourably as well. Halo effect is most likely to occur when concrete information about the perceived target is missing or we are not sufficiently motivated to search for it. Instead, we use our general impression of the person to fill in the missing information.

primacy effect
A perceptual error in which we quickly form an opinion of people based on the first information we receive about them.

- *Primacy effect*—This is our tendency to quickly form an opinion of people based on the first information we receive about them.[34] This rapid perceptual organization and interpretation occurs because we need to make sense of the world around us. The problem is that first impressions—particularly negative first impressions— are difficult to change. After categorizing someone, we tend to select subsequent information that supports our first impression and screen out information that opposes that impression.

© Scott Adams/Distributed by United Features Syndicate, Inc.

recency effect
A perceptual error in which the most recent information dominates our perception of others.

- *Recency effect*—This perceptual bias occurs when the most recent information dominates our perceptions.[35] This effect is most common when making an evaluation involving complex information, particularly among people with limited experience. For instance, auditors must digest large volumes of information in their judgments about financial documents, and the most recent information received prior to the decision tends to get weighted more heavily than information received at the beginning of the audit. Similarly, when supervisors evaluate the performance of employees over the previous year, the most recent performance information dominates the evaluation because it is the most easily recalled.

false-consensus effect
A perceptual error in which we overestimate the extent to which others have beliefs and characteristics similar to our own.

- *False-consensus effect*—Sometimes called the "similar to me" effect, false-consensus effect is a widely observed bias in which we overestimate the extent to which others have beliefs and characteristics similar to our own.[36] Employees who are thinking of quitting their job believe that a large percentage of their co-workers are also thinking about quitting. This bias occurs to some extent because we associate with others who are similar and selectively remember information that is consistent with our own views. We also believe "everyone does it" to reinforce our self-concept regarding behaviours that do not have a positive image (quitting, parking illegally, etc.).

IMPROVING PERCEPTIONS

We can't bypass the perceptual process, but we should make every attempt to minimize perceptual biases and distortions. Three potentially effective ways to improve perceptions include awareness of perceptual bias, self-awareness, and meaningful interaction.

AWARENESS OF PERCEPTUAL BIASES

One of the most obvious and widely practised ways to reduce perceptual biases is by knowing that they exist. For example, diversity awareness training tries to minimize discrimination by making people aware of systemic discrimination as well as prejudices that occur through stereotyping. This training also attempts to dispel myths about people from various cultural and demographic groups. Awareness of perceptual biases can reduce these biases to some extent by making people more mindful of their thoughts and actions. However, awareness has only a limited effect.[37] For example, self-fulfilling prophecy training informs managers about this perceptual bias and encourages them to engage in more positive rather than negative self-fulfilling prophecies, yet research has found that managers continue to engage in negative self-fulfilling prophecies after they complete the training program.

IMPROVING SELF-AWARENESS

A more powerful way to minimize perceptual biases is to provide evidence that the individual's own behaviour and decisions reflect these biases. A powerful example is the Implicit Association Test (IAT), which detects subtle race, age, and gender bias by associating positive and negative words with specific demographic groups.[38] Many people are much more vigilant about their stereotypes and prejudices after discovering that their test results show a personal bias against older people or individuals from different ethnic backgrounds. For example, Jennifer Smith-Holladay was surprised to learn after taking the IAT that she is biased in favour of white people, a group to which she belongs, and in favour of heterosexuals, a group to which she does not belong. "I discovered that I not only have some ingroup favouritism lurking in my subconscious, but also possess some internalized oppression in terms of my sexuality." Smith-Holladay says this revelation will make her more aware of personal biases and to minimize their application in decision making. "In the case of my own subconscious ingroup favouritism for white people, for example, my charge is to be colour-conscious, not colour-blind, and to always explicitly consider how race may affect behaviours and decisions," she says.[39]

More generally, people tend to reduce their perceptual biases by "knowing themselves"—increasing awareness of their own values, beliefs, and prejudices.[40] The **Johari Window** is a popular model for understanding how co-workers can increase their mutual understanding.[41] Developed by Joseph Luft and Harry Ingram (hence the name Johari), this model divides information about you into four "windows"— open, blind, hidden, and unknown—based on whether your own values, beliefs, and experiences are known to you and to others (see Exhibit 3.4). The *open area* includes information about you that is known both to you and to others. The *blind area* refers to information that is known to others but not to you. For example, your colleagues might notice that you are self-conscious and awkward when meeting the company chief executive, but you are unaware of this fact. Information known to you but unknown to others is found in the *hidden area*. Finally, the *unknown area* includes your values, beliefs, and experiences that aren't known to you or others.

> **Johari Window**
> A model of mutual understanding that encourages disclosure and feedback to increase our own open area and reduce the blind, hidden, and unknown areas.

EXHIBIT 3.4   The Johari Window model of self-awareness and mutual understanding

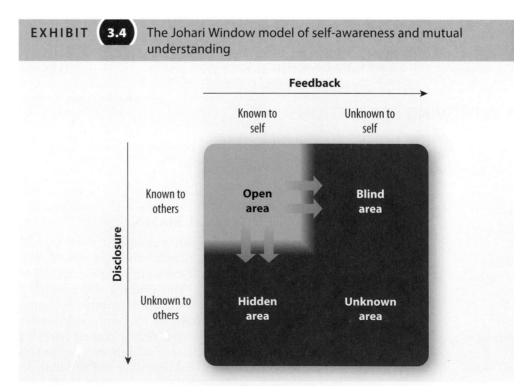

Source: Based on J. Luft, *Group Processes* (Palo Alto, CA: Mayfield, 1984).

The main objective of the Johari Window is to increase the size of the open area so that both you and colleagues are aware of your perceptual limitations. This is partly accomplished by reducing the hidden area through *disclosure*— informing others of your beliefs, feelings, and experiences that may influence the work relationship.[42] The open area also increases through *feedback* from others about your behaviours. This information helps you to reduce your blind area, because co-workers often see things in you that you do not see. Finally, the combination of disclosure and feedback occasionally produces revelations about information in the unknown area.

MEANINGFUL INTERACTION

contact hypothesis
A theory stating that the more we interact with someone, the less we rely on stereotypes to understand that person.

While the Johari Window relies on dialogue, self-awareness and mutual understanding can also improve through *meaningful interaction*.[43] This statement is based on the **contact hypothesis**, which states that, under certain conditions, people who interact with each other will be less prejudiced or perceptually biased against each other. Simply spending time with members of other groups can improve your understanding and opinion of that person to some extent. But the contact hypothesis effect is much stronger under specific conditions. First, participants should have close and frequent interaction working toward a shared goal where they need to rely on each other (i.e., cooperate rather than compete with each other). Everyone should have equal status in that context and should be engaged in a meaningful task. An hour-long social gathering between executives and front-line employees does not satisfy these conditions. On the other hand, meaningful interaction does occur when senior executives, such as Canada Post CEO Moya Greene, work in front-line jobs (see opening story to this chapter). These activities tend to improve perceptions of executives and employees because executives minimize status differences with other staff, cooperate toward a common goal, and have close and frequent interaction with front-line employees.

empathy
A person's understanding of and sensitivity to the feelings, thoughts, and situation of others.

Meaningful interaction does more than reduce our reliance on stereotypes. It also potentially improves empathy towards others. **Empathy** refers to a person's understanding of and sensitivity to the feelings, thoughts, and situation of others.[44] You have empathy when actively visualizing the other person's situation and feeling that person's emotions in that situation. Empathizing with others improves our sensitivity to external causes of another person's performance and behaviour, thereby reducing fundamental attribution error. A supervisor who imagines what it's like to be a single mother, for example, would become more sensitive to the external causes of lateness and other events among these employees.

The perceptual process represents the filter through which information passes from the external environment to our brain. As such, it is really the beginning of the learning process, which we discuss next.

LEARNING IN ORGANIZATIONS

learning
A relatively permanent change in behaviour (or behaviour tendency) that occurs as a result of a person's interaction with the environment.

Learning is a relatively permanent change in behaviour (or behaviour tendency) that occurs as a result of a person's interaction with the environment. Learning occurs when the learner behaves differently. For example, we can see that you have "learned" computer skills when you operate the keyboard and software more quickly than before. Learning occurs when interaction with the environment leads to behaviour change. This means that we learn through our senses, such as through study, observation, and experience.

tacit knowledge
Knowledge embedded in our actions and ways of thinking, and transmitted only through observation and experience.

Some of what we learn is *explicit knowledge*, such as reading information in this book. However, explicit knowledge is really only the tip of the knowledge iceberg. Most of what we know is **tacit knowledge**.[45] Tacit knowledge is not documented; rather, it is acquired through observation and direct experience. For example, airline pilots learn to operate commercial jets more by watching experts and practising on flight simulators than through lectures. They acquire tacit knowledge by directly experiencing the complex interaction of behaviour with the machine's response.

Three perspectives of learning tacit and explicit knowledge are reinforcement, social learning, and direct experience. Each perspective offers a different angle for understanding the dynamics of learning.

BEHAVIOUR MODIFICATION: LEARNING THROUGH REINFORCEMENT

behaviour modification
A theory that explains learning in terms of the antecedents and consequences of behaviour.

One of the oldest perspectives on learning, called **behaviour modification** (also known as *operant conditioning* and *reinforcement theory*), takes the rather extreme view that learning is completely dependent on the environment. Behaviour modification does not question the notion that thinking is part of the learning process, but it views human thoughts as unimportant intermediate stages between behaviour and the environment. The environment teaches us to alter our behaviours so that we maximize positive consequences and minimize adverse consequences.[46]

A-B-Cs of Behaviour Modification   The central objective of behaviour modification is to change behaviour (B) by managing its antecedents (A) and consequences (C). This process is nicely illustrated in the A-B-C model of behaviour modification, shown in Exhibit 3.5.[47]

Antecedents are events preceding the behaviour, informing employees that certain behaviours will have particular consequences. An antecedent may be a sound from your computer signalling that an email has arrived or a request from your supervisor to complete a specific task by tomorrow. These antecedents let employees know that a particular action will produce specific consequences. Notice that antecedents do not cause behaviours. The computer sound doesn't cause us to open our email. Rather, the sound is a cue telling us that certain consequences are likely to occur if we engage in certain behaviours. In behaviour modification, *consequences* are events following a particular behaviour that influence its future occurrence. Generally speaking, people tend to repeat behaviours that are followed by pleasant consequences and are less likely to repeat behaviours that are followed by unpleasant consequences or no consequences at all.

Contingencies of Reinforcement   Behaviour modification identifies four types of consequences, called the *contingencies of reinforcement*, which increase, maintain, or reduce the probability that behaviour will be repeated.[48]

• *Positive reinforcement*—occurs when the *introduction* of a consequence *increases or maintains* the frequency or future probability of a specific behaviour. Receiving a bonus after successfully completing an important project is considered positive

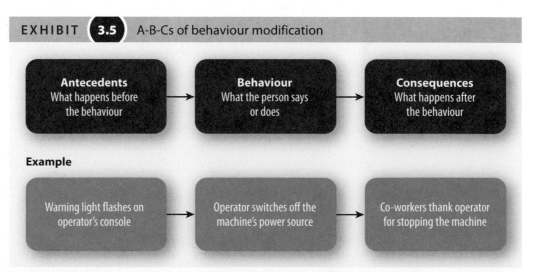

EXHIBIT 3.5   A-B-Cs of behaviour modification

Antecedents What happens before the behaviour	**Behaviour** What the person says or does	**Consequences** What happens after the behaviour

Example

Warning light flashes on operator's console	Operator switches off the machine's power source	Co-workers thank operator for stopping the machine

Sources: Adapted from T. K. Connellan, *How to Improve Human Performance*, (New York: Harper & Row, 1978), p. 50; F. Luthans and R. Kreitner, *Organizational Behaviour Modification and Beyond*, (Glenview, IL: Scott, Foresman, 1985), pp. 85–88.

reinforcement because it typically increases the probability that you will use those behaviours in the future.

- *Punishment*—occurs when a consequence decreases the frequency or future probability of a behaviour. This consequence typically involves introducing something that employees try to avoid. For instance, most of us would consider a demotion or being ostracized by our co-workers as forms of punishment.[49]

- *Negative reinforcement*—occurs when the removal or avoidance of a consequence increases or maintains the frequency or future probability of a specific behaviour. Supervisors apply negative reinforcement when they stop criticizing employees whose substandard performance has improved. When the criticism is withheld, employees are more likely to repeat behaviours that improved their performance. Notice that negative reinforcement is not punishment. Whereas punishment extinguishes behaviour by introducing a negative consequence, negative reinforcement actually reinforces behaviour by removing the negative consequence.

- *Extinction*—occurs when the target behaviour decreases because no consequence follows it. In this respect, extinction is a do-nothing strategy. Generally, behaviour that is no longer reinforced tends to disappear; it becomes extinct. For instance, research suggests that performance tends to decline when managers stop congratulating employees for their good work.[50]

Which contingency of reinforcement should be used in the learning process? In most situations, positive reinforcement should follow desired behaviours and extinction (do nothing) should follow undesirable behaviours. This approach is preferred because punishment and negative reinforcement generate negative emotions and attitudes toward the punisher (e.g., supervisor) and organization. However, some form of punishment (dismissal, suspension, demotion, etc.) may be necessary for extreme behaviours, such as deliberately hurting a co-worker or stealing inventory. Indeed, research suggests that, under certain conditions, punishment maintains a sense of fairness.[51]

Schedules of Reinforcement   Along with the types of reinforcement, the frequency and timing of those reinforcers also influence employee behaviours.[52] These reinforcement schedules can be continuous or intermittent. The most effective reinforcement schedule for learning new tasks is *continuous reinforcement*—providing positive reinforcement after every occurrence of the desired behaviour. Employees learn desired behaviours quickly and, when the reinforcer is removed, extinction also occurs very quickly.

The best schedule for reinforcing learned behaviour is a *variable ratio schedule* in which employee behaviour is reinforced after a variable number of times. Salespeople experience variable ratio reinforcement because they make a successful sale (the reinforcer) after a varying number of client calls. They might make four unsuccessful calls before receiving an order on the fifth one, then make 10 more calls before receiving the next order, and so on. The variable ratio schedule makes behaviour highly resistant to extinction because it is never expected at a particular time or after a fixed number of accomplishments.

Behaviour Modification in Practice   Everyone practises behaviour modification in one form or another. We thank people for a job well done, are silent when displeased, and sometimes try to punish those who go against our wishes. Behaviour modification also occurs in various formal programs to reduce absenteeism, improve task performance, encourage safe work behaviours, and have a healthier lifestyle.[53] For example, ExxonMobil's Fawley refinery in the U.K. introduced a "Behave Safely Challenge" program in which supervisors rewarded employees and contractors on the spot when they exhibited good safety behaviour or intervened to improve the safe behaviour of co-workers. These rewards were a form of positive reinforcement using a variable ratio schedule (safe work behaviours were reinforced after a variable number of times that they occurred).[54]

Although a natural part of human interaction, behaviour modification has a number of limitations when applied strategically in organizational settings. One limitation is "reward inflation," in which the reinforcer is eventually considered an entitlement. For this reason, most behaviour modification programs must run infrequently and for a short duration. Another concern is that the variable ratio schedule of reinforcement tends to create a lottery-style reward system, which is unpopular to people who dislike gambling. But probably the most significant problem is behaviour modification's radical view that behaviour is learned only through personal interaction with the environment.[56] This view is no longer accepted; instead, learning experts recognize that people also learn by observing others and thinking logically about possible consequences. This learning through observation process is explained by social learning theory.

SOCIAL LEARNING THEORY: LEARNING BY OBSERVING

LO8

Social learning theory states that much learning occurs by observing others and then modelling the behaviours that lead to favourable outcomes and avoiding behaviours that lead to punishing consequences.[57] This form of learning occurs in three ways: behaviour modelling, learning behaviour consequences, and self-reinforcement.

> **social learning theory**
> A theory stating that much learning occurs by observing others and then modelling the behaviours that lead to favourable outcomes and avoiding behaviours that lead to punishing consequences.

- *Behaviour modelling*—People learn by observing the behaviours of a role model on the critical task, remembering the important elements of the observed behaviours, and then practising those behaviours.[58] This is a valuable form of learning because tacit knowledge and skills are mainly acquired through observation and practice. As an example, it is difficult to document or explain in a conversation all of the steps necessary to bake professional quality bread. Student chefs also need to observe the master baker's subtle behaviours. Behavioural modelling also increases self-efficacy because people gain more self-confidence after seeing someone else perform the task. This is particularly true when observers identify with the model, such as someone who is similar in age, experience, gender, and related features.

- *Learning behaviour consequences*—People learn the consequences of behaviour through logic and observation, not just through direct experience. They logically anticipate consequences after completing a task well or poorly. They also learn behavioural consequences by observing the experiences of other people. Consider the employee who observes a co-worker receiving a stern warning for working in an unsafe manner. This event would reduce the observer's likelihood of engaging in unsafe behaviours because he or she has learned to anticipate a similar reprimand following those behaviours.[59]

> **self-reinforcement**
> Occurs whenever an employee has control over a reinforcer but doesn't "take" it until completing a self-set goal.

- *Self-reinforcement*—**Self-reinforcement** occurs whenever an employee has control over a reinforcer but doesn't "take" it until completing a self-set goal.[60] For example, you might be thinking about having a snack after you finish reading the rest of this chapter. Raiding the refrigerator is a form of self-induced positive reinforcement for completing this reading assignment. Self-reinforcement takes many forms, such as taking a short walk, watching a movie, or simply congratulating yourself for completing the task.

LEARNING THROUGH EXPERIENCE

Along with behaviour modification and social learning, employees learn through direct experience. In fact, most tacit knowledge and skills are acquired through experience as well as observation. Generally, experiential learning begins with engagement with the environment, then reflecting on that experience and forming theories about how the world around us works. This is followed by experimentation, in which we find out how well the newly formed theories work.[61] Experiential learning requires all of these steps, although people tend to prefer one step more than the others.

One of the most important ingredients for learning through experience is that the organization should possess a strong **learning orientation**.[62] This means that they value learning opportunities and, in particular, the generation of new knowledge while employees perform their jobs. If an employee initially fails to perform a task, then the experience might still be a valuable learning opportunity. In other words, a learning orientation culture rewards experimentation and recognizes mistakes as a natural part of the learning process. It encourages employees to take reasonable risks to ultimately discover new and better ways of doing things.

Organizations achieve a learning orientation culture by rewarding experimentation and accepting reasonable failures. They encourage employees to question long-held assumptions or mental models and to actively "unlearn" practices that are no longer ideal. Without a learning orientation, mistakes are hidden and problems are more likely to escalate or re-emerge later. It's not surprising, then, that one of the most frequently mentioned lessons from the best performing manufacturers is to expect mistakes. "[Mistakes] are a source of learning and will improve operations in the long run," explains an executive at Lockheed Martin. "[They] foster the concept that no question is dumb, no idea too wild, and no task or activity is irrelevant."[63]

> **learning orientation**
> A culture in which the organization rewards experimentation, accepts reasonable mistakes, and encourages employees to question long-held assumptions about past practices.

FROM INDIVIDUAL TO ORGANIZATIONAL LEARNING

LO9

One of the most popular contemporary perspectives of organizational effectiveness is *organizational learning*, which was defined in Chapter 1 as any structured activity that improves an organization's capacity to acquire, share, and use knowledge in ways that improve its survival and success. Organizational learning is heavily dependent on individual learning, but the "capacity" to acquire, share, and use knowledge means that companies establish systems, structures, and organizational values that support the knowledge management process.[64]

- *Knowledge acquisition*—This includes extracting information and ideas from the external environment as well as through insight. One of the fastest and most powerful ways to acquire knowledge is by hiring individuals or acquiring entire companies. Knowledge also enters the organization when employees learn from external sources, such as discovering new resources from suppliers or becoming aware of new trends from clients. A third knowledge acquisition strategy is through experimentation. Companies receive knowledge through insight as a result of research and other creative processes.

- *Knowledge sharing*—This aspect of organizational learning involves distributing knowledge to others across the organization. Although typically associated with computer intranets and digital repositories of knowledge, knowledge sharing also occurs through informal online or face-to-face communication.[65] Most social learning (such as behavioural modelling) and experiential learning are forms of knowledge sharing because the learning is transferred from one employee to another.

- *Knowledge use*—The competitive advantage of knowledge comes from applying it in ways that add value to the organization and its stakeholders. To do this, employees must realize that the knowledge is available and that they have enough freedom to apply it. This requires a culture that supports the learning process.

This chapter has introduced two fundamental activities in human behaviour in the workplace: perceptions and learning. These activities involve receiving information from the environment, organizing it, and acting on it as a learning process. Our knowledge about perceptions and learning in the workplace lays the foundation for the next chapter, which looks at workplace emotions and attitudes.

CHAPTER SUMMARY

Perception involves selecting, organizing, and interpreting information to make sense of the world around us. Perceptual organization engages categorical thinking—the mostly nonconscious process of organizing people and objects into preconceived categories that are stored in our long-term memory. Mental models—internal representations of the external world—also help us to make sense of incoming stimuli.

Social identity theory explains how we perceive people through categorization, homogenization, and differentiation. Stereotyping is a derivative of social identity theory, in which people assign traits to others based on their membership in a social category. Stereotyping economizes mental effort, fills in missing information, and enhances our self-perception and social identity. However, it also lays the foundation for prejudice and systemic discrimination.

The attribution process involves deciding whether an observed behaviour or event is caused mainly by the person (internal factors) or the environment (external factors). Attributions are decided by perceptions of the consistency, distinctiveness, and consensus of the behaviour. This process helps us to link together the various pieces of our world in cause-effect relationships, but it is also subject to attribution errors, including fundamental attribution error and self-serving bias.

Self-fulfilling prophecy occurs when our expectations about another person cause that person to act in a way that is consistent with those expectations. Essentially, our expectations affect our behaviour toward the target person, which then affects that person's opportunities and attitudes, which then influences his or her behaviour. Self-fulfilling prophecies tend to be stronger at the beginning of the relationship (such as when employees first join the department), when several people hold the expectations toward the employee, and when the employee has a history of low achievement.

Four other perceptual errors commonly noted in organizations are halo effect, primacy effect, recency effect, and false-consensus effect. We can minimize these and other perceptual problems through awareness of perceptual bias, self-awareness, and meaningful interaction.

Learning is a relatively permanent change in behaviour (or behaviour tendency) that occurs as a result of a person's interaction with the environment. Much of what we learn is tacit knowledge, which is embedded in our actions without conscious awareness.

The behaviour modification perspective of learning states that behaviour change occurs by altering its antecedents and consequences. Antecedents are environmental stimuli that provoke (not necessarily cause) behaviour. Consequences are events following behaviour that influence its future occurrence. Consequences include positive reinforcement, punishment, negative reinforcement, and extinction. The schedules of reinforcement also influence behaviour.

Social learning theory states that much learning occurs by observing others and then modelling those behaviours that seem to lead to favourable outcomes and avoiding behaviours that lead to punishing consequences. It also recognizes that we often engage in self-reinforcement. Behaviour modelling is effective because it transfers tacit knowledge and enhances the observer's confidence in performing the task.

Many companies now use experiential learning because employees do not acquire tacit knowledge through formal classroom instruction. Experiential learning is supported by a learning orientation, which occurs when companies reward experimentation, accept reasonable mistakes, and encourage employees to question long-held assumptions.

Organizational learning is any structured activity that improves an organization's capacity to acquire, share, and use knowledge in ways that improve its survival and success. Organizations acquire knowledge through individual learning and experimentation. Knowledge sharing occurs mainly through various forms of communication and training. Knowledge use occurs when employees realize that the knowledge is available and that they have enough freedom to apply it.

KEY TERMS

attribution process, p. 58

behaviour modification, p. 66

categorical thinking, p. 56

contact hypothesis, p. 65

empathy, p. 65

false-consensus effect, p. 63

fundamental attribution error, p. 60

halo effect, p. 62

Johari Window, p. 64

learning, p. 65

learning orientation, p. 69

mental models, p. 56

perception, p. 54

primacy effect, p. 62

recency effect, p. 63

selective attention, p. 54

self-fulfilling prophecy, p. 61

self-reinforcement, p. 68

self-serving bias, p. 60

social learning theory, p. 68

stereotyping, p. 57

tacit knowledge, p. 65

CRITICAL THINKING QUESTIONS

1. Several years ago, senior executives at energy company CanOil wanted to acquire an exploration company (HBOG) that was owned by another energy company, AmOil. Rather than face a hostile takeover and unfavourable tax implications, CanOil's two top executives met with the CEO of AmOil to discuss a friendly exchange of stock to carry out the transaction. AmOil's chief executive was previously unaware of CanOil's plans and, as the meeting began, the AmOil executive warned that he was there merely to listen. The CanOil executives were confident that AmOil wanted to sell HBOG because energy legislation at the time made HBOG a poor investment for AmOil. AmOil's CEO remained silent for most of the meeting, which CanOil executives interpreted as an implied agreement to proceed to buy AmOil stock on the market. But when CanOil launched the stock purchase a month later, AmOil's CEO was both surprised and outraged. He thought he had given the CanOil executives the cold shoulder, remaining silent to show his disinterest in the deal. The misunderstanding nearly bankrupted CanOil because AmOil reacted by protecting its stock. What perceptual problem(s) likely occurred that led to this misunderstanding?

2. What mental models do you have about attending a college or university lecture? Are these mental models helpful? Could any of these mental models hold you back from achieving the full benefit of the lecture?

3. Do you define yourself in terms of the university or college you attend? Why or why not? What are the implications of your answer for your university or college?

4. During a diversity management session, a manager suggests that stereotypes are a necessary part of working with others. "I have to make assumptions about what's in the other person's head, and stereotypes help me do that," she explains. "It's better to rely on stereotypes than to enter a working relationship with someone from another culture without any idea of what they believe in!" Discuss the merits of and problems with the manager's statement.

5. Describe how a manager or coach could use the process of self-fulfilling prophecy to enhance an individual's performance.

6. Describe a situation in which you used behaviour modification to influence someone's behaviour. What specifically did you do? What was the result?

7. Why are organizations moving toward the use of experiential approaches to learning? What conditions are required for success?

8. BusNews Corp. is the leading stock market and business news service. Over the past two years, BusNews has experienced increased competition from other news providers. These competitors have brought in the Internet and other emerging computer technologies to link customers with information more quickly. There is little knowledge within BusNews about how to use these computer technologies. Based on the knowledge acquisition processes for knowledge management, explain how BusNews might gain the intellectual capital necessary to become more competitive in this respect.

CASE STUDY 3.1

Hy Dairies, Ltd.

Syd Gilman read the latest sales figures with a great deal of satisfaction. The vice-president of marketing at Hy Dairies, Ltd., a large Canadian milk products manufacturer, was pleased to see that the marketing campaign to improve sagging sales of Hy's gourmet ice cream brand was working. Sales volume and market share of the product had increased significantly over the past two quarters compared with the previous year.

The improved sales of Hy's gourmet ice cream could be credited to Rochelle Beauport, who was assigned to the gourmet ice cream brand last year. Beauport had joined Hy less than two years ago as an assistant brand manager after leaving a similar job at a food products firm. She was one of the few visible minority women in marketing management at Hy Dairies and had a promising career with the company. Gilman was pleased with Beauport's work and tried to let her know this in the annual performance reviews. He now had an excellent opportunity to reward her by offering the recently vacated position of market research coordinator. Although technically only a lateral transfer with a modest salary increase, the marketing research coordinator job would give Beauport broader experience in some high-profile work, which would enhance her career with Hy Dairies. Few people were aware that Gilman's own career had been boosted by working as marketing research coordinator at Hy several years before.

Rochelle Beauport had also seen the latest sales figures on Hy's gourmet ice cream and was expecting Gilman's call to meet with her that morning. Gilman began the conversation by briefly mentioning the favourable sales figures, and then explained that he wanted Beauport to take the marketing research coordinator job. Beauport was shocked by the news. She enjoyed brand management and particularly the challenge involved with controlling a product that directly affected the company's profitability. Marketing research coordinator was a technical support position—a "backroom" job—far removed from the company's bottom-line activities. Marketing research was not the route to top management in most organizations, Beauport thought. She had been sidelined.

After a long silence, Beauport managed a weak "Thank you, Mr. Gilman." She was too bewildered to protest. She wanted to collect her thoughts and reflect on what she had done wrong. Also, she did not know her boss well enough to be openly critical.

Gilman recognized Beauport's surprise, which he naturally assumed was her positive response to hearing of this wonderful career opportunity. He, too, had been delighted several years earlier about his temporary transfer to marketing research to round out his marketing experience. "This move will be good for both you and Hy Dairies," said Gilman as he escorted Beauport from his office.

Beauport was preoccupied with several tasks that afternoon, but was able to consider the day's events that evening. She was one of the top women and few visible minorities in brand management at Hy Dairies and feared that she was being sidelined because the company didn't want women or visible minorities in top management. Her previous employer had made it quite clear that women "couldn't take the heat" in marketing management and tended to place women in technical support positions after a brief term in lower brand management jobs. Obviously Syd Gilman and Hy Dairies were following the same game plan. Gilman's comments that the coordinator job would be good for her was just a nice way of saying that Beauport couldn't go any further in brand management at Hy Dairies.

Beauport now faced the difficult decision of whether to confront Gilman and try to change Hy Dairies' sexist and possibly racist practices or to leave the company.

Discussion Questions

1. Apply your knowledge of stereotyping and social identity theory to explain what went wrong here.

2. What other perceptual error is apparent in this case study?

3. What can organizations do to minimize misperceptions in these types of situations?

 CLASS EXERCISE 3.2

The Learning Exercise

Purpose	This exercise is designed to help you understand how the contingencies of reinforcement in behaviour modification affect learning.
Materials	Any objects normally available in a classroom will be acceptable for this activity.
Instructions (Large or small class)	The instructor will ask for three volunteers, who are then briefed outside the classroom. The instructor will spend a few minutes briefing the remaining students in the class about their duties. Then, one of the three volunteers will enter the room to participate in the exercise. When completed, the second volunteer enters the room and participates in the exercise. When completed, the third volunteer enters the class and participates in the exercise.

For students to gain the full benefit of this exercise, no other information will be provided here. However, your instructor will have more details at the beginning of this fun activity.

WEB EXERCISE 3.3

Stereotyping in Corporate Annual Reports

Purpose   This exercise is designed to help you diagnose evidence of stereotyping and corporate role models that minimize stereotyping in corporate annual reports.

Materials   Students need to complete their research for this activity prior to class, including selecting a publicly traded company and downloading the past four or more years of its fully illustrated annual reports.

Instructions   The instructor may have students work alone or in groups for this activity. Students will select a company that is publicly traded and makes its annual reports available on the company website. Ideally, annual reports for at least the past four years should be available, and these reports should be presented in the final illustrated format (typically PDF replicas of the original hard copy report).

Students will closely examine images in the selected company's recent annual reports in terms of how women, visible minorities, and older employees and clients are presented. Specifically, students should be prepared to discuss and provide details in class regarding:

1. The percentage of images showing (i.e., visual representations of) women, visible minorities, and older workers and clients. Students should also be sensitive to the size and placement of these images on the page and throughout the annual report.

2. The roles in which women, visible minorities, and older workers and clients are depicted. For example, are women shown more in traditional or non-traditional occupations and nonwork roles in these annual reports?

3. If several years of annual reports are available, pick one that is a decade or more old and compare its visual representation of and role depiction of women, visible minorities, and older employees and clients.

If possible, pick one of the most blatantly stereotypic illustrations you can find in these annual reports to show in class, either as a hard copy printout or as a computer projection.

www.mcgrawhill.ca/olc/mcshane

SELF-ASSESSMENT EXERCISE 3.4

How Much Perceptual Structure Do You Need?

Purpose This self-assessment is designed to help you to estimate your personal need for perceptual structure.

Instructions Read each of the statements below and decide how much you agree with each according to your attitudes, beliefs, and experiences. Then use the scoring key in Appendix B of this book to calculate your results. It is important for you to realize that there are no "right" or "wrong" answers to these questions. This self-assessment is completed alone so that students rate themselves honestly without concerns of social comparison. However, class discussion will focus on the meaning of need for structure in terms of how we engage differently in the perceptual process at work and in other settings.

Personal Need for Structure Scale						
To what extent do you agree or disagree with each of these statements about yourself?	Strongly Agree	Moderately Agree	Slightly Agree	Slightly Disagree	Moderately Disagree	Strongly Disagree
1. It upsets me to go into a situation without knowing what I can expect from it.	☐	☐	☐	☐	☐	☐
2. I'm not bothered by things that interrupt my daily routine.	☐	☐	☐	☐	☐	☐
3. I enjoy being spontaneous.	☐	☐	☐	☐	☐	☐
4. I find that a well-ordered life with regular hours makes my life tedious.	☐	☐	☐	☐	☐	☐
5. I find that a consistent routine enables me to enjoy life more.	☐	☐	☐	☐	☐	☐
6. I enjoy having a clear and structured mode of life.	☐	☐	☐	☐	☐	☐
7. I like to have a place for everything and everything in its place.	☐	☐	☐	☐	☐	☐
8. I don't like situations that are uncertain.	☐	☐	☐	☐	☐	☐
9. I hate to change my plans at the last minute.	☐	☐	☐	☐	☐	☐
10. I hate to be with people who are unpredictable.	☐	☐	☐	☐	☐	☐
11. I enjoy the exhilaration of being in unpredictable situations.	☐	☐	☐	☐	☐	☐
12. I become uncomfortable when the rules in a situation are not clear.	☐	☐	☐	☐	☐	☐

Source: M. M. Thompson, M. E. Naccarato, and K. E. Parker, "Assessing Cognitive Need: The Development of the Personal Need for Structure and the Personal Fear of Invalidity Scales," Paper presented at the Annual meeting of the Canadian Psychological Association, Halifax, Nova Scotia (1989).

 Go to the Online Learning Centre at www.mcgrawhill.ca/olc/mcshane to complete the following interactive self-assessments.

 SELF-ASSESSMENT EXERCISE 3.5

Cognitive Empathy Questionnaire

Empathy is an important perceptual ability in social relations, but the degree to which people empathize varies considerably. This self-assessment provides an estimate of one form of empathy, known as cognitive empathy or perspective-taking. This means that it measures the level of cognitive awareness of another person's situational and individual circumstances. To complete this scale, indicate the degree to which each of the statements presented does or does not describe you very well. You need to be honest with yourself to obtain a reasonable estimate of your level of perspective taking. The results show your relative position along the perspective-taking continuum and the general meaning of this score.

SELF-ASSESSMENT EXERCISE 3.6

Emotional Empathy Questionnaire

Empathy is an important perceptual ability in social relations, but the degree to which people empathize varies considerably. This self-assessment provides an estimate of one form of empathy, known as emotional empathy. This refers to the extent that you are able to experience the emotions or feelings of the other person. To complete this scale, indicate the degree to which each of the statements presented does or does not describe you very well. You need to be honest with yourself to obtain a reasonable estimate of your level of emotional empathy. The results show your relative position along the emotional empathy continuum and the general meaning of this score.

iStudy—Available 24/7 with instant feedback so you can study when you want, how you want, and where you want. Visit www.istudyob.ca to register—take practice quizzes, run interactive scenarios, practice concepts, and much more. Also visit the Student Online Learning Centre for additional study tools.

CHAPTER 4

Workplace Emotions, Attitudes, and Stress

You know the fun is about to begin at Suntech Optics when employees spot the pineapple wearing sunglasses. The bespectacled fruit is mascot for the North Vancouver-based eyewear supplier's Have Fun Team, which is responsible for creating various forms of workplace levity. Employees might discover a puzzle on their desk, with a prize awarded to the person who first solves it. Dozens of stuffed bears are brought to work on Bring Your Teddy Bear to Work Day. Halloween is a special treat as staff dress up for the occasion and show off their pumpkin carving skills. "We try to infuse having fun into our whole corporate culture," says Suntech manager Deborah Peck. "It's one of our core strategies. It's part of our life."

Fun at work? It sounds like an oxymoron. But in order to attract and keep valuable talent, companies are finding creative ways to generate positive emotions in the workplace. At Myers Norris Penny (MNP), western Canada's largest accounting firm, fun includes employee barbecues, sporting events, and end-of-tax-season parties. "Every firm says it has a positive work environment; MNP really does," claims Mia Gross, a senior manager in MNP's Calgary office.

Well-known for creating a fun environment for customers, WestJet Airlines Ltd. extends this experience to its own staff. For example, this photo shows WestJet CEO Sean Durfy tossing a butter cream cupcake up to pilot Gordon Simmons, who is hanging out the cockpit window. Durfy and his entire executive team showed up at Calgary International Airport to distribute the treats to WestJet's 280 staff.

Another fun-focused company is Tri Fit Inc. in Oakville, Ontario. Boasting one of the industry's lowest turnover rates, the fitness, health, and wellness company holds five all-day staff meetings each year, which includes opening a "treasure chest" filled with sports equipment and health-related items distributed to exemplary employees. "It's amazing, the chatter, the laughter, the excitement about opening the treasure chest," says Marsden. "They [employees] love it."[1]

Having fun is part of the culture at WestJet, including this attempt by CEO Sean Durfy to toss a cupcake up to pilot Gordon Simmons. Photo by Greg Fulmes; article: "WestJet Banks on its Brand" by Gina Teel, December 28, 2007, Calgary Herald. Reprinted with permission of The Calgary Herald.

Suntech Optics, WestJet, Myers Norris Penny, Tri Fit, and many other Canadian firms are discovering that emotions and attitudes make a difference in individual behaviour and well-being, as well as in the organization's performance and customer service. Over the past decade, the field of organizational behaviour has experienced a major shift in thinking about workplace emotions, so this chapter begins by introducing the concept and explaining why researchers are so eager to discover how emotions influence attitudes and behaviour. Next, we consider the dynamics of emotional labour, followed by the popular topic of emotional intelligence. The specific work attitudes of job satisfaction and organizational commitment are then discussed, including their association with various employee behaviours and work performance. Organizational commitment is strongly influenced by the psychological contract, so the final section of this chapter looks briefly at the topic of work-related stress, including the stress experience, three prominent stressors, individual differences in stress, and ways to combat excessive stress.

EMOTIONS IN THE WORKPLACE

LO1

Emotions have a profound effect on almost everything we do in the workplace. This is a strong statement, and one that you would rarely find a decade ago in organizational behaviour research or textbooks. Until recently, OB experts assumed that a person's thoughts and actions are governed primarily by conscious reasoning (called *cognition*). Yet, groundbreaking neuroscience discoveries have revealed that our perceptions, attitudes, decisions, and behaviour are influenced by both cognition and emotion, and that the latter often has the greater influence.[2]

emotions
Physiological, behavioural, and psychological episodes experienced toward an object, person, or event that create a state of readiness.

Emotions are physiological, behavioural, and psychological episodes experienced toward an object, person, or event that create a state of readiness.[3] These "episodes" are very brief events that typically subside or occur in waves lasting from milliseconds to a few minutes. Emotions are directed toward someone or something. For example, we experience joy, fear, anger, and other emotional episodes toward tasks, customers, or a software program we are using. This contrasts with *moods*, which are less intense emotional states that are not directed toward anything in particular.[4]

Emotions are experiences. They represent changes in our physiological state (e.g., blood pressure, heart rate), psychological state (e.g., ability to think clearly), and behaviour (e.g., facial expression). These emotional reactions are involuntary and often occur without our awareness. This is a particularly important point because people often think about "getting emotional" when the subject of emotions is mentioned. In reality, you experience emotions every minute, but aren't even aware of most of them. Finally, emotions put us in a state of readiness. When we get worried, for example, our heart rate and blood pressure increase to make our body better prepared to engage in fight or flight. Strong emotions also trigger our conscious awareness of a threat or opportunity in the external environment.[5]

There are dozens of emotions, and experts organize them in terms of whether they are positive or negative as well as how much they activate us (demand our attention). Anger is a negative emotion that generates a high level of activation, whereas feeling relaxed is a pleasant emotion that has fairly low activation. Emotions generate a global evaluation (called *core affect*) that something is good or bad, helpful or harmful, to be approached or avoided.[6]

"Biosensors. The whole company knows instantly when I'm displeased."

EMOTIONS, ATTITUDES, AND BEHAVIOUR

To understand how emotions influence our thoughts and behaviour in the workplace, we first need to know about atti-

attitudes
The cluster of beliefs, assessed feelings, and behavioural intentions toward a person, object, or event (called an *attitude object*).

tudes. **Attitudes** represent the cluster of beliefs, assessed feelings, and behavioural intentions toward a person, object, or event (called an *attitude object*).[7] Attitudes are *judgments*, whereas emotions are *experiences*. In other words, attitudes involve conscious logical reasoning, whereas emotions operate as events, often without our awareness. We also experience most emotions briefly, whereas our attitude toward someone or something is more stable over time.

Until recently, attitude experts described attitudes in terms of its three cognitive components illustrated on the left side of Exhibit 4.1: beliefs, feelings, and behavioural intentions. Now, we have good evidence that a parallel emotional process is also at work, shown on the right side of the exhibit.[8] Using attitude toward mergers as an example, let's look more closely at this model, beginning with the traditional cognitive perspective of attitudes.

- *Beliefs*—These are your established perceptions about the attitude object—what you believe to be true. For example, you might believe that mergers reduce job security for employees in the merged firms. Or you might believe that mergers increase the company's competitiveness in this era of globalization. These beliefs are perceived facts that you acquire from past experience and other forms of learning.

- *Feelings*—Feelings represent your positive or negative evaluations of the attitude object. Some people think mergers are good; others think they are bad. Your like or dislike of mergers represents your assessed feelings. According to the traditional cognitive perspective of attitudes (left side of the model), feelings are calculated from your beliefs about mergers. If you believe that mergers typically have negative consequences such as layoffs and organizational politics, then you will form nega-

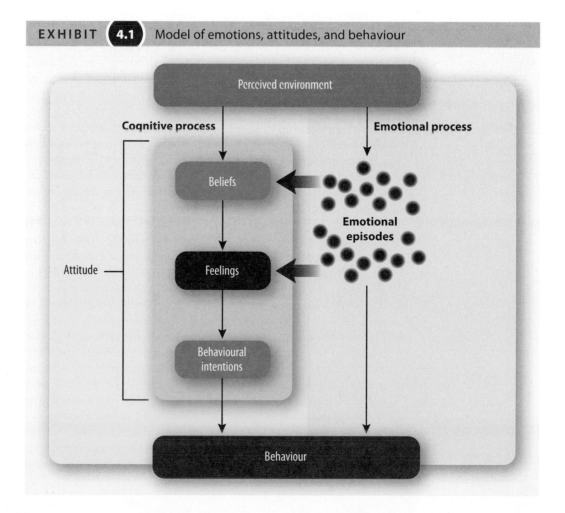

EXHIBIT 4.1   Model of emotions, attitudes, and behaviour

tive feelings towards mergers in general or about a specific planned merger in your organization.

- *Behavioural intentions*—Intentions represent your motivation to engage in a particular behaviour with respect to the attitude object.[9] Upon hearing that the company will merge with another organization, you might become motivated to look for a job elsewhere, or possibly to complain to management about the merger decision. Your feelings toward mergers motivates your behavioural intentions, and which actions you choose depends on your past experience, self-concept (values, personality), and social norms of appropriate behaviour.

The model in Exhibit 4.1 also illustrates that behavioural intentions directly predict behaviour. However, whether your intentions translate into behaviour depends on all four elements of the MARS model, such as opportunity and ability to act. Attitudes are also more likely to influence behaviour when they are strong, meaning that they are anchored by strong emotions.

How Emotions Influence Attitudes and Behaviour   Along with the cognitive process, emotions play a central role in forming and changing employee attitudes.[10] As the right side of Exhibit 4.1 illustrates, this process also begins with perceptions. Specifically, the emotional components of our brain quickly and imprecisely tag emotional markers to incoming information based on whether that information supports or threatens our innate drives. These are not calculated feelings; they are automatic and unconscious emotional responses based on very thin slices of sensory information.[11]

Returning to the example of your attitude toward mergers, you might experience excitement, worry, nervousness, or happiness upon learning that your company intends to merge with a competitor. The large dots on the right side of Exhibit 4.1 illustrate the numerous emotional episodes you experience upon hearing the merger announcement, subsequent thinking about the merger, discussion with co-workers about the merger, and so on. These emotions are transmitted to the logical reasoning process, where they swirl around and influence our logical thinking about the attitude object.[12] Thus, while consciously evaluating whether the merger is good or bad, your emotions have already formed an opinion, which then sways your conscious evaluation. In fact, we often deliberately "listen in" on our emotions to help us consciously decide whether to support or oppose something.[13] If you experience mainly positive emotions whenever you think about or discuss the merger, then these positive emotional episodes will lean your logical reasoning toward positive feelings regarding the merger.

The dual cognitive-emotional attitude process helps us to understand why Suntech Optics and many other companies want their employees to experience plenty of positive emotional episodes each day. Job satisfaction is shaped by the almost continuous bombardment of emotional experiences people have at work. Those who experience more positive emotions tend to have more favourable attitudes toward their jobs, even when they aren't consciously aware of many of these emotional experiences. And when they do think about how they feel about their job, they listen in on the emotions regenerated from past positive or negative events in the workplace.

The influence of both cognitive reasoning and emotions on attitudes is most apparent when they disagree with each other. Everyone occasionally experiences this mental tug-of-war, sensing that something isn't right even though they can't think of any logical reason to be concerned. This conflicting experience indicates that our logical analysis of the situation (left side of Exhibit 4.1) can't identify reasons to support the automatic emotional reaction (right side of Exhibit 4.1).[14] Should we pay attention to our emotional response or our logical analysis? This question is not easy to answer, but some studies indicate that while executives tend to make quick decisions based on their gut feelings (emotional response), the best decisions tend to occur when they spend time logically evaluating the situation.[15] Thus, we should pay attention to both the cognitive and emotional side of the attitude model, and hope they agree with each other most of the time!

One last comment about Exhibit 4.1: Notice the arrow from the emotional episodes to behaviour? This indicates that people have direct behavioural reactions to their emotions. Even low intensity emotions automatically change your facial expressions. High intensity emotions can have a more powerful effect, which is apparent when an upset employee bangs his/her fist on the desk or an overjoyed colleague embraces someone nearby. These actions are not carefully thought out. They are automatic emotional responses that serve as coping mechanisms in that situation.[16]

Cognitive Dissonance   Emotions and attitudes usually lead to behaviour, but the opposite sometimes occurs through the process of **cognitive dissonance**.[17] Cognitive dissonance occurs when we perceive an inconsistency between our beliefs, feelings, and behaviour. When this inconsistency violates our self-concept, it generates emotions that motivate us to change one or more of these elements. Behaviour is usually the most difficult element to change, particularly when it is known to everyone, was done voluntarily, and can't be undone. Thus, we usually change our beliefs and feelings to reduce the inconsistency.

> **cognitive dissonance**
> Occurs when we perceive an inconsistency between our beliefs, feelings, and behaviour.

Emotions and Personality   Our coverage of the dynamics of workplace emotions wouldn't be complete unless we mentioned that emotions are also partly determined by a person's personality, not just workplace experiences.[18] Some people experience positive emotions as a natural trait. These people are generally extroverted—outgoing, talkative, sociable, and assertive (see Chapter 2). In contrast, other people have a personality with a tendency to experience more negative emotions. Positive and negative emotional traits affect a person's attendance, turnover, and long-term work attitudes. For example, several studies—including a recent analysis of employees at Transport Canada—have found that people with a negative emotional trait have lower levels of job satisfaction. Another Canadian study reported that employees with a negative emotional trait experience higher levels of job burnout.[19] While these positive and negative personality traits have some effect, other research concludes that the actual situation in which people work has a noticeably stronger influence on their attitudes and behaviour.[20]

MANAGING EMOTIONS AT WORK

The Elbow Room Café is packed and noisy on this Saturday morning. A customer at the Vancouver restaurant half shouts across the room for more coffee. A passing waiter scoffs: "You want more coffee, get it yourself!" The customer only laughs. Another diner complains loudly that he and his party are running late and need their food. This time, restaurant manager Patrick Savoie speaks up: "If you're in a hurry, you should have gone to McDonald's." The diner and his companions chuckle. To the uninitiated, the Elbow Room Café is an emotional basket case, full of irate guests and the rudest staff on Canada's West Coast. But it's all a performance—a place where guests can enjoy good food and play out their emotions about dreadful customer service. "It's almost like coming to a theatre," says Savoie, who spends much of his time inventing new ways to insult the clientele.[21]

Whether giving the most insulting service at Elbow Room Café or the friendliest service at WestJet Airlines, people are expected to manage their emotions in the workplace. They must conceal their frustration when serving an irritating customer, display compassion to an ill patient, and hide their boredom in a long meeting with senior management. These are all forms of **emotional labour**—the effort, planning, and control needed to express organizationally desired emotions during interpersonal transactions.[22] Almost everyone is expected to abide by *display rules* on the job; these are norms requiring us to display specific emotions and to hide other emotions. Emotional labour is higher in jobs requiring a variety of emotions (e.g., anger as well as joy) and more intense emotions (e.g., showing delight rather than smiling weakly), as well as where interaction with clients is frequent and for a longer duration. Emotional

> **emotional labour**
> The effort, planning, and control needed to express organizationally desired emotions during interpersonal transactions.

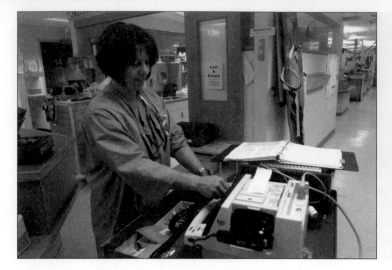

Managing the Emotional Roller Coaster of Emergency Nursing

"Emergency nurses are a very special breed," says Suzanne Stringer (shown here), a charge nurse in the emergency facility at Regina General Hospital. "They can be a nurse to family members who have just lost their loved one to a tragic episode and then have to flip gears in 30 seconds and look at someone who has just sprained their ankle. All day, it's a roller coaster of emotions." Although their true emotions may include the extremes of sorrow, relief, helplessness, and joyfulness, Springer and other emergency room nurses are expected to manage their emotions to suit the situation. They must display calm concern to a patient with serious injuries, compassion to grieving family members, and caring optimism to a frightened child. Little wonder that emotional exhaustion is a real risk in the nursing profession.[23] *Bryan Schlosser/Regina Leader-Post*

labour also increases when employees must precisely rather than casually abide by the display rules.[24]

EMOTIONAL DISPLAY NORMS ACROSS CULTURES

How much we are expected to hide or reveal our true emotions in public depends to some extent on the culture in which we live. Cultural values in some countries—particularly Ethiopia, Korea, Japan, and Austria—expect people to subdue their emotional expression and minimize physical contact with others. Even voice intonation tends to be monotonic. In other countries—notably Kuwait, Egypt, Spain, and Russia—cultural values allow or encourage open display of one's true emotions. People are expected to be transparent in revealing their thoughts and feelings, dramatic in their conversational tones, and animated in their use of nonverbal behaviours to get their message across. These cultural variations in emotional display can be quite noticeable. One survey reported that 83 percent of Japanese believe it is inappropriate to get emotional in a business context, compared with 40 percent of Americans, 34 percent of French, and only 29 percent of Italians. In other words, Italians are more likely to accept or tolerate people who display their true emotions at work, whereas this would be considered rude or embarrassing in Japan.[25]

EMOTIONAL DISSONANCE

Emotional labour can be challenging for most of us because it is difficult to conceal true emotions and to display the emotions required by the job. Joy, sadness, worry and other emotions automatically activate a complex set of facial muscles that are difficult to prevent, and equally difficult to fake. Pretending to be cheerful or concerned requires adjustment and coordination of several specific facial muscles and body positions. Meanwhile, our true emotions tend to reveal themselves as subtle gestures, usually without our awareness. More often than not, observers see when we are faking and sense that we feel a different emotion.[26]

emotional dissonance
The conflict between required and true emotions.

Emotional labour also creates conflict between required and true emotions, called **emotional dissonance**. The larger the gap between the required and the true emotions, the more employees tend to experience stress, job burnout, and psychological separation from self.[27] Hiring people with a natural tendency to display the emotions required for the job can minimize this emotional dissonance. For example, Container Store expects employees to display positive emotions on the job, so its unofficial motto is "Grouchy People Need Not Apply." The owner of Flagworks Inc., the Calgary-based manufacturer of in-store signage and flags, takes a similar view: "If you're not happy, we don't put up with you," she says.[28]

Emotional dissonance is also minimized through *deep acting* rather than *surface acting*.[29] People engage in surface acting when they try to modify their behaviour to be consistent with required emotions but continue to hold different internal feelings. For instance, we force a smile while greeting a customer who we consider rude. Deep acting involves changing true emotions to match the required emotions. Rather than feeling irritated by a rude customer, you might view your next interaction with that person as an opportunity to test your sales skills. This change in perspective can potentially generate more positive emotions next time you meet that difficult customer, which produces friendlier displays of emotion. However, deep acting also requires considerable emotional intelligence, which we discuss next.

EMOTIONAL INTELLIGENCE

 LO3

emotional intelligence (EI)
The ability to monitor our own and others' feelings and emotions, to discriminate between them, and to use this information to guide our thinking and actions.

Air Canada is looking beyond flying skills when choosing new pilots. All new pilots are also evaluated by their scores on an emotional intelligence test. Pilots are team leaders of the on-board crew and need to work effectively with staff on the ground, so they must have the ability to understand and manage their own emotions as well as the emotions of others. "If you have to interact well with other people, these [emotional intelligence tests] are instruments that we can use during the selection process to identify people that have these enhanced skills," says Capt. Dave Legge, vice-president of Air Canada flight operations. "At the end of the day, we want to have a better idea of who we're hiring."[30]

Air Canada is one of many organizations discovering that **emotional intelligence (EI)** can significantly improve individual, team, and organizational effectiveness. EI includes a set of *abilities* to perceive and express emotion, assimilate emotion in thought, understand and reason with emotion, and regulate emotion in oneself and others.[31] One popular model, shown in Exhibit 4.2, organizes EI into four dimensions representing the recognition of emotions in ourselves and in others, as well as the regulation of emotions in ourselves and in others.[32] These four dimensions are also found in other models of EI, but experts disagree on the definitive list of abilities representing EI. For example, the authors of the model shown here include a list of "abilities" for each cell, but others warn that the list includes personality traits and personal values (e.g., achievement, optimism) as well as task outcomes (e.g., teamwork, inspirational leadership).[33]

- *Self-awareness*—Self-awareness refers to perceiving and understanding the meaning of your own emotions. You are more sensitive to subtle emotional responses to events and understand their message. Self-aware people are better able to eavesdrop

EXHIBIT 4.2   Dimensions of emotional intelligence

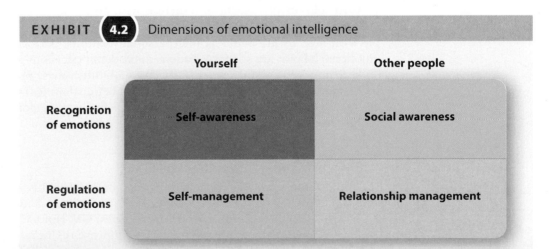

Sources: D. Goleman, R. Boyatzis, and A. McKee, *Primal Leadership* (Boston: Harvard Business School Press, 2002), Chapter 3; D. Goleman, "An EI-Based Theory of Performance," in C. Cherniss and D. Goleman, (Eds.), *The Emotionally Intelligent Workplace* (San Francisco: Jossey-Bass, 2001), p. 28.

in on their emotional responses to specific situations and to use this awareness as conscious information.[34]

- *Self-management*—Self-management refers to managing our own emotions, something that we all do to some extent. We keep disruptive impulses in check. We try not to feel angry or frustrated when events go against us. We try to feel and express joy and happiness toward others when the occasion calls for these emotional displays. We try to create a second wind of motivation later in the work day. Notice that self-management goes beyond displaying behaviours that represent desired emotions in a particular situation. It includes actually generating or suppressing emotions. In other words, the deep acting described earlier requires high levels of the self-management component of emotional intelligence.

- *Social awareness*—Social awareness is the ability to perceive and understand the emotions of other people. To a large extent, this ability is represented by *empathy*— having understanding and sensitivity to the feelings, thoughts, and situation of others (see Chapter 3). This includes understanding another person's situation, experiencing the other person's emotions, and knowing his or her needs even though unstated. Social awareness extends beyond empathy to include being organizationally aware, such as sensing office politics and understanding social networks.

- *Relationship management*—This dimension of EI refers to managing other people's emotions. This includes consoling people who feel sad, emotionally inspiring your team members to complete a class project on time, getting strangers to feel comfortable working with you, and managing dysfunctional emotions among staff who experience conflict with customers or other employees. Some emotional intelligence experts link this component of emotional intelligence to a wide variety of interpersonal activities, but we must remember that relationship management is restricted to managing other people's emotions, whereas working effectively with other people extends to other competencies.

These four dimensions of emotional intelligence form a hierarchy.[35] Self-awareness is the lowest level of EI because it is a prerequisite for the other three dimensions but does not require the other dimensions. Self-management and social awareness are necessarily above self-awareness in the EI hierarchy. You can't manage your own emotions (self-management) if you aren't good at knowing your own emotions (self-awareness). Relationship management is the highest level of EI because it requires all three other dimensions. In other words, we require a high degree of emotional intelligence to master relationship management because this set of competencies requires sufficiently high levels of self-awareness, self-management, and social awareness.

Most jobs involve social interaction with co-workers or external stakeholders, so employees need emotional intelligence to work effectively. Research indicates that people with high EI are better at interpersonal relations, perform better in jobs requiring emotional labour, are superior leaders, make better decisions involving social exchanges, and are more successful in many aspects of job interviews. Teams whose members have high emotional intelligence initially perform better than teams with low EI.[36] However, emotional intelligence does not improve some forms of performance, such as tasks that require minimal social interaction.[37]

IMPROVING EMOTIONAL INTELLIGENCE

Emotional intelligence is associated with some personality traits, as well as with the emotional intelligence of one's parents, but it can also be learned in adulthood to some extent.[38] As GLOBAL Connections 4.1 describes, GM Holden in Australia developed an emotional intelligence training program to improve relations among employees.[39] Sony Europe also incorporates emotional intelligence training in its executive development program, including an exercise where leaders keep a journal of their emotional experiences throughout a week of work. One study reported that business students scored higher on emotional intelligence after taking an undergraduate interpersonal skills

global connections 4.1

GM Holden Revs Up Emotional Intelligence

General Motors carefully selected staff for its new GM Holden production facility at Port Melbourne, Australia, but it wasn't long before the project unravelled due to infighting and interpersonal tensions. Consultants called in to analyze the problems offered the following solution: employees need to improve their emotional intelligence. With this advice, the 30 plant design team members and more than 300 other employees completed a detailed assessment of their emotional intelligence. The automaker then introduced a variety of training modules targeting different aspects of emotional intelligence, such as effective self-expression, understanding others, and controlling emotions.

Some staff were skeptical about these touchy-feely seminars, so GM Holden evaluated the program to see whether employee scores improved and behaviour changed. The company discovered that employee scores on the emotional intelligence test improved by almost 50 percent, and that employees became much more cooperative and diplomatic in their behaviour. "It has greatly improved communication within the team and with other teams outside the plant," says GM Holden quality systems engi-

GM Holden reduced infighting and interpersonal tensions by teaching staff to improve their emotional intelligence. © 2008 General Motors and Wieck Media Services, Inc.

neer Vesselka Vassileva. Some employees also note that it has improved their interpersonal behaviour outside the workplace. "I'm not so aggressive or assertive," says manufacturing engineer Alf Moore. "I feel better and it's helped me at home."[40]

course.[41] Employees can improve EI by receiving personal coaching and frequent feedback on their interpersonal behaviour, and by practising interpersonal skills. Emotional intelligence also increases with age; it is part of the process called maturity. Overall, emotional intelligence offers considerable potential, but we also have a lot to learn about its measurement and effects on people in the workplace.

So far, this chapter has introduced the model of emotions and attitudes, as well as emotional intelligence as the means by which we manage emotions in the workplace. The next two sections of this chapter introduce the concepts of job satisfaction and organizational commitment. These two attitudes are so important in our understanding of workplace behaviour that some experts suggest that together they should be called "overall job attitude."[42]

JOB SATISFACTION

job satisfaction
A person's evaluation of his or her job and work context.

Job satisfaction, a person's evaluation of his or her job and work context, is probably the most studied attitude in organizational behaviour.[43] It is an *appraisal* of the perceived job characteristics, work environment, and emotional experiences at work. Satisfied employees have a favourable evaluation of their job, based on their observations and emotional experiences. Job satisfaction is best viewed as a collection of attitudes about different aspects of the job and work context. You might like your co-workers but be less satisfied with workload, for instance.

How satisfied are Canadians at work? Most surveys indicate that between 80 and 90 percent of Canadians are moderately or very satisfied overall with their jobs. This is similar to satisfaction levels a decade ago. Most global survey results over the past decade indicate that Canadian job satisfaction levels are higher than in most other countries.

One recent global poll reported that Canadians rate their job and workplace higher than do employees in most other countries. However, Canada ranked only 18th out of 28 countries in terms of job satisfaction in another survey of 70,000 employees (10,000 of whom were Canadians). Even in the latter study, the majority of Canadians indicated that they are satisfied at work. In most global surveys, employees in Denmark, India, Mexico, and the United States tend to report the highest levels of job satisfaction.[44]

Can we conclude from these results that Canadians are happy at work? Possibly, but not as much as these statistics suggest. The problem is that surveys often use a single direct question, such as "How satisfied are you with your job?" Many dissatisfied employees are reluctant to reveal their feelings in a direct question because this is tantamount to admitting that they made a poor job choice and are not enjoying life. One indication that the overall satisfaction ratings are inflated is that nearly half of all of Canadians say they would abandon their employer if offered a comparable job elsewhere! Another indication is that employees rate almost all aspects of the job lower than their overall satisfaction.[45]

LO4 JOB SATISFACTION AND WORK BEHAVIOUR

Annette Verschuren, president of Home Depot Canada, pays a lot of attention to job satisfaction. "I can tell you within two seconds of entering a store whether morale is good," says Verschuren. The main reason for her interest is that job satisfaction is a key driver to corporate success. "With an unhappy workforce you have nothing and you will never be great," Verschuren warns.[46]

Home Depot Canada, Fours Seasons Hotels and Resorts, and many other Canadian firms pay close attention to job satisfaction. In some firms, executive bonuses depend partly on employee satisfaction ratings. The reason for this attention is simple: Job satisfaction affects many of the individual behaviours introduced in Chapter 1. A useful template to organize and understand the consequences of job dissatisfaction is the **exit-voice-loyalty-neglect (EVLN) model.** As the name suggests, the EVLN model identifies four ways that employees respond to dissatisfaction:[47]

> **exit-voice-loyalty-neglect (EVLN) model**
> The four ways, as indicated in the name, that employees respond to job dissatisfaction.

- *Exit*—Exit refers to leaving the organization, transferring to another work unit, or at least trying to exit the dissatisfying situation. The traditional view is that job dissatisfaction builds over time and is eventually strong enough to motivate employees to search for better work opportunities elsewhere. This is likely true to some extent, but the most recent opinion is that specific "shock events" quickly energize employees to think about and engage in exit behaviour. For example, the emotional reaction you experience to an unfair management decision or a conflict episode with a co-worker motivates you to look at job ads and speak to friends about job opportunities where they work. This begins the process of redefining your self-concept more in terms of another company rather than your current employer.[48]

- *Voice*—Voice refers to any attempt to change, rather than escape from, the dissatisfying situation. Voice can be a constructive response, such as recommending ways for management to improve the situation, or it can be more confrontational, such as by filing formal grievances or forming a coalition to oppose a decision.[49] In the extreme, some employees might engage in counterproductive behaviours to get attention and force changes in the organization.

- *Loyalty*—In the original version of this model, loyalty was not an outcome of dissatisfaction. Rather, it determined whether people chose exit or voice (i.e., high loyalty resulted in voice; low loyalty produced exit).[50] More recent writers describe loyalty as an outcome, but in various and somewhat unclear ways. Generally, they suggest that "loyalists" are employees who respond to dissatisfaction by patiently waiting—some say they "suffer in silence"—for the problem to work itself out or get resolved by others.[51]

- *Neglect*—Neglect includes reducing work effort, paying less attention to quality, and increasing absenteeism and lateness. It is generally considered a passive activity that has negative consequences for the organization.

Which of the four EVLN alternatives do employees use? It depends on the person and situation.[52] One determining factor is the person's self-concept. Some people avoid the self-image as a complainer, whereas others view themselves very much as taking action when they dislike a work situation. This self-concept relates to personal and cultural values as well as personality. For example, people with a high conscientiousness personality are less likely to engage in neglect and more likely to engage in voice. Past experience also influences which EVLN action is applied. Employees who were unsuccessful with voice in the past are more likely to engage in exit or neglect when experiencing job dissatisfaction in the future. Another factor is loyalty, as it was originally intended. Specifically, employees are more likely to quit when they have low loyalty to the company, and are more likely to engage in voice when they have high loyalty. Finally, the response to dissatisfaction depends on the situation. Employees are more likely to use the exit option when there are more job alternatives, for example.

LO5 **Job Satisfaction and Performance**   For almost a century, OB researchers have challenged the popular belief that "a happy worker is a productive worker." For most of that time, they concluded that job satisfaction has a minimal effect on job performance. Now, the evidence suggests that the popular saying may be correct after all; there is a *moderate* relationship between job satisfaction and job performance. In other words, happy workers really are more productive workers *to some extent*.[53] Even with a moderate association between job satisfaction and performance, there are a few underlying reasons why the relationship isn't even stronger. One argument is that general attitudes (such as job satisfaction) don't predict specific behaviours very well. As we learned with the EVLN model, job dissatisfaction can lead to a variety of outcomes rather than lower job performance (neglect). Some employees continue to work productively while they complain (voice), look for another job (exit), or patiently wait for the problem to be fixed (loyalty).

A second explanation is that job performance leads to job satisfaction (rather than vice versa), but only when performance is linked to valued rewards. Higher performers receive more rewards and, consequently, are more satisfied than low-performing employees who receive fewer rewards. The connection between job satisfaction and performance isn't stronger because many organizations do not reward good performance. The third explanation is that job satisfaction influences employee motivation, but doesn't affect performance in jobs where employees have little control over their job output (such as assembly line work).

Job Satisfaction and Customer Satisfaction   Wegmans Food Markets in the United States and HCL Technologies in India have the same unusual motto: Employees first, customers second. Both firms definitely put employees on top of the stakeholder list, but why not customers first? Their rationale is that customer satisfaction follows from employee satisfaction. In other words, it is difficult to keep customers happy if employee morale is low. "It just seems common sense to me that if you start with a happy, well-motivated workforce, you're much more likely to have happy customers," suggests Virgin Group founder Sir Richard Branson.[54]

Organizational behaviour research generally agrees that job satisfaction has a positive effect on customer service.[55] There are two main reasons for this relationship. First, employees are usually in a more positive mood when they feel satisfied with their job and working conditions. Employees in a good mood display friendliness and positive emotions more naturally and frequently, which create positive emotions for customers. Second, satisfied employees are less likely to quit their jobs, so they have better knowledge and skills to serve clients. Lower turnover also gives customers the same employees to serve them, so there is more consistent service. There is some evidence that customers build their loyalty to specific employees, not to the organization, so keeping employee turnover low tends to build customer loyalty.[56]

Before leaving the topic of job satisfaction, we should mention that job satisfaction does more than improve work behaviours and customer satisfaction. Job satisfaction is

Happy Employees = Happy Customers

Outback Steakhouse, Inc. has become a phenomenal success story in North America's competitive restaurant industry. In 1988, Outback's four partners each opened a restaurant in Tampa, Florida, based on popular images of casual lifestyle and tucker (food) in the land Down Under. Today, Outback's 65,000 employees work in 1,100 restaurants around the United States and Canada. While the Australian theme launched the company's success, Outback founder and CEO says the quality of staff deserves as much credit. Long before scholars pointed out that satisfied employees provide better customer service, Outback was applying this principle. "Outback's theory of success is that you hire the right people and take care of them," explained founder Chris Sullivan and three colleagues in a recent journal article. The company hires and creates a culture that supports energized employees who stay with the company and provide excellent service. This service makes customers happy, which brings them back and refers Outback to friends. The result of such customer satisfaction is higher sales, which improve company profits.[57]
Photo courtesy of Outback Steakhouse

also an ethical issue that influences the organization's reputation in the community. People spend a large portion of their time working in organizations, and many societies now expect companies to provide work environments that are safe and enjoyable. Indeed, employees in several countries closely monitor ratings of the best companies to work for, an indication that employee satisfaction is a virtue worth considerable goodwill to employers. This virtue is apparent when an organization has low job satisfaction. The company tries to hide this fact and, when morale problems become public, corporate leaders are usually quick to improve the situation.

ORGANIZATIONAL COMMITMENT

LO6

organizational (affective) commitment
The employee's emotional attachment to, identification with, and involvement in a particular organization.

During the mid-1800s, Samuel Cunard founded Cunard Lines, the greatest steamship line ever to cover the Atlantic Ocean. The energetic Nova Scotian was able to make ship transportation dependable and safe, long before it was thought possible, by having the best ships, officers, and crew. He insisted on safety before profits and, by listening to his technical experts, was able to introduce the latest innovations. Above all, Cunard had the quaint notion that if you picked people well, paid them well, and treated them well, they would return the favour with loyalty and pride.[58]

More than 150 years later, Samuel Cunard's assumptions about organizational commitment still hold true. **Organizational commitment** refers to the employee's emotional attachment to, identification with, and involvement in a particular organization.[59] This definition refers specifically to *affective commitment* because it is an emotional attachment—our feelings of loyalty—to the organization. Organizational (affective) commitment differs from **continuance commitment**, which is a calculative attachment.[60] Employees have high continuance commitment when they do not particularly identify with the organization where they work but feel bound to remain there because it would be too costly to quit. In other words, they choose to stay because the calculated (typically financial) value of staying is higher than the value of working somewhere else. You can tell someone has high calculative commitment when they say: "I hate this place but can't afford to quit!" This reluctance to quit may be due to the risk of losing a large bonus by leaving early or because they are well established in the community where they work.[61]

continuance commitment
An employee's calculative attachment to the organization, whereby an employee is motivated to stay only because leaving would be costly.

CONSEQUENCES OF ORGANIZATIONAL COMMITMENT

Organizational (affective) commitment can be a significant competitive advantage.[62] Loyal employees are less likely to quit their jobs and be absent from work. They also have higher work motivation and organizational citizenship, as well as somewhat higher job performance. Organizational commitment also improves customer satisfaction because long-tenure employees have better knowledge of work practices, and clients like to do business with the same employees. One warning is that employees with very high loyalty tend to have high conformity, which results in lower creativity. There are also cases of dedicated employees who violated laws to defend the organization. However, most companies suffer from too little rather than too much employee loyalty.

While affective commitment is beneficial, research suggests that continuance commitment can be dysfunctional. In fact, employees with high levels of continuance commitment tend to have *lower* performance ratings and are *less* likely to engage in organizational citizenship behaviours! Furthermore, unionized employees with high continuance commitment are more likely to use formal grievances, whereas employees with high affective commitment engage in more constructive problem solving when employee–employer relations sour.[63] Although some level of financial connection may be necessary, employers should not confuse continuance commitment with employee loyalty. Employers still need to win employees' hearts (affective commitment) beyond tying them financially to the organization (continuance commitment).

LO7

BUILDING ORGANIZATIONAL COMMITMENT

There are almost as many ways to increase organizational (affective) commitment as there are topics in this textbook, but the following list is most prominent in the literature.

- *Justice and support*—Affective commitment is higher in organizations that fulfill their obligations to employees and abide by humanitarian values, such as fairness, courtesy, forgiveness, and moral integrity. These values relate to the concept of organizational justice that we discuss in the next chapter. Similarly, organizations that support employee well-being tend to cultivate higher levels of loyalty in return.[64]

- *Shared values*—The definition of affective commitment refers to a person's identification with the organization, and that identification is highest when employees believe their values are congruent with the organization's dominant values. Also, employees experience more comfort and predictability when they agree with the values underlying corporate decisions. This comfort increases their motivation to stay with the organization.[65]

- *Trust*—**Trust** refers to positive expectations one person has toward another person in situations involving risk.[66] Trust means putting faith in the other person or group. It is also a reciprocal activity: To receive trust, you must demonstrate trust. Employees identify with and feel obliged to work for an organization only when they trust its leaders. This explains why layoffs are one of the greatest blows to employee loyalty—by reducing job security, companies reduce the trust employees have in their employer and the employment relationship.[67]

- *Organizational comprehension*—Affective commitment is a person's identification with the company, so it makes sense that this attitude is strengthened when employees understand the company, including its past, present, and future. Thus, loyalty tends to increase with open and rapid communication to and from corporate leaders, as well as with opportunities to interact with co-workers across the organization.[68]

- *Employee involvement*—Employee involvement increases affective commitment by strengthening the employee's social identity with the organization. Employees feel that they are part of the organization when they take part in decisions that guide the organization's future. Employee involvement also builds loyalty because giving this power is a demonstration of the company's trust in its employees.

Organizational commitment and job satisfaction represent two of the most often studied and discussed attitudes in the workplace. Each is linked to emotional episodes and cognitive judgments about the workplace and relationship with the company. Emotions also play an important role in another concept that is on everyone's mind these days: stress. The final section of this chapter provides an overview of work-related stress and how it can be managed.

trust
Positive expectations one person has toward another person in situations involving risk.

WORK-RELATED STRESS AND ITS MANAGEMENT

LO8

Stephanie Lirette never seems to have enough time. The single mother, who works as casting co-ordinator for an ad agency in Montreal, rushes to drop off and pick up her young daughter from childcare. She often skips lunch and coffee breaks in order to complete all the work that needs to get done. And although the workday is officially from 9 to 5, last-minute projects make those normal hours more fiction than reality. "All of my friends seem to be in the same boat, too," says Lirette. "Everybody is doing overtime, going in early in the morning or on the weekend. We're all stressed out."[69]

Stephanie Lirette and her friends are experiencing a complex phenomenon related to emotions, called **stress**.[70] Stress is an adaptive response to a situation that is perceived as challenging or threatening to the person's well-being.[71] Stress produces physiological changes to prepare us for "fight or flight"—to defend the threat or flee from it. Specifically, our heart rate increases, muscles tighten, breathing speeds up, and perspiration increases. Our body also moves more blood to the brain, releases adrenaline and other hormones, fuels the system by releasing more glucose and fatty acids, activates systems that sharpen our senses, and conserves resources by shutting down our immune system.

Stress has become a pervasive experience in the daily lives of Canadians. Three out of four Canadians (and a similar percentage of people in Germany, the United States, Australia, and the United Kingdom) say they frequently or sometimes feel stress in their daily lives. In Canada, the workplace is the most common source of that stress, followed by finances. In contrast, only 61 percent of Spaniards frequently or sometimes feel stressed. And in Mexico, more than half of those surveyed claim they never feel stressed. Statistics Canada reports that more than one-quarter of Canadians say they experience high levels of stress each day. This level jumps to 37 percent among men and 43 percent among women in management jobs.[72]

We often hear about stress as a negative experience. This is known as *distress*—the degree of physiological, psychological, and behavioural deviation from healthy functioning. However, some level of stress—called *eustress*—is also a necessary part of life because it activates and motivates people to achieve goals, change their environments, and succeed in life's challenge.[73] Our focus will be on the causes and management of distress, because it has become a chronic problem in many societies.

stress
An adaptive response to a situation that is perceived as challenging or threatening to the person's well-being.

GENERAL ADAPTATION SYNDROME

The stress experience was first documented 50 years ago by Dr. Hans Selye, the Montreal-based pioneer in stress research. Selye determined that people have a fairly consistent physiological response to stressful situations. This response, called the **general adaptation syndrome,** is an automatic defence system to help us cope with environmental demands. It occurs through the three stages shown in Exhibit 4.3.[74] The *alarm reaction* stage occurs when a threat or challenge activates the physiological stress responses that were noted earlier. The individual's energy level and coping effectiveness decrease in response to the initial shock. The second stage, *resistance*, activates various biochemical, psychological, and behavioural mechanisms that give us more energy and engage coping mechanisms to overcome or remove the source of stress. During this process, some elements of the body's immune system are suppressed, while others operate in more erratic or less effective ways. This explains why people are more likely to catch a cold or other illness when they experience prolonged stress.

People have a limited resistance capacity and, if the source of stress persists, they will eventually move into the third stage, *exhaustion*. Most of us are able to remove the source of stress or remove ourselves from that source before becoming too exhausted. However, people who frequently reach exhaustion have increased risk of long-term physiological and psychological damage.[75]

general adaptation syndrome
A model of the stress experience, consisting of three stages: alarm reaction, resistance, and exhaustion.

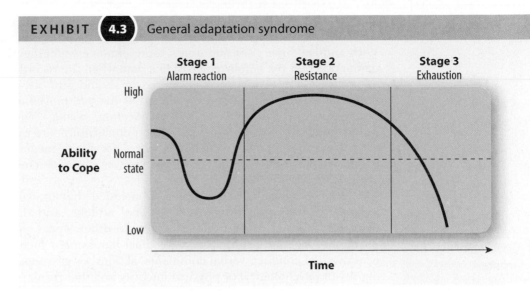

EXHIBIT 4.3 General adaptation syndrome

Source: Adapted from H. Selye, *The Stress of Life* (New York: McGraw-Hill, 1956).

CONSEQUENCES OF DISTRESS

Stress takes its toll on the human body.[76] Many people experience tension headaches, muscle pain, and related problems mainly due to muscle contractions from the stress response. Studies have found that high stress levels also contribute to cardiovascular disease, including heart attacks and strokes. They also produce various psychological consequences, such as job dissatisfaction, moodiness, depression, and lower organizational commitment. Furthermore, various behavioural outcomes have been linked to high or persistent stress, including lower job performance, poor decision making, and increased workplace accidents and aggressive behaviour. Most people react to stress through 'fight or flight,' so increased absenteeism is another outcome because it is a form of flight.[77]

job burnout
The process of emotional exhaustion, depersonalization, and reduced personal accomplishment resulting from prolonged exposure to stress.

Job Burnout **Job burnout** is a particular stress consequence that refers to the process of emotional exhaustion, cynicism, and reduced feelings of personal accomplishment.[78] *Emotional exhaustion*, the first stage, is characterized by a lack of energy, tiredness, and a feeling that one's emotional resources are depleted. This is followed by *cynicism* (also called *depersonalization*), which is characterized by an indifferent attitude toward work, emotional detachment from clients, cynicism about the organization, and tendency to strictly follow rules and regulations rather than adapt to the needs of others. The final stage of burnout, called *reduced personal accomplishment*, refers to feelings of diminished confidence in the ability to perform the job well. In these situations, employees develop a sense of learned helplessness as they no longer believe that their efforts make a difference.

STRESSORS: THE CAUSES OF STRESS

stressors
Any environmental conditions that place a physical or emotional demand on the person.

Before identifying ways to manage work-related stress, we must first understand its causes, known as stressors. **Stressors** include any environmental conditions that place a physical or emotional demand on the person.[79] There are numerous stressors in the workplace and in life generally. In this section, we'll highlight three of the most common stressors: harassment and incivility, workload, and lack of task control.

Harassment and Incivility A family therapist at the Children's Aid Society of Cape Breton-Victoria had a history of anxiety attacks, which worsened after his new supervisor became irritated and critical of his recordkeeping. The supervisor eventually called a meeting in which he accused the employee of unprofessional practice. With another supervisor and union representative watching, the supervisor repeatedly demanded that the employee provide a date when the records would be caught up; the employee kept replying that the supervisor should give *him* a date. The argument got more heated and almost became violent as the two moved aggressively closer to each other. Abruptly, the employee left the meeting, saying, "You may intimidate a lot of these young people around here, but you don't intimidate me!" Too shaken to get any work done, the employee went home, where his wife immediately sent him to the doctor to address his anxiety attack. The employee was suspended for a week, but then went on stress leave for several months.[80]

The Nova Scotia Court of Appeal concluded that the supervisor's behaviour was aggressive, his complaints were personal attacks, and the meeting was intended to embarrass and debase the employee. In other words, the supervisor engaged in **psychological harassment**. Psychological harassment includes repeated and hostile or unwanted conduct, verbal comments, actions, or gestures, that affect an employee's dignity or psychological or physical integrity and that result in a harmful work environment for the employee. This covers a broad landscape of behaviours, from threats and bullying to subtle yet persistent forms of incivility.[81]

Psychological harassment has become such a problem that some European governments explicitly prohibit it in the workplace. The Quebec government, which recently passed the first workplace anti-harassment legislation in North America, received over 2,500 complaints in the first year alone! Psychological harassment also permeates throughout workplaces in other countries. For example, two-thirds of Americans think people are less civil today than 20 years ago; 10 percent say they witness incivility daily in their workplaces and are targets of that abuse at least once each week. More than half of U.K. human resource managers and Australian lawyers say they have been bullied or intimidated.[82]

Sexual harassment is a type of harassment in which a person's employment or job performance is conditional on unwanted sexual relations (called *quid pro quo*), and/or the person experiences sexual conduct from others (such as posting sexually explicit material) that unreasonably interferes with work performance or creates an intimidating, hostile, or offensive working environment (called *hostile work environment*). Less than 10 percent of complaints received by human rights commissions across Canada involve sexual harassment in the workplace, but surveys indicate that a higher percentage of women (and a few men) experience this stressor each year. Sexual harassment is more common where the organizational culture tolerates this behaviour and where policies are lacking.

psychological harassment
Repeated and hostile or unwanted conduct, verbal comments, actions, or gestures that affect an employee's dignity or psychological or physical integrity and that result in a harmful work environment for the employee.

sexual harassment
Unwelcome conduct of a sexual nature that detrimentally affects the work environment or leads to adverse job-related consequences for its victims.

Work Overload   A half-century ago, social scientists predicted that technology would allow employees to enjoy a 15-hour work week at full pay by 2030.[83] So far, it hasn't turned out that way. Canadians experience considerable *work overload*—working more hours and more intensely during those hours than they can reasonably cope. Nearly one-quarter of Canadian employees work more than 50 hours per week, compared with only 10 percent a decade ago. Equally significant, Canadians are working more *unofficial* hours. Surveys indicate that 81 percent of Canadians accept business calls at home, 65 percent check their work email after hours, and 59 percent check their work voicemail after hours. This work overload is also the main cause of work-family conflicts, because overworked employees have insufficient time to satisfy their nonwork roles of being a parent, spouse, and so forth.[84]

Why do employees work such long hours? One explanation is the combined effects of technology and globalization. "Everyone in this industry is working harder now because of email, wireless access, and globalization," says Christopher Lochhead, chief marketing officer of Mercury Interactive, a California-based consulting firm. "You can't even get a rest on the weekend." A second cause, according to a recent study, is that many people are caught up in consumerism; they want to buy more goods and services, which requires more income through longer work hours. A third reason, called the "ideal worker norm," is that professionals expect themselves and others to work longer work

Blackberry Addiction

Nick Salaysay (shown in this photo) admits that his work routinely gets mixed in with his personal time. "I have a BlackBerry, so I check my email a lot when I'm supposed to be on vacation," says the Calgary lawyer. Salaysay also acknowledges that having work spill over into his time off "really annoys my girlfriend." Amy Schulman is another dedicated Black-Berry user. The New York City lawyer recalls that "the BlackBerry was at first a significant intrusion on family life," but she can't resist how the device helps her to process several hundred emails each day. As a consolation, Schulman says she usually avoids looking at her emails while dining with her family "and I try not to look at it in movie theatres." Although Nick Salaysay and Amy Schulman are comfortable using their BlackBerrys during family time, research indicates that the increased workload and work preoccupation caused by these devices can result in the additional stress of relationship and marital problems. One law report recently warned that employers who issue Blackberrys could also incur liability of stress-related illnesses as the devices keep employees on an "electronic leash."[85] *Photo by Mikael Kjellstrom; article "Hard-working Canadians Find it Tough to Disconnect" by Theresa Taylor, May 18, 2008, Calgary Herald. Reprinted with permission of The Calgary Herald.*

hours. For many, toiling away far beyond the normal workweek is a badge of honour, a symbol of their superhuman capacity to perform above others.[86] This badge of honour is particularly serious in several (but not all) Asian countries, to the point where "death from overwork" is now part of the common language (*karoshi* in Japanese and *guolaosi* in Chinese). For example, two young faculty members at China's top engineering school died suddenly, apparently from exhaustion and overwork.[87]

Low Task Control   As a private driver for an executive in Jakarta, Eddy knows that traffic jams are a way of life in Indonesia's largest city. "Jakarta is traffic congestion," he complains. "All of the streets in the city are crowded with vehicles. It is impossible to avoid this distressing fact every day." Eddy's boss complains when traffic jams make him late for appointments, which makes matters even more stressful.[88] Eddy and many other people experience stress due to a lack of task control. Along with driving through congested traffic, low task control occurs where the work is paced by a machine, the job involves monitoring equipment, or the work schedule is controlled by someone else. Computers, cellphones, and other technology also increase stress by limiting a person's control of time and privacy.[89]

The degree to which low task control is a stressor increases with the burden of responsibility the employee must carry. Assembly line workers have low task control, but their stress can also be fairly low if their level of responsibility is also low. In contrast, sports coaches are under immense pressure to win games (high responsibility), yet have little control over what happens on the playing field (low task control). Similarly, Eddy (the Jakarta driver) is under pressure to get his employer to a particular destination on time (high responsibility), yet he has little control over traffic congestion (low task control).

LO9

INDIVIDUAL DIFFERENCES IN STRESS

People have different stress experiences when exposed to the same stressor due to unique personal characteristics. One reason is that they have different threshold levels of resistance to the stressor. Those who exercise and have healthy lifestyles have a larger store of energy to cope with high stress levels. A second reason for different stress responses is that people use different coping strategies, some of which are more effective than others. Research suggests that employees who try to ignore or deny the existence of a stressor suffer more in the long run than those who try to find ways to weaken the stressor and seek social support.[90]

A third reason why some people experience less stress than others is that they have higher resilience.[91] **Resilience** is the capability of individuals to cope successfully in the face of significant change, adversity, or risk. Those with high resilience are able to withstand adversity as well as recover more quickly from it. Resilient people possess personality traits (such as high extroversion and low neuroticism) that generate more optimism, confidence, and positive emotions. Resilience also involves specific competencies and behaviours to respond and adapt more effectively to stressors. Research indicates that resilient people have higher emotional intelligence and good problem-solving skills. They also apply productive coping strategies, such as analyzing the sources of stress and finding ways to neutralize these problems.[92]

While resilience helps people to withstand stress, another personal characteristic—workaholism—attracts more stressors and weakens the capacity to cope with them. The classic **workaholic** (also called *work addict*) is highly involved in work, feels compelled or driven to work because of inner pressures, and has a low enjoyment of work. Workaholics are compulsive and preoccupied with work, often to the exclusion and detriment of personal health, intimate relationships, and family.[93] Classic workaholics are more prone to job stress and have significantly higher scores on depression, anxiety, and anger.[94]

> **resilience**
> The capability of individuals to cope successfully in the face of significant change, adversity, or risk.

> **workaholic**
> A person who is highly involved in work, feels compelled to work, and has a low enjoyment of work.

MANAGING WORK-RELATED STRESS

Not long ago, Koh Ching Hong would dutifully arrive at work around 7:30 in the morning and stay until 10 at night. The managing director of Fuji Xerox in Singapore would continue working back home for a few more hours, sending off emails listing tasks to be completed by employees "first thing in the morning." Eventually, Koh realized that the relentless pace was defeating a higher purpose. "It came to a point that the people whom I worked so hard to provide for, my family, weren't getting to see me," says the father of three children. Today, Koh is out of the office by 6:30 p.m. and shoos his staff out at the same time. Fuji Xerox also gives staff the opportunity to work from home as well as flexibility regarding when they want to begin and end their work day.[95]

Koh Ching Hong was fortunate. He was able to change his work habits and improve conditions for his 500 employees before matters got worse. Unfortunately, many of us deny the existence of our stress until it is too late. This avoidance strategy creates a vicious cycle because the failure to cope with stress becomes another stressor on top of the one that created the stress in the first place. To prevent this vicious cycle, employers and employees need to apply one or more of the stress management strategies described below: remove the stressor, withdraw from the stressor, change stress perceptions, control stress consequences, and receive social support.[96]

Many Ways to Remove the Stressor   Removing the stressor usually begins by identifying areas of high stress and determining its main causes. Canada Post recently introduced a Web-based stress test that helps employees determine whether they need help. Ericsson Canada conducts an annual survey that includes a stress index. Executives at the telecommunications company use the index to identify departments where stress problems may be developing. "We look at those scores and if there appears to be a problem in a particular group, we put in action plans to try and remedy and improve the work situation that may be causing the stress," explains an Ericsson executive.[97]

There are many ways to remove stressors, but some of the more common actions involve assigning employees to jobs that match their skills and preferences, reducing excessive workplace noise, having a complaint system and corrective action against harassment, and giving employees more control over the work process. Work/life balance initiatives also fall into this category, such as offering flexible work schedules, job sharing, telecommuting, personal leave, and childcare support.[98]

Getting a Life at Propaganda

Josh Holmes (third from right in front) has fond memories of working at Electronic Arts (EA), but admits that the long hours at the electronic games company were stressful. "From the minute I joined [EA], I put every waking hour of my day into my work...It definitely took its toll," says Holmes. After 10 years at EA, Holmes decided to quit to follow his heart and fulfill a long-time dream of starting his own studio. "We had done a lot of really long gruelling hours. I know I was thinking that there's got to be a way to do things a little differently." In their quest for a less stressful electronic games company, Holmes and three other senior EA staff formed Propaganda Games (now a creative centre within Disney's video game division). The Vancouver-based company is considered unique in the industry because it espouses not just creativity and risk taking, but also plenty of work/life balance. "We want you to come into the studio, do great work, then get out and live your life," says Propaganda's website. "We foster a start-up attitude without the start-up stress."[99] © Disney Enterprises, Inc.

Withdraw from the Stressor A study of a police and emergency response services department in Western Canada found that leisure time significantly improves the ability to cope with work-related stress.[100] Leisure time includes vacations, days off, and (in a few firms) sabbaticals. But even while at work, companies create environments where employees can withdraw temporarily. For instance, Lighthouse Publishing in Bridgewater, N.S., offers employees massage sessions every month. At TeleTech's call centre in Orillia, Ontario, employees can retreat to a cyber café near the cafeteria, which features a soothing tropical desert island mural painted by employees.[101]

Change Stress Perceptions Earlier, we learned that employees experience different stress levels because they have different levels of resilience, including self-confidence and optimism. Consequently, corporate leaders need to look at ways for employees to improve their self-concept so that job challenges are not perceived as threatening. A study of newly hired accountants reported that personal goal setting and self-reinforcement can also reduce the stress that people experience when they enter new work settings. Humour can also improve optimism and create positive emotions by taking some psychological weight off the situation.[102]

Control Stress Consequences Companies can reduce the adverse consequences of high stress by ensuring that employees maintain healthy lifestyles.[103] Some companies provide onsite fitness centres or subsidize the cost of offsite fitness centres. A few firms, such as AstraZeneca, encourage employees to practise relaxation and meditation techniques during the workday. Others, such as the Town of Richmond Hill, Ontario, offer more comprehensive wellness programs that educate and support employees in better nutrition and fitness, regular sleep, and other good health habits. Many employers also offer employee assistance programs—counselling services that help employees overcome personal or organizational stressors and adopt more effective coping mechanisms. These programs typically help employees resolve marital, financial, or work-related troubles, but some counselling also varies with the industry. For instance, Vancouver City Savings Credit Union has an award-winning program that counsels employees following a bank robbery. There are more than 200 bank robberies in Vancouver each year, and Vancity's program dramatically reduces the time employees require for recovery compared to employees in other financial institutions.[104]

Receive Social Support   Social support occurs when co-workers, supervisors, family members, friends, and others, provide emotional and/or informational support to buffer the stress experience. It potentially improves the person's resilience (particularly their optimism and self-confidence) because support makes people feel valued and worthy. Social support also provides information to help employees interpret, comprehend, and possibly remove the stressor. For instance, social support might reduce a new employee's stress because co-workers describe ways to handle difficult customers. Seeking social support is called a "tend and befriend" response to stress, and research suggests that women often follow this route rather than the "fight-or-flight" response mentioned earlier.[105]

Employee emotions, attitudes, and stress influence employee behaviour mainly through motivation. Recall, for instance, that behavioural intentions are judgments or expectations about the motivation to engage in a particular behaviour. The next chapter introduces the prominent theories of employee motivation as well as applied practices that increase and support motivation.

CHAPTER SUMMARY

Emotions are physiological, behavioural, and psychological episodes experienced toward an object, person, or event that create a state of readiness. Emotions differ from attitudes, which represent the cluster of beliefs, feelings, and behavioural intentions toward a person, object, or event. Beliefs are a person's established perceptions about the attitude object. Feelings are positive or negative evaluations of the attitude object. Behavioural intentions represent a motivation to engage in a particular behaviour with respect to the target.

Attitudes have traditionally been described as a purely rational process in which beliefs predict feelings, which predict behavioural intentions, which predict behaviour. We now know that emotions have an equal or greater influence. This dual process is apparent when we internally experience a conflict between what logically seems good or bad and what we emotionally feel is good or bad in a situation. Emotions also affect behaviour directly. Behaviour sometimes influences our subsequent attitudes through cognitive dissonance.

Emotional labour refers to the effort, planning, and control needed to express organizationally desired emotions during interpersonal transactions. This is more common in jobs requiring a variety of emotions and more intense emotions, as well as where interaction with clients is frequent and for a long duration. Cultures also differ in the norms of displaying or concealing a person's true emotions. Emotional dissonance occurs when required and true emotions are incompatible with each other. Deep acting can minimize this dissonance, as can the practice of hiring people with a natural tendency to display desired emotions.

Emotional intelligence is the ability to perceive and express emotion, assimilate emotion in thought, understand and reason with emotion, and regulate emotion in oneself and others. This concept includes four components arranged in a hierarchy: self-awareness, self-management, social awareness, and relationship management. Emotional intelligence can be learned to some extent, particularly through personal coaching.

Job satisfaction represents a person's evaluation of his or her job and work context. The exit-voice-loyalty-neglect model outlines four possible consequences of job dissatisfaction. Job satisfaction has a moderate relationship with job performance and with customer satisfaction. Affective organizational commitment (loyalty) refers to the employee's emotional attachment to, identification with, and involvement in a particular organization. This contrasts with continuance commitment, which is a calculative bond with the organization. Companies build loyalty through justice and support, shared values, trust, organizational comprehension, and employee involvement.

Stress is an adaptive response to a situation that is perceived as challenging or threatening to the person's well-being. The stress experience, called the general adaptation syndrome, involves moving through three stages: alarm, resistance, and exhaustion. Stressors are the causes of stress and include any environmental conditions that place a physical or emotional demand on the person. Three stressors that have received considerable attention are harassment and incivility, work overload, and low task control.

Two people exposed to the same stressor may experience different stress levels. Many interventions are available to manage work-related stress, including removing the stressor, withdrawing from the stressor, changing stress perceptions, controlling stress consequences, and receiving social support

KEY TERMS

attitudes, p. 79

cognitive dissonance, p. 81

continuance commitment, p. 88

emotional dissonance, p. 82

emotional intelligence (EI), p. 83

emotional labour, p. 81

emotions, p. 78

exit-voice-loyalty-neglect (EVLN) model, p. 86

general adaptation syndrome, p. 90

job burnout, p. 91

job satisfaction, p. 85

organizational (affective) commitment, p. 88

psychological harassment, p. 92

resilience, p. 94

sexual harassment, p. 92

stress, p. 90

stressors, p. 91

trust, p. 89

workaholic, p. 94

CRITICAL THINKING QUESTIONS

1. A recent study reported that instructors at colleges and universities are frequently required to engage in emotional labour. Identify the situations in which emotional labour is required for this job. In your opinion, is emotional labour more troublesome for college instructors or for 911 operators?

2. "Emotional intelligence is more important than cognitive intelligence in influencing an individual's success." Do you agree or disagree with this statement? Support your perspective.

3. Describe a time when you effectively managed someone's emotions. What happened? What was the result?

4. "Happy employees create happy customers." Explain why this statement might be true, and identify conditions in which it might not be true.

5. What factors influence an employee's organizational loyalty?

6. Is being a full-time college or university student a stressful role? Why or why not? Contrast your response with other students' perspectives.

7. Two recent university graduates join the same major newspaper as journalists. Both work long hours and have tight deadlines to complete their stories. They are under constant pressure to scout out new leads and be the first to report new controversies. One journalist is increasingly fatigued and despondent and has taken several days of sick leave. The other is getting the work done and seems to enjoy the challenges. Use your knowledge of stress to explain why these two journalists are reacting differently to their jobs.

8. A senior official of a labour union stated: "All stress management does is help people cope with poor management. [Employers] should really be into stress reduction." Discuss the accuracy of this statement.

CASE STUDY 4.1

Conestoga-Rovers and Associates

At first glance, the thick, hardcover books featured prominently in the reception area of Conestoga-Rovers and Associates in Waterloo, Ontario, have the appearance of dry legal volumes. Then you notice the word "Yearbook" inscribed in large, gold letters across their covers; a peek inside reveals a vividly photographed encapsulation of the company's unspoken, but well understood, work hard–play hard mantra. Within their pages, hundreds of photographs capture smiling, laughing, and often zanily dressed Conestoga-Rovers employees engaged in any number of social events, clubs, and activities that play an integral role in the company's culture.

There are plenty of events to choose from. Hardly a weekend goes by when a group of employees is not engaged in some social event, be it jet-boating on the Niagara River, taking a bus trip to a Buffalo Bills football game, celebrating Roverfest (a massive annual bash for employees and their families), or indulging in a death-by-chocolate night.

Conestoga-Rovers and Associates has forged an exemplary reputation for its expertise in the fields of engineering, the environment, construction, and information technology.

But its employees, some 450 in Waterloo alone, will tell you the company's dynamic social side, along with a range of unique employee perks, also makes it a great place to work and grow, both professionally and socially. Not surprisingly, Conestoga-Rovers has been identified as one of the best places to work in the Waterloo Region.

In addition to an extremely active social committee, the company boasts an on-site day-care centre—The Butterfly Learning Centre—that was launched in 2001, just months after Dianne Freeman, a senior project manager with the company's air quality group, suggested it. "You always go in and ask for the whole dream but you usually only get a window," says Freeman. "[Company president Ed Roberts] offered the whole dream and it was overwhelming."

Another valued Conestoga-Rovers perk is company-paid vacations for employees and their families after 10 years of service. Freeman and her family went to New Zealand, courtesy of the company, five years ago. Last year alone, 44 other 10-year employees were rewarded with similarly ambitious vacations.

"The only thing we have is our employees," says Conestoga-Rovers vice-president Ian Richardson. "Without happy, engaged employees we don't have anything." Richardson also acknowledges that creating a positive work environment helps to recruit top talent: "Our employees know the kind of place they work in. We wanted to let others know a little more about what goes on here."

Discussion Questions

1. Why does Conestoga-Rovers and Associates and other companies try to create a positive work environment?

2. How does this company manage to provide events and perks that employees value?

3. Is it possible that employees can have too much fun at work?

Source: Gary Nyp, "Where Dreams Sometimes Come True," *Kitchener-Waterloo Record*, October 13, 2007, p. E1.

CLASS EXERCISE 4.2

Strengths-Based Coaching

Purpose   To help students practise a form of interpersonal development built on the dynamics of positive emotions.

Materials   None

Background   Several chapters in this book introduce and apply the emerging philosophy of *positive organizational behaviour*, which suggests that focusing on the positive rather than negative aspects of life will improve organizational success and individual well-being. An application of positive OB is strengths-based or appreciative coaching, in which the coach focuses on the person's strengths rather than weaknesses, and helps to realize his or her potential. As part of any coaching process, the coach listens to the employee's story and uses questions and suggestions to help that person redefine his/her self-concept and perceptions of the environment. Listening and probing for information (rather than telling the person a solution or direction) is a key process of effective coaching. The instructions below identify specific information and issues that the coach and coachee will discuss.

Instructions (Small class)
- *Step 1*: Form teams of four people. One team can have six people if the class does not have multiples of four. For odd-numbered class sizes, one person may be an observer. Divide into pairs in which one person is coach and the other coachee. Ideally for this exercise, the coach and coachee should have *little* knowledge of each other.

- *Step 2*: Coachees will describe something about themselves in which they excel and for which they like to be recognized. This competency might be work related, but not necessarily. It would be a personal achievement or ability that is close to their self-concept (how they define themselves). The coach listens, but also prompts more details from the coachee using "probe" questions ("Tell me more about that"; "What did you do next?"; "Could you explain that further, please?"; "What else can you remember about that event?"). As the coachee's story develops, the coach will guide the coachee to identify ways to leverage this strength. For example, the pair would explore situational barriers to practising the coachee's strength as well as aspects of this strength that requires further development. The strength may also be discussed as a foundation for the coachee to develop strengths in other related ways. The session should end with some discussion of the coachee's goals and action plans. The first coaching session can be any length of time specified by the instructor, but 15 to 25 minutes is typical for each coaching session.

- *Step 3*: After completing the first coaching session, regroup so that each pair has different partners than in the first pair (i.e., if pairs are A-B and C-D in session 1, then pairs are A-C and B-D in session 2). The coaches become coachees to their new partner in session 2.

- *Step 4*: The class will debrief regarding the emotional experience of discussing personal strengths, the role of self-concept in emotions and attitudes, the role of managers and co-workers in building positive emotions in people, and the value and limitations of strengths-based coaching.

Note: For further information about strengths-based coaching, see: Sara L. Orem, Jacqueline Binkert, and Ann L. Clancy, *Appreciative Coaching* (San Francisco: Jossey-Bass, 2007); Marcus Buckingham and C. Coffman, *First, Break All the Rules* (New York: Simon & Schuster, 1999).

TEAM EXERCISE 4.3

Stage Fright!

Purpose   This exercise is designed to help you to diagnose a common stressful situation and determine how stress management practices apply to this situation.

Background   Stage fright—including the fear of public speaking—is one of the most stressful experiences many people have in everyday life. According to some estimates, nearly three-quarters of us frequently get stage fright, even when speaking or acting in front of a small audience. Stage fright is an excellent topic for this team activity on stress management because the psychological and physiological symptoms of stage fright are really symptoms of stress. In other words, stage fright is the stress experience in a specific context involving a public audience. Based on the personal experiences of team members, your team is asked to identify the symptoms of stage fright and to determine specific stress management activities that effectively combat stage fright.

Instructions   - *Step 1*: Students are organized into teams, typically four to six students per team. Ideally, each team should have one or more people who acknowledge that they have experienced stage fright.

- *Step 2*: Each team's first task is to identify the symptoms of stage fright. The best way to organize these symptoms is to look at the three categories of stress outcomes described in the textbook: physiological, psychological, and behavioural. The specific stage fright symptoms may be different from the stress outcomes described in the textbook, but the three broad categories would be relevant. Teams should be prepared to identify several symptoms and to present one or two specific examples of stage fright symptoms based on personal experiences of team members. (Please remember that individual students are not required to describe their experiences to the entire class.)

- *Step 3*: Each team's second task is to identify specific strategies people could or have applied to minimize stage fright. The five categories of stress management presented in the textbook will likely provide a useful template in which to organize the specific stage fright management activities. Each team should document several strategies to minimize stage fright and be able to present one or two specific examples to illustrate some of these strategies.

- *Step 4*: The class will congregate to hear each team's analysis of symptoms and solutions to stage fright. This information will then be compared to the stress experience and stress management practices, respectively.

 **TEAM EXERCISE 4.4**

Ranking Jobs on Their Emotional Labour

Purpose   This exercise is designed to help you understand the jobs in which people tend to experience higher or lower degrees of emotional labour.

Instructions
- *Step 1*: Individually rank order the extent that the jobs listed below require emotional labour. In other words, assign a "1" to the job you believe requires the most effort, planning, and control to express organizationally desired emotions during interpersonal transactions. Assign a "10" to the job you believe requires the least amount of emotional labour. Mark your rankings in column 1.

- *Step 2*: The instructor will form teams of four or five members and each team will rank order the items based on consensus (not simply averaging the individual rankings). These results are placed in column 2.

- *Step 3*: The instructor will provide expert ranking information. This information should be written in column 3. Then, students calculate the differences in columns 4 and 5.

- *Step 4*: The class will compare the results and discuss the features of jobs with high emotional labour.

Occupational Emotional Labour Scoring Sheet				
Occupation	(1) Individual Ranking	(2) Team Ranking	(3) Expert Ranking	(4) Absolute Difference of 1 and 3	(5) Absolute Difference of 2 and 3
Bartender					
Cashier					
Dental hygienist					
Insurance adjuster					
Lawyer					
Librarian					
Postal clerk					
Registered nurse					
Social worker					
Television announcer					
			TOTAL		

(The lower the score, the better)   Your score   Team score

SELF-ASSESSMENT EXERCISE 4.5

Are You Committed to Your School?

Purpose	This self-assessment is designed to help you understand the concept of organizational commitment and to assess your commitment to the college or university you are currently attending.
Overview	The concept of commitment is as relevant to students enrolled in college or university courses as it is to employees working in various organizations. This self-assessment adapts a popular organizational commitment instrument so it refers to your commitment as a student to the school where you are attending this program.
Instructions	Read each of the statements below and circle the response that best fits your personal belief. Then use the scoring key in Appendix B of this book to calculate your results. This self-assessment is completed alone so that students rate themselves honestly without concerns of social comparison. However, class discussion will focus on the meaning of the different types of organizational commitment and how well this scale applies to the commitment of students toward the college or university they are attending.

School Commitment Scale						
To what extent do you agree or disagree with each of these statements?	Strongly Agree	Moderately Agree	Slightly Agree	Neutral	Slightly Disagree	Moderately Disagree	Strongly Disagree
1. I would be very happy to complete the rest of my education at this school.	☐	☐	☐	☐	☐	☐	☐
2. One of the difficulties of leaving this school is that there are few alternatives.	☐	☐	☐	☐	☐	☐	☐
3. I really feel as if this school's problems are my own.	☐	☐	☐	☐	☐	☐	☐
4. Right now, staying enrolled at this school is a matter of necessity as much as desire.	☐	☐	☐	☐	☐	☐	☐
5. I do not feel a strong sense of belonging to this school.	☐	☐	☐	☐	☐	☐	☐
6. It would be very hard for me to leave this school right now even if I wanted to.	☐	☐	☐	☐	☐	☐	☐
7. I do not feel emotionally attached to this school.	☐	☐	☐	☐	☐	☐	☐
8. Too much of my life would be disrupted if I decided to move to a different school now.	☐	☐	☐	☐	☐	☐	☐
9. I do not feel like part of the "family" at this school.	☐	☐	☐	☐	☐	☐	☐
10. I feel that I have too few options to consider leaving this school.	☐	☐	☐	☐	☐	☐	☐
11. This school has a great deal of personal meaning for me.	☐	☐	☐	☐	☐	☐	☐
12. If I had not already put so much of myself into this school, I might consider completing my education elsewhere.	☐	☐	☐	☐	☐	☐	☐

Source: Adapted from: J. P. Meyer, N. J. Allen, and C. A. Smith, "Commitment to Organizations and Occupations: Extension and Test of a Three-Component Model," *Journal of Applied Psychology*, 78 (1993), pp. 538–551.

www.mcgrawhill.ca/olc/mcshane

 Go to the Online Learning Centre at www.mcgrawhill.ca/olc/mcshane to complete the following interactive self-assessments.

 SELF-ASSESSMENT EXERCISE 4.6

What is Your Emotional Personality?

This self-assessment is designed to help you understand mood states or personality traits of emotions and to assess your own mood or emotion personality. This self-assessment consists of several words representing various emotions that you might have experienced. For each word presented, indicate the extent to which you have felt this way generally across all situations **over the past six months**. You need to be honest with yourself to obtain a reasonable estimate of your mood state or personality trait on these scales. The results provide an estimate of your level on two emotional personality scales. This instrument is widely used in research, but it is only an estimate. You should not assume that the results are accurate without a more complete assessment by a trained professional.

SELF-ASSESSMENT EXERCISE 4.7

Are You a Workaholic?

This self-assessment is designed to help you identify the extent to which you are a workaholic. This instrument presents several statements, and asks you to indicate the extent to which each statement is true of your work habits. You need to be honest with yourself to obtain a reasonable estimate of your level of workaholism.

SELF-ASSESSMENT EXERCISE 4.8

How Resilient Are You?

This self-assessment is designed to help you estimate your personal level of resilience. Please indicate the extent that each statement in this instrument is true for you **over the past month**. It is important for you to realize that there are no "right" or "wrong" answers to these questions. This self-assessment is completed alone so that you can complete this instrument honestly without concerns of social comparison. However, class discussion will focus on the meaning of resilience and how it relates to workplace stress.

SELF-ASSESSMENT EXERCISE 4.9

Are You Stressed?

This self-assessment is designed to help you estimate your perceived general level of stress. The items in this scale ask you about your feelings and thoughts during the last month. In each case, indicate how often you felt or thought a certain way. You need to be honest with yourself to obtain a reasonable estimate of your general level of stress.

www.mcgrawhill.ca/olc/mcshane

SELF-ASSESSMENT EXERCISE 4.10

How Do You Cope with Stressful Situations?

This self-assessment is designed to help you identify the type of coping strategy you prefer to use in stressful situations. This scale lists a variety of things you might do when faced with a stressful situation. You are asked how often you tend to react in these ways. You need to be honest with yourself to obtain a reasonable estimate of your preferred coping strategy.

[istudy]

¡Interact ¡Learn ¡Succeed

iStudy—Available 24/7 with instant feedback so you can study when you want, how you want, and where you want. Visit www.istudyob.ca to register—take practice quizzes, run interactive scenarios, practice concepts, and much more. Also visit the Student Online Learning Centre for additional study tools.

www.mcgrawhill.ca/olc/mcshane

CHAPTER 5

Foundations of Employee Motivation

Robert Meggy understands the importance of employee motivation for business success. "When I set out 25 years ago to turn around a box manufacturing company in receivership, the focus quickly became the employees," explains Meggy, who has turned Vancouver-based Great Little Box Company Ltd. (GLBC) into a strong competitor in the corrugated box industry. "It is clear that happy and motivated employees are the key to success and longevity."

To motivate staff, Meggy relies on a combination of challenging goals, open-book feedback, valued rewards that are distributed fairly, and plenty of appreciation and recognition in between. The company has a "Big Outrageous eXtravaganza (BOX)" goal representing a stretch profit target for the forthcoming year. If the BOX goal is achieved, all of GLBC's 170 employees receive a week-long company-paid tropical vacation. Employees are also motivated more frequently through open-book meetings where they see the company's financial results for the previous month and receive a bonus cheque representing a share of that month's profits. The same amount of bonus is distributed to everyone, which most staff say is fair. "I certainly believe in fair pay," says Meggy. "You don't have to be the best paying but you do have to be fair."

Meggy also motivates his staff by paying from $10 to $1,000 at monthly meetings for generating ideas that improve operations. Equally important, anyone can participate in one of several task forces focused on improving sales, reducing costs, or improving employee well-being. "We are always into improving what we do, and this motivates middle management and sales people to put ideas on the table," Meggy explains. "It has really helped our growth."

Altogether, these activities have produced a workforce that is motivated and highly engaged in their work. It has also contributed to GLBC's standing as the best company to work for in British Columbia, one of the top-rated companies to work for in Canada, and one of Canada's best-managed companies. "Over the years we have made it a priority to engage employees, provide them with the information they need and empower them to make decisions," says Meggy.[1]

Great Little Box Company motivates its employees through goal setting, fair pay, and recognition, resulting in a highly engaged workforce. "It is clear that happy and motivated employees are the key to success and longevity," says CEO Robert Meggy. *Photo courtesy of Great Little Box Company Ltd.*

motivation
The forces within a person that affect the direction, intensity, and persistence of voluntary behaviour.

employee engagement
The employee's emotional and cognitive motivation, self-efficacy to perform the job, a clear understanding of his or her role in the organization's vision, and a belief that he or she has the resources to perform their job done.

Stretch goals, open-book feedback, fairness in rewards, and various celebrations for good performance are designed to maintain and improve employee motivation at Great Little Box Company (GLBC). This motivation has sustained the company's performance in a difficult market and has helped it to become one of the best places to work in Canada. Recall from Chapter 2 that **motivation** refers to the forces within a person that affect the direction, intensity, and persistence of voluntary behaviour.[2] Motivated employees are willing to exert a particular level of effort (intensity), for a certain amount of time (persistence), toward a particular goal (direction). Motivation is one of the four essential drivers of individual behaviour and performance. It is also closely related to the increasingly popular concept of employee engagement. For example, GLBC CEO Robert Meggy refers to employee engagement when speaking about the company's success through its effective workforce.

Employee engagement has been popularized by practitioners without much theoretical foundation or collaborative development. Consequently, its meaning varies across studies and its distinction from job satisfaction, organizational commitment, and other concepts is uncertain. Even so, most writers describe employee engagement as an emotional and cognitive motivation, a desire to perform beyond narrowly defined job duties, a high level of absorption in the work (i.e., getting "carried away"), and a strong self-efficacy to perform the work.[3] Putting these pieces together, we define employee engagement as the employee's emotional and cognitive motivation, self-efficacy to perform the job, a clear understanding of his or her role in the organization's vision, and a belief that he or she has the resources to perform their job. You might notice that this definition relates to the four cornerstones of individual behaviour and performance identified in the MARS model (see Chapter 2); motivation, ability, role perceptions, and situational factors. Employee engagement is about one's beliefs and emotional responses to these conditions that create high performance.

Employee motivation and engagement are important for a company's success (and likely employee well-being), yet these have been elusive goals. Most employers—92 percent of them, according to one major survey—say that motivating employees has become more challenging. Several consulting reports paint a similarly bleak portrait of employee engagement in Canada and elsewhere. One recent study found that 23 percent of Canadian employees are engaged, slightly above the global average of 21 percent, whereas fully one-quarter were "disenchanted" (fairly low engagement) and 7 percent were "disengaged" (below the global averages of 30 percent and 8 percent, respectively).[4] Some writers suggest that globalization, information technology, corporate restructuring, and other changes have potentially undermined the levels of trust and commitment necessary to motivate employees beyond minimum standards.[5] Others point out that companies have not adjusted to the changing needs and expectations of new workforce entrants. According to one report, more than 40 percent of employees aged 25 to 34 sometimes or frequently feel demotivated compared to 30 percent of 35- to 44-year-olds and just 18 percent of 45- to 54-year olds.[6]

This chapter introduces the core theories and concepts of employee motivation. We begin by distinguishing drives and needs and explaining how people reshape their needs through their self-concept and personal characteristics. Maslow's needs hierarchy is described, followed by an explanation why this popular theory and other needs hierarchy theories do not fit reality. McClelland's learned needs theory is then introduced, followed by the emerging (but well-founded in neuroscience and psychological research) four-drives theory. Next, we turn our attention to the popular rational decision model of employee motivation, called expectancy theory. This is followed by discussion of the key elements of goal setting and feedback. In the final section, we look at organizational justice, including the dimensions and dynamics of equity theory and procedural justice.

DRIVES, NEEDS, AND EMPLOYEE MOTIVATION

Motivation is defined as "forces" within a person, but what are these forces? We need to have some understanding of these prime movers of individual effort in order to make sense of various motivation theories. Unfortunately, many writers conveniently avoid this topic, resulting in a stream of confusing phrases such as innate drives, learned needs, motivations, instincts, secondary drives, and primary needs.[7] Therefore, we begin this chapter by defining drives and needs, and how these concepts relate to individual goals and behaviour.

drives
Neural states that energize individuals to correct deficiencies or maintain an internal equilibrium.

Drives (also called *primary needs*, *fundamental needs*, or *innate motives*) are hard-wired characteristics of the brain that energize individuals to correct deficiencies or maintain an internal equilibrium.[8] They serve as the 'prime movers' of behaviour by activating emotions, which put us in a state of readiness to act. Although typically overlooked in organizational behaviour, emotions play a central role in motivation.[9] In fact, both words (emotion and motivation) come from the same Latin word, *movere*, which means "to move." Drive theories popular a half-century ago ultimately failed because they limited drives to physiological essentials, such as hunger and thirst. Now, experts conclude that people also have non-physiological drives, such as the drive for social interaction, to understand the immediate environment, as well as to defend oneself against physiological and psychological harm.[10] In short, to the best of our knowledge, drives and emotions represent the primary sources of employee motivation.

needs
Goal-directed forces that people experience.

We define **needs** as goal-directed forces that people experience. Drives produce emotions, whereas needs represent the motivational force of those emotions channelled toward particular goals to correct deficiencies or imbalances. Consider the following example: Everyone has a drive to bond—an inherent need to be associated with other people to some degree. This drive to bond generates negative emotions when we are rejected by others or lack social interaction over time, and generates positive emotions when accepted by others. However, two people may experience different needs for belongingness even when they have identical levels of social interaction. Some people develop a strong need to visit friends whereas others are less motivated to do so.

Exhibit 5.1 explains why this difference occurs. The left side of the model shows that the individual's self-concept (including personality and values), social norms, and past experience amplify or suppress emotions, which results in stronger or weaker needs.[11] People who define themselves as very sociable would have a strong need for social interaction if alone for a while, whereas people who view themselves as less sociable would experience a less intense need to socialize over that same time. These individual differences also explain, as we shall discover later in this chapter, why needs can be "learned" to some extent. Essentially, people form self-concepts of having high or low achievement orientation, high or low social needs, and so forth.

Self-concept, social norms, and past experience do more than adjust the level of drive-based emotions. The right side of Exhibit 5.1 shows that these individual characteristics also regulate a person's decisions and behaviour. If you have a strong desire for social companionship, you probably wouldn't walk up to strangers and start talking to them because it is contrary to most social norms of behaviour. Similarly, suppose that you dislike your boss's decision to assign you to a particular project. In some companies

EXHIBIT 5.1   Drives, needs, and behaviour

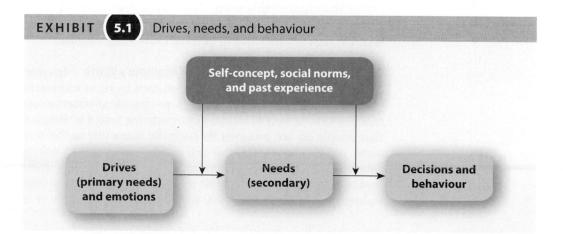

and cultures, openly expressing disagreement with the boss is acceptable, whereas it is strongly discouraged in others. Your self-concept of being forthright or avoiding conflict also influences your motivation to confront your boss on this matter.

We have presented this detail about needs and drives for a few reasons.[12] First, as mentioned, motivation theories use the terms drives, needs, and motivations so loosely that they make it difficult to compare theories, so it is important to settle this confusion at the outset. Second, the field of organizational behaviour has been woefully slow to acknowledge the central role of emotions in employee motivation, which will be apparent when reviewing most motivation theories in this chapter. Third, Exhibit 5.1 provides a useful template to understand various motivation theories. In fact, you will see pieces of this theory when we discuss four-drive theory, expectancy theory, and other concepts in this chapter. The remainder of this section describes theories that try to explain the dynamics of drives and needs. Later theories in this chapter explain how experiences—such as expectancies, feedback, and work experiences—influence the motivation process.

LO2 MASLOW'S NEEDS HIERARCHY THEORY

Maslow's needs hierarchy theory

A motivation theory of needs arranged in a hierarchy, whereby people are motivated to fulfill a higher need as a lower one becomes gratified.

By far, the most widely known theory of human motivation is **Maslow's needs hierarchy theory**. Developed by psychologist Abraham Maslow in the 1940s, the model condenses and integrates the long list of needs that had been studied previously into a hierarchy of five basic categories (from lowest to highest; see Exhibit 5.2):[13]

Physiological—the need for food, air, water, shelter, etc.

Safety needs—the need for a secure and stable environment and the absence of pain, threat, or illness.

Belongingness/love—the need for love, affection, and interaction with other people.

Esteem—the need for self-esteem through personal achievement as well as social esteem through recognition and respect from others.

Self-actualization—the need for self-fulfi llment, realization of one's potential.

Along with these five categories, Maslow identified the desire to know and the desire for aesthetic beauty as two innate drives that do not fit within the hierarchy.

Maslow's list represents drives (primary needs) because they are described as innate and universal. According to Maslow, we are motivated simultaneously by several needs, but the strongest source is the lowest unsatisfied need at the time. As the person satisfies a lower level need, the next higher need in the hierarchy becomes the primary motivator and remains so even if never satisfied. Physiological needs are initially the most important and people are motivated to satisfy them first. As they become gratified, the desire for safety emerges as the strongest motivator. As safety needs are satisfied, belongingness needs become most important, and so forth. The exception to this need fulfillment process is self-actualization; as people experience self-actualization, they desire more rather than less of this need. Thus, while the bottom four groups are *deficiency needs* because they become activated when unfulfilled, self-actualization is known as a *growth need* because it continues to develop even when fulfilled.

Limitations and Contributions of Maslow's Work   In spite of its popularity, Maslow's needs hierarchy theory has been dismissed by most motivation experts.[14] Maslow developed the theory based only on his professional observations and was later surprised that it was so widely accepted before anyone tested it! Empirical studies have concluded that people do not progress through the hierarchy as the theory predicts. For example, some people strive more for self-esteem before their belongingness needs have been satisfied. The theory also assumes that needs priorities shift over a long time, whereas needs priorities rise and fall far more frequently with the situation. A person's needs for status, food, social interaction, and so forth, change daily or weekly, not every few years.

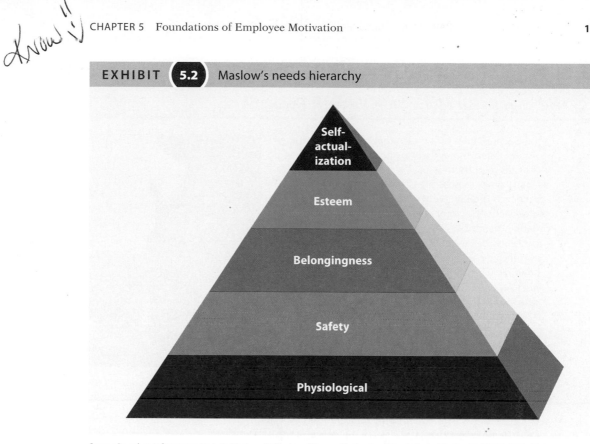

EXHIBIT **5.2** Maslow's needs hierarchy

Source: Based on information in: A. H. Maslow, "A Theory of Human Motivation," *Psychological Review* 50 (1943): 370–396.

As GLOBAL Connections 5.1 describes, companies around the world routinely motivate all staff through recognition. These examples illustrate that people regularly need—and are motivated to receive—respect and belongingness in the workplace.

Although needs hierarchy theory has failed the reality test, Maslow deserves credit for bringing a more holistic, humanistic, and positive approach to the study of human motivation. First, Maslow brought a more holistic perspective by introducing the notion that needs are related to each other and, consequently, should be studied together. Prior to the needs hierarchy model, motivation experts had splintered needs or drives into dozens of categories, each studied in isolation using nontypical subjects (usually animals or people with severe psychological dysfunctions).[15] Maslow argued that isolating narrowly defined needs and drives was inappropriate because human behaviour is typically initiated by more than one of these needs or drives with varying degrees of influence on that behaviour.

Second, Maslow brought a more humanistic perspective to the study of motivation. At a time when most researchers thought of human instincts as direct drivers of human motivation and behaviour, Maslow suggested that higher order needs are influenced by personal and social influences, not just instincts. In other words, he was among the first to recognize that human thoughts (including self-concept, social norms, past experience) play a role in motivation. Third, Maslow brought a more positive perspective of employee motivation by focusing on need gratification rather than only need deprivation. In particular, he popularized the previously developed concept of self-actualization, suggesting that people are naturally motivated to reach their potential and that organizations and societies need to be structured to help people continue and develop this motivation.[16] This view of employee motivation, which was novel at the time, has become the foundation of **positive organizational behaviour** (a variation of *positive psychology*), which focuses on building positive qualities and traits within individuals or institutions as opposed to focusing on just trying to fix what might be wrong with them.

positive organizational behaviour

A perspective of organizational behaviour that focuses on building positive qualities and traits within individuals or institutions as opposed to focusing on what is wrong with them.

🌐 global connections 5.1

Never Enough Motivation through Recognition

David Gachuru lives by a motto that motivates employees with much more than money: "If an employee's work calls for a thumbs-up, I will appreciate him or her as many times as possible." Translating this advice into practice is a daily event for the general manager of Sarova Panafric Hotel in Nairobi, Kenya. In addition to thanking staff personally and through emails, Gachuru holds bi-monthly meetings where top performing employees are congratulated and receive paid holidays with their family. Employee achievements are also celebrated in the hotel's newsletter, which is distributed to guests as well as to employees.

Sarova Panafric Hotel and other firms are returning to good old-fashioned praise and recognition to regularly motivate staff. Good thing, because recent surveys in several countries identify lack of praise, recognition, or appreciation as a major reason why employees are demotivated, unsatisfied, or decide to find work elsewhere. For instance, based on 1,000 exit interviews, the Small Firms Association (SMA) recently reported that lack of recognition was a top reason why Irish employees quit their jobs. "Increasingly people need to feel that their contribution is valued," suggests SMA director Patricia Callan. "If people do not feel important, they are not motivated to stay."

The challenge of recognition is to "catch" employees doing extraordinary work or showing organizational citizenship. To this end, many companies have turned to peer recognition, in which co-workers show their appreciation and document this praise so the company can offer financial rewards. An example is ScotiaBank's award-winning Applause program, in which employees use a special website to identify peers or teams who have

Panafric Hotel in Nairobi, Kenya, motivates its employees through plenty of praise and recognition. *Photo courtesy of Sarova, Panafric Hotel in Nairobi, Kenya*

demonstrated the five Applause Principles: integrity, respect, commitment, insight, and spirit. The name of the submitter as well as the name of individuals being recognized are entered into monthly sweepstakes. In a recent year, ScotiaBank staff submitted more than 500,000 peer recognition certificates.

The Ritz Carlton Hotel in Kuala Lumpur applies a similar peer recognition process using First Class Cards. A Ritz Carlton Kuala Lumpur manager explains that "congratulatory messages or words of appreciation are written down by any member of the team to another and even as far as from the hotel and corporate senior leaders. This serves as a motivational aspect of the work environment."[17]

In other words, this approach emphasizes building on strengths rather than trying to correct weaknesses.[18]

WHAT'S WRONG WITH NEEDS HIERARCHY MODELS?

ERG theory
A needs hierarchy theory consisting of three fundamental needs—existence, relatedness, and growth.

Maslow's theory is not the only attempt to map employee needs onto a single hierarchy. Another hierarchy model, called **ERG theory**, re-organizes Maslow's five groups into three—existence, relatedness, and growth.[19] Unlike Maslow's theory, which only explained how people progress up the hierarchy, ERG theory also describes how people regress down the hierarchy when they fail to fulfill higher needs. ERG theory seems to explain human motivation somewhat better than Maslow's needs hierarchy, but that's mainly because it is easier to cluster human needs around ERG's three categories than Maslow's five categories. Otherwise, the research indicates that ERG theory only marginally improves our understanding of human needs.[20]

Why have Maslow's needs hierarchy, ERG theory, and other needs hierarchies largely failed to explain the dynamics of employee needs? The most glaring explanation is that people don't fit into a single needs hierarchy. Some people place social status at the top of their personal hierarchy; others consider personal development and growth an ongoing priority over social relations or status. There is increasing evidence that needs hierarchies are unique to each person, not universal, because needs are strongly influenced by each individual's self-concept, including personal values and social identity. If your most important values lean toward stimulation and self-direction, you probably pay more attention to self-actualization needs. If power and achievement are at the top of your value system, then status needs will likely be at the top of your needs hierarchy. This connection between values and needs suggests that a needs hierarchy is unique to each person and can possibly change over time, just as values change over a lifetime.[21]

LEARNED NEEDS THEORY

Earlier in this chapter we said that drives (primary needs) are innate whereas needs are shaped, amplified, or suppressed through self-concept, social norms, and past experience. Maslow noted that individual characteristics influence the strength of higher order needs, such as the need to belong. However, psychologist David McClelland further investigated this idea that need strength can be altered through social influences. In particular, he recognized that a person's needs can be strengthened through reinforcement, learning, and social conditions. McClelland examined three of these "learned" needs: achievement, power, and affiliation.[22]

Need for Achievement (nAch)   People with a strong need for achievement (nAch) want to accomplish reasonably challenging goals through their own effort. They prefer working alone rather than in teams and they choose tasks with a moderate degree of risk (i.e., neither too easy nor impossible to complete). High nAch people also desire unambiguous feedback and recognition for their success. Money is a weak motivator, except when it provides feedback and recognition.[23] In contrast, employees with a low nAch perform their work better when money is used as an incentive. Successful entrepreneurs tend to have a high nAch, possibly because they establish challenging goals for themselves and thrive on competition.[24]

Need for Affiliation (nAff)   Need for affiliation (nAff) refers to a desire to seek approval from others, conform to their wishes and expectations, and avoid conflict and confrontation. People with a strong nAff try to project a favourable image of themselves. They tend to actively support others and try to smooth out workplace conflicts. High nAff employees general work well in coordinating roles to mediate conflicts, and in sales positions where the main task is cultivating long-term relations. However, they tend to be less effective at allocating scarce resources and making other decisions that potentially generate conflict. People in decision-making positions must have a relatively low need for affiliation so that their choices and actions are not biased by a personal need for approval.[25]

Need for Power (nPow)   People with a high need for power (nPow) want to exercise control over others and are concerned about maintaining their leadership position. They frequently rely on persuasive communication, make more suggestions in meetings, and tend to publicly evaluate situations more frequently. McClelland pointed out that there are two types of nPow. Those who enjoy their power for its own sake, use it to advance personal interests, and wear their power as a status symbol have *personalized power*. Others mainly have a high need for *socialized power* because they desire power as a means to help others.[26] McClelland argues that effective leaders should have a high need for socialized rather than personalized power. They must have a high degree of altruism and social responsibility and be concerned about the consequences of their own actions on others.

Learning Needs   McClelland's research supported his theory that needs can be learned (more accurately, strengthened or weakened), so he developed training programs for this purpose. In his achievement motivation program, trainees write achievement-oriented stories and practise achievement-oriented behaviours in business games. They also complete a detailed achievement plan for the next two years and form a reference group with other trainees to maintain their newfound achievement motive style.[27] These programs seem to work. Participants attending a need for achievement course in India subsequently started more new businesses, had greater community involvement, invested more in expanding their businesses, and employed twice as many people as nonparticipants. Research on similar achievement-motive courses for North American small-business owners reported dramatic increases in the profitability of the participants' businesses. In essence, these programs attempt to alter the individual's self-concept or experiences such that they amplify or suppress related drive-generated emotions.

LO4   FOUR-DRIVE THEORY

four-drive theory
A motivation theory based on the innate drives to acquire, bond, learn, and defend that incorporates both emotions and rationality.

One of the central messages of this chapter is that emotions play a significant role in employee motivation. This view is supported by a groundswell of research in neuroscience, but is almost completely absent from contemporary motivation theories in organizational behaviour. Also, social scientists in several fields (psychology, anthropology, etc.) increasingly agree that human beings have several hard-wired drives, including social interaction, learning, and dominance. One of the few theories to apply this emerging knowledge is **four-drive theory**.[28] Developed by Harvard Business School professors Paul Lawrence and Nitin Nohria, four-drive theory states that everyone has the drive to acquire, bond, learn, and defend:

- *Drive to acquire*—This is the drive to seek, take, control, and retain objects and personal experiences. The drive to acquire extends beyond basic food and water; it includes enhancing one's self-concept through relative status and recognition in society.[29] Thus, it is the foundation of competition and the basis of our need for esteem. Four-drive theory states that the drive to acquire is insatiable because the purpose of human motivation is to achieve a higher position than others, not just to fulfill one's physiological needs.

- *Drive to bond*—This is the drive to form social relationships and develop mutual caring commitments with others. It also explains why people form social identities by aligning their self-concept with various social groups (see Chapter 2). It may also explain why people who lack social contact are more prone to serious health problems.[30] The drive to bond motivates people to cooperate and, consequently, is a fundamental ingredient in the success of organizations and the development of societies.

- *Drive to learn*—This is the drive to satisfy our curiosity, to know and understand ourselves and the environment around us.[31] When observing something that is inconsistent with or beyond our current knowledge, we experience a tension that motivates us to close that information gap. In fact, studies in the 1950s involving Canadian students revealed that people who are removed from any novel information will crave even boring information; the drive to learn generated such strong emotions that these students eventually craved for month-old stock reports![32] The drive to learn is related to the higher order needs of growth and self-actualization described earlier.

- *Drive to defend*—This is the drive to protect ourselves physically and socially. Probably the first drive to develop, it creates a "fight-or-flight" response in the face of personal danger. The drive to defend goes beyond protecting our physical self. It includes defending our relationships, our acquisitions, and our belief systems.

These four drives are innate and universal, meaning that they are hardwired in our brains and are found in all human beings. They are also independent of each other. There is no hierarchy of drives, so one drive is neither dependent on nor inherently inferior or superior to another drive. Four-drive theory also states that these four drives are a complete set—there are no other fundamental drives excluded from the model.

Another key feature is that three of the four drives are "proactive"—we regularly try to fulfill them. Only the drive to defend is reactive—it is triggered by threat. Thus, any notion of fulfilling drives is temporary, at best.

How Drives Influence Employee Motivation   Along with its list of core drives, four-drive theory draws from current neuroscience knowledge to explain how drives translate into goal-directed effort. To begin with, recall from previous chapters that the information we receive is quickly and nonconsciously tagged with emotional markers that subsequently shape our logical analysis of the situation.[33] According to four-drive theory, these four drives determine which emotions are tagged to incoming stimuli. If you arrive at work one day to see a stranger sitting in your office chair, you might quickly experience worry, curiosity, or both. These emotions are automatically created by one or more of the four drives. In this example, the emotions produced are likely strong enough to demand your attention and motivate you to act on this observation.

Most of the time, we aren't aware of our emotional experiences because they are subtle and fleeting. However, emotions do become conscious experiences when they are sufficiently strong or when we experience conflicting emotions. Under these circumstances, our mental skill set relies on social norms, past experience, and personal values to direct the motivational force of our emotions to useful and acceptable goals that address the source of those emotions (see Exhibit 5.3). In other words, the emotions generated by the four drives motivate us to act, and our mental skill set chooses courses of action that are acceptable to society and our own moral compass.[34] This is similar to the process described at the beginning of this chapter, namely that drives produce emotions; our self-concept, social norms, and past experience translate these emotions into goal-directed needs, and these individual characteristics also translate needs into decisions and behaviour.

Evaluating Four-Drive Theory   Although four-drive theory was introduced very recently, it is based on a deep foundation of research that dates back more than three decades. The drives have been identified from psychological and anthropological studies. The translation of drives into goal-directed behaviour originates from considerable research on emotions and neural processes. The theory avoids the assumption that everyone has the same needs hierarchy, and explains why needs vary from one person to

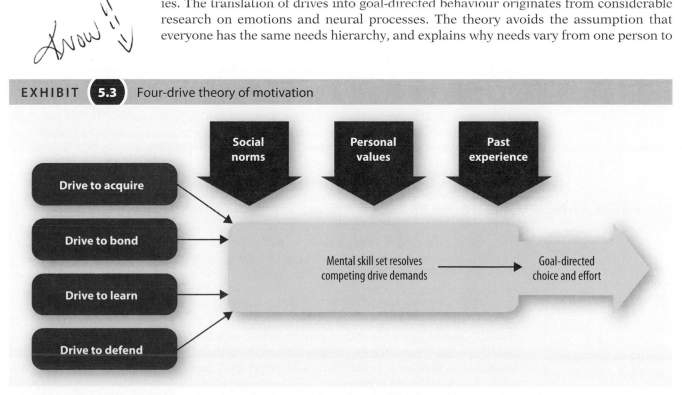

EXHIBIT 5.3   Four-drive theory of motivation

Source: Based on information in P. R. Lawrence and N. Nohria, *Driven: How Human Nature Shapes Our Choices* (San Francisco: Jossey-Bass, 2002).

the next. Notice, too, that four-drive theory is both holistic (it integrates several drives) and humanistic (it acknowledges the role of human thought and social influences rather than just instinct). Maslow had identified these two principles as important features of a motivation theory. Four-drive theory also provides a much clearer understanding about the role of emotional intelligence in employee motivation and behaviour. Employees with high emotional intelligence are more sensitive to competing demands from the four drives, are better able to avoid impulsive behaviour from those drives, and can judge the best way to act to fulfill those drive demands in a social context.

Even with its well-researched foundations, four-drive theory is far from complete. First, most experts would argue that one or two other drives exist that should be included. Second, social norms, personal values, and past experience probably don't represent the full set of individual characteristics that translate emotions into goal-directed effort. For example, other elements of self-concept beyond personal values, such as personality and social identity, likely play a significant role in translating drives into needs, and needs into decisions and behaviour.

Practical Implications of Four-Drive Theory   The main recommendation from four-drive theory is to ensure that individual jobs and workplaces provide a balanced opportunity to fulfill the drive to acquire, bond, learn, and defend.[35] There are really two recommendations here. The first is that the best workplaces for employee motivation and well-being offer conditions that help employees to fulfill all four drives. Employees continually seek fulfillment of their innate drives, so successful companies provide sufficient rewards, learning opportunities, social interaction, and so forth for all employees.

The second recommendation is that fulfillment of these four drives must be kept in "balance"; that is, organizations should avoid too much or too little opportunity to fulfill each drive. The reason for this advice is that the four drives counterbalance each other. The drive to bond counterbalances the drive to acquire; the drive to defend counterbalances the drive to learn. An organization that energizes the drive to acquire without the drive to bond may eventually suffer from organizational politics and dysfunctional conflict. Change and novelty in the workplace will aid the drive to learn, but too much of it will trigger the drive to defend to such an extent that employees become territorial and resistant to change. Thus, the workplace should offer enough opportunity to keep all four drives in balance.

These recommendations partly explain why Great Little Box Company, described at the beginning of this chapter, has a motivated workforce and is rated as one of the best places to work. Employees have opportunities to achieve, to learn, and to bond. In fact, CEO Robert Meggy insists that socializing with co-workers distinguishes employees who connect with the company from those who are unlikely to remain. "If they [employees] don't go to social events, it usually means they're not interested in the people they work with," he explained a few years ago. "And if you're not interested in that, you're not interested in the company, because the people make up everything."[36]   ·

EXPECTANCY THEORY OF MOTIVATION

LO5

expectancy theory
A motivation theory based on the idea that work effort is directed towards behaviours that people believe will lead to desired outcomes.

The theories described so far mainly explain the internal origins of employee motivation. But how do these drives and needs translate into specific effort and behaviour? Four-drive theory recognizes that social norms, personal values, and past experience direct our effort, but doesn't offer any more detail. **Expectancy theory**, on the other hand, offers an elegant model based on rational logic to predict the chosen direction, level, and persistence of motivation. Essentially, the theory states that work effort is directed toward behaviours that people believe will lead to desired outcomes. In other words, we are motivated to achieve the goals with the highest expected payoff.[37] As illustrated in Exhibit 5.4, an individual's effort level depends on three factors: effort-to-performance (E-to-P) expectancy, performance-to-outcome (P-to-O) expectancy, and outcome valences. Employee motivation is influenced by all three components of the expectancy theory model. If any component weakens, motivation weakens.

Know !!

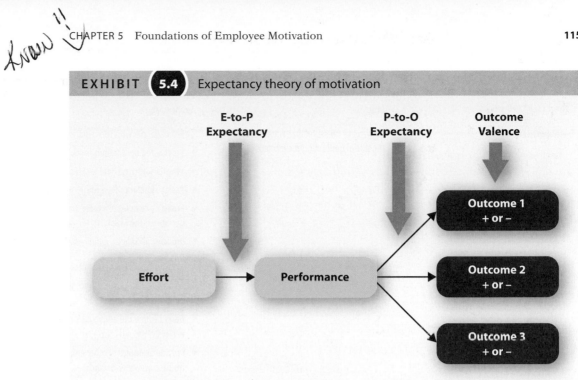

EXHIBIT **5.4**   Expectancy theory of motivation

- *E-to-P Expectancy*   This refers to the individual's perception that his or her effort will result in a particular level of performance. In some situations, employees may believe that they can unquestionably accomplish the task (a probability of 1.0). In other situations, they expect that even their highest level of effort will not result in the desired performance level (a probability of 0.0). In most cases, the E-to-P expectancy falls somewhere between these two extremes.

- *P-to-O Expectancy*—This is the perceived probability that a specific behaviour or performance level will lead to particular outcomes. In extreme cases, employees may believe that accomplishing a particular task (performance) will definitely result in a particular outcome (a probability of 1.0), or they may believe that this outcome will have no effect on successful performance (a probability of 0.0). More often, the P-to-O expectancy falls somewhere between these two extremes.

- *Outcome Valences*—A valence is the anticipated satisfaction or dissatisfaction that an individual feels toward an outcome. It ranges from negative to positive. (The actual range doesn't matter; it may be from –1 to +1, or from –100 to +100.) An outcome valence represents a person's anticipated satisfaction with the outcome.[38] Outcomes have a positive valence when they are consistent with our values and satisfy our needs; they have a negative valence when they oppose our values and inhibit need fulfillment.

EXPECTANCY THEORY IN PRACTICE

One of the appealing characteristics of expectancy theory is that it provides clear guidelines for increasing employee motivation.[39] Several practical applications of expectancy theory are listed in Exhibit 5.5 and described below.

Increasing E-to-P Expectancies   E-to-P expectancies are influenced by the individual's belief that he or she can successfully complete the task. Some companies increase this can-do attitude by assuring employees that they have the necessary competencies, clear role perceptions, and necessary resources to reach the desired levels of performance. Matching employees to jobs based on their abilities and clearly communicating the tasks required for the job is an important part of this process. Similarly, E-to-P expectancies are learned, so behavioural modelling and supportive feedback (positive reinforcement) typically strengthen the individual's belief that he/she is able to perform the task.

EXHIBIT 5.5   Practical applications of expectancy theory

Expectancy Theory Component	Objective	Applications
E→P expectancies	To increase the belief that employees are capable of performing the job successfully	• Select people with the required skills and knowledge. • Provide required training and clarify job requirements. • Provide sufficient time and resources. • Assign simpler or fewer tasks until employees can master them. • Provide examples of similar employees who have successfully performed the task. • Provide coaching to employees who lack self-confidence.
P→O expectancies	To increase the belief that good performance will result in certain (valued) outcomes	• Measure job performance accurately. • Clearly explain the outcomes that will result from successful performance. • Describe how the employee's rewards were based on past performance. • Provide examples of other employees whose good performance has resulted in higher rewards.
Outcome valences	To increase the expected value of outcomes resulting from desired performance	• Distribute rewards that employees value. • Individualize rewards. • Minimize the presence of countervalent outcomes.

Increasing P-to-O Expectancies   The most obvious ways to improve P-to-O expectancies are to measure employee performance accurately and distribute more valued rewards to those with higher job performance. P-to-O expectancies are perceptions, so employees need to know how higher performance will result in higher rewards. This occurs by explaining how specific rewards are connected to specific past performance, and by using examples, anecdotes, and public ceremonies to illustrate when behaviour has been rewarded.

Increasing Outcome Valences   Everyone has unique values and experiences, which translates into different needs at different times. Consequently, individualizing rather than standardizing rewards and other performance outcomes is an important ingredient in employee motivation. At the same time, leaders need to watch out for countervalent outcomes—consequences with negative valences that reduce rather than enhance employee motivation. For example, peer pressure may cause some employees to perform their jobs at the minimum standard even though formal rewards and the job itself would otherwise motivate them to perform at higher levels.

Overall, expectancy theory is a useful model that explains how people rationally figure out the best direction, intensity, and persistence of effort. It has been tested in a variety of situations and predicts employee motivation in different cultures.[40] However, critics have a number of concerns with how the theory has been tested. Another concern is that expectancy theory ignores the central role of emotion in employee effort and behaviour. The valence element of expectancy theory captures some of this emotional process, but only peripherally.[41]

GOAL SETTING AND FEEDBACK

LO6

Walk into almost any customer contact centre (i.e., call centre) in Canada—whether its Intuit Canada's centre in Edmonton or Rogers' customer care centre in Moncton—and you will notice that work activities are dominated by goal setting and plenty of feedback.[42] In fact, a typical contact centre manager's job includes establishing "performance goals for all service department employees, and monitor performance on a continual basis." Contact centre performance is judged on several metrics—called key performance indicators (KPIs)—such as average time to answer the call, length of time per call, and abandon rates (customers who hang up before the call is handled by a customer service representative). Some contact centres have large electronic boards showing how many customers are waiting, the average time they have been waiting, and the average time before someone talks to them. A few even have "emotion detection" software, which translates words and voice intonation into a measure of the customer's level of happiness or anger during the telephone conversation![43]

goal setting
The process of motivating employees and clarifying their role perceptions by establishing performance objectives.

Goal setting is the process of motivating employees and clarifying their role perceptions by establishing performance objectives. It potentially improves employee performance in two ways: (1) by stretching the intensity and persistence of effort and (2) by giving employees clearer role perceptions so that their effort is channelled toward behaviours that will improve work performance. Goal setting is more complex than simply telling someone to "do your best." Instead, it requires several specific characteristics. Some consultants refer to these as SMART goals, but the acronym doesn't quite capture all of the key variables identified by goal-setting research. The six key characteristics include: specific goals, relevant goals, challenging goals, goal commitment, participation in goal formation (sometimes), and goal feedback.[44]

- *Specific goals*—Employees put more effort into a task when they work toward specific goals rather than "do your best" targets. Specific goals have measurable levels of change over a specific and relatively short timeframe, such as "within the next six months, reduce average call pick-up time from 35 to 25 seconds." Specific goals communicate more precise performance expectations, so employees can direct their effort more efficiently and reliably.

- *Relevant goals* Goals must also be relevant to the individual's job and within his or her control. For example, a goal to reduce waste materials would have little value if employees don't have much control over waste in the production process.

- *Challenging goals*—Challenging goals (rather than easy ones) cause people to raise the intensity and persistence of their work effort and to think through information more actively. They also fulfill a person's achievement or growth needs when the goal is achieved. General Electric, Goldman Sachs, and many other organizations emphasize *stretch goals*. These goals don't just stretch a person's abilities and motivation;

The Missing Link in Pay and Performance

One of the clearest messages from expectancy theory is that motivation increases when employees see a clear link between their performance and valued rewards (pay, recognition, promotions, etc.). Many companies have attempted to follow this principle by introducing more performance-based rewards, yet the performance-to-outcome linkage remains foggy to most staff. One recent survey reported that only one-quarter of the 10,000 Canadian employees surveyed said they regularly receive rewards for a job well done. Approximately 30 percent claimed that they are rarely or never rewarded based on their performance. This is consistent with another survey which reported that only 27 percent of Canadian employees say there is a clear link between their job performance and pay. At first glance, the P-to-O connection seems to be somewhat stronger in the United States, where 41 percent say that employees at their company who perform their job well receive more money than those who perform their job poorly. However, this statistic hides a significant gap between managers' and employees' perceptions. While 56 percent of managers in that study believe that employees are paid more for doing a better job, only 32 percent of nonmanagement employees agreed with this statement.[45] © Ryan McVay/Photodisc/Getty Images

they are goals that people don't even know how to reach, so they need to be creative to achieve them.

- *Goal commitment*—Ideally goals should be challenging without being so difficult that employees lose their motivation to achieve them.[46] This is the same as the E-to-P expectancy that we learned about in the section on expectancy theory. The lower the E-to-P expectancy that the goal can be accomplished, the less committed (motivated) the employee is to the goal.

- *Goal participation* (sometimes)—Goal setting is usually (but not always) more effective when employees participate in setting goals.[47] Participation potentially increases goal commitment compared to goals set alone by the supervisor. Participation may also improve goal quality, because employees have valuable information and knowledge that may not be known to those who initially formed the goal.

- *Goal feedback*—Feedback is another necessary condition for effective goal setting.[48] Feedback is any information that lets us know whether we have achieved the goal or are properly directing our effort toward it. Feedback redirects our effort, but it potentially also fulfills our growth needs.

To illustrate the value of these goal characteristics, recall the opening story to this chapter, which described how Robert Meggy at Great Little Box Company motivates employees through goal setting. Every year, Meggy establishes a specific BOX target goal—a stretch goal because it requires innovative thinking to achieve. Individuals and teams also have performance objectives to achieve for each project or job to be completed. Every month through open-book meetings, employees see the company's financial results, which is feedback about the company's progress toward that annual goal as well as monthly performance targets. Feedback is so central to goal setting that we will look more closely at it next.

CHARACTERISTICS OF EFFECTIVE FEEDBACK

Whirlpool Corp. employees complained they weren't getting enough feedback from their bosses, so the appliance manufacturer asked managers to meet with their immediate subordinates quarterly rather than the previous schedule of every six months. Jeffrey Davidoff, head of marketing for Whirlpool's North American consumer brands, has taken the feedback frequency even further; he meets with his eight direct reports for up to 45 minutes every two weeks. "I'm noticing much better results," Mr. Davidoff says.[49]

Whirlpool managers are discovering that feedback is an important practice in employee motivation and performance. Along with clarifying role perceptions and improving employee skills and knowledge, feedback motivates when it is constructive and when employees have a strong self-efficacy.[50] As with goal setting, feedback should be *specific* and *relevant*. In other words, the information should include specific metrics (e.g., sales increased by 5 percent last month) rather than vague information, and must relate to the individual's behaviour rather than to conditions beyond the individual's control. Feedback should also be *timely*; the information should be available soon after the behaviour or results occur so employees see a clear association between their actions and the consequences.

Effective feedback is also *sufficiently frequent*. How frequent is "sufficiently"? The answer depends on at least two things. One consideration is the employee's knowledge and experience with the task. Feedback is a form of reinforcement, so employees working on new tasks should receive more frequent corrective feedback because they require more guidance and reinforcement (see Chapter 3). Employees who perform familiar tasks can receive less frequent feedback. The second factor is how long it takes to complete the task. Feedback is necessarily less frequent in jobs with a long cycle time (e.g., executives and scientists) than in jobs with a short cycle time (e.g., grocery store cashiers). The final characteristic of effective feedback is that it should be *credible*. Employees are more likely to accept feedback (particularly corrective feedback) from trustworthy and credible sources.

Real-time Feedback Sparks Competitive Spirit at Nova Chemicals

To improve its manufacturing excellence, Nova Chemicals introduced computer technology that monitors in real time the plant's operational capacity, depicted as a gently flowing green line, and actual production output, shown as a red squiggly line. What executives at the Calgary-based company didn't anticipate was that this information sparked a new level of competitive spirit among Nova's plant operators. Almost immediately, the plant's operations staff saw the two lines as a computer game, in which the green line was the goal and the red line was the feedback that could be changed by tweaking the plant's equipment. In bouts of friendly rivalry, employees tried to see who could keep the red squiggly line as close as possible to the plant's maximum capacity, the flowing green line. "In effect, they were kind of competing with each other to see who could push the plant that much harder within its constraints," says Alan Schrob, director of Nova's manufacturing excellence program. "It goes back to the idea that putting this information in front of folks is going to drive different behaviours. And if we can do this through data that allows people to act immediately, then that's our key objective."[51] *Photo courtesy of Nova Chemicals*

SOURCES OF FEEDBACK

Feedback can originate from nonsocial or social sources. Nonsocial sources provide feedback without someone communicating that information. Employees at contact centres view electronic displays showing how many callers are waiting and the average time they have been waiting. Nova Chemicals operators receive real-time feedback from a computer screen showing the plant's actual production output compared to its theoretical production capacity. Corporate intranets now allow many executives to receive feedback instantaneously on their computer, usually in the form of graphic output on an executive dashboard. Almost half of Microsoft employees use a dashboard to monitor project deadlines, sales, and other metrics. Microsoft CEO Steve Ballmer regularly reviews dashboard results in one-on-one meetings with his seven business leaders. "Every time I go to see Ballmer, it's an expectation that I bring my dashboard with me," says the head of the Microsoft Office division.[52]

Multisource (360-Degree) Feedback   Erik Djukastein felt that he needed feedback on his leadership skills to improve morale and engagement among his employees. However, going to his boss for performance feedback wasn't possible because Djukastein owns the company, Victoria, B.C.-based Contech Electronics. Instead, he asked all 20 managers and employees to anonymously complete a written report about his strengths and weaknesses. "It was illuminating and scary looking at the results—when your staff says you don't follow through on your commitments, that hurts," Djukastein admits.

"But the good news is that it enabled me to open my eyes to things that were instrumental in changing my mental attitude."[53]

Contech Electronics is one of many organizations that has introduced **multisource** or **360-degree feedback** to improve employee performance. As the name implies, multisource feedback is information about an employee's performance collected from a full circle of people, including subordinates, peers, supervisors, and customers. Nearly half of Canada's largest firms use multisource feedback, typically for managers rather than to nonmanagement employees.[54] Multisource feedback tends to provide more complete and accurate information than feedback from a supervisor alone. It is particularly useful when the supervisor is unable to observe the employee's behaviour or performance throughout the year. Lower level employees also feel a greater sense of fairness and open communication when they are able to provide upward feedback about their boss's performance.[55]

However, multisource feedback also creates challenges. Having several people review so many other people can be expensive and time-consuming. With multiple opinions, the 360-degree process can also produce ambiguous and conflicting feedback, so employees may require guidance to interpret the results. A third concern is that peers may provide inflated rather than accurate feedback to avoid conflicts over the forthcoming year. A final concern is that critical feedback from many people can create a stronger emotional reaction than if the critical judgment originates from just one person (your boss). "Initially you do take it personally," admits a manager at software maker Autodesk. "[360-degree feedback] is meant to be constructive, but you have to internally battle that."[56]

Choosing Feedback Sources   With so many sources of feedback—multisource feedback, executive dashboards, customer surveys, equipment gauges, nonverbal communication from your boss, and so on—which one works best under which conditions? The preferred feedback source depends on the purpose of the information. To learn about their progress toward goal accomplishment, employees usually prefer nonsocial feedback sources, such as computer printouts or feedback directly from the job. This is because information from nonsocial sources is considered more accurate than information from social sources. Corrective feedback from nonsocial sources is also less damaging to self-esteem. This is probably just as well because social sources tend to delay negative information, leave some of it out, and distort the bad news in a positive way.[57] When employees want to improve their self-image, they seek out positive feedback from social sources. It feels better to have co-workers say that you are performing the job well than to discover this from a computer screen.

EVALUATING GOAL SETTING AND FEEDBACK

Goal setting represents one of the "tried and true" theories in organizational behaviour, so much so that a recent survey of professors identified it as one of the top OB theories in terms of validity and usefulness.[58] In partnership with goal setting, feedback also has an excellent reputation for improving employee motivation and performance. At the same time, putting goal setting into practice is far from perfect.[59] One concern is that goal setting tends to focus employees on a narrow subset of measurable performance indicators while ignoring aspects of job performance that are difficult to measure. The saying, "What gets measured, gets done" applies here. A second problem is that when tied to financial rewards, many employees are motivated to make their goals easy (while making the boss think they are difficult) so they have a higher probability of the bonus or pay increase. As a former chief executive at Ford once quipped: "At Ford, we hire very smart people. They quickly learn how to make relatively easy goals look difficult!"[60] A third problem is that setting performance goals is effective in established jobs, but seems to interfere with the learning process in new, complex jobs. Thus, we need to be careful not to apply goal setting where an intense learning process is occurring.

---

multisource (360-degree) feedback Information about an employee's performance collected from a full circle of people, including subordinates, peers, supervisors, and customers.

ORGANIZATIONAL JUSTICE

When Robert Meggy first introduced a profit sharing plan at Great Little Box Company, he felt that the size of the profit sharing bonus should correspond to the person's position and seniority in the organization. "It used to be a program based on seniority and a number of other variables but there were a number of complaints about that," Meggy recalls. "Now that it's equal across the board, we don't have that problem."[61] In other words, employees didn't think the bonus distribution system was fair, something that Meggy considers vital to a successful company. "I certainly believe in fair pay," says Meggy. "You don't have to be the best paying but you do have to be fair."

distributive justice
Perceived fairness in the outcomes we receive relative to our contributions and the outcomes and contributions of others.

Most organizational leaders know that treating employees fairly is both morally correct and good for employee motivation, loyalty, and well-being. Yet, feelings of injustice are regular occurrences in the workplace. To minimize these incidents, we need to first understand that there are two forms of organizational justice: distributive justice and procedural justice.[62] **Distributive justice** refers to perceived fairness in the outcomes we receive relative to our contributions and the outcomes and contributions of others. **Procedural justice**, on the other hand, refers to fairness of the procedures used to decide the distribution of resources.

procedural justice
Perceived fairness of the procedures used to decide the distribution of resources.

LO7

 Know !!

EQUITY THEORY

The first thing we usually think about and experience in situations of injustice is distributive injustice   the belief (and its emotional response) that the distribution of pay and other outcomes is unfair. What is considered "fair" varies with each person and situation. We apply an *equality principle* when we believe that everyone in the group should receive the same outcomes (such as the profit sharing bonus at Great Little Box Company). The *need principle* is applied when we believe that those with the greatest need should receive more outcomes than others with less need. The *equity principle* infers that people should be paid in proportion to their contribution. The equity principle is the most common distributive justice rule in organizational settings, so let's look at it in more detail.

equity theory
A theory that explains how people develop perceptions of fairness in the distribution and exchange of resources.

To explain how the equity principle operates, OB scholars developed **equity theory**, which says that employees determine feelings of equity by comparing their own outcome/input ratio to the outcome/input ratio of some other person.[63] The outcome/input ratio is the value of the outcomes you receive divided by the value of inputs you provide in the exchange relationship. Inputs include such things as skill, effort, reputation, performance, experience, and hours worked. Outcomes are what employees receive from the organization in exchange for the inputs, such as pay, promotions, recognition, preferential treatment, or preferred jobs in the future.

Equity theory states that we compare our outcome/input ratio with a *comparison other*.[64] The comparison other may be another person or group of people in the same job, another job, or another organization. Some research suggests that employees frequently collect information on several referents to form a "generalized" comparison other.[65] For the most part, however, the comparison other varies from one person to the next and is not easily identifiable.

People develop feelings of equity or inequity by comparing their own outcome/input ratio with the comparison other's ratio. Exhibit 5.6 diagrams the three equity evaluations. In the equity condition, people believe that their outcome/input ratio is similar to the ratio of the comparison other. People experience underreward inequity when they believe their ratio is lower than the comparison other's ratio. Overreward inequity occurs when people believe their ratio of outcomes/inputs is higher than the comparison other's ratio. However, overreward inequity isn't as common as underreward inequity because people change their perceptions to justify the higher outcomes.

EXHIBIT 5.6 Equity theory model

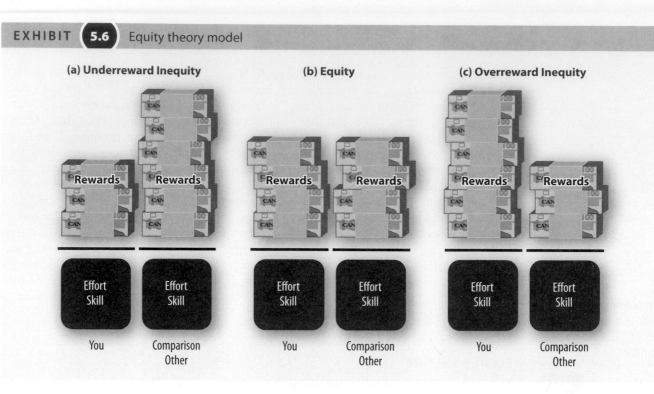

(a) Underreward Inequity   **(b) Equity**   **(c) Overreward Inequity**

Rewards   Rewards   Rewards   Rewards   Rewards   Rewards

Effort Skill   Effort Skill   Effort Skill   Effort Skill   Effort Skill   Effort Skill

You   Comparison Other   You   Comparison Other   You   Comparison Other

Inequity and Employee Motivation   How does the equity evaluation relate to employee motivation? The answer is that feelings of inequity generate negative emotions and, as we have pointed out throughout this chapter, emotions are the engines of motivation. In the case of inequity, people are motivated to reduce the emotional tension. Here are the main ways that people correct inequity feelings when they are underrewarded compared to a co-worker (comparison other):[66]

- *Reduce our inputs*—perform at a lower level, give fewer helpful suggestions, engage in less organizational citizenship behaviour

- *Increase our outcomes*—ask for a pay increase, make unauthorized use of company resources

- *Increase the comparison other's inputs*—subtly ask the better off co-worker to do a larger share of the work to justify his/her higher pay or other outcomes

- *Reduce comparison other's outcomes*—ask the boss to stop giving favourable treatment to the co-worker

- *Change our perceptions*—believe the co-worker really is doing more (e.g., working longer hours), or that the higher outcomes (e.g., better office) he/she receives really aren't so much better than what you get

- *Change the comparison other*—compare yourself to someone else closer to your situation (job duties, pay scale)

- *Leave the field*—avoid thinking about the inequity by keeping away from the office where the co-worker is located, taking more sick leave, moving to another department, or quitting the job

Although the categories remain the same, people who feel overreward inequity would, of course, act differently. For example, overrewarded employees don't usually reduce the inequity tension by working harder. Instead, they might encourage the co-worker to work at a more leisurely pace

"O.K., if you can't see your way to giving me a pay raise, how about giving Parkerson a pay cut?"

or, equally likely, change their perceptions to justify why they are given more favourable outcomes. As the late Canadian author Pierre Berton once said: "I was underpaid for the first half of my life. I don't mind being overpaid for the second half."[67]

Individual Differences: Equity Sensitivity

equity sensitivity
An individual's outcome/input preferences and reaction to various outcome/input ratios.

Thus far, we have described equity theory as though everyone has the same feelings of inequity in a particular situation. The reality, however, is that people vary in their **equity sensitivity**, that is, their outcome/input preferences and reaction to various outcome/input ratios.[68] At one end of the equity sensitivity continuum are the "Benevolents"—people who are tolerant of situations where they are underrewarded. They might still prefer equal outcome/input ratios, but they don't mind if others receive more than they do for the same inputs. In the middle are people who fit the standard equity theory model. These "Equity Sensitives" want their outcome/input ratio to be equal to the outcome/input ratio of the comparison other. Equity sensitives feel increasing inequity as the ratios become different. At the other end are the "Entitleds." These people feel more comfortable in situations where they receive proportionately more than others. They might accept having the same outcome/input ratio as others, but they would prefer receiving more than others performing the same work.

Evaluating Equity Theory

Equity theory is widely studied and quite successful at predicting various situations involving feelings of workplace injustice.[69] However, equity theory isn't so easy to put into practice because it doesn't identify the "comparison other" and doesn't indicate which inputs or outcomes are most valuable to each employee. The best solution here is for leaders to know their employees well enough to minimize the risk of inequity feelings. Open communication is also the key, so employees can let decision makers know when they feel their decisions are unfair. A second problem is that equity theory accounts for only some of our feelings of fairness or justice in the workplace. Experts now say that procedural justice is at least as important as distributive justice.

LO8

PROCEDURAL JUSTICE

Recall that procedural justice refers to fairness of the procedures used to decide the distribution of resources. How do companies improve procedural justice?[70] A good place to start is by giving employees "voice" in the process; encourage them to present their facts and perspectives on the issue. Voice also provides a "value-expressive" function;

Costco Wholesale CEO Keeps Executive Pay Equitable

John Pierpont Morgan, who in the 1800s founded the financial giant now called J.P. Morgan Chase, warned that no CEO should earn more than 20 times an average worker's pay. That advice didn't stop James L. Dimon, the current CEO of J.P. Morgan Chase, from recently earning $51 million in salary, bonus, and stock gains during his first year in the top job. That's more than 1,700 times the pay of the average employee in the United States. Costco Wholesale chief executive Jim Sinegal (shown in this photo) thinks such a large wage gap is blatantly unfair and can lead to long-term employee motivation problems. "Having an individual who is making 100 or 200 or 300 times more than the average person working on the floor is wrong," says Sinegal, who co-founded the wholesale club company. With annual salary and bonus of $550,000, Sinegal ranks as one of the lowest paid executives, even though Costco is one of North America's largest retailers and its employees among the highest paid in the industry.[71] *AP Images/ Atsushi Tsukada*

employees tend to feel better after having an opportunity to speak their mind. Procedural justice is also higher when the decision maker is perceived as unbiased, relies on complete and accurate information, applies existing policies consistently, and has listened to all sides of the dispute. If employees still feel unfairness in the allocation of resources, these feelings tend to weaken if the company has a way of appealing the decision to a higher authority.

Finally, people usually feel better when they are treated with respect and are given a full explanation of the decision. If employees believe a decision is unfair, refusing to explain how the decision was made could fuel those feelings of inequity. For instance, one Canadian study found that nonwhite nurses who experienced racism tended to file grievances only after experiencing disrespectful treatment in their attempt to resolve the racist situation. Another study reported that employees with repetitive strain injuries were more likely to file workers' compensation claims after experiencing disrespectful behaviour from management. A third recent study noted that employees have stronger feelings of injustice when the manager has a reputation of treating people unfairly most of the time.[72]

Consequences of Procedural Injustice   Procedural justice has a strong influence on a person's emotions and motivation. Employees tend to experience anger toward the source of the injustice, which generates various response behaviours that scholars categorize as either withdrawal or aggression.[73] Notice how these response behaviours are similar to the fight-or-flight responses described earlier in the chapter regarding situations that activate our drive to defend. Research suggests that being treated unfairly threatens our self-concept and social status, particularly when others see that we have been unjustly treated. Consequently, employees retaliate to restore their self-concept and reinstate their status and power in the relationship with the perpetrator of the injustice. Employees also engage in these counterproductive behaviours to educate the decision maker, thereby trying to minimize the likelihood of future injustices.[74]

CHAPTER SUMMARY

Motivation refers to the forces within a person that affect his or her direction, intensity, and persistence of voluntary behaviour in the workplace. Drives (also called primary needs) are neural states that energize individuals to correct deficiencies or maintain an internal equilibrium. They are the "prime movers" of behaviour by activating emotions, which put us in a state of readiness to act. Needs—goal-directed forces that people experience—are shaped by the individual's self-concept (including personality and values), social norms, and past experience.

Maslow's needs hierarchy groups needs into a hierarchy of five levels and states that the lowest needs are initially most important, but higher needs become more important as the lower ones are satisfied. Although very popular, the theory lacks research support, as does ERG theory, which attempted to overcome some of the limitations in Maslow's needs hierarchy. Both models assume that everyone has the same hierarchy, whereas the emerging evidence suggests that needs hierarchies vary from one person to the next based on their personal values.

McClelland's learned needs theory argues that needs can be strengthened through learning. The three needs studied in this respect have been need for achievement, need for power, and need for affiliation. Four-drive theory states that everyone has four innate drives—the drive to acquire, bond, learn, and defend. These drives activate emotions that we regulate through a skill set that considers social norms, past experience, and personal values. The main recommendation from four-drive theory is to ensure that individual jobs and workplaces provide a balanced opportunity to fulfill the four drives.

Expectancy theory states that work effort is determined by the perception that effort will result in a particular level of performance (E-to-P expectancy), the perception that a specific behaviour or performance level will lead to specific outcomes (P-to-O expectancy), and the valences that the person feels for those outcomes. The E-to-P expectancy increases by improving the employee's ability and confidence to perform the job. The P-to-O expectancy increases by measuring performance accurately, distributing higher rewards to better performers, and showing employees that rewards are performance-based. Outcome valences increase by finding out what employees want and using these resources as rewards.

Goal setting is the process of motivating employees and clarifying their role perceptions by establishing performance objectives. Goals are more effective when they are specific, relevant, and challenging; have employee commitment; and are accompanied by meaningful feedback. Participative goal setting is important in some situations.

Effective feedback is specific, relevant, timely, credible, and sufficiently frequent.

Organizational justice consists of distributive justice (perceived fairness in the outcomes we receive relative to our contributions and the outcomes and contributions of others) and procedural justice (fairness of the procedures used to decide the distribution of resources). Equity the-ory has four elements: outcome/input ratio, comparison other, equity evaluation, and consequences of inequity. The theory also explains what people are motivated to do when they feel inequitably treated. Along with equity of the distribution of resources, companies need to con-sider fairness in the process of making resource allocation decisions.

KEY TERMS

distributive justice, p. 121

drives, p. 107

employee engagement, p. 106

equity sensitivity, p. 123

equity theory, p. 121

ERG theory, p. 110

expectancy theory, p. 114

four-drive theory, p. 112

goal setting, p. 117

Maslow's needs hierarchy theory, p. 108

motivation, p. 106

multisource (360-degree) feedback, p. 120

needs, p. 107

positive organizational behaviour, p. 109

procedural justice, p. 121

CRITICAL THINKING QUESTIONS

1. Four-drive theory is conceptually different from Maslow's needs hierarchy theory (as well as ERG the-ory) in several ways. Describe these differences. At the same time, needs are based on drives, so the four drives should parallel the seven needs that Maslow identi-fied (five in the hierarchy and two additional needs). Map Maslow's needs onto the four drives in four-drive theory.

2. Learned needs theory states that needs can be strength-ened or weakened. How might a company strengthen the achievement needs of its management team?

3. Exhibit 5.1 illustrates how a person's drives and needs result in decisions and behaviour. Explain where expec-tancy theory of motivation fits into this model.

4. Use all three components of expectancy theory to explain why some employees are motivated to show up for work during a severe storm whereas others make no effort to leave their home.

5. Two friends who have just completed an organizational behaviour course at another university inform you that employees must fulfill their need for self-esteem and social esteem before they can reach their full potential through self-actualization. What theory are these friends referring to? How does this statement differ from what you learned about that theory in this textbook?

6. Using your knowledge of the characteristics of effective goals, establish two meaningful goals related to your performance in this class.

7. Several service representatives are upset that the newly hired representative with no previous experience will be paid $3,000 a year above the usual starting salary in the pay range. The department manager explained that the new hire would not accept the entry-level rate, so the company raised the offer by $3,000. All five reps currently earn salaries near the top of the scale ($15,000 higher than the new recruit), although they all started at the minimum starting salary a few years earlier. Use equity theory to explain why the five service represen-tatives feel inequity in this situation.

8. Organizational injustice can occur in the classroom as well as in the workplace. Identify classroom situations in which you experienced feelings of injustice. What can instructors do to maintain an environment that fosters both distributive and procedural justice?

CASE STUDY 5.1

Vêtements Ltée

By Steven L McShane, The University of Western Australia

Vêtements Ltée is a chain of men's retail clothing stores located throughout the province of Quebec, Canada. Two years ago, the company introduced new incentive systems for both store managers and sales employees. Store managers in each store receive a salary with annual merit increases based on sales above targeted goals, store appearance, store inventory management, customer feedback, and several other performance measures. Some of this information (e.g., store appearance) is gathered during visits by senior management, while other information is based on company records (e.g., sales volume).

Sales employees are paid a fixed salary plus a commission based on the percentage of sales credited to that employee over the pay period. The commission represents about 30 percent of a typical paycheque and is intended to encourage employees to actively serve customers and to increase sales volume. Because returned merchandise is discounted from commissions, sales employees are discouraged from selling products that customers do not really want.

Soon after the new incentive systems were introduced, senior management began to receive complaints from store managers regarding the performance of their sales staff. They observed that sales employees tended to stand near the store entrance waiting to "tag" customers as their own. Occasionally, sales staff would argue over "ownership" of the customer. Managers were concerned that this aggressive behaviour intimidated some customers. It also tended to leave some parts of the store unattended by staff.

Many managers were also concerned about inventory duties. Previously, sales staff would share responsibility for restocking inventory and completing inventory reorder forms. Under the new compensation system, however, few employees were willing to do these essential tasks. On several occasions, stores have faced stock shortages because merchandise was not stocked or reorder forms were not completed in a timely manner. Potential sales have suffered from empty shelves when plenty of merchandise was available in the back storeroom or at the warehouse. The company's new automatic inventory system could reduce some of these problems, but employees must still stock shelves and assist in other aspects of inventory management.

Store managers have tried to correct the inventory problem by assigning employees to inventory duty, but this has created resentment among the employees selected. Other managers have threatened sales staff with dismissals if they do not do their share of inventory management. This strategy has been somewhat effective when the manager is in the store, but staff members sneak back onto the floor when the manager is away. It has also hurt staff morale, particularly relations with the store manager.

To reduce the tendency of sales staff to hoard customers at the store entrance, some managers have assigned employees to specific areas of the store. This has also created some resentment among employees stationed in areas with less traffic or lower-priced merchandise. Some staff have openly complained of lower paycheques because they have been placed in a slow area of the store or have been given more than their share of inventory duties.

CLASS EXERCISE 5.2

What do Employees Value the Most?

Purpose   This class exercise is designed to help you understand the characteristics and contingencies of employee needs in the workplace

Instructions (Large Class)

- *Step 1:* The table below lists in alphabetical order 14 characteristics of the job or work environment. Working alone, use the far left column to rank order these characteristics in terms of how important they are to you personally. Write in "1" beside the most important characteristic, "2" for the second most important, and so on through to "14" for the least important characteristic on this list.

- *Step 2:* In the second column, rank order these characteristics in the order that you think human resource managers believe are important for their employees.

- *Step 3:* The instructor asks students with a show of hands (or using classroom technology) to identify the top ranked options.

- *Step 4:* The instructor will provide results of a recent large-scale survey of employees. When these results are presented, identify the reasons for any noticeable differences. Relate these difference to your understanding of the emerging view of employee needs and drives in work settings.

Instructions (Small Class) Same as above for previous steps.

- *Step 5:* Students are assigned to teams, where they compare their rank order results and explain their ranking. Rationale for different rankings are noted and discussed with the entire class. Students should pay close attention to different needs, self-concepts, and various forms of diversity (culture, profession, age, etc.) to identify possible explanations for variation of results across students.

Importance to YOU	What HR Managers Believe are Important to Employees	
_____	_____	Autonomy and independence
_____	_____	Benefits (health care, dental, etc.)
_____		Career development opportunities
_____	_____	Communication between employees and senior mgt
	_____	Compensation/pay
	_____	Feeling safe in the work environment
_____	_____	Flexibility to balance work/life issues
_____	_____	Job security
_____	_____	Job specific training
_____	_____	Management recognition of employee job performance
_____	_____	Opportunities to use skills/abilities
_____	_____	Organization's commitment to professional development
_____	_____	Relationship with immediate supervisor
	_____	The work itself

 **TEAM EXERCISE 5.3**

A Question of Feedback

Purpose This exercise is designed to help you understand the importance of feedback, including problems that occur with imperfect communication in the feedback process.

Materials The instructor will distribute a few pages of exhibits to one person on each team. The other students will require a pencil with eraser and blank paper. Movable chairs and tables in a large area are helpful.

Instructions (Small Class)

- *Step 1:* The class is divided into pairs of students. Each pair is ideally located in a private area, away from other students and where one person can write. One student is given the pages of exhibits from the instructor. The other student in each pair is not allowed to see these exhibits.

- *Step 2:* The student holding the materials will describe each of the exhibits and the other student's task is to accurately replicate each exhibit. The pair of students can compare the replication with the original at the end of each drawing. They may also switch roles for each exhibit, if they wish. If roles are switched, the instructor must distribute exhibits separately to each student so that they are not seen by the other person. Each exhibit has a different set of limitations, as described below:

    Exhibit 1: The student describing the exhibit cannot look at the other student or his/her diagram. The student drawing the exhibit cannot speak or otherwise communicate with the person describing the exhibit.

    Exhibit 2: The student describing the exhibit may look at the other student's diagram. However, he/she may only say "Yes" or "No" when the student drawing the diagram asks a specific question. In other words, the person presenting the information can only use these words for feedback and only when asked a question by the writer.

    Exhibit 3: (optional—if time permits) The student describing the exhibit may look at the other student's diagram and may provide any feedback at any time to the person replicating the exhibit.

- *Step 3*: The class will gather to debrief this exercise. This may include discussion on the importance of feedback, and the characteristics of effective feedback for individual motivation and learning.

Instructions (Large Class)

Some parts of this exercise are possible in large classes. Here is one variation:

- *Step 1:* Students are asked to prepare for the exercise by having a pen/pencil and paper ready.

- *Step 2:* One student volunteers to provide instructions from the front of the class regarding Exhibit 1. The volunteer receives the first exhibit and describes it to the class, while other students try to replicate the exhibit. When finished, the exhibit is shown to the class on a transparency or computer projection.

- *Step 3:* For Exhibit 2, one student volunteers to provide instructions and a few other students serve as feedback helpers. The helpers have a copy of Exhibit 2, which they may view but cannot show to students doing the drawing. The helpers are dispersed to various parts of the room to provide feedback to a group of students under their care (if the class has 100 students, then the exercise might have five helpers, each responsible for feedback to 20 students). Helpers can only say "Yes" or "No," but they may point to specific locations of the student's drawing when uttering these words (because these helpers provide feedback to many students). Throughout this activity, the student describing the exhibit must NOT stop his or her description. After the speaker has finished and drawings are completed, the helpers might be asked to select the most accurate drawing among those within their domain. Students who drew these accurate depictions might be asked to discuss their experience with feedback.

SELF-ASSESSMENT EXERCISE 5.4

What Needs are Most Important to You?

Although everyone has the same innate drives, our secondary or learned needs vary based on our self-concept. This self-assessment provides an estimate of your need strength on selected secondary needs. Read each of the statements below and check the response that you believe best reflects your position regarding each statement. Then use the scoring key in Appendix B to calculate your results. To receive a meaningful estimate of your need strength, you need to answer each item honestly and with reflection to your personal experiences. Class discussion will focus on the meaning of the needs measured in this self-assessment as well as their relevance in the workplace.

Personal Needs Questionnaire					
How accurately do each of the following statements describe you?	Very Accurate Description of Me	Moderately Accurate	Neither Accurate nor Inaccurate	Moderately Inaccurate	Very Inaccurate Description of Me
1. I would rather be myself than be well thought of.	☐	☐	☐	☐	☐
2. I'm the type of person who never gives up.	☐	☐	☐	☐	☐
3. When the opportunity occurs, I want to be in charge.	☐	☐	☐	☐	☐
4. I try not to say things that others don't like to hear.	☐	☐	☐	☐	☐
5. I find it difficult to talk about my ideas if they are contrary to group opinion.	☐	☐	☐	☐	☐
6. I tend to take control of things.	☐	☐	☐	☐	☐
7. I am not highly motivated to succeed.	☐	☐	☐	☐	☐
8. I usually disagree with others only if I know my friends will back me up.	☐	☐	☐	☐	☐
9. I try to be the very best at what I do.	☐	☐	☐	☐	☐
10. I seldom make excuses or apologize for my behaviour.	☐	☐	☐	☐	☐
11. If anyone criticizes me, I can take it.	☐	☐	☐	☐	☐
12. I try to outdo others.	☐	☐	☐	☐	☐
13. I seldom change my opinion when people disagree with me.	☐	☐	☐	☐	☐
14. I try to achieve more than what others have accomplished.	☐	☐	☐	☐	☐
15. To get along and be liked, I tend to be what people expect me to be.	☐	☐	☐	☐	☐

Sources: Adapted from instruments described and/or presented in: L. R. Goldberg, J. A. Johnson, H. W. Eber, R. Hogan, M. C. Ashton, C. R. Cloninger, & H. C. Gough (2006), "The International Personality Item Pool and the Future of Public-Domain Personality Measures," *Journal of Research in Personality*, 40, 84–96; H. J. Martin (1984), "A Revised Measure of Approval Motivation and Its Relationship to Social Desirability," *Journal of Personality Assessment*, 48, 508–19.

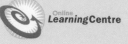 Go to the Online Learning Centre at www.mcgrawhill.ca/olc/mcshane to complete the following interactive self-assessments.

SELF-ASSESSMENT EXERCISE 5.5

How Strong is Your Need for Growth?

Abraham Maslow's needs hierarchy theory distinguished between deficiency needs and growth needs. Deficiency needs become activated when unfulfilled, such as the need for food or belongingness. Growth needs, on the other hand, continue to develop even when temporarily fulfilled. Maslow identified self-actualization as the only category of growth needs. Research has found that Maslow's needs hierarchy theory overall doesn't fit reality, but specific elements such as the concept of growth needs remain valid concepts. This self-assessment is designed to estimate your level of growth need strength. This instrument asks you to consider what it is about a job that is most important to you. Please indicate which of the two jobs you personally would prefer if you had to make a choice between them. In answering each question, assume that everything else about the jobs is the same. Pay attention only to the characteristics actually listed.

SELF-ASSESSMENT EXERCISE 5.6

How Sensitive Are You to Inequity?

Some people experience stronger or weaker feelings of unfairness in specific situations. This self-assessment estimates your level of equity sensitivity. Read each of the statements in this questionnaire and indicate the response that you believe best reflects your position regarding each statement. This exercise is completed alone so students assess themselves honestly without concerns of social comparison. However, class discussion will focus on equity theory and the effect of equity sensitivity on perceptions of fairness in the workplace.

iStudy—Available 24/7 with instant feedback so you can study when you want, how you want, and where you want. Visit www.istudyob.ca to register—take practice quizzes, run interactive scenarios, practice concepts, and much more. Also visit the Student Online Learning Centre for additional study tools.

¡Interact ¡Learn ¡Succeed

www.mcgrawhill.ca/olc/mcshane

CHAPTER 6

Applied Performance Practices

LEARNING OBJECTIVES

After reading this chapter, you should be able to:

LO1 Discuss the advantages and disadvantages of the four reward objectives.

LO2 Identify several team- and organizational-level performance based rewards.

LO3 Describe five ways to improve reward effectiveness.

LO4 Discuss the advantages and disadvantages of job specialization.

LO5 Diagram the job characteristics model of job design.

LO6 Identify three strategies to improve employee motivation through job design.

LO7 Define empowerment and identify strategies to support empowerment.

LO8 Describe the five elements of self-leadership.

LO9 Identify specific personal and work environment influences on self-leadership.

Over the past two decades, Bethlehem Steel, Stelco, and other steel industry giants have disappeared or are under bankruptcy protection. Meanwhile, Nucor Inc. has become one of the largest steel companies in North America, including its recent acquisition of Toronto-based Harris Steel Group Inc. Even with more than 14,000 employees (including 2,500 with Harris in Canada), Nucor remains nimble, highly competitive, and profitable. What's Nucor's secret to success? To a large extent, the company's competitive advantage is its reliance on performance-based rewards, empowerment, and self-leadership.

Nucor employees typically earn well above the industry average, but most of that pay is variable—it depends on team and organization performance. Base pay is around $10 per hour, but employees often earn an additional $15 to $20 an hour in bonuses. Nucor's team-based bonus system also includes penalties. If employees catch a bad batch of steel before it leaves the mini-mill, they lose their bonus for that shipment. But if a bad batch makes its way to the customer, the team loses three times its usual bonus. A profit-sharing bonus (recently more than $15,000) on top of the fixed and bonus pay further motivates Nucor employees to keep mills running and to discover ways to improve steel quality and output.

Along with rewarding performance, Nucor gives employees the freedom and flexibility to make the best decisions for their mini-mill. Nucor's head office has only 65 people, leaving most decisions to management and employees at the plant level. This level of autonomy creates feelings of empowerment beyond most other organizations. For instance, when the electrical grid failed at one of Nucor's mini-mills, three Nucor electricians from other mills immediately took their weekend off to get the stricken mill running again. Nucor management didn't tell these three to help; they flew or drove to the site on their own because they knew their effort could make a huge difference to Nucor's success. While remarkable in most companies, this is just a routine example at Nucor. "It happens daily," says a Nucor executive.[1]

Nucor has survived and thrived in the turbulent steel industry through the benefits of applied performance practices. *Photo courtesy of Nucor Corporation*

Nucor's success is a testament to the organizational behaviour benefits of rewards, job design, empowerment, and self-leadership. This chapter looks at each of these applied performance practices. The chapter begins with an overview of financial reward practices, including the different types of rewards and how to implement rewards effectively. Next, we look at the dynamics of job design, including specific job design strategies to motivate employees. We then consider the elements of empowerment as well as conditions that support empowerment. The final part of this chapter explains how employees manage their own performance through self-leadership.

FINANCIAL REWARD PRACTICES

Know various kinds of rewards.

Financial rewards are probably the oldest—and certainly the most fundamental—applied performance practice in organizational settings. At the most basic level, financial rewards represent a form of exchange; employees provide their labour, skill, and knowledge in return for money and benefits from the organization. From this perspective, money and related rewards align employee goals with organizational goals.

However, financial rewards do much more than pay employees back for their contributions to organizational objectives. One study reported that pay has multiple meanings to Canadian managers.[2] It is a symbol of success, a reinforcer and motivator, a reflection of one's performance, and a source of reduced anxiety. Some writers suggest that rewards (such as bonuses) are more valued when they are bestowed to few rather than many people. This occurs because the reward gives those who receive it a degree of social distinction, which is consistent with the drive to acquire introduced in Chapter 5. Furthermore, with the ongoing debate about the importance of pay, several experts now believe that pay is a much more important motivator than was previously believed.[3]

The value and meaning of money also varies considerably from one person to the next. One large-scale survey revealed that men in almost all 43 countries studied attach more importance or value to money than do women. This result is consistent with public opinion polls reporting that money has a higher priority for men than for women, particularly as a symbol of power and status.[4] Cultural values also seem to influence the meaning and value of money. People in countries with high power distance (such as China and Japan) tend to have a high respect and priority for money, whereas people in countries with a strong egalitarian culture (such as Denmark, Austria, and Israel) are discouraged from openly talking about money or displaying their personal wealth.[5]

Financial rewards come in many forms, which can be organized into the four specific objectives identified in Exhibit 6.1: membership and seniority, job status, competencies, and performance.

LO1

MEMBERSHIP- AND SENIORITY-BASED REWARDS

Membership- and seniority-based rewards (sometimes called "pay for pulse") represent the largest part of most paycheques. Some employee benefits, such as free or discounted meals in the company cafeteria, remain the same for everyone, whereas others increase with seniority. For example, employees at Better Beef Ltd. (one of Canada's largest meat processing companies) receive an additional $1,000 for each year of seniority. Many Asian companies distribute a "13th month" bonus, which every employee expects to receive each year no matter how well the company performed over the previous year. And although many Japanese firms have shifted to performance-based pay, others have retained or returned to wage scales based on the employee's age. "Even during that period [when the employee's performance is below expectations], we raise salaries according to their age," says Tokai Rubber Industries Ltd. president Akira Fujii.[6]

These membership and seniority-based rewards potentially attract job applicants (particularly those who desire predictable income) and reduce turnover. However, they do not directly motivate job performance; on the contrary, they discourage poor performers from seeking out work better suited to their abilities. Instead, the good performers are lured to better-paying jobs. Some of these rewards are also golden hand-

EXHIBIT 6.1 Reward objectives, advantages, and disadvantages			
Reward Objective	**Sample Rewards**	**Advantages**	**Disadvantages**
Membership/ Seniority	• Fixed pay • Most employee benefits • Paid-time off	• May attract applicants • Minimizes stress of insecurity • Reduces turnover	• Doesn't directly motivate performance • May discourage poor performers from leaving • Golden handcuffs may undermine performance
Job status	• Promotion-based pay increase • Status-based benefits	• Tries to maintain internal equity • Minimizes pay discrimination • Motivates employees to compete for promotions	• Encourages hierarchy which may increase costs and reduce responsiveness • Reinforces status differences • Motivates job competition and exaggerated job worth
Competencies	• Pay increase based on competency • Skill-based pay	• Improves workforce flexibility • Tends to improve quality • Consistent with employability	• Subjective measurement of competencies • Skill-based pay plans are expensive
Task performance	• Commissions • Merit pay • Gainsharing • Profit sharing • Stock options	• Motivates task performance • Attracts performance-oriented applicants • Organizational rewards create an ownership culture • Pay variability may avoid layoffs during downturns	• May weaken job content motivation • May distance reward giver from receiver • May discourage creativity • Tends to address symptoms, not underlying causes of behaviour

cuffs which, as we learned in Chapter 4, can potentially weaken job performance by creating continuance commitment.

JOB STATUS-BASED REWARDS

Almost every organization rewards employees to some extent based on the status or worth of the jobs they occupy. According to one estimate, three-quarters of Canadian firms use **job evaluation** methods to estimate job worth. Most job evaluation methods give higher value to jobs that require more skill and effort, have more responsibility, and have more difficult working conditions.[7] Aside from receiving higher pay, employees with more valued jobs sometimes receive larger offices, company-paid vehicles, and other perks.

Job status-based rewards maintain feelings of equity (that people in higher valued jobs should get higher pay) and motivate employees to compete for promotions. However, at a time when companies are trying to be more cost efficient and responsive to the external environment, job status-based rewards potentially do the opposite by encouraging bureaucratic hierarchy. These rewards also reinforce a status mentality, whereas Generation-X and Generation-Y employees expect a more egalitarian workplace. Furthermore, status-based pay potentially motivates employees to compete with each other for higher status jobs and to raise the value of their own jobs by exaggerating job duties and hoarding resources.[8]

job evaluation
Systematically evaluating the worth of jobs within an organization by measuring their required skill, effort, responsibility, and working conditions.

COMPETENCY-BASED REWARDS

Some firms have shifted from job status to competency-based rewards. For instance, the RCMP rewards some staff based on the number of competencies they have acquired. Employees now receive pay increases within each pay band partly based on how well they have acquired new knowledge and skills.[9] *Skill-based pay* is a variation of competency-based rewards in which employees are rewarded for the number of skill modules mastered and, consequently, on the number of jobs they can perform.

Competency-based rewards improve workforce flexibility by motivating employees to learn a variety of skills and thereby perform a variety of jobs. Product or service quality tends to improve because employees with multiple skills are more likely to understand the work process and know how to improve it. Competency-based rewards are also consistent with employability because they reward employees who continuously learn skills that will keep them employed. However, competency and skill-based plans have been criticized for a number of reasons. They are often over-designed, making it difficult to communicate these plans to employees. Competency definitions are often vague, which raises questions about fairness when relying on these definitions to award pay increases. Skill-based pay systems measure specific skills, so they are usually more objective. However, they are expensive because employees spend more time learning new tasks.[10]

PERFORMANCE-BASED REWARDS

Performance-based rewards (also called *variable pay plans*) have existed since Babylonian days in the 20th century B.C., but their popularity has increased dramatically over the past couple of decades. According to the Conference Board of Canada, 83 percent of Canadian firms have at least one form of performance-based reward for some groups of employees, although this is much lower (56 percent) among public sector organizations.[11] Here is an overview of some of the most popular individual, team, and organizational performance-based rewards.

Individual Rewards   Many employees receive individual bonuses or awards for accomplishing a specific task or exceeding annual performance goals. Real estate agents and other salespeople typically earn *commissions*, in which their pay increases with sales volume. Piece rate systems reward employees based on the number of units produced. For example, lawn care staff at The Lawn Mowgul earn a form of piece rate (called "piecemeal") based on the number of yards cut; housekeeping staff in some British hotels earn a piece rate for each room they clean (about $3 per room).[12]

LO2

Team Rewards   Over the past two decades, many organizations have shifted their focus from individuals to teams. Consequently, employees in these companies are finding a larger part of their total paycheque determined by team performance. As was described at the beginning of this chapter, Nucor employees at each mini-mill are organized into teams, and individuals earn bonuses based on the volume and quality of the team's output. At Spruceland Millworks in Acheson, Alberta, team members receive a small bonus and can go home early if they surpass the team's daily production target early.

Spruceland Profits from High-Performance Rewards

Spruceland Millworks, a remanufacturer of mouldings, decking, and other niche lumber products, is a high-performance workplace that rewards individual, team, organization-level performance. When teams at the Acheson, Alberta, company achieve their daily production target early, they can take the rest of the day off and receive a bonus for exceeding the daily objective. Management also encourages innovation and individual initiative by handing out gift certificates on the spot when they see an employee doing a great job. But probably the company's biggest motivator is that the company provides an all-expense-paid trip to a resort destination when employees achieve a challenging annual production and profitability target. For example, the company recently flew every employee and many family members to Puerto Vallarta, Mexico, for a week. Each employee receives between one and four tickets for the trip, depending on their years of service with the company. "I've always strongly believed my job is to recognize people and reward their efforts, and that they go home at night feeling significant," says Spruceland founder Ben Sawatzky, shown here with a few of the company's 130 employees.[13]
© Bruce Edwards, Edmonton Journal

gainsharing plans
Team-based rewards that calculate bonuses from the work unit's cost savings and productivity improvement.

Gainsharing plans are a form of team-based compensation that calculates bonuses from the work unit's cost savings and productivity improvement. At Whole Foods Market, for instance, each department within a store is run by a team with a monthly payroll budget. If payroll money is unspent at the end of the month, the surplus is divided among members of that Whole Foods' team. Gainsharing plans tend to improve team dynamics, knowledge sharing, and pay satisfaction. They also create a reasonably strong link between effort and performance because much of the cost reduction and labour efficiency is within the team's control.

Organizational Rewards Although gainsharing plans are typically set up for teams, some companies aim these productivity improvement plans at an organizational level. At Syncrude Canada, for example, employees share productivity gains every three months related to the unit cost per barrel of oil produced, energy consumed per barrel produced, and safety performance. Even in quarters where employees reduce production costs and energy consumption, they will not receive the bonus if the company experiences a fatality, a major environmental incident, or a serious safety error.[14] Although rare, one of the more interesting organizational-level incentives is taking the entire workforce on an all-expenses-paid vacation if they achieve challenging performance goals. Great Little Box Company, which was described in Chapter 5, offers this incentive. Spruceland Millworks also has such a reward, which has resulted in companywide trips for the entire staff in 18 of the past 25 years.

profit-sharing plans
A reward system that pays bonuses to employees based on the previous year's level of corporate profits.

Some organizations have a **profit-sharing plan**, in which employees earn bonuses based on the previous year's level of corporate profits. The opening vignette to this chapter mentioned that Nucor employees earn a profit-sharing bonus on top of their fixed pay and team bonuses. Specifically, the steelmaker distributes 10 percent of its earnings before taxes to employees each year, which recently amounted to more than $17,000 per employee.[15] A different form of organizational-level reward is the **employee share ownership plan (ESOP)**. ESOPs encourage employees to buy company shares, usually at a discounted price or a no-interest loan. For instance, Calgary-based WestJet Airlines encourages employees to buy shares of the company by matching their contributions up to an annual limit based on the employee's salary. ESOPs potentially motivate and reward employees through dividends and market appreciation of those shares.

employee share ownership plans (ESOP)
A reward system that encourages employees to buy shares of the company.

share options
A reward system that gives employees the right to purchase company shares at a future date at a predetermined price.

While ESOPs involve purchasing company shares, **share options** give employees the right to purchase shares from the company at a future date at a predetermined price up to a fixed expiry date. For example, Cell-Loc Location Technologies Inc, a Calgary-based developer of wireless location technologies, recently offered its executives and employees share options in which each person could purchase a specific amount of the company's shares at 15 cents per share at least two years and at most five years in the future. If the company's shares are worth more than 15 cents on Toronto's TSX Venture Exchange in two years, employees can purchase some or all of the shares granted to them from the company at 15 cents and immediately sell them at the higher price on the stock exchange (or hold on to those shares if they wish). If the share price is less than 15 cents two years from now, then employees would wait until the price rises significantly above that amount. If the stock never rises above 15 cents over the five years, then they are "out of the money" and employees would just let the options expire. The intention of share options is to motivate employees to make the company more profitable, which would raise the company's share price and thereby allow them to reap the value above the exercise price of the share options.[16]

balanced scorecard (BSC)
A reward system that pays bonuses for improved results on a composite of financial, customer, internal process, and employee factors.

An increasingly popular organizational-level reward strategy, called **balanced scorecard (BSC)**, is a goal-oriented performance measurement system that rewards people (typically executives) for improving performance on a composite of financial, customer, and internal processes, as well as employee factors. The better the improvements measured across these dimensions, the larger the bonus awarded. Nova Scotia Power, Royal Bank of Canada, Sun Life Financial, and other Canadian organizations apply some variation of BSC, usually to reward and direct the performance of management staff, although some also reward nonmanagement employees. For instance, KT (formerly Korea Telecom) relied on BSC to transform the former government-owned telephone

Hugo Stays Boss with Balanced Scorecard

In the highly competitive fashion industry, Hugo Boss Industries commands an impressive brand image and market share (30 percent for business suits in some markets). This success is due in part to a balanced scorecard that captures diverse performance measures across the Swiss company's various product groups. "You can't expect miracles, and no tool is going to do the job," concedes Werner Lackas, HBI's head of operations. "But the scorecard serves a very important purpose in focusing attention on the things that are being measured and where we are trying to go." Lackas explains that the scorecard gives HBI managers and employees "a pretty rigid skeleton" within which to be flexible and creative. The scorecard, which includes a range of hard (e.g., return on capital) and soft (e.g., staff development and satisfaction) objectives, is the foundation of performance bonuses received by all of HBI's 350 employees and managers.[17] *Wolfgang von Brauchitsch/Bloomberg News/Landov*

company into a more competitive business after privatization. "It guided our employees with clear direction and balanced perspectives," says Song Young-han, KT's executive senior vice president. "By gathering all the employees around BSC, we were able to concentrate our foundation for the performance-oriented organization culture."[18]

Evaluating Organizational-level Rewards   How effective are organizational-level rewards? ESOPs, share options, and balanced scorecards tend to create an "ownership culture" in which employees feel aligned with the organization's success. Balanced scorecards have the added benefit of aligning rewards to several specific measures of organizational performance. However, BSC is potentially more subjective and requires a particular corporate culture in order for it to be implemented effectively. Profit sharing tends to create less ownership culture, but it has the advantage of automatically adjusting employee compensation with the firm's prosperity, thereby reducing the need for layoffs or negotiated pay reductions during recessions.[19]

The main problem with ESOPs, share options, and profit sharing (less so with balanced scorecards) is that employees often perceive a weak connection between individual effort and corporate profits or the value of company shares. Even in small firms, the company's share price or profitability is influenced by economic conditions, competition, and other factors beyond the employee's immediate control. This low individual performance-to-outcome expectancy weakens employee motivation. Another concern is that some companies use ESOPs as a replacement for employee pension plans. This is a risky strategy because the pension funds lack diversification. If the company goes bankrupt, employees lose both their jobs and a large portion of their retirement nest egg.[20]

LO3

IMPROVING REWARD EFFECTIVENESS

Performance-based rewards have come under attack over the years for discouraging creativity, distancing management from employees, distracting employees from the meaningfulness of the work itself, and being quick fixes that ignore the true causes of poor performance. While these issues have kernels of truth under specific circumstances, they do not necessarily mean that we should abandon performance-based pay. On the contrary, as the high performance work practices perspective of organizational effectiveness advises (see Chapter 1), the top performing companies are more likely to have performance-based rewards.[21] Reward systems do motivate most employees, but only under the right conditions. Here are some of the more important strategies to improve reward effectiveness.

Link Rewards to Performance   Behaviour modification theory (Chapter 3) and expectancy theory (Chapter 5) both recommend that employees with better performance should be rewarded more than those with poorer performance. Unfortunately, as was emphasized in Chapter 5, this simple principle seems to be unusually difficult to apply. Few employees see a relationship between job performance and the amount of pay they and co-workers receive. A Gallup survey at a U.S. telecommunications company revealed an equally devastating observation: management's evaluation of 5,000 customer service employees was uncorrelated with the performance ratings that customers gave those employees. "Whatever behaviour the managers were evaluating were irrelevant to the customers," concluded Gallup executives. "The managers might as well have been rating the employees' shoe sizes, for all the customers cared."[22]

How can companies improve the pay–performance linkage? Inconsistencies and bias can be minimized by introducing gainsharing, ESOPs, and other plans that use objective performance measures. Where subjective measures of performance are necessary, companies should rely on multiple sources of information, such as 360-degree feedback. Companies also need to apply rewards soon after the performance occurs, and in a large enough dose (such as a bonus rather than pay increase) so employees experience positive emotions when they receive the reward.[23]

Ensure that Rewards are Relevant Companies need to align rewards with performance within the employee's control. The more employees see a "line of sight" between their daily actions and the reward, the more they are motivated to improve performance. Wal-Mart applies this principle by rewarding bonuses to top executives based on the company's overall performance, whereas frontline employees earn bonuses based on the sales volume of the store where they work. Reward systems also need to correct for situational factors. Salespeople in one region may have higher sales because the economy is stronger there than elsewhere, so sales bonuses need to be adjusted for these economic factors.

Use Team Rewards for Interdependent Jobs Team rewards should be used rather than individual rewards when employees work in highly interdependent jobs because it is difficult to measure individual performance in these situations. Nucor relies on team-based bonuses for this reason; steelmaking is a team effort, so employees earn bonuses based on team performance. Team rewards also encourage cooperation, which is more important when work is highly interdependent. A third benefit of team rewards is that they tend to support employee preferences for team-based work. One concern, however, is that employees (particularly the most productive employees) in Canada and many other low-collectivism cultures prefer rewards based on their individual performance rather than team performance.[24]

Ensure that Rewards are Valued It seems obvious that rewards work best when they are valued. Yet companies sometimes make false assumptions about what employees want, with unfortunate consequences. The solution, of course, is to ask employees what they value. Campbell Soup did this several years ago at its Canadian distribution centres. Executives thought the employees would ask for more money in a special team reward program. Instead, distribution staff said the most valued reward was a leather jacket with the Campbell Soup logo on the back. These leather jackets cost much less yet were worth much more than the financial bonus the company had otherwise intended to distribute.[25]

Watch Out for Unintended Consequences Performance-based reward systems sometimes have an unexpected—and undesirable—effect on employee behaviours. Consider the pizza company that decided to reward its drivers for on-time delivery. The plan got more hot pizzas to customers on time, but it also increased the accident rates of its drivers because the incentive motivated them to drive recklessly.[26] Connections 6.1 describes a few other examples where reward systems had unintended consequences. The solution here is to carefully think through the consequences of rewards and, where possible, test incentives in a pilot project before applying them across the organization.

Financial rewards come in many forms and, as was mentioned at the outset of this section, influence employees in complex ways. But money isn't the only thing that motivates people to join an organization and perform effectively. "The reward of doing

connections 6.1

When Rewards Go Wrong

There is an old saying that "what gets rewarded, gets done." But what companies reward isn't always what they had intended for employees to do. Here are a few dramatic examples:[27]

- Stock options are supposed to motivate executives to improve corporate performance. Instead, they seem to motivate some leaders to inflate share values through dodgy accounting practices. Recent research estimates that for every 25 percent increase in stock options awarded to executives, the risk of fraud rises by 68 percent. The companies with the largest corporate frauds in recent years have, on average, eight times as many options as similar companies that did not experience fraud.

- Integrated steel companies often rewarded managers for increased labour efficiency. The lower the labour hours required to produce a tonne of steel, the larger the manager's bonus. Unfortunately, steel firms usually didn't count the work of outside contractors in the formula, so the reward system motivated managers to hire expensive contractors in the

production process. By employing more contractors, the cost of production actually increased, not decreased.

- Toyota rewards its dealerships based on customer satisfaction surveys, not just car sales. What Toyota discovered, however, is that this motivates dealers to increase satisfaction scores, not customer satisfaction. One Toyota dealership received high ratings because it offered free detailing to every customer who returned a "Very Satisfied" survey. The dealership even had a special copy of the survey showing clients which boxes to check off. This increased customer ratings, but not customer satisfaction.

- Donnelly Mirrors (now part of Canada's Magna International empire) introduced a gainsharing plan that motivated employees to reduce labour but not material costs. Employees at the automobile parts manufacturer knew they worked faster with sharp grinding wheels, so they replaced the expensive diamond wheels more often. This action reduced labour costs, thereby giving employees the gainsharing bonus. However, the labour savings were easily offset by much higher costs for diamond grinding wheels.

a job well is in having done the job," says Richard Currie, who built Loblaws into one of the top 10 mass retailing companies in the world and is currently Chancellor of the University of New Brunswick. "The money is a by-product."[28] In other words, companies motivate employees mainly by designing interesting and challenging jobs, which is discussed next.

JOB DESIGN PRACTICES

job design
The process of assigning tasks to a job, including the interdependency of those tasks with other jobs.

How do you build a better job? That question has challenged organizational behaviour experts as well as psychologists, engineers, and economists for a few centuries. Some jobs have very few tasks and usually require very little skill. Other jobs are immensely complex and require years of experience and learning to master them. From one extreme to the other, jobs have different effects on work efficiency and employee motivation. The challenge, at least from the organization's perspective, is to find the right combination so work is performed efficiently but employees are motivated and engaged.[29] This challenge requires careful **job design**—the process of assigning tasks to a job, including the interdependency of those tasks with other jobs. A job is a set of tasks performed by one person. To understand this issue more fully, let's begin by describing early job design efforts aimed at increasing work efficiency through job specialization.

 LO4

JOB DESIGN AND WORK EFFICIENCY

Chrysler Corp. outsources European manufacturing of its popular minivan to Magna Steyr, a subsidiary of Canada's Magna International. On average, employees assigned to Magna Steyr's Chrysler minivan assembly line in Graz, Austria, take 3 minutes to attach their assigned pieces to the chassis before repeating their work on the next vehicle. Meanwhile, employees assembling the same vehicle at Chrysler's own assembly plants in North America, have an average job cycle time of 64.5 seconds.[30] The difference isn't

job specialization
The result of division of labour in which each job includes a subset of the tasks required to complete the product or service.

that Austrian employees take longer. Rather, Chrysler's North American employees are assigned fewer tasks. They have a higher degree of **job specialization**.

Job specialization occurs when the work required to build an automobile—or any other product or service—is subdivided into separate jobs assigned to different people. Each resulting job includes a narrow subset of tasks, usually completed in a short "cycle time." Cycle time is the time required to complete the task before starting over with a new work unit. Employees at Chrysler's minivan assembly operations in North America have an average cycle time of 64.5 seconds, which means they repeat the same set of tasks about 58 times each hour and probably about 230 times before they take a meal break.

Why would companies divide work into such tiny bits? The simple answer is that job specialization improves work efficiency. In fact, the economic benefits of dividing work into specialized jobs have been described and applied for at least two millennia. More than 2,300 years ago, the Chinese philosopher Mencius and Greek philosopher Plato noted that division of labour improves work efficiency. In A.D. 1436, the waterways of Venice became an assembly line loading 10 galleons in just six hours. More than 200 years ago, economist Adam Smith described a small factory where 10 pin makers collectively produced as many as 48,000 pins per day because they performed specialized tasks, such as straightening, cutting, sharpening, grinding, and whitening the pins. In contrast, Smith explained that if these 10 people worked alone producing complete pins, they would collectively manufacture no more than 200 pins per day.[31]

One reason why job specialization potentially increases work efficiency is that employees have fewer tasks to juggle and therefore spend less time changing activities. They also require fewer physical and mental skills to accomplish the assigned work, so less time and resources are needed for training. A third reason is that employees practise their tasks more frequently with shorter work cycles, so jobs are mastered quickly. A fourth reason why work efficiency increases is that employees with specific aptitudes or skills can be matched more precisely to the jobs for which they are best suited.[32]

Know

scientific management
Systematically partitioning work into its smallest elements and standardizing tasks to achieve maximum efficiency.

Scientific Management   One of the strongest advocates of job specialization was Frederick Winslow Taylor, an American industrial engineer who introduced the principles of **scientific management** in the early 1900s.[33] Scientific management consists of a toolkit of activities. Some of these interventions—training, goal setting, and work incentives—are common today but were rare until Taylor popularized them. However, scientific management is mainly associated with high levels of job specialization and standardization of tasks to achieve maximum efficiency.

According to Taylor, the most effective companies have detailed procedures and work practices developed by engineers, enforced by supervisors, and executed by employees. Even the supervisor's tasks should be divided: one person manages operational efficiency, another manages inspection, and another is the disciplinarian. Taylor and other industrial engineers demonstrated that scientific management significantly improves work efficiency. No doubt, some of the increased productivity can be credited to the training, goal setting, and work incentives, but job specialization quickly became popular in its own right.

Frederick Taylor and his contemporaries focused on how job specialization reduces labour "waste" by improving the mechanical efficiency of work (i.e., matching skills, faster learning, less switch-over time). Yet, they didn't seem to notice how this extreme job specialization adversely affects employee attitudes and motivation. Some jobs—such as assembling Chrysler minivans—are so specialized that they may soon become tedious, trivial, and socially isolating. Employee turnover and absenteeism tend to be higher in specialized jobs with very short time cycles. Companies sometimes have to pay higher wages to attract job applicants to this dissatisfying, narrowly defined work.[34]

Job specialization often reduces work quality because employees see only a small part of the process. As one observer of an automobile assembly line work reports: "Often [employees] did not know how their jobs related to the total picture. Not knowing, there was no incentive to strive for quality—what did quality even mean as it related to a bracket whose function you did not understand?"[35]

Equally important, Taylor's reliance on job specialization to improve employee performance ignores the motivational potential of jobs. As jobs become specialized, the work tends to become easier to perform but less motivating. As jobs become more complex, work motivation increases but the ability to master the job decreases. Maximum job performance occurs somewhere between these two extremes, where most people can eventually perform the job tasks efficiently, yet the work is interesting.

JOB DESIGN AND WORK MOTIVATION

Industrial engineers may have overlooked the motivational effect of job characteristics, but it is now the central focus of many job design changes. Organizational behaviour scholar Frederick Herzberg is credited with shifting the spotlight when he introduced **motivator-hygiene theory** in the 1950s.[36] Motivator-hygiene theory proposes that employees experience job satisfaction when they fulfill growth and esteem needs (called motivators), and they experience dissatisfaction when they have poor working conditions, job security, and other factors categorized as lower order needs (called hygienes). Herzberg argued that only characteristics of the job itself motivate employees, whereas the hygiene factors merely prevent dissatisfaction. It might seem obvious to us today that the job itself is a source of motivation, but it was radical thinking when Herzberg proposed the idea.

Motivator-hygiene theory has been soundly rejected due to lack of research support, but Herzberg's ideas generated new thinking about the motivational potential of the job itself.[37] Out of subsequent research emerged the **job characteristics model**, shown in Exhibit 6.2. The job characteristics model identifies five core job dimensions that produce three psychological states. Employees who experience these psychological states tend to have higher levels of internal work motivation (motivation from the work itself), job satisfaction (particularly satisfaction with the work itself), and work effectiveness.[38]

Core Job Characteristics   The job characteristics model identifies five core job characteristics. Under the right conditions, employees are more motivated and satisfied when jobs have higher levels of these characteristics.

- *Skill variety*—**Skill variety** refers to the use of different skills and talents to complete a variety of work activities. For example, sales clerks who normally only serve customers might be assigned the additional duties of stocking inventory and changing storefront displays.

- *Task identity*—**Task identity** is the degree to which a job requires completion of a whole or identifiable piece of work, such as assembling an entire broadband modem rather than just soldering in the circuitry.

- *Task significance*—**Task significance** is the degree to which the job affects the organization and/or larger society. For instance, many employees at Medtronic, the Minneapolis-based maker of pacemakers and other medical equipment, have high job specialization, yet 86 percent say their work has special meaning and 94 percent feel pride in what they accomplish. The reason for their high task significance is that they attend seminars that show how the products they manufacture save lives. "We have patients who come in who would be dead if it wasn't for us," says a Medtronic production supervisor.[39]

- *Autonomy*—Jobs with high levels of **autonomy** provide freedom, independence, and discretion in scheduling the work and determining the procedures to be used to complete the work. In autonomous jobs, employees make their own decisions rather than relying on detailed instructions from supervisors or procedure manuals.

- *Job feedback*—Job feedback is the degree to which employees can tell how well they are doing based on direct sensory information from the job itself. Airline pilots can tell how well they land their aircraft and road crews can see how well they have prepared the road bed and laid the asphalt.

---

motivator-hygiene theory
Herzberg's theory stating that employees are primarily motivated by growth and esteem needs, not by lower-level needs.

job characteristics model
A job design model that relates the motivational properties of jobs to specific personal and organizational consequences.

LO5

skill variety
The extent to which employees must use different skills and talents to perform tasks within their job.

task identity
The degree to which a job requires completion of a whole or an identifiable piece of work.

task significance
The degree to which the job has a substantial impact on the organization and/or larger society.

autonomy
The degree to which a job gives employees the freedom, independence, and discretion to schedule their work and determine the procedures used in completing it.

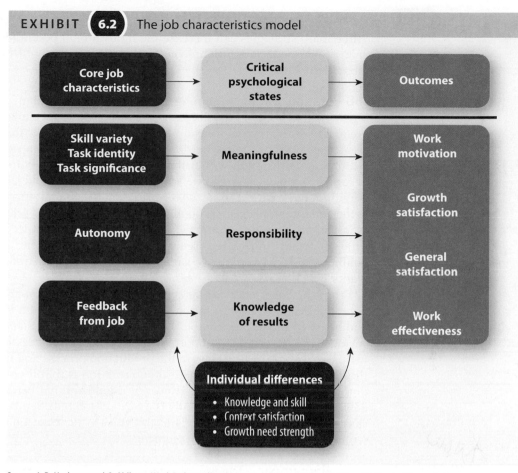

EXHIBIT 6.2 The job characteristics model

Source: J. R. Hackman and G. Oldham, *Work Redesign* (Reading, MA: Addison-Wesley, 1980), p. 90. Used with permission.

Critical Psychological States   The five core job characteristics affect employee motivation and satisfaction through three critical psychological states shown above in Exhibit 6.2. One of these psychological states is *experienced meaningfulness*—the belief that one's work is worthwhile or important. Skill variety, task identity, and task significance directly contribute to the job's meaningfulness. If the job has high levels of all three characteristics, employees are likely to feel that their job is highly meaningful. The meaningfulness of a job drops as one or more of these characteristics declines.

Work motivation and performance increase when employees feel personally accountable for the outcomes of their efforts. Autonomy directly contributes to this feeling of *experienced responsibility*. Employees must be assigned control of their work environment to feel responsible for their successes and failures. The third critical psychological state is *knowledge of results*. Employees want information about the consequences of their work effort. Knowledge of results can originate from co-workers, supervisors, or clients. However, job design focuses on knowledge of results from the work itself.

Individual Differences   Job design doesn't increase work motivation for everyone in every situation. Employees must have the required skills and knowledge to master the more challenging work. Otherwise, job design tends to increase stress and reduce job performance. The original model also suggests that increasing the motivational potential of jobs will not motivate employees who are dissatisfied with their work context (e.g., working conditions, job security) or who have a low growth need strength. However, research findings have been mixed, suggesting that employees might be motivated by job design no matter how they feel about their job context or how high or low they score on growth needs.[40]

LO6

JOB DESIGN PRACTICES THAT MOTIVATE

Three main strategies can increase the motivational potential of jobs: job rotation, job enlargement, and job enrichment. This section also identifies two ways to implement job enrichment.

Job Rotation   At the beginning of this topic on job design, we mentioned that assembly line employees at Chrysler have a high degree of specialization. Chrysler executives are aware of the motivational and physiological problems that this repetitive work can create, so they have introduced a policy where employees work in teams and rotate to a different workstation within that team every few hours. **Job rotation** is the practice of moving employees from one job to another. "The whole idea of job rotation makes a big difference," says Chrysler's vice president of manufacturing. "The job naturally gets better, quality improves, throughput improves." Chrysler reported significant improvements in productivity and morale within the first year of its job rotation program. Job rotation offers "important ergonomic benefits to workers, improvements in product quality, and higher employee satisfaction," says a senior manager at one of Chrysler's plants.[41]

> **job rotation**
> The practice of moving employees from one job to another.

From the experience at Chrysler and many other companies, we can identify three potential benefits of job rotation. First, it minimizes health risks from repetitive strain and heavy lifting because employees use different muscles and physical positions in the various jobs. Second, it supports multiskilling (employees learn several jobs), which increases workforce flexibility in the production process and in finding replacements for those on vacation. A third benefit of job rotation is that it potentially reduces the boredom of highly repetitive jobs. However, organizational behaviour experts continue to debate whether job rotation really is a form of job redesign because the jobs remain the same; they are still highly specialized. Critics argue that job redesign requires changes within the job, such as job enlargement.

know

> **job enlargement**
> Increasing the number of tasks employees perform within their job.

Job Enlargement   **Job enlargement** adds tasks to an existing job. This might involve combining two or more complete jobs into one, or just adding one or two more tasks to an existing job. Either way, skill variety increases because there are more tasks to perform. Video journalists represent a clear example of an enlarged job. As Exhibit 6.3 illustrates, a traditional news team consists of a camera operator, a sound and lighting specialist, and the journalist who writes and presents or narrates the story. One video journalist performs all of these tasks.

Job enlargement significantly improves work efficiency and flexibility. However, research suggests that simply giving employees more tasks won't affect motivation, performance, or job satisfaction. Instead, these benefits result only when skill variety is combined with more autonomy and job knowledge.[42] In other words, employees are

EXHIBIT 6.3 Job enlargement of video journalists

Traditional news team

Employee 1
Operates camera

Employee 2
Operates sound

Employee 3
Reports story

Video journalist

- Operates camera
- Operates sound
- Reports story

motivated when they perform a variety of tasks *and* have the freedom and knowledge to structure their work to achieve the highest satisfaction and performance. These job characteristics are at the heart of job enrichment.

> **job enrichment**
> Occurs when employees are given more responsibility for scheduling, coordinating, and planning their own work.

Job Enrichment

Job enrichment occurs when employees are given more responsibility for scheduling, coordinating, and planning their own work.[43] Generally, people in enriched jobs experience higher job satisfaction and work motivation, along with lower absenteeism and turnover. Productivity is also higher when task identity and job feedback are improved. Product and service quality tend to improve because job enrichment increases the jobholder's felt responsibility and sense of ownership over the product or service.[44]

One way to increase job enrichment is by combining highly interdependent tasks into one job. This *natural grouping* approach is reflected in the video journalist job. Video journalist was earlier described as an enlarged job, but it is also an example of job enrichment because it naturally groups tasks together to complete an entire product (i.e., a news clip). By forming natural work units, jobholders have stronger feelings of responsibility for an identifiable body of work. They feel a sense of ownership and, therefore, tend to increase job quality. Forming natural work units increases task identity and task significance because employees perform a complete product or service and can more readily see how their work affects others.

A second job enrichment strategy, called *establishing client relationships*, involves putting employees in direct contact with their clients rather than using the supervisor as a go-between. By being directly responsible for specific clients, employees have more information and can make decisions affecting those clients.[45] Establishing client relationships also increases task significance because employees see a line-of-sight connection between their work and consequences for customers. This was apparent among medical secretaries at a large regional hospital in Sweden after the hospital reduced its workforce by 10 percent and gave the secretaries expanded job duties. Although these employees experienced more stress from the higher workloads, some of them also felt more motivated and satisfied because they now had direct interaction with patients. "Before, I never saw a patient; now they have a face," says one medical secretary. "I feel satisfied and pleased with myself; you feel someone needs you."[46]

Forming natural task groups and establishing client relationships are common ways to enrich jobs, but the heart of the job enrichment philosophy is to give employees more autonomy over their work. This basic idea is at the core of one of the most widely mentioned—and often misunderstood—practices, known as empowerment.

EMPOWERMENT PRACTICES

LO7

> **empowerment**
> A psychological concept in which people experience more self-determination, meaning, competence, and impact regarding their role in the organization.

When Clive Beddoe co-founded WestJet Airlines, he wanted to create an organization where employees had the freedom to serve customers rather than follow strict rules. Beddoe explains that most other airlines in the world have a military mindset. "You see it even in their flight uniforms and the autocratic way their companies behave," points out Beddoe, who recently stepped down as WestJet's CEO. "Manuals and polices have to be followed exactly and, while that's necessary in the cockpit, it's not the best way when it comes to customer service." Beddoe emphasizes that WestJet is the opposite. "Here, we empower our employees and encourage them to be free-thinking and to do whatever it takes in whatever way they feel it's appropriate to solve customer problems."[47]

Empowerment is a term that has been loosely tossed around in corporate circles and has been the subject of considerable scholarly debate. However, the most widely accepted definition is that empowerment is a psychological concept represented by four dimensions: self-determination, meaning, competence, and impact of the individual's role in the organization. Empowerment consists of all four dimensions. If any dimension weakens, the employee's sense of empowerment will weaken.[48]

- *Self-determination*—Empowered employees feel that they have freedom, independence, and discretion over their work activities.

- *Meaning*—Employees who feel empowered care about their work and believe that what they do is important.

- *Competence*—Empowered people are confident about their ability to perform the work well and have a capacity to grow with new challenges.

- *Impact*—Empowered employees view themselves as active participants in the organization; that is, their decisions and actions have an influence on the company's success.

SUPPORTING EMPOWERMENT

Chances are that you have heard corporate leaders say they are "empowering" the workforce. What these executives really mean is that they are changing the work environment to support empowerment.[49] Numerous individual, job design, and organizational or work context factors support empowerment. At the individual level, employees must possess the necessary competencies to be able to perform the work as well as handle the additional decision-making requirements.[50] Job characteristics clearly influence the degree to which people feel empowered.[51] Employees are much more likely to experience self-determination when working in jobs with a high degree of autonomy and minimal bureaucratic control. They experience more meaningfulness when working in jobs with high levels of task identity and task significance. They experience more self-confidence when working in jobs that allow them to receive feedback about their performance and accomplishments.

Several organizational and work context factors also influence empowerment. Employees experience more empowerment in organizations where information and other resources are easily accessible. Empowerment also requires a learning orientation culture. In other words, empowerment flourishes in organizations that appreciate the value of the employee learning and that accept reasonable mistakes as a natural part of the learning process. Furthermore, empowerment requires corporate leaders who trust employees and are willing to take the risks that empowerment creates. As Clive Beddoe said recently when stepping aside as WestJet CEO: "It's amazing what people can do when you trust and empower them because 99.9 percent of the time they will amaze you in terms of what they can achieve."[52]

With the right individuals, job characteristics, and organizational environment, empowerment can have a noticeable effect on motivation and performance. For instance, a study of Canadian bank employees concluded that empowerment improved customer service and tended to reduce conflict between employees and their supervisors. A study of Canadian nurses reported that empowerment is associated with higher trust in management, which ultimately influences job satisfaction, belief and acceptance of organi-

Kambuku Empowerment

Kambuku is the name of one of the largest tusked elephants in Africa. It is also the symbolic title for a "people focused, value added" initiative that has transformed Pretoria Portland Cement (PPC) into a performance-oriented company and one of South Africa's best employers. The company had a long way to go to reach its goal. A few years ago, PPC was a top-down, autocratic organization where managers gave "oodles of supervision and checking that people do the right things," recalls PPC chief executive John Gomersall. Now, he says, "we have passed the ownership to the people." Departments and teams are given much more autonomy. Company leaders seek out employee ideas, offer continuous training, and reward teams and individuals for their performance. "We attribute our ongoing success and strength to the fact that every employee in the company has the opportunity to make a contribution and be recognized for their input to achieving success," says chief operating officer Orrie Fenn. "Empowered employees ensure a committed workforce, which eventually translates into sustainable business performance."[53] *Photo courtesy of Pretoria Portland Cement Company*

zational goals and values, and effective organizational commitment. Empowerment also tends to increase personal initiative because employees identify with and assume more psychological ownership of their work.[54]

SELF-LEADERSHIP PRACTICES

LO8

What is the most important characteristic that companies look for in their employees? Leadership potential, ability to work in a team, and good communication skills are important, but a survey of 800 British employers concludes that they don't top the list. Instead, the most important employee characteristic is self-motivation. Rick Emberley can identify with these survey results. The co-founder of Bristol Group, one of Atlantic Canada's largest and most successful marketing communications companies, believes that the best performing businesses prosper when employees manage their own motivation and performance. "Hire self-motivated, independent-thinking people who don't require constant supervision on the front end, and who don't require constant back-slapping on the back end," advises Emberley.[55]

Most of the concepts introduced in Chapter 5 and in this chapter have assumed that corporate leaders do things to motivate employees. Certainly, these theories and practices are valuable, but they overlook the fact that the most successful employees ultimately motivate and manage themselves. In other words, they engage in self-leadership.

self-leadership
The process of influencing oneself to establish the self-direction and self-motivation needed to perform a task.

Self-leadership refers to the process of influencing oneself to establish the self-direction and self-motivation needed to perform a task.[56] This concept includes a toolkit of behavioural activities borrowed from social learning theory and goal setting. It also includes constructive thought processes that have been extensively studied in sports psychology. Overall, self-leadership takes the view that individuals mostly regulate their own actions through these behavioural and cognitive (thought) activities.

SELF-LEADERSHIP STRATEGIES

Although self-leadership consists of several processes, the five main activities are identified in Exhibit 6.4. These elements, which generally follow each other in a sequence, are personal goal setting, constructive thought patterns, designing natural rewards, self-monitoring, and self-reinforcement.[57]

Personal Goal Setting   The first step in self-leadership is to set goals for your own work effort. This applies the ideas learned in Chapter 5 on goal setting, such as identifying goals that are specific, relevant, and challenging. The main difference is that self-leadership involves setting goals alone, rather than having them assigned by or jointly decided with a supervisor. Research suggests that employees are more focused and perform better when they set their own goals, particularly in combination with other self-leadership practices.[58]

self-talk
Talking to ourselves about our own thoughts or actions for the purpose of increasing our self-confidence and navigating through decisions in a future event.

Constructive Thought Patterns   Before beginning a task and while performing it, employees should engage in positive (constructive) thoughts about that work and its accomplishment. In particular, employees are more motivated and better prepared to accomplish a task after they have engaged in positive self-talk and mental imagery.

Positive Self-talk.   Do you ever talk to yourself? Most of us do, according to a major study of Canadian university students.[59] **Self-talk** refers to any situation in which we

EXHIBIT 6.4   Elements of self-leadership

| Personal goal setting | Constructive thought patterns | Designing natural rewards | Self-monitoring | Self-reinforcement |

talk to ourselves about our own thoughts or actions. Some of this internal communication assists the decision-making process, such as weighing the advantages of a particular choice. Self-leadership is mostly interested in evaluative self-talk, in which you evaluate your capabilities and accomplishments.

The problem is that most evaluative self-talk is negative; we criticize much more than encourage or congratulate ourselves. Negative self-talk undermines our confidence and potential to perform a particular task. In contrast, positive self-talk creates a "can-do" belief and thereby increases motivation by raising our effort-to-performance expectancy. We often hear that professional athletes "psyche" themselves up before an important event. They tell themselves that they can achieve their goal and that they have practised enough to reach that goal. They are motivating themselves through self-talk.

mental imagery
Mentally practising a task and visualizing its successful completion.

Mental Imagery.   You've probably heard the phrase "I'll cross that bridge when I come to it!" Self-leadership takes the opposite view. It suggests that we need to mentally practise a task and imagine successfully performing it beforehand. This process, known as mental imagery, has two parts. One part involves mentally practising the task, anticipating obstacles to goal accomplishment, and working out solutions to those obstacles before they occur. By mentally walking through the activities required to accomplish the task, we begin to see problems that may occur. We can then imagine what responses would be best for each contingency.[60]

While one part of mental imagery helps us to anticipate things that could go wrong, the other part involves visualizing successful completion of the task. We imagine the experience of completing the task and the positive results that follow. You might imagine yourself being promoted to your boss's job, receiving a prestigious award, or taking time off work. This visualization increases goal commitment and motivates us to complete the task effectively. This is the strategy that Tony Wang applies to motivate himself. "Since I am in sales, I think about the reward I get for closing new business—the commission cheque—and the things it will allow me to do that I really enjoy," explains Wang. "Or I think about the feeling I get when I am successful at something and how it makes me feel good, and use that to get me going."[61]

Designing Natural Rewards   Self-leadership recognizes that employees actively craft their jobs. To varying degrees, they can alter tasks and work relationships to make the work more motivating.[62] One way to build natural rewards into the job is to alter the way a task is accomplished. People often have enough discretion in their jobs to make slight changes to suit their needs and preferences. For instance, you might try out a new software program to design an idea, rather than sketch the image with pencil. By using the new software, you are making more challenging and appealing a task that may have otherwise been mundane.

Self-Monitoring   Self-monitoring is the process of keeping track at regular intervals of one's progress toward a goal using naturally occurring feedback. Some people can receive feedback from the job itself, such as a lawn maintenance crew that can see how they are improving the appearance of their client's property. But many of us are unable to observe our work output so readily. Instead, many people need to design feedback systems. Salespeople might arrange to receive monthly reports on sales levels in their territory. Production staff might have gauges or computer feedback systems installed so they can see how many errors are made on the production line. Research suggests that people who have control over the timing of performance feedback perform their tasks better than those with feedback assigned by others.[63]

Self-Reinforcement   Self-leadership includes the social learning theory concept of self-reinforcement. Self-reinforcement occurs whenever an employee has control over a reinforcer but doesn't "take" the reinforcer until completing a self-set goal.[64] A common example is taking a break after reaching a predetermined stage of your work. The work break is a self-induced form of positive reinforcement. Self-reinforcement also occurs when you decide to do a more enjoyable task after completing a task that you dislike. For example, after slogging through a difficult report, you might decide to spend time doing a more pleasant task, such as catching up on industry news by scanning websites.

EFFECTIVENESS OF SELF-LEADERSHIP

Self-leadership is shaping up to be a valuable applied performance practice in organizational settings. A respectable body of research shows consistent support for most elements of self-leadership. Self-set goals and self-monitoring increased the frequency of wearing safety equipment among employees in a mining operation. Airline employees who received constructive thought training experienced better mental performance, enthusiasm, and job satisfaction than co-workers who did not receive this training. Mental imagery helped supervisors and process engineers in a pulp and paper mill to transfer what they learned in an interpersonal communication skills class back to the job.[65] Studies in Canada and elsewhere also indicate that constructive thought processes improve individual performance in cycling, hockey goaltending, ice skating, soccer, and other sports. Indeed, studies show that almost all Olympic athletes rely on mental rehearsal and positive self-talk to achieve their performance goals.[66]

LO9 SELF-LEADERSHIP CONTINGENCIES

As with most other forms of organizational behaviour, self-leadership is more or less likely to occur depending on the person and the situation. With respect to individual differences, preliminary research suggests that self-leadership behaviours are more frequently found in people with higher levels of conscientiousness and extroversion. Some writers also suggest that people with a positive self-concept evaluation (i.e., self-esteem, self-efficacy, and internal locus of control) are more likely to apply self-leadership strategies.[67]

Although the research is still very sparse, it is likely that the extent to which employees engage in self-leadership strategies also depends on the work environment. In particular, employees require some degree of autonomy to engage in some or most aspects of self-leadership. They probably also feel more confident with self-leadership when their boss is empowering rather than controlling, and where there is a high degree of trust between them. Employees are also more likely to engage in self-monitoring in companies that emphasize continuous measurement of performance.[68] Overall, self-leadership promises to be an important concept and practice for improving employee motivation and performance.

CHAPTER SUMMARY

Money and other financial rewards are a fundamental part of the employment relationship, but their value and meaning varies from one person to the next. Organizations reward employees for their membership and seniority, job status, competencies, and performance. Membership-based rewards may attract job applicants and seniority-based rewards reduce turnover, but these reward objectives tend to discourage turnover among those with the lowest performance. Rewards based on job status try to maintain internal equity and motivate employees to compete for promotions. However, they tend to encourage bureaucratic hierarchy, support status differences, and motivate employees to compete and hoard resources. Competency-based rewards are becoming increasingly popular because

they improve workforce flexibility and are consistent with the emerging idea of employability. However, they tend to be subjectively measured and can result in higher costs as employees spend more time learning new skills.

Awards/bonuses, commissions, and other individual performance-based rewards have existed for centuries and are widely used. Many companies are shifting to team-based rewards such as gainsharing plans and to organizational rewards such as employee share ownership plans (ESOPs), share options, profit sharing, and balanced scorecards (BSC). ESOPs and share options create an ownership culture, but employees often perceive a weak connection between individual performance and the organizational reward.

Financial rewards have a number of limitations, but reward effectiveness can be improved in several ways. Organizational leaders should ensure that rewards are linked to work performance, rewards are aligned with performance within the employee's control, team rewards are used where jobs are interdependent, rewards are valued by employees, and rewards have no unintended consequences.

Job design refers to the process of assigning tasks to a job, including the interdependency of those tasks with other jobs. Job specialization subdivides work into separate jobs for different people. This increases work efficiency because employees master the tasks quickly, spend less time changing tasks, require less training, and can be matched more closely with the jobs best suited to their skills. However, job specialization may reduce work motivation, create mental health problems, lower product or service quality, and increase costs through discontentment, absenteeism, and turnover.

Contemporary job design strategies reverse job specialization through job rotation, job enlargement, and job enrichment. The job characteristics model is a template for job redesign that specifies core job dimensions, psychological states, and individual differences. Organizations introduce job rotation to reduce job boredom, develop a more flexible workforce, and reduce the incidence of repetitive strain injuries. Two ways to enrich jobs are clustering tasks into natural groups and establishing client relationships.

Empowerment is a psychological concept represented by four dimensions: self-determination, meaning, competence, and impact regarding the individual's role in the organization. Individual characteristics seem to have a minor influence on empowerment. Job design is a major influence, particularly autonomy, task identity, task significance, and job feedback. Empowerment is also supported at the organizational level through a learning orientation culture, sufficient information and resources, and corporate leaders who trust employees.

Self-leadership is the process of influencing oneself to establish the self-direction and self-motivation needed to perform a task. This includes personal goal setting, constructive thought patterns, designing natural rewards, self-monitoring, and self-reinforcement. Constructive thought patterns include self-talk and mental imagery. Self-talk refers to any situation in which a person talks to himself or herself about his or her own thoughts or actions. Mental imagery involves mentally practising a task and imagining successfully performing it beforehand.

KEY TERMS

autonomy, p. 140

balanced scorecard (BSC), p. 135

employee share ownership plans (ESOP), p. 135

empowerment, p. 143

gainsharing plans, p. 135

job characteristics model, p. 140

job design, p. 138

job enlargement, p. 142

job enrichment, p. 143

job evaluation, p. 133

job rotation, p. 142

job specialization, p. 139

mental imagery, p. 146

motivator-hygiene theory, p. 140

profit-sharing plans, p. 135

scientific management, p. 139

self-leadership, p. 145

self-talk, p. 145

share options, p. 135

skill variety, p. 140

task identity, p. 140

task significance, p. 140

CRITICAL THINKING QUESTIONS

1. As a consultant, you have been asked to recommend either a gainsharing plan or a profit-sharing plan for employees who work in the four regional distribution and warehousing facilities of a large retail organization. Which reward system would you recommend? Explain your answer.

2. You are a member of a team responsible for developing performance measures for your college or university department or faculty unit based on the balanced scorecard approach. Identify one performance measurement for each of the following factors: financial, customer satisfaction, internal processes, and employee performance.

3. Okanagan Tire Corporation redesigned its production facilities around a team-based system. However, the company president believes that employees will not be motivated unless they receive incentives based on their individual performance. Give three explanations why Okanagan Tire should introduce team-based rather than individual rewards in this setting.

4. What can organizations do to increase the effectiveness of financial rewards?

5. Most of us have watched pizzas being made while waiting in a pizzeria. What level of job specialization do you usually notice in these operations? Why does this high or low level of specialization exist? If some pizzerias have different levels of specialization than others, identify the contingencies that might explain these differences.

6. Can a manager or supervisor "empower" an employee? Discuss fully.

7. Describe a time when you practised self-leadership to successfully perform a task. With reference to each step in the self-leadership process, describe what you did to achieve this success.

8. Can self-leadership replace formal leadership in an organizational setting?

www.mcgrawhill.ca/olc/mcshane

CASE STUDY 6.1

And the Award for Best Commercial Goes To…

As the Canadian subsidiary of one of the world's largest consumer products companies, Procter & Gamble (P&G) Canada is continually on the lookout for the best ways to motivate its staff. One of these motivational highlights is the company's in-house awards night, in which P&G Canada's 100 marketing staff vie for 10 Canadian Business Building Marketing Awards—three for individual excellence and seven for team execution. The team awards include best initiative, best overall marketing plan, best product innovation, best marketing innovation, best turnaround brand, best test-and-learn (i.e., best learning either from success or failure), and best search-and-reapply (in which marketing from another country is applied successfully in Canada).

"Our objectives were to inspire, celebrate, and reward the organization," says Chris Laird, P&G Canada's associate marketing director of fabric and home care, who coordinated the most recent awards event. Laird and other associate marketing directors screened more than 60 marketing projects across the company's many brands, including Tide, Pampers, Swiffer, Crest, Gillette, Pringles, and Pantene. Eventually, they formed a list of three or four nominees for each of the 10 categories.

The three individual winners were chosen by a nine-member team of senior marketers. The seven team category winners, on the other hand, were determined during the awards night based on votes from the audience, which included P&G Canada marketing staff, nearly three dozen agency partners, and numerous senior executives from P&G's Canadian and global headquarters. Voting via text message, the audience mainly took into account each project's business results (share growth and return on investment). However, they were also treated to two-minute video presentations that each shortlisted team created with their agencies over the previous two months to showcase their project during the awards event.

"The winners just get the glory and a statue, but it's a pretty big deal," Laird emphasizes. "It's really our one shot a year to get the whole marketing organization together outside of the typical training sessions and celebrate the great work that's been done." Laird adds that these awards motivate staff to be more innovative. "It's a big company that can at times be siloed, and the awards are a great way to share and reapply and get everybody's creative juices going."

Discussion Questions

1. In what ways would Procter & Gamble Canada's awards event likely improve the organization's effectiveness?

2. Evaluate P&G's awards event against the five strategies for improving reward effectiveness.

Source: Adapted from M. Dickie, "The (Real) Best Work of the Year," *Strategy*, January 2, 2008, p. 14.

TEAM EXERCISE 6.2

Is Student Work Enriched?

Purpose   This exercise is designed to help you to learn how to measure the motivational potential of jobs and to evaluate the extent that jobs should be further enriched.

Instructions (Small Class)   Being a student is like a job in several ways. You have tasks to perform and someone (such as your instructor) oversees your work. Although few people want to be students most of their lives (the pay rate is too low!), it may be interesting to determine how enriched your job is as a student.

- *Step 1*: Students are placed into teams (preferably four or five people).

www.mcgrawhill.ca/olc/mcshane

- *Step 2*: Working alone, each student completes both sets of measures in this exercise. Then, using the guidelines below, they individually calculate the score for the five core job characteristics as well as the overall motivating potential score for the job.

- *Step 3*: Members of each team compare their individual results. The group should identify differences of opinion for each core job characteristic. They should also note which core job characteristics have the lowest scores and recommend how these scores could be increased.

- *Step 4*: The entire class will now meet to discuss the results of the exercise. The instructor may ask some teams to present their comparisons and recommendations for a particular core job characteristic.

Instructions (Large Class)

- *Step 1*: Working alone, each student completes both sets of measures in this exercise. Then, using the guidelines below, they individually calculate the score for the five core job characteristics as well as the overall motivating potential score for the job.

- *Step 2*: Using a show of hands or classroom technology, students indicate their results for each core job characteristics. The instructor will ask for results for several bands across the range of the scales. Alternatively, students can complete this activity prior to class and submit their results through online classroom technology. Later, the instructors will provide feedback to the class showing the collective results (i.e., distribution of results across the range of scores).

- *Step 3*: Where possible, the instructor might ask students with very high or very low results to discuss their views with the class.

Job Diagnostic Survey							
Circle the number on the right that best describes student work.	Very Little			Moderately			Very Much
1. To what extent does student work permit you to decide on your own how to go about doing the work?	1	2	3	4	5	6	7
2. To what extent does student work involve doing a whole or identifiable piece of work, rather than a small portion of the overall work process?	1	2	3	4	5	6	7
3. To what extent does student work require you to do many different things, using a variety of your skills/talents?	1	2	3	4	5	6	7
4. To what extent are the results of your work as a student likely to significantly affect the lives and well-being of other people (e.g., within your school, your family, society)?	1	2	3	4	5	6	7
5. To what extent does working on student activities provide information about your performance?	1	2	3	4	5	6	7

Circle the number on the right that best describes student work.	Very Inaccurate			Uncertain			Very Accurate
6. Being a student requires me to use a number of complex and high-level skills	1	2	3	4	5	6	7
7. Student work is arranged so that I do NOT have the chance to do an entire piece of work from beginning to end.	7	6	5	4	3	2	1
8. Doing the work required of students provides many chances for me to figure out how well I am doing.	1	2	3	4	5	6	7
9. The work students must do is quite simple and repetitive.	7	6	5	4	3	2	1
10. The work of a student is one where a lot of other people can be affected by how well the work gets done.	1	2	3	4	5	6	7
11. Student work denies me any chance to use my personal initiative or judgment in carrying out the work.	7	6	5	4	3	2	1
12. Student work provides me the chance to completely finish the pieces of work I begin.	1	2	3	4	5	6	7
13. Doing student work by itself provides very few clues about whether or not I am performing well.	7	6	5	4	3	2	1
14. As a student, I have considerable opportunity for independence and freedom in how I do the work.	1	2	3	4	5	6	7
15. The work I perform as a student is NOT very significant or important in the broader scheme of things.	7	6	5	4	3	2	1

Calculating The Motivating Potential Score

Scoring Core Job Characteristics: Use the following set of calculations to estimate the motivating potential score for the job of being a student. Use your answers from the Job Diagnostic Survey that you completed above.

Skill Variety (SV)	$\dfrac{\text{Question } 3 + 6 + 9}{3}$ = _____	*Autonomy*	$\dfrac{\text{Question } 1 + 11 + 14}{3}$ = _____
Task Identity (TI)	$\dfrac{\text{Question } 2 + 7 + 12}{3}$ = _____	*Job Feedback*	$\dfrac{\text{Question } 5 + 8 + 13}{3}$ = _____
Task Significance (TS)	$\dfrac{\text{Question } 4 + 10 + 15}{3}$ = _____		

Calculating Motivating Potential Score (MPS): Use the following formula and the results above to calculate the motivating potential score. Notice that skill variety, task identity, and task significance are averaged before being multiplied by the score for autonomy and job feedback.

$$\left(\frac{SV + TI + TS}{3}\right) \times \text{Autonomy} \times \text{Job Feedback}$$

$$\left(\frac{\underline{\quad} + \underline{\quad} + \underline{\quad}}{3}\right) + \underline{\quad} + \underline{\quad} = \underline{\quad}$$

 SELF-ASSESSMENT EXERCISE 6.3

What is Your Attitude Toward Money?

Purpose   This exercise is designed to help you to understand the types of attitudes toward money and to assess your attitude toward money.

Instructions   Read each of the statements below and circle the response that you believe best reflects your position regarding each statement. Then use the scoring key in Appendix B to calculate your results. This exercise is completed alone so students assess themselves honestly without concerns of social comparison. However, class discussion will focus on the meaning of money, including the dimensions measured here and other aspects of money that may have an influence on behaviour in the workplace.

Money Attitude Scale					
To what extent do you agree or disagree that. . .	Strongly Agree	Agree	Neutral	Disagree	Strongly Disagree
1. I sometimes purchase things because I know they will impress other people.	5	4	3	2	1
2. I regularly put money aside for the future.	5	4	3	2	1
3. I tend to get worried about decisions involving money.	5	4	3	2	1
4. I believe that financial wealth is one of the most important signs of a person's success.	5	4	3	2	1
5. I keep a close watch on how much money I have.	5	4	3	2	1
6. I feel nervous when I don't have enough money.	5	4	3	2	1
7. I tend to show more respect to people who are wealthier than I am.	5	4	3	2	1
8. I follow a careful financial budget.	5	4	3	2	1
9. I worry about being financially secure.	5	4	3	2	1
10. I sometimes boast about my financial wealth or how much money I make.	5	4	3	2	1
11. I keep track of my investments and financial wealth.	5	4	3	2	1
12. I usually say "I can't afford it," even when I can afford something.	5	4	3	2	1

Sources: Adapted from J. A. Roberts and C. J. Sepulveda, "Demographics and Money Attitudes: A Test of Yamauchi and Templer's (1982) Money Attitude Scale in Mexico," *Personality and Individual Differences*, 27 (July 1999), pp. 19–35; K. Yamauchi and D. Templer, "The Development of a Money Attitudes Scale," *Journal of Personality Assessment*, 46 (1982), pp. 522–528.

 Go to the Online Learning Centre at www.mcgrawhill.ca/olc/mcshane to complete the following interactive self-assessments.

 SELF-ASSESSMENT EXERCISE 6.4

How Well Do You Practise Self-Leadership?

This exercise is designed to help you understand self-leadership concepts and to assess your self-leadership tendencies. Self-leadership is the process of influencing oneself to establish the self-direction and self-motivation needed to perform a task. Please indicate the extent to which each statement in this instrument describes you very well or does not describe you at all. Complete each item honestly to get the best estimate of your score on each self-leadership dimension.

 SELF-ASSESSMENT EXERCISE 6.5

Are You Empowered as a Student?

Empowerment is a concept that applies to people in a variety of situations. This instrument is specifically adapted to your position as a student at this college or university. Indicate the extent to which you agree or disagree with each statement in this instrument, then request the results, which provide an overall score as well as scores on each of the four dimensions of empowerment. Complete each item honestly to get the best estimate of your level of empowerment.

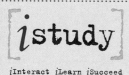

iStudy—Available 24/7 with instant feedback so you can study when you want, how you want, and where you want. Visit www.istudyob.ca to register—take practice quizzes, run interactive scenarios, practice concepts, and much more. Also visit the Student Online Learning Centre for additional study tools.

CHAPTER 7

Decision Making and Creativity

Dylan Hansen enjoys his regular job as a computer software developer at GenoLogics Life Sciences Software Inc., but some of his favourite times are "hack days." Hack days are occasions in which staff at the Victoria-based developer of biological research computer software can work on anything innovative that interests them, even if it doesn't benefit the company. The day ends with a show-and-tell session, with the most creative "hacks" winning prizes. Hansen recently designed an applet that notifies him when new music is posted on the Internet. That hack is far removed from GenoLogics' product range, but hack days are important because they boost creativity and learning. "This really gets your brain going" says Hansen.

Effective decision making and creativity are so important that GenoLogics also holds GenoPalooza, an annual full-day event where its 50 employees attend seminars to improve their creativity, decision making, and organizational skill. For example, a recent GenoPalooza conference included workshops on using humour to help drive innovation, how to influence others in the decision-making process, and how to improve decision making through systems thinking. Other activities that crank up the creative potential of employees include Lunch and Laughs every Friday, cooking classes, frequent recreational events, and participation in fund-raising activities (such as the BC Cancer Foundation's Canary Derby, shown in this photo).

GenoLogics also strengthens its decision-making process through employee involvement. In fact, GenoLogics human resources manager Brandie Yarish describes the company as an easy-going workplace that relies on a lot of consensus-based decision making. "It's a flat, open organization," says Yarish. "The best ideas come from everyone." GenoLogics CEO, Michael Ball, agrees, saying that the company benefits by giving employees "free rein" to discover better ideas.[1]

GenoLogics encourages lots of creativity and employee involvement. Some of that creativity is apparent in the Victoria-based company's fund-raising activities, including participation in the BC Cancer Foundation's Canary Derby (shown here with CEO Michael Ball in the driver's seat). © *Debra Brash/Times Colonist*

decision making
A conscious process of making choices among alternatives with the intention of moving toward some desired state of affairs.

To keep pace with customer requirements and new discoveries, GenoLogics requires a workforce that is actively engaged in decision making and creativity. **Decision making** is a conscious process of making choices among alternatives with the intention of moving toward some desired state of affairs.[2] This chapter begins by outlining the rational choice paradigm of decision making. Then, we examine this perspective more critically by recognizing how people identify problems and opportunities, choose among alternatives, and evaluate the success of their decisions differently from the rational model. Bounded rationality, escalation of commitment, and intuition are three of the more prominent topics in this section. Next, we explore the role of employee involvement in decision making, including the benefits of involvement and the factors that determine the optimal level of involvement. The final section of this chapter examines the factors that support creativity in decision making, including characteristics of creative people, work environments that support creativity, and creativity activities.

RATIONAL CHOICE PARADIGM OF DECISION MAKING

rational choice paradigm
A deeply held perspective that people should or actually do make decisions based on pure logic or rationality.

How do people make decisions in organizations? For most of written history, philosophers, economists, and other scholars in Western societies have stated or assumed that people should or actually do make decisions based on pure logic or rationality. This **rational choice paradigm** was established 2,500 years ago when Plato and his contemporaries in ancient Greece raised logical debate and reasoning to a fine art. A few centuries later, Greek and Roman Stoics insisted that one should always "follow where reason leads" rather than fall victim to passion and emotions. About 400 years ago, Descartes and other European philosophers emphasized that the ability to make logical decisions is one of the most important accomplishments of human beings. In the 1700s, Scottish philosophers proposed that the best choice is the one that offers the "greatest good for the greatest number." This eventually evolved into the ethical principle of utilitarianism as well as maximization, which is at the heart of contemporary economics. By the 1900s, social scientists and mathematicians had developed elegant rational choice models and formulae that are now embedded in operations research, economics, and other decision sciences.[3]

Exhibit 7.1 illustrates the rational choice process.[4] The first step is to identify the problem or recognize an opportunity. A problem is a deviation between the current and the desired situation—the gap between "what is" and "what ought to be." This deviation is a symptom of more fundamental root causes that need to be corrected.[5] An opportunity is a deviation between current expectations and a potentially better situation that was not previously expected. In other words, decision makers realize that some decisions may produce results beyond current goals or expectations.

The second step involves deciding how to process the decision.[6] One issue is whether the decision maker has enough information or needs to involve others in the process. Later in this chapter, we'll examine the contingencies of employee involvement in the decision. Another issue is whether the decision is programmed or nonprogrammed. *Programmed decisions* follow standard operating procedures; they have been resolved in the past, so the optimal solution has already been identified and documented. In contrast, *nonprogrammed decisions* require all steps in the decision model because the problems are new, complex, or ill-defined. The third step is to identify and develop a list of possible solutions. This usually begins by searching for ready-made solutions, such as practices that have worked well on similar problems. If an acceptable solution cannot be found, then decision makers need to design a custom-made solution or modify an existing one.

subjective expected utility
A rational choice calculation of the expected satisfaction or positive emotion experienced by choosing a specific alternative in a decision.

The fourth step in the rational choice decision process is to choose the alternative with the highest **subjective expected utility**.[7] Subjective expected utility refers to the probability (expectation) of satisfaction (utility) for each alternative. Rational decision makers will choose the alternative with the highest expected utility—the one that offers the greatest level of happiness. Figuring out which alternative produces the most happiness is incredibly complex because it requires the decision maker to estimate (a) the

EXHIBIT 7.1   Rational choice decision-making process

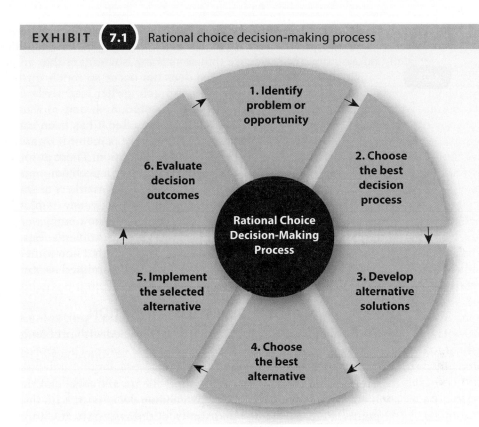

probability of all outcomes relating to each alternative and (b) the happiness that will be experienced from each outcome. Still, the rational choice paradigm assumes that everyone does this calculation with ease.

The fifth step in the rational choice decision process is to implement the selected alternative. Rational choice experts have little to say about this step because they assume implementation occurs without any problems. This is followed by the sixth step, evaluating whether the gap has narrowed between "what is" and "what ought to be." Ideally, this information should come from systematic benchmarks, so that relevant feedback is objective and easily observed.

PROBLEMS WITH THE RATIONAL CHOICE PARADIGM

The rational choice paradigm seems so logical, yet it is rarely practised in reality. One reason is that the model assumes people are efficient and logical information processing machines. But as we will discuss over the next few pages, people have difficulty recognizing problems; they cannot (or will not) simultaneously process the huge volume of information needed to identify the best solution; and they have difficulty recognizing when their choices have failed. The second reason why the rational model doesn't fit reality is that it focuses on logical thinking and completely ignores the fact that emotions also influence— perhaps even dominate—the decision-making process. As we shall discover in this chapter, emotions both support and interfere with our quest to make better decisions.[8] With these points in mind, let's look again at each step in the rational decision-making process, but with more detail about what really happens.

IDENTIFYING PROBLEMS AND OPPORTUNITIES

When Albert Einstein was asked how he would save the world in one hour, he replied that the first 55 minutes should be spent defining the problem and the last 5 minutes solving it.[9] Einstein's point is that problem identification is not just the first step in decision making; it is arguably the most important step. But problems and opportunities do not appear on our desks as well-labelled objects. Instead, decision makers translate information into evidence that something is wrong or that an opportunity is available.

This translation of evidence does not occur so much through systematic conscious evaluation of the facts; it begins much earlier and without conscious deliberation. Recall from earlier chapters (i.e., Chapters 3, 4, and 5) that people form preferences as soon as they receive information, not after it has been carefully analyzed.[10] Specifically, we evaluate information as soon as we perceive it by attaching emotional markers (anger, caution, delight, etc.) to that information. These automatic emotional responses determine whether you perceive something as a problem, opportunity, or irrelevant. For example, employees form an opinion of new co-workers as soon as they first meet them, and this initial impression influences how quickly new employees are viewed as successful (opportunities) or failures (problems). If the new employee is viewed negatively, then any instances of failure are quickly labelled as problems. But if co-workers form a positive initial impression of a new employee, then that newcomer's failures are less likely to be viewed as problems—they are ignored or dismissed as temporary setbacks.

PROBLEMS WITH PROBLEM IDENTIFICATION

The problem identification stage is, itself, filled with problems. Here are five of the most widely recognized concerns:[11]

Stakeholder Framing   Employees, clients, and other stakeholders with vested interests try to "frame" the situation by persuading decision makers that the available information points to a problem, an opportunity, or does not have any importance at all. This framing of facts tends to short-circuit the decision maker's full assessment of the situation.

Perceptual Defence   People sometimes block out bad news as a coping mechanism. Their brain refuses to see information that threatens their self-concept. This phenomenon is not true for everyone. Some people inherently avoid negative information, whereas others are more sensitive to it. Recent studies also report that people are more likely to disregard danger signals when they have limited control over the situation.[12] For example, an investigation of the space shuttle Columbia disaster revealed that NASA managers rejected suggestions and evidence that the shuttle and its seven crew members were in trouble.

Mental Models   Mental models—visual or relational images in our mind of the external world—are vital to help us understand and navigate in our surrounding environment. Unfortunately, mental models also blind us from seeing unique problems or opportunities. If an idea doesn't fit the existing mental model of how things should work, then the idea is dismissed as unworkable or undesirable. Movie studio executives have a long history of missed opportunities because they reject scripts that don't fit their mental model of a successful film. For example, Nia Vardalos wrote a comedy screenplay based on incidents involving her Greek-Canadian family in Winnipeg, but none of Hollywood's literary agents were interested in her work. Undeterred, Vardalos turned the script into a successful one-woman show in Los Angeles. After watching the show, actors Rita Wilson and Tom Hanks supported her on making a movie. But even with Hanks on board, every Hollywood studio rejected the script. HBO agreed to provide a paltry US$2.5 million "as a favour" to Hanks. With a budget of only $5 million, *My Big Fat Greek Wedding* became one of the highest grossing independent films of all time. The screenplay that no one in Hollywood wanted was also nominated for an Oscar.[13]

Decisive Leadership   Studies report that people view leaders as more effective decision makers when they are decisive.[14] This includes quickly forming an opinion whether an event signals a problem or opportunity. Consequently, eager to look effective, many leaders quickly announce problems or opportunities before having an opportunity to logically assess the situation. The result, according to research, is more often a poorer

No Problem, Houston?

In February 2003, the NASA space shuttle *Columbia* disintegrated during re-entry, kill-ing all seven crew members. The disintegration was technically caused by a hole in the left wing created when a large piece of foam debris struck the wing during lift-off. However, a special accident investigation board concluded that NASA's middle manage-ment continually resisted attempts to recognize that the *Columbia* was in trouble, and therefore made no attempt to prevent loss of life. For example, photos from military satellites would have determined whether the foam caused serious wing damage. But when a team of engineers requested these photos, NASA management shot back an email just 26 minutes later rejecting the request without explanation. Managers also questioned tests suggesting that a chunk of foam debris could cause wing damage, yet were quick to accept a faulty test showing that the foam could not damage the wing. In addition, the accident board reported that NASA managers criticized those who believed that a problem existed. One engineer was called "alarmist"; NASA's lead flight director said that the "rationale was lousy" in a report submitted by an engineering team concerned about the wing damage. In one meeting, *Columbia's* lead flight director candidly admitted: "I don't think there is much we can do, so you know it's not really a factor during the flight because there isn't much we can do about it."[15] *The Canadian Press (Chris O'Meara)*

decision than if more time had been devoted to identifying the problem and evaluating the alternatives.

Solution-focused Problems   Various studies have found that decision makers often find a solution almost as soon as the problem is identified.[16] Indeed, you will sometimes hear people define problems in terms of their pet solutions, such as "The problem is that we need more control over our suppliers." This solution-focused identification of problems occurs because it provides comforting closure to the otherwise ambiguous and uncertain nature of problems. People with a strong need for cognitive closure (those who feel uncomfortable with ambiguity) are particularly prone to solution-focused problems. Some decision makers take this solution focus a step further by seeing all problems as solutions that have worked well for them in the past, even though they were applied under different circumstances. Again, the familiarity of past solutions makes the current problem less ambiguous or uncertain.

IDENTIFYING PROBLEMS AND OPPORTUNITIES MORE EFFECTIVELY

Recognizing problems and opportunities will always be a challenge, but the process can be improved through awareness of these perceptual and diagnostic limitations. By keep-ing in mind that mental models restrict a person's perspective of the world, decision makers are more motivated to consider other perspectives of reality. A second method of minimizing perceptual and diagnostic weaknesses is to discuss the situation with colleagues. GenoLogics, described at the beginning of this chapter, involves everyone in decision making partly because blind spots in problem identification are more easily identified by hearing how others perceive certain information and diagnose problems. Opportunities also become apparent when outsiders explore this information from their different mental models. Third, leaders require considerable willpower to resist appear-ing decisive when a more thoughtful examination of the situation should occur. Finally, successful decision makers experience "divine discontent." They are never satisfied with the status quo, and this aversion to complacency creates a mindset that more actively searches for problems and opportunities. Toyota Canada applies divine discontent, even though its parent company has become the world's largest automaker. "We're paranoid against arrogance," explains Toyota Canada president Ray Tanguay. "'Not good enough' are key words for us."[17]

EVALUATING AND CHOOSING ALTERNATIVES

LO3

According to the rational choice paradigm of decision making, people rely on logic to evaluate and choose alternatives. This paradigm assumes that decision makers have well-articulated and agreed-on organizational goals, that they efficiently and simultaneously process facts about all alternatives and the consequences of those alternatives, and that they choose the alternative with the highest payoff.

Nobel Prize–winning organizational scholar Herbert Simon questioned these assumptions a half-century ago. He argued that people engage in **bounded rationality** because they process limited and imperfect information and rarely select the best choice.[18] Simon and other OB experts demonstrated that how people evaluate and choose alternatives differs from the rational choice paradigm in several ways, as illustrated in Exhibit 7.2. These differences are so significant that even economists have shifted from rational choice to bounded rationality assumptions in their theories. Let's look at these differences in terms of goals, information processing, and maximization.

bounded rationality
Processing limited and imperfect information and satisficing rather than maximizing when choosing between alternatives.

PROBLEMS WITH GOALS

The rational choice paradigm assumes that organizational goals are clear and agreed-upon. In fact, these conditions are necessary to identify "what ought to be" and, therefore, provide a standard against which each alternative is evaluated. Unfortunately, organizational goals are often ambiguous or in conflict with each other. One survey reported that 25 percent of managers and employees felt decisions are delayed because of difficulty agreeing on what they want the decision to achieve.[19]

EXHIBIT 7.2 Rational choice assumptions versus organizational behaviour findings about choosing alternatives

Rational choice paradigm assumptions	Observations from organizational behaviour
Goals are clear, compatible, and agreed upon.	Goals are ambiguous, in conflict, and lack full support.
Decision makers can calculate all alternatives and their outcomes.	Decision makers have limited information-processing abilities.
Decision makers evaluate all alternatives simultaneously.	Decision makers evaluate alternatives sequentially.
Decision makers use absolute standards to evaluate alternatives.	Decision makers evaluate alternatives against an implicit favourite.
Decision makers use factual information to choose alternatives.	Decision makers process perceptually distorted information.
Decision makers choose the alternative with the highest payoff.	Decision makers choose the alternative that is good enough (satisficing).

PROBLEMS WITH INFORMATION PROCESSING

The rational choice paradigm also makes several assumptions about the human capacity to process information. It assumes that decision makers can process information about all alternatives and their consequences, whereas this is not possible in reality. Instead, people evaluate only a few alternatives and only some of the main outcomes of those alternatives.[20] For example, there may be dozens of computer brands to choose from and dozens of features to consider, yet people typically evaluate only a few brands and a few features.

A related problem is that decision makers typically evaluate alternatives sequentially rather than all at the same time. As a new alternative comes along, it is immediately compared to an **implicit favourite**—an alternative that the decision maker prefers and is used as a comparison against which other choices are judged. When choosing a new computer system, for example, people typically have an implicit favourite brand or model in their heads which they use to compare against the others. This sequential process of comparing alternatives against an implicit favourite occurs even when decision makers aren't consciously aware that they are doing this.[21]

Although inherent in human decision making, the implicit favourite comparison process often undermines effective decision making because people distort information to favour their implicit favourite over the alternative choices. They tend to ignore problems with the implicit favourite and advantages of the alternative. Decision makers also overweight factors where the implicit favourite is better and underweight areas where the alternative is superior.[22] This effect was observed in a study of Canadian auditing students who had to decide in a case study whether the company had significant financial problems. Those who decided that the company did have significant problems distorted the available information to make those problems appear worse. Students who felt the financial problems were not significant enough to report in a formal audit minimized any reference to the negative information in their case reports.[23]

> **implicit favourite**
> A preferred alternative that the decision maker uses repeatedly as a comparison.

PROBLEMS WITH MAXIMIZATION

Decision makers tend to select the alternative that is acceptable or "good enough," rather than the one with the highest payoff (i.e., the highest subjective expected utility). In other words, they engage in **satisficing** rather than maximizing. Satisficing occurs because it isn't possible to identify every alternative, and information about available alternatives is imperfect or ambiguous. Satisficing also occurs because, as mentioned already, decision makers tend to evaluate alternatives sequentially, not all at the same time. They evaluate each alternative against the implicit favourite and eventually select an option that scores above a subjective minimum point considered to be good enough to satisfy their needs or preferences.[24]

> **satisficing**
> Selecting a solution that is satisfactory or 'good enough,' rather than optimal or 'the best.'

EVALUATING OPPORTUNITIES

Opportunities are just as important as problems, but what happens when an opportunity is "discovered" is quite different from the process of problem solving. According to a recent study of decision failures, decision makers do not evaluate several alternatives when they find an opportunity; after all, the opportunity *is* the solution, so why look for others! An opportunity is usually experienced as an exciting and rare revelation, so decision makers tend to have an emotional attachment to the opportunity. Unfortunately, this emotional preference motivates decision makers to apply the opportunity and short-circuit any detailed evaluation of it.[25]

Know

LO4

EMOTIONS AND MAKING CHOICES

Herbert Simon and many other experts have presented plenty of evidence that people do not evaluate alternatives nearly as well as is assumed by the rational choice paradigm. However, they neglected to mention another glaring weakness with rational choice: it completely ignores the effect of emotions in human decision making. Just as both the

Emotional Intelligence

rational and emotional brain centres alert us to problems, they also influence our choice of alternatives. Emotions affect the evaluation of alternatives in three ways.

Emotions Form Early Preferences   The emotional marker process described earlier in this chapter as well as in previous chapters (Chapters 3 through 5) determines our preferences for each alternative. Our brain very quickly attaches specific emotions to information about each alternative, and our preferred alternative is strongly influenced by those initial emotional markers. Of course, logical analysis also influences which alternative we choose, but it requires strong logical evidence to change our initial preferences (initial emotional markers). But even logical analysis depends on emotions to sway our decision. Specifically, neuroscientific evidence says that information produced from logical analysis is also tagged with emotional markers, which then motivates us to choose or avoid a particular alternative. Ultimately, emotions, not rational logic, energize us to make the preferred choice. In fact, people with damaged emotional brain centres have difficulty making choices.

Emotions Change the Decision Evaluation Process   A considerable body of literature indicates that moods and specific emotions influence the *process* of evaluating alternatives. For instance, we pay more attention to details when in a negative mood, possibly because a negative mood signals that there is something wrong that requires attention. When in a positive mood, on the other hand, we pay less attention to details and rely on a more programmed decision routine. Research also suggests that decision makers rely on stereotypes and other shortcuts to speed up the choice process when they experience anger. Anger also makes them more optimistic about the success of risky alternatives whereas the emotion of fear tends to make them less optimistic.[26] Overall, emotions shape *how* we evaluate information, not just which choice we select.

Emotions as Information When Evaluating Alternatives   The third way that emotions influence the evaluation of alternatives is through a process called "emotions as information." Marketing experts have found that we listen in on our emotions to provide guidance when making choices.[27] You might think of this as a temporary improvement in emotional intelligence. Most emotional experiences remain below the level of conscious awareness, but people tend to be more sensitive to these subtle emotions—they temporarily increase their self-awareness dimension of emotional intelligence—when making a decision.

When buying a new car, for example, you not only logically evaluate each vehicle's features; you also try to gauge your emotions when visualizing what it would be like to own each of the alternative cars on your list of choices. Even if you have solid information about the quality of each vehicle on key features (purchase price, fuel efficiency, maintenance costs, resale value, etc.), you are swayed by your emotional reaction to each vehicle and actively try to sense that emotional response when thinking about it. Some people pay more attention to these gut feelings, and personality tests such as the Myers-Briggs Type Indicator (see Chapter 2) identify those who listen in on their emotions more than others.[28] But all of us use our emotions as information to some degree. This phenomenon ties directly into our next topic, intuition.

LO5

INTUITION AND MAKING CHOICES

Greg McDonald felt uneasy about a suspicious-looking crack in the rock face, so the veteran Potash Corp. of Saskatchewan miner warned a co-worker to stay away from the area. "There was no indication there was anything wrong—just a little crack," McDonald recalled. A few minutes later, the ceiling in that mine shaft 1,000 metres underground caved in. Fortunately, the co-worker heeded McDonald's advice. "If he had been there, he would be dead," McDonald said in an interview following a near-sleepless night after the incident.[29]

The gut instinct that helped Greg McDonald save his co-worker's life is known as **intuition**—the ability to know when a problem or opportunity exists and to select the

intuition
The ability to know when a problem or opportunity exists and to select the best course of action without conscious reasoning.

best course of action without conscious reasoning.[30] Intuition is both an emotional experience and a rapid nonconscious analytic process. As was mentioned in the previous section, the gut feelings we experience are emotional signals that have enough intensity to make us consciously aware of them. These signals warn us of impending danger, such as a dangerous mine wall, or motivate us to take advantage of an opportunity. Some intuition also directs us to preferred choices relative to other alternatives in that situation.

All gut feelings are emotional signals, but not all emotional signals are intuition. The key distinction is that intuition involves rapidly comparing our observations against deeply held patterns learned through experience.[31] These templates represent tacit knowledge that has been implicitly acquired over time. They are mental models that help us to understand whether the current situation is good or bad depending how well that situation fits our mental model. When a template fits or doesn't fit the current situation, emotions are produced that motivate us to act. Greg McDonald's years of experience produced mental templates of unsafe rock faces that matched what he saw on that fateful day. Studies have also found that chess masters receive emotional signals when they sense an opportunity through quick observation of a chessboard. When given the opportunity to think about the situation, chess masters can explain why they see a favourable move on the chessboard. However, their intuition signals the opportunity long before this rational analysis takes place.

As mentioned, some emotional signals are not intuition. As a result, some experts warn that we should not trust our gut feelings. The problem is that emotional responses are not always based on well-grounded mental models. Instead, they occur when we compare the current situation to more remote templates, which may or may not be relevant. A new employee might feel confident about relations with a supplier, whereas an experienced employee senses potential problems. The difference is that the new employee relies on templates from other experiences or industries that might not work well in this situation. Thus, whether the emotions we experience in a situation represent intuition or not depends largely on our level of experience in that situation.

So far, intuition has been described as an emotional experience (gut feeling) and a process in which we compare the current situation with well-established templates of the mind. Intuition also relies on *action scripts*—programmed decision routines that speed up our response to pattern matches or mismatches.[32] Action scripts effectively shorten the decision-making process by jumping from problem identification to selection of a solution. In other words, action scripting is a form of programmed decision making. These action scripts are generic, so we need to consciously adapt them to the specific situation.

MAKING CHOICES MORE EFFECTIVELY

It is very difficult to get around the human limitations of making choices, but a few strategies help to minimize these concerns. One important discovery is that decisions tend to have a higher failure rate when leaders are decisive rather than contemplative about the available options. Of course, decisions can also be ineffective when leaders take too long to make a choice, but research indicates that a lack of logical evaluation of alternatives is a greater concern. By systematically assessing alternatives against relevant factors, decision makers minimize the implicit favourite and satisficing problems that occur when relying on general subjective judgments. This recommendation does not suggest that we ignore intuition; rather, it suggests that we do so in combination with careful analysis of relevant information.[33]

A second piece of advice is that we need to be constantly aware that decisions are influenced by both rational and emotional processes. With this awareness, some decision makers deliberately revisit important issues so they look at the information in different moods and have allowed their initial emotions to subside. For example, if you sense that your team is feeling somewhat too self-confident when making an important competitive decision, you might decide to have them revisit the decision a few days later when they are thinking more critically.

scenario planning
A systematic process of thinking about alternative futures and what the organization should do to anticipate and react to those environments.

Another strategy is **scenario planning,** which is a disciplined method for imagining possible futures. It typically involves thinking about what would happen if a significant environmental condition changed, and what the organization should do to anticipate and react to such an outcome.[34] As an example, when BASF Canada formed an innovation team on sustainable growth, the unit held a scenario planning session that anticipated the future of Canada's housing industry and its product needs. "We asked ourselves questions around what the housing industry could be like 25 years from now, in terms of energy efficiency, aesthetics, and new products—basically everything from the roof down to the foundations," says BASF sales manager Kay Schaltz.[35] Scenario planning is a useful vehicle for choosing the best solutions under possible scenarios long before they occur, because alternative courses of action are evaluated without the pressure and emotions that occur during real emergencies.

IMPLEMENTING DECISIONS

Implementing decisions is often skipped over in most writing about the decision-making process. Yet leading business writers emphasize that execution—translating decisions into action—is one of the most important and challenging tasks of leaders. A recent survey of 3,600 managers identified the "drive for results" as one of the five most important competencies of effective managers. This evidence is backed up by Larry Bossidy's experience leading thousands of managers. "When assessing candidates, the first thing I looked for was energy and enthusiasm for execution," says the former CEO of Honeywell and Allied Signal. The art and science of implementing decisions will be covered more fully in later chapters, particularly those on leadership and organizational change.[36]

EVALUATING DECISION OUTCOMES

postdecisional justification
The tendency for people to support their selected alternative in a decision by forgetting or downplaying the negative features of the selected alternative, emphasizing its positive features, and doing the opposite for alternatives not selected.

Contrary to the rational choice paradigm, decision makers aren't completely honest with themselves when evaluating the effectiveness of their decisions. One concern is that after making a choice, decision makers tend to support their choice by forgetting or downplaying the negative features of the selected alternative and emphasizing its positive features. This perceptual distortion, known as **postdecisional justification**, results from the need to maintain a positive self-concept.[37] Postdecisional justification gives people an excessively optimistic evaluation of their decisions, but only until they receive very clear and undeniable information to the contrary. Unfortunately, it also inflates the decision maker's initial evaluation of the decision, so reality often comes as a painful shock when objective feedback is finally received.

ESCALATION OF COMMITMENT

escalation of commitment
The tendency to repeat an apparently bad decision or allocate more resources to a failing course of action.

A second problem when evaluating decision outcomes is **escalation of commitment**—the tendency to repeat an apparently bad decision or allocate more resources to a failing course of action.[38] One example of escalation occurred when Tokyo's Metropolitan Transport Bureau promised to build a 32-kilometre high-speed subway loop under the city in record time and at enormous profit. Instead, the multi-billion dollar project was seriously over-budget, more than three years overdue, and won't be profitable until 2040, if ever. In Canada, British Columbia Ferry Services (BC Ferries) ordered the design and construction of three catamaran-style ferries for its route between the city of Vancouver and Vancouver Island. These "PacifiCats" were supposed to travel faster than conventional ferries and cost $210 million "right down to the toilet paper." Instead, costs ballooned to nearly $500 million. The Darlington nuclear power plant in Ontario had an estimated cost of $2 billion (although some claim the estimate was $5 billion), but the project eventually spent more than $14 billion. This huge debacle prompted the Ontario government to deregulate the electricity industry and split Ontario Hydro into two operating companies. Ironically, a former CEO of Ontario Hydro (now Hydro One) warned that Darlington and other megaprojects invite escalating commitment because "once you commit to them, there's very little you can do to reverse that commitment."[39]

Irish Health under re-PPARS

In the mid-1990s, executives at five health boards across Ireland decided to develop a common payroll system, called PPARS (payroll, payment, and related systems). Using well-established SAP software, the project would be done in three years at a total estimated cost of CAD$14 million. Health department officials were enthusiastic about PPARS' many benefits, but four years later the system was still far from completion even though costs had more than doubled to $25 million. Asked in 2002 to evaluate the project, Hay Associates concluded that PPARS was worth continuing, even if only to recoup the funds spent so far. The catch, however, was that the government needed to fork over another $120 million, which it agreed. By 2005, Ireland's finance department was sounding alarm bells that PPARS' costs had spiralled out of control and the operational parts of the system were error-prone. The most embarrassing example was a health department employee who received a $1.5-million paycheque one week. The Irish government halted rollout of PPARS, yet senior health officials remained confident in its success, ordering staff as late as May 2007 to "realize the benefits" of the system. PPARS was officially axed in July 2007. The estimated cost of the failed project: somewhere between $250 and $350 million.[40] © *Irish Times Ltd.*

LO6

Causes of Escalating Commitment The four main reasons why people are led deeper and deeper into failing projects include self-justification, prospect theory effect, perceptual blinders, and closing costs.

- *Self-justification*—Individuals are motivated to maintain their course of action when they have a high need to justify their decision. This self-justification is particularly evident when decision makers are personally identified with the project and have staked their reputations to some extent on the project's success.[41] The Irish government's PPARS project (see photo) likely experienced escalation to some degree for this reason. The reputations of government politicians and health board officials depended on the success of PPARS, and pouring more money into the project symbolized their continued support and evidence that the decision was a wise one.

- *Prospect theory effect*—You would think that people dislike losing $50 just as much as they like receiving $50, but that isn't true for most of us. The negative emotions we experience when losing a particular amount are stronger than the positive emotions we experience when gaining the same amount. Consequently, we are more willing to take risks to avoid losses than to increase our gains. This effect, called **prospect theory**, is a second explanation for escalation of commitment. Stopping a project is a certain loss, which is more painful to most people than the uncertainty of success associated with continuing to fund the project. Given the choice, decision makers choose the less painful option.[42]

- *Perceptual blinders*—Escalation of commitment sometimes occurs because decision makers do not see the problems soon enough. They nonconsciously screen out or explain away negative information to protect self-esteem. Serious problems initially look like random errors along the trend line to success. Even when they see that something is wrong, the information is sufficiently ambiguous that it can be misinterpreted or justified.

- *Closing costs*—Even when a project's success is in doubt, decision makers will persist because the costs of ending the project are high or unknown. Terminating a major project may involve large financial penalties, a bad public image, or personal political costs. This effect was apparent when a former premier of Ontario was asked why he didn't shut down the Darlington nuclear plant project. "I don't think anybody can look at a situation with . . . $7 billion in the ground and just cavalierly write it off," he replied.[43]

These four conditions make escalation of commitment look irrational. Usually it is, but there are exceptions. Studies suggest that throwing more money into a failing project is sometimes a logical attempt to further understand an ambiguous situation. This strategy is essentially a variation of testing unknown waters. By adding more resources,

prospect theory
An effect in which losing a particular amount is more disliked than gaining the same amount.

the decision maker gains new information about the effectiveness of these funds, which provides more feedback about the project's future success. This strategy is particularly common where the project has high closing costs.[44]

EVALUATING DECISION OUTCOMES MORE EFFECTIVELY

One of the most effective ways to minimize escalation of commitment and postdecisional justification is to ensure that the people who made the original decision are not the same people who later evaluate that decision. This separation of roles minimizes the self-justification effect because the person responsible for evaluating the decision is not connected to the original decision. A second strategy is to publicly establish a preset level at which the decision is abandoned or re-evaluated. This is similar to a stop-loss order in the stock market, whereby the stock is sold if it falls below a certain price. The problem with this solution is that conditions are often so complex that it is difficult to identify an appropriate point to abandon a project.[45]

A third strategy is to find a source of systematic and clear feedback.[46] For example, the estimated cost of Scotland's new parliament buildings was £50 million (CAD$80 million), but its final cost soared to £440 million. To some extent, these cost overruns might have been smaller if the Scottish government had received less ambiguous or less distorted information from civil servants about the true costs of the project during the first few years. (In fact, civil servants hid some of these costs from elected officials.)[47] A fourth strategy to improve the decision evaluation process is to involve several people in the evaluation. Co-workers continuously monitor each other and might notice problems sooner than someone working alone on the project. Employee involvement offers these and other benefits to the decision-making process, as we learn next.

EMPLOYEE INVOLVEMENT IN DECISION MAKING

LO7

The opening vignette to this chapter describes GenoLogics Life Sciences Software Inc. as a company that involves employees in organizational decisions. In this world of rapid change and increasing complexity, leaders rarely have enough information to make the best decision alone, so executives at GenoLogics and other organizations rely on the knowledge and multiple perspectives of employees to more effectively solve problems or realize opportunities. "The Information Age has brought us into a democratic age, an age of participation and influence," says Traci Fenton, founder and CEO of WorldBlu, a consulting firm that specializes in employee involvement and organizational democracy.[48]

employee involvement
The degree to which employees influence how their work is organized and carried out.

Employee involvement (also called *participative management*) refers to the degree to which employees influence how their work is organized and carried out.[49] Every organization has some form and various levels of employee involvement. At the lowest level, participation involves asking employees for information. They do not make recommendations and might not even know what the problem is about. At a moderate level of involvement, employees are told about the problem and provide recommendations to the decision maker. At the highest level of involvement, the entire decision-making process is handed over to employees. They identify the problem, choose the best alternative, and implement their choice.

BENEFITS OF EMPLOYEE INVOLVEMENT

For the past half-century, organizational behaviour scholars have advised that employee involvement potentially improves decision-making quality and commitment.[50] Involving employees potentially improves decision quality by recognizing problems more quickly and defining them more accurately. Employees are, in many respects, the sensors of the organization's environment. When the organization's activities misalign with customer expectations, employees are usually the first to know. Employee involvement ensures that everyone in the organization is quickly alerted to these problems.[51]

Employee Involvement Keeps Thai Carbon Black in the Black

Thai Carbon Black, which makes the black colouring agent in tires, inks, and many other products, views all of its employees as problem solvers. "The 'can do' attitude of every employee is important," says Subburaman Srinivasan, president of the Thai–Indian joint venture. Each year, the staff submits over 600 productivity improvement suggestions, placing their ideas in one of the little red boxes located around the site. Participatory management meetings are held every month, where employees are encouraged to come up with new ideas on ways to improve day-to-day operations. For instance, the company cut its transport costs by more than 10 percent after employees developed a special shipping bag allowing packers to stuff more product into the same volume. Thanks in part to this emphasis on employee involvement, Thai Carbon Black is one of the few companies outside Japan to receive the Deming Prize for total quality management. It has also received the Thailand Quality Class award, *Forbes* magazine's recognition as one of the best managed companies, and Hewitt Associates' ranking as one of the best employers in Asia and Thailand.[52] *OnAsia Images/Yvan Cohen*

Employee involvement can also potentially improve the number and quality of solutions generated. In a well-managed meeting, team members create synergy by pooling their knowledge to form new alternatives. In other words, several people working together can potentially generate more and better solutions than the same people working alone. A third benefit is that employee involvement often improves the likelihood of choosing the best alternative. This occurs because the decision is reviewed by people with diverse perspectives and a broader representation of values.[53]

Along with improving decision quality, employee involvement tends to strengthen employee commitment to the decision. Rather than viewing themselves as agents of someone else's decision, staff members feel personally responsible for its success. It also has positive effects on employee motivation, satisfaction, and turnover. A recent study reported that employee involvement also increases skill variety, feelings of autonomy, and task identity, all of which increase job enrichment and potentially employee motivation. Participation is also a critical practice in organizational change because employees are more motivated to implement the decision and less likely to resist changes resulting from the decision. Brian Scudamore, CEO of Vancouver-based 1-800-GOT-JUNK?, explains: "Everybody at 1-800-GOT-JUNK? has an opportunity to express their ideas for growth and improvement of our business and we all share best practices. As a result, our people take pride in the work they do every day, and our customers reap the benefits."[54]

LO8

CONTINGENCIES OF EMPLOYEE INVOLVEMENT

If employee involvement is so wonderful, why don't leaders leave all decisions to employees? The answer is that the optimal level of employee involvement depends on the situation. The employee involvement model, shown in Exhibit 7.3, lists four contingencies: decision structure, source of decision knowledge, decision commitment, and risk of conflict in the decision process.

- *Decision structure*—At the beginning of this chapter, we learned that some decisions are programmed, whereas others are nonprogrammed. Programmed decisions are less likely to need employee involvement because the solutions are already worked out from past incidents. In other words, the benefits of employee involvement increase with the novelty and complexity of the problem or opportunity.

- *Source of decision knowledge*—Subordinates should be involved in some level of decision making when the leader lacks sufficient knowledge and subordinates have additional information to improve decision quality. In many cases, employees are closer to customers and production activities, so they often know where the company can save money, improve product or service quality, and realize opportunities. This

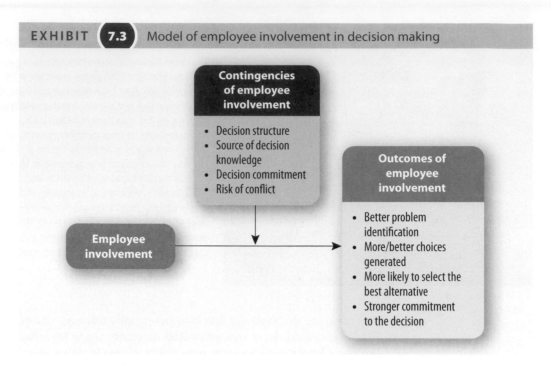

EXHIBIT 7.3 Model of employee involvement in decision making

is particularly true for complex decisions where employees are more likely to possess relevant information.[55]

- *Decision commitment*—Participation tends to improve employee commitment to the decision. If employees are unlikely to accept a decision made without their involvement, then some level of participation is usually necessary.

- *Risk of conflict*—Two types of conflict undermine the benefits of employee involvement. First, if employee goals and norms conflict with the organization's goals, then only a low level of employee involvement is advisable. Second, the degree of involvement depends on whether employees will reach agreement on the preferred solution. If conflict is likely, then high involvement (i.e., where employees make the decision alone) would be difficult to achieve.

Employee involvement is an important component of the decision-making process. To make the best decisions, we need to involve people who have the most valuable information and who will increase commitment to implement the decision. Another important component of decision making is creativity, which we discuss next.

CREATIVITY

From "hack days" to GenoPalooza conferences, GenoLogics Life Sciences Software Inc. makes creativity a top priority. As was described in the opening vignette to this chapter, the Victoria-based company actively engages employees in organizational decisions, and relies on their creativity to identify new software applications and improvements. **Creativity** is the development of original ideas that make a socially recognized contribution.[56] Although there are unique conditions for creativity that we discuss over the next few pages, it is really part of the decision-making process described earlier in the chapter. We rely on creativity to find problems, identify alternatives, and implement solutions. Creativity is not something saved for special occasions. It is an integral part of decision making.

Exhibit 7.4 illustrates one of the earliest and most influential models of creativity.[57] Although there are other models of the creative process, many of them overlap with the model presented here. The first stage is preparation—the person's or team's effort to acquire knowledge and skills regarding the problem or opportunity. Preparation

creativity
The development of original ideas that make a socially recognized contribution.

LO9

Know !!

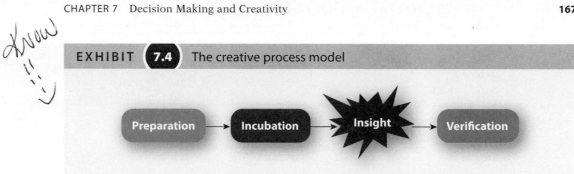

EXHIBIT 7.4 The creative process model

Based on: Graham Wallas, *The Art of Thought* (New York: Harcourt Brace Jovanovich, 1926).

involves developing a clear understanding of what you are trying to achieve through a novel solution, then actively studying information seemingly related to the topic.

The second stage, called incubation, is the period of reflective thought. We put the problem aside, but our mind is still working on it in the background.[58] The important condition here is to maintain a low-level awareness by frequently revisiting the problem. Incubation does not mean that you forget about the problem or issue. Incubation assists **divergent thinking**—reframing the problem in a unique way and generating different approaches to the issue. This contrasts with *convergent thinking*—calculating the conventionally accepted "right answer" to a logical problem. Divergent thinking breaks us away from existing mental models so we can apply concepts or processes from completely different areas of life. Consider the following classic example: Years ago, the experimental light bulbs in Thomas Edison's lab kept falling off their fixtures until a technician wondered whether the threaded caps that screwed down tightly on kerosene bottles would work on light bulbs. They did, and the design remains to this day.[59]

Insight, the third stage of creativity, refers to the experience of suddenly becoming aware of a unique idea.[60] Insight is often visually depicted as a light bulb, but a better image would be a brief flash of light or perhaps a briefly flickering candle because these bits of inspiration are fleeting and can be quickly lost if not documented. For this reason, many creative people keep a journal or notebook nearby at all times, so that they can jot down these ideas before they disappear. Also, these flickering ideas don't keep a particular schedule; they might come to you at any time of day or night. Insights are merely rough ideas. Their usefulness still requires verification through detailed logical evaluation and experimentation. Thus, although verification is labelled the final stage of creativity, it is really the beginning of a long process of discovery, further creativity, and ultimately decision making.

divergent thinking
Reframing the problem in a unique way and generating different approaches to the issue.

LO10

CHARACTERISTICS OF CREATIVE PEOPLE

Everyone is creative, but some people have a higher potential for creativity. Four of the main characteristics that give individuals more creative potential are intelligence, persistence, knowledge/experience, and a cluster of personality traits and values representing independent imagination. First, creative people have above-average intelligence to synthesize information, analyze ideas, and apply their ideas.[61] Like the fictional sleuth Sherlock Holmes, creative people recognize the significance of small bits of information and are able to connect them in ways that no one else could imagine. Then, they have the capacity to evaluate the potential usefulness of their ideas.

Although intelligence helps people to discover new ideas, an equally (or more) important characteristic is the person's persistence to seek out these ideas through trial and error in the face of resistance. In other words, creative potential includes the persistence of trying out more ideas, whereas less creative people give up sooner. Creative people have persistence because they have a higher need for achievement, a strong motivation from the task itself, and a moderate or high degree of self-esteem. In support of this, a recent study reported that Canadian inventors have higher levels of confidence and optimism than do people in the general population, and these traits motivate inventors to continue working on and investing in a project after receiving diagnostic advice to quit.[62]

Persistence Becomes the Cure for Peptic Ulcers

Barry Marshall (left) and Robin Warren (right) faced plenty of doubters when they first proposed that peptic ulcers are brought on by specific bacteria. The prevailing belief was that these ulcers are caused by weak stomach linings, gastric acid, and unhealthy diets. Few believed that bacteria could survive, let alone thrive, in the highly acidic stomach environment. Marshall and Warren's research supported the bacteria theory, but their paper was initially rejected because none of the reviewers believed the findings! The paper was eventually published after a British researcher replicated the results in his lab. Bacteria experts soon embraced the theory, but most stomach ulcer experts remained skeptical. To further convince the doubters, Marshall ingested the bacteria into his healthy stomach and developed symptoms within a few days. "It took 10 years and there was a lot of opposition," recalls one expert. "[But Marshall] had this enormous self-belief that what he'd found was right." Marshall and Warren were recently awarded the Nobel Prize in medicine for their discovery. Fittingly, the Nobel committee acknowledged their "tenacity and a prepared mind challenging prevailing dogmas."[63] *Anders Wiklund/Reuters/Landov*

Inventor Thomas Edison highlighted the importance of persistence when he famously said that genius is 1 percent inspiration and 99 percent perspiration. Edison and his staff discovered hundreds of ways NOT to build a light bulb before they got it right!

A third feature of creative people is that they possess sufficient knowledge and experience on the subject.[64] Creativity experts explain that discovering new ideas requires knowledge of the fundamentals. For example, 1960s rock group The Beatles produced most of their songs only after they had played together for several years. They developed extensive experience singing and adapting the music of other people before their creative talents soared.

Although knowledge and experience may be important in one sense, they can also undermine creativity because people develop mental models that lead to "mindless behaviour," whereby they stop questioning their assumptions.[65] This explains why some corporate leaders like to hire people from other industries and areas of expertise. For instance, Geoffrey Ballard, founder of Vancouver-based Ballard Power Systems, hired a chemist to develop a better battery. When the chemist protested that he didn't know anything about batteries, Ballard replied: "That's fine. I don't want someone who knows batteries. They know what won't work."[66] Ballard explained that he wanted to hire people who would question and investigate avenues to which experts had long ago closed their minds. The point here is that knowledge/experience is a double-edged sword. It is an important prerequisite for creativity, but too much routinization of that knowledge and experience can cause people to be less investigative.

The fourth characteristic of creative people is that they possess a cluster of personality traits and values representing independent imagination. This cluster includes high openness to experience, a Big Five personality dimension described in Chapter 2 that represents the extent to which a person is imaginative, curious, sensitive, open-minded, and original. This cluster also includes the personal values of self-direction (creativity, independent thought) and stimulation (excitement, challenge), which combine to form openness to change—representing the motivation to pursue innovative ways (see Chapter 2). Another personal characteristic in this cluster is a relatively low need for affiliation. People are more creative when they have less need for social approval and have a somewhat (but not necessarily very) high degree of nonconformity. Due to these characteristics, creative people are less embarrassed when they make mistakes and remain motivated to explore ideas even when others criticize them for their persistence. Studies disagree on the extent to which openness to experience, self-direction and stimulation, and low need for affiliation influence creativity, but they generally agree that these personality traits and values influence one's creative potential under some circumstances.[67]

ORGANIZATIONAL CONDITIONS SUPPORTING CREATIVITY

Intelligence, persistence, knowledge/experience, and independent imagination represent a person's creative potential, but the extent to which they actually practise creativity depends on a work environment that supports the creative process.[68] Before describing these contextual influences on creativity, we need to point out that different combinations of situations can equally support creativity; there isn't one best work environment.[69] With this caveat in mind, here are some of the conditions that seem to unleash creative potential.

One of the most important conditions that supports creative practice is the extent to which the organization has a learning orientation; that is, leaders recognize that employees make reasonable mistakes as part of the creative process. Motivation from the job itself is another important condition for creativity.[70] Employees tend to be more creative when they believe their work has a substantial effect on the organization and/or larger society (i.e., task significance) and when they have the freedom to pursue novel ideas without bureaucratic delays (i.e., autonomy). Creativity is about changing things, and change is possible only when employees have the authority to experiment. More generally, jobs encourage creativity when they are challenging and aligned with the employee's competencies.

Along with supporting a learning orientation and intrinsically motivating jobs, companies foster creativity through open communication and sufficient resources. They also provide a reasonable level of job security, which explains why creativity suffers during times of downsizing and corporate restructuring.[71] Some companies support the reflection stage of creativity by designing nontraditional work spaces. Toronto-based advertising agency Grip Limited followed this route by installing a bright red slide and

Creativity in Aisle 3

Canadian Tire has a secret weapon in the highly competitive battle for customers: an innovation room that sparks creativity. The innovation room features a canoe, sun deck, Lego building blocks, crayons, and a tree that looks like it has spouted ski poles, skateboards, and other Canadian Tire products. One creative team used the innovation room to design a solar-lit tent, which is now one of the retailer's big sellers. Rather than working alone, the solar-tent team invited friends, family, and anyone else with an interest in camping to join them in the innovation room. "It's really about unlocking and unleashing creativity and getting people to just let loose and dream a little and have fun," explains a Canadian Tire senior vice president. "It's a process that usually ends up with some very unique and different products and concepts."[72] *The Canadian Press (Steve White)*

a fire pole to descend to the lower area, as well as a lounge pit that looks like a hot tub (complete with beer on tap) and a board room fashioned after a refrigerator. These features produce a fun environment that apparently inspires creative staff.[73]

To some degree, creativity also improves with support from leaders and co-workers. One Canadian study reported that effective product champions provide enthusiastic support for new ideas. Other studies suggest that co-worker support can improve creativity in some situations, whereas competition among co-workers improves creativity in other situations.[74] Similarly, it isn't clear how much pressure should be exerted on employees to produce creative ideas. Extreme time pressures are well-known creativity inhibitors, but lack of pressure doesn't seem to produce the highest creativity, either.

ACTIVITIES THAT ENCOURAGE CREATIVITY

Along with hiring people with strong creative potential and providing a work environment that supports creativity, organizations have introduced numerous activities that help employees to think more creatively. One set of activities encourages employees to redefine the problem. This occurs when we revisit old projects that have been set aside. After a few months of neglect, these projects might be seen in new ways.[75] Another strategy involves asking people unfamiliar with the issue (preferably with different expertise) to explore the problem with you. You would state the objectives and give some facts, then let the other person ask questions to further understand the situation. By verbalizing the problem, listening to questions, and hearing what others think, you are more likely to form new perspectives on the issue.[76]

A second set of creativity activities, known as *associative play*, range from art classes to impromptu storytelling and acting. For example, British media giant OMD sends employees to two-day retreats in the countryside where they play grapefruit croquet, chant like medieval monks, and pretend to be dog collars. "Being creative is a bit like an emotion; we need to be stimulated," explains Harriet Frost, one of OMD's specialists in building creativity. "The same is true for our imagination and its ability to come up with new ideas. You can't just sit in a room and devise hundreds of ideas."[77]

Another associative play activity, called *morphological analysis*, involves listing different dimensions of a system and the elements of each dimension, then looking at each combination. This encourages people to carefully examine combinations that initially seem nonsensical. Tyson Foods, the world's largest poultry producer, applied this activity to identify new ways to serve chicken for lunch. The marketing and research team assigned to this task focused on three categories: occasion, packaging, and taste. Next, the team worked through numerous combinations of items in the three categories. This created unusual ideas, such as cheese chicken pasta (taste) in pizza boxes (packaging) for concessions at baseball games (occasion). Later, the team looked more closely at the feasibility of these combinations and sent them to customer focus groups for further testing.[78]

Other activities that encourage creativity in organizations are various forms of *cross-pollination*.[79] Cross-pollination occurs when people from different areas of the organization exchange ideas. Radical Entertainment, the Vancouver-based computer games developer, practises cross-pollination through its monthly "game fair" day, in which teams show off their products and make presentations to other teams in the organization. IDEO, the California-based product design company, has a similar effect by mixing together employees from different past projects so they share new knowledge with each other.

Cross-pollination highlights the fact that creativity rarely occurs alone. Some creative people may be individualistic, but most creative ideas are generated through teams and informal social interaction. This probably explains why Jonathon Ive, the award-winning designer of Apple Computer products, always refers to his team's creativity rather than his own. "The only time you'll hear [Jonathan Ive] use the word 'I' is when he's naming some of the products he helped make famous: iMac, iBook, iPod," says one writer.[80] The next chapter turns our attention to the main concepts in team effectiveness, as well as ways to improve team decision making and creativity.

CHAPTER SUMMARY

Decision making is a conscious process of making choices among one or more alternatives with the intention of moving toward some desired state of affairs. The rational choice paradigm of decision making includes identifying problems and opportunities, choosing the best decision style, developing alternative solutions, choosing the best solution, implementing the selected alternative, and evaluating decision outcomes.

Stakeholder framing, perceptual defence, mental models, decisive leadership, and solution-oriented focus affect our ability to identify problems and opportunities. We can minimize these challenges by being aware of the human limitations and discussing the situation with colleagues.

Evaluating and choosing alternatives is often challenging because organizational goals are ambiguous or in conflict, human information processing is incomplete and subjective, and people tend to satisfice rather than maximize. Decision makers also short-circuit the evaluation process when faced with an opportunity rather than a problem. Emotions shape our preferences for alternatives and the process we follow to evaluate alternatives. We also listen in to our emotions for guidance when making decisions. This latter activity relates to intuition—the ability to know when a problem or opportunity exists and to select the best course of action without conscious reasoning. Intuition is both an emotional experience and a rapid unconscious analytic process that involves both pattern matching and action scripts.

People generally make better choices by systematically evaluating alternatives. Scenario planning can help to make future decisions without the pressure and emotions that occur during real emergencies.

Postdecisional justification and escalation of commitment make it difficult to accurately evaluate decision outcomes. Escalation is mainly caused by self justification, the prospect theory effect, perceptual blinders, and closing costs. These problems are minimized by separating decision choosers from decision evaluators, establishing a preset level at which the decision is abandoned or re-evaluated, relying on more systematic and clear feedback about the project's success, and involving several people in decision making.

Employee involvement (or participation) refers to the degree that employees influence how their work is organized and carried out. The level of participation may range from an employee providing specific information to management without knowing the problem or issue, to complete involvement in all phases of the decision process. Employee involvement may lead to higher decision quality and commitment, but several contingencies need to be considered, including the decision structure, source of decision knowledge, decision commitment, and risk of conflict.

Creativity is the development of original ideas that make a socially recognized contribution. The four creativity stages are preparation, incubation, insight, and verification. Incubation assists divergent thinking, which involves reframing the problem in a unique way and generating different approaches to the issue.

Four of the main features of creative people are intelligence, persistence, knowledge/experience, and inventive thinking style. Creativity is also strengthened for everyone when the work environment supports a learning orientation, the job has high intrinsic motivation, the organization provides a reasonable level of job security, and project leaders provide appropriate goals, time pressure, and resources. Three types of activities that encourage creativity are redefining the problem, associative play, and cross-pollination.

KEY TERMS

bounded rationality, p. 158

creativity, p. 166

decision making, p. 154

divergent thinking, p. 167

employee involvement, p. 164

escalation of commitment, p. 162

implicit favourite, p. 159

intuition, p. 160

postdecisional justification, p. 162

prospect theory, p. 163

rational choice paradigm, p. 154

satisficing, p. 159

scenario planning, p. 161

subjective expected utility, p. 154

CRITICAL THINKING QUESTIONS

1. A management consultant is hired by a manufacturing firm to determine the best site for its next production facility. The consultant has had several meetings with the company's senior executives regarding the factors to consider when making the recommendation. Discuss the decision-making problems that might prevent the consultant from choosing the best site location.

2. You have been asked to personally recommend a new travel agency to handle all airfare, accommodation, and related travel needs for your organization of 500 staff. One of your colleagues, who is responsible for the company's economic planning, suggests that the best travel agent could be selected mathematically by inputting the relevant factors for each agency and the weight (importance) of each factor. What decision-making approach is your colleague recommending? Is this recommendation a good idea in this situation? Why or why not?

3. Intuition is both an emotional experience and an unconscious analytic process. One problem, however, is that

www.mcgrawhill.ca/olc/mcshane

not all emotions signalling that there is a problem or opportunity represent intuition. Explain how we would know if our "gut feelings" are intuition or not, and if not intuition, suggest what might be causing them.

4. A developer received financial backing for a new business financial centre along a derelict section of the waterfront, a few miles from the current downtown area of a large European city. The idea was to build several high-rise structures, attract large tenants to those sites, and have the city extend transportation systems out to the new centre. Over the next decade, the developer believed that others would build in the area, thereby attracting the regional or national offices of many financial institutions. Interest from potential tenants was much lower than initially predicted and the city did not build transportation systems as quickly as expected. Still, the builder proceeded with the original plans. Only after financial support was curtailed did the developer reconsider the project. Using your knowledge of escalation of commitment, discuss three possible reasons why the developer was motivated to continue with the project.

5. Ancient Book Company has a problem with new book projects. Even when others are aware that a book is far behind schedule and may engender little public interest, sponsoring editors are reluctant to terminate contracts with authors whom they have signed. The result is that editors invest more time with these projects than on more fruitful projects. As a form of escalation of commitment, describe two methods that Ancient Book Company can use to minimize this problem.

6. Employee involvement applies just as well to the classroom as to the office or factory floor. Explain how student involvement in classroom decisions typically made by the instructor alone might improve decision quality. What potential problems may occur in this process?

7. Think of a time when you experienced the creative process. Maybe you woke up with a brilliant (but usually sketchy and incomplete) idea, or you solved a baffling problem while doing something else. Describe this incident to your class and explain how the experience followed the creative process.

8. Two characteristics of creative people are that they have relevant experience and are persistent in their quest. Does this mean that people with the most experience and the highest need for achievement are the most creative? Explain your answer.

CASE STUDY 7.1

Employee Involvement Cases

Case 1: The Sugar Substitute Research Decision

You are the head of research and development (R&D) for a major beer company. While working on a new beer product, one of the scientists in your unit seems to have tentatively identified a new chemical compound that has few calories but tastes closer to sugar than current sugar substitutes. The company has no foreseeable need for this product, but it could be patented and licensed to manufacturers in the food industry.

The sugar substitute discovery is in its preliminary stages and would require considerable time and resources before it would be commercially viable. This means that it would necessarily take some resources away from other projects in the lab. The sugar substitute project is beyond your technical expertise, but some of the R&D lab researchers are familiar with that field of chemistry. As with most forms of research, it is difficult to determine the amount of research required to further identify and perfect the sugar substitute. You do not know how much demand is expected for this product. Your department has a decision process for funding projects that are behind schedule. However, there are no rules or precedents about funding projects that would be licensed but not used by the organization.

The company's R&D budget is limited and other scientists in your work group have recently complained that they require more resources and financial support to get their projects completed. Some of these other R&D projects hold promise for future beer sales. You believe that most researchers in the R&D unit are committed to ensuring the company's interests are achieved.

Case 2: Coast Guard Cutter Decision Problem

You are the captain of a 72-metre Coast Guard cutter, with a crew of 16, including officers. Your mission is general at-sea search and rescue. At 2:00 this morning, while en route to your home port after a routine 28-day patrol, you received word from the nearest Coast Guard station that a small plane had crashed 100 kilometres offshore. You obtained all the available information concerning the location of the crash, informed your crew of the mission, and set a new course at maximum speed for the scene to commence a search for survivors and wreckage.

You have now been searching for 20 hours. Your search operation has been increasingly impaired by rough seas, and there is evidence of a severe storm building. The atmospherics associated with the deteriorating weather have made communications with the Coast Guard station impossible. A decision must be made shortly about whether to abandon the search and place your vessel on a course that would ride out the storm (thereby protecting the vessel and your crew, but relegating any possible survivors to almost certain death from exposure) or to continue a potentially futile search and the risks it would entail.

Before losing communications, you received an update weather advisory concerning the severity and duration of the storm. Although your crew members are extremely conscientious about their responsibility, you believe that they would be divided on the decision of leaving or staying.

Discussion Questions (for both cases)

1. To what extent should your subordinates be involved in this decision? Select one of the following levels of involvement:

   - *No involvement*: You make the decision alone without any participation from subordinates.

   - *Low involvement*: You ask one or more subordinates for information relating to the problem, but you don't ask for their recommendations and might not mention the problem to them.

   - *Medium involvement*: You describe the problem to one or more subordinates (alone or in a meeting) and ask for any relevant information as well as their recommendations on the issue. However, you make the final decision, which might or might not reflect their advice.

   - *High involvement*: You describe the problem to subordinates. They discuss the matter, identify a solution without your involvement (unless they invite your ideas), and implement that solution. You have agreed to support their decision.

2. What factors led you to choose this level of employee involvement rather than the others?

3. What problems might occur if less or more involvement occurred in this case (where possible)?

Sources: The Sugar Substitute Research Decision is written by Steven L. McShane, copyright © 2002. The Coast Guard Cutter case is adapted from V. H. Vroom and A. G. Jago, *The New Leadership: Managing Participation in Organizations* (Englewood Cliffs, N.J.: Prentice Hall, 1988). Copyright © 1987 V. H. Vroom and A. G. Jago. Used with permission of the authors.

TEAM EXERCISE 7.2

Where in the World Are We?

Purpose This exercise is designed to help you understand the potential advantages of involving others in decisions rather than making decisions alone.

Materials Students require an unmarked copy of the map of Canada with grid marks (Exhibit 2). Students are not allowed to look at any other maps or use any other materials. The instructor will provide a list of communities located somewhere on Exhibit 2. The instructor will also provide copies of the answer sheet after students have individually and in teams estimated the locations of communities.

Instructions
- *Step 1*: Write down in Exhibit 1 the list of communities identified by your instructor. Then, working alone, estimate the location in Exhibit 2 of these communities, all of which are in Canada. For example, mark a small "1" in Exhibit 2 on the spot where you believe the first community is located. Mark a small "2" where you think the second community is located, and so on. Please be sure to number each location clearly and with numbers small enough to fit within one grid space.

- *Step 2*: The instructor will organize students into approximately equal sized teams (typically five or six people per team). Working with your team members, reach a consensus on the location of each community listed in Exhibit 1. The instructor might provide teams with a separate copy of this map, or each member can identify the team's numbers using a different coloured pen on their individual maps. The team's decision for each location should occur by consensus, not voting or averaging.

- *Step 3*: The instructor will provide or display an answer sheet, showing the correct locations of the communities. Using this answer sheet, students will count the minimum number of grid squares between the location they individually marked and the true location of each community. Write the number of grid squares in the second column of Exhibit 1, then add up the total. Next, count the minimum number of grid squares between the location the team marked and the true location of each community. Write the number of grid squares in the third column of Exhibit 1, then add up the total.

- *Step 4*: The instructor will ask for information about the totals and the class will discuss the implication of these results for employee involvement and decision making.

EXHIBIT 1 List of Selected Communities in Canada			
Number	**Community**	**Individual distance in grid units from the true location**	**Team distance in grid units from the true location**
1			
2			
3			
4			
5			
6			
7			
8			
		Total:	Total:

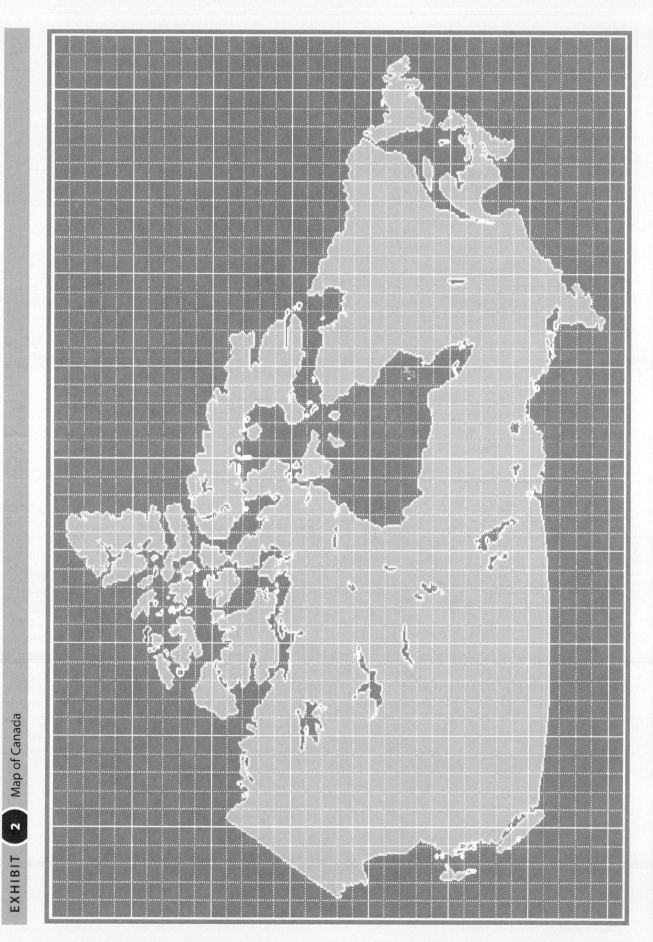

EXHIBIT 2   Map of Canada

www.mcgrawhill.ca/olc/mcshane

TEAM EXERCISE 7.3

Winter Survival Exercise

Purpose   This exercise is designed to help you understand the potential advantages of involving others in decisions rather than making decisions alone.

Instructions
- *Step 1*: Read the "Situation" below. Then, working alone, rank order the 12 items shown in the chart below according to their importance to your survival. In the "Individual Ranking" column, indicate the most important item with "1," going through to "12" for the least important. Keep in mind the reasons why each item is or is not important.

- *Step 2*: The instructor will divide the class into small teams (four to six people). Each team will rank order the items in the second column. Team rankings should be based on consensus, not simply averaging the individual rankings.

- *Step 3*: When the teams have completed their rankings, the instructor will provide the expert's ranking, which can be entered in the third column.

- *Step 4*: Each student will compute the absolute difference (i.e., ignore minus signs) between the individual ranking and the expert's ranking, record this information in column four, and sum the absolute values at the bottom of column four.

- *Step 5*: In column five, record the absolute difference between the team's ranking and the expert's ranking, and sum these absolute scores at the bottom. A class discussion will follow regarding the implications of these results for employee involvement and decision making.

Situation   You have just crash-landed somewhere in the woods of southern Manitoba or possibly northern Minnesota. It is 11:32 a.m. in mid-January. The small plane in which you were travelling crashed on a small lake. The pilot and copilot were killed. Shortly after the crash, the plane sank completely into the lake with the pilot's and copilot's bodies inside. Everyone else on the flight escaped to dry land and without serious injury.

The crash came suddenly before the pilot had time to radio for help or inform anyone of your position. Since your pilot was trying to avoid the storm, you know the plane was considerably off course. The pilot announced shortly before the crash that you were 72 kilometres north-west of a small town that is the nearest known habitation.

You are in a wilderness area made up of thick woods broken by many lakes and rivers. The snow depth varies from above the ankles in windswept areas to more than knee-deep where it has drifted. The last weather report indicated that the temperature would reach minus 15 degrees Celsius in the daytime and minus 26 degrees at night. There are plenty of dead wood and twigs in the area around the lake. You and the other surviving passengers are dressed in winter clothing appropriate for city wear—suits, pantsuits, street shoes, and overcoats. While escaping from the plane, your group salvaged the 12 items listed in the chart below. You may assume that the number of persons in the group is the same as the number in your group, and that you have agreed to stay together.

	Step 1 Your individual ranking	Step 2 Your team's ranking	Step 3 Survival expert's ranking	Step 4 Difference between steps 1 and 3	Step 5 Difference between steps 2 and 3
Winter Survival Tally Sheet					
Items					
Ball of steel wool					
Newspapers					
Compass					
Hand axe					
Cigarette lighter					
45-calibre pistol					
Section air map					
Canvas					
Shirt and pants					
Can of shortening*					
Whiskey					
Chocolate bars					
			Total		
				Your score	Team score

(The lower the score, the better)

Source: Adapted from "Winter Survival" in D. Johnson and F. Johnson, *Joining Together*, 3rd ed. (Englewood Cliffs, N.J.: Prentice Hall, 1984).
*A solid animal or vegetable fat product used in cooking.

 CLASS EXERCISE 7.4

The Hopping Orange

Purpose   This exercise is designed to help students understand the dynamics of creativity and team problem solving.

Instructions   You will be placed in teams of six students. One student serves as the official timer for the team and must have a watch, preferably with a stopwatch timer. The instructor will give each team an orange (or similar object) with a specific task involving use of the orange. The objective is easily understand and non-threatening, and will be described by the instructor at the beginning of the exercise. Each team will have a few opportunities to achieve the objective more efficiently. To maximize the effectiveness of this exercise, no other information is provided here.

www.mcgrawhill.ca/olc/mcshane

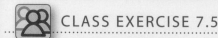 **CLASS EXERCISE 7.5**

Creativity Brainbusters

Purpose   This exercise is designed to help students understand the dynamics of creativity and team problem solving.

Instructions
(Large or small class)   The instructor describes the problem and, working alone, students figure out the solution. When enough time has past, the instructor may then ask specific students who think they have the solution to describe (or show using an overhead transparency) their answer. The instructor will review the solutions and discuss the implications of this exercise. In particular, be prepared to discuss what you needed to solve these puzzles and what may have prevented you from solving them more quickly (or at all).

1. Double Circle Problem

Draw two circles, one inside the other, with a single line and with neither circle touching the other (as shown below). In other words, you must draw both of these circles without lifting your pen (or other writing instrument).

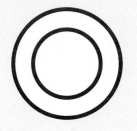

2. Nine Dot Problem

Below are nine dots. Without lifting your pencil, draw no more than four straight lines that pass through all nine dots.

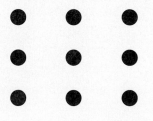

3. Nine Dot Problem Revisited

Referring to the nine dot exhibit above, describe how, without lifting your pencil, you could pass a pencil line through all dots with three (3) or fewer straight lines.

4. Word Search

In the following line of letters, cross out five letters so that the remaining letters, without altering their sequence, spell a familiar English word.

CFRIVEELATETITEVRSE

5. Burning Ropes

You have two pieces of rope of unequal lengths and a box of matches. In spite of their different lengths, each piece of rope takes one hour to burn; however, parts of each rope burn at unequal speeds. For example, the first half of one piece might burn in 10 minutes. Use these materials to accurately determine when 45 minutes has elapsed.

SELF-ASSESSMENT EXERCISE 7.6

Do You Have a Creative Personality?

Purpose   This self-assessment is designed to help you measure the extent to which you have a creative personality.

Instructions   Listed below is an adjective checklist with 30 words that may or may not describe you. Put a check mark in the box beside the words that you think accurately describe you. Please **DO NOT** mark the boxes for words that do not describe you. When finished, you can score the test using the scoring key in Appendix B. This exercise is completed alone so students assess themselves without concerns of social comparison. However, class discussion will focus on how this scale might be applied in organizations, and the limitations of measuring creativity in work settings.

Adjective Checklist					
Affected	☐	Honest	☐	Reflective	☐
Capable	☐	Humorous	☐	Resourceful	☐
Cautious	☐	Individualistic	☐	Self-confident	☐
Clever	☐	Informal	☐	Sexy	☐
Commonplace	☐	Insightful	☐	Sincere	☐
Confident	☐	Intelligent	☐	Snobbish	☐
Conservative	☐	Inventive	☐	Submissive	☐
Conventional	☐	Mannerly	☐	Suspicious	☐
Dissatisfied	☐	Narrow interests	☐	Unconventional	☐
Egotistical	☐	Original	☐	Wide interests	☐

Source: Adapted from and based on information in H. G. Gough and A. B. Hellbrun, Jr., *The Adjective Check List Manual* (Palo Alto, CA: Consulting Psychologists Press, 1965).

 Go to the Online Learning Centre at www.mcgrawhill.ca/olc/mcshane to complete the following interactive self-assessments.

 SELF-ASSESSMENT EXERCISE 7.7

How Creative Are You?

This self-assessment takes the form of a self-scoring quiz. It consists of 12 questions that require divergent thinking to identify the correct answers. For each question, enter your answer in the space provided. When finished, look at the correct answer for each question, along with the explanation for that answer.

SELF-ASSESSMENT EXERCISE 7.8

What is Your Preferred Decision-Making Style?

People have different styles of decision making that are reflected in how they identify problems or opportunities and make choices. This self-assessment estimates your decision-making style through a series of statements describing how individuals go about making important decisions. Please indicate whether you agree or disagree with each statement. Answer each item as truthfully as possible so that you get an accurate estimate of your decision-making style. This exercise is completed alone so students assess themselves honestly without concerns of social comparison. However, class discussion will focus on the decision-making style that people prefer in organizational settings.

PART TWO VIDEO CASE STUDIES

Case 1   Workplace Bias

Wal-Mart is known for its low prices, but many former and current female employees claim the company also has discriminatory low pay and promotional opportunities for women. This video program presents the views of several women who have joined in one of the largest class action sex discrimination lawsuits in history. They claim that qualified women at Wal-Mart receive fewer promotions than their male counterparts. Others say they were fired for launching a sexual harassment complaint. The program describes statistics showing that male district managers earn significantly more than their female counterparts.

Discussion Questions

1. Use your knowledge of social identity theory, stereotyping, and prejudice to explain how sex discrimination might exist at Wal-Mart and in other large retail organizations. Be sure to note any evidence described in this program to support your explanation.

2. If you were a senior manager at Wal-Mart and believed that some of these complaints are due to stereotyping and other biases among middle managers, what interventions would you recommend to correct these biases?

Case 2   Employee Loyalty

CBC ⊚

Not so long ago, companies offered secure employment. In return, workers showed their loyalty by remaining with one company for most of their careers. Not any more! This CBC video program illustrates how dramatically times have changed. Joel Baglole received an internship at the Toronto Star and later was offered a full-time job. Baglole happily accepted the position, but quit six weeks later when the prestigious Wall Street Journal offered him a job. Baglole explains why he has no obligation to be loyal to the Toronto Star, whereas Toronto Star publisher John Honderich believes that loyalty is important and should be expected. This program also examines ways that the Toronto Star and other companies try to increase employee loyalty.

Discussion Questions

1. Which, if any, of the five strategies to build organizational commitment would be effective in this situation involving Joel Baglole?

2. Explain how Joel Baglole's psychological contract is influenced by organizational loyalty in this situation.

Case 3   Pike Place Fish Market

Fifteen years ago, Pike Place Fish Market in Seattle had unhappy employees and was in financial trouble. Rather than close shop, owner John Yokoyama sought help from consultant Jim Bergquist to improve his leadership and energize the workforce. Rather than rule as a tyrant, Yokoyama learned how to actively involve employees in the business. Soon, staff felt more empowered and gained more enjoyment from their work. They also began to actively have fun at work, including setting goals as a game, throwing fish to each other as sport, and pretending they are "world famous." Today, thanks to these and other strategies described in this video case, Pike Place *is* world famous. The little shop has become a tourist attraction and customers from California to New York call in orders.

Discussion Questions

1. Based on the model of emotions and attitudes in Chapter 4, explain how the changes at Pike Place Fish Market improved job satisfaction and reduced turnover. How did these attitude changes affect customer satisfaction?

2. Goal setting is discussed as an important activity at Pike Place. Evaluate the effectiveness of this goal-setting process in the context of the characteristics of effective goals described in Chapter 5 of this textbook.

3. How is coaching applied at Pike Place, and how does this coaching influence employee performance?

Case 4   Stress in Japan

Stress from overwork has become an epidemic in Japan. This video program consists of two segments that illustrate the degree to which some Japanese employees are overworked, as well as the consequences of their overwork. The first segment follows a typical day of a Japanese manager, from his two-hour morning commute to his late night working hours. The program also shows how he is under constant pressure to improve efficiency, and experiences a heavy burden and responsibility to do better. The second segment describes how *karoshi*—death from overwork—took the life of 23-year-old Yoshika. It reconstructs Yoshika's work life as a graphic artist up to the time when she died suddenly on the job due to a brain hemorrhage.

Discussion Questions

1. Identify the various sources of stress (i.e., stressors) that the Japanese manager in the first segment likely experiences each day. Does he do anything to try to manage his stress?

2. What conditions led up to the *karoshi* death of Yoshika? Are these conditions commonly found in the country where you live?

Case 5   Balancing Work and Life

CBC ◉

Work/life balance is the hottest topic among human resource executives these days, and for good reason. Most Canadians have a serious lack of balance, which is costing employers plenty. Companies have introduced several practices to minimize the damage to time-stressed staff, such as fitness programs, career breaks, daycare centres, flextime, job sharing, telework, and so on. But a major Canadian study has reported that Canadians are still stressed. University of Guelph professor Peter Hausdorf says that part of the problem is that employers don't want to deal with the main cause of poor work/life balance: workload. Carleton University professor Linda Duxbury asks how companies can afford not to help employees maintain a work/life balance. This CBC video program investigates these and other issues regarding work/life balance among Canadian employees.

www.mcgrawhill.ca/olc/mcshane

Discussion Questions

1. Explain how companies that encourage work/life balance might be more successful than those pushing more hours of work out of their staff.

2. Looking through other chapters in this book, identify topics that might explain why work/life balance is linked to employee performance and workplace productivity.

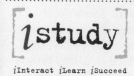

iStudy—Available 24/7 with instant feedback so you can study when you want, how you want, and where you want. Visit www.istudyob.ca to register—take practice quizzes, run interactive scenarios, practice concepts, and much more. Also visit the Student Online Learning Centre for additional study tools.

Team Dynamics

When Whole Foods Market opened stores in Toronto and Vancouver a few years ago, the organic food retailer wasn't just looking for staff with good customer service skills. It was looking for people who also worked well in teams. Every Whole Foods Market store is divided into about 10 teams, such as the prepared-foods team, the cashier/front-end team, and the seafood team. Teams are "self-directed" because team members make the decisions about their work unit with minimal interference from management.

"Each team is . . . responsible for managing its own business," explains Whole Foods Market co-founder John Mackey. "It gets a profit-and-loss statement, it's responsible for managing inventory, labour productivity, gross margins; and its members are responsible for many of the product-placement decisions." Whole Foods Market introduced a team-based structure when it was founded in 1980. The idea came from the then-popular Japanese management books, which espoused the value of teamwork. Even today with almost 200 stores employing 40,000 people in the United States, Canada, and the United Kingdom, Whole Foods Market remains true to its team-based structure.

Along with making departmental decisions, Whole Foods Market teams decide on whether new hires get to remain as permanent team members. After a recruit is temporarily employed for 30 to 45 days, team members vote on whether the individual should become a permanent member; at least two thirds must vote in favour for the recruit to join the team permanently. Team members take these hiring decision seriously because their monthly bonuses are based on team performance. Every four weeks, the company calculates each team's performance against goals and cost efficiencies. When the team finds ways to work more effectively, the unused budget is divided among them. This team bonus can add up to hundreds of extra dollars in each paycheque.[1]

Whole Foods Market relies on teams (including the employees shown here at its Toronto store) to more effectively serve customers and fulfill employee needs. © *Whole Foods Market*®

Several factors explain why Whole Foods Market has become a retail success story and one of the best places to work, but the company's focus on teams is clearly one of those factors. This emphasis on teamwork extends to most industries. All production employees at General Cable Corp.'s manufacturing plant in Moose Jaw, Saskatchewan, work in self-directed teams. To help them improve productivity, employees receive production data and financial performance measures, as well as weekly reports on scrap, defects, and expenses. Hotel Dieu Grace Hospital in Windsor and more than two dozen other hospitals throughout Ontario have set up critical care outreach teams, consisting of specially trained doctors and nurses who stabilize patients prior to their arrival at the hospital. Ford Motor Company's legal department was recently identified as one of the best legal departments in North America, partly because almost everything the department does is achieved through project teams.[2]

This chapter begins by defining teams and examining the reasons why organizations rely on teams and why people join informal groups in organizational settings. Several types of teams are described, including the increasing prevalence of self-directed teams and virtual teams. A large segment of this chapter examines a model of team effectiveness, which includes team and organizational environment, team design, and the team processes of development, norms, cohesion, and trust. The final section of this chapter looks at the challenges and strategies for making better decisions in teams.

TEAMS AND INFORMAL GROUPS

LO1

teams
Groups of two or more people who interact and influence each other, are mutually accountable for achieving common goals associated with organizational objectives, and perceive themselves as a social entity within an organization.

Teams are groups of two or more people who interact and influence each other, are mutually accountable for achieving common goals associated with organizational objectives, and perceive themselves as a social entity within an organization.[3] This definition has a few important components worth repeating. First, all teams exist to fulfill some purpose, such as assembling a product, providing a service, designing a new manufacturing facility, or making an important decision. Second, team members are held together by their interdependence and need for collaboration to achieve common goals. All teams require some form of communication so members can coordinate and share common objectives. Third, team members influence each other, although some members may be more influential than others regarding the team's goals and activities. Finally, a team exists when its members perceive themselves to be a team.

Exhibit 8.1 briefly describes various types of teams in organizations. Some teams are permanent, while others are temporary; some are responsible for making products or providing services, while others exist to make decisions or share knowledge. Each type of team has been created deliberately to serve an organizational purpose. Some teams, such as skunkworks teams, are not initially sanctioned by management, yet are called "teams" because members work toward an organization objective.

INFORMAL GROUPS

Although most of our attention in this chapter is on formal teams, employees also belong to informal groups. All teams are groups, but many groups do not satisfy our definition of teams. Groups include people assembled together whether or not they have any interdependence or organizationally focused objective. The friends you meet for lunch are an *informal group*, but wouldn't be called a team because they have little or no interdependence (each person could just as easily eat lunch alone) and no organizationally mandated purpose (which is why they are "informal"). Instead, they exist primarily for the benefit of their members. Although the terms are used interchangeably, "teams" has largely replaced "groups" in the language of business when referring to employees who work together to complete tasks.[4]

LO2

People join informal groups for several reasons. One reason is that human beings are social animals. Our drive to bond is hardwired through evolutionary development, which creates a need to belong to informal groups.[5] This is evident by the fact that people invest considerable time and effort forming and maintaining social relation-

EXHIBIT 8.1   Types of teams in organizations

Team Type	Description
Departmental teams	Employees have similar or complementary skills located in the same unit of a functional structure; usually minimal task interdependence because each person works with employees in other departments.
Production/service/leadership teams	Typically multiskilled (employees have diverse competencies), team members collectively produce a common product/service or make ongoing decisions; production/service teams typically have an assembly line type of interdependence, whereas leadership teams tend to have tight interactive (reciprocal) interdependence.
Self-directed teams	Similar to production/service teams except (1) they are organized around work processes that complete an entire piece of work requiring several interdependent tasks, and (2) they have substantial autonomy over the execution of those tasks (i.e., they usually control inputs, flow, and outputs with little or no supervision).
Advisory teams	Teams that provide recommendations to decision makers; includes committees, advisory councils, work councils, and review panels; may be temporary, but often permanent, some with frequent rotation of members.
Task force (project) teams	Usually multiskilled, temporary teams whose assignment is to solve a problem, realize an opportunity, or design a product or service.
Skunkworks	Multiskilled teams that are usually located away from the organization and relatively free of its hierarchy; often initiated by an entrepreneurial team leader who borrows people and resources (*bootlegging*) to design a product or service.
Virtual teams	Teams whose members operate across space, time, and organizational boundaries and are linked through information technologies to achieve organizational tasks; may be a temporary task force or permanent service team.
Communities of practice	May be informal groups, but increasingly formal teams bound together by shared expertise and passion for a particular activity or interest; main purpose is to share information; often rely on information technologies as main source of interaction (i.e., a specific form of virtual team).

ships without any special circumstances or ulterior motives. A second explanation is provided by social identity theory, which states that individuals define themselves by their group affiliations. Thus, we join groups—particularly those viewed favourably by others and that are similar to our existing values—because they shape and reinforce our self-concept.[6]

A third reason why people are motivated to form informal groups is that they accomplish tasks that cannot be achieved by individuals working alone. For example, employees will sometimes create a group to oppose organizational changes because the group collectively has more power than individuals complaining alone. A fourth explanation for informal groups is that in stressful situations we are comforted by the mere presence of other people and are therefore motivated to be near them. When in danger, people congregate near each other even though it serves no protective purpose. Similarly, employees tend to mingle more often when hearing rumours that the company might be acquired by a competitor.[7]

ADVANTAGES AND DISADVANTAGES OF TEAMS

When 1,760 Canadian professionals were recently asked about their work, 86 percent agreed that working in teams is more important to business success today than it was five years ago. This is certainly true in scientific research; a recent study of almost 20 million research publications reported that the percentage of journal articles written by teams rather than individuals has increased substantially over the past five decades. Furthermore, team-based articles had a much higher number of subsequent citations, which suggests that journal article quality is higher when written by teams than individuals.[8]

Why is teamwork so important? The answer to this question has a long history, dating back to research on British coal mining in the 1940s and the Japanese economic miracle of the 1970s.[9] These early studies and a huge number of investigations since then have revealed that *under the right conditions*, teams make better decisions, develop

GM Holden's Secret Skunkworks

In the late 1990s, eight designers at General Motor's small development centre in Australia secretly worked on a souped-up coupe, something that was missing from GM's line-up. "It had to stay quiet," recalls Michael Simcoe (shown in this photo), who led the clandestine skunkworks group. "It wasn't an official Holden (GM's Australian company) project and management hadn't asked us to produce a coupe. It was all after hours work; people stayed on at the office instead of going straight home at night and they even came in on weekends to make it happen." The project was so secret that the family room wall at one team member's home was used to complete the first full-size line drawings. When GM Holden executives were notified, they excitedly supported the project, which eventually became the Monaro in Australia and the Pontiac GTO in the United States. Members of the skunkworks team are now working with their American colleagues on a new version of the Camaro; Simcoe is now global head of new car design at General Motors headquarters in Detroit.[10] © *Peter Braig/Fairfaxphotos*

better products and services, and create a more engaged workforce compared with employees working alone.[11] Similarly, team members can quickly share information and coordinate tasks, whereas these processes are slower and prone to more errors in traditional departments led by supervisors. Teams typically provide superior customer service because they provide more breadth of knowledge and expertise to customers than individual "stars" can offer.

In many situations, people are potentially more motivated when working in teams than alone.[12] One reason for this motivation is that, as we mentioned a few paragraphs ago, employees have a drive to bond and are motivated to fulfill the goals of groups to which they belong. This motivation is particularly strong when the team is part of the employee's social identity. Second, people are more motivated in teams because they are accountable to fellow team members, who monitor performance more closely than a traditional supervisor. This is particularly true where the team's performance depends on the worst performer, such as on an assembly line where how fast the product is assembled depends on the speed of the slowest employee. Third, under some circumstances, performance improves when employees work near others because co-workers become benchmarks of comparison. Employees are also motivated to work harder because of apprehension that their performance will be compared to others' performance.

THE TROUBLE WITH TEAMS

In spite of the many benefits of teams, they are not always as effective as individuals working alone.[13] Teams are usually better suited to work that is sufficiently complex, such as designing a building or auditing a company's financial records. Under these circumstances, one person rarely has all the necessary knowledge and skills. Instead, the work is performed more efficiently by dividing its tasks into more specialized roles, with people in those specialized roles coordinating with each other. In contrast, work is typically performed more effectively by individuals alone when they have all the necessary knowledge and skills and the work cannot be divided into specialized tasks or is not complex enough to benefit from specialization. Even where the work can and should be specialized, a team structure might not be necessary if the tasks performed by several people require minimal coordination.

process losses
Resources (including time and energy) expended toward team development and maintenance rather than the task.

The main problem with teams is that they have additional costs called **process losses**—resources (including time and energy) expended toward team development and maintenance rather than the task.[14] It is much easier for someone to coordinate his or her own actions than with other people. As we will learn in this chapter, to perform well, team members need to agree and have mutual understanding of their goals, the strategy to accomplish those goals, their specific roles, and informal rules of conduct.[15] Developing and maintaining these team requirements divert time and energy away from performing the work. The process loss problem is particularly apparent when more staff are added or replace others on the team. Team performance suffers when a team adds members, because those employees need to learn how the team operates and how to coordinate efficiently with other team members. The software industry even has a name for this. **Brooks's law** (also called the "mythical man-month") says that adding more people to a late software project only makes it later!

> **Brooks's law**
> Also called the "mythical man-month," this principle says that adding more people to a late software project only makes it later.

> **social loafing**
> Occurs when people exert less effort (and usually perform at a lower level) when working in groups than when working alone.

Social Loafing   Perhaps the best-known limitation of teams is the risk of productivity loss due to **social loafing**. Social loafing occurs when people exert less effort (and usually perform at a lower level) when working in teams than when working alone.[16] It is most likely to occur in large teams where individual output is difficult to identify. In particular, employees tend to put out less effort when the team produces a single output, such as solving a customer's problem. Under these conditions, employees aren't as worried that their individual performance will be noticed. There is less social loafing when each team member's contribution becomes more noticeable, such as by reducing the size of the team or measuring each team member's performance. Social loafing is also less likely to occur when the task is interesting, because individuals are more motivated by the work itself to perform their duties. Social loafing is also less common when the team's objective is important, possibly because individuals experience more pressure from co-workers to perform well. Finally, social loafing occurs less frequently among members who value team membership and believe in working toward the team's objectives.[17]

In summary, teams can be very powerful forces for competitive advantage, or they can be much more trouble than they are worth, so much so that job performance and morale decline when employees are placed in teams. This leads to the questions: When are teams valuable, and what conditions can improve team effectiveness? The next few sections of this chapter address these questions.

A MODEL OF TEAM EFFECTIVENESS

Let's begin by clarifying the meaning of team effectiveness. A team is called effective when it (a) achieves its objectives, (b) helps individual team members to fulfill their needs, and (c) is able to maintain the commitment of its members so the team does not fall apart.[18] The team's survival also refers to the ability to secure sufficient resources and find a benevolent environment in which to operate.

Why are some teams effective while others fail? This question has challenged organizational researchers for some time and, as you might expect, numerous models of team effectiveness have been proposed over the years.[19] Exhibit 8.2 presents the model of team effectiveness that pulls together the main concepts on team effectiveness and will be examined closely over the next several pages. Although this model shows how the concepts relate to each other, it is best viewed as a template of several theories. For example, the team effectiveness model refers to team composition and team cohesion, both of which have specific theories and models to explain how those concepts operate.

ORGANIZATIONAL AND TEAM ENVIRONMENT

The organizational and team environment represents all of the factors beyond the team's boundaries that influence its effectiveness. Team members tend to work together more effectively when they are at least partly rewarded for team performance.[20] For instance, part of an employee's paycheque at Whole Foods Market is determined by the team's productivity. Communication systems can influence team effectiveness, particularly in

EXHIBIT **8.2**   Team effectiveness model

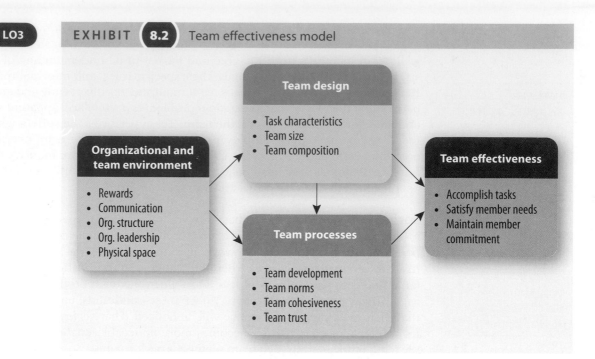

virtual teams, which are highly dependent on information technologies to coordinate work. Another environmental factor is the organizational structure; teams flourish when organized around work processes because it increases interaction among team members. High-performance teams also depend on organizational leaders who provide support and strategic direction while team members focus on operational efficiency and flexibility.[21]

Along with these conditions, the physical layout of the team's workspace can make a difference. Celestica, Inc., the Toronto-based third-party electronic equipment manufacturer, found that one of the best ways to support teams and lean manufacturing (minimize waste) was by replacing the straight-line assembly line with a clustered production arrangement in which members of each team work more closely in U-shaped work cells.[22]

TEAM DESIGN ELEMENTS

Along with setting up a team-friendly environment, leaders need to carefully design the team itself, including task characteristics, team size, team composition, and team roles.

TASK CHARACTERISTICS

What type of work is best for teams? As we noted earlier, teams operate better than individuals working alone on work that is sufficiently complex, such as launching the business in a new market, developing a computer operating system, or constructing a bridge. Complex work requires skills and knowledge beyond the competencies of one person. Teams are particularly well suited when this complex work can be divided into more specialized roles, and people in those specialized roles require frequent coordination with each other. Some evidence also suggests that teams work best with well structured tasks because it is easier to coordinate work among several people.[23] The challenge, however, is to find tasks with the uncommon combination of being both well structured and complex.

One task characteristic that is particularly important for teams is **task interdependence**—the extent that team members must share materials, information, or expertise in order to perform their jobs.[24] Aside from complete independence, there are three

task interdependence
The extent that team members must share materials, information, or expertise in order to perform their jobs.

levels of task interdependence, as illustrated in Exhibit 8.3. _Pooled interdependence_ produces minimal interdependence, such as when team members share machinery, administrative support, budget, or some other resource from a common source. Interdependence is higher under _sequential interdependence_, in which the output of one person is the direct input for another person or unit. The relationship among employees on an assembly line is an example of sequential interdependence. _Reciprocal interdependence_, in which work output is exchanged back and forth among individuals, produces the highest degree of interdependence. Employees with reciprocal interdependence should almost always be organized into teams to facilitate coordination in their interwoven relationship.

The general rule is that the higher the level of task interdependence, the greater the need for teams rather than individuals working alone. A team structure helps employees to coordinate better because they have more opportunity to communicate. High task interdependence also motivates most people to be part of the team. However, the rule that a team should be formed when employees have high interdependence applies when team members have the same task goals, such as serving the same clients or collectively assembling the same product. When team members have different goals (such as serving different clients) but must depend on other team members (high task interdependence) to achieve those unique goals, teamwork might create excessive conflict. Under these circumstances, the company should try to reduce the level of interdependence or rely on supervision as a buffer or mediator among employees.

TEAM SIZE

What is the ideal size for a team? One popular (but untested) rule is that the optimal team size is somewhere between five to seven people. Others have recently argued that tasks are getting so complex that many teams need to have more than 100 members![25] Unfortunately, the former piece of advice is oversimplistic and the latter seems to have lost sight of the meaning and dynamics of real teams. The general rule is that teams should be large enough to provide the necessary competencies and perspectives to

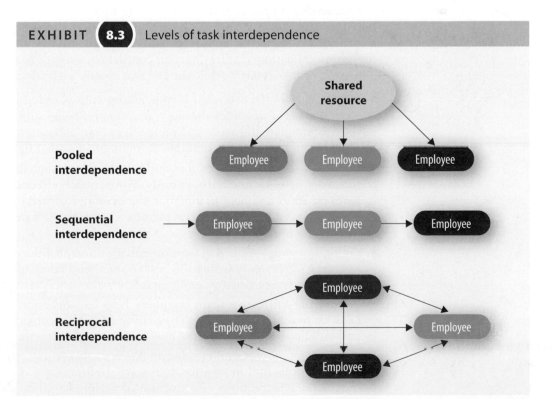

EXHIBIT 8.3   Levels of task interdependence

perform the work, yet small enough to maintain efficient coordination and meaningful involvement of each member.[26] As a Sun Microsystems executive explains: "You need to have a balance between having enough people to do all the things that need to be done, while keeping the team small enough so that it is cohesive and can make decisions effectively and speedily."[27] Small teams (say, less than a dozen members) operate effectively because they have less process loss. Members also tend to identify more with smaller teams because they get to know their teammates (which improves trust) and have more influence on the group's norms and goals.

def. of a team

Should companies have 100-person teams if the task is highly complex? The answer is that a group this large probably isn't a team, even if management calls it one. A team exists when its members interact and influence each other, are mutually accountable for achieving common goals associated with organizational objectives, and perceive themselves as a social entity within an organization. It is very difficult for everyone in a 100-person work unit to influence each other and experience enough cohesion to perceive themselves as team members. Whole Foods was aware that real teams are much smaller when the company opened its huge store in New York City's Columbus Circle. The store had 140 cashiers—far too many people for one cashier team—so Whole Foods divided the group into teams with a dozen employees each. All cashiers meet as one massive group every month to discuss production issues, but the smaller teams work effectively on a day-to-day basis.[28]

TEAM COMPOSITION

Choosing a new team member is too important a decision at Whole Foods Market to be left to management. Instead, as this chapter's opening vignette noted, new hires are approved for permanent employment by their teammates. Royal Dutch/Shell is also serious about selecting job applicants who have excellent team skills. As GLOBAL Connections 8.1 describes, the global energy giant hosts a special five-day exercise in Europe, North America, Asia, and the Middle East to observe how well participants work under pressure with others from diverse backgrounds.

To work effectively in a team, employees must have more than technical skills and self-leadership to perform their own work; they must also be able and willing to support team dynamics. The most frequently mentioned characteristics or behaviours of effective team members are categorized below as the five 'C's: cooperating, coordinating, communicating, comforting, and conflict resolving. The first three mainly (but not entirely) are task-related, while the last two mostly assist team maintenance:[29]

1. • *Cooperating*—Effective team members are willing and able to work together rather than alone. This includes sharing resources and being sufficiently adaptive or flexible to accommodate the needs and preferences of other team members, such as re-scheduling use of machinery so another team member with a tighter deadline can use it.

2. • *Coordinating*—Effective team members actively manage the team's work so it is performed efficiently and harmoniously. For example, effective team members keep the team on track and help to integrate the work performed by different members. This typically requires effective team members to know the work of other team members, not just their own.

3. • *Communicating*—Effective team members transmit information freely (rather than hoarding), efficiently (using the best channel and language), and respectfully (minimizing arousal of negative emotions). They also listen actively to co-workers.

4. • *Comforting*—Effective team members help co-workers to maintain a positive and healthy psychological state. They show empathy, provide psychological comfort, and build co-worker feelings of confidence and self-worth.

5. • *Conflict resolving*—Conflict is inevitable in social settings, so effective team members have the skills and motivation to resolve dysfunctional disagreements among team members. This requires effective use of various conflict handling styles as well as diagnostic skills to identify and resolve the structural sources of conflict.

global connections 8.1

Royal Dutch/Shell Finds Team Players in Gourami

Royal Dutch/Shell (Shell) discovered long ago that a job interview isn't the best way to determine a job applicant's technical skills, nor how well he or she works in a team environment. That's why the global energy company launched the Shell Gourami Business Challenge a decade ago in Europe and very recently in the United States, Asia, and the Middle East. The five-day event involves several dozen engineering and business university students who are split into several teams representing different departments (exploration, refining, manufacturing, finance, etc.). Teams initially develop a business plan for their own department; later, they must merge the departmental plans into an organization-wide business strategy. On the final day, the multi-team's strategy is presented to Gourami's board of directors, which consists of senior level executives from Shell.

Shell leaders emphasize that the Gourami event is more like an audition than a competition because the company hires as many participants as it thinks are qualified. Throughout the event, Shell assessors evaluate students' technical knowledge and skills, but they equally observe how effectively they worked in diverse teams. The need for team skills is quickly apparent to most participants. Maureen Valencia, a business student from the Philippines who attended the Asian Gourami exercise, admitted feeling some initial tension because the Australians were "more straightforward and tell you right away if you're doing something right or wrong."

Team skills were also vital to help students work with people from different specializations. "Coming from a business background, it's most difficult to understand the engineering aspect of the oil industry," admitted Arpan Shah, a University of Texas finance student who attended

Royal Dutch/Shell has found a better way to identify the team skills of prospective job applicants by observing business and engineering students in the Shell Gourami Business Challenge. *AP Images/The Canadian Press (Michael Stravato)*

the Gourami exercise in Rancho Mirage, California. "We have to work together so that both sides understand each other."

Claire Gould, a British mechanical engineering student who attended the European session, also noticed the challenges and potential of teamwork with people from other disciplines. "Dealing with the 'real-life' challenges of Gourami made us all aware of the value of other skills and aptitudes and the need to work as a team," says Gould.[30] "It was a really positive experience to work with so many different types of personalities from such diverse cultures," says Tom Arnott, a mechatronics engineering student from the University of New South Wales in Australia. "I learned how cultural aspects can affect the way a team works together, and how to handle working with an international group."

 These characteristics of effective team members are associated with conscientiousness and extroversion personality traits, as well as with emotional intelligence. Furthermore, the old saying "one bad apple spoils the barrel" seems to apply to teams; one team member who lacks these teamwork competencies may undermine the dynamics of the entire team.[31]

Another important dimension of team composition is diversity.[32] Teams whose members have diverse knowledge, skills, and perspectives are generally more effective in situations involving complex problems requiring innovative solutions. One reason is that people from different backgrounds see a problem or opportunity from different perspectives. A second reason is that they usually have a broader knowledge base. A third reason favouring teams with diverse members is that they provide better representation of the team's constituents, such as other departments or clients from similarly diverse backgrounds. However, diverse employees take longer to become a high-performing team. They are also more susceptible to "faultlines"—hypothetical dividing lines that may split a team into subgroups along gender, ethnic, professional, or other dimensions. Faultlines increase the risk of dysfunctional conflict and other behaviours that undermine team effectiveness.

TEAM PROCESSES

The third set of elements in the team effectiveness model, collectively known as team processes, includes team development, norms, cohesion, and trust. These represent characteristics of the team that continuously evolve.

LO5

TEAM DEVELOPMENT

A few years ago, the National Transportation Safety Board (NTSB) studied the circumstances under which airplane cockpit crews were most likely to have accidents and related problems. What they discovered was startling: 73 percent of all incidents took place on the crew's first day, and 44 percent occurred on the crew's very first flight together. This isn't an isolated example. NASA studied fatigue of pilots after returning from multiple-day trips. Fatigued pilots made more errors in the NASA flight simulator, as one would expect. But the NASA researchers didn't expect the discovery that fatigued crews who had worked together made fewer errors than did rested crews who had not yet flown together.[33]

The NTSB and NASA studies reveal that team members must resolve several issues and pass through several stages of development before emerging as an effective work unit. They need to get to know and trust each other, understand and agree upon their respective roles, discover appropriate and inappropriate behaviours, and learn how to coordinate with each other. The longer that team members work together, the better they develop common or complementary mental models, mutual understanding, and effective performance routines to complete the work.

Exhibit 8.4 presents a popular model that captures many team development activities.[34] The model shows teams moving systematically from one stage to the next, while the dashed lines illustrate that teams might fall back to an earlier stage of development as new members join or other conditions disrupt the team's maturity. *Forming*, the first stage of team development is a period of testing and orientation in which members learn about each other and evaluate the benefits and costs of continued membership. People tend to be polite, will defer to authority, and try to find out what is expected of them and how they will fit into the team. The *storming* stage is marked by interpersonal conflict as members become more proactive and compete for various team roles. Members try to establish norms of appropriate behaviour and performance standards.

During the *norming* stage, the team develops its first real sense of cohesion as roles are established and a consensus forms around group objectives and a common or complementary team-based mental model. By the *performing* stage, team members have learned to efficiently coordinate and resolve conflicts. In high-performance teams, members are highly cooperative, have a high level of trust in each other, are committed to group objectives, and identify with the team. Finally, the *adjourning* stage occurs when the team is about to disband. Team members shift their attention away from task orientation to a relationship focus.

The five-stage model is consistent with what students experience on team projects (as one Canadian study found), but it is far from a perfect representation of the team development process.[35] For instance, it does not show that some teams remain in a particular stage longer than others. It also blurs two distinct processes during team development: membership and competence.[36] The membership development process occurs as employees make the transition from viewing the team as something "out there" to something that is part of them. In other words, team development occurs when employees shift their view of the team from "them" to "us." This relates to becoming familiar with the team, making it part of their social identity, and shaping the team to better fit their ideal. The other process—developing team competence—includes several changes related to team learning. Team members develop habitual routines that increase work efficiency. They also form shared or complementary mental models regarding team resources, goals and tasks, social interaction, and characteristics of other team members.[37]

Know

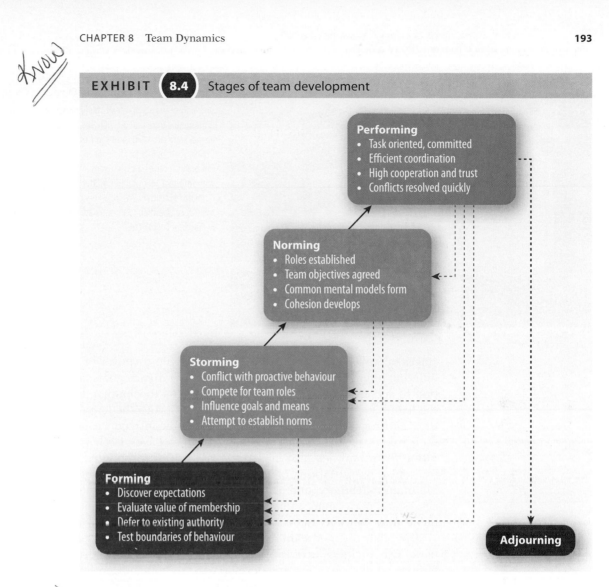

EXHIBIT 8.4   Stages of team development

Performing
- Task oriented, committed
- Efficient coordination
- High cooperation and trust
- Conflicts resolved quickly

Norming
- Roles established
- Team objectives agreed
- Common mental models form
- Cohesion develops

Storming
- Conflict with proactive behaviour
- Compete for team roles
- Influence goals and means
- Attempt to establish norms

Forming
- Discover expectations
- Evaluate value of membership
- Defer to existing authority
- Test boundaries of behaviour

Adjourning

role
A set of behaviours that people are expected to perform because they hold certain positions in a team and organization.

Team Roles   An important part of the team development process is forming and reinforcing team roles. A **role** is a set of behaviours that people are expected to perform because they hold certain positions in a team and organization.[38] In a team setting, some roles help the team achieve its goals; other roles maintain relationships within the team. Some team roles are formally assigned to specific people. For example, team leaders are usually expected to initiate discussion, ensure that everyone has an opportunity to present their views, and help the team reach agreement on the issues discussed.

Team members are typically assigned specific roles as a job responsibility. Yet, throughout the continuous team development process, people vary their formal roles to suit their personality and values as well as the wishes of other team members. Furthermore, many roles exist informally, such as being a cheerleader, initiator of new ideas, or an adviser that encourages the group to soberly rethink their actions. These informal roles are shared among team members, but many are eventually associated with specific team members. Again, this informal role assignment process is influenced by each team member's personal preferences (personality and values) as well as through negotiated dynamics with other team members.[39]

team building
Formal activities intended to improve the development and functioning of a work team.

Accelerating Team Development through Team Building   Team development, including sorting out team roles, takes time, so many companies try to speed up the process through team-building activities. **Team building** refers to formal activities intended to improve the development and functioning of a work team.[40] It can help new teams, but it is more commonly applied to existing teams that have regressed to earlier

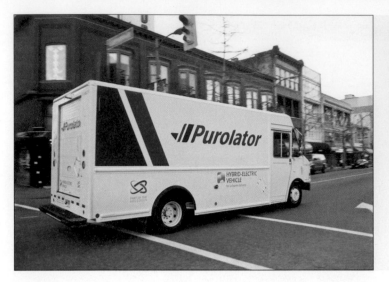

Purolator's Team Building Obstacle Course

One of the most popular team-building activities at Purolator Courier Ltd. is the annual truck rodeo, where the Canadian company's top courier drivers navigate cube vans and semi-trucks through a tight obstacle course. Drivers score points for their speed and safe handling of the vehicle. The top driver receives a cash award. Most of the 100 participants continue with informal team building after the event. "It's a bit novel," says a Purolator executive. "We're a very competitive group and this combines friendly competition with camaraderie and teamwork."[41] *Photo Courtesy of Purolator Courier Ltd.*

stages of team development due to membership turnover or loss of focus. Some team-building interventions clarify the team's performance goals, increase the team's motivation to accomplish these goals, and establish a mechanism for systematic feedback on the team's goal performance. Others try to improve the team's problem-solving skills. A third category of team building clarifies and reconstructs each member's perceptions of their role as well as the role expectations they have of other team members. Role definition team building also helps the team to develop shared mental models—common internal representations of the external world, such as how to interact with clients, maintain machinery, and engage in meetings. Research studies indicate that team processes and performance depend on how well teammates share common mental models about how they should work together.[42]

A popular form of team building is aimed at improving relations among team members. This includes activities that help team members learn more about each other, build trust in each other, and develop ways to manage conflict within the team. Popular interventions such as wilderness team activities, paintball wars, and obstacle course challenges are typically offered to build trust. "If two colleagues hold the rope for you while you're climbing 10 metres up, that is truly team building," explains Jan Antwerpes, a partner in a German communications consulting firm.[43]

Although team-building activities are popular, their success is less certain than many claim.[44] One problem is that team-building activities are used as general solutions to general team problems. A better approach is to begin with a sound diagnosis of the team's health, then select team-building interventions that address weaknesses.[45] Another problem is that team building is applied as a one-shot medical inoculation that every team should receive when it is formed. In truth, team building is an ongoing process, not a three-day jumpstart.[46] Finally, we must remember that team building occurs on the job, not just on an obstacle course or in a national park. Organizations should encourage team members to reflect on their work experiences and to experiment with just-in-time learning for team development.

② TEAM NORMS

norms
The informal rules and shared expectations that groups establish to regulate the behaviour of their members.

Norms are the informal rules and shared expectations that groups establish to regulate the behaviour of their members. Norms apply only to behaviour, not to private thoughts or feelings. Furthermore, norms exist only for behaviours that are important to the team.[47] Norms are enforced in various ways. Co-workers grimace if we are late for a meeting or make sarcastic comments if we don't have our part of the project completed on time. Norms are also directly reinforced through praise from high-status members, more access to valued resources, or other rewards available to the team. But team members often conform to prevailing norms without direct reinforcement or punishment because they identify with the group and want to align their behaviour with the team's values. The more closely the person's social identity is connected to the group, the more the individual is motivated to avoid negative sanctions from that group.[48]

LO6

How Team Norms Develop   Norms develop as soon as teams form because people need to anticipate or predict how others will act. Even subtle events during the team's formation, such as how team members initially greet each other and where they sit in the first meetings, can initiate norms that are later difficult to change. Norms also form as team members discover behaviours that help them function more effectively (such as the need to respond quickly to email). In particular, a critical event in the team's history can trigger formation of a norm or sharpen a previously vague one. A third influence on team norms is the past experiences and values that members bring to the team. If members of a new team value work/life balance, then norms are likely to develop that discourage long hours and work overload.[49]

Preventing and Changing Dysfunctional Team Norms   Team norms often become deeply anchored, so the best way to avoid norms that undermine organizational success or employee well-being is to establish desirable norms when the team is first formed. One way to do this is to clearly state desirable norms as soon as the team is created. Another approach is to select people with appropriate values. If organizational leaders want their teams to have strong safety norms, then they should hire people who already value safety and clearly identify the importance of safety when the team is formed.

The suggestions so far refer to new teams, but how can organizational leaders maintain desirable norms in older teams? First, as one recent study affirmed, leaders often have the capacity to alter existing norms.[50] By speaking up or actively coaching the team, they can often subdue dysfunctional norms while developing useful norms. Team-based reward systems can also weaken counterproductive norms; however, studies report that employees might continue to adhere to a dysfunctional team norm (such as limiting output) even though this behaviour reduces their paycheque. Finally, if dysfunctional norms are deeply ingrained and the previous solutions don't work, it may be necessary to disband the group and replace it with people having more favourable norms.

③ **TEAM COHESION**

team cohesion
The degree of attraction people feel toward the team and their motivation to remain members.

Team cohesion refers to the degree of attraction people feel toward the team and their motivation to remain members. It is a characteristic of the team, including the extent to which its members are attracted to the team, are committed to the team's goals or tasks, and feel a collective sense of team pride.[51] Thus, team cohesion is an emotional experience, not just a calculation of whether to stay or leave the team. It exists when team members make the team part of their social identity.

LO7

Influences on Team Cohesion   Several factors influence team cohesion: member similarity, team size, member interaction, difficult entry, team success, and external competition or challenges. For the most part, these factors reflect the individual's social identity with the group and beliefs about how team membership will fulfill personal needs.

- *Member Similarity*—For more than 2,000 years, philosophers and researchers have observed that people with similar backgrounds and values are more comfortable and attractive to each other. In team settings, this similarity–attraction effect means that teams have higher cohesion—or become cohesive more quickly—when members are similar to each other. Diversity tends to undermine cohesion, but this depends on the type of diversity, however. For example, teams consisting of people from different job groups seem to gel together just as well as teams of people from the same job.[52]

- *Team Size*—Smaller teams tend to have more cohesion than larger teams because it is easier for a few people to agree on goals and coordinate work activities. However, small teams have less cohesion when they lack enough members to perform the required tasks.

- *Member Interaction*—Teams tend to have more cohesion when team members interact with each other fairly regularly. This occurs when team members perform highly interdependent tasks and work in the same physical area.

- *Somewhat Difficult Entry*—Teams tend to have more cohesion when entry to the team is restricted. The more elite the team, the more prestige it confers on its members, and the more they tend to value their membership in the unit. At the same time, research suggests that severe initiations can weaken team cohesion because of the adverse effects of humiliation, even for those who successfully endure the initiation.[53]

- *Team Success*—Cohesion is both emotional and instrumental, with the latter referring to the notion that people feel more cohesion to teams that fulfill their needs and goals. Consequently, cohesion increases with the team's level of success.[54] Furthermore, individuals are more likely to attach their social identity to successful teams than to those with a string of failures.

- *External Competition and Challenges*—Team cohesion tends to increase when members face external competition or a valued objective that is challenging. This might include a threat from an external competitor or friendly competition from other teams. Employees value their membership on the team because of its ability to overcome the threat of competition, and as a form of social support. However, cohesion can dissipate when external threats are severe because these threats are stressful and cause teams to make less effective decisions.[55]

Consequences of Team Cohesion   Every team must have some minimal level of cohesion to maintain its existence. People who belong to high-cohesion teams are motivated to maintain their membership and to help the team perform effectively. Compared to low-cohesion teams, high-cohesion team members spend more time together, share

A Lighthouse Built on High Cohesion

The staff at Lighthouse Publishing in Bridgewater, Nova Scotia, are a highly cohesive group that successfully keeps its much larger competitors off-guard. "Lighthouse staff members [have] kept us independent in the face of stiff competition and corporate takeovers," says Lighthouse president Lynn Hennigar. Its weekly newspaper, the *Bridgewater Bulletin*, is judged as best in class for Atlantic Canada and one of the top five across Canada. In all, the company has received more than two dozen awards in recent years. Lighthouse's mostly female staff often demonstrate their cohesion when faced with new challenges. For instance, the team performed above any reasonable expectations when the press broke down, which threatened to delay getting the paper out on time. On another occasion, when putting together an interactive CD-ROM promoting Nova Scotia tourism, Lighthouse staff displayed skills that Hennigar admits she didn't even know about. "Lighthouse succeeds because of its multi-talented, highly dedicated team of employees," says Hennigar. "It's a team that embraces change."[56] *Courtesy of Atlantic Business Magazine and Lighthouse Publishing. Photo by Robert Hirtle*

information more frequently, and are more satisfied with each other. They provide each other with better social support in stressful situations.[57]

Members of high-cohesion teams are generally more sensitive to each other's needs and develop better interpersonal relationships, thereby reducing dysfunctional conflict. When conflict does arise, members tend to resolve these differences swiftly and effectively. With better cooperation and more conformity to norms, high-cohesion teams usually perform better than low-cohesion teams.[58] However, as Exhibit 8.5 illustrates, this relationship only holds true when team norms are compatible with organizational values and objectives. Cohesion motivates employees to perform at a level more consistent with team norms, so when those norms conflict with the organization's success (such as when norms support high absenteeism or acting unethically), high cohesion will reduce team performance.[59]

LO8

TEAM TRUST

trust
A psychological state comprising the intention to accept vulnerability based on positive expectations of the intent or behaviour of another person.

Any relationship—including the relationship among team members—depends on a certain degree of trust.[60] **Trust** is a psychological state comprising the intention to accept vulnerability based on positive expectations of the intent or behaviour of another person. A high level of trust occurs when others affect you in situations where you are at risk, but you believe they will not harm you. Trust includes both your beliefs and conscious feelings about the relationship with other team members. In other words, a person both logically evaluates the situation as trustworthy and feels that it is trustworthy.[61] Trust can also be understood in terms of the foundation of that trust. From this perspective, people trust others based on three foundations: calculus, knowledge, and identification (see Exhibit 8.6).

- *Calculus-based trust* represents a logical calculation that other team members will act appropriately because they face sanctions if their actions violate reasonable expectations.[62] It offers the lowest potential trust and is easily broken by a violation of expectations. Generally, calculus-based trust alone cannot sustain a team's relationship, because it relies on deterrence.

- *Knowledge-based trust* is based on the predictability of another team member's behaviour. Even if we don't agree with a particular team member's actions, his or her consistency generates some level of trust. Knowledge-based trust also relates to

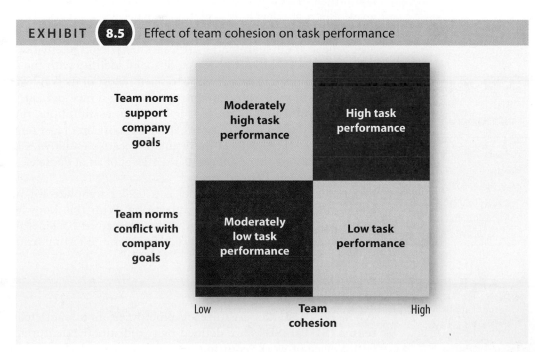

EXHIBIT 8.5   Effect of team cohesion on task performance

Team norms support company goals — Moderately high task performance / High task performance

Team norms conflict with company goals — Moderately low task performance / Low task performance

Low ——— Team cohesion ——— High

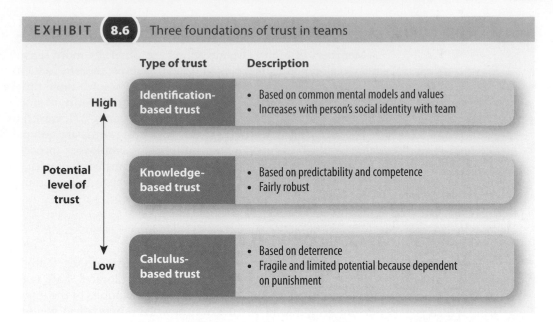

EXHIBIT 8.6   Three foundations of trust in teams

	Type of trust	Description
High ↑	**Identification-based trust**	• Based on common mental models and values • Increases with person's social identity with team
Potential level of trust	**Knowledge-based trust**	• Based on predictability and competence • Fairly robust
Low ↓	**Calculus-based trust**	• Based on deterrence • Fragile and limited potential because dependent on punishment

confidence in the other person's ability or competence, such as when you trust a physician.[63] Knowledge-based trust offers a higher potential level of trust and is more stable because it develops over time.

- *Identification-based trust* is based on mutual understanding and an emotional bond among team members. It occurs when team members think, feel, and act like each other. High-performance teams exhibit this level of trust because they share the same values and mental models. Identification-based trust is potentially the strongest and most robust of all three types of trust. The individual's self-concept is based partly on membership in the team and he/she believes their values highly overlap, so any transgressions by other team members are quickly forgiven. People are more reluctant to acknowledge a violation of this high-level trust because it strikes at the heart of their self-image.

Dynamics of Team Trust   Employees typically join a team with a moderate or high level—not a low level—of trust in their new co-workers. The main explanation for the initially high trust (called *swift trust*) in organizational settings is that people usually believe their teammates are reasonably competent (knowledge-based trust) and they tend to develop some degree of social identity with the team (identification-based trust). Even when working with strangers, most of us display some level of trust, if only because it supports our self-concept of being a nice person.[64] However, trust is fragile in new relationships because it is based on assumptions rather than well-established experience. Consequently, recent studies report that trust tends to decrease rather than increase over time. This is unfortunate because employees become less forgiving and less cooperative toward others as their level of trust decreases, which undermines team and organizational effectiveness.[65]

The team effectiveness model is a useful template for understanding how teams work—and don't work—in organizations. With this knowledge in hand, let's briefly investigate two types of teams that have received considerable attention amongst OB experts and practitioners: self-directed teams and virtual teams.

self-directed teams (SDTs)

Cross-functional work groups organized around work processes, that complete an entire piece of work requiring several interdependent tasks, and that have substantial autonomy over the execution of those tasks.

SELF-DIRECTED TEAMS

Whole Foods Market organizes its employees not just into teams, but into **self-directed teams (SDTs)**. SDTs are defined by two distinctive features.[66] First, they complete an entire piece of work requiring several interdependent tasks. This type of work arrange-

ment clusters the team members together while minimizing interdependence and interaction with employees outside the team. The result is a close-knit group that depends on each other to accomplish their individual tasks. For example, employees in the prepared foods team at a Whole Foods store would naturally work more closely with each other than with members of other teams.

The second distinctive feature of SDTs is that they have substantial autonomy over the execution of their tasks. In particular, these teams plan, organize, and control work activities with little or no direct involvement of a higher status supervisor. At Whole Foods Market, for example, every store team "gets a profit-and-loss statement, it's responsible for managing inventory, labour productivity, gross margins; and its members are responsible for many of the product-placement decisions," says Whole Foods co-founder and CEO John Mackey.[68]

Self-directed teams are found in several Canadian industries, ranging from petrochemical plants to aircraft parts manufacturing. Almost all of the top-rated manufacturing firms in North America rely on SDTs.[69] This popularity of SDTs is consistent with research indicating that they potentially increase both productivity and job satisfaction. For instance, one study found that car dealership service shops that organize employees into SDTs were significantly more profitable than shops where employees work without a team structure. Another study reported that both short- and long-term measures of customer satisfaction increased after street cleaners in a German city were organized into SDTs.[70]

LO9   **SUCCESS FACTORS FOR SELF-DIRECTED TEAMS**

Self-directed teams probably would add value in most organizations, but several conditions must be in place to realize their benefits.[71] In addition to managing the team dynamics issues described earlier in this chapter, SDTs operate best when they are responsible for an entire work process, such as making an entire product or providing a service. This organization around a work process keeps each team sufficiently independent from other teams, yet demands a relatively high degree of interdependence among employees within the team.[72] SDTs should also have sufficient autonomy to organize and coordinate their work. This autonomy allows them to respond more quickly and effectively to client and stakeholder demands. It also motivates team members through feelings of empowerment. Finally, SDTs are more successful when the work site and technology support coordination and communication among team members and increases job enrichment.[73] Too often, management calls a group of employees a "team," yet the work layout, assembly line structure, and other technologies isolate employees from each other.

VIRTUAL TEAMS

Denis Chamberland admits that he had trouble recognizing most of his colleagues when he worked at Accenture. That's because Chamberland was chief legal counsel in Toronto for the global consulting firm, whereas his boss and co-workers operated out of London, Chicago, and other far-flung locations. "There were many people who I worked with for years and never actually met. In many cases, I never even talked to them on the phone," says Chamberland, who is now a partner at a Toronto law firm.[74]

Denis Chamberland has had plenty of experience with the growing trend toward **virtual teams**. Virtual teams are teams whose members operate across space, time, and organizational boundaries and are linked through information technologies to achieve organizational tasks.[75] Virtual teams differ from traditional teams in two ways: (1) they are not usually co-located (work in the same physical area), and (2) due to their lack of co-location, members of virtual teams depend primarily on information technologies rather than face-to-face interaction to communicate and coordinate their work effort.

According to one estimate, more than 60 percent of employees in professions are members of a virtual team at some point during the year. In global companies such as IBM, almost everyone in knowledge work is part of a virtual team. One reason why virtual teams have become so widespread is that information technologies have made it easier than ever before to communicate and coordinate with people at a distance.[76] The shift from production-based to knowledge-based work is a second reason why virtual teamwork is feasible. It isn't yet possible to make a product when team members are located apart, but most of us are now in jobs that mainly process knowledge.

Information technologies and knowledge-based work make virtual teams *possible*, but organizational learning and globalization are two reasons why they are increasingly *necessary*. Virtual teams represent a natural part of the organizational learning process because they encourage employees to share and use knowledge where geography limits more direct forms of collaboration. Globalization makes virtual teams increasingly necessary because employees are spread around the planet rather than around one city. Thus, global businesses depend on virtual teamwork to leverage their human capital.

> **virtual teams**
> Teams whose members operate across space, time, and organizational boundaries and are linked through information technologies to achieve organizational tasks.

SUCCESS FACTORS FOR VIRTUAL TEAMS

Virtual teams have all of the challenges of traditional teams along with the complications of distance and time. Fortunately, OB researchers have been keenly interested in virtual teams, and their studies are now yielding ways to improve virtual team effectiveness.[77] First, along with the list of team competencies described earlier in this chapter, members of successful virtual teams require the ability to communicate easily through technology, strong self-leadership skills to motivate and guide their behaviour without peers or bosses nearby, and higher emotional intelligence so they can decipher the feelings of teammates from email and other limited communication media. Second, studies have found that leaders typically impose technology on virtual teams rather than allow them to adopt technology that suits their needs at a particular time. The best situation occurs where virtual teams have a toolkit of communication vehicles (email, virtual white boards, video conferencing, etc.), which gain and lose importance over different parts of the project.

The final recommendation is that virtual team members should meet face-to-face fairly early in the team development process. This idea may seem contradictory to the entire notion of virtual teams, but so far, no technology has replaced face-to-face interaction for high-level bonding and mutual understanding. For instance, when IBM Canada formed a virtual team to build an electronic customer-access system for Shell Canada, employees from both firms began with an "all hands" face-to-face gathering to assist the team development process. The two firms also made a rule that the dispersed team members should have face-to-face contact at least once every six weeks throughout the project. Without this, "after about five or six weeks we found some of that communication would start to break down," says Sharon Hartung, the IBM co-manager for the project.[78]

TEAM DECISION MAKING

Self-directed teams, virtual teams, and practically all other groups are expected to make decisions. Under certain conditions, teams are more effective than individuals at identifying problems, choosing alternatives, and evaluating their decisions. To leverage these benefits, however, we first need to understand the constraints on effective team decision making. Then, we look at specific team structures that try to overcome these constraints.

LO10

CONSTRAINTS ON TEAM DECISION MAKING

Anyone who has spent enough time in the workplace can reel off several ways in which teams stumble in decision making. The four most common problems are time constraints, evaluation apprehension, pressure to conform, and groupthink.

Time Constraints   There's a saying that "committees keep minutes and waste hours." This reflects the fact that teams take longer than individuals to make decisions.[79] Unlike individuals, teams require extra time to organize, coordinate, and maintain relationships. The larger the group, the more time is required to make a decision. Team members need time to learn about each other and build rapport. They need to manage an imperfect communication process so that there is sufficient understanding of each other's ideas. They also need to coordinate roles and rules of order within the decision process.

Another time-related constraint found in most team structures is that only one person can speak at a time.[80] This problem, known as **production blocking**, undermines idea generation in several ways. First, team members need to listen in on the conversation to find an opportune time to speak up, and this monitoring makes it difficult for them to concentrate on their own ideas. Second, ideas are fleeting, so the longer they wait to speak up, the more likely these flickering ideas will die out. Third, team members might remember their fleeting thoughts by concentrating on them, but this causes them to pay less attention to the conversation. By ignoring what others are saying, team members miss other potentially good ideas as well as the opportunity to convey their ideas to others in the group.

production blocking
A time constraint in team decision making due to the procedural requirement that only one person may speak at a time.

Evaluation Apprehension   Individuals are reluctant to mention ideas that seem silly because they believe (often correctly) that other team members are silently evaluating them.[81] This **evaluation apprehension** is based on the individual's desire to create a favourable self-presentation and need to protect self-esteem. It is most common in meetings attended by people with different levels of status or expertise, or when members formally evaluate each other's performance throughout the year (as in 360-degree feedback). Creative ideas often sound bizarre or illogical when first presented, so evaluation apprehension tends to discourage employees from mentioning them in front of co-workers.

evaluation apprehension
Occurs when individuals are reluctant to mention ideas that seem silly because they believe (often correctly) that other team members are silently evaluating them.

Pressure to Conform   Team cohesion leads employees to conform to the team's norms. This control keeps the group organized around common goals, but it may also cause team members to suppress their dissenting opinions, particularly when a strong team norm is related to the issue. When someone does state a point of view that violates the majority opinion, other members might punish the violator or try to persuade him or her that the opinion is incorrect. Conformity can also be subtle. To some extent, we depend on the opinions that others hold to validate our own views. If co-workers don't agree with us, then we begin to question our own opinions even without overt peer pressure.

groupthink
The tendency of highly cohesive groups to value consensus at the price of decision quality.

(A) Groupthink   **Groupthink** is the tendency of highly cohesive groups to value consensus at the price of decision quality.[82] Groupthink goes beyond the problem of conformity by focusing on how decisions go awry when team members try to maintain harmony. This desire for harmony exists as a group norm and is most apparent when team members have a strong social identity with the group. Along with a desire for harmony, group-think supposedly occurs when the team is isolated from outsiders, the team leader is opinionated (rather than impartial), the team is under stress due to an external threat, the team has experienced recent failures or other decision-making problems, and the team lacks clear guidance from corporate policies or procedures.

The term "groupthink" is now part of everyday language, so much so that some experts worry that it commonly refers to almost any problem in team decision making. Meanwhile, scholarly studies have found that the symptoms of groupthink do not cluster together as the concept assumes; some of these characteristics actually tend to improve rather than undermine decision making in some situations. Although many cases of groupthink have been documented, a recent study found that this evidence is illusory because observers retrospectively make sense of bad decisions by incorrectly perceiving evidence of groupthink.[83]

In spite of the problems with the concept of groupthink, some of its specific elements continue to be relevant because they explain specific problems with team decision making. One of these elements, conformity, was described above as a concern. Another important element is the team's overconfidence. Studies consistently report that highly confident teams have a false sense of invulnerability, which makes them less attentive in decision making than are moderately confident teams.[84]

LO11

TEAM STRUCTURES TO IMPROVE DECISION MAKING

There is plenty of research revealing problems with team decision making, but several solutions also emerge from these bad-news studies. Team members need to be confident in their decision making, but not so confident that they collectively feel invulnerable. This calls for team norms that encourage critical thinking as well as team membership with sufficient diversity. Checks and balances need to be in place to prevent one or two people from dominating the discussion. The team should also be large enough to possess the collective knowledge to resolve the problem, yet small enough that the team doesn't consume too much time or restrict individual input.

Team structures also help to minimize the problems described over the previous few pages. Four structures potentially improve team decision making in team settings: constructive conflict, brainstorming, electronic brainstorming, and nominal group technique.

(?) Constructive Conflict   A popular way to improve team decision making at Corning Inc. is to assign promising ideas to two-person teams, who spend up to four months analyzing the feasibility of their assigned idea. The unique feature about this process is that the team is deliberately designed so that one person is from marketing, while the other has technical expertise. This oil-and-water combination sometimes ruffles feathers, but it seems to generate better ideas and evaluations. "We find great constructive conflict this way," says Deborah Mills, who leads Corning's early-stage marketing team.[85]

**constructive conflict
(also known as *task or cognitive conflict*)**
Occurs when people focus their discussion on the issue while maintaining respectfulness for people having other points of view.

Constructive conflict (also known as *task or cognitive conflict*) occurs when people focus their discussion on the issue while maintaining respectfulness for people having other points of view. This conflict is called "constructive" because different viewpoints are encouraged so that ideas and recommendations can be clarified, redesigned, and tested for logical soundness. The main advantage of this debate is that it presents different points of view, which encourages everyone to re-examine their assumptions and logic. The main challenge with constructive conflict is that healthy debate too often slides into personal attacks, which may explain why the evidence of constructive conflict on team decision making is inconsistent.[86] We will explore this issue further in Chapter 11, along with specific strategies to minimize the emotional effects of conflict while maintaining constructive debate.

Brainstorming

brainstorming
A freewheeling, face-to-face meeting where team members aren't allowed to criticize, but are encouraged to speak freely, generate as many ideas as possible, and build on the ideas of others.

Brainstorming tries to leverage the creative potential of teams by establishing four simple rules: (1) speak freely—describe even the craziest ideas; (2) don't criticize others or their ideas; (3) provide as many ideas as possible—the quality of ideas increases with the quantity of ideas; and (4) build on the ideas that others have presented. These rules are supposed to encourage divergent thinking while minimizing evaluation apprehension and other team dynamics problems. Lab studies using university students concluded many years ago that brainstorming isn't so effective, largely because production blocking and evaluation apprehension still interfere with team dynamics.[88]

However, brainstorming may be more beneficial than the earlier studies indicated.[89] The earlier lab studies measured the number of ideas generated, whereas recent investigations within companies using brainstorming indicate that this team structure results in more *creative* ideas, which is the main reason why companies use brainstorming. Also, evaluation apprehension is less of a problem in high-performing teams that embrace a learning orientation culture than for students brainstorming in lab experiments. Another overlooked advantage of brainstorming is that participants interact and participate directly, thereby increasing decision acceptance and team cohesion. Finally, brainstorming sessions often spread enthusiasm, which tends to generate more creativity. Overall, while brainstorming might not always be the best team structure, it seems to be more valuable than some of the earlier research studies indicated.

Electronic Brainstorming

electronic brainstorming
A recent form of brainstorming that relies on networked computers to submit and share creative ideas.

Electronic brainstorming is a recent form of brainstorming that relies on networked computers to submit and share creative ideas. After receiving the question or issue, participants enter their ideas using special computer software. The ideas are distributed anonymously to other participants, who are encouraged to piggyback on those ideas. Team members eventually vote electronically on the ideas presented. Face-to-face discussion usually follows. Electronic brainstorming can be quite effective at generating creative ideas with minimal production blocking, evaluation apprehension, or conformity problems.[90] Despite these numerous advantages, electronic brainstorming seems to be too structured and technology-bound for some executives. Some leaders may also feel threatened by the honesty of statements generated through this process and by their limited ability to control the discussion.

Nominal Group Technique

nominal group technique
A variation of traditional brainstorming that tries to combine the benefits of team decision making without the problems mentioned earlier.

Nominal group technique is a variation of traditional brainstorming that tries to combine the benefits of team decision making without the problems mentioned earlier.[91] The method is called nominal because participants form a group in name only during two of its three stages. After the problem is described, team members silently and independently write down as many solutions as they can. In the second stage, participants describe their solutions to the other team members, usually in a round-robin format. As with brainstorming, there is no criticism or debate, although members are encouraged to ask for clarification of the ideas presented. In the third stage, participants silently and independently rank order or vote on each proposed solution. Nominal group technique tends to generate a higher number and better quality of ideas compared with traditional interacting and possibly brainstorming groups.[92] Due to its high degree of structure, nominal group technique usually maintains a high task orientation and relatively low potential for conflict within the team. However, production blocking and evaluation apprehension still occur to some extent.

CHAPTER SUMMARY

Teams are groups of two or more people who interact and influence each other, are mutually accountable for achieving common goals associated with organizational objectives, and perceive themselves as a social entity within an organization. All teams are groups, because they consist of people with a unifying relationship; not all groups are teams, because some groups do not exist to serve organizational objectives.

People join informal groups (and are motivated to be on formal teams) for four reasons: (1) people have an innate drive to bond, (2) group membership is an inherent ingredient in a person's self-image, (3) some personal goals are accomplished better in groups, and (4) individuals are comforted in stressful situations by the mere presence of other people. Teams have become popular because they tend to make better decisions, support the knowledge management process, and provide superior customer service. People also tend to be more motivated working in teams. However, teams are not always as effective as individuals working alone. Process losses and social loafing are two particular concerns that drag down team performance.

Team effectiveness includes the team's ability to achieve its objectives, fulfill the needs of its members, and maintain its survival. The model of team effectiveness considers the team and organizational environment, team design, and team processes. Three team design elements are task characteristics, team size, and team composition. Teams tend to be better suited for complex work and where tasks among employees have high interdependence. Teams should be large enough to perform the work, yet small enough for efficient coordination and meaningful involvement. Effective teams are composed of people with the competencies and motivation to perform tasks in a team environment. Team member diversity has advantages and disadvantages for team performance.

Teams develop through the stages of forming, storming, norming, performing, and eventually adjourning. Within these stages are two distinct team development processes: membership and team competence. Team development can be accelerated through team building—any formal activity intended to improve the development and functioning of a work team. Teams develop norms to regulate and guide member behaviour. These norms may be influenced by initial experiences, critical events, and the values and experiences that team members bring to the group. Team cohesion—the degree of attraction people feel toward the team and their motivation to remain members—increases with member similarity, smaller team size, higher degree of interaction, somewhat difficult entry, team success, and external challenges. Cohesion increases team performance when the team's norms are congruent with organizational goals. Trust is a psychological state comprising the intention to accept vulnerability based on positive expectations of the intent or behaviour of another person. People trust others based on three foundations: calculus, knowledge, and identification.

Self-directed teams (SDTs) complete an entire piece of work requiring several interdependent tasks, and they have substantial autonomy over the execution of their tasks. SDTs operate best when they are responsible for an entire work process, when they have sufficient autonomy to organize and coordinate their work, and when the technology supports coordination and communication among team members and increases job enrichment.

Members of virtual teams operate across space, time, and organizational boundaries and are linked through information technologies to achieve organizational tasks. Virtual teams are more effective when their members have certain competencies (communicating through technology, self-leadership, and higher emotional intelligence), where the team has the freedom to choose the preferred communication channels, and where virtual team members meet face-to-face fairly early in the team development process.

Team decisions are impeded by time constraints, evaluation apprehension, conformity to peer pressure, and groupthink (specifically overconfidence). Four structures potentially improve decision making in team settings: constructive conflict, brainstorming, electronic brainstorming, and nominal group technique.

KEY TERMS

brainstorming, p. 203
Brooks's law, p. 187
constructive conflict (task conflict or cognitive conflict), p. 202
electronic brainstorming, p. 203
evaluation apprehension, p. 201
groupthink, p. 202

nominal group technique, p. 203
norms, p. 194
process losses, p. 186
production blocking, p. 201
role, p. 193
self-directed teams (SDTs), p. 198
social loafing, p. 187

task interdependence, p. 188
team building, p. 193
team cohesion, p. 195
teams, p. 184
trust, p. 197
virtual teams, p. 200

CRITICAL THINKING QUESTIONS

1. Informal groups exist in almost every form of social organization. What types of informal groups exist in your classroom? Why are students motivated to belong to these informal groups?

2. The late management guru Peter Drucker said: "The now-fashionable team in which everybody works with everybody on everything from the beginning rapidly is becoming a disappointment." Discuss three problems associated with teams.

3. You have been put in charge of a cross-functional task force that will develop enhanced Internet banking services for retail customers. The team includes representatives from marketing, information services, customer service, and accounting, all of whom will move to the same location at headquarters for three months. Describe the behaviours you might observe during each stage of the team's development.

4. You have just been transferred from the Regina office to the Saskatoon office of your company, a national sales organization of electrical products for developers and contractors. In Regina, team members regularly called customers after a sale to ask whether the products arrived on time and whether they are satisfied. But when you moved to the Saskatoon office, no one seemed to make these follow-up calls. A recently hired co-worker explained that other co-workers discouraged her from making those calls. Later, another co-worker suggested that your follow-up calls were making everyone else look lazy. Give three possible reasons why the norms in Saskatoon might be different from those in the Regina office, even though the customers, products, sales commissions, and other characteristics of the workplace are almost identical.

5. You have been assigned to a class project with five other students, none of whom you have met before. To what extent would team cohesion improve your team's performance on this project? What actions would you recommend to build team cohesion among student team members in this situation?

6. Suppose that you were put in charge of a virtual team where each member is located in different cities around the country or region. What tactics could you use to build and maintain team trust, as well as minimize the decline in trust that often occurs in teams?

7. You are responsible for convening a major event in which senior officials from several provincial governments will try to come to agreement on environmental issues. It is well known that some officials posture so they appear superior, whereas others are highly motivated to solve the environmental problems that cross adjacent provinces. What team decision-making problems are likely to be apparent in this government forum, and what actions can you take to minimize these problems?

8. Truro Technologies wants to use brainstorming with its employees and customers to identify new uses for its technology. Advise Truro's president about the potential benefits of brainstorming, as well as its potential limitations.

www.mcgrawhill.ca/olc/mcshane

CASE STUDY 8.1

The Shipping Industry Accounting Team

For the past five years, I have been working at McKay, Sanderson, and Smith Associates, a mid-sized accounting firm in Halifax that specializes in commercial accounting and audits. My particular speciality is accounting practices for shipping companies, ranging from small fishing fleets to a couple of the big firms with ships on the St. Lawrence Seaway.

About 18 months ago, McKay, Sanderson, and Smith Associates became part of a large merger involving two other accounting firms across Canada. These firms have offices in Montreal, Ottawa, Toronto, Calgary, and Vancouver. Although the other two accounting firms were much larger than McKay, all three firms agreed to avoid centralizing the business around one office in Toronto. Instead, the new firm—called Goldberg, Choo, and McKay Associates—would rely on teams across the country to "leverage the synergies of our collective knowledge" (an often-cited statement from the managing partner soon after the merger).

The effect of the merger affected me a year ago when my boss (a senior partner and vice-president of the merger firm) announced that I would be working more closely with three people from the other two firms to become the firm's new shipping industry accounting team. The other "team members" were Rochelle in Montreal, Thomas in Toronto, and Brad in Vancouver. I had met Rochelle briefly at a meeting in Montreal during the merger, but have never met Thomas or Brad, although knew that they were shipping accounting professionals at the other firms.

Initially, the shipping "team" activities involved emailing each other about new contracts and prospective clients. Later, we were asked to submit joint monthly reports on accounting statements and issues. Normally, I submitted my own monthly reports, which summarize activities involving my own clients. Coordinating the monthly report with three other people took much more time, particularly since different accounting documentation procedures across the three firms were still being resolved. It took numerous emails and a few telephone calls to work out a reasonable monthly report style.

During this aggravating process, it became apparent—to me at least—that this "teams" business was costing me more time than it was worth. Moreover, Brad in Vancouver didn't have a clue as to how to communicate with the rest of us. He rarely replied to emails. Instead, he often used the telephone voice mail system, which resulted in lots of telephone tag. Brad arrives at work at 9 a.m. in Vancouver (and is often late!), which is early afternoon in Halifax. I typically have a flexible work schedule from 7:30 a.m. to 3:30 p.m., so I can chauffeur my kids after school to sports and music lessons. So Brad and I have a window of less than three hours to share information.

The biggest nuisance with the shipping specialist accounting team started two weeks ago when the firm asked the four of us to develop a new strategy for attracting more shipping firm business. This new strategic plan is a messy business. Somehow, we have to share our thoughts on various approaches, agree on a new plan, and write a unified submission to the managing partner. Already, the project is taking most of my time just writing and responding to emails, and talking in conference calls (which none of us did much before the team formed).

Thomas and Rochelle have already had two or three "misunderstandings" via email about their different perspectives on delicate matters in the strategic plan. The worst of these disagreements required a conference call with all of us to resolve. Except for the most basic matters, it seems that we can't understand each other, let alone agree on key issues. I have come to the conclusion that I would never want Brad to work in my Halifax office (thank goodness, he's on the other side of the country). While Rochelle and I seem to agree on most points, the overall team can't form a common vision or strategy. I don't know how Rochelle, Thomas, or Brad feel, but I would be quite happy to work somewhere that did not require any of these long-distance team headaches.

Discussion Questions

1. What type of team was formed here? Was it necessary, in your opinion?

2. Use the team effectiveness model and related information in this chapter to identify the strengths and weaknesses of this team's environment, design, and processes.

3. Assuming that these four people must continue to work as a team, recommend ways to improve the team's effectiveness.

Copyright © 2004. Steven L. McShane.

www.mcgrawhill.ca/olc/mcshane

CASE STUDY 8.2

The Philanthropic Team-Builder

To kick-off the post-merger integration of Molson and Coors breweries, the top dozen executives from both companies wanted to accelerate their team development. But rather than the usual team building in the woods or with a challenging in-house activity, the Molson Coors leaders spent a full day helping build a house for Habitat for Humanity. "We quickly got past the idea of a ropes course or golf outing," recalls Samuel D. Walker, Molson Coors' chief legal officer. "We really wanted something where we would give back to one of the communities where we do business." According to Walker, the volunteering experience exceeded everyone's expectations. "We had to unload this truck full of cement roof tiles. We actually had to figure out how to have kind of a bucket line, handing these very heavy tiles from one person to the next. That's the ultimate team-building exercise."

The Molson Coors executive team's experience with team building through volunteerism has since spread throughout the company. In particular, Molson Canada's operations have changed how they support communities and how they engage employees in team building to support that process. "Traditionally, you have someone in charge of philanthropy [who made decisions about] donating money," says Scott Ewart, chief of legal and public affairs at Molson Canada. "We wanted our customers and employees to feel that we were doing the right thing." A survey of customers and staff revealed that Molson's should be donating more to help young adults to develop active lifestyles, new skills, and healthy communities.

Along with aligning corporate donations more closely to stakeholder preferences, Molson now actively encourages employee involvement in these philanthropic projects through an in-house volunteer program. Rather than meeting on the golf course or a corporate retreat, employees participate in team-building exercises such as painting youth hostels and refurbishing cabins at children's cancer camps in Quebec and Alberta.

This movement toward team building through volunteerism has not only helped Molson Coors employees to form more functional teams; it has also had a positive effect on morale. The percentage of employees who said they were 'extremely satisfied' with Molson as a place to work increased from 62 percent to 78 percent in the year after the volunteering initiative was introduced. "The results were swift and positive," Ewart recalls. This initiative has also made the company a more attractive employer of choice. "To attract and retain the right people today, you simply can't say we're going to train you or we're going to give you a good salary, or whatever," explains Molson Coors CEO Kevin Boyce. "They are looking for more. They are looking for a company they can feel good about."

Discussion Questions

1. What type of team building best describes these volunteering activities?

2. Explain how the corporate social responsibility element of volunteering contributes to team building.

3. Along with team building, in what other ways do these volunteering activities improve organizations?

Sources: Martha C. White, "Doing Good on Company Time," *New York Times*, May 8, 2007; Hollie Shaw, "Doing the Right Thing," *National Post*, June 15, 2007; Michael Kane, "Companies Find New Ways to Celebrate," *Vancouver Sun*, December 1, 2007.

www.mcgrawhill.ca/olc/mcshane

 **TEAM EXERCISE 8.3**

Team Tower Power

Purpose   This exercise is designed to help you understand team roles, team development, and other issues in the development and maintenance of effective teams.

Materials   The instructor will provide enough Lego pieces or similar materials for each team to complete the assigned task. All teams should have an identical (or very similar) amount and type of pieces. The instructor will need a measuring tape and stopwatch. Students may use writing materials during the design stage (Stage 2 below). The instructor will distribute a "Team Objectives Sheet" and "Tower Specifications Effectiveness Sheet" to all teams.

Instructions   • *Step 1*: The instructor will divide the class into teams. Depending on class size and space available, teams may have between four to seven members, but all should be approximately equal size.

• *Step 2*: Each team is given 20 minutes to design a tower that uses only the materials provided, is freestanding, and provides an optimal return on investment. Team members may wish to draw their tower on paper or flip chart to assist the tower's design. Teams are free to practise building their tower during this stage. Preferably, teams are assigned to their own rooms so the design can be created privately. During this stage, each team will complete the Team Objectives Sheet distributed by the instructor. This sheet requires the Tower Specifications Effectiveness Sheet, also distributed by the instructor.

• *Step 3*: Each team will show the instructor that it has completed its Team Objectives Sheet. Then, with all teams in the same room, the instructor will announce the start of the construction phase. The time elapsed for construction will be closely monitored and the instructor will occasionally call out time elapsed (particularly if there is no clock in the room).

• *Step 4*: Each team will advise the instructor as soon as it has completed its tower. The team will write down the time elapsed that the instructor has determined. It may be asked to assist the instructor by counting the number of blocks used and height of the tower. This information is also written on the Team Objectives Sheet. Then, the team calculates its profit.

• *Step 5*: After presenting the results, the class will discuss the team dynamics elements that contribute to team effectiveness. Team members will discuss their strategy, division of labour (team roles), expertise within the team, and other elements of team dynamics.

Source: Several published and online sources describe variations of this exercise, but there is no known origin to this activity.

www.mcgrawhill.ca/olc/mcshane

SELF-ASSESSMENT EXERCISE 8.4

What Team Roles Do You Prefer?

Purpose   This self-assessment is designed to help you identify your preferred roles in meetings and similar team activities.

Instructions   Read each of the statements below and circle the response that you believe best reflects your position regarding each statement. Then use the scoring key in Appendix B to calculate your results for each team role. This exercise is completed alone so students assess themselves honestly without concerns of social comparison. However, class discussion will focus on the roles that people assume in team settings. This scale only assesses a few team roles.

Team Roles Preferences Scale					
Circle the number that best reflects your position regarding each of these statements.	Does Not Describe Me at All	Does Not Describe Me Very Well	Describes Me Somewhat	Describes Me Well	Describes Me Very Well
1. I usually take responsibility for getting the team to agree on what the meeting should accomplish.	1	2	3	4	5
2. I tend to summarize to other team members what the team has accomplished so far.	1	2	3	4	5
3. I'm usually the person who helps other team members overcome their disagreements.	1	2	3	4	5
4. I try to ensure that everyone gets heard on issues.	1	2	3	4	5
5. I'm usually the person who helps the team determine how to organize the discussion.	1	2	3	4	5
6. I praise other team members for their ideas more than do others in the meetings.	1	2	3	4	5
7. People tend to rely on me to keep track of what has been said in meetings.	1	2	3	4	5
8. The team typically counts on me to prevent debates from getting out of hand.	1	2	3	4	5
9. I tend to say things that make the group feel optimistic about its accomplishments.	1	2	3	4	5
10. Team members usually count on me to give everyone a chance to speak.	1	2	3	4	5
11. In most meetings, I am less likely than others to "put down" the ideas of teammates.	1	2	3	4	5
12. I actively help teammates to resolve their differences in meetings.	1	2	3	4	5
13. I actively encourage quiet team members to describe their ideas on each issue.	1	2	3	4	5
14. People tend to rely on me to clarify the purpose of the meeting.	1	2	3	4	5
15. I like to be the person who takes notes or minutes of the meeting.	1	2	3	4	5

Go to the Online Learning Centre at www.mcgrawhill.ca/olc/mcshane to complete the following interactive self-assessments.

SELF-ASSESSMENT EXERCISE 8.5

Are You a Team Player?

How much do you like working in teams? Some of us avoid teams wherever possible; others tolerate team work; still others thrive in team environments. This exercise is designed to help you estimate the extent to which you are positively predisposed to work in teams. Read each statement in this scale and indicate the extent to which you agree or disagree with that statement. This exercise is completed alone so students assess themselves honestly without concerns of social comparison. However, class discussion will focus on the characteristics of individuals who are more or less compatible with working in teams.

SELF-ASSESSMENT EXERCISE 8.6

How Trusting Are You?

Trust is a psychological state comprising the intention to accept vulnerability based on positive expectations of the intent or behaviour of another person. While trust varies from one situation to the next, some people have a higher or lower propensity to trust. In other words, some people are highly trusting of others, even when first meeting them, whereas others have difficulty trusting anyone, even over a long time. This self-assessment provides an estimate of your propensity to trust. Indicate your preferred response to each statement, being honest with yourself for each item. This self-assessment is completed alone, although class discussion will focus on the meaning of propensity to trust, why it varies from one person to the next, and how it affects teamwork.

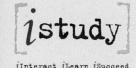

iStudy—Available 24/7 with instant feedback so you can study when you want, how you want, and where you want. Visit www.istudyob.ca to register—take practice quizzes, run interactive scenarios, practice concepts, and much more. Also visit the Student Online Learning Centre for additional study tools.

CHAPTER 9

Communicating in Teams and Organizations

Imagine IBM chief executive Samuel Palmisano speaking to a throng of 7,000 employees with Beijing's famous Forbidden City towering behind him. Does this scenario sound a bit too fantastic to be real? Well, Palmisano *was* recently in Beijing speaking face-to-face to about 2,000 staff in an auditorium, but he also communicated part of his talk to another 5,000 IBMers globally through his avatar (graphic character representing a person) in front of a virtual version of the Forbidden City on the Second Life website.

Second Life, an online world where individuals can cruise around various islands, is becoming one of IBM's venues for sharing information. Along with Palmisano's virtual town hall meeting, IBMers have held hundreds of virtual meetings at a large boardroom that IBM created on its Second Life islands. Canadian labour unions have also discovered the communication value of Second Life. Several union leaders recently picketed IBM's islands in support of the company's Italian workers, who had their annual performance bonus forfeited. Canadian Auto Workers national communications representative Angelo DiCaro was particularly impressed by how Second Life can quickly and economically bring people together from around the world. "Being able to do it in this alternate reality, it was fascinating," he says.

Although Second Life accommodates audio and video communication, most interaction around IBM's virtual islands—whether formal meetings or union protests relies on written text messages. Unlike instant messaging text chats, however, the avatars add a personal touch that improves the communication experience. "There's a sense that you're actually at the meeting," explains Chuck Hamilton, director of IBM's centre for advanced learning. "If I stop moving my mouse, eventually my avatar will slump forward (fall asleep), and the other people in the room will say, 'Hey, Chuck, are you still there?'"[1]

Standing in front of Beijing's Forbidden City, IBM chief executive Sam Palmisano communicates through his Second Life avatar to several thousand employees worldwide. *Courtesy of International Business Machines Corporation. Unauthorized use not permitted.*

Information technologies have transformed how we communicate in organizations, yet we may still be at the beginning of this revolution. Wire cablegrams and telephones introduced a century ago are giving way to email, instant messaging, Weblogs, podcasting, and virtual reality social networking. Each of these inventions creates fascinating changes in how people communicate with each other in the workplace, as well as new opportunities to improve organizational effectiveness and employee well-being.

communication
The process by which information is transmitted and *understood* between two or more people.

Communication refers to the process by which information is transmitted and *understood* between two or more people. We emphasize the word 'understood' because transmitting the sender's intended meaning is the essence of good communication. This chapter begins by discussing the importance of effective communication and outlining a model of the communication process. Next, we identify types of communication channels, including computer-mediated communication, followed by factors to consider when choosing a communication medium. This chapter then identifies barriers to effective communication. This is followed by an overview of ways to communicate in organizational hierarchies and the pervasive organizational grapevine.

THE IMPORTANCE OF COMMUNICATION

LO1

Effective communication is vital to all organizations, so much so that no company could exist without it. The reason? In Chapter 1 we defined organizations as groups of people who work interdependently toward some purpose. People can only work interdependently through communication. Communication is the vehicle through which people clarify their expectations and coordinate work, which allows them to achieve organizational objectives more efficiently and effectively. Chester Barnard, a telecommunications CEO and a respected pioneer in organizational behaviour theory, stated this point back in 1938: "An organization is born when there are individuals who are able to communicate."[2]

Communication is also an important instrument for organizational learning and decision making. Chapter 1 explained that one perspective of organizational effectiveness is organizational learning, which refers to the firm's capacity to acquire, share, use, and store valuable knowledge. These processes depend on various forms of communication. Effective communication minimizes "silos of knowledge," a situation in which knowledge is cloistered rather than distributed to those who require the information to make better decisions and perform their jobs more effectively.[3] IBM improves organizational learning through various informal and computer-mediated communication media. For instance, when Vancouver-based IBM consultant Currie Boyl, wanted expertise for a Canadian client, he tapped into the company's "Small Blue" search engine, which quickly identifies people with various forms of expertise throughout the company.[4]

Communication also aids employee well-being.[5] Employees cope better when co-workers communicate information that helps to manage the situation, such as describing proper work procedures or how to remain on good terms with the boss. However, the communication process itself is critical to personal well-being because it fulfills the drive to bond and validates the individual's worth and identity. Social interaction is so important that people who experience social isolation are much more susceptible to colds, cardiovascular disease, and other physical and mental illnesses.[6] Communicating with others is partially the means through which individuals define themselves, that is, maintain their social identity. This occurs even in the virtual world of Second Life. "In Second Life we gather and mingle before the meeting, and when it finishes, some people stop and talk again," explains Ian Hughes, an IBM employee who attends these virtual meetings as a pudgy avatar with spiky green hair. "We start to form social networks and the kinds of bonds you make in real life."[7]

A MODEL OF COMMUNICATION

The communication model presented in Exhibit 9.1 provides a useful "conduit" metaphor for thinking about the communication process.[8] According to this model, com-

LO2

EXHIBIT **9.1**   The communication process model

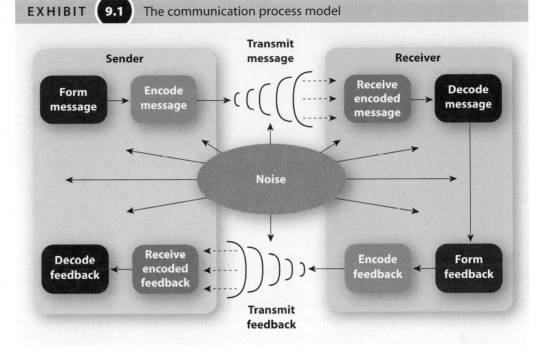

munication flows through channels between the sender and receiver. The sender forms a message and encodes it into words, gestures, voice intonations, and other symbols or signs. Next, the encoded message is transmitted to the intended receiver through one or more communication channels (media). The receiver senses the incoming message and decodes it into something meaningful. Ideally, the decoded meaning is what the sender had intended.

In most situations, the sender looks for evidence that the other person received and understood the transmitted message. This feedback may be a formal acknowledgment, such as "Yes, I know what you mean," or indirect evidence from the receiver's subsequent actions. Notice that feedback repeats the communication process. Intended feedback is encoded, transmitted, received, and decoded from the receiver to the sender of the original message. This model recognizes that communication is not a free-flowing conduit. Rather, the transmission of meaning from one person to another is hampered by *noise*—the psychological, social, and structural barriers that distort and obscure the sender's intended message. If any part of the communication process is distorted or broken, the sender and receiver will not have a common understanding of the message.

INFLUENCES ON EFFECTIVE ENCODING AND DECODING

The communication model suggests that communication effectiveness depends on the ability of sender and receiver to efficiently and accurately encode and decode information. Experts have identified four factors that influence the efficiency and effectiveness of this process.[9] One factor is whether both parties have similar "codebooks"—dictionaries of symbols, language, gestures, idioms, and other tools used to convey information. With similar codebooks, the communication participants are able to encode and decode more accurately because they both have the same or similar meaning. Having similar codebooks also improves communication efficiency because there is less need for redundancy (such as saying the same thing in different ways) and less need for confirmation feedback ("So, you are saying that…?").

A second factor influencing the encoding-decoding process is the extent to which both parties have similar mental models about the context of the information. Mental models are internal representations of the external world that allow us to visualize elements of a setting and relationships among those elements (see Chapter 3). When sender and receiver have common mental models, they share a common understanding of the context relating to the information, so less communication is necessary. For instance, two NASA astronauts familiar with the space shuttle would be able to communicate information about a specific piece of equipment in the shuttle much more quickly and accurately than if an astronaut tried to communicate the same information to someone who was unfamiliar with the intricacies of the space shuttle.

A third factor is familiarity with the message topic. As people become more familiar with the subject matter, they develop more efficient or colourful scripts to describe the subject. This is similar to the effect of job training or sports practice. The more experience and practice gained at communicating a subject, the more one learns how to effectively transmit that information to others. Finally, the effectiveness of the encoding-decoding process depends on the sender and receiver's proficiency with the communication channel. If you learn that a co-worker doesn't work well with email, you might try to improve communication effectiveness by telephoning that person more often instead of sending emails.[10]

COMMUNICATION CHANNELS

A critical part of the communication model is the channel or medium through which information is transmitted. There are two main types of channels: verbal and nonverbal. Verbal communication includes any spoken or written means of transmitting meaning through words. Nonverbal communication, which we discuss later, is any part of communication that does not use words.

VERBAL COMMUNICATION

Different forms of verbal communication should be used in different situations. Face-to-face interaction is usually better than written methods for transmitting emotions and persuading the receiver. This is because nonverbal cues accompany oral communications, such as voice intonations and use of silence. Furthermore, face-to-face interaction provides the sender with immediate feedback from the receiver and the opportunity to adjust the emotional tone of the message accordingly. Written communication is more appropriate for recording and presenting technical details. This is because ideas are easier to follow when written down than when communicated orally. Traditionally, written communication has been slow to develop and transmit, but electronic mail, Weblogs, and other computer-mediated communication channels have significantly improved written communication efficiency.

COMPUTER-MEDIATED COMMUNICATION

Two decades ago, computer-mediated communication was a novel development. Today, it seems that many of us rely more on this medium than the old-fashioned options. By far, the most widely used of these is electronic mail (email), which has revolutionized the way we communicate in organizational settings. Email has become the medium of choice in most workplaces because messages are quickly written, edited, and transmitted. Information can be appended and conveyed to many people with a simple click of a mouse. Email is asynchronous (messages are sent and received at different times), so there is no need to coordinate a communication session. Email software has also become an efficient filing cabinet.[11] Employees increasingly rely on email to filter, store, sort, and search messages and attachments far more quickly than is possible with paper-based memos.

Email tends to be the preferred medium for coordinating work (e.g., confirming deadlines with a co-worker's schedule) and for sending well-defined information for decision making. It often increases the volume of communication and significantly alters the flow of that information within groups and throughout the organization.[12]

Specifically, it reduces some face-to-face and telephone communication but increases communication with people further up the hierarchy. Some social and organizational status differences still exist with email,[13] but they are somewhat less apparent than in face-to-face communication. By hiding age, race, and other features, email reduces stereotype biases. However, it also tends to increase reliance on stereotypes when we are already aware of the other person's personal characteristics.[14]

LO3

Problems with Email   In spite of the wonders of email, anyone who has used this communication medium knows that it has its limitations. Here are the top four complaints:

1. *Poor medium for communicating emotions*. People rely on facial expressions and other nonverbal cues to interpret the emotional meaning of words; email lacks this parallel communication channel. Senders try to clarify the emotional tone of their messages by using expressive language ("Wonderful to hear from you!"), highlighting phrases in boldface or quotation marks, and inserting graphic faces (called emoticons or "smileys") representing the desired emotion. These actions help, but do not replace the full complexity of real facial expressions, voice intonation, and hand movements.[15]

2. *Reduces politeness and respect*. Email messages are often less diplomatic than written letters because individuals can post email messages before their emotions subside. Also, email has low social presence (which makes it more impersonal), so people are more likely to write things that would never be said verbally in face-to-face conversation. These "flaming" emails are aggravated by misinterpretation of the emotional tone of the message. Fortunately, research has found that flaming decreases as teams move to later stages of development and when explicit norms and rules of communication are established.[16]

3. *Poor medium for ambiguous, complex, and novel situations*. Email requires a moderate level of mutual understanding between the sender and receiver. Coordinating through email in ambiguous, complex, and novel situations, on the other hand, requires communication channels that quickly send a larger volume of information and offer equally rapid feedback. "I've stopped using email volleys where you just keep going back and forth and back and forth and nothing is going in the right

Admiral Reduces the Flame on Emails

Executives at Admiral Insurance are concerned that the electronic communication medium is making staff at the Welsh company less polite to each other and to customers. "It is much easier to have a row by email than it is face to face, and people are often ruder as a result," says Admiral spokesperson Justin Beddows. "Orders can be issued out and people can be quite abrupt because they feel protected by the distance the email provides. But once an abusive email is sent out, there is no getting it back and it can cause a rift that cannot be resolved easily." Along with reminding employees of email's limitations as a communication medium, Admiral executives occasionally try to wean staff from email dependence. "We hold 'no email days' to encourage people to get off their backsides and visit people face to face," says Beddows.[17] *Courtesy of Admiral Insurance*

direction," says a manager at the Irving Oil refinery in Saint John, NB. By talking face-to-face or by telephone in these complex situations, the manager has discovered that he is "coming up with much better outcomes and a much better understanding of an issue."[18] In other words, when the issue gets messy, stop emailing and start talking, preferably face-to-face.

4. *Contributes to information overload.* Email contributes to information overload, which we'll discuss in more detail later in this chapter.[19] An estimated 22.3 trillion emails are now transmitted annually, up from just 1.1 trillion in 1998. According to one survey, professionals spend an average of two hours per day processing email. The email glut occurs because messages can be easily created and copied to many people without much effort. The number of email messages will probably decrease as people become more familiar with it, but to date email volume continues to rise. To reduce email overload and encourage more face-to-face interaction, Toronto-based Loblaw Companies Limited has introduced "no-email Wednesdays." Staff were initially skeptical about the plan, but many now enjoy Wednesdays more than most other days. "It just sort of unburdens you. You look forward to Wednesdays," says Liz Margles, Loblaws' vice-president of communications.[20]

Social Networking Communication   The opening story to this chapter described how IBM is experimenting with innovative forms of computer-mediated communication. In fact, while email likely remains the most popular medium, IBMers have flocked to computer-mediated technologies that support *social networking.*[21] Social networking sites such as Facebook and LinkedIn are rapidly becoming part of popular culture. University students rate Facebook as the second most "in" thing (iPods were number one); Canadians top the list of Facebook users. These technologies allow people to form communities around friendships, common interests, expertise, and other themes, resulting in closer interaction in the communication experience. Indeed, some social networking technologies—online forums and instant messaging are two examples—gain value and potential when more people are clustered and linked to the technology.[22]

Yet just as corporate leaders stumbled their way through the first stage of the Internet revolution (Web 1.0) over the past two decades, many are fighting rather than leveraging the potential of this second stage (called Web 2.0). For example, the City of Toronto banned access to Facebook and other social networking sites after it discovered that two percent of employees were making excessive use of the company's Internet resources (including visits to Facebook).[23]

Meanwhile, some firms are being proactive by experimenting with ways to transform social networking technologies into a form of communication with employees and other stakeholders. Scott Baldwin, who counts himself as one of the early members of Facebook (he signed up soon after Facebook opened in 2004), sees the potential of social networking websites. The manager of Web services at North Shore Credit Union (NSCU) in North Vancouver created a Facebook page to promote the credit union's products and engage the community. This site has had some success for those purposes, but Baldwin discovered that its biggest fans are current and former employees. In other words, employees may be ready for social networking as a source of communication and information sharing.[24]

As you might have guessed from the opening vignette, IBM is an active adopter of social networking technologies. In addition to using Second Life for employee and customer interaction, the company created Beehive, a corporate version of Facebook, where employees can post their profiles, photos, interests, and comments about work or other aspects of their lives. Beehive (and other Facebook look-alikes) create an opportunity for employees to bond with co-workers as well as discover sources of diverse knowledge throughout the company. IBM has also been at the forefront of **wikis**— collaborative Web spaces in which anyone in a group can write, edit, or remove material from the website. IBM introduced wikis just a few years years ago, but already has 20,000 of them, involving 100,000 employees. Wikis are discussed in more detail later in this chapter.

wikis
Collaborative Web spaces in which anyone in a group can write, edit, or remove material from the website.

NONVERBAL COMMUNICATION

Nonverbal communication includes facial gestures, voice intonation, physical distance, and even silence. This communication channel is necessary where noise or physical distance prevents effective verbal exchanges and the need for immediate feedback precludes written communication. But even in quiet face-to-face meetings, most information is communicated nonverbally. Rather like a parallel conversation, nonverbal cues signal subtle information to both parties, such as reinforcing their interest in the verbal conversation or demonstrating their relative status in the relationship.[25]

Nonverbal communication differs from verbal (i.e., written and spoken) communication in a couple of ways. First, it is less rule-bound than verbal communication. We receive plenty of formal training on how to understand spoken words, but very little on understanding the nonverbal signals that accompany those words. Consequently, nonverbal cues are generally more ambiguous and susceptible to misinterpretation. At the same time, many facial expressions (such as smiling) are hardwired and universal, thereby providing the only reliable means of communicating across cultures.

The other difference between verbal and nonverbal communication is that the former is typically conscious, whereas most nonverbal communication is automatic and nonconscious. We normally plan the words we say or write, but we rarely plan every blink, smile, or other gesture during a conversation. Indeed, as we just mentioned, many of these facial expressions communicate the same meaning across cultures because they are hardwired nonconscious or preconscious responses to human emotions.[26] For example, pleasant emotions cause the brain centre to widen the mouth, whereas negative emotions produce constricted facial expressions (squinting eyes, pursed lips, etc.).

Emotional Contagion   One of the most fascinating effects of emotions on nonverbal communication is the phenomenon called **emotional contagion,** which is the automatic process of 'catching' or sharing another person's emotions by mimicking that person's facial expressions and other nonverbal behaviour. Consider what happens when you see a co-worker accidentally bang his or her head against a filing cabinet. Chances are, you wince and put your hand on your own head as if you had hit the cabinet. Similarly, while listening to someone describe a positive event, you tend to smile and exhibit other emotional displays of happiness. While some of our nonverbal communication is planned, emotional contagion represents nonconscious behaviour—we automatically mimic and synchronize our nonverbal behaviours with other people.[27]

>
> **emotional contagion**
> The automatic and nonconscious tendency to mimic and synchronize one's own nonverbal behaviours with those of other people.

Emotional contagion serves three purposes. First, mimicry provides continuous feedback, communicating that we understand and empathize with the sender. To consider the significance of this, imagine employees remaining expressionless after watching a co-worker bang his or her head! The lack of parallel behaviour conveys a lack of understanding or caring. Second, mimicking the nonverbal behaviours of other people seems to be a way of receiving emotional meaning from those people. If a co-worker is angry with a client, your tendency to frown and show anger while listening helps you share that emotion more fully. In other words, we receive meaning by expressing the sender's emotions as well as by listening to the sender's words.

The third function of emotional contagion is to fulfill the drive to bond that was described in Chapter 5. Social solidarity is built out of each member's awareness of a collective sentiment. Through nonverbal expressions of emotional contagion, people see others share the same emotions that they feel. This strengthens team cohesiveness by providing evidence of member similarity.[28]

CHOOSING THE BEST COMMUNICATION MEDIUM

Which communication channel is most appropriate in a particular situation? Two important sets of factors to consider are (a) social acceptance and (b) media richness. Let's look first at social acceptance—how well the communication medium is approved and supported by the organization, teams, and individuals.[29] One factor in social acceptance is the organization's and team's norms regarding the use of specific communication channels. Norms partly explain why telephone conversations are more common among staff in some firms, whereas email or instant messaging is the medium of choice in other organizations. Some companies expect employees to meet face-to-face, whereas meetings and similar conversations are rare events elsewhere. Norms also shape the use of communication media for people in specific positions. For instance, front-line employees are more likely to write an email and less likely to telephone or personally visit the company's CEO.

A second social acceptance factor is individual preferences for specific communication channels.[30] You may have discovered that a co-worker prefers email rather than voice mail, or wants to meet in person more than you think is necessary. These preferences are due to personality traits as well as previous experience and reinforcement with particular channels. A third social acceptance factor to consider is the symbolic meaning of a channel. Some communication channels are viewed as impersonal whereas others are more personal; some are considered professional whereas others are casual; some are "cool" whereas others are not. To illustrate the importance of a channel's symbolic meaning, consider stories about corporate leaders who use emails or cell-phone text messages to tell employees that they are fired or laid off. These actions make front-page headlines because email and text messages are considered inappropriate (too impersonal) for transmission of that particular information.[31]

MEDIA RICHNESS

media richness
The medium's data-carrying capacity, that is, the volume and variety of information that can be transmitted during a specific time.

Along with social acceptance, people select communication media based on their **media richness**. Media richness refers to the medium's data-carrying capacity—the volume and variety of information that can be transmitted during a specific time.[32] Exhibit 9.2 illustrates various communication channels arranged in a hierarchy of richness, with

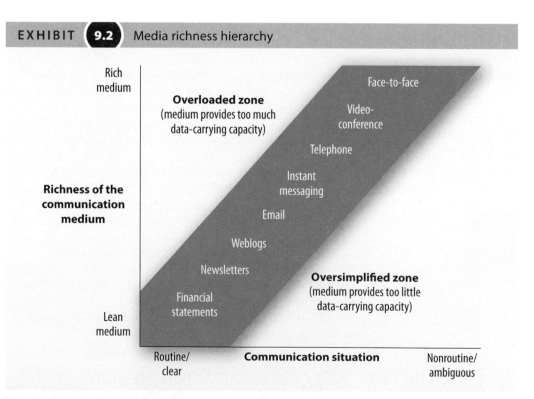

EXHIBIT 9.2   Media richness hierarchy

Source: Based on R. Lengel and R. Daft, "The Selection of Communication Media as an Executive Skill," *Academy of Management Executive* 2, no. 3 (August, 1988), p. 226; R. L. Daft and R. H. Lengel, "Information Richness: A New Approach to Managerial Behaviour and Organization Design," *Research in Organizational Behaviour*, 1984, p. 199.

face-to-face interaction at the top and lean data-only reports at the bottom. A communication channel has high richness when it is able to convey multiple cues (such as both verbal and nonverbal information), allows timely feedback from receiver to sender, allows the sender to customize the message to the receiver, and makes use of complex symbols (such as words and phrases with multiple meanings). Face-to-face communication is at the top of media richness because it allows us to communicate both verbally and nonverbally at the same time, to receive feedback almost immediately from the receiver, to quickly adjust our message and style, and to use complex language such as metaphors and idioms (e.g., "spilling the beans").

According to media richness theory, rich media are better than lean media when the communication situation is nonroutine and ambiguous. In nonroutine situations (such as an unexpected and unusual emergency), the sender and receiver have little common experience, so they need to transmit a large volume of information with immediate feedback. Lean media work well in routine situations because the sender and receiver have common expectations through shared mental models. Ambiguous situations also require rich media because the parties must share large amounts of information with immediate feedback to resolve multiple and conflicting interpretations of their observations and experiences.[34] Choosing the wrong medium reduces communication effectiveness. When the situation is routine or clear, using a rich medium—such as holding a special meeting—would seem like a waste of time. On the other hand, if a unique and ambiguous issue is handled through email or another lean medium, then issues take longer to resolve and misunderstandings are more likely to occur.

Evaluating Media Richness Theory   Research generally supports the relevance of media richness for traditional channels (face-to-face, written memos, etc.). However, the evidence is mixed when computer-mediated communication channels are studied. Three factors seem to override or blur the medium's richness:

1. *The ability to multi-communicate.* Unlike most traditional communication channels, particularly those with high media richness, emerging technologies allow employees to multi-communicate—engage in two or more communication events at the same time.[35] For example, you might be instant messaging with a client while simultaneously listening to a discussion at a large meeting. Similarly, people routinely scan Web pages while carrying on telephone conversations. The reduced sensory demand for most forms of computer-mediated communication allow employees to exchange information through multiple channels at the same time, possibly resulting in as

much information processing as occurs through one traditional channel with high media richness (e.g., a face-to-face one-on-one conversation).

2. *More varied proficiency levels.* Some experts point out that the richness of a computer-mediated communication channel is not fixed; some people can "push" more information through the channel because of their higher proficiency. Experienced BlackBerry users, for instance, can whip through messages in a flash, whereas new users struggle to type email notes and organize incoming messages. In contrast, there is less variation in the ability to communicate through traditional channels (e.g., casual conversation, memos) because most of us develop good levels of proficiency throughout life and possibly through hardwired evolutionary development.[36]

3. *Social distractions of rich channels.* Channels with higher media richness tend to have higher social interaction. But the social dynamics of rich media tend to distract people from efficiently processing the message content.[37] Instead, the sender and receiver focus on their relative status, and engage in activities that maintain their self-worth and status. This social distraction reduces efficiency at transmitting and receiving information, which sometimes makes rich media less effective than leaner media that have less social interaction.

COMMUNICATION BARRIERS (NOISE)

LO6   In spite of the best intentions of sender and receiver to communicate, several barriers (called "noise" earlier in Exhibit 9.1) inhibit the effective exchange of information. As author George Bernard Shaw wrote, "The greatest problem with communication is the illusion that it has been accomplished." One barrier is the imperfect perceptual process of both sender and receiver. As receivers, we don't listen as well as senders assume, and our needs and expectations influence what signals get noticed and ignored. We aren't any better as senders, either. Some studies suggest that we have difficulty stepping out of our own perspectives and stepping into the perspectives of others, so we overestimate how well other people understand the message we are communicating.[38]

Even if the perceptual process is well tuned, messages sometimes get filtered on their way up or down the corporate hierarchy. Filtering may involve deleting or delaying negative information or using less harsh words so the message sounds more favourable.[39] Filtering is most common where the organization rewards employees who communicate mainly positive information and among employees with strong career mobility aspirations.

Language issues can be huge sources of communication noise because sender and receiver might not have the same "codebook." They might not speak the same language, or might have different meanings for particular words and phrases. For example, a French executive might call an event a "catastrophe" as a casual exaggeration, whereas someone in Germany usually interprets this word literally as an earth-shaking event.[40] Jargon, which includes specialized words and phrases for specific occupations or groups, is designed to improve communication efficiency. However, it has the opposite effect when senders transmit jargon to people who do not possess the jargon codebook.

Even when both people speak the same language and codebook, they might interpret words and phrases differently. For example, do you know what someone means when they ask "Can you close the door?" Some people might assume the sender is telling you to shut the door. But the question might be asking whether you are physically able to shut the door, whether the door is designed such that it can be shut, or whether shutting the door is permitted.[41]

The ambiguity of language isn't always dysfunctional noise.[42] Corporate leaders sometimes rely on metaphors and other vague language to describe ill-defined or complex ideas. Ambiguity is also used to avoid conveying or creating undesirable emotions. For example, one study reported that people rely on more ambiguous language when communicating with people who have different values and beliefs. In these situations, ambiguity minimizes the risk of conflict.

INFORMATION OVERLOAD

Start with a daily avalanche of email, then add in voice mail, cellphone text messages, PDF file downloads, Web pages, hard copy documents, instant messages, blogs, wikis, and other sources of incoming information. Together, you have created a perfect recipe for **information overload**.[43] Information overload occurs when the volume of information received exceeds the person's capacity to get through it. Employees have a certain *information processing capacity*—the amount of information that they are able to process in a fixed unit of time. At the same time, jobs have a varying *information load*— the amount of information to be processed per unit of time. Information overload creates noise in the communication system because information gets overlooked or misinterpreted when people can't process it fast enough. The result is poorer quality decisions as well as higher workplace stress.[44]

information overload Occurs when the volume of information received exceeds the person's capacity to get through it.

Information overload problems can be minimized by increasing our information processing capacity, reducing the job's information load, or through a combination of both. Studies suggest that employees often increase their information processing capacity by temporarily reading faster, scanning through documents more efficiently, and removing distractions that slow information processing speed. Time management also increases information processing capacity. When information overload is temporary, information processing capacity can increase by working longer hours. Information load can be reduced by buffering, omitting, and summarizing. Buffering involves having incoming communication filtered, usually by an assistant. Omitting occurs when we decide to overlook messages, such as using software rules to redirect emails from distribution lists to folders that we never look at. An example of summarizing would be where we read executive summaries rather than the full report.

CROSS-CULTURAL AND GENDER COMMUNICATION

As globalization and cultural diversity increase, you can be sure that cross-cultural communication problems will also increase.[45] Language is the most obvious cross-cultural communications challenge. Words are easily misunderstood in verbal communication, either because the receiver has a limited vocabulary or the sender's accent distorts the usual sound of some words. Voice intonation is another cross-cultural communication barrier. How loudly, deeply, and quickly people speak vary across cultures, and these voice intonations send secondary messages that have different meaning in different cultures.

Communication includes silence, but its use and meaning varies from one culture to another.[46] One study estimated that silence and pauses represented 30 percent of conversation time between Japanese doctors and patients, compared to only 8 percent of the time between North American doctors and patients. In Japan, silence symbolizes respect and indicates that the listener is thoughtfully contemplating what has just been said.[47] Similarly, Japanese people usually stop talking when they are interrupted, whereas talking over the other person's speech is more common in some other countries, such as Brazil. Indeed, Brazilians are more likely to view interruptions as evidence that the other person is involved in the conversation!

NONVERBAL DIFFERENCES

Nonverbal communication represents another potential area for misunderstanding across cultures. Many nonconscious or involuntary nonverbal cues (such as smiling) have the same meaning around the world, but deliberate gestures often have different interpretations. For example, most of us shake our head from side to side to say "No," but a variation of head shaking means "I understand" to many people in India. Filipinos raise their eyebrows to give an affirmative answer, yet Arabs interpret this expression (along with clicking one's tongue) as a negative response. Most Canadians are taught to maintain eye contact with the speaker to show interest and respect, whereas some First

Nations groups and Australian Aborigines, among others, learn at an early age to show respect by looking down when an older or more senior person is talking to them.[49]

GENDER DIFFERENCES IN COMMUNICATION

LO7

Men and women have similar communication practices, but there are subtle distinctions that can occasionally lead to misunderstanding and conflict. One distinction is that men are more likely than women to view conversations as negotiations of relative status and power. They assert their power by directly giving advice to others (e.g., "You should do the following") and using combative language. There is also evidence that men dominate the talk time in conversations with women, as well as interrupt more and adjust their speaking style less than do women.[50]

Men engage in more "report talk," in which the primary function of the conversation is impersonal and efficient information exchange. Women also do report talk, particularly when conversing with men, but conversations among women have a higher incidence of relationship building through "rapport talk." Women make more use of indirect requests ("Do you think you should…?"), apologize more often, and seek advice from others more quickly than do men. Finally, research fairly consistently indicates that women are more sensitive than men to nonverbal cues in face-to-face meetings.[51] Together, these conditions can create communication conflicts. Women who describe problems get frustrated that men offer advice rather than rapport, whereas men become frustrated because they can't understand why women don't appreciate their advice.

IMPROVING INTERPERSONAL COMMUNICATION

LO8

Effective interpersonal communication depends on the sender's ability to get the message across and the receiver's performance as an active listener. In this section, we outline these two essential features of effective interpersonal communication.

GETTING YOUR MESSAGE ACROSS

This chapter began with the statement that effective communication occurs when the other person receives and understands the message. To accomplish this difficult task, the sender must learn to empathize with the receiver, repeat the message, choose an appropriate time for the conversation, and be descriptive rather than evaluative.

- *Empathize*—Recall from earlier chapters that empathy is a person's ability to understand and be sensitive to the feelings, thoughts, and situation of others. In conversations, this involves putting yourself in the receiver's shoes when encoding the message. For instance, be sensitive to words that may be ambiguous or trigger the wrong emotional response.

- *Repeat the message*—Rephrase the key points a couple of times. The saying "Tell them what you're going to tell them; tell them; then tell them what you've told them" reflects this need for redundancy.

- *Use timing effectively*—Your message competes with other messages and noise, so find a time when the receiver is less likely to be distracted by these other matters.

- *Be descriptive*—Focus on the problem, not the person, if you have negative information to convey. People stop listening when the information attacks their self-esteem. Also, suggest things the listener can do to improve, rather than point to him or her as a problem.

ACTIVE LISTENING

"Nature gave people two ears but only one tongue, which is a gentle hint that they should listen more than they talk."[52] To follow this advice, we need to recognize that listening is a process of actively sensing the sender's signals, evaluating them accurately, and responding appropriately. These three components of listening—sensing, evaluating, and responding—reflect the listener's side of the communication model described at the beginning of this chapter. Listeners receive the sender's signals, decode them as intended, and provide appropriate and timely feedback to the sender (see Exhibit 9.3). Active listeners constantly cycle through sensing, evaluating, and responding during the conversation and engage in various activities to improve these processes.[53]

Sensing   Sensing is the process of receiving signals from the sender and paying attention to them. Active listeners improve sensing in three ways. First, they postpone

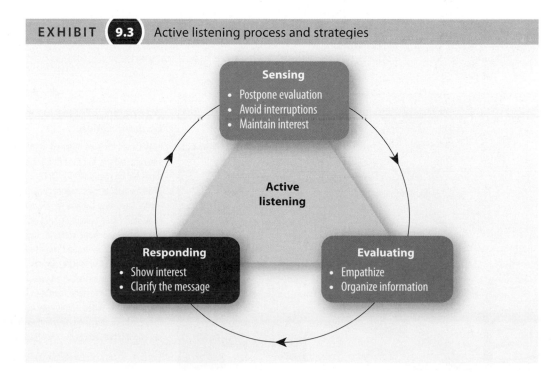

EXHIBIT 9.3   Active listening process and strategies

Sensing
- Postpone evaluation
- Avoid interruptions
- Maintain interest

Active listening

Responding
- Show interest
- Clarify the message

Evaluating
- Empathize
- Organize information

evaluation by not forming an opinion until the speaker has finished. Second, they avoid interrupting the speaker's conversation. Third, they remain motivated to listen to the speaker.

Evaluating   This component of listening includes understanding the message meaning, evaluating the message, and remembering the message. To improve their evaluation of the conversation, active listeners empathize with the speaker—they try to understand and be sensitive to the speaker's feelings, thoughts, and situation. Evaluation also improves by organizing the speaker's ideas during the communication episode.

Responding   Responding, the third component of listening, is feedback to the sender, which motivates and directs the speaker's communication. Active listeners accomplish this by maintaining sufficient eye contact and sending back channel signals (e.g., "I see"), both of which show interest. They also respond by clarifying the message—rephrasing the speaker's ideas at appropriate breaks ("So you're saying that . . . ?").

IMPROVING COMMUNICATION THROUGHOUT THE HIERARCHY

LO9

So far, we have focused on "micro-level" issues in the communication process, namely, the dynamics of sending and receiving information between two employees or a small cluster of people. But in this era where knowledge is competitive advantage, corporate leaders also need to maintain an open flow of communication up, down, and across the organization. In this section, we discuss three communication strategies: workspace design, blogs/wikis/e-zines, and direct communication with top management

WORKSPACE DESIGN

The ability and motivation to communicate is partially influenced by the physical space in which employees work.[54] The location and design of hallways, offices, cubicles, and communal areas (cafeterias, elevators) all shape whom we speak to as well as the frequency of that communication. Pixar Animation Studios has leveraged the power of workspaces by constructing a campus in Emeryville, Calif. that clusters teams and encourages more casual communication among team members. At the same time, the campus encourages happenstance interactions with people on other teams. Pixar executives call this the "bathroom effect," because team members must leave their isolated pods to fetch their mail, have lunch, or visit the restroom.[55]

Waving the Red Flag in Open-Office Communication

eBay Canada has an open-concept office to encourage communication and camaraderie, but the noise can be distracting. "Our employees sometimes bid on items on eBay and when it gets down to the final seconds of an auction, tension mounts and the bidder often shouts out in excitement," says eBay Canada spokeswoman, Alexandra Brown. Fortunately, eBay staff found a solution that seems to work. When employees need quiet time they drape colourful bandanas across the top of their desks, on desk lamps, or around their heads, which communicates to others "QUIET PLEASE!" To reduce some of the distractions and stress associated with open-space offices, everyone also turns off the audio alert signal for incoming email messages and uses wireless headsets rather than hands-free handsets. When employees need privacy to do undisturbed work, they can book and bring their laptops into meeting rooms that have intranet and Internet access.[56] © *National Post/Peter Redman*

A popular workspace strategy is to replace traditional offices with open space arrangements, where all employees (including management) work in the same open area. One recent convert to open space is design and innovation firm, CONTINUUM. "We do not have doors," explains a continuum executive. "It's structured that way to stimulate conversation and to allow people to work collaboratively. Anyone from the chief operating officer to our interns shares space and sits next to each other. You can stop in and have a conversation with anyone, anytime you want."[57] People do communicate more with fewer walls, but research also suggests that open-office design potentially increases employee stress due to noise, distractions, and loss of privacy.[58] The challenge is to balance privacy and noise reduction with opportunities for social interaction.

WIKIS, BLOGS, AND E-ZINES

For decades, employees have received official company news through hard copy newsletters and magazines. Many firms still use these communication devices, but most have supplemented or replaced them completely with Web-based or PDF format newsletters, called *e-zines*. E-zines can prepare and distribute company news quickly, but employees are increasingly skeptical of information that has been screened and packaged by management. In response, some adventurous firms are encouraging employees to write any news they see fit on their own online journals, called Weblogs or blogs. IBM is a pioneer in this area through BlogCentral, an inward-facing (i.e., for IBM employees' eyes only) blog-hosting service where several thousand employees blog about their own news of the week. A search engine helps staff find important information on any of the several thousand blogs.

Earlier in this chapter we introduced wikis as an emerging form of corporate social networking. Wikis are collaborative Web spaces in which anyone in a group can write, edit, or remove material from the website. Wikipedia, the popular online encyclopedia, is a massive public example of a wiki. Wikis hold considerable promise for organizational communication because they are democratic, collaborative social networking spaces that rapidly document new knowledge. IBM introduced wiki technology a few years ago in the form of WikiCentral, which is now used by more than one-third of its employees. One of IBM's many wiki projects involved accumulating ideas and issues from several employees about a new patent policy within IBM. "Wikis are good for project management, for to-do's, status reports, creating an issues log—you're always up to date," explains Brad Kasell, an IBM manager for emerging technologies. "There's no collating reports from everyone at the end of the week for an update." The accuracy of wikis depends on the quality of participants, but Kasell says that errors are quickly identified by IBM's online community.[59]

DIRECT COMMUNICATION WITH TOP MANAGEMENT

"The best fertilizer in any field is that of the farmer's footsteps!" This old Chinese saying means that farms are most successful when the farmers spend time in the fields directly observing the crop's development. In an organizational context, this means that to fully understand the issues, senior executives need to get out of the executive suite and meet directly with employees at all levels and on their turf. Nearly 40 years ago, people at Hewlett-Packard coined a phrase for this communication strategy: **management by walking around (MBWA)**. A few corporate leaders, such as Brian Scudamore, founder and CEO of Vancouver-based 1-800-Got-Junk?, take this practice further by getting rid of their own office altogether. "I don't have my own office, and I very often move around to different departments for a day at a time," says Scudamore.[60]

Along with MBWA, executives communicate more directly with employees through "town hall meetings." 1-800-Got-Junk? holds these sessions, where large groups of employees hear about company news directly from the key decision makers. At a typical 1-800-Got-Junk? town hall meeting, leaders report to all staff on developments in their departments, after which staff are encouraged to share their thoughts and ideas. Some

management by walking around (MBWA)
A communication practice in which executives get out of their offices and learn from others in the organization through face-to-face dialogue.

Kowloon Shangri-La's 'State of the Hotel' Meetings

Communicating with employees can be a challenge when the organization is a large hotel that operates around the clock. But these conditions haven't prevented senior management at Kowloon Shangri-La from holding "state of the hotel" meetings with all 700 staff twice each year. Two sessions are held—one in the morning, the other in the afternoon—so all employees at the Hong Kong hotel can attend without leaving the hotel short staffed. General manager Mark Heywood conducts no holds barred sessions in which employees are updated on the hotel's financial performance, upcoming events, and renovations. "It's a chance to communicate about the good, the bad and the ugly," says Heywood. "We don't just share good news and positive things." He also outlines his vision for the hotel and reinforces its "one team—one way" culture.[61] *Photo courtesy of Kowloon Shangri-La Hotel*

executives also conduct employee roundtable forums to hear opinions from a small representation of staff about various issues. All of these direct communication strategies potentially minimize filtering because executives listen directly to employees. They also help executives acquire a deeper meaning and quicker understanding of internal organizational problems. A third benefit of direct communication is that employees might have more empathy for decisions made further up the corporate hierarchy.

COMMUNICATING THROUGH THE GRAPEVINE

grapevine
An unstructured and informal network founded on social relationships rather than organizational charts or job descriptions.

No matter how much corporate leaders try to communicate through e-zines, blogs, wikis, MBWA, and other means, employees will still rely on the oldest communication channel: the corporate **grapevine**. The grapevine is an unstructured and informal network founded on social relationships rather than organizational charts or job descriptions. What do employees think about the grapevine? Surveys of employees in two U.S. firms—one in Florida, the other in California—found that almost all employees use the grapevine, but very few of them prefer this source of information. The Californian survey also reported that only one-third of employees believe grapevine information is credible. In other words, employees turn to the grapevine when they have few other options.[62]

GRAPEVINE CHARACTERISTICS

Research conducted several decades ago reported that the grapevine transmits information very rapidly in all directions throughout the organization. The typical pattern is a cluster chain, whereby a few people actively transmit rumours to many others. The grapevine works through informal social networks, so it is more active where employees have similar backgrounds and are able to communicate easily. Many rumours seem to have at least a kernel of truth, possibly because they are transmitted through media-rich communication channels (e.g., face to face) and employees are motivated to communicate effectively. Nevertheless, the grapevine distorts information by deleting fine details and exaggerating key points of the story.[63]

Some of these characteristics might still be true, but other features of the grapevine would have changed due to the dramatic effects of information technologies in the workplace. Email, social networking sites, and blogs have replaced the traditional water cooler as sources of gossip. For example, several sites on Facebook are devoted to how employees and customers feel about Tim Hortons Inc. If something happens at the popular Oakville, Ontario restaurant chain, more people find out faster than ever before from these websites. In addition to altering the speed and network of corporate grapevines, information technologies have expanded these networks around the globe, not just around the next cubicle.

LO10   GRAPEVINE BENEFITS AND LIMITATIONS

Should the grapevine be encouraged, tolerated, or quashed? The difficulty in answering this question is that the grapevine has both benefits and limitations.[64] One benefit, as was mentioned earlier, is that employees rely on the grapevine when information is not available through formal channels. It is also the main conduit through which organizational stories and other symbols of the organization's culture are communicated. A third benefit of the grapevine is that this social interaction relieves anxiety. This explains why rumour mills are most active during times of uncertainty.[65] Finally, the grapevine is associated with the drive to bond. Being a recipient of gossip is a sign of inclusion, according to evolutionary psychologists. Trying to quash the grapevine is, in some respects, an attempt to undermine the natural human drive for social interaction.[66]

While the grapevine offers these benefits, it is not a preferred communication medium. Grapevine information is sometimes so distorted that it escalates rather than reduces employee anxiety. Furthermore, employees develop more negative attitudes toward the organization when management is slower than the grapevine in communicating information. What should corporate leaders do with the grapevine? The best advice seems to be to listen to the grapevine as a signal of employee anxiety, then correct the cause of this anxiety. Some companies also listen to the grapevine and step in to correct blatant errors and fabrications. Most important, corporate leaders need to view the grapevine as a competitor, and meet this challenge by directly informing employees of news before it spreads throughout the grapevine.

CHAPTER SUMMARY

Communication refers to the process by which information is transmitted and *understood* between two or more people. Communication supports work coordination, organizational learning, decision making, and employee well-being. The communication process involves forming, encoding, and transmitting the intended message to a receiver, who then decodes the message and provides feedback to the sender. Effective communication occurs when the sender's thoughts are transmitted to and understood by the intended receiver. Four ways to improve this process is for both sender and receiver to have common codebooks of symbols, to share common mental models, to be familiar with the message topic, and to be proficient with the communication channel.

The two main types of communication channels are verbal and nonverbal. Various forms of computer-mediated communication are widely used in organizations, with email the most popular. Although efficient and a useful filing cabinet, email is relatively poor at communicating emotions; it tends to reduce politeness and respect; it is an inefficient medium for communicating in ambiguous, complex, and novel situations; and it contributes to information overload. Social networking communication, such as Facebook-like websites, wikis, and virtual reality platforms, are also gaining popularity as forms of communica-

tion. Nonverbal communication includes facial gestures, voice intonation, physical distance, and even silence. Unlike verbal communication, nonverbal communication is less rule-bound and is mostly automatic and unconscious.

The most appropriate communication medium partly depends on social acceptance factors, including organization and team norms, individual preferences, for specific communication channels, and the symbolic meaning of a channel. A communication medium should also be chosen for its data-carrying capacity (media richness). Nonroutine and ambiguous situations require rich media. However, we also need to recognize that lean media allow people to multi-communicate, that the capacity of computer-mediated communication is varied due to the proficiency of individual users, and that social distractions can reduce the efficient processing of information in high media richness channels.

Several barriers create noise in the communication process. People misinterpret messages because of perceptual biases. Some information is filtered out as it gets passed up the hierarchy. Jargon and ambiguous language are barriers when the sender and receiver have different interpretations of the words and symbols used. People also screen out or misinterpret messages due to information overload. These problems are often amplified in cross-cultural settings because of language barriers and differences in meaning of nonverbal cues. There are also some communication differences between men and women, such as the tendency for men to exert status and engage in report talk in conversations, whereas women use more rapport talk and are more sensitive than are men to nonverbal cues.

To get a message across, the sender must learn to empathize with the receiver, repeat the message, choose an appropriate time for the conversation, and be descriptive rather than evaluative. Listening includes sensing, evaluating, and responding. Active listeners support these processes by postponing evaluation, avoiding interruptions, maintaining interest, empathizing, organizing information, showing interest, and clarifying the message.

Some companies try to encourage communication through workspace design, as well as through wikis, blogs, and e-zines, Some executives also meet directly with employees, either through management by walking around (MBWA) or other arrangements, to facilitate communication across the organization.

In any organization, employees rely on the grapevine, particularly during times of uncertainty. The grapevine is an unstructured and informal network founded on social relationships rather than organizational charts or job descriptions. Although early research identified several unique features of the grapevine, some of these features may be changing as the Internet plays an increasing role in grapevine communication.

KEY TERMS

communication, p. 212
emotional contagion, p. 217
grapevine, p. 226

information overload, p. 221
management by walking around (MBWA), p. 225

media richness, p. 218
wikis, p. 216

CRITICAL THINKING QUESTIONS

1. You have been hired as a consultant to improve communication between engineering and marketing staff in a large high-technology company. Use the communication model and the four ways to improve that process to devise strategies to improve communication effectiveness among employees between these two work units.

2. A company in a country that is just entering the information age intends to introduce electronic mail for office staff at its three buildings located throughout the city. Describe two benefits as well as two potential problems that employees will likely experience with this medium.

3. Instant messaging has become increasingly popular in organizations over the past few years. What are the advantages and disadvantages of this communication medium?

4. Senior management at a consumer goods company wants you to investigate the feasibility of using a virtual reality platform (such as Second Life) for monthly

online meetings involving its three-dozen sales managers located in several cities and countries. Use the social acceptance and media richness factors described in this chapter to identify information you need to consider when conducting this evaluation.

5. Under what conditions, if any, do you think it is appropriate to use email to notify an employee that he or she has been laid off or fired? Why is email usually considered an inappropriate channel to convey this information?

6. Explain why men and women are sometimes frustrated with each other's communication behaviours.

7. In your opinion, has the introduction of email and other information technologies increased or decreased the amount of information flowing through the corporate grapevine? Explain your answer.

8. Wikis are collaborative websites where anyone in the group can post, edit, or delete any information. Where might this communication technology be most useful in organizations?

CASE STUDY 9.1

Communicating with the Millenials

The Millenials (Generation Y, born between 1980 and 1995) have arrived in the workplace, and they are bringing new ways to communicate. Surveys report that this generation lives by computer and cellphone communication. Three out of four GenYs use instant messaging; 15 percent of them are logged on to IM 24/7! Most GenYs either have a space on a social network site such as Facebook, or frequent these sites where they have friends. These digital natives also get most of their news from the Internet rather than from TV or newspapers.

"Employers are going to find this generation communicates differently. They IM (instant message), send text messages, and can't live without a cellphone," says Dave O'Brien, regional manager of Berbee, a company that helps businesses with their information technology needs. Frank Albi, president of Inacom, a technology and business consulting firm, agrees. "The way they (Millenials) exchange information is vastly different. It's all about IMs and text messages—nice and short."

Albi also notes that Millenials are much more active in multi-communicating. "You can be on the phone with someone and easily instant message someone who you see is online to answer a question or share an idea with," Albi says. However, managers also worry that too much of this multi-communication isn't work-related. "There's a fine line about what can be allowed at work and what can't," suggests Steve Hoeft, a recruiting manager at Time Warner Cable. "Instant messaging is very popular, but if it's affecting their work, that's when there's a problem."

Corporate leaders at BT, Britain's largest telecommunications company, are also aware that Millenials (and to some extent GenX employees) live in different communication channels from Baby Boomers. "Young people in BT communicate much more informally and in real-time," says Richard Dennison, BT's intranet and channel strategy manager. "They're not intimidated by hierarchy or status; to them BT is flat." Dennison adds that Generation Y employees want bite-size information, not long treatises.

Dennison also emphasizes that, more than previous generations, Millenials demand authentic communication, not marketing hype. "Corporate speak won't cut it anymore," Dennison warns. "First, people won't read it—if they ever did—and second, people won't believe it—if they ever did." Dennison also notices that if GenYs get corporate babble, they find ways to let the source know that it lacks authenticity. Remember, this is the generation that has always had a place to write comments after reading the original message.

From these observations, you might think that executive blogs are the answer to GenY communication needs. Not so, argues Dennison. "Force all our senior managers to blog? My experience is that the more senior a manager is, the less likely they'll be able to blog successfully." He adds that executives have too little time to nurture a blog, and they tend to have communication experts who want to meddle (thereby undermining the blog's authenticity).

So how can the company's top dogs communicate effectively with Millenial employees? At BT, the chief executive has held 90-minute online Web chats with BT staff every six weeks. This medium works well for young BT employees because the communication is in real time and authentic—the questions aren't screened and the CEO's answers aren't edited. "Thousands of people participate in these chats and it has helped to build up a significant amount of trust" in the CEO, says Dennison. These online Web chats also work well with BT executives because they represent a fixed chunk of time and provide direct contact with the concerns and issues facing employees throughout the hierarchy.

Discussion Questions

1. Take a poll of your class (at least, the GenX and GenY members). At school or work, how many regularly (e.g., daily or every few days) send or receive information (not entertainment) using (a) cellphone text messages, (b) email, (c) visiting/authoring social network sites (e.g., Facebook), (d) watching/creating online videos (e.g., YouTube), (e) instant messages (such as MSN), (f) reading/writing blogs?

2. Even within this generation, there are different preferences for communication media. After conducting the poll above, ask students who don't regularly use one or more of these methods why they don't like that particular communication medium. Ask those who very often use these sources to give their point of view.

3. Companies have been slow and reluctant to adopt social networking sites, online videos, and similar forms of communication. If you were a senior manager, how would you introduce these communication technologies in the workplace to share information and knowledge more effectively?

Sources: MaryBeth Matzek, "R U on 2 Gen Y?" *Marketplace*, September 4, 2007, p. 10; Richard Dennison, "Encouraging BT's Authentic Voice of Leadership," *Strategic Communication Management* 12, no. 2 (2008), p. 12.

CASE STUDY 9.2

The Trouble with Arthur

By Beth Gilbert, University of New Brunswick, St. John

Arthur is a talented, smart, and energetic student in the co-op program of a business faculty. He is involved in a variety of organizations, both on and off campus, and in many ways the co-op staff are proud to have him as one of their students. However, Arthur is constantly missing commitments, such as attendance at professional development seminars, classes, and networking sessions. Also, although he is positive and outgoing, he is somewhat aggressive and expects accommodations to be made for him and other students. Even some students are starting to get irritated with him. The proverbial "last straw" occurs when Arthur misses a job interview and the employer is very annoyed. Missing a job interview reflects badly on Arthur and on the entire program.

Numerous, previous efforts at influencing Arthur's behaviour by using traditional approaches such as discussion, reasoning, positive reinforcement, coercion, threats, etc. have not been successful. Although the director is furious with Arthur (as she has been so many times in the past), she forces herself to sit down, reflect on the situation, and develop a plan. The director has been teaching and conducting research in the areas of emotional intelligence and effective communications for several years, and considered herself to be reasonably skilled in these areas. However, after reflecting on her difficulties with Arthur, she realizes that she has not been applying the principles of these concepts to this situation. Because Arthur makes a contribution in many positive ways, the program does not want to lose him, but missing commitments cannot be tolerated any longer. The director of the co-op program asks Arthur to come to her office to discuss the situation. Arthur arrives at the director's office and in "true Arthur style" pounds aggressively on the door. The director decides that she had better apply the concepts that she had been researching. Clearly, the more traditional approaches have not been effective.

Discussion Questions

1. What are some possible reasons that the director of the co-op program had not used the principles of active listening and emotional intelligence, even though she had been doing research in the field and teaching about it to students and managers?

2. Why do you think that the more traditional approaches have not been working? Why do you think that Arthur has been behaving as he has?

3. Why doesn't the director simply expel Arthur from the program?

4. How might the situation be improved if active listening and emotional intelligence are applied appropriately? Specifically, what might the director do? Discuss fully. Do you think that the director is likely to change Arthur's behaviour? What are the risks?

TEAM EXERCISE 9.3

Analyzing the Blogosphere

Purpose This exercise is designed to help you understand the dynamics of corporate blogs as a way to communicate around organizations.

Instructions This activity is usually conducted in between classes as a homework assignment. The instructor will divide the class into teams (although this can also be conducted as individuals). Each team will identify a corporate blog (written by a company or government executive and aimed for customers, employees, or the wider community). The team will analyze content on the selected blog and answer the following questions for class (preferably with brief samples where applicable).

1. Who is the main intended audience of the selected blog?

2. To what extent do you think this blog attracts the interest of its intended audience? Explain.

3. What are the main topics in recent postings about this organization? Are they mostly good or bad news? Why?

 TEAM EXERCISE 9.4

Active Listening Exercise

Mary Gander, Winona State University

Purpose   This exercise is designed to help you understand the dynamics of active listening in conversations and to develop active listening skills.

Instructions   For each of the four vignettes presented here, student teams (or students working individually) will compose three statements that demonstrate active listening. Specifically, one statement will indicate that you show empathy for the situation; the second will ask for clarification and detail in a nonjudgmental way; and the third statement will provide nonevaluative feedback to the speaker. Here are details about each of these three types of responses:

> **Showing empathy: acknowledge feelings.** Sometimes it sounds like a speaker wants you to agree with him or her, but in reality the speaker mainly wants you to understand how he or she feels. "Acknowledging feelings" involves taking in the speaker's statements while looking at the "whole message" including body language, tone of voice, and level of arousal, and trying to determine what emotion the speaker is conveying. Then you let the speaker know that you realize what he or she is feeling by acknowledging it in a sentence.

> **Asking for clarification and detail while withholding your judgment and own opinions.** This conveys that you are trying to understand and not just trying to push your opinions onto the speaker. To formulate a relevant question in asking for more clarification, you will have to listen carefully to what the speaker says. Frame your question as someone trying to understand in more detail; often asking for a specific example is useful. This also helps the speaker evaluate his or her own opinions and perspective.

> **Providing non-evaluative feedback: feeding back the message you heard.** This will allow the speaker to determine if he or she conveyed the message to you and will help prevent troublesome miscommunication. It will also help the speaker become more aware of how he or she is coming across to another person (self-evaluation). Just think about what the speaker is conveying; paraphrase it in your own words, and say it back to the speaker (without judging the correctness or merit of what was said), asking him or her if that is what was meant.

After teams (or individual students) have prepared the three statements for each vignette, the instructor will ask them to present their statements and explain how these statements satisfy the active listening criteria.

www.mcgrawhill.ca/olc/mcshane

Vignette #1

A colleague stops by your desk and says, "I am tired of the lack of leadership around here. The boss is so wishy-washy, he can't get tough with some of the slackers around here. They just keep milking the company, living off the rest of us. Why doesn't management do something about these guys? And *you* are always so supportive of the boss; he's not as good as you make him out to be."

Develop three statements that respond to the speaker in this vignette by (a) showing empathy, (b) seeking clarification, and (c) providing nonevaluative feedback.

Vignette #2

Your co-worker stops by your cubicle; her voice and body language show stress, frustration, and even some fear. You know she has been working hard and has a strong need to get her work done on time and done well. You are trying to concentrate on some work and have had a number of interruptions already. She just abruptly interrupts you and says, "This project is turning out to be a mess. Why can't the other three people on my team quit fighting with each other?"

Develop three statements that respond to the speaker in this vignette by (a) showing empathy, (b) seeking clarification, and (c) providing nonevaluative feedback.

Vignette #3

One of your subordinates is working on an important project. He is an engineer who has good technical skills and knowledge and was selected for the project team because of that. He stops by your office and appears to be quite agitated: his voice is loud and strained, and his face has a look of bewilderment. He says, "I'm supposed to be working with four other people from four other departments on this new project, but they never listen to my ideas and seem to hardly know I'm at the meeting!"

Develop three statements that respond to the speaker in this vignette by (a) showing empathy, (b) seeking clarification, and (c) providing nonevaluative feedback.

Vignette #4

Your subordinate comes into your office in a state of agitation, asking if she can talk to you. She is polite and sits down. She seems calm and does not have an angry look on her face. However, she says, "It seems like you consistently make up lousy schedules; you are unfair and unrealistic in the kinds of assignments you give certain people, me included. Everyone else is so intimidated they don't complain, but I think you need to know that this isn't right and it's got to change."

Develop three statements that respond to the speaker in this vignette by (a) showing empathy, (b) seeking clarification, and (c) providing nonevaluative feedback.

www.mcgrawhill.ca/olc/mcshane

 TEAM EXERCISE 9.5

Cross-Cultural Communication Game

Purpose   This exercise is designed to develop and test your knowledge of cross-cultural differences in communication and etiquette.

Materials   The instructor will provide one set of question/answer cards to each pair of teams.

Instructions
- *Step 1*: The class is divided into an even number of teams. Ideally, each team would have three students. (Two- or four-student teams are possible if matched with an equal-sized team.) Each team is then paired with another team and the paired teams (team "A" and Team "B") are assigned a private space away from other matched teams.

- *Step 2*: The instructor will hand each pair of teams a stack of cards with the multiple choice questions face down. These cards have questions and answers about cross-cultural differences in communication and etiquette. No books or other aids are allowed.

- *Step 3*: The exercise begins with a member of Team A picking up one card from the top of the pile and asking the question on that card to members of Team B. The information given to Team B includes the question and all alternatives listed on the card. Team B has 30 seconds after the question and alternatives have been read to give an answer. Team B earns one point if the correct answer is given. If Team B's answer is incorrect, however, Team A earns that point. Correct answers to each question are indicated on the card and, of course, should not be revealed until the question is correctly answered or time is up. Whether or not Team B answers correctly, it picks up the next card on the pile and reads it to members of Team A. In other words, cards are read alternatively to each team. This procedure is repeated until all of the cards have been read or time has elapsed. The team receiving the most points wins.

Important note: The textbook provides very little information pertaining to the questions in this exercise. Rather, you must rely on past learning, logic, and luck to win.

www.mcgrawhill.ca/olc/mcshane

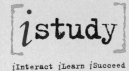

SELF-ASSESSMENT EXERCISE 9.6

Are You An Active Listener?

Purpose   This self-assessment is designed to help you determine your strengths and weaknesses on various dimensions of active listening.

Instructions   Think back to face-to-face conversations you have had with a co-worker or client in the office, hallway, factory floor, or other setting. Indicate the extent that each item below describes your behaviour during those conversations. Answer each item as truthfully as possible so that you get an accurate estimate of where your active listening skills need improvement. Then use the scoring key in Appendix B to calculate your results for each scale. This exercise is completed alone so students assess themselves honestly without concerns of social comparison. However, class discussion will focus on the important elements of active listening.

Active Listening Skills Inventory				
Circle the best response to the right that indicates the extent to which each statement describes you when listening to others.	Not at All	A Little	Somewhat	Very Much
1. I keep an open mind about the speaker's point of view until he or she has finished talking.	☐	☐	☐	☐
2. While listening, I mentally sort out the speaker's ideas in a way that makes sense to me.	☐	☐	☐	☐
3. I stop the speaker and give my opinion when I disagree with something he or she has said.	☐	☐	☐	☐
4. People can often tell when I'm not concentrating on what they are saying.	☐	☐	☐	☐
5. I don't evaluate what a person is saying until he or she has finished talking.	☐	☐	☐	☐
6. When someone takes a long time to present a simple idea, I let my mind wander to other things.	☐	☐	☐	☐
7. I jump into conversations to present my views rather than wait and risk forgetting what I wanted to say.	☐	☐	☐	☐
8. I nod my head and make other gestures to show I'm interested in the conversation.	☐	☐	☐	☐
9. I can usually keep focused on what people are saying to me even when they don't sound interesting.	☐	☐	☐	☐
10. Rather than organizing the speaker's ideas, I usually expect the person to summarize them for me.	☐	☐	☐	☐
11. I always say things like "I see" or "uh-huh" so people know that I'm really listening to them.	☐	☐	☐	☐
12. While listening, I concentrate on what is being said and regularly organize the information.	☐	☐	☐	☐
13. While the speaker is talking, I quickly determine whether I like or dislike his or her ideas.	☐	☐	☐	☐
14. I pay close attention to what people are saying even when they are explaining something I already know.	☐	☐	☐	☐
15. I don't give my opinion until I'm sure the other person has finished talking.	☐	☐	☐	☐

iStudy—Available 24/7 with instant feedback so you can study when you want, how you want, and where you want. Visit www.istudyob.ca to register—take practice quizzes, run interactive scenarios, practice concepts, and much more. Also visit the Student Online Learning Centre for additional study tools.

istudy

¡Interact ¡Learn ¡Succeed

www.mcgrawhill.ca/olc/mcshane

CHAPTER 10

Power and Influence
in the Workplace

LEARNING OBJECTIVES

After reading this chapter, you should be able to:

LO1 Define power and countervailing power.

LO2 Describe the five sources of power in organizations.

LO3 Explain how information relates to power in organizations.

LO4 Discuss the four contingencies of power.

LO5 Summarize the effects of power on the power-holder's own performance and well-being.

LO6 Summarize the eight types of influence tactics.

LO7 Discuss three contingencies to consider when deciding which influence tactic to use.

LO8 Distinguish influence from organizational politics.

LO9 Describe the organizational conditions and personal characteristics that support organizational politics.

LO10 Identify ways to minimize organizational politics.

Denise Revine's review was supposed to uncover more efficient uses of the RCMP's human resources budget. Instead, the human resources director discovered misappropriations that would shake the foundations of the law enforcement agency: pension funds were being siphoned off for questionable and unrelated operating expenses, including excessive payments to family members. Two auditor reports later confirmed Revine's findings.

Revine informed her boss, Chief Superintendent Fraser Macauley, who reported the preliminary evidence to the RCMP's ethics adviser. Soon after, Macauley was asked to brief RCMP Commissioner Giuliano Zaccardelli on this matter. To Macauley's surprise, the RCMP Commissioner accused Macauley of hiding this wrongdoing, and soon after transferred him to the Department of National Defence "so he could learn from his mistake." A Canadian government investigation into the RCMP pension affair concluded that Zaccardelli's claims against Macauley were unfounded. Equally important, it concluded that the transfer scuttled Macauley's career and sent "a message throughout the organization that one brings bad news to the Commissioner at one's peril."

Revine submitted her final report a few months after her boss's fateful meeting with the RCMP Commissioner. A few months later, after 33 years of RCMP employment, her job was declared surplus during a human resources department restructuring. When a HR staff member tried to find work for Revine in other departments, his boss warned: "No, don't touch her!" The Canadian government investigation concluded that some members of the RCMP executive were "using the restructuring process in the Human Resources Branch to try to force [Revine] out of the organization." According to the Canadian government report, at least three other RCMP officers apparently suffered career setbacks or were forced into retirement due to pressure from the RCMP's top brass.

The Canadian government's independent investigator noted significantly that the RCMP Commissioner "enjoyed the status and privileges of his office," often "reminding people that 'I am the Commissioner.'" The investigation concluded that the RCMP suffered from this "absolute power exercised by the Commissioner," and that the solution is restructuring "aimed at whittling down the power of the Commissioner."[1]

Subversive power, influence, and politics derailed the careers of RCMP human resources director Denise Revine, her boss Chief Superintendent Fraser Macauley (both shown here), as well as other RCMP staff who tried to discover and report wrongdoing in RCMP pension fund expenditures. *Jean Levac/Ottawa Citizen Reprinted by permission*

The Canadian government's independent investigation, along with separate Parliamentary committee meetings, reveal the extent to which some members of the RCMP's senior executive abused their power, used aggressive influence tactics, and engaged in organizational politics to suppress or subvert evidence of wrongdoing. Some RCMP executives may have taken these actions to hide their own inappropriate actions; other executives likely used their power and influence in a perverse attempt to protect the RCMP's public image. Although this story illustrates the dark side of power and influence, these concepts are equally relevant to ethical conduct and organizational performance. In fact, some OB experts point out that power and influence are inherent in all organizations. They exist in every business and in every decision and action.

This chapter unfolds as follows: First, we define power and present a basic model depicting the dynamics of power in organizational settings. The chapter then discusses the five bases of power, as well as information as a power base. Next, we look at the contingencies necessary to translate those sources into meaningful power. The latter part of this chapter examines the various types of influence in organizational settings as well as the contingencies of effective influence strategies. The final section of this chapter looks at situations in which influence becomes organizational politics, as well as ways of minimizing dysfunctional politics.

THE MEANING OF POWER

LO1

power
The capacity of a person, team, or organization to influence others.

Power is the capacity of a person, team, or organization to influence others.[2] Power is not the act of changing someone's attitudes or behaviour; it is only the potential to do so. People frequently have power they do not use; they might not even know they have power. Also power is not a personal feeling of power. You might feel powerful or think you have power over someone else, but this is not power unless you actually have the capacity to influence that person. The most basic prerequisite of power is that one person or group believes it is dependent on another person or group for a resource of value.[3] This relationship, shown in Exhibit 10.1, occurs where Person A has power over Person B by controlling something that Person B wants. You might have power over others by controlling a desired job assignment, useful information, important resources, or even the privilege of being associated with you! However, power requires the *perception* of dependence, so people might gain power by convincing others that they have something of value, whether or not they actually control that resource. Thus, power exists when others believe that you control resources they want.

countervailing power
The capacity of a person, team, or organization to keep a more powerful person or group in the exchange relationship.

Although dependence is a key element of power relationships, it is really more accurate to say that the parties are *interdependent*.[4] In Exhibit 10.1, Person A dominates in the power relationship, but Person B also has some **countervailing power**—enough

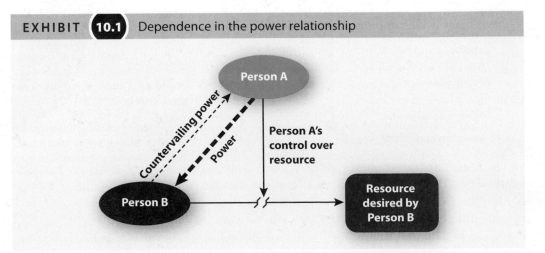

EXHIBIT 10.1   Dependence in the power relationship

Person A

Countervailing power

Power

Person A's control over resource

Person B

Resource desired by Person B

power to keep Person A in the exchange relationship and ensure that they use their dominant power judiciously. For example, executives have power over subordinates by controlling their job security and promotional opportunities. At the same time, employees have countervailing power by possessing skills and knowledge to keep production humming and customers happy, something that executives can't accomplish alone. Finally, the power relationship depends on some minimum level of trust. Trust indicates a level of expectation that the more powerful party will deliver the resource. For example, you trust your employer to give you a paycheque at the end of each pay period. Even those in extremely dependent situations will usually walk away from the relationship if they lack a minimum level of trust in the more powerful party.

A MODEL OF POWER IN ORGANIZATIONS

Power involves more than just dependence. As we see in Exhibit 10.2, the model of power includes both power sources and contingencies. It indicates that power is derived from five sources: legitimate, reward, coercive, expert, and referent. The model also indicates that these sources yield power only under certain conditions. The four contingencies of power include the employee's or department's substitutability, centrality, discretion, and visibility. Finally, as we will discuss later, the type of power applied affects the type of influence the powerholder has over the other person or work unit.

SOURCES OF POWER IN ORGANIZATIONS

LO2

Power derives from several sources and a few contingencies that determine the potential of those power sources.[5] Three sources of power—legitimate, reward, and coercive—originate mostly from the powerholder's formal position or informal role. In other words, the person is granted these power bases formally by the organization or informally

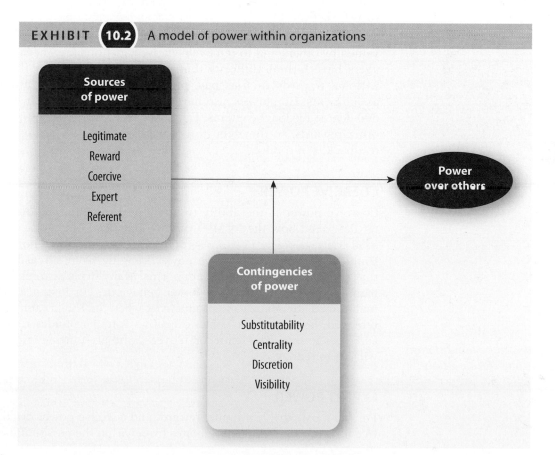

EXHIBIT 10.2   A model of power within organizations

by co-workers. Two other sources of power—expert and referent—originate from the powerholder's own characteristics; that is, they bring these power bases to the organization. Sources of power are resources that help the dependent person directly or indirectly achieve his or her goals. For example, your expertise is a source of power when others need that expertise to accomplish their objectives.

LEGITIMATE POWER

legitimate power
An agreement among organizational members that people in certain roles can request certain behaviours of others.

Legitimate power is an agreement among organizational members that people in certain roles can request certain behaviours of others. This perceived right originates from formal job descriptions as well as informal rules of conduct. This legitimate power extends to employees, not just managers. For example, an organization might give employees the right to request customer files if this information is required for their job. Legitimate power depends on more than job descriptions. It also depends on mutual agreement from those expected to abide by this authority. Your boss's power to make you work overtime partly depends on your agreement to this authority. Thus, legitimate power operates within a "zone of indifference"—the range within which people are willing to accept someone else's authority.[6]

The size of this zone of indifference (and, consequently, the magnitude of legitimate power) increases with the extent that the powerholder is trusted and makes fair decisions. Some people are also more obedient than others to authority, particularly those who value conformity and tradition. People in high power distance cultures (i.e., those who accept an unequal distribution of power) also tend to have higher obedience to authority compared with people in low power distance cultures. The organization's culture represents a third factor. A 3M scientist might continue to work on a project after being told by superiors to stop working on it because the 3M culture supports an entrepreneurial spirit, which includes ignoring your boss's authority from time to time.[7]

REWARD POWER

Reward power is derived from the person's ability to control the allocation of rewards valued by others and to remove negative sanctions (i.e., negative reinforcement). Managers have formal authority that gives them power over the distribution of organizational rewards such as pay, promotions, time off, vacation schedules, and work assignments. Employees also have reward power over their bosses through the use of 360-degree feedback systems. Employee feedback affects supervisors' promotions and other rewards, so they tend to behave differently toward employees after 360-degree feedback is introduced.

COERCIVE POWER

Coercive power is the ability to apply punishment. The opening story to this chapter described how the RCMP Commissioner and likely other senior RCMP executives used coercive power to suppress and remove employees who had revealed wrongdoing. Employees also have coercive power, ranging from sarcasm to ostracism, to ensure that co-workers conform to team norms. Many firms also rely on the coercive power of team members to control co-worker behaviour. For instance, when asked how AirAsia maintained attendance and productivity when the Kuala Lumpur-based discount airline removed the time clocks, chief executive Tony Fernandes replied: "Simple. Peer pressure sees to that. The fellow employees, who are putting their shoulders to the wheel, will see to that."[8]

EXPERT POWER

For the most part, legitimate, reward, and coercive power originate from the position.[9] In contrast, expert power originates from within the person. It is an individual's or work unit's capacity to influence others by possessing knowledge or skills that they value. The power of expertise is apparent when observing how people respond to authority figures.[10] In one classic study, for example, a researcher posing as a hospital physician telephoned on-duty nurses to prescribe a specific dosage of medicine to a hospitalized patient. None of the nurses knew the person calling, and hospital policy forbade them from accepting treatment by telephone. Furthermore, the medication was unauthorized and the prescription was twice the maximum daily dose. Yet, almost all 22 nurses who received the telephone call followed the "doctor's" orders until stopped by researchers.

This doctor-nurse study is a few decades old, but the power of expertise remains strong today, sometimes with tragic consequences. Most recently, the Canadian justice system discovered that the expert testimony of a famous Canadian pathologist was far from accurate in more than a dozen cases, resulting in the conviction of innocent people. The pathologist's reputation as a renowned authority was the main reason why his often-weak evidence was rarely questioned. "Experts in a courtroom—we give great deference to experts," says the chairman of the Canadian Council of Criminal Defence Lawyers when explaining why the pathologist's testimony was so readily accepted.[11]

REFERENT POWER

referent power
The capacity to influence others based on an identification with and respect for the powerholder.

People have **referent power** when others identify with them, like them, or otherwise respect them. Like expert power, referent power comes from within the person. It is largely a function of the person's interpersonal skills and tends to develop slowly. Referent power is usually associated with charismatic leadership. Experts have difficulty agreeing on the meaning of *charisma*, but it is most often described as a form of interpersonal attraction whereby followers ascribe almost magical powers to the charismatic individual.[12] Some experts describe charisma as a special "gift" or trait within the charismatic person, while others say it is mainly in the eyes of the beholder. However, all agree that charisma produces a high degree of trust, respect, and devotion towards the charismatic individual.

LO3

INFORMATION AND POWER

Information is power.[13] In one form, people gain information power when they control (through legitimate power) the flow of information to others. Employees are ultimately dependent on these information gatekeepers to release the information required to perform their jobs. Furthermore, by deciding what information is distributed to whom, those who control information flow also control perceptions of the situation by releasing information favouring one perspective more than another.[14] This right to control information flow is a form of legitimate power and is most common in highly bureaucratic firms. The wheel formation in Exhibit 10.3 depicts this highly centralized control over information flow. The all-channels structure, on the other hand, depicts a situation where no one has control over the flow of information. The former would occur when information must flow through your boss to you, whereas the latter occurs when information is distributed to many people, such as co-workers in a self-directed team.

The other form of information power relates to the ability to cope with organizational uncertainties. This coping capability, which is a form of expert power, includes a person's or work team's skill or knowledge to effectively address environmental uncertainties affecting the organization. The ability to cope with uncertainty is valuable because organizations are more effective when they can operate in predictable environments. A groundbreaking study of Canadian breweries and container companies identified three general strategies to help organizations cope with uncertainty. These coping strategies are arranged in a hierarchy of importance, with the first being the most powerful:[15]

- *Prevention*—The most effective strategy is to prevent environmental changes from occurring. For example, financial experts acquire power by preventing the organization from experiencing a cash shortage or defaulting on loans.

EXHIBIT 10.3 Power through the control of information

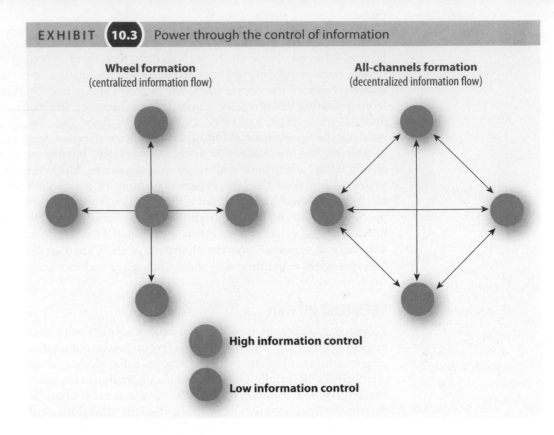

Wheel formation
(centralized information flow)

All-channels formation
(decentralized information flow)

High information control

Low information control

- *Forecasting*—The next best strategy is to predict environmental changes or variations. In this respect, trendspotters and other marketing specialists gain power by predicting changes in consumer preferences.
- *Absorption*—People and work units also gain power by absorbing or neutralizing the impact of environmental shifts as they occur. An example is the ability of maintenance crews to come to the rescue when machines break down and the production process stops.

CONTINGENCIES OF POWER

LO4

Let's say that you have expert power because of your ability to forecast and possibly even prevent dramatic changes in the organization's environment. Does this expertise mean that you are influential? Not necessarily. As we saw earlier in Exhibit 10.2, power bases generate power only under certain conditions. Four important contingencies of power are substitutability, centrality, discretion, and visibility.[16]

SUBSTITUTABILITY

substitutability
A contingency of power referring to the availability of alternatives.

Substitutability refers to the availability of alternatives. Power is strongest when someone has a monopoly over a valued resource. Conversely, power decreases as the number of alternative sources of the critical resource increases. If you—and no one else—has expertise across the organization on an important issue, you would be more powerful than if several people in your company possess this valued knowledge. Substitutability refers not only to other sources that offer the resource, but also to substitutions of the resource itself. For instance, labour unions are weakened when companies introduce technologies that replace the need for their union members. Technology is a substitute for employees and, consequently, reduces union power.

Nonsubstitutability is strengthened by controlling access to the resource. Professions and labour unions gain power by controlling knowledge, tasks, or labour to perform important activities. For instance, the medical profession is powerful because it controls who can perform specific medical procedures. Labour unions that dominate an industry effectively control access to labour needed to perform key jobs. Employees become nonsubstitutable when they possess knowledge (such as operating equipment or serving clients) that is not documented or readily available to others. Nonsubstitutability also occurs when people differentiate their resource from the alternatives. Some people claim that consultants use this tactic. They take skills and knowledge that many consulting firms can provide and wrap them into a package (with the latest buzz words, of course) so that it looks like a service that no one else can offer.

CENTRALITY

centrality

A contingency of power referring to the degree and nature of interdependence between the powerholder and others.

Centrality refers to the degree and nature of interdependence between the powerholder and others.[18] Think about your own centrality for a moment: If you decided not to show up for work or school tomorrow, how many people would be affected, and how much time would pass before they are affected? If you have high centrality, most people in the organization would be adversely affected by your absence, and they would be affected quickly. For example, airline pilots have high centrality because their actions affect many people, and those actions affect others very quickly.

DISCRETION

The freedom to exercise judgment—to make decisions without referring to a specific rule or receiving permission from someone else—is another important contingency of power in organizations. Consider the plight of first-line supervisors. It may seem that they have legitimate, reward, and coercive power over employees, but this power is often curtailed by specific rules. The lack of discretion makes supervisors less powerful than their positions would indicate. "Middle managers are very much 'piggy-in-the-middle,'" complains a middle manager at Britain's National Health System. "They have little power, only what senior managers are allowed to give them."[19] More generally, research indicates that managerial discretion varies considerably across industries, and that managers with an internal locus of control are viewed as more powerful because they behave as though they have discretion in their job (even if they don't).[20]

VISIBILITY

Several years ago as a junior copywriter at advertising agency Chiat/Day, Mimi Cook submitted an idea for a potential client to her boss, who then presented it to co-founder Jay Chiat. Chiat was thrilled with the concept, but Cook's boss "never mentioned the idea came from me," recalls Cook. Cook confronted her boss, who claimed the oversight was unintentional. But when a similar incident occurred a few months later, Cook left the agency for another firm.[21]

Mimi Cook, who has since progressed to associate creative director at another ad agency, knows that power does not flow to unknown people in the organization. Those who control valued resources or knowledge will yield power only when others are aware of these power bases, in other words, when it is visible. One way to increase visibility is to take people-oriented jobs and work on projects that require frequent interaction with senior executives. "You can take visibility in steps," advises an executive at a pharmaceutical firm. "You can start by making yourself visible in a small group, such as a staff meeting. Then when you're comfortable with that, seek out larger arenas."[22]

Employees also gain visibility by being, quite literally, visible. Some people strategically locate themselves in more visible offices, such as those closest to the elevator or staff coffee room. People often use public symbols as subtle (and not-so-subtle) cues to make their power sources known to others. Many professionals display their educational diplomas and awards on office walls to remind visitors of their expertise. Medical professionals wear white coats with a stethoscope around their neck to symbolize their legitimate and expert power in hospital settings. Other people play the game of "face time"—spending more time at work and showing that they are working productively.

SOCIAL NETWORKING AND POWER

"It's not what you know, but who you know that counts!" This often-heard statement reflects the fact that employees get ahead not just by developing their competencies, but by *networking*—cultivating social relationships with others to accomplish one's goals. Networking increases a person's power in three ways. First, networks represent a critical component of **social capital**—the knowledge and other resources available to people or social units (teams, organizations) due to a durable network that connects them to others. Networks consist of people who trust each other, which increases the flow of knowledge among those within the network. The more you network, the more likely you will receive valuable information that increases your expert power in the organization.[23]

Second, people tend to identify more with partners within their own networks, which increases referent power among people within each network. This network-based referent power may lead to more favourable decisions by others in the network. Finally, effective networkers are better known by others in the organization, so their talents are more readily recognized. This power increases when networkers place themselves in strategic positions in the network, thereby gaining centrality.[24] For example, an individual might be regarded as the main person who distributes information in the network or who keeps the network connected through informal gatherings.

Social networks are natural elements of the informal organization, yet they can create a formidable barrier to those who are not actively connected to it.[25] Women are often excluded from powerful networks because they do not participate in golf games and other male-dominated social events. That's what Deloitte and Touche executives discovered when they investigated why so many junior female employees left the accounting and consulting firm before reaching partnership level. Deloitte and Touche now relies on mentoring, formal women's network groups, and measurement of career progress to ensure that female staff members have the same career development opportunities as their male colleagues.[26]

social capital
The knowledge and other resources available to people or social units (teams, organizations) due to a durable network that connects them to others.

LO5

CONSEQUENCES OF POWER

How does power affect the powerholder? We partly answered this question earlier in this book when describing *empowerment*—an individual's feelings of self-determination, meaning, competence, and impact in the organization. Under the right conditions, employees who receive more power feel more empowered. This feeling of empowerment tends to increase employee motivation, job satisfaction, organizational commitment, and job performance. In addition, research suggests that as people become more powerful, they are more goal directed and tend to act on their environment rather than hide from it.

At the same time, increasing power over others can potentially undermine an individual's effectiveness and interpersonal relations. Some studies have found that people who have (or believe they have) more power over others are more likely to cling to stereotypes, have more difficulty empathizing, and generally have less accurate perceptions compared with people with less power. They also engage in more automatic rather than mindful thinking, possibly because powerful people are less concerned about the consequences of their actions.[27] These findings may explain the widely criticized decisions and actions of former RCMP Commissioner, including his response to the pension fund abuses described at the beginning of this chapter.[28]

INFLUENCING OTHERS

Up to this point, we have focused on the sources and contingencies of power. But power is only the capacity to influence others. It represents the potential to change someone's attitudes and behaviour. **Influence**, on the other hand, refers to any behaviour that attempts to alter someone's attitudes or behaviour.[29] Influence is power in motion. It applies one or more power bases to get people to alter their beliefs, feelings, and activities. Consequently, our interest in the remainder of this chapter is on how people use power to influence others.

Influence tactics are woven throughout the social fabric of all organizations. This is because influence is an essential process through which people coordinate their effort and act in concert to achieve organizational objectives. Indeed, influence is central to the definition of leadership. Influence operates down, across, and up the corporate hierarchy. Executives ensure that subordinates complete required tasks. Employees influence co-workers to help them with their job assignments. Subordinates engage in upward influence tactics so corporate leaders make decisions compatible with subordinates' needs and expectations.

influence
Any behaviour that attempts to alter someone's attitudes or behaviour.

LO6

TYPES OF INFLUENCE TACTICS

Organizational behaviour researchers have devoted considerable attention to the various types of influence tactics found in organizational settings. They do not agree on a definitive list of influence tactics, but the most commonly identified are listed in Exhibit 10.4 and described over the next few pages.[30] The first five are known as "hard" influence tactics because they force behaviour change through position power (legitimate, reward, and coercion). The latter three—ingratiation and impression management, persuasion, and exchange—are called "soft" tactics because they rely more on personal sources of power (referent, expert) and appeal to the target person's attitudes and needs.

Silent Authority The silent application of authority occurs where someone complies with a request because of the requester's legitimate power as well as the target person's role expectations. We often refer to this condition as *deference to authority*.[31] This deference occurs when you comply with your boss's request to complete a particular task. If the task is within your job scope and your boss has the right to make this request, then this influence strategy operates without negotiation, threats, persuasion, or other tactics. Silent authority is the most common form of influence in high power distance cultures.[32]

EXHIBIT 10.4   Types of influence tactics in organizations

Influence Tactic	Description
Silent authority	Influencing behaviour through legitimate power without explicitly referring to that power base
Assertiveness	Actively applying legitimate and coercive power by applying pressure or threats
Information control	Explicitly manipulating someone else's access to information for the purpose of changing their attitudes and/or behaviour
Coalition formation	Forming a group that attempts to influence others by pooling the resources and power of its members
Upward appeal	Gaining support from one or more people with higher authority or expertise
Persuasion	Using logical arguments, factual evidence, and emotional appeals to convince people of the value of a request
Ingratiation/impression management	Attempting to increase liking by, or perceived similarity to, some targeted person
Exchange	Promising benefits or resources in exchange for the target person's compliance

Assertiveness   In contrast to silent authority, assertiveness might be called "vocal authority" because it involves actively applying legitimate and coercive power to influence others. Assertiveness includes persistently reminding the target of his or her obligations, frequently checking the target's work, confronting the target, and using threats of sanctions to force compliance. Assertiveness typically applies or threatens to apply punishment if the target does not comply. Explicit or implicit threats range from job loss to losing face by letting down the team. Extreme forms of assertiveness include blackmailing colleagues, such as by threatening to reveal the other person's previously unknown failures unless he or she complies with your request. Referring to the opening story to this chapter, evidence suggests that senior RCMP executives relied on various forms of assertiveness to suppress investigation of pension fund abuses.

Information Control   Information control involves explicitly manipulating others' access to information for the purpose of changing their attitudes and/or behaviour. With limited access to potentially valuable information, others are at a disadvantage. The opening story on RCMP pension fund abuses suggests that information control was used as an influence tactic. One investigator told a parliamentary committee: "I was met with inaction, delays, roadblocks, obstruction and lies." He pointed to the RCMP's top leaders as the source of this information control.[33] According to one major survey, almost half of employees believe co-workers keep others in the dark about work issues if it helps their own cause. Employees also influence executive decisions by screening out (filtering) information flowing up the hierarchy. One study found that CEOs influence their board of directors by selectively feeding and withholding information.[34]

coalition
A group that attempts to influence people outside the group by pooling the resources and power of its members.

Coalition Formation   When people lack sufficient power alone to influence others in the organization, they might form a **coalition** of people who support the proposed change. A coalition is influential in three ways.[35] First, it pools the power and resources of many people, so the coalition potentially has more influence than any number of people operating alone. Second, the coalition's mere existence can be a source of power by symbolizing the legitimacy of the issue. In other words, a coalition creates a sense that the issue deserves attention because it has broad support. Third, coalitions tap into the power of the social identity process introduced in Chapter 2. A coalition is essentially an informal group that advocates a new set of norms and behaviours. If the coalition has a broad-based membership (i.e., its members come from various parts of the organization), then other employees are more likely to identify with that group and, consequently, accept the ideas the coalition is proposing.

Upward Appeal   The opening vignette to this chapter mentions that other RCMP officers left the force because they attempted to uncover pension fund wrongdoing. One of these people, Staff Sgt. Ron Lewis, was the RCMP staff relations representative for headquarters and had received information before most other people about suspicious activity in human resources, including nepotism and pension fund mismanagement. When RCMP top brass failed to launch an investigation, Lewis threatened to take his information to Canada's political leaders and to the public. This tactic, called **upward appeal**, involves calling upon higher authority or expertise, or symbolically relying on these sources to support the influencer's position. Lewis's threat of upward appeal influenced RCMP leaders enough to fire two human resources managers close to the pension fund scheme, but not to investigate further. Unfortunately for Lewis, there was apparently no response from Canada's political leaders (including the minister responsible for the RCMP) when he attempted to inform these higher authorities.[36]

> **upward appeal**
> A type of influence in which someone with higher authority or expertise is called upon in reality or symbolically to support the influencer's position.

Along with seeking out support from higher sources, upward appeal occurs when relying on the authority of the firm's policies or values. By reminding others that your request is consistent with the organization's overarching goals, you are implying support from senior executives without formally involving them.

Persuasion   **Persuasion** is one of the most effective influence strategies for career success. The ability to present facts, logical arguments, and emotional appeals to change another person's attitudes and behaviour is not just an acceptable way to influence others; in many societies, it is a noble art and a quality of effective leaders. The effectiveness of persuasion as an influence tactic depends on characteristics of the persuader, message content, communication medium, and the audience being persuaded.[37] People are more persuasive when listeners believe they have expertise and credibility, such as when the persuader does not seem to profit from the persuasion attempt and demonstrates this by acknowledging other counter-arguments to the position.

> **persuasion**
> Presenting facts, logical arguments, and emotional appeals to change another person's attitudes and behaviour.

The message is more important than the messenger when the issue is important to the audience. Persuasive message content acknowledges several points of view so the audience does not feel cornered by the speaker. The message should also be limited to a few strong arguments, which are repeated a few times, but not too frequently. The message should use emotional appeals (such as graphically showing the unfortunate consequences of a bad decision), but only in combination with logical arguments and specific recommendations to overcome the threat. Finally, message content is more

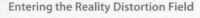

Entering the Reality Distortion Field

Wearing his trademark black turtleneck and faded jeans, Apple Computer co-founder and CEO Steve Jobs is famous for stirring up crowds with evangelical fervour as he draws them into his "reality distortion field." A reality distortion field occurs when people are caught in Steve Jobs's visionary headlights. Apple Computer manager Bud Tribble borrowed the phrase from the TV series *Star Trek* to describe Jobs's overwhelming persuasiveness. "In his presence, reality is malleable," Tribble explained to newly hired Andy Hertzfeld in 1981. "He [Steve Jobs] can convince anyone of practically anything. It wears off when he's not around, but it makes it hard to have realistic schedules." As one journalist wrote: "[Reality distortion field] refers, of course, to Jobs's incredible ability to turn anyone—even skeptical reporters—into near-mindless fanboys. Reality distortion wears off, but not before a blizzard of uncritical media coverage of what frequently are routine announcements."[38] © *Kimberly White/CORBIS*

inoculation effect
A persuasive communication strategy of warning listeners that others will try to influence them in the future and that they should be wary about the opponent's arguments.

persuasive when the audience is warned about opposing arguments. This **inoculation effect** causes listeners to generate counter-arguments to the anticipated persuasion attempts, which makes the opponent's subsequent persuasion attempts less effective.[39]

Two other considerations when persuading people are the medium of communication and characteristics of the audience. Generally, persuasion works best in face-to-face conversations and through other media-rich communication channels. The personal nature of face-to-face communication increases the persuader's credibility, and the richness of this channel provides faster feedback that the influence strategy is working. With respect to audience characteristics, it is more difficult to persuade people who have high self-esteem and intelligence, as well as those whose targeted attitudes are strongly connected to their self-identity.[40]

Ingratiation and Impression Management

ingratiation
Any attempt to increase liking by, or perceived similarity to, some targeted person.

Silent authority, assertiveness, information control, coalitions, and upward appeals are somewhat (or very!) forceful ways to influence other people. In contrast, a very "soft" influence tactic is **ingratiation**—any attempt to increase liking by, or perceived similarity to, some targeted person.[41] Ingratiation comes in several flavours. For example, employees might flatter their boss in front of others, demonstrate that they have similar attitudes as their boss (e.g., agreeing with the boss's proposal), and ask their boss for advice. Ingratiation is one of the more effective influence tactics at boosting a person's career success (i.e., performance appraisal feedback, salaries, and promotions).[42] However, people who engage in high levels of ingratiation are less (not more) influential and less likely to get promoted.[43] The explanation for the contrasting evidence is that those who engage in too much ingratiation are viewed as insincere and self-serving. The terms "apple polishing" and "brown-nosing" are applied to those who ingratiate to excess or in ways that suggest selfish motives for the ingratiation.

impression management
The practice of actively shaping our public images.

Ingratiation is part of a larger influence tactic known as impression management. **Impression management** is the practice of actively shaping our public images.[44] These public images might be crafted as being important, vulnerable, threatening, or pleasant. For the most part, employees routinely engage in pleasant impression management behaviours to satisfy the basic norms of social behaviour, such as the way they dress and how they behave toward colleagues and customers. Impression management is a common strategy for people trying to get ahead in the workplace. In fact, career professionals encourage people to develop a personal "brand"; that is, to demonstrate and symbolize a distinctive competitive advantage.[45] Just as running shoes and soft drinks have brand images that represent an expectation, successful individuals build a personal brand in which they deliver valued knowledge or skills. Furthermore, people who are

Building a Personal Brand

Only 22, Kendal Harazny has already built a personal brand as an influential business student, entrepreneur, and future leader. He runs a successful global-event ticket brokerage with 11 employees while studying full-time at the University of Alberta, and is involved in student and local business organizations including the Business Student's Association and the Junior Chamber of Commerce. Kendal recently served as External Chair of RoundTable, a chance for leading companies such as EnCana, Price WaterhouseCoopers, TELUS, CIBC, and the Chartered Accountants of Alberta to recruit, inform, and understand 250 of Canada's elite student leaders from 31 business schools across the country. The students took part in a series of workshops, keynote addresses, and academic competitions over the course of a weekend. One of the features of the most recent RoundTable conference was an opportunity for these student leaders to present five and 10-year plans for the telecommunications sector that will assist Telus in fine-tuning their future.[46] *Rick MacWilliam, Edmonton Journal*

adept at personal branding rely on impression management through distinctive personal characteristics. Former Canadian Prime Minister Pierre Trudeau engaged in this distinctive impression management by wearing a red rose in his lapel.

Unfortunately, a few individuals carry impression management beyond ethical boundaries by exaggerating their credentials and accomplishments on their resume. For instance, a Lucent Technologies executive lied about having a PhD from Stanford University and hid his criminal past involving forgery and embezzlement. Ironically, the executive was Lucent's director of recruiting![47] One of the most elaborate misrepresentations occurred a few years ago when a Singaporean entrepreneur sent out news releases claiming to be a renowned artificial intelligence researcher, the author of several books, and the recipient of numerous awards from MIT and Stanford University (one of the awards was illustrated on his website). These falsehoods were so convincing that the entrepreneur almost received a real award, the "Internet Visionary of the Year" at the Internet World Asia Industry Awards.[48]

Exchange   Exchange activities involve the promise of benefits or resources in exchange for the target person's compliance with your request. This tactic also includes reminding the target person of past benefits or favours with the expectation that he or she will now make up for that debt. The norm of reciprocity is a central and explicit theme in exchange strategies. According to the norm of reciprocity, individuals are expected to help those who have helped them.[49] Negotiation is also an integral part of exchange influence activities. For instance, you might negotiate with your boss for a day off in return for working a less desirable shift at a future date. Networking is another form of exchange as an influence strategy. Active networkers build up "exchange credits" by helping colleagues in the short-term for reciprocal benefits in the long term.

Networking as an influence strategy is a deeply ingrained practice in several cultures. The Chinese term *guanxi* refers to special relationships and active interpersonal connectedness. It is based on traditional Confucian values of helping others without expecting future repayment. However, some writers suggest that the original interpretation and practice of guanxi has shifted to include implicit long-term reciprocity, which can slip into cronyism. As a result, some Asian governments are discouraging guanxi-based decisions, preferring more arm's-length transactions in business and government decisions.[50]

CONSEQUENCES AND CONTINGENCIES OF INFLUENCE TACTICS

Now that the main influence strategies have been described, you are probably asking: Which ones are best? The best way to answer this question is to identify the three ways that people react when others try to influence them: resistance, compliance, or commitment.[51] *Resistance* occurs when people or work units oppose the behaviour desired by the influencer and, consequently refuse, argue, or delay engaging in the behaviour. *Compliance* occurs when people are motivated to implement the influencer's request at a minimal level of effort and for purely instrumental reasons. Without external sources to prompt the desired behaviour, it would not occur. *Commitment* is the strongest response to influence, whereby people identify with the influencer's request and are highly motivated to implement it even when extrinsic sources of motivation are no longer present.

Generally, people react more favourably to "soft" tactics than to "hard" tactics (see Exhibit 10.5). Soft influence tactics rely on personal power bases (expert and referent power), which tend to build commitment to the influencer's request. In contrast, hard tactics rely on position power (legitimate, reward, and coercion), so they tend to produce compliance or, worse, resistance. Hard tactics also tend to undermine trust, which can hurt future relationships.

Apart from the general preference for soft rather than hard tactics, the most appropriate influence strategy depends on a few contingencies. One obvious contingency is which sources of power are strongest. Those with expertise tend to have more influence using persuasion, whereas those with a strong legitimate power base are usually more

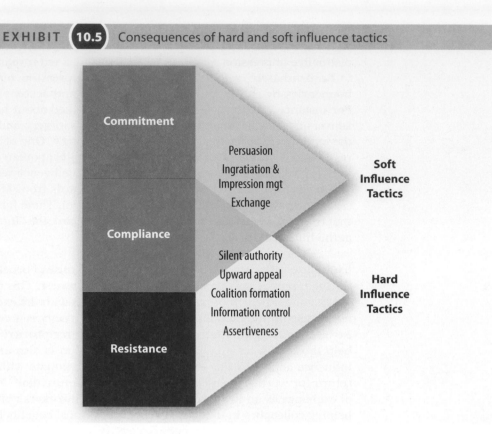

EXHIBIT 10.5 Consequences of hard and soft influence tactics

successful applying silent authority.[52] A second contingency is whether the person being influenced is higher, lower, or at the same level in the organization. As an example, employees may face adverse career consequences by being too assertive with their boss. Meanwhile, supervisors who engage in ingratiation and impression management tend to lose the respect of their staff.

Finally, the most appropriate influence tactic depends on personal, organizational, and cultural values.[53] People with a strong power orientation might feel more comfortable using assertiveness, whereas those who value conformity might feel more comfortable with upward appeals. At an organizational level, firms with a competitive culture might encourage more use of information control and coalition formation, whereas companies with a learning orientation would likely encourage more influence through persuasion. The preferred influence tactics also vary across societal cultures. Research indicates that ingratiation is much more common among managers in Canada and the United States than in Hong Kong, possibly because this tactic disrupts the more distant roles that managers and employees expect in high power distance cultures.

INFLUENCE TACTICS AND ORGANIZATIONAL POLITICS

LO8

organizational politics
Behaviours that others perceive as self-serving tactics for personal gain at the expense of other people and possibly the organization.

You might have noticed that organizational politics has not been mentioned yet, even though some of the practices or examples described over the past few pages are usually considered political tactics. The phrase was carefully avoided because, for the most part, organizational politics is in the eye of the beholder. You might perceive a co-worker's attempt to influence the boss as normal behaviour, whereas someone else might perceive the co-worker's tactic as brazen organizational politics.

This perceptual issue explains why OB experts increasingly discuss influence tactics as behaviours and organizational politics as perceptions.[54] The influence tactics described earlier are perceived as **organizational politics** when observers view the tactics as self-serving behaviours at the expense of others and sometimes contrary to the interests of the entire organization or work unit. Of course, some tactics are so blatantly selfish that almost everyone views them as political. But in most situations, there is no consensus that a person is being "political." When employees perceive many incidents of organizational politics, the result is lower job satisfaction, organizational commitment, and organizational citizenship, as well as high levels of work-related stress.[55] And when political tactics really are self-serving, such as occurred at National Australia Bank's foreign currency options desk (see GLOBAL Connections 10.1), they divert resources away from the organization's effective functioning and potentially threaten the company's survival.

LO9   CONDITIONS SUPPORTING ORGANIZATIONAL POLITICS

Organizational politics flourishes under the right conditions.[56] One of those conditions is scarce resources. When budgets are slashed, people rely on political tactics to safeguard their resources and maintain the status quo. Office politics also flourishes when resource allocation decisions are ambiguous, complex, or lack formal rules. This occurs because decision makers are given more discretion over resource allocation, so potential recipients of those resources use political tactics to influence the factors that should be considered in the decision. Organizational change encourages political behaviours for this reason. Change creates uncertainty and ambiguity as the company moves from an

---

global connections 10.1

NAB's Rogue Politics

For three long days, junior trader Dennis Gentilin received the cold shoulder from his boss, Luke Duffy. As head of National Australia Bank's (NAB) foreign currency options desk in Melbourne, Duffy was angry that Gentilin notified Duffy's boss that Duffy was carrying forward trading losses (called smoothing), which was recently prohibited. On the fourth day, Duffy launched into a tirade: "I felt like...killing someone the other day," Duffy apparently said pointedly to Gentilin. "If you want to stay in the team, I demand loyalty and don't want you going to Dillon [Duffy's boss] about what's happening in the team."

Gentilin later told authorities that, due to their expertise, Duffy and other senior traders were "untouchables" who were given free rein at NAB. "They just created this power base where they were laws unto themselves," claims Gentilin. Duffy also mocked and intimidated employees into submission. He referred to one of NAB's traders in London as "the London stench boy" because the London trader "was always making a stink about things." Duffy warned a junior trader Vanessa McCallum not to cross him, saying that another employee who had done so was now making bread for a living. When testifying against Duffy in court, the junior trader recalled: "My greatest fear was, if nothing is wrong, I'm going to have to leave the desk because you had to be loyal to Luke."

But something did go very wrong. When Duffy's team bet against a rising Australian dollar, they began an escalating series of cover-ups, including creation

National Australia Bank rogue trader Luke Duffy (shown here after sentencing) and his colleagues created losses of CAD$300 million, thanks in part to Duffy's political tactics.
© Craig Abraham/Fairfax Photos

of fictitious trades to offset the losses. The unrestrained power and influence of Duffy and other senior traders in Melbourne and London kept everyone in line, resulting in more than 800 breaches of the bank's trading limits. Gentilin and McCallum eventually notified senior management, but by then the damage had been done. Within a year, the rogue team had amassed CAD$300 million in losses. Duffy and three other traders were jailed for securities violations. The chief executive and chairman of National Australia Bank lost their jobs.[57]

old set of rules and practices to a new set. During these times, employees apply political strategies to protect their valued resources, position, and self-concept.[58]

Personal Characteristics   Several personal characteristics affect a person's motivation to engage in self-serving behaviour.[59] This includes a strong need for personal as opposed to socialized power. Those with a need for personal power seek power for its own sake and try to acquire more power. Some individuals have strong **Machiavellian values**. Machiavellianism is named after Niccolò Machiavelli, the sixteenth-century Italian philosopher who wrote *The Prince*, a famous treatise about political behaviour. People with high Machiavellian values are comfortable with getting more than they deserve, and they believe that deceit is a natural and acceptable way to achieve this goal. They seldom trust co-workers and tend to use cruder influence tactics, such as bypassing one's boss or being assertive, to get their own way.[60] GLOBAL Connections 10.1, presented on the previous page, suggests that National Australia Bank's rogue trader displayed Machiavellian characteristics, including rough assertiveness and controlling information.

> **Machiavellian values**
> The belief that deceit is a natural and acceptable way to influence others.

LO10

Minimizing Organizational Politics and its Consequences   The conditions that fuel organizational politics also give us some clues about how to control dysfunctional political activities.[61] One strategy to keep organizational politics in check is to introduce clear rules and regulations to specify the use of scarce resources. Organizational politics can become a problem during times of organizational change, so politics can be minimized through effective organizational change practices. Leaders also need to actively manage group norms to curtail self-serving influence activities. In particular, they can support organizational values that oppose political tactics, such as altruism and customer-focus. One of the most important strategies is for leaders to become role models of organizational citizenship rather than symbols of successful organizational politicians.

Along with minimizing organizational politics, companies can limit the adverse effects of political perceptions by giving employees more control over their work and keeping them informed of organizational events. Research has found that employees who are kept informed of what is going on in the organization and who are involved in organizational decisions are less likely to experience organizational politics, which results in less stress, job dissatisfaction, and absenteeism.

CHAPTER SUMMARY

Power is the capacity to influence others. It exists when one party perceives that he or she is dependent on the other for something of value. However, the dependent person must also have countervailing power—some power over the dominant party—to maintain the relationship.

There are five power bases. Legitimate power is an agreement among organizational members that people in certain roles can request certain behaviours of others. Reward power is derived from the ability to control the allocation of rewards valued by others and to remove negative sanctions. Coercive power is the ability to apply punishment. Expert power is the capacity to influence others by possessing knowledge or skills that they value. People have referent power when others identify with them, like them, or otherwise respect them. Information plays an important role in organizational power. Employees gain power by controlling the flow of information that others need and by being able to cope with uncertainties related to important organizational goals.

Four contingencies determine whether these power bases translate into real power. Individuals and work units are more powerful when they are non-substitutable, that is, there is a lack of alternatives. Employees, work units, and organizations reduce substitutability by controlling tasks, knowledge, and labour, and by differentiating themselves from competitors. A second contingency is centrality. People have more power when they have high centrality, that is, the number of people affected is large and people are quickly affected by their actions. Discretion, the third contingency of power, refers to the freedom to exercise judgment. Power increases when people have freedom to use their power. The fourth contingency, visibility, refers to the idea that power increases to the extent that a person's or work unit's competencies are known to others.

Social networking involves cultivating social relationships with others to accomplish one's goals. This activity increases an individual's social capital, which strengthens expert power, referent power, visibility, and possibly centrality. Power has both beneficial and adverse consequences for individuals. On the positive side, empowerment strengthens their well-being and effectiveness. On the negative side, research indicates that when people become more powerful, their perceptual and decision-making skills can suffer.

Influence refers to any behaviour that attempts to alter someone's attitudes or behaviour. The most widely studied influence tactics are silent authority, assertiveness, information control, coalition formation, upward appeal, persuasion, ingratiation and impression management, and exchange. "Soft" influence tactics such as friendly persuasion and subtle ingratiation are more acceptable than "hard" tactics such as upward appeal and assertiveness. However, the most appropriate influence tactic also depends on the influencer's power base; whether the person being influenced is higher, lower, or at the same level in the organization; and personal, organizational, and cultural values regarding influence behaviour.

Organizational politics refers to influence tactics that others perceive to be self-serving behaviours at the expense of others and sometimes contrary to the interests of the entire organization or work unit. Organizational politics is more prevalent when scarce resources are allocated using complex and ambiguous decisions and when the organization tolerates or rewards political behaviour. Individuals with a high need for personal power and strong Machiavellian values have a higher propensity to use political tactics.

Organizational politics can be minimized by providing clear rules for resource allocation, establishing a free flow of information, using education and involvement during organizational change, supporting team norms and a corporate culture that discourages dysfunctional politics, and having leaders who role model organizational citizenship rather than political savvy.

KEY TERMS

centrality, p. 241

coalition, p. 244

countervailing power, p. 236

impression management, p. 246

influence, p. 243

ingratiation, p. 246

inoculation effect, p. 246

legitimate power, p. 238

Machiavellian values, p. 250

organizational politics, p. 248

persuasion, p. 245

power, p. 236

referent power, p. 239

social capital, p. 242

substitutability, p. 240

upward appeal, p. 245

CRITICAL THINKING QUESTIONS

1. What role does countervailing power play in the power relationship? Give an example of your own encounter with countervailing power at school or work.

2. Several years ago, the major league baseball players association went on strike in September, just before the World Series started. The players' contract expired at the beginning of the season (March), but they held off the strike until September when they would lose only one-sixth of their salaries. In contrast, a September strike would hurt the owners financially because they earn a larger portion of their revenue during the playoffs. As one player explained: "If we strike next spring, there's nothing stopping [the club owners] from letting us go until next June or July because they don't have that much at stake." Use your knowledge of the sources and contingencies of power to explain why the baseball players association had more power in negotiations by walking out in September rather than March.

3. You have just been hired as a brand manager of toothpaste for a large consumer products company. Your job mainly involves encouraging the advertising and production groups to promote and manufacture your product more effectively. These departments aren't under your direct authority, although company procedures indicate that they must complete certain tasks requested by brand managers. Describe the sources of power you can use to ensure that the advertising and production departments will help you make and sell toothpaste more effectively.

4. How does social networking increase a person's power? What social networking strategies could you initiate now to potentially enhance your future career success?

5. List the eight influence tactics described in this chapter in terms of how they are used by students to influence their course instructors. Which influence tactic is applied most often? Which is applied least often, in your opinion? To what extent is each influence tactic considered legitimate behaviour or organizational politics?

6. How do cultural differences affect the following influence factors: (a) silent authority and (b) upward appeal?

7. A few years ago, the CEO of Apple Computer invited Steve Jobs (who was not associated with the company at the time) to serve as a special adviser and raise morale among Apple employees and customers. While doing this, Jobs spent more time advising the CEO on how to cut costs, redraw the organizational chart, and hire new people. Before long, most of the top people at Apple were Jobs's colleagues, who began to systematically evaluate and weed out teams of Apple employees. While publicly supporting Apple's CEO, Jobs privately criticized him and, in a show of nonconfidence, sold 1.5 million shares of Apple stock he had received. This action caught the attention of Apple's board of directors, who soon after decided to replace the CEO with Steve Jobs. The CEO claimed Jobs was a conniving back-stabber who used political tactics to get his way.

Others suggest that Apple would be out of business today if he hadn't taken over the company. In your opinion, were Steve Jobs's actions examples of organizational politics? Justify your answer.

8. This book frequently emphasizes that successful companies engage in organizational learning. How do political tactics interfere with organizational learning objectives?

CASE STUDY 10.1

The Rise and Fall of WorldCom

Edmonton-born Bernie Ebbers built WorldCom, Inc. (now part of Verizon, Inc.) into one of the world's largest telecommunications firms. Yet he and chief financial officer (CFO) Scott Sullivan have become better known for creating a massive corporate accounting fraud that led to the largest bankruptcy in U.S. history. Two investigative reports and subsequent court cases concluded that WorldCom executives were responsible for billions in fraudulent or unsupported accounting entries. How did this mammoth accounting scandal occur without anyone raising the alarm? Evidence suggests that Ebbers and Sullivan held considerable power and influence that prevented accounting staff from complaining, or even knowing, about the fraud.

Ebbers's inner circle held tight control over the flow of all financial information. The geographically dispersed accounting groups were discouraged from sharing information. Ebbers's group also restricted distribution of company-level financial reports and prevented sensitive reports from being prepared at all. Accountants didn't even have access to the computer files where some of the largest fraudulent entries were made. As a result, employees had to rely on Ebbers's executive team to justify the accounting entries that were requested.

Another reason why employees complied with questionable accounting practices was that CFO Scott Sullivan wielded immense personal power. He was considered a "whiz kid" with impeccable integrity who had won the prestigious "CFO Excellence Award." Thus, when Sullivan's office asked staff to make questionable entries, some accountants assumed Sullivan had found an innovative—and legal—accounting loophole. If Sullivan's influence didn't work, other executives took a more coercive approach. Employees cited incidents where they were publicly berated for questioning headquarters' decisions and intimidated if they asked for more information. When one employee at a branch refused to alter an accounting entry, WorldCom's controller threatened to fly in from WorldCom's Mississippi headquarters to make the change himself. The employee changed the entry.

Ebbers had similar influence over WorldCom's board of directors. Sources indicate that his personal charisma and intolerance of dissension produced a passive board that rubber-stamped most of his recommendations. As one report concluded: "The Board of Directors appears to have embraced suggestions by Mr. Ebbers without question or dissent, even under circumstances where its members now readily acknowledge they had significant misgivings regarding his recommended course of action."

Discussion Questions

1. What power bases did Bernie Ebbers and Scott Sullivan rely on to get their way with accounting fraud?

2. What influence tactics did Bernie Ebbers and Scott Sullivan use to control employees and the company's board?

3. Did Bernie Ebbers and Scott Sullivan engage in organizational politics? Explain your answer.

Sources: United States Bankruptcy Court, Southern District of New York. *In Re: WorldCom, Inc., et al., Debtors*. Chapter 11 Case No. 02-15533 (Ajg) Jointly Administered Second Interim Report of Dick Thornburgh, Bankruptcy Court Examiner, June 9, 2003; Report of Investigation by the Special Investigative Committee of the Board of Directors of WorldCom, Inc. Dennis R. Beresford, Nicholas Deb. Katzenbach, C.B. Rogers, Jr., Counsel, Wilmer, Cutler & Pickering, Accounting

Advisors, Pricewaterhousecoopers LLP, March 31, 2003. Also see: T. Catan et al., "Before the Fall," *Financial Times (London)*, December 19, 2002, p. 17; J. O'Donnell and A. Backover, "Ebbers' High-Risk Act Came Crashing Down on Him," *USA Today*, December 12, 2002, p. B1; C. Stern, "Ebbers Dominated Board, Report Says," *Washington Post*, November 5, 2002, p. E1; D. S. Hilzenrath, "How a Distinguished Roster of Board Members Failed to Detect Company's Problems," *Washington Post*, June 16, 2003, p. E1; S. Pulliam and A. Latour, "Lost Connection," *Wall Street Journal*, January 12, 2005, p. A1; S. Rosenbush, "Five Lessons of the Worldcom Debacle," *Business Week Online*, March 16, 2005.

TEAM EXERCISE 10.2

Budget Deliberations

By Sharon Card

Purpose   This exercise is designed to help you understand some of the power dynamics and influence tactics that occur across hierarchical levels in organizations.

Materials   This activity works best where one small room leads to a larger room, which leads to a larger area.

Instructions   These exercise instructions are based on a class size of about 30 students. The instructor may adjust the size of the first two groups slightly for larger classes. The instructor will organize students as follows: A few (three or four) students are assigned the position of executives. They are preferably located in a secluded office or corner of a large classroom. Another six to eight students are assigned positions as middle managers. These people will ideally be located in an adjoining room or space, allowing privacy for the executives. The remaining students represent the non-management employees in the organization. They are located in an open area outside the executive and management rooms.

Rules   Members of the executive group are free to enter the space of either the middle management or non-management groups and to communicate whatever they wish, whenever they wish. Members of the middle management group may enter the space of the nonmanagement group whenever they wish, but must request permission to enter the executive group's space. The executive group can refuse the middle management group's request. Members of the nonmanagement group are not allowed to disturb the top group in any way unless specifically invited by members of the executive group. The nonmanagement group does have the right to request permission to communicate with the middle management group. The middle management group can refuse the lower group's request.

Task   Your organization is in the process of preparing a budget. The challenge is to balance needs with the financial resources. Of course, the needs are greater than the resources. The instructor will distribute a budget sheet showing a list of budget requests and their costs. Each group has control over a portion of the budget and must decide how to spend the money over which they have control. Non-management has discretion over a relatively small portion and the executive group has discretion over the greatest portion. The exercise is finished when the organization has negotiated a satisfactory budget, or until the instructor calls time out. The class will then debrief with the following questions and others the instructor might ask.

Discussion Questions
1. What can we learn from this exercise about power in organizational hierarchies?
2. How is this exercise similar to relations in real organizations?
3. How did students in each group feel about the amount of power they held?
4. How did they exercise their power in relations with the other groups?

SELF-ASSESSMENT EXERCISE 10.3

What's Your Approach to Upward Influence?

Purpose   This exercise is designed to help you understand several ways of influencing people up the organizational hierarchy as well as estimate your preferred upward influence tactics.

Instructions   Read each of the statements below and circle the response that you believe best indicates how often you engaged in that behaviour over the past six (6) months. Then use the scoring key in Appendix B to calculate your results. This exercise is completed alone so students assess themselves honestly without concerns of social comparison. However, class discussion will focus on the types of influence in organizations and the conditions under which particular influence tactics are most and least appropriate.

Upward Influence Scale					
How often in the past six months have you engaged in the behaviours?	Never	Seldom	Occasionally	Frequently	Almost Always
1. I obtain the support of my co-workers in persuading my manager to act on my request.	1	2	3	4	5
2. I offer an exchange in which I will do something that my manager wants if he or she will do what I want.	1	2	3	4	5
3. I act very humble and polite while making my request.	1	2	3	4	5
4. I appeal to higher management to put pressure on my manager.	1	2	3	4	5
5. I remind my manager of how I have helped him or her in the past and imply that now I expect compliance with my request.	1	2	3	4	5
6. I go out of my way to make my manager feel good about me, before asking him or her to do what I want.	1	2	3	4	5
7. I use logical arguments in order to convince my manager.	1	2	3	4	5
8. I have a face-to-face confrontation with my manager in which I forcefully state what I want.	1	2	3	4	5
9. I act in a friendly manner toward my manager before making my request.	1	2	3	4	5
10. I present facts, figures, and other information to my manager in support of my position.	1	2	3	4	5
11. I obtain the support and cooperation of my subordinates to back up my request.	1	2	3	4	5
12. I obtain the informal support of higher management to back me.	1	2	3	4	5
13. I offer to make a personal sacrifice such as giving up my free time if my manager will do what I want.	1	2	3	4	5
14. I very carefully explain to my manager the reasons for my request.	1	2	3	4	5
15. I verbally express my anger to my manager in order to get what I want.	1	2	3	4	5
16. I use a forceful manner; I try such things as demands, the setting of deadlines, and the expression of strong emotion.	1	2	3	4	5
17. I rely on the chain of command—on people higher up in the organization who have power over my supervisor.	1	2	3	4	5
18. I mobilize other people in the organization to help me in influencing my supervisor.	1	2	3	4	5

Source: R. C. Ringer and R. W. Boss, "Hospital Professional's Use of Upward Influence Tactics," *Journal of Managerial Issues,* 12 (Spring 2000), pp. 92-109; C. Schriesheim and T. Hinkin, "Influence Tactics Used by Subordinates: A Theoretical and Empirical Analysis and Refinement of the Kipnis, Schmidt, and Wilkinson Subscales," *Journal of Applied Psychology,* 75 (1990), pp. 246–257.

www.mcgrawhill.ca/olc/mcshane

 Go to the Online Learning Centre at www.mcgrawhill.ca/olc/mcshane to complete the following interactive self-assessments.

 SELF-ASSESSMENT EXERCISE 10.4

Do You Have a Guanxi Orientation?

Guanxi, which is translated as interpersonal connections, is an important element of doing business in China and some other Asian countries with strong Confucian cultural values. Guanxi is based on traditional Confucian values of helping others without expecting future repayment. This instrument estimates your guanxi orientation; that is, the extent to which you accept and apply guanxi values. This self-assessment is completed alone so that students rate themselves honestly without concerns of social comparison. However, class discussion will focus on the meaning of guanxi and its relevance for organizational power and influence.

SELF-ASSESSMENT EXERCISE 10.5

How Machiavellian Are You?

Machiavellianism is named after Niccolo Machiavelli, the sixteenth-century Italian philosopher who wrote *The Prince,* a famous treatise about political behaviour. Out of Machiavelli's work emerged this instrument that estimates the degree to which you have a Machiavellian personality. Indicate the extent to which you agree or disagree that each statement in this instrument describes you. Complete each item honestly to get the best estimate of your level of Machiavellianism.

SELF-ASSESSMENT EXERCISE 10.6

Does Your School Behave Politically?

Organizations have been called "political arenas"—environments where political tactics are common because decisions are ambiguous and resources are scarce. This instrument estimates the degree to which you believe the school where you attend classes has a politicized culture. This scale consists of several statements that might or might not describe the school where you are attending classes. These statements refer to the administration of the school, not the classroom. Please indicate the extent to which you agree or disagree with each statement.

istudy
¡Interact ¡Learn ¡Succeed

iStudy—Available 24/7 with instant feedback so you can study when you want, how you want, and where you want. Visit www.istudyob.ca to register—take practice quizzes, run interactive scenarios, practice concepts, and much more. Also visit the Student Online Learning Centre for additional study tools.

CHAPTER 11

Conflict and Negotiation in the Workplace

"I'm not going to be the type of person who's going to sit around and do nothing if there's nothing to do," says Tennyson Cho, a 22-year-old Queen's University commerce graduate who was recently hired by Westwind Partners, a small Toronto-based private investment bank. Although Cho is willing to put in the long hours that his job demands, he has no qualms about acknowledging that he plans to "learn as much as I can" and then move on to another firm. Highly confident organizational newcomers sometimes find their enthusiasm receives skepticism or even hostility from older employees.

Baby boomer managers also have work expectations that sometimes clash with expectations held by their younger subordinates. One oft-cited complaint is that younger employees demand clear assignments as well as frequent task clarification and feedback, whereas their baby boomer bosses expect new hires to take initiative without close supervision. Ambiguous rules can also result in conflict between younger and more seasoned employees. For example, baby boomers sometimes grumble when new employees attend meetings wearing edgy clothing with exposed body piercings, or request Fridays off so they can go to the beach.

To minimize multigenerational conflict, many companies have developed training programs and guidelines that establish common expectations and norms. For instance, Ernst & Young employs dozens of young interns throughout its Canadian operations every summer. Recognizing that these students work closely with older staff, the accounting firm has introduced a special program that alerts the newcomers to multigenerational differences. One topic, "Strategies to Connect with Baby Boomers," offers the following advice: It is probably not a good time to request time off, even for a volunteer commitment, just after your boss says that his or her team of young staff is "spending too much time text-messaging each other and listening to iPods."[1]

Technologically savvy and ambitious, Generation Y employees' attributes and attitudes toward work have the potential to induce generational conflicts in the workplace.
© J.P. Moczulaki

One of the facts of life is that people hold different points of view. They have unique values hierarchies, develop unique perceptions of reality through learning and reinforcement, and establish different goals and priorities from those of co-workers. At the same time, organizations are living systems that demand dynamic rather than static relationships among employees. In other words, employees at Ernst & Young, Westwind Partners, and other companies need to frequently agree on new work arrangements, revise the company's strategic direction, and re-negotiate the allocation of scarce resources required to perform their jobs.

Given that people do not have identical viewpoints, this dynamic relationship necessarily leads to conflict. **Conflict** is a process in which one party perceives that its interests are being opposed or negatively affected by another party.[2] It may occur when one party obstructs or plans to obstruct another's goals in some way. For example, baby boomer managers experience conflict with Gen X or Gen Y employees who spend a lot of time text messaging, believing that this interferes with the manager's goal of completing departmental deadlines on time. Text-messaging employees experience conflict with their boss because they view this form of communication as a valuable way to network, keep informed, and (contrary to the boss's opinion) achieve departmental objectives. Conflict is ultimately based on perceptions; it exists whenever one party *believes* that another might obstruct its efforts, whether or not the other party actually intends to do so.

This chapter investigates the dynamics of conflict in organizational settings. We begin by considering the age-old question: Is conflict good or bad? Next, we describe the conflict process and examine in detail the main factors that cause or amplify conflict. The five styles of handling conflict are then described, followed by a discussion of the structural approaches to conflict management. The last two sections of this chapter introduce two procedures for resolving conflict: negotiation and third-party resolution.

> **conflict**
> A process in which one party perceives that its interests are being opposed or negatively affected by another party.

IS CONFLICT GOOD OR BAD?

LO1

For most of the past century, conflict was widely regarded as undesirable and counter-productive.[3] This is illustrated in Exhibit 11.1a, where the downward line shows that as the level of conflict increases, conflict outcomes get worse. According to this view, even moderately low levels of disagreement tatter the fabric of workplace relations and sap energy away from productive activities. Conflict with one's supervisor not only wastes productive time; it violates the hierarchy of command and questions the efficient assignment of authority (where managers made the decisions and employees followed them).

Although the "conflict is bad" perspective is now considered oversimplistic, numerous studies report that some levels of conflict do produce lower job satisfaction, team cohesion, and information sharing; biased perceptions and decisions; and higher levels of organizational politics, stress, and turnover.[4] Conflict distracts employees from their work and, in some cases, motivates them to withhold valuable knowledge and other resources. People who experience conflict are less motivated to communicate or try to understand the other party, which further escalates conflict as each side increasingly relies on distorted perceptions and stereotypes. One Canadian survey estimates that 42 percent of a manager's time is spent dealing with workplace conflict, and that conflict triggers most voluntary and involuntary employee turnover.[5]

By the 1950s and 1960s, a few writers questioned the "conflict is bad" perspective, suggesting instead that there is an optimal level of conflict—too little and too much conflict is bad for organizational effectiveness. This upside down U-shaped relationship—shown in Exhibit 11.1b—gained wide acceptance in the 1970s and remains popular today.[6] Various studies have reported that a moderate level of conflict produces several favourable outcomes. One outcome is improved decision making. Conflict energizes people to debate issues and evaluate alternatives more thoroughly. The debate tests the logic of arguments and encourages participants to re-examine their basic assumptions about the problem and its possible solution. Another apparent benefit of moderate conflict is that it prevents organizations from stagnating and becoming nonresponsive to

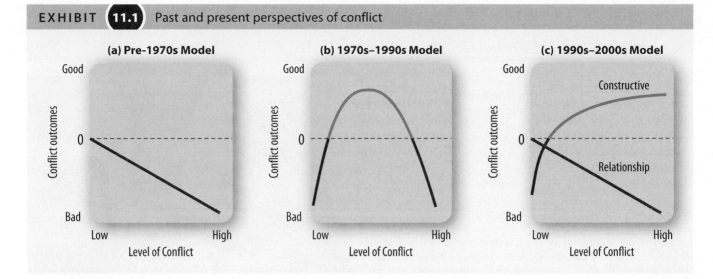

EXHIBIT 11.1   Past and present perspectives of conflict

their external environment. This reflects our earlier observation that conflict occurs in organizations because they are living systems. Moderate levels of conflict are inevitable and necessary in dynamic organizations; conflict episodes occur when employees try to keep the organization responsive to the needs of customers and other stakeholders.[7] A third benefit, which we learned in the chapter on teams, is that conflict with people outside the team potentially increases cohesion within the team. People are more motivated to work together when faced with an external threat, such as conflict with people outside the team.

THE EMERGING VIEW: CONSTRUCTIVE AND RELATIONSHIP CONFLICT

The upside down U-shaped model of conflict was replaced in the 1990s by the perspective that there are actually two types of conflict with opposing consequences (see Exhibit 11.1c).[8] **Constructive conflict** (also known as *task or cognitive conflict*) occurs when people focus their discussion on the issue while maintaining respectfulness for people having other points of view. This conflict is called "constructive" because different viewpoints are encouraged so that ideas and recommendations can be clarified, redesigned, and tested for logical soundness. By keeping the debate focused on the task and logic, participants can re-examine their assumptions and beliefs about the problem and possible solutions without triggering the drive to defend and its associated negative emotions and ego-defence mechanism behaviours. Teams and organizations that have very low levels of constructive conflict are less effective, but there is also likely an upper limit to the level of intensity of constructive conflict.[9] Former Intel employees Logan Shrine and Bob Coleman, described in GLOBAL Connections 11.1, were critical of the company's conflict episodes because that conflict may be more intense than is beneficial.

In contrast to constructive conflict, **relationship conflict** (also known as *socioemotional, affective, or destructive conflict*), occurs when people view their differences as personal attacks rather than attempts to resolve an issue. The attention is on interpersonal incompatibilities such as "personality clashes" rather than legitimate differences of opinion regarding tasks or decisions. Employees try to undermine another person's argument by questioning the competency of the person presenting that argument. Attacking a person's credibility or displaying an aggressive response toward him or her triggers defence mechanisms and a competitive orientation. The subjects of those verbal attacks become less motivated to communicate and share information, making it more difficult for everyone to discover common ground and ultimately resolve the conflict. The parties then rely on more distorted perceptions and stereotypes which, as we noted on the previous page, tend to further escalate the conflict.

constructive conflict
Occurs when people focus their discussion on the issue while maintaining respectfulness for people having other points of view.

relationship conflict
Occurs when people view their differences as personal attacks rather than attempts to resolve an issue.

global connections 11.1

Constructive Confrontation Inside Intel

Former Goldman Sachs president John Thornton has had his share of executive debates, but even he was surprised by the animated discussion that permeates Intel, the chipmaker where Thornton is a member of the board. "It can be kind of shocking at first," says Thornton, recalling his first few Intel meetings. "You realize quickly that [Intel managers] practise a form of honesty that borders on brutality." Intel co-founder and former chairman Andy Grove nurtured this culture of conflict—called constructive confrontation—many years ago when he noticed that meetings generate better ideas when staff actively debate rather than politely defer to ideas that others put forward. The practice is so important that new Intel employees are taught the fine art of confrontation through supervised debates and role plays.

Andy Grove emphasizes that conflict is constructive only under specific circumstances. "Constructive confrontation does not mean being loud, unpleasant or rude, and it is not designed to affix blame," warns Grove. "The essence of it is to attack a problem by speaking up in a businesslike way." If you target the other person, then the benefits of constructive debate disintegrate. But some people claim that Intel's constructive confrontation never was very constructive. Instead, like John Thornton, some staff also experience a heavy dose of relationship conflict. "I

Constructive conflict is part of Intel's culture, but some people say the computer chip-maker's task-focused discussion includes plenty of relationship conflict. *Christopher Bissell/Getty Images*

can tell you unequivocally that constructive confrontation was a licence for a**holes to be a**holes and express themselves," says former Intel employee Logan Shrine, who co-authored a book with Bob Coleman on Intel's changing culture. "Intel's culture is dysfunctional and anomalous to what's considered acceptable behaviour in any other corporation."[10]

LO3

Separating Constructive from Relationship Conflict   The idea that there are two types of conflict—constructive and relationship—leads to the logical conclusion that we should encourage constructive conflict for better decision making and minimize relationship conflict in order to avoid dysfunctional emotions and behaviours. This recommendation sounds good in theory, but recent evidence suggests that separating these two types of conflict isn't easy. Most of us experience some degree of relationship conflict during or after any constructive debate.[11] In other words, any attempt to engage in constructive conflict, no matter how calmly and rationally, may still sow the seeds of relationship conflict. The stronger the level of debate and the more the issue is tied to the individual's social identity or need fulfillment, the higher the chance that the constructive conflict will evolve into (or mix with) relationship conflict. As GLOBAL Connections 11.1 describes, Intel staff and visitors experience relationship conflict, even though they are taught the fine art of constructive debate.

Fortunately, conflict management experts have identified three strategies that potentially minimize the level of relationship conflict during constructive conflict episodes.[12]

- *Emotional Intelligence.* Relationship conflict is less likely to occur, or is less likely to escalate, when team members have high levels of emotional intelligence. Emotionally intelligent employees are better able to regulate their emotions during debate, which reduces the risk of escalating perceptions of interpersonal hostility. People with high emotional intelligence are also more likely to view a co-worker's emotional reaction as valuable information about that person's needs and expectations, rather than as a personal attack.

- *Cohesive Team.* Relationship conflict is suppressed when the conflict occurs within a highly cohesive team. The longer people work together, get to know each other, and develop mutual trust, the more latitude they give to each other to show emotions without being personally offended. Strong cohesion also allows each person to know about and anticipate the behaviours and emotions of his or her teammates. Another benefit is that cohesion produces a stronger social identity with the group, so team members are motivated to avoid escalating relationship conflict during otherwise emotionally turbulent discussions.

- *Supportive Team Norms.* Various team norms can hold relationship conflict at bay during constructive debate. When team norms encourage openness, for instance, team members learn to appreciate honest dialogue without personally reacting to any emotional display during the disagreements.[13] Other norms might discourage team members from displaying negative emotions toward co-workers. Team norms also encourage tactics that diffuse relationship conflict when it first appears. For instance, research has found that teams with low relationship conflict use humour to maintain positive group emotions, which offsets negative feelings team members might develop toward some co-workers during debate.

CONFLICT PROCESS MODEL

LO4 Now that we have outlined the history and current knowledge about conflict and its outcomes, let's look at the model of the conflict process, shown in Exhibit 11.2.[14] This model begins with the sources of conflict, which we will describe in more detail in the next section. At some point, the sources of conflict lead one or both parties to perceive that conflict exists. They become aware that one party's statements and actions are incompatible with their own goals. These perceptions usually interact with emotions experienced about the conflict.[15] Conflict perceptions and emotions manifest themselves in the decisions and behaviours of one party toward the other. These *conflict episodes* may range from subtle nonverbal behaviours to warlike aggression. Particularly when people experience high levels of conflict emotions, they have difficulty finding the words and expressions that communicate effectively without further irritating the relationship.[16] Conflict is also manifested by the style each side uses to resolve the conflict. Some people tend to avoid the conflict whereas others try to defeat those with opposing views.

Exhibit 11.2 shows arrows looping back from manifest conflict to conflict perceptions and emotions. These arrows illustrate that the conflict process is really a series of episodes that potentially cycle into conflict escalation.[17] It doesn't take much to start this

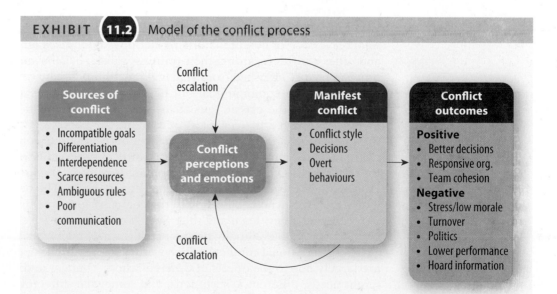

EXHIBIT 11.2 Model of the conflict process

- **Sources of conflict**
  - Incompatible goals
  - Differentiation
  - Interdependence
  - Scarce resources
  - Ambiguous rules
  - Poor communication

Conflict escalation

Conflict perceptions and emotions

Conflict escalation

- **Manifest conflict**
  - Conflict style
  - Decisions
  - Overt behaviours

- **Conflict outcomes**
  - **Positive**
    - Better decisions
    - Responsive org.
    - Team cohesion
  - **Negative**
    - Stress/low morale
    - Turnover
    - Politics
    - Lower performance
    - Hoard information

conflict cycle—just an inappropriate comment, a misunderstanding, or action that lacks diplomacy. These behaviours cause the other party to perceive that conflict exists. Even if the first party did not intend to demonstrate conflict, the second party's response may create that perception.

STRUCTURAL SOURCES OF CONFLICT IN ORGANIZATIONS

LO5

The conflict model starts with the sources of conflict, and it is vital that we understand these sources to effectively diagnose conflict episodes, or to identify strategies that will generate more conflict. The six main conditions that cause conflict in organizational settings are incompatible goals, differentiation, interdependence, scarce resources, ambiguous rules, and communication problems.

① INCOMPATIBLE GOALS

Microsoft Corp. has been highly successful with its host of products and services, yet various sources conclude that the company suffers from vicious infighting across product groups. "Pretty much across the board people are saying that Microsoft is dysfunctional," concludes one industry analyst. "They are not cooperating across business groups." One of the major sources of this conflict is that some work units have incompatible goals with other units. For example, the MSN group had developed desktop search software which would compete against Google Desktop. However, Microsoft's Windows group opposed release of the MSN software because the Windows group had developed similar software for its Vista operating system. The MSN group also fought against the Office people over MSN's desire to connect their online calendar with the calendar in Office. The Office group balked because "then MSN could cannibalize Office," says an employee who recently left Microsoft. "Windows and Office would never let MSN have more budget or more control."[18]

The battles between Microsoft MSN and Windows work units illustrate how goal incompatibility—where the goals of one person or department seem to interfere with another person's or department's goals—can be a source of conflict in organizations.[19] MSN's goal of competing against Google with desktop search software threatened the Windows group's goals of launching new features in Microsoft Vista. MSN's goal of providing users with better calendar integration threatened the Microsoft Office group's product territory, which might undermine its profitability or control over the calendar feature.

② DIFFERENTIATION

Another source of conflict is differentiation—differences among people, departments, and other entities regarding their training, values, beliefs, and experiences. Differentiation can be distinguished from goal incompatibility because two people or departments may agree on a common goal but have profound differences in how to achieve that goal. Consider the classic tension between employees from two companies brought together through a merger. Staff in each organization fight over the "right way" to do things because of their unique experiences in the separate companies. A Canadian retail clothing chain experienced another variation of differentiation-based conflict when the founder and CEO hired several senior managers from larger organizations to strengthen the experience levels of its senior management group. The new managers soon clashed with executives who had been with the company for some time. "We ended up with an old team and a new team and they weren't on the same wavelength," explains the company owner, who eventually fired most of the new managers.

Intergenerational conflicts, which were described in the opening story to this chapter, are largely due to the effects of differentiation. Younger and older employees have different needs, different expectations, and somewhat different values, which sometimes

produces conflicting preferences and actions. One recent poll reported that four out of ten Canadians believe a multigenerational workplace adds some challenges to the job. "These different generations have grown up experiencing significantly different events that have shaped their values and beliefs," explains Gabriel Bouchard, vice-president and general manager of online employment site Monster Canada. "As diverse generations cross paths on the job, we sometimes see a clash of attitudes, ethics, values, and behaviours."[21]

Information technology also maintains differentiation because without face-to-face experiences, employees have more difficulty forming common mental models and norms. For instance, recent investigations indicate that virtual teams have a high incidence of conflict because technology makes it difficult for them to form common experiences and perspectives.[22]

③ INTERDEPENDENCE

Conflict tends to increase with the level of interdependence. Interdependence exists when team members must share common inputs to their individual tasks, need to interact in the process of executing their work, or receive outcomes (such as rewards) that are partly determined by the performance of others.[23] Higher interdependence increases the risk of conflict because there is a greater chance that each side will disrupt or interfere with the other side's goals.[24]

Other than complete independence, employees tend to have the lowest risk of conflict when working with others in a pooled interdependence relationship. Pooled interdependence occurs where individuals operate independently except for reliance on a common resource or authority (see Chapter 8). The potential for conflict is higher in sequential interdependence work relationships, such as an assembly line. The highest risk of conflict tends to occur in reciprocal interdependence situations. With reciprocal interdependence, employees are highly dependent on each other and, consequently, have a higher probability of interfering with each other's work and personal goals.

④ SCARCE RESOURCES

Resource scarcity generates conflict because each person or unit requiring the same resource necessarily undermines others who also need that resource to fulfill their goals. Consider the lively debates among employees at Intel, described in earlier GLOBAL Connections 11.1. These conflict episodes occur partly because there aren't enough financial, human capital, and other resources for everyone to accomplish their goals, so employees need to justify why they should receive the resources. The more resources one project receives, the fewer resources that another project will have to accomplish its goals.

⑤ AMBIGUOUS RULES

Ambiguous rules—or the complete lack of rules—breed conflict. This occurs because uncertainty increases the risk that one party intends to interfere with the other party's goals. Ambiguity also encourages political tactics and, in some cases, employees enter a free-for-all battle to win decisions in their favour. This explains why conflict is more common during mergers and acquisitions. Employees from both companies have conflicting practices and values, and few rules have developed to minimize the manoeuvring for power and resources.[25] When clear rules exist, on the other hand, employees know what to expect from each other and have agreed to abide by those rules.

⑥ COMMUNICATION PROBLEMS

Conflict often occurs due to the lack of opportunity, ability, or motivation to communicate effectively. Let's look at each of these causes. First, when two parties lack the opportunity to communicate, they tend to rely more on stereotypes to understand the other party in the conflict. Unfortunately, stereotypes are sufficiently subjective that emotions can negatively distort the meaning of an opponent's actions, thereby escalating perceptions of conflict. Second, some people lack the necessary skills to communicate in a diplomatic, nonconfrontational manner. When one party communicates its disagreement arrogantly, opponents are more likely to heighten their perception of the conflict. This may lead the other party to reciprocate with a similar response, which further escalates the conflict.[26]

A third problem is that the perception of conflict reduces motivation to communicate. Relationship conflict is uncomfortable, so people avoid interacting with others in a conflicting relationship. Unfortunately, less communication can further escalate the conflict because there is less opportunity to empathize with the opponent's situation and opponents are more likely to rely on distorted stereotypes of the other party. In fact, conflict tends to further distort these stereotypes through the process of social identity (see Chapter 2). We begin to see competitors less favourably so that our self-concept remains strong during these uncertain times.[27]

INTERPERSONAL CONFLICT HANDLING STYLES

LO6

The six structural conditions described above set the stage for conflict, and these sources lead to conflict perceptions and emotions which, in turn, motivate people to take some sort of action to address the conflict. Dating back to the forward-thinking views of management scholar Mary Parker Follett in the 1920s, organizational behaviour experts have identified several conflict handling styles. The number of styles identified by conflict experts has varied over the years, but most common are variations of the five-category model shown in Exhibit 11.3 and described below.[28]

win–win orientation
The belief that the parties will find a mutually beneficial solution to their disagreement.

win–lose orientation
The belief that conflicting parties are drawing from a fixed pie, so the more one party receives, the less the other party will receive.

- *Problem solving*—Problem solving tries to find a mutually beneficial solution for both parties. This is known as the **win–win orientation** because people using this style believe that the resources at stake are expandable rather than fixed if the parties work together to find a creative solution. Information sharing is an important feature of this style because both parties collaborate to identify common ground and potential solutions that satisfy everyone involved.

- *Forcing*—Forcing tries to win the conflict at the other's expense. People who use this style typically have a **win–lose orientation**—they believe the parties are drawing from a fixed pie, so the more one party receives, the less the other party will receive. Consequently, this style relies on some of the "hard" influence tactics described in Chapter 10, particularly assertiveness, to get one's own way.

- *Avoiding*—Avoiding tries to smooth over or avoid conflict situations altogether. It represents a low concern for both self and the other party; in other words, avoiders try to suppress thinking about the conflict. For example, some employees will rearrange their work area or tasks to minimize interaction with certain co-workers.[29]

- *Yielding*—Yielding involves giving in completely to the other side's wishes, or at least cooperating with little or no attention to your own interests. This style involves making unilateral concessions and unconditional promises, as well as offering help with no expectation of reciprocal help.

- *Compromising*—Compromising involves looking for a position in which your losses are offset by equally valued gains. It involves matching the other party's concessions, making conditional promises or threats, and actively searching for a middle ground between the interests of the two parties.

CHOOSING THE BEST CONFLICT HANDLING STYLE

Probably everyone has a preferred conflict handling style. You might have a tendency toward avoiding or yielding because disagreement makes you feel uncomfortable and is inconsistent with your self-concept as someone who likes to get along with everyone. Or you might prefer the compromising and forcing strategies because they reflect your strong need for achievement and to control your environment. In general, people gravitate toward one or two preferred conflict handling styles that match their personality, personal and cultural values, and past experience. For example, studies have found that people in Confucian cultures prefer non-confrontational conflict handling styles (e.g., avoidance) because this approach is consistent with the cultural value of harmony. People in Canada, the United States and similar Western cultures, on the other hand, are generally more comfortable with the forcing approach (although it is still less popular than other styles).[30] Some research reports gender differences in conflict handling tendencies, with the problem solving and compromising styles preferred by women more often than by men.[31]

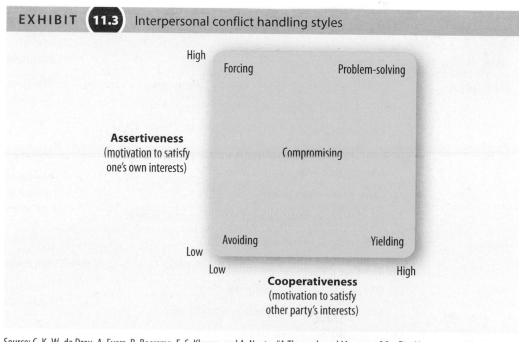

EXHIBIT 11.3   Interpersonal conflict handling styles

Source: C. K. W. de Dreu, A. Evers, B. Beersma, E. S. Kluwer, and A. Nauta, "A Theory-based Measure of Conflict Management Strategies in the Workplace," *Journal of Organizational Behaviour*, 22 (2001), pp. 645–68. For other variations of this model, see: T. L. Ruble and K. Thomas, "Support for a Two-Dimensional Model of Conflict Behaviour," *Organizational Behaviour and Human Performance*, 16 (1976), p. 145. Also see: R. R. Blake, H. A. Shepard, and J. S. Mouton, *Managing Intergroup Conflict in Industry* (Houston: Gulf Publishing, 1964); M. A. Rahim, "Toward a Theory of Managing Organizational Conflict," *International Journal of Conflict Management* 13, no. 3 (2002), pp. 206–235.

However, most people recognize that they should use different conflict handling styles in different situations.[32] In other words, the best style varies with the situation.[33] Exhibit 11.4 summarizes the main contingencies, as well as problems with using each conflict handling style. Problem solving has long been identified as the preferred conflict handling style where possible because dialogue and clever thinking helps people to break out of the limited boundaries of their opposing alternatives to find an integrated solution where both gain value. In addition, recent studies report that problem solving improves long-term relationships, reduces stress, and minimizes emotional defensiveness and other indications of relationship conflict.[34] However, problem solving is the best choice of conflict handling only when there is some potential for mutual gains, which is more likely to occur when the issue is complex, and when the parties have enough trust, openness, and time to share information. If problem solving is used under the wrong conditions, there is an increased risk that the other party will take advantage of the information you have openly shared.

You might think that avoiding is an ineffective conflict management strategy, but it is actually the best approach where conflict has become emotionally charged or where negotiating has a higher cost than the benefits of conflict resolution.[35] At the same time, conflict avoidance is often ineffective because it doesn't resolve the conflict and may increase the other party's frustration. The forcing style of conflict resolution is usually inappropriate because research indicates that it generates relationship conflict more quickly or intensely than other conflict handling styles. However, forcing may be necessary where you know you are correct (e.g., the other party's position is unethical or based on obviously flawed logic), the dispute requires a quick solution, or the other party would take advantage of a more cooperative conflict handling style.

The yielding style may be appropriate when the other party has substantially more power, the issue is not as important to you as to the other party, and you aren't confident that your position has the best value or logical consistency. On the other hand, yielding behaviours may give the other side unrealistically high expectations, thereby motivating them to seek more from you in the future. In the long run, yielding may produce more

EXHIBIT 11.4	Conflict handling style contingencies and problems	
Conflict Handling Style	**Preferred Style When...**	**Problems with this Style**
Problem solving	Interests are not perfectly opposing (i.e., not actually win–lose) Parties have trust, openness, and time to share information The issues are complex	Sharing information that the other party might use to their advantage
Forcing	You have a deep conviction about your position (e.g., believe other person's behaviour is unethical) Dispute requires a quick solution The other party would take advantage of more cooperative strategies	Highest risk of relationship conflict May damage long-term relations, reducing future problem solving
Avoiding	Conflict has become too emotionally charged Cost of trying to resolve the conflict outweighs the benefits	Doesn't usually resolve the conflict May increase other party's frustration
Yielding	Other party has substantially more power Issue is much less important to you than to the other party The value and logic of your position isn't as clear	Increases other party's expectations in future conflict episodes
Compromising	Parties have equal power Time pressure to resolve the conflict Parties lack trust/openness for problem solving	Sub-optimal solution where mutual gains are possible

NHLPA Stick Handles the Extremes of Conflict Handling

Former National Hockey League Players' Association (NHLPA) boss Bob Goodenow (left in photo) was called the Darth Vader of hockey. He relied on a forcing style that catapulted NHL player salaries into the stratosphere, but also soured relations with the NHL commissioner and team owners, resulting in cancellation of an entire NHL season. Goodenow stepped down after the cancelled season, replaced by Montreal-born Ted Saskin (right in photo), who promised a more diplomatic problem-solving approach. "I just think that in any business you need a spirit of cooperation to move forward, and I think Ted Saskin will handle that well," said NHL board of governors chairman Harley Hotchkiss when Saskin was appointed NHLPA executive director. But Saskin may have been too cozy with the NHL team owners and too mistrusting of the players he represented. Some players opposed Saskin's appointment, so the NHL Commissioner's staff allegedly gave Saskin the names of players who were conspiring against him. Saskin allegedly had the emails of these conspiring players monitored so he could anticipate their actions against him. When news of the email monitoring went public, Saskin was fired. Replacing Saskin is Paul Kelly, who so far has been careful not to display too much yielding or forcing in his dealings with the NHL Commissioner.[36] *AP Images/The Canadian Press (Adrian Wyld)*

conflict rather than resolve it. The compromising style may be best when there is little hope for mutual gain through problem solving, both parties have equal power, and both are under time pressure to settle their differences. However, we rarely know for certain that mutual gains are not available, so entering a conflict with the compromising style may cause the parties to overlook better solutions.

STRUCTURAL APPROACHES TO CONFLICT MANAGEMENT

LO7

Conflict management styles refer to how we approach the other party in a conflict situation. But conflict management also involves altering the underlying structural causes of potential conflict. The main structural approaches are emphasizing superordinate goals, reducing differentiation, improving communication and understanding, reducing task interdependence, increasing resources, and clarifying rules and procedures.

EMPHASIZING SUPERORDINATE GOALS

One of the oldest recommendations for resolving conflict is to seek out and find common goals.[37] In organizational settings, this typically takes the form of a **superordinate goal,** which is any goal that both conflicting parties value and whose attainment is beyond the resources and effort of either party alone.[38] By increasing commitment to corporate-wide goals, employees pay less attention to competing individual or departmental-level goals, which reduces their perceived conflict with co-workers. By establishing a common frame of reference, they also potentially reduce the problem of differentiation. For example, research indicates that the most effective executive teams frame their decisions as superordinate goals that rise above each executive's departmental or divisional goals.[39]

superordinate goal
Any goal that both conflicting parties value and whose attainment is beyond the resources and effort of either party alone.

REDUCING DIFFERENTIATION

Another way to minimize dysfunctional conflict is to reduce the differences that produce the conflict in the first place. The more employees think they have common backgrounds or experiences with co-workers, the more motivated they are to coordinate their activities and resolve conflict through constructive discussion with those co-workers.[40] One way to increase this commonality is by creating common experiences. The Manila Diamond Hotel in the Philippines accomplishes this by rotating staff across different departments. Multinational peacekeeping forces reduce differentiation among troops from the representative nations by providing opportunities for them to socialize and engage in common activities, including eating together.[41]

IMPROVING COMMUNICATION AND UNDERSTANDING

A third way to resolve dysfunctional conflict is to give the conflicting parties more opportunities to communicate and understand each other. This recommendation relates back to the contact hypothesis described in Chapter 3. Specifically, the more meaningful interaction we have with someone, the less we rely on stereotypes to understand that person.[42] There are two warnings, however. First, communication and understanding interventions should be applied only *after* differentiation between the two sides has been reduced or where differentiation is already sufficiently low. If perceived differentiation remains high, attempts to manage conflict through dialogue might escalate rather than reduce relationship conflict. The reason is that when forced to interact with people who we believe are quite different and in conflict with us, we tend to select information that reinforces that view.[43] Thus, communication and understanding interventions are effective only when differentiation is sufficiently low.

The second warning is that people in collectivist and high power distance cultures are less comfortable with the practice of resolving differences through direct and open communication.[44] As noted earlier, people in Confucian cultures prefer an avoidance conflict management style because it is the most consistent with harmony and face-saving. Direct communication is a high-risk strategy because it easily threatens the need to save face and maintain harmony.

REDUCING INTERDEPENDENCE

Conflict increases with the level of interdependence so minimizing dysfunctional conflict might involve reducing the level of interdependence between the parties. If cost effective, this can occur by dividing the shared resource so that each party has exclusive use at different times. Sequentially or reciprocally interdependent jobs might be combined so that they form a pooled interdependence. For example, rather than having one employee serve customers and another operate the cash register, each employee could handle both customer activities alone. Buffers also help to reduce interdependence between people. Buffers include resources, such as adding more inventory between

Drumming Out Conflict

With increasing diversity and geographic dispersion, employees require a vehicle to reduce their differentiation and improve mutual understanding. For some companies, that vehicle is a drum circle, an ensemble of far-flung employees with little or no percussion experience who literally learn to develop a common beat using a variety of drums. "Companies, like music, are made up of a variety of different rhythms," explains Danny Aaron, president of Vancouver-based Drum Cafe Canada, shown in this photo with musician and master facilitator Mbuyiselp Ncapayi. "You can have sales, marketing, accounting. You can have Vancouver, Calgary, and Toronto. But as long as those different rhythms can play to that same beat—the foundation—and can listen to each other—the communication—then as an organization they can make music." Drum circles have been so effective in some firms that Toyota USA and McDonnell Douglas send a random group of employees through their internal drum circle sessions each week. "Drumming cuts across language and cultural barriers," says Paul Houle, a Toronto-based professional percussionist who has facilitated drum circles for Black & Decker Canada, TD Bank, and many other firms. "It has a primal energy that brings everyone together—without Power Point presentations."[45] © *Lyle Stafford*

people who perform sequential tasks. Organizations also use human buffers—people who serve as intermediaries between interdependent people or work units who do not get along through direct interaction.

INCREASING RESOURCES

An obvious way to reduce conflict caused by resource scarcity is to increase the amount of available resources. Corporate decision makers might quickly dismiss this solution because of the costs involved. However, they need to carefully compare these costs with the costs of dysfunctional conflict arising out of resource scarcity.

CLARIFYING RULES AND PROCEDURES

Conflicts that arise from ambiguous rules can be minimized by establishing rules and procedures. Armstrong World Industries, Inc., applied this strategy when consultants and information systems employees clashed while working together on development of a client–server network. Information systems employees at the flooring and building materials company thought they should be in charge, whereas consultants believed they had the senior role. Also, the consultants wanted to work long hours and take Fridays off to fly home, whereas Armstrong employees wanted to work regular hours. The company reduced these conflicts by having both parties agree on specific responsibilities and roles. The agreement also assigned two senior executives at the company to establish rules if future disagreements arose.[46]

Rules establish changes to the terms of interdependence, such as an employee's hours of work or a supplier's fulfillment of an order. In most cases, the parties affected by these rules are involved in the process of deciding these terms of interdependence. Thus, by redefining the terms of interdependence, the strategy of clarifying rules involves negotiation, which we discuss next.

RESOLVING CONFLICT THROUGH NEGOTIATION

negotiation

The process whereby two or more conflicting parties attempt to resolve their divergent goals by redefining the terms of their interdependence.

Think back through yesterday's events. Maybe you had to work out an agreement with other students about what tasks to complete for a team project. Chances are that you shared transportation with someone, so you had to clarify the timing of the ride. Then perhaps there was the question of who made dinner. Each of these daily events created potential conflict, and they were resolved through negotiation. **Negotiation** occurs whenever two or more conflicting parties attempt to resolve their divergent goals by redefining the terms of their interdependence. In other words, people negotiate when they think that discussion can produce a more satisfactory arrangement (at least for them) in their exchange of goods or services.

As you can see, negotiation is not an obscure practice reserved for labour and management bosses when hammering out a collective agreement. Everyone negotiates, every day. Most of the time, you don't even realize that you are in negotiations. Negotiation is particularly evident in the workplace because employees work interdependently with each other. They negotiate with their supervisors over next month's work assignments, with customers over the sale and delivery schedules of their product, and with co-workers over when to have lunch. And yes, they occasionally negotiate with each other in labour disputes and workplace agreements.

Some writers suggest that negotiations are more successful when the parties adopt a problem-solving style, whereas others caution that this conflict handling style is sometimes costly.[47] We know that any win–lose style (forcing, yielding, etc.) is unlikely to produce the optimal solution, because the parties have not shared information necessary to discover a mutually satisfactory solution. On the other hand, we must be careful about openly adopting a problem-solving style until mutual trust has been established.

The concern with the problem-solving style is that information is power, so information sharing gives the other party more power to leverage a better deal if the opportunity occurs. Skilled negotiators often adopt a cautious problem-solving style at the outset by sharing information slowly and determining whether the other side will reciprocate. In this respect, they try to establish trust with the other party.[48] They switch to one of the win–lose styles only when it becomes apparent that a win–win solution is not possible or the other party is unwilling to share information with a cooperative orientation.

BARGAINING ZONE MODEL OF NEGOTIATIONS

The negotiation process moves each party along a continuum with an area of potential overlap called the *bargaining zone*.[49] Exhibit 11.5 displays one possible bargaining zone situation. This linear diagram illustrates a purely win–lose situation—one side's gain will be the other's loss. However, the bargaining zone model can also be applied to situations in which both sides potentially gain from the negotiations. As this model illustrates, the parties typically establish three main negotiating points. The *initial offer point* is the team's opening offer to the other party. This may be its best expectation or a pie-in-the-sky starting point. The *target point* is the team's realistic goal or expectation for a final agreement. The *resistance point* is the point beyond which the team will make no further concessions.

The parties begin negotiations by describing their initial offer point for each item on the agenda. In most cases, the participants know that this is only a starting point that will change as both sides offer concessions. In win–lose situations, neither the target nor the resistance point is revealed to the other party. However, people try to discover the other side's resistance point because this knowledge helps them determine how much they can gain without breaking off negotiations. When the parties have a win–win orientation, on the other hand, the objective is to find a creative solution that keeps everyone close to their initial offer points. They hope to find an arrangement by which each side loses relatively little value on some issues and gains significantly more on other issues.

LO8

SITUATIONAL INFLUENCES ON NEGOTIATIONS

The effectiveness of negotiating depends on both the situation and the behaviours of the negotiators. Four of the most important situational factors are location, physical setting, time, and audience.

Location It is easier to negotiate on your own turf because you are familiar with the negotiating environment and are able to maintain comfortable routines.[50] Also, there is

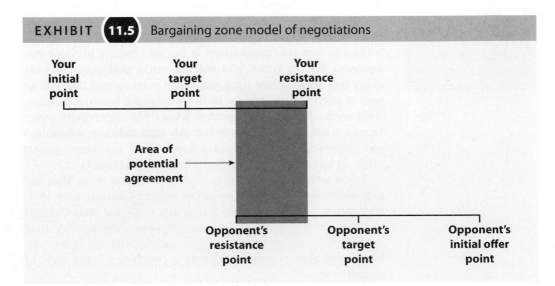

EXHIBIT 11.5   Bargaining zone model of negotiations

no need to cope with travel-related stress or depend on others for resources during the negotiation. Of course, you can't walk out of negotiations as easily when on your own turf, but this is usually a minor issue. Considering these strategic benefits of home turf, many negotiators agree to neutral territory. Phone calls, videoconferences, and other forms of information technology potentially avoid territorial issues, but skilled negotiators usually prefer the media richness of face-to-face meetings. Frank Lowy, co-founder of retail property giant Westfield Group says that phone calls are "too cold" for negotiating. "From a voice I don't get all the cues I need. I go by touch and feel and I need to see the other person."[51]

Physical Setting   The physical distance between the parties and formality of the setting can influence their orientation toward each other and the disputed issues. So can the seating arrangements. People who sit face to face are more likely to develop a win–lose orientation toward the conflict situation. In contrast, some negotiation groups deliberately intersperse participants around the table to convey a win–win orientation. Others arrange the seating so that both parties face a white board, reflecting the notion that both parties face the same problem or issue.

Time Passage and Deadlines   The more time people invest in negotiations, the stronger is their commitment to reaching an agreement. This increases the motivation to resolve the conflict, but it also fuels the escalation of commitment problems described in Chapter 7. For example, the more time put into negotiations, the stronger the tendency to make unwarranted concessions so that the negotiations do not fail.

Time deadlines may be useful to the extent that they motivate the parties to complete negotiations. However, time pressures are usually a liability in negotiations.[52] One problem is that time pressure inhibits a problem-solving conflict management style, because the parties have less time to exchange information or present flexible offers. Negotiators under time pressure also process information less effectively, so they have less creative ability to discover a win–win solution to the conflict. There is also anecdotal evidence that negotiators make excessive concessions and soften their demands more rapidly as the deadline approaches.

Audience Characteristics   Most negotiators have audiences—anyone with a vested interest in the negotiation outcomes, such as executives, other team members, or the general public. Negotiators tend to act differently when their audience observes the negotiation or has detailed information about the process, compared to situations in which the audience sees only the end results.[53] When the audience has direct surveillance over the proceedings, negotiators tend to be more competitive, less willing to make concessions, and more likely to engage in political tactics against the other party. This "hardline" behaviour shows the audience that the negotiator is working for their interests. With their audience watching, negotiators also have more interest in saving face.

L09

NEGOTIATOR SKILLS

Negotiator skills play an important role in resolving conflict. Four of the most important skills are preparing and setting goals, gathering information, communicating effectively, and making concessions.

- *Preparation and goal setting*—Research consistently reports that people have more favourable negotiation results when they prepare for the negotiation and set goals.[54] In particular, negotiators should carefully think through their initial offer, target, and resistance points. They need to consider alternative strategies in case the negotiation fails. Negotiators also need to check their underlying assumptions, as well as goals and values. Equally important is the need to research what the other party wants from the negotiation. "You have to be prepared every which way about the people, the subject, and your fallback position," advises Paul Tellier, who has served as Canada's top civil servant as well as CEO of Bombardier Inc. "Before walking into the room for the actual negotiation, I ask my colleagues to throw some curve balls at me," he says.[55]

- *Gathering information*—"Seek to understand before you seek to be understood." This popular philosophy from management guru Stephen Covey applies to effective negotiations. It means that we should spend more time listening closely to the other party and asking for details.[56] One way to improve the information-gathering process is to have a team of people participate in negotiations. Asian companies tend to have large negotiation teams for this purpose.[57] With more information about the opponent's interests and needs, negotiators are better able to discover low-cost concessions or proposals that will satisfy the other side.

- *Communicating effectively*—Effective negotiators communicate in a way that maintains effective relationships between the parties. Specifically, they minimize socioemotional conflict by focusing on issues rather than people. Effective negotiators also avoid irritating statements such as "I think you'll agree that this is a generous offer." Third, effective negotiators are masters of persuasion. They structure the content of their message so it is accepted by others, not merely understood.[58]

- *Making concessions*—Concessions are important because they (1) enable the parties to move toward the area of potential agreement, (2) symbolize each party's motivation to bargain in good faith, and (3) tell the other party of the relative importance of the negotiating items.[59] How many concessions should you make? This varies with the other party's expectations and the level of trust between you. For instance, many Chinese negotiators are wary of people who change their position during the early stages of negotiations. Similarly, some writers warn that Russian negotiators tend to view concessions as a sign of weakness, rather than a sign of trust.[60] Generally, the best strategy is to be moderately tough and give just enough concessions to communicate sincerity and motivation to resolve the conflict.[61] Being too tough can undermine relations between the parties; giving too many concessions implies weakness and encourages the other party to use power and resistance.

THIRD-PARTY CONFLICT RESOLUTION

LO10

third-party conflict resolution
Any attempt by a relatively neutral person to help the parties resolve their differences.

Most of this chapter has focused on people directly involved in a conflict, yet many disputes in organizational settings are resolved with the assistance of the manager responsible for the feuding parties, or some other third party. **Third-party conflict resolution** is any attempt by a relatively neutral person to help the parties resolve their differences. There are generally three types of third-party dispute resolution activities: arbitration, inquisition, and mediation. These activities can be classified by their level of control over the process and control over the decision (see Exhibit 11.6).[62]

- *Arbitration*—Arbitrators have high control over the final decision, but low control over the process. Executives engage in this strategy by following previously agreed rules of due process, listening to arguments from the disputing employees, and making a binding decision. Arbitration is applied as the final stage of grievances by unionized employees, but it is also becoming more common in nonunion conflicts.

- *Inquisition*—Inquisitors control all discussion about the conflict. Like arbitrators, they have high decision control because they choose the form of conflict resolution. However, they also have high process control because they choose which information to examine and how to examine it, and they generally decide how the conflict resolution process will be handled.

- *Mediation*—Mediators have high control over the intervention process. In fact, their main purpose is to manage the process and context of interaction between the disputing parties. However, the parties make the final decision about how to resolve their differences. Thus, mediators have little or no control over the conflict resolution decision.

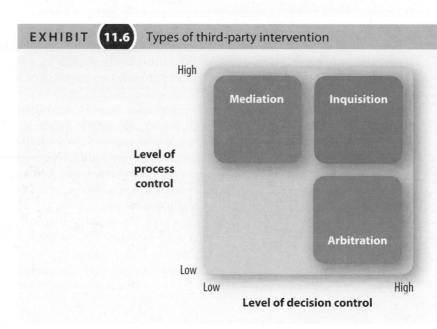

EXHIBIT **11.6** Types of third-party intervention

CHOOSING THE BEST THIRD-PARTY INTERVENTION STRATEGY

Team leaders, executives, and co-workers regularly intervene in disputes between employees and departments. Sometimes they adopt a mediator role; other times they serve as arbitrators. However, research suggests that people in positions of authority (e.g., managers) usually adopt an inquisitional approach whereby they dominate the intervention process as well as make a binding decision.[63] Managers prefer the inquisition approach because it is consistent with the decision-oriented nature of managerial jobs, gives them control over the conflict process and outcome, and tends to resolve disputes efficiently.

However, the inquisitional approach to third-party conflict resolution is usually the least effective in organizational settings.[64] One problem is that leaders who take an inquisitional role tend to collect limited information about the problem, so their imposed decision may produce an ineffective solution to the conflict. Also, employees often view inquisitional procedures and outcomes as unfair because they have little control over this approach.

RBC's Ombuds Office

RBC, Canada's largest financial institution, employs more than 8,000 people who manage other people throughout the organization. They have an important role in maintaining employee morale and engagement, which includes addressing conflicts when they occur. But what happens when the manager is part of the conflict or doesn't provide the level of assistance an employee expects? RBC's solution is an Employee Ombudsman, who serves as a confidential and impartial resource to help employees manage and resolve workplace conflicts. Each year, more than 1,000 RBC employees contact the employee ombudsman for coaching and mediation to solve workplace problems.[65] *The Canadian Press (Sean Vokey)*

Which third-party intervention is most appropriate in organizations? The answer partly depends on the situation, such as the type of dispute, the relationship between the manager and employees, and cultural values such as power distance.[66] But generally speaking, for everyday disputes between two employees, the mediation approach is usually best because this gives employees more responsibility for resolving their own differences. The third-party representative merely establishes an appropriate context for conflict resolution. Although not as efficient as other strategies, mediation potentially offers the highest level of employee satisfaction with the conflict process and outcomes.[67] When employees cannot resolve their differences, arbitration seems to work best because the predetermined rules of evidence and other processes create a higher sense of procedural fairness. Moreover, arbitration is preferred where the organization's goals should take priority over individual goals.

Whether resolving conflict through third-party dispute resolution or direct dialogue, we need to recognize that many solutions come from the sources of conflict that were identified earlier in this chapter. This may seem obvious, but in the heat of conflict, people often focus on each other rather than the underlying causes. Recognizing these conflict sources is the role of effective leadership, which is discussed in the next chapter.

CHAPTER SUMMARY

Conflict is the process in which one party perceives that its interests are being opposed or negatively affected by another party. For many years, conflict was viewed as undesirable and counterproductive. There is evidence that conflict can produce undesirable outcomes such as lower job satisfaction, team cohesion, and knowledge sharing as well as higher organizational politics and turnover. However, experts later formed the opinion that organizations suffer from too little as well as too much conflict. Research reports that moderate conflict can improve decision making, organizational responsiveness to the environment, and team cohesion (when conflict is with sources outside the team).

The current perspective involves distinguishing constructive from relationship conflict. The former focuses on issues and a logical evaluation of ideas, whereas the latter pays attention to interpersonal incompatibilities and flaws. Although the ideal would be to encourage constructive conflict and minimize relationship conflict, relationship conflict tends to emerge in most constructive conflict episodes. However, relationship conflict is less likely to dominate when the parties are emotionally intelligent, have a cohesive team, and have supportive team norms.

The conflict process model begins with the five structural sources of conflict: incompatible goals, differentiation (different values and beliefs), interdependence, scarce resources, ambiguous rules, and communication problems. These sources lead one or more parties to perceive a conflict and to experience conflict emotions. This, in turn, produces manifest conflict, such as behaviours toward the other side. The conflict process often escalates through a series of episodes.

Organizational behaviour experts have identified several conflict handling styles: problem solving, forcing, avoiding, yielding, and compromising. People who use problem solving have a win–win orientation. Others, particularly forcing, assume a win–lose orientation. In general, people gravitate toward one or two preferred conflict handling styles that match their personality, personal and cultural values, and past experience. However, the best style depends on various characteristics of the situation.

Structural approaches to conflict management include emphasizing superordinate goals, reducing differentiation, improving communication and understanding, reducing interdependence, increasing resources, and clarifying rules and procedures.

Negotiation occurs whenever two or more conflicting parties attempt to resolve their divergent goals by redefining the terms of their interdependence. Negotiations are influenced by several situational factors, including location, physical setting, time passage and deadlines, and audience. Important negotiator behaviours include preparation and goal setting, gathering information, communicating effectively, and making concessions.

Third-party conflict resolution is any attempt by a relatively neutral person to help the parties resolve their differences. The three main forms of third-party dispute resolution are mediation, arbitration, and inquisition. Managers tend to use an inquisition approach, although mediation and arbitration are more appropriate, depending on the situation.

KEY TERMS

conflict, p. 258

constructive conflict, p. 259

negotiation, p. 269

relationship conflict, p. 259

superordinate goal, p. 267

third-party conflict resolution, p. 272

win–lose orientation, p. 264

win–win orientation, p. 264

CRITICAL THINKING QUESTIONS

1. Distinguish constructive conflict from relationship conflict and explain how to apply the former with minimal levels of the latter.

2. The chief executive officer of Creative Toys, Inc. read about cooperation in Japanese companies and vowed to bring this same philosophy to the company. The goal is to avoid all conflict, so that employees will work cooperatively and be happier at Creative Toys. Discuss the merits and limitations of the CEO's policy.

3. Conflict among managers emerged soon after a French company acquired a Swedish firm. The Swedes perceived the French management as hierarchical and arrogant, whereas the French thought the Swedes were naive, cautious, and lacking an achievement orientation. Describe ways to reduce dysfunctional conflict in this situation.

4. This chapter describes three levels of interdependence that exist in interpersonal and intergroup relationships. Identify examples of these three levels in your work or school activities. How do these three levels affect potential conflict for you?

5. Jane has just been appointed as purchasing manager of Tacoma Technologies Corp. The previous purchasing manager, who recently retired, was known for his "winner-take-all" approach to suppliers. He continually fought for more discounts and was skeptical about any special deals that suppliers would propose. A few suppliers refused to do business with Tacoma Technologies, but senior management was confident that the former purchasing manager's approach minimized the company's costs. Jane wants to try a more collaborative approach to working with suppliers. Will her approach work? How should she adopt a more collaborative approach in future negotiations with suppliers?

6. You are a special assistant to the commander-in-chief of a peacekeeping mission to a war-torn part of the world. The unit consists of a few thousand peacekeeping troops from Canada, the United States, France, India, and four other countries. The troops will work together for approximately one year. What strategies would you recommend to improve mutual understanding and minimize conflict among these troops?

7. The chief operating officer (COO) has noticed that production employees in the company's Mexican manufacturing operations are unhappy with some of the production engineering decisions engineers made in the company's headquarters in Toronto. At the same time, the engineers complain that production employees aren't applying their engineering specifications correctly and don't understand why those specifications were put in place. The COO believes that the best way to resolve this conflict is to have a frank and open discussion between some of the engineers and employees representing the Mexican production crew. This open dialogue approach worked well recently among managers in the company's Toronto headquarters, so should work equally well between the engineers and production staff. Based on your knowledge of communication and mutual understanding as a way to resolve conflict, discuss the COO's proposal.

8. Describe the inquisitional approach to resolve disputes between employees and departments. Discuss its appropriateness in organizational settings including the suitability of its use with a multigenerational workforce.

www.mcgrawhill.ca/olc/mcshane

CASE STUDY 11.1

Tamarack Industries

By David J. Cherrington, Brigham Young University

Tamarack Industries manufactures motor boats primarily used for water skiing. During the summer months, a third production line is normally created to help meet the heavy summer demand. This third line is usually created by assigning the experienced workers to all three lines and hiring college and university students who are home for summer vacation to complete the crews. In the past, however, experienced workers resented having to break up their teams to form a third line. They also resented having to work with a bunch of kids and complained that they were slow and arrogant.

The foreman, Dan Jensen, decided to try a different strategy this summer and have all the students work on the new line. He asked Mark Allen to supervise the new crew because Mark claimed that he knew everything about boats and could perform every job "with my eyes closed." Mark was happy to accept the new job and participated in selecting his own crew. Mark's crew was called "the Geek Team" because most of the students were computer savvy and talked frequently about the latest electronic gadgets.

Mark spent many hours in training to get his group running at full production. The students learned quickly, and by the end of June their production rate was up to standard, with an error rate that was only slightly above normal. To simplify the learning process, Dan Jensen assigned the Geek Team long production runs that generally consisted of 30 to 40 identical units. Thus the training period was shortened and errors were reduced. Shorter production runs were assigned to the experienced teams.

By the middle of July, a substantial rivalry had been created between the Geek Team and the older workers. At first, the rivalry was good-natured. But after a few weeks, the older workers became resentful of the remarks made by the students. The Geek Team often met its production schedules with time to spare at the end of the day for goofing around. It wasn't uncommon for someone from the Geek Team to go to another line pretending to look for materials just to make demeaning comments. The experienced workers resented having to perform all the shorter production runs and began to retaliate with sabotage. They would sneak over during breaks and hide tools, dent materials, install something crooked, and in other small ways do something that would slow production for the Geek Team.

Dan felt good about his decision to form a separate crew of students, but when he heard reports of sabotage and rivalry, he became very concerned. Because of complaints from the experienced workers, Dan equalized the production so that all of the crews had similar production runs. The rivalry, however, did not stop. The Geek Team continued to finish early and flaunt their performance in front of the other crews.

One day the Geek Team suspected that one of their assemblies was going to be sabotaged during the lunch break by one of the experienced crews. By skillful deception, they were able to substitute an assembly from the other experienced line for theirs. By the end of the lunch period, the Geek Team was laughing wildly because of their deception, while one experienced crew was very angry with the other one.

Dan Jensen decided that the situation had to be changed and announced that the job assignments between the different crews would be shuffled. The employees were told that when they appeared for work the next morning, the names of the workers assigned to each crew would be posted on the bulletin board. The announcement was not greeted with much enthusiasm, and Mark Allen decided to stay late to try to talk Dan out of his idea. Mark didn't believe the rivalry was serious enough for this type of action, and he suspected that many of the students would quit if their team was broken up.

Discussion Questions

1. What are the signs (symptoms) of conflict in this case?

2. Use the conflict model to (a) identify the structural causes of conflict and (b) discuss the escalation of conflict described in this case.

3. If you were Dan Jensen, what action would you take in this situation?

CLASS EXERCISE 11.2

The Contingencies of Conflict Handling

Gerard A. Callanan and David F. Perri, West Chester University Of Pennsylvania

Purpose This exercise is designed to help you understand the contingencies of applying conflict handling styles in organizational settings.

Instructions

- *Step 1:* Participants will read each of the five scenarios presented below and select the most appropriate response from among the five alternatives. Each scenario has a situationally correct response.

- *Step 2 (Optional):* The instructor may ask each student to complete the Dutch Test for Conflict Handling self-assessment in this chapter (Self-Assessment 11.4) or a similar instrument. This instrument will provide an estimate of your preferred conflict handling style.

- *Step 3:* As a class, participants give their feedback on the responses to each of the scenarios, with the instructor guiding discussion on the contextual factors embodied in each scenario. For each scenario, the class should identify the response selected by the majority. In addition, participants will discuss how they decided on the choices they made and the contextual factors they took into account in making their selections.

- *Step 4:* Students will compare their responses to the five scenarios with their results from the conflict handling self-assessment. Discussion will focus on the extent to which each person's preferred conflict-handling style influenced their alternatives in this activity, and the implications of this style preference for managing conflict in organizations.

Scenario #1

Setting You are a manager of a division in the accounting department of a large Canadian bank. Nine exempt-level analysts and six unionized clerical staff report to you. Recently, one of your analysts, Jane Wilson, has sought the bank's approval for tuition reimbursement for the cost of an evening MBA program specializing in leadership. The bank normally encourages employees to seek advanced degrees on a part-time basis. Indeed, through your encouragement, nearly all of the members of your staff are pursuing additional schoolwork. You consult the bank's policy manual and discover that two approvals are necessary for reimbursement—yours and that of the manager of training and development, Kathy Gordon. Further, the manual states that approval for reimbursement will only be granted if the coursework is "reasonably job related." Based on your review of the matter, you decide to approve Jane's request for reimbursement. However, Kathy Gordon rejects it outright by claiming that coursework in organizational behaviour is not related to an accounting analyst position. She states that the bank will only reimburse the analyst for a degree in either accounting or finance. In your opinion, however, the interpersonal skills and insights to be gained from an MBA degree specializing in leadership are job related and can also benefit the employee in future assignments. The analyst job requires interaction with a variety of individuals at different levels in the organization, and it is important that interpersonal and communication skills be strong.

After further discussion it becomes clear that you and Kathy Gordon have opposite views on the matter. Since both of you are at the same organization level and have equal status, it appears that you are at an impasse. Although the goal of reimbursement is important, you are faced with other pressing demands on your time. In addition, the conflict has diverted the attention of your work group away from its primary responsibilities. Because the school term is about to begin, it is essential that you and Kathy Gordon reach a timely agreement to enable Jane to pursue her coursework.

www.mcgrawhill.ca/olc/mcshane

Action Alternatives
for Scenario #1

Please indicate your first (1) and second (2) choices from among the following alternatives by writing the appropriate number in the space provided.

Action Alternatives	Ranking (1st & 2nd)
1. You go along with Kathy Gordon's view and advise Jane Wilson to select either accounting or finance as a major for her MBA.	_____
2. You decide to withdraw from the situation completely, and tell Jane to work it out with Kathy Gordon on her own.	_____
3. You decide to take the matter to those in higher management levels and argue forcefully for your point of view. You do everything in your power to ensure that a decision will be made in your favour.	_____
4. You decide to meet Kathy Gordon halfway in order to reach an agreement. You advise Jane to pursue her MBA in accounting or finance, but also recommend she minor in leadership by taking electives in that field.	_____
5. You decide to work more closely with Kathy Gordon by attempting to get a clear as well as flexible policy written that reflects both of your views. Of course, this will require a significant amount of your time	_____

Scenario #2

Setting

You are the vice president of a relatively large division (80 employees) in a medium-sized consumer products company. Due to the recent turnover of minority staff, your division has fallen behind in meeting the company's goal for employment equity hiring. Because of a scarcity of qualified minority candidates, it appears that you may fall further behind in achieving stated employment equity goals.

Although you are aware of the problem, you believe that the low level of minority hiring is due to increased attrition in minority staff as well as the lack of viable replacement candidates. However, the employment equity officer believes that your hiring criteria are too stringent, resulting in the rejection of minority candidates with the basic qualifications to do the job. You support the goals and principles of employment equity; however, you are concerned that the hiring of less-qualified candidates will weaken the performance of your division. The employment equity officer believes that your failure to hire minority employees is damaging to the company in the short term because corporate goals will not be met, and in the long term because it will restrict the pool of minority candidates available for upward mobility. Both of you regard your concerns as important. Further, you recognize that both of you have the company's best interests in mind and that you have a mutual interest in resolving the conflict.

Action Alternatives
for Scenario #2

Please indicate your first (1) and second (2) choices from among the following alternatives by writing the appropriate number in the space provided.

Action Alternatives	Ranking (1st & 2nd)
1. You conclude that the whole problem is too complex an issue for you to handle right now. You put it on the "back burner" and decide to reconsider the problem at a later date.	_____
2. You believe that your view outweighs the perspective of the employment equity officer. You decide to argue your position more vigorously and hope that your stance will sway the employment equity officer to agree with your view.	_____
3. You decide to accept the employment equity officer's view. You agree to use less stringent selection criteria and thereby hire more minority employees.	_____
4. You give in to the employment equity officer somewhat by agreeing to relax your standards a little bit. This would allow slightly more minority hiring (but not enough to satisfy the employment equity goal) and could cause a small reduction in the overall performance of your division.	_____
5. You try and reach a consensus that addresses each of your concerns. You agree to work harder at hiring more minority applicants and request that the employment equity officer agree to help find the most qualified minority candidates available.	_____

Scenario #3

Setting You are the manager in charge of the financial reporting section of a large insurance company. It is the responsibility of your group to make periodic written and oral reports to senior management regarding the company's financial performance. The company's senior management has come to rely on your quick and accurate dissemination of financial data as a way to make vital decisions in a timely fashion. This has given you a relatively high degree of organizational influence. You rely on various operating departments to supply you with financial information according to a pre-established reporting schedule.

In two days, you must make your quarterly presentation to the company's board of directors. However, the Claims department has failed to supply you with several key pieces of information that are critical to your presentation. You check the reporting schedule and realize that you should have had the information two days ago. When you call Bill Jones, the Claims department manager, he informs you that he cannot possibly have the data to you within the next two days. He states that other pressing work has a higher priority. Although you explain the critical need for this data, he is unwilling to change his position. You believe that your presentation is vital to the company's welfare and explain this to Bill Jones. Although Bill has less status than you, he has been known to take advantage of individuals who are unwilling or unable to push their point of view. With your presentation less than two days away, it is critical that you receive information from the Claims department within the next 24 hours.

Action Alternatives for Scenario #3 Please indicate your first (1) and second (2) choices from among the following alternatives by writing the appropriate number in the space provided.

Action Alternatives	Ranking (1st & 2nd)
1. Accept the explanation from Bill Jones and try to get by without the figures by using your best judgment as to what they would be.	_____
2. Tell Bill Jones that unless you have the data from his department on your desk by tomorrow morning, you will be forced to go over his head to compel him to give you the numbers.	_____
3. Meet Bill Jones halfway by agreeing to receive part of the needed figures and using your own judgment on the others.	_____
4. Try to get your presentation postponed until a later date, if possible.	_____
5. Forget about the short-term need for information and try to achieve a longer term solution, such as adjusting the reporting schedule to better accommodate your mutual needs.	_____

Scenario #4

Setting You are the production manager of a medium-sized building products company. You control a production line that runs on a three-shift basis. Recently, Ted Smith, the materials handling manager, requested you to accept a different packaging of the raw materials for the production process than what has been customary. He states that new machinery he has installed makes it much easier to provide the material in 45-kilogram sacks instead of the 22-kilogram bags that you currently receive. Ted further explains that the provision of the material in the 22-kilogram bags would put an immense strain on his operation, and he therefore has a critical need for you to accept the change. You know that accepting materials in the new packaging will cause some minor disruption in your production process, but should not cause long-term problems for any of the three shifts. However, you are a little annoyed by the proposed change because Ted did not consult with you before he installed the new equipment. In the past, you and he have been open in your communication. You do not think that this failure to consult you represents a change in your relationship.

Because you work closely with Ted, it is essential that you maintain the harmonious and stable working relationship that you have built over the past few years. In addition, you may need some help from him in the future, since you already know that your operation will have special material requirements in about two months. You also know that Ted has influence at higher levels of the organization.

Action Alternatives for Scenario #4

Please indicate your first (1) and second (2) choices from among the following alternatives by writing the appropriate number in the space provided.

Action Alternatives	Ranking (1st & 2nd)
1. Agree to accept the raw material in the different format.	_____
2. Refuse to accept the material in the new format because it would cause a disruption in your operation.	_____
3. Propose a solution where you accept material in the new format during the first shift, but not during the second and third.	_____
4. Tell Ted Smith that you do not wish to deal with the issue at this time, but that you will consider his request and get back to him at a later date.	_____
5. You decide to tell Ted Smith of your concern regarding his failure to consult with you before installing new equipment. You inform him that you wish to find longer term solutions to the conflict between you.	_____

Scenario #5

Setting

You are employed as supervisor of the compensation and benefits section in the human resources department of a medium-sized pharmaceutical company. Your staff of three clerks is responsible for maintaining contacts with the various benefits providers and answering related questions from the company's employees. Your section shares clerical, word processing, and copier resources with the training and development section of the department. Recently, a disagreement has arisen between you and Beth Hanson, the training and development supervisor, over when the clerical staff should take their lunches. Beth would like the clerical staff to take their lunches an hour later to coincide with the time most of her people go to lunch. You know that the clerical employees do not want to change their lunchtimes. Further, the current time is more convenient for your staff.

At this time, you are hard-pressed to deal with the situation. You have an important meeting with the provider of dental insurance in two days. It is critical that you are well prepared for this meeting, and these other tasks are a distraction.

Action Alternatives for Scenario #5

Please indicate your first (1) and second (2) choices from among the following alternatives by writing the appropriate number in the space provided.

Action Alternatives	Ranking (1st & 2nd)
1. Take some time over the next day and propose a solution whereby three days a week the clerical employees take their lunch at the earlier time and two days at the later.	_____
2. Tell Beth Hanson you will deal with the matter in a few days, after you have addressed the more pressing issues.	_____
3. Let Beth Hanson have her way by agreeing to a later lunch hour for the clerical staff.	_____
4. Flat out tell Beth Hanson that you will not agree to a change in the clerical employees' lunchtime.	_____
5. Devote more time to the issue. Attempt to achieve a broad-based consensus with Beth Hanson that meets her needs as well as yours and those of the clerical employees.	_____

Source: G. A. Callanan and D. F. Perri, "Teaching Conflict Management Using a Scenario-Based Approach," *Journal of Education for Business*, 81 (Jan/Feb 2006), pp. 131–139.

TEAM EXERCISE 11.3

Ugli Orange Role Play

Purpose   This exercise is designed to help you understand the dynamics of interpersonal and intergroup conflict as well as the effectiveness of negotiation strategies under specific conditions.

Materials   The instructor will distribute roles for Dr. Roland, Dr. Jones, and a few observers. Ideally, each negotiation should occur in a private area away from other negotiations.

Instructions

- *Step 1:* The instructor will divide the class into an even number of teams of three people each, with one participant left over for each team formed (e.g., six observers if there are six teams). One-half of the teams will take the role of Dr. Roland and the other half will be Dr. Jones. The instructor will distribute roles after these teams have been formed.

- *Step 2:* Members within each team are given 10 minutes (or other time limit stated by the instructor) to learn their roles and decide negotiating strategy.

- *Step 3:* After reading their roles and discussing strategy, each Dr. Jones team is matched with a Dr. Roland team to conduct negotiations. Observers will receive observation forms from the instructor, and two observers will be assigned to watch the paired teams during prenegotiations and subsequent negotiations.

- *Step 4:* As soon as Roland and Jones reach agreement or at the end of the time allotted for the negotiation (which ever comes first), the Roland and Jones teams report to the instructor for further instruction.

- *Step 5:* At the end of the exercise, the class will congregate to discuss the negotiations. Observers, negotiators, and instructors will then discuss their observations and experiences and the implications for conflict management and negotiation.

NOTE: This exercise was developed by Robert J. House, Wharton Business School, University of Pennsylvania. A similar activity is also attributed to earlier writing by R. R. Blake and J. S. Mouton.

www.mcgrawhill.ca/olc/mcshane

SELF-ASSESSMENT EXERCISE 11.4

The Dutch Test for Conflict Handling

Purpose   This self-assessment is designed to help you identify your preferred conflict management style.

Instructions   Read each of the statements below and circle the response that you believe best reflects your position regarding each statement. Then use the scoring key in Appendix B to calculate your results for each conflict management style. This exercise is completed alone so students assess themselves honestly without concerns of social comparison. However, class discussion will focus on the different conflict management styles and the situations in which each is most appropriate.

Dutch Test for Conflict Handling					
When I have a conflict at work, I do the following:	Not at All				Very Much
1. I give in to the wishes of the other party.	1	2	3	4	5
2. I try to realize a middle-of-the-road solution.	1	2	3	4	5
3. I push my own point of view.	1	2	3	4	5
4. I examine issues until I find a solution that really satisfies me and the other party.	1	2	3	4	5
5. I avoid confrontation about our differences.	1	2	3	4	5
6. I concur with the other party.	1	2	3	4	5
7. I emphasize that we have to find a compromise solution.	1	2	3	4	5
8. I search for gains.	1	2	3	4	5
9. I stand for my own and other's goals and interests.	1	2	3	4	5
10. I avoid differences of opinion as much as possible.	1	2	3	4	5
11. I try to accommodate the other party.	1	2	3	4	5
12. I insist we both give in a little.	1	2	3	4	5
13. I fight for a good outcome for myself.	1	2	3	4	5
14. I examine ideas from both sides to find a mutually optimal solution.	1	2	3	4	5
15. I try to make differences loom less severe.	1	2	3	4	5
16. I adapt to the parties' goals and interests.	1	2	3	4	5
17. I strive whenever possible towards a fifty-fifty compromise.	1	2	3	4	5
18. I do everything to win.	1	2	3	4	5
19. I work out a solution that serves my own as well as other's interests as good as possible.	1	2	3	4	5
20. I try to avoid a confrontation with the other.	1	2	3	4	5

Source: C. K. W. de Dreu, A. Evers, B. Beersma, E. S. Kluwer, and A. Nauta, "A Theory-based Measure of Conflict Management Strategies in the Workplace," *Journal of Organizational Behaviour*, 22 (2001), pp. 645–68.

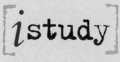

iStudy—Available 24/7 with instant feedback so you can study when you want, how you want, and where you want. Visit www.istudyob.ca to register—take practice quizzes, run interactive scenarios, practice concepts, and much more. Also visit the Student Online Learning Centre for additional study tools.

CHAPTER 12

Leadership in Organizational Settings

LEARNING OBJECTIVES

After reading this chapter, you should be able to:

LO1 Define leadership and shared leadership.

LO2 List the main competencies of effective leaders and discuss the limitations of this leadership perspective.

LO3 Describe the people-oriented and task-oriented leadership styles.

LO4 Outline the path-goal theory of leadership.

LO5 Summarize leadership substitutes theory.

LO6 Distinguish transformational leadership from transactional and charismatic leadership.

LO7 Describe the four elements of transformational leadership.

LO8 Describe the implicit leadership perspective.

LO9 Discuss similarities and differences in the leadership styles of women and men.

As a young accordion player, stiltwalker, and fire-eater from Quebec City, Guy Laliberté founded Cirque du Soleil in 1984. But that was 80 million spectators ago. His unique vision to blend cultures, artistic expression, and acrobatic disciplines has resulted in a globally recognized brand that employs almost 4,000 employees and artists from over 40 countries. Laliberté personally guides the creative team—"every new show starts with a concept from Cirque founder Guy Laliberté." "We sit and create it from a blank page," says set designer Stephane Roy. "We are inventing a world that we do not know exists." Laliberté's unique leadership style provides the team with both direction and freedom to be creative and innovative. After his initial involvement for a new show, a creative team spends a year working out the concept. In the second year, small teams, or creative cells guide all aspects, however, before the launch, Laliberté is once again highly involved "thrashing out last-minute refinements."

Although he never graduated from high school, Laliberté's intelligence and business acumen have made him a highly regarded and wealthy business leader in Canada. As sole proprietor of Cirque, "all major decisions still begin and end with him." Rather than employ a traditional board of directors, Laliberté put together a small advisory board consisting of a handful of Canada's most highly regarded business leaders.

In addition to extensive global travel, Laliberté maintains knowledge of the business and keeps current through a team of young people, called the "Trend Group." The Trend Group meets with him every three months to create a stimulating environment for sharing: "What is new in the multimedia field? What's new in dance, acrobatics, music?" Laliberté is also known for his decisiveness, being willing to abandon projects when the need arises—like Quebec's government-owned Cirque-themed casino and hotel complex that presented a "political debate that could have damaged the Cirque's brand value." Laliberté's leadership motivation also involves benefiting society. He recently created the ONE DROP Foundation with the vision to fight world poverty by creating sustainable access to safe water.[1]

Guy Laliberté, founder of Cirque du Soleil, is known for his bold vision and passionate style of leadership that motivates and inspires employees to continuously push the limits of creativity and artistic expression. *AP Images/ The Canadian Press (Kevork Djansezian)*

WHAT IS LEADERSHIP?

The world is changing, and so is our concept of leadership. Gone is the image of a command-and-control boss. Also gone is the more recent view that leaders are front-and-centre charismatic heroes. Instead, as is apparent with Cirque du Soleil co-founder Guy Laliberté in the opening vignette, leadership is about values, vision, enabling, and coaching. A few years ago, 54 leadership experts from 38 countries reached a consensus that **leadership** is about influencing, motivating, and enabling others to contribute toward the effectiveness and success of the organizations of which they are members.[2] Leaders apply various forms of influence—from subtle persuasion to direct application of power—to ensure that followers have the motivation and role clarity to achieve specified goals. Leaders also arrange the work environment—such as allocating resources and altering communication patterns—so that employees can achieve corporate objectives more easily.

> **leadership**
> Influencing, motivating, and enabling others to contribute toward the effectiveness and success of the organizations of which they are members.

SHARED LEADERSHIP

Leadership isn't restricted to the executive suite. Anyone in the organization may be a leader in various ways and at various times.[3] This view is known as **shared leadership** or the *leaderful organization*. With shared leadership, "leadership" is plural, not singular. It doesn't operate out of one formally assigned position or role. Instead, a team or work unit may have several leaders at the same time. One team member might champion the introduction of new technology while a co-worker keeps the work unit focused on its key performance indicators. These conditions call for a higher level of collaboration among employees because the shared leadership roles are affirmed by the team rather than formally assigned. Employees perform leadership roles because co-workers support them for their initiative. Furthermore, shared leadership lacks formal authority, so influence occurs mainly by involving and receiving commitment from co-workers.

> **shared leadership**
> The view that leadership is broadly distributed rather than assigned to one person, such that people within the team and organization lead each other.

To understand the meaning of shared leadership, consider W. L. Gore & Associates, which has no formal (called *vertical*) leaders at all.[4] Instead, the company's 7,000 associates work with champions of projects and other initiatives because they are willing to follow them. "There is no positional power," explains a Gore team leader. "You are only a leader if teams decide to respect and follow you." Diane Davidson discovered this extreme version of shared leadership when the newly hired apparel industry sales executive asked her "starting sponsor" to identify her boss. The sponsor replied that she has no boss and eventually advised her to "stop using the B-word." Davidson initially thought the company must have formal managers who downplayed their position, but she soon realized that Gore really is a shared leadership organization. "Your team is your boss, because you don't want to let them down," says Davidson. "Everyone's your boss, and no one's your boss." In fact, when Gore employees are asked in annual surveys "Are you a leader?" more than 50 percent of them answer "Yes."

Shared leadership is essential at Gore and other organizations that have no formal leadership roles, but it exists in all organizations.[5] Even with a formal manager performing important duties, a department or division benefits when employees also champion various objectives. Every moment of responsibility can be a shared leadership occasion. For instance, Patty Shapiro & Associates holds weekly meetings to move the business forward and keep staff informed. But company founder Patty Shapiro chairs the meetings only once every 10 weeks. The recruitment and training company's nine employees take turns the other weeks, including setting the agenda and bringing new information to the others. Shapiro says that some employees are nervous with this responsibility while others reveal their innate leadership potential. "I want everyone in my company to have a chance to be a leader," says Shapiro.[6]

The Leaderful Community of St. Magloire

Thanks to shared leadership, the small community of St. Magloire, Quebec reversed population decline and kept its only school open. When the Quebec government threatened to close the school, Francine Bond and Julie Bercier (left two in this photo), along with a handful of other residents, rallied to attract newcomers to the community. Many initially doubted the success of such a bold initiative, but Bond's and Bercier's persistent optimism inspired neighbours to participate in a new resident welcoming program and to support newspaper campaigns that promoted St. Magloire's healthy lifestyle. In the first year, these activities attracted 54 people, including enough children to keep the school open. Although formal leaders—including the village mayor and school administrators—played important roles, Bercier, Bond, and others became leaders by providing the passion and vision of what the small community could become with enough ingenuity and effort.[7] *Passion-FM Radio Bellechasse*

Leadership is one of the most researched, and possibly the most complex, topics in organizational behaviour. This has resulted in an enormous volume of leadership literature, most of which can be organized into five perspectives: competency, behavioural, contingency, transformational, and implicit.[8] Although some of these perspectives are currently more popular than others, each helps us to more fully understand this complex issue. This chapter explores each of these five perspectives of leadership. In the final section, we also consider cross-cultural and gender issues in organizational leadership.

COMPETENCY PERSPECTIVE OF LEADERSHIP

LO2

Since the beginning of recorded civilization, people have been interested in the personal characteristics that distinguish great leaders from the rest of us.[9] In the sixth century B.C.E., the Chinese philosopher Lao-tzu described effective leaders as selfless, honest, fair, and hardworking. The Greek philosopher Plato claimed that great leaders have wisdom and a superior capacity for logical thinking. For the past century, hundreds of leadership studies have tried to empirically identify the traits of effective leaders. However, a major review in the late 1940s concluded that no consistent list of traits could be distilled from this research. This conclusion was revised a decade later, suggesting that a few traits are associated with effective leaders.[10] These paltry findings caused many scholars to give up their search for personal characteristics that distinguish effective leaders.

Over the past two decades, leadership researchers and consultants have returned to the notion that effective leaders possess specific personal characteristics.[11] The earlier research was apparently plagued by methodological problems, lack of theoretical foundation, and inconsistent definitions of leadership. The emerging work has identified several leadership *competencies;* that is, skills, knowledge, aptitudes, and other personal characteristics that lead to superior performance (see Chapter 2). The main categories of leadership competencies are listed in Exhibit 12.1 and described below.[12]

- *Personality*—Most of the Big Five personality dimensions (see Chapter 2) are associated with effective leadership to some extent, but the strongest predictors are high levels of extroversion (outgoing, talkative, sociable, and assertive) and conscientiousness (careful, dependable, and self-disciplined). With high extroversion, effective leaders are comfortable having an influential role in social settings. With higher conscientiousness, effective leaders set higher personal goals for themselves, are more motivated, and have higher performance expectations.

EXHIBIT 12.1   Competencies of effective leaders

Leadership Competency	Description
Personality	Higher levels of extroversion (outgoing, talkative, sociable, and assertive) and conscientiousness (careful, dependable, and self-disciplined).
Self-concept	The leader's self-beliefs and positive self-evaluation about his/her own leadership skills and ability to achieve objectives.
Drive	The leader's inner motivation to pursue goals.
Integrity	The leader's truthfulness and tendency to translate words into deeds.
Leadership motivation	The leader's need for socialized power to accomplish team or organizational goals.
Knowledge of the business	The leader's tacit and explicit knowledge about the company's environment, enabling the leader to make more intuitive decisions.
Cognitive and practical intelligence	The leader's above average cognitive ability to process information (cognitive intelligence) and ability to solve real-world problems by adapting to, shaping, or selecting appropriate environments (practical intelligence).
Emotional intelligence	The leader's ability to monitor his or her own and others' emotions, discriminate among them, and use the information to guide his or her thoughts and actions.

- *Self-concept*—Successful leaders have a positive self-evaluation, including high self-esteem, self-efficacy, and internal locus of control (see Chapter 2).[13] They are confident in their leadership skills and ability to achieve objectives. These leaders also have a complex, internally consistent, and clear self-concept. They know themselves and act consistently with that self-concept. These characteristics are essential for *authentic leadership*, which refers to how well leaders know themselves (they have a clear self-concept) and act in accordance with that self-concept (consistency with one's values).[14]

- *Drive*—Related to high conscientiousness and positive self-concept, successful leaders have a high need for achievement (see Chapter 5). This drive represents the inner motivation that leaders possess to pursue their goals and encourage others to move forward with theirs. Drive inspires inquisitiveness, an action-orientation, and boldness to take the organization or team into uncharted waters. In fact, Larry Bossidy, the former CEO of Honeywell and Allied Signal, says that drive is so important for leadership that "if you have to choose between someone with a staggering IQ...and someone with a lower IQ who is absolutely determined to succeed, you'll always do better with the second person."[15]

- *Integrity*—Integrity refers to truthfulness and consistency of words and actions, which is related to honesty and ethics. Leaders have a high moral capacity to judge dilemmas based on sound values and to act accordingly. Notice that integrity is ultimately based on the leader's values, which provide an anchor for consistency. Several large-scale studies have reported that integrity and honesty are the most important characteristics of effective leaders.[16] Unfortunately, recent surveys report that many employees don't trust their leaders and don't think they have integrity.[17]

- *Leadership motivation*—Effective leaders are motivated to lead others. They have a strong need for *socialized power*, meaning that they want power as a means to accomplish organizational objectives and similar good deeds. This contrasts with a need for *personalized power*, which is the desire for power for personal gain or for the thrill one might experience from wielding power over others (see Chapter 5).[18] Leadership motivation is also necessary because even in collegial firms, leaders are in contests for positions further up the hierarchy. Effective leaders thrive rather than wither in the face of this competition.[19]

- *Knowledge of the business*—Effective leaders possess tacit and explicit knowledge of the business environment in which they operate.

- *Cognitive and practical intelligence*—Leaders have above-average cognitive ability to process enormous amounts of information. Leaders aren't necessarily geniuses; rather, they have superior ability to analyze a variety of complex alternatives and opportunities. Furthermore, leaders have practical intelligence; they are able to use their knowledge of the business to solve real-world problems by adapting to, shaping, or selecting appropriate environments. Unlike cognitive intelligence, which is assessed by performance on clearly defined problems with sufficient information and usually one best answer, practical intelligence refers to performance in real-world settings, where problems are poorly defined, information is missing, and more than one solution may be plausible.[20]

- *Emotional intelligence*—Effective leaders have a high level of emotional intelligence.[21] They are able to perceive and express emotion, assimilate emotion in thought, understand and reason with emotion, and regulate emotion in themselves and others (see Chapter 4).

COMPETENCY PERSPECTIVE LIMITATIONS AND PRACTICAL IMPLICATIONS

Although the competency perspective is gaining popularity (again), it has a few limitations.[22] First, it assumes that all effective leaders have the same personal characteristics that are equally important in all situations. This is probably a false assumption; leadership is far too complex to have a universal list of traits that apply to every condition. Some competencies might not be important all the time. Second, alternative combinations of competencies may be equally successful; two people with different sets of competencies might be equally good leaders. Third, the leadership competencies perspective views leadership as something within a person, yet experts emphasize that leadership is relational. People are effective leaders because of their favourable relationship with followers, so effective leaders cannot be identified without considering the quality of these relationships.[23]

As we will learn later in this chapter, several leadership researchers have also warned that some personal characteristics might only influence our perception that someone is a leader, not whether the individual really makes a difference to the organization's success. People who exhibit self-confidence, extroversion, and other traits are called leaders because they fit our stereotype of an effective leader. Or we might see a successful person, call that person a leader, and then attribute unobservable traits that we consider essential for great leaders.

The competency perspective of leadership does not necessarily imply that leadership is a talent that you acquire at birth rather than develop through life. On the contrary, competencies only indicate leadership *potential*, not leadership performance. People with these characteristics become effective leaders only after they have developed and mastered the necessary leadership behaviours. Those with somewhat lower leadership competencies may become very effective leaders because they have leveraged their potential more fully.

BEHAVIOURAL PERSPECTIVE OF LEADERSHIP

LO3

In the 1940s and 1950s, leadership experts at several universities launched an intensive research investigation to answer the question: What behaviours make leaders effective? Questionnaires were administered to subordinates, asking them to rate their supervisors on a large number of behaviours. These studies distilled two clusters of leadership behaviours from literally thousands of leadership behaviour items.[24]

One cluster represents people-oriented behaviours. This includes showing mutual trust and respect for subordinates, demonstrating a genuine concern for their needs, and having a desire to look out for their welfare. Leaders with a strong people-oriented style listen to employee suggestions, do personal favours for employees, support their interests when required, and treat employees as equals. The other cluster represents a task-oriented leadership style and includes behaviours that define and structure work roles. Task-oriented leaders assign employees to specific tasks, clarify their work duties and procedures, ensure that they follow company rules, and push them to reach their performance capacity. They establish stretch goals and challenge employees to push beyond those high standards.

CHOOSING TASK- VERSUS PEOPLE-ORIENTED LEADERSHIP

Should leaders be task-oriented or people-oriented? This is a difficult question to answer because each style has its advantages and disadvantages. Recent evidence suggests that both styles are positively associated with leader effectiveness, but differences are often apparent only in very high or very low levels of each style. Generally, absenteeism, grievances, turnover, and job dissatisfaction are higher among employees who work with supervisors with very low levels of people-oriented leadership. Job performance is lower among employees who work for supervisors with low levels of task-oriented leadership.[25] Research suggests that university students value task-oriented instructors because they want clear objectives and well-prepared lectures that abide by the unit's objectives.[26]

One problem with the behavioural leadership perspective is that the two categories are broad generalizations that mask specific behaviours within each category. For instance, task-oriented leadership includes planning work activities, clarifying roles, and monitoring operations and performance. Each of these clusters of activities is fairly distinct and likely has different effects on employee well-being and performance. A second concern is that the behavioural approach assumes high levels of both styles are best in all situations. In reality, the best leadership style depends on the situation.[27] On a positive note, the behavioural perspective lays the foundation for two of the main leadership styles—people-oriented and task-oriented—found in many contemporary leadership theories. These contemporary theories adopt a contingency perspective, which is described next.

CONTINGENCY PERSPECTIVE OF LEADERSHIP

path-goal leadership theory
A contingency theory of leadership based on the expectancy theory of motivation that relates several leadership styles to specific employee and situational contingencies.

LO4

servant leadership
The view that leaders serve followers, rather than vice versa; they help employees fulfill their needs and are coaches, stewards, and facilitators of employee performance.

The contingency perspective of leadership is based on the idea that the most appropriate leadership style depends on the situation. Most (although not all) contingency leadership theories assume that effective leaders must be both insightful and flexible.[28] They must be able to adapt their behaviours and styles to the immediate situation. This isn't easy to do, however. Leaders typically have a preferred style. It takes considerable effort for leaders to choose and enact different styles for different situations. As we noted earlier, leaders must have high emotional intelligence, so they can diagnose the circumstances and match their behaviours accordingly.

PATH-GOAL THEORY OF LEADERSHIP

Several contingency theories have been proposed over the years, but **path-goal leadership theory** has withstood scientific critique better than the others. The theory has its roots in the expectancy theory of motivation (see Chapter 5).[29] Early research incorporated expectancy theory into the study of how leader behaviours influence employee perceptions of expectancies (paths) between employee effort and performance (goals). Out of this early work was born path-goal theory as a contingency leadership model.

Path-goal theory states that effective leaders ensure that employees who perform their jobs well receive more valued rewards than those who perform poorly. Effective leaders also provide the information, support, and other resources necessary to help employees complete their tasks.[30] In other words, path-goal theory advocates **servant leadership**.[31] Servant leaders do not view leadership as a position of power; rather, they are coaches, stewards, and facilitators. Leadership is an obligation to understand employee needs and to facilitate their work performance. Servant leaders ask, "How can

I help you?" rather than expect employees to serve them. "The role of the leader is to create environments where others can do great work—and then to get out of the way," suggests Microsoft executive Steve Vamos. Similarly, when Financial Planning Association president Jim Barnash was recently asked about his leadership style, he replied: "I try to live a servant-leader's life, which means being more interested in your needs than my needs."[32]

Path-Goal Leadership Styles   Exhibit 12.2 presents the path-goal theory of leadership. This model specifically highlights four leadership styles and several contingency factors leading to three indicators of leader effectiveness. The four leadership styles are:[33]

- *Directive*—These are clarifying behaviours that provide a psychological structure for subordinates. The leader clarifies performance goals, the means to reach those goals, and the standards against which performance will be judged. It also includes judicious use of rewards and disciplinary actions. Directive leadership is the same as task-oriented leadership described earlier and echoes our discussion in Chapter 2 on the importance of clear role perceptions in employee performance.

- *Supportive*—These behaviours provide psychological support for subordinates. The leader is friendly and approachable; makes the work more pleasant; treats employees with equal respect; and shows concern for the status, needs, and well-being of employees. Supportive leadership is the same as people-oriented leadership described earlier and reflects the benefits of social support to help employees cope with stressful situations.

- *Participative*—These behaviours encourage and facilitate subordinate involvement in decisions beyond their normal work activities. The leader consults with employees, asks for their suggestions, and takes these ideas into serious consideration before making a decision. Participative leadership relates to involving employees in decisions.

- *Achievement-oriented*—These behaviours encourage employees to reach their peak performance. The leader sets challenging goals, expects employees to perform at their highest level, continuously seeks improvement in employee performance, and shows a high degree of confidence that employees will assume responsibility and accomplish challenging goals. Achievement-oriented leadership applies goal-setting theory as well as positive expectations in self-fulfilling prophecy.

EXHIBIT 12.2   Path-goal leadership theory

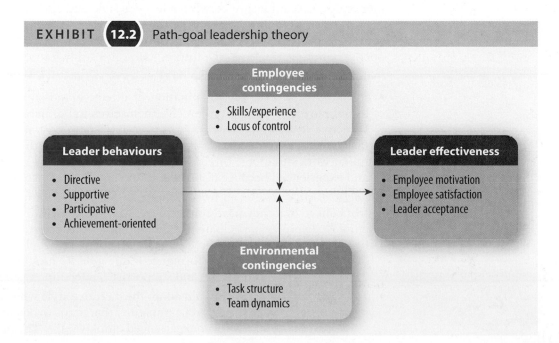

People-Oriented Leader Takes Britain's Top Spot

What does it take to be voted the best boss in Great Britain? You will likely find the answer by watching Bruce Draper at work. Recently named Britain's best boss, Draper exemplifies the people-oriented leadership style, according to staff at Geo-technical Instruments where he served as Managing Director at the time of the award. (Draper is now Director at Sword Scientific Ltd.) "Bruce cared about his staff," said one employee. "He appeared friendly, approachable, and kind and made sure everyone was content in their job." Fiona Cannon, head of equality and diversity at Lloyds TSB, the financial institution that co-sponsored the award, says that people-oriented leadership is vital in organizations today. "Having a good boss can make a huge difference, not only to the success of a business but also to the happiness and well-being of those who work for them." She adds: "Bruce Draper particularly stood out from the crowd."[34] © *Anita Maric/News Team International*

The path-goal model contends that effective leaders are capable of selecting the most appropriate behavioural style (or styles) for that situation. Leaders might simultaneously use two or more styles. For example, they might be both supportive and participative in a specific situation.

Contingencies of Path-Goal Theory   As a contingency theory, path-goal theory states that each of these four leadership styles will be effective in some situations but not in others. The path-goal leadership model specifies two sets of situational variables that moderate the relationship between a leader's style and effectiveness: (1) employee characteristics and (2) characteristics of the employee's work environment. Several contingencies have already been studied within the path-goal framework, and the model is open for more variables in the future.[35] However, only four contingencies are reviewed here (see Exhibit 12.3).

- *Skill and experience*—A combination of directive and supportive leadership is best for employees who are (or perceive themselves to be) inexperienced and unskilled.[36] Directive leadership gives subordinates information about how to accomplish the task, whereas supportive leadership helps them cope with the uncertainties of unfamiliar work situations. Directive leadership is detrimental when employees are skilled and experienced because it introduces too much supervisory control.

- *Locus of control*—Recall from Chapter 2 that people with an internal locus of control believe that they have control over their work environment. Consequently, these employees prefer participative and achievement-oriented leadership styles and may become frustrated with a directive style. In contrast, people with an external locus of control believe that their performance is due more to luck and fate, so they tend to be more satisfied with directive and supportive leadership.

- *Task structure*—Leaders should adopt the directive style when the task is nonroutine, because this style minimizes role ambiguity that tends to occur in these complex work situations (particularly for inexperienced employees).[37] The directive style is ineffec-

EXHIBIT 12.3	Selected contingencies of path-goal theory			
	Directive	Supportive	Participative	Achievement-oriented
Employee contingencies				
Skill/experience	Low	Low	High	High
Locus of control	External	External	Internal	Internal
Environmental contingencies				
Task structure	Nonroutine	Routine	Nonroutine	???
Team dynamics	Negative norms	Low cohesion	Positive norms	???

tive when employees have routine and simple tasks because the manager's guidance serves no purpose and may be viewed as unnecessarily close control. Employees in highly routine and simple jobs may require supportive leadership to help them cope with the tedious nature of the work and lack of control over the pace of work. Participative leadership is preferred for employees performing nonroutine tasks because the lack of rules and procedures gives them more discretion to achieve challenging goals. The participative style is ineffective for employees in routine tasks because they lack discretion over their work.

- *Team dynamics*—Cohesive teams with performance-oriented norms act as a substitute for most leader interventions. High team cohesion substitutes for supportive leadership, whereas performance oriented team norms substitute for directive and possibly achievement-oriented leadership. Thus, when team cohesiveness is low, leaders should use the supportive style. Leaders should apply a directive style to counteract team norms that oppose the team's formal objectives. For example, the team leader may need to use legitimate power if team members have developed a norm to "take it easy" rather than get a project completed on time.

Path-goal theory has received more research support than other contingency leadership models, but the evidence is far from complete. A few contingencies (i.e., task structure) have limited research support. Other contingencies and leadership styles in the path-goal leadership model haven't been investigated at all (as noted by the question marks in Exhibit 12.3).[38] Another concern is that as path-goal theory expands, the model may become too complex for practical use. Few people would be able to remember all the contingencies and appropriate leadership styles for those contingencies. In spite of these limitations, path-goal theory remains a relatively robust contingency leadership theory.

OTHER CONTINGENCY THEORIES

At the beginning of this chapter we noted that numerous leadership theories have developed over the years. Most of them are found in the contingency perspective of leadership. Some overlap with the path-goal model in terms of leadership styles, but most use simpler and more abstract contingencies. We will very briefly mention only two here because of their popularity and historical significance to the field.

situational leadership theory (SLT)
A commercially popular but poorly supported leadership model, stating that effective leaders vary their style (telling, selling, participating, delegating) with the "readiness" of followers.

Situational Leadership Theory One of the most popular contingency theories among practitioners is the **situational leadership theory (SLT)** also called life-cycle theory of leadership, developed by Paul Hersey and Ken Blanchard.[39] SLT suggests that effective leaders vary their style with the "readiness" of followers. (An earlier version of the model called this "maturity.") Readiness refers to the employee's or work team's ability and willingness to accomplish a specific task. Ability refers to the extent that the follower has the skills and knowledge to perform the task without the leader's guidance. Willingness refers to the follower's motivation and commitment to perform the assigned task. The model compresses these distinct concepts into a single situational condition.

The situational leadership model also identifies four leadership styles—telling, selling, participating, and delegating—that Hersey and Blanchard distinguish in terms of the amount of directive and supportive behaviour provided. For example, "telling" has high task behaviour and low supportive behaviour. The situational leadership model has four quadrants with each quadrant showing the leadership style that is most appropriate under different circumstances.

In spite of its popularity, several studies and at least three reviews have concluded that the situational leadership model lacks empirical support.[40] Only one part of the model apparently works, namely that leaders should use "telling" (i.e., directive style) when employees lack motivation and ability. (Recall that is also documented in path-goal theory.) The model's elegant simplicity is attractive and entertaining, but most parts don't represent reality very well.

Fiedler's Contingency Model

Fiedler's contingency model

Developed by Fred Fiedler, this early contingency leadership model suggests that leader effectiveness depends on whether the person's natural leadership style is appropriately matched to the situation.

Fiedler's contingency model, developed by Fred Fiedler and his associates, is the earliest contingency theory of leadership.[41] According to this model, leader effectiveness depends on whether the person's natural leadership style is appropriately matched to the situation. The theory examines two leadership styles that essentially correspond to the previously described people-oriented and task-oriented styles. Unfortunately, Fiedler's model relies on a questionnaire that does not measure either leadership style very well.

Fiedler's model suggests that the best leadership style depends on the level of *situational control*; that is, the degree of power and influence that the leader possesses in a particular situation. Situational control is affected by three factors in the following order of importance: leader-member relations, task structure, and position power.[42] Leader-member relations refers to how much employees trust and respect the leader and are willing to follow his or her guidance. Task structure refers to the clarity or ambiguity of operating procedures. Position power is the extent to which the leader possesses legitimate, reward, and coercive power over subordinates. These three contingencies form the eight possible combinations of *situation favourableness* from the leader's viewpoint. Good leader-member relations, high task structure, and strong position power create the most favourable situation for the leader because he or she has the most power and influence under these conditions.

Fiedler has gained considerable respect for pioneering the first contingency theory of leadership. However, his theory has fared less well. As mentioned, the leadership style scale used by Fiedler has been widely criticized. There is also no scientific justification for placing the three situational control factors in a hierarchy. Moreover, the concept of leader-member relations is actually an indicator of leader effectiveness (as in path-goal theory) rather than as a situational factor. Finally, the theory considers only two leadership styles whereas other models present a more complex and realistic array of behaviour options. These concerns explain why the theory has limited empirical support.[43]

Changing the Situation to Match the Leader's Natural Style

Fiedler's contingency model may have become a historical footnote, but it does make an important and lasting contribution by suggesting that leadership style is related to the individual's personality and, consequently, is relatively stable over time. Leaders might be able to alter their style temporarily, but they tend to use a preferred style in the long term. More recent scholars have also proposed that leadership styles are "hard-wired" more than most contingency leadership theories assume.[44]

If leadership style is influenced by a person's personality, then organizations should engineer the situation to fit the leader's dominant style, rather than expect leaders to change their style with the situation. A directive leader might be assigned inexperienced employees who need direction rather than seasoned people who work less effectively under a directive style. Alternatively, companies might transfer supervisors to workplaces where their dominant style fits best. For instance, directive leaders might be parachuted into work teams with counterproductive norms, whereas leaders who prefer a supportive style should be sent to departments in which employees face work pressures and other stressors.

LO5

LEADERSHIP SUBSTITUTES

leadership substitutes
A theory identifying contingencies that either limit the leader's ability to influence subordinates or make that particular leadership style unnecessary.

So far, we have looked at theories that recommend using different leadership styles in various situations. But one theory, called **leadership substitutes**, identifies conditions that either limit the leader's ability to influence subordinates or make that particular leadership style unnecessary. The literature identifies several conditions that possibly substitute for task-oriented or people-oriented leadership. For example, performance-based reward systems keep employees directed toward organizational goals, so they might replace or reduce the need for task-oriented leadership. Task-oriented leadership is also less important when employees are skilled and experienced. These propositions are similar to path-goal leadership theory, namely that directive leadership is unnecessary—and may be detrimental—when employees are skilled or experienced.[45]

Some research suggests that effective leaders help team members learn to lead themselves through leadership substitutes; in other words, co-workers substitute for leadership in high involvement team structures.[46] Co-workers instruct new employees, thereby providing directive leadership. They also provide social support, which reduces stress among fellow employees. Teams with norms that support organizational goals may substitute for achievement-oriented leadership, because employees encourage (or pressure) co-workers to stretch their performance levels.[47]

Self-leadership—the process of influencing oneself to establish the self-direction and self-motivation needed to perform a task (see Chapter 6)—is another possible leadership substitute.[48] Employees with high self-leadership set their own goals, reinforce their own behaviour, maintain positive thought processes, and monitor their own performance, thereby managing both personal motivation and abilities. As employees become more proficient in self-leadership, they presumably require less supervision to keep them focused and energized toward organizational objectives.

The leadership substitutes model has intuitive appeal, but the evidence so far is mixed. Some studies show that a few substitutes do replace the need for task or people-oriented leadership, but others do not. The difficulties of statistically testing for leadership substitutes may account for some problems, but a few writers contend that the limited support is evidence that leadership plays a critical role regardless of the situation.[49] At this point, we can conclude that a few conditions such as self-directed work teams, self-leadership, and reward systems might reduce the importance of task or people-oriented leadership, but probably won't completely replace leaders in these roles.

TRANSFORMATIONAL PERSPECTIVE OF LEADERSHIP

When Teresa Cascioli was recruited to lead Lakeport Beverage Corp. a few years ago, the Hamilton, Ontario-based brewer was in bankruptcy protection and about to shut its doors. In spite of the grim situation, Cascioli and her investment partners had a vision that Lakeport could be a successful company. They shut the plant for two months to complete a massive overhaul of the manufacturing process, and reduced costs by removing several middle management positions. Cascioli and her new management team also generated competitive optimism that resonated with employees. "We brought a sense of urgency to this place that was never here before," she says. Lakeport's fortunes started to rebound by the end of the first year, but the company really hit its stride when it introduced its now-famous "$24 for 24" strategy—selling a case of beer for a loonie per bottle. Lakeport's market share surged while national and regional brewers stumbled. Rather than fight this tough competitor, Molson's recently bought the company.[50]

By any measure, Teresa Cascioli is a transformational leader. Through her vision, communication, and actions, she transformed Lakeport Beverage Corp. into a more effective organization. Transformational leaders such as Teresa Cascioli, Guy Laliberté (Cirque du Soleil), Rick George (Suncor), Terry Matthews (Mitel and Newbridge Networks), Glenn Cooke (Cooke Aquaculture), and Isadore Sharp (Four Seasons Hotels and Resorts) dot the Canadian landscape. These leaders are agents of change. They create, communicate, and model a shared vision for the team or organization, and inspire followers to strive for that vision.[51]

TRANSFORMATIONAL VERSUS TRANSACTIONAL LEADERSHIP

Transformational leadership differs from **transactional leadership**.[52] The leadership literature offers a confusing array of definitions for transactional leadership, but we shall define it as helping organizations achieve their current objectives more efficiently, such as by linking job performance to valued rewards and ensuring that employees have the resources needed to get the job done. The contingency and behavioural theories described earlier adopt the transactional perspective because they focus on leader behaviours that improve employee performance and satisfaction. You might think of transactional leadership as "managing," or "doing things right" because the focus is on improving employee performance and well-being.[53] In contrast, transformational leadership is about "leading"—changing the organization's strategies and culture so that they have a better fit with the surrounding environment. Transformational leaders are change agents who energize and direct employees to a new set of corporate values and behaviours.

Organizations require both transactional and transformational leadership.[54] Transactional leadership improves organizational efficiency, whereas transformational leadership steers companies onto a better course of action. Transformational leadership is particularly important in organizations that require significant alignment with the external environment. Unfortunately, too many leaders get trapped in the daily managerial activities that represent transactional leadership.[55] They lose touch with the transformational aspect of effective leadership. Without transformational leaders, organizations stagnate and eventually become seriously misaligned with their environments.

TRANSFORMATIONAL VERSUS CHARISMATIC LEADERSHIP

Another topic that has generated some confusion and controversy is the distinction between transformational and charismatic leadership.[56] Many researchers either use the words interchangeably, as if they have the same meaning, or view charismatic leadership as an essential ingredient of transformational leadership. Others take this view further by suggesting that charismatic leadership is the highest degree of transformational leadership.

However, the emerging view, which this book adopts, comes from a third group of experts who contend that charisma is distinct from transformational leadership. These academics point out that charisma is a personal trait or relational quality that provides referent power over followers, whereas transformational leadership is a set of behaviours that people use to lead the change process.[57] Charismatic leaders might be transformational leaders; indeed, their personal power through charisma is a tool to change the behaviour of followers. However, some research points out that charismatic or "heroic" leaders easily build allegiance in followers, but do not necessarily change the organization. Other research suggests that charismatic leaders produce dependent followers, whereas transformational leaders have the opposite effect—they build follower empowerment, which tends to reduce dependence on the leader. For example, one study reported a negative relationship between charismatic leadership and the self-efficacy of followers.[58]

The main point here is that transformational leaders are not necessarily charismatic. Alan G. Lafley, the CEO of Proctor & Gamble, is not known for being charismatic,

transformational leadership
A leadership perspective that explains how leaders change teams or organizations by creating, communicating, and modelling a vision for the organization or work unit, and inspiring employees to strive for that vision.

transactional leadership
Leadership that helps organizations achieve their current objectives more efficiently, such as linking job performance to valued rewards and ensuring that employees have the resources needed to get the job done.

but has transformed the household goods company like no leader in recent memory. Similarly, IBM CEO Sam Palmisano speaks with humility, yet continues to drive IBM's success. "I don't have much curb appeal," Palmisano says of his minimal charisma, adding that IBM has more than 300,000 brilliant people to help drive the organization. "I just try to lead them and get them to come together around a common point of view," he explains.[60] In other words, Palmisano and Lafley lead by applying transformational leadership behaviours.

LO7   ELEMENTS OF TRANSFORMATIONAL LEADERSHIP

There are several descriptions of transformational leadership, but most include the following four elements: creating a strategic vision, communicating the vision, modelling the vision, and building commitment toward the vision.

Creating a Strategic Vision   The opening vignette to this chapter highlighted the leadership of Cirque du Soleil co-founder Guy Laliberté. One of Laliberté's many strengths as a leader is his uncanny ability to establish a vision of the company's future state that engages employees and establishes near-impossible, yet ultimately achievable objectives. Laliberté and other transformational leaders shape a strategic vision of a realistic and attractive future that bonds employees together and focuses their energy toward a superordinate organizational goal.[61] A shared strategic vision represents the substance of transformational leadership. It reflects a future for the company or work unit that is ultimately accepted and valued by organizational members. "In essence, leadership is about dreaming the impossible and helping followers achieve the same," says Nandan Nilekani, CEO of India's information technology giant, Infosys. "Moreover, the dream has to be built on sound and context-invariant values to sustain the enthusiasm and energy of people over a long time."[62]

Strategic vision creates a "higher purpose" or superordinate goal that energizes and unifies employees.[63] A strategic vision might originate with the leader, but it is just as likely to emerge from employees, clients, suppliers, or other stakeholders. A shared strategic vision plays an important role in organizational effectiveness.[64] Visions offer the motivational benefits of goal setting, but are compelling future states that bond employees and motivate them to strive for those objectives. Visions are typically described in a way that distinguishes them from the current situation, yet makes the goal both appealing and achievable.

Communicating the Vision If vision is the substance of transformational leadership, then communicating that vision is the process. Canadian CEOs say that the most important leadership qualities are being able to build and share their vision for the organization. "Part of a leader's role is to set the vision for the company and to communicate that vision to staff to get their buy-in," explains Dave Anderson, president of WorkSafeBC (the Workers' Compensation Board of British Columbia).[66]

Transformational leaders communicate meaning and elevate the importance of the visionary goal to employees. They frame messages around a grand purpose with emotional appeal that captivates employees and other corporate stakeholders. Framing helps transformational leaders establish a common mental model so that the group or organization will act collectively toward the desirable goal.[67]

Transformational leaders bring their visions to life through symbols, metaphors, stories, and other vehicles that transcend plain language. Metaphors borrow images of other experiences, thereby creating richer meaning of the vision that has not yet been experienced. When George Cohen, the ebullient CEO of McDonald's Canada, faced the difficult challenge of opening restaurants in Moscow, he frequently reminded his team members that they were establishing "hamburger diplomacy." And in the mid-1800s, when ocean transportation was treacherous, Samuel Cunard emphasized that he was creating an "ocean railway." At the time, railroads provided one of the safest forms of transportation, and Cunard's metaphor reinforced the notion to employees and passengers alike that Cunard Steamship Lines, which at the time was based in Halifax, Nova Scotia, would provide equally safe transportation across the Atlantic Ocean."[68]

Modelling the Vision Transformational leaders not only talk about a vision; they enact it. They "walk the talk" by stepping outside the executive suite and doing things that symbolize the vision.[69] They are also reliable and persistent in their actions, thereby legitimizing the vision and providing further evidence that they can be trusted. "The example you set at the top is probably the most important thing a CEO does in terms of what you ask people to do," says Calgary-based Suncor CEO Rick George. "You have got to walk that same line yourself."[70]

Leaders walk the talk through significant events such as visiting customers, moving their offices closer to employees, and holding ceremonies to destroy outdated policy manuals. However, they also alter mundane activities—meeting agendas, dress code, executive schedules—so they are more consistent with the vision and its underlying values. Modelling the vision is important because employees and other stakeholders are executive watchers who look for behaviours that symbolize values and expectations. The greater the consistency between the leader's words and actions, the more employees will believe and follow the leader. Walking the talk also builds employee trust because it is partly determined by the consistency of the person's actions.

Building Commitment toward the Vision   Transforming a vision into reality requires employee commitment. Transformational leaders build this commitment in several ways. Their words, symbols, and stories build a contagious enthusiasm that energizes people to adopt the vision as their own. Leaders demonstrate a 'can do' attitude by enacting their vision and staying on course. Their persistence and consistency reflect an image of honesty, trust, and integrity. Finally, leaders build commitment by involving employees in the process of shaping the organization's vision.

EVALUATING THE TRANSFORMATIONAL LEADERSHIP PERSPECTIVE

Transformational leaders do make a difference. Subordinates are more satisfied and have higher affective organizational commitment under transformational leaders. They also perform their jobs better, engage in more organizational citizenship behaviours, and make better or more creative decisions. One study of Canadian bank branches also reported that organizational commitment and financial performance seem to increase where the branch manager completed a transformational leadership training program.[71]

Transformational leadership is currently the most popular leadership perspective, but it faces a number of challenges. One problem is that some writers engage in circular logic by defining transformational leadership in terms of the leader's success.[72] They suggest that leaders are transformational when they successfully bring about change, rather than whether they engage in certain behaviours we call transformational. Another concern is that transformational leadership is usually described as a universal rather than contingency-oriented model. Only very recently have writers begun to explore the idea that transformational leadership is more appropriate in some situations than others.[73] For instance, transformational leadership is probably more valuable when organizations need to adapt than when environmental conditions are stable. Preliminary evidence suggests that the transformational leadership perspective is relevant across cultures. However, there may be specific elements of transformational leadership, such as the way visions are formed and communicated, that are more appropriate in North America than other cultures.

IMPLICIT LEADERSHIP PERSPECTIVE

LO8

The competency, behaviour, contingency, and transformational leadership perspectives make the basic assumption that leaders 'make a difference.' Certainly, there is evidence that senior executives do influence organizational performance. However, leadership also involves followers' perceptions about the characteristics and influence of people they call leaders. This perceptual perspective of leadership is collectively called **implicit leadership theory**.[74]

PROTOTYPES OF EFFECTIVE LEADERS

Implicit leadership theory consists of two related concepts. The main part of this theory states that everyone has *leadership prototypes*—preconceived beliefs about the features and behaviours of effective leaders. These prototypes, which develop through socialization within the family and society,[75] shape our expectations and acceptance of others as leaders, which in turn affect our willingness to serve as followers. In other words, we are more willing to allow someone to influence us as a leader if that person looks and acts like our prototype of a leader. For example, one recent study established that inherited personality characteristics significantly influence the perception that someone is a leader in a leaderless situation.[76] These leadership prototypes not only support a per-

implicit leadership theory
A theory stating that people evaluate a leader's effectiveness in terms of how well that person fits preconceived beliefs about the features and behaviours of effective leaders (leadership prototypes), and that they tend to inflate the influence of leaders on organizational events.

son's role as leader; they also form or influence our perception of the leader's effectiveness. If the leader looks like and acts consistently with our prototype, then we are more likely to believe that the leader is effective.[77] This prototype comparison process occurs because people have an inherent need to quickly evaluate people as leaders, yet leadership effectiveness is often ambiguous and might not be apparent for a long time.

THE ROMANCE OF LEADERSHIP

Along with relying on implicit prototypes of effective leaders, followers tend to distort their perception of the influence that leaders have on the environment. This "romance of leadership" effect exists because in most cultures people want to believe that leaders make a difference. There are two basic reasons for this belief.[78] First, leadership is a useful way for us to simplify life events. It is easier to explain organizational successes and failures in terms of the leader's ability than by analyzing a complex array of other forces. Second, there is a strong tendency in Canada and other Western cultures to believe that life events are generated more from people than from uncontrollable natural forces.[79] This illusion of control is satisfied by believing that events result from the rational actions of leaders. In other words, employees feel better believing that leaders make a difference, so they actively look for evidence that this is so.

One way that followers support their perceptions that leaders make a difference is through fundamental attribution error (see Chapter 3). Research has found that (at least in Western cultures) leaders are given credit or blame for the company's success or failure because employees do not readily see the external forces that also influence these events. Leaders reinforce this belief by taking credit for organizational successes.[80]

The implicit leadership perspective provides valuable advice to improve leadership acceptance. It highlights the fact that leadership is a perception of followers as much as the actual behaviours and formal roles of people calling themselves leaders. Potential leaders must be sensitive to this fact, understand what followers expect, and act accordingly. Individuals who do not make an effort to fit leadership prototypes will have more difficulty bringing about necessary organizational change.

CROSS-CULTURAL AND GENDER ISSUES IN LEADERSHIP

Along with the five perspectives of leadership presented throughout this chapter, cultural values and practices affect what leaders do. Culture shapes the leader's values and norms, which influence his or her decisions and actions. These cultural values also shape the expectations that followers have of their leaders. An executive who acts inconsistently with cultural expectations is more likely to be perceived as an ineffective leader. Furthermore, leaders who deviate from those values may experience various forms of influence to get them to conform to the leadership norms and expectations of that society. In other words, implicit leadership theory described in the previous section of this chapter explains differences in leadership practices across cultures.

LO9

With respect to gender, studies in field settings have generally found that male and female leaders do not differ in their levels of task-oriented or people-oriented leadership. The main explanation is that real-world jobs require similar behaviour from male and female job incumbents.[81] However, women do adopt a participative leadership style more readily than their male counterparts. One possible reason is that, compared to boys, girls are often raised to be more egalitarian and less status oriented, which is consistent with being participative. There is also some evidence that women have somewhat better interpersonal skills than men, and this translates into their relatively greater use of the participative leadership style. A third explanation is that subordinates expect female leaders to be more participative, based on their own gender stereotypes, so female leaders comply with follower expectations to some extent.

Several recent surveys report that women are rated higher than men on the emerging leadership qualities of coaching, teamwork, and empowering employees.[82] Yet research also suggests that women are evaluated negatively when they try to apply the full range of leadership styles, particularly more directive and autocratic approaches. Thus, ironically, women may be well suited to contemporary leadership roles, yet they often continue to face limitations of leadership through the gender stereotypes and prototypes of leaders held by followers.[83] Overall, both male and female leaders must be sensitive to the fact that followers have expectations about how leaders should act, and negative evaluations may go to leaders who deviate from those expectations.

CHAPTER SUMMARY

Leadership is defined as the ability to influence, motivate, and enable others to contribute toward the effectiveness and success of the organizations of which they are members. Leaders use influence to motivate followers, and arrange the work environment so that they do the job more effectively. Leaders exist throughout the organization, not just in the executive suite.

The competency perspective tries to identify the characteristics of effective leaders. Recent writing suggests that leaders have specific personality characteristics, positive self-concept, drive, integrity, leadership motivation, knowledge of the business, cognitive and practical intelligence, and emotional intelligence. The behavioural perspective of leadership identifies two clusters of leader behaviour: people-oriented and task-oriented. People-oriented behaviours include showing mutual trust and respect for subordinates, demonstrating a genuine concern for their needs, and having a desire to look out for their welfare. Task-oriented behaviours include assigning employees to specific tasks, clarifying their work duties and procedures, ensuring they follow company rules, and pushing them to reach their performance capacity.

The contingency perspective of leadership takes the view that effective leaders diagnose the situation and adapt their style to fit that situation. The path-goal model is the prominent contingency theory that identifies four leadership styles—directive, supportive, participative, and achievement-oriented—and several contingencies relating to the characteristics of the employee and of the situation.

Two other contingency leadership theories include the situational leadership theory and Fiedler's contingency theory. Research support is quite weak for both theories. However, a lasting element of Fiedler's theory is the idea that leaders have natural styles and, consequently, companies need to change the leader's environment to suit their style. Another theory, leadership substitutes, identifies contingencies that either limit the leader's ability to influence subordinates or make that particular leadership style unnecessary.

Transformational leaders create a strategic vision, communicate that vision through framing and use of metaphors, model the vision by 'walking the talk' and acting consistently, and build commitment toward the vision. This contrasts with transactional leadership, which involves linking job performance to valued rewards and ensuring that employees have the resources needed to get the job done. The contingency and behavioural perspectives adopt the transactional view of leadership.

According to the implicit leadership perspective, people have leadership prototypes, which they use to evaluate the leader's effectiveness. Furthermore, people form a romance of leadership; they want to believe that leaders make a difference, so they engage in fundamental attribution error and other perceptual distortions to support this belief in the leader's impact.

Cultural values also influence the leader's personal values, which in turn influence his or her leadership practices. Women generally do not differ from men in the degree of people-oriented or task-oriented leadership. However, female leaders more often adopt a participative style. Research also suggests that people evaluate female leaders based on gender stereotypes, which may result in higher or lower ratings.

KEY TERMS

Fiedler's contingency model, p. 292
implicit leadership theory, p. 297
leadership, p. 284
leadership substitutes, p. 293

path-goal leadership theory, p. 288
servant leadership, p. 288
shared leadership, p. 284

situational leadership theory
  (SLT), p. 291
transactional leadership, p. 294
transformational leadership, p. 294

CRITICAL THINKING QUESTIONS

1. Why is it important for top executives to value and support leadership demonstrated at all levels of the organization?

2. Find two newspaper ads for management or executive positions. What leadership competencies are mentioned in these ads? If you were on the selection panel, what methods would you use to identify these competencies in job applicants?

3. Consider your favourite teacher. What people-oriented and task-oriented leadership behaviours did he or she use effectively? In general, do you think students prefer an instructor who is more people-oriented or task-oriented? Explain your preference.

4. Your employees are skilled and experienced customer service representatives who perform nonroutine tasks, such as solving unique customer problems or special needs with the company's equipment. Use path-goal theory to identify the most appropriate leadership style(s) you should use in this situation. Be sure to fully explain your answer and discuss why other styles are inappropriate.

5. Transformational leadership is a popular perspective of leadership. However, it is far from perfect. Discuss the limitations of transformational leadership.

6. This chapter distinguished charismatic leadership from transformational leadership. Yet, charisma is identified by most employees and managers as a characteristic of effective leaders. Why is charisma commonly related to leadership? In your opinion, are the best leaders charismatic? Why or why not?

7. Identify a current political leader (e.g., prime minister, president, governor, mayor) and his or her recent accomplishments. Now, using the implicit leadership perspective, think of ways that these accomplishments of the leader may be overstated. In other words, explain why they may be due to factors other than the leader.

8. You hear two people debating the merits of women as leaders. One person claims that women make better leaders than do men because women are more sensitive to their employees' needs and involve them in organizational decisions. The other person counters that although these leadership styles may be increasingly important, most women have trouble gaining acceptance as leaders when they face tough situations in which a more autocratic style is required. Discuss the accuracy of the comments made in this discussion.

CASE STUDY 12.1

Profitel Inc.

By Steven L McShane, The University of Western Australia

As a formerly government-owned telephone monopoly, Profitel enjoyed many decades of minimal competition. Even today as a publicly traded enterprise, the company's almost exclusive control over telephone copper wiring across the country keeps its profit margins above 40 percent. Competitors in telephone and DSL broadband continue to rely on Profitel's wholesale business, which generates substantially more profit than similar wholesale services in many other countries. However, Profitel has stiff competition in the cellular telephone business, and other emerging technologies (voice-over-Internet) threaten Profitel's dominance. Based on these threats, Profitel's board of directors decided to hire an outsider as the new chief executive.

Although several qualified candidates expressed an interest in Profitel's top job, the board selected Lars Peeters, who had been CEO for six years of a publicly traded European telephone company, followed by a brief stint as CEO of a cellular telephone company in the United States until it was acquired by a larger firm. Profitel's board couldn't believe its good fortune; Peeters brought extensive industry knowledge and global experience, a high-octane energy level, self-confidence, decisiveness, and congenial yet strongly persuasive interpersonal style. He also had a unique "presence," which caused people to pay attention and respect his leadership. The board was also impressed with Peeters strategy to bolster Profitel's profit margins. This included heavy investment in the latest wireless broadband technology (for both cellular telephone and computer Internet) before competitors could gain a foothold, cutting costs through layoffs and reduction of peripheral services, and putting pressure on government to deregulate its traditional and emerging businesses. When Peeters described his strategy to the board, one board member commented that this was the same strategy Peeters used in his previous two CEO postings. Peeters dismissed the comment, saying that each situation is unique.

Peeters lived up to his reputation as a decisive executive. Almost immediately after taking the CEO job at Profitel, he hired two executives from the European company where he previously worked. Together over the next two years they cut the workforce by 5 percent and rolled out the new wireless broadband technology for cellphones and Internet. Costs increased somewhat due to downsizing expenses and the wireless technology rollout. Profitel's wireless broadband subscriber list grew quickly because, in spite of its very high prices, the technology faced limited competition and Profitel was pushing customers off the older technology to the new network. Profitel's customer satisfaction ratings fell, however. A national consumer research group reported that Profitel's broadband offered the country's worst value. Employee morale also declined due to layoffs and the company's public image problems. Some industry experts also noted that Profitel selected its wireless technology without evaluating the alternative emerging wireless technology, which has been gaining ground in other countries. Peeters's aggressive campaign against government regulation also had unintended consequences. Rather than convincing the government to reduce the amount of regulation imposed on Profitel, Peeters's scathing attacks made Profitel look even more arrogant in the eyes of both customers and government leaders.

Profitel's board was troubled by the company's lacklustre share price, which had declined 20 percent since Peeters was hired. Some board members also worried that the company had bet on the wrong wireless technology and that subscription levels would stall far below the number necessary to achieve the profits stated in Peeters's strategic plan. This concern came closer to reality when a foreign owned competitor won a $1-billion government contract to improve broadband services in regional areas of the country. Profitel's proposal for that regional broadband upgrade specified high prices and limited corporate investment, but Peeters was confident Profitel would be awarded the contract because of its market dominance and existing infrastructure with the new wireless network. When the government decided otherwise, Profitel's board fired Peeters along with two executives he had hired from the European company where he previously worked. Now, the board had to figure out what went wrong and how to avoid this problem in the future.

Discussion Questions

1. Which perspective(s) of leadership best explains the problems experienced in this case? Analyze the case using concepts discussed in that leadership perspective.

2. What can organizations do to minimize the leadership problems discussed above?

Copyright © 2008. Steven L. McShane.

CASE STUDY 12.2

The Staff Sergeant's Leadership Dilemma

By James Buchkowsky, Saskatchewan Institute of Science and Technology

Donna Lindsay, staff sergeant and commander of a Canadian regional police force detachment, just learned that she was not getting a replacement for a constable who had recently retired. Lindsay's superintendent said, "Hiring freezes are in effect until the next budget year, so you'll have to figure out a way for the other constables to pick up the work." Donna spent the rest of the day deciding how to divide the work among the other officers in her detachment.

The next morning at the daily briefing session, Donna announced the hiring freeze and that the constable position would not be replaced. She explained how she had divided the job into seven categories so that one constable would be responsible for each. Donna then informed the officers of the additional work that would be added to their duties. During the rest of the session, Donna couldn't help notice that many weren't reacting favourably to the announced assignments.

The next day, one constable, Earl, was waiting for her at her office door. "Why did you assign me to deal with the media?" he asked. "I hate being in front of a camera. Can't you tell someone else they have to do this?"

Before long another staff member, Joe, was at Donna's door. "Can't you reassign the travelling presentations to someone else? I have a wife and young children. This detachment covers a large area with small communities, and asking me to travel all over is really unfair to my family."

By the end of the day, the seven constables had produced seven complaints. Donna re-examined the tasks and duties, attempted to juggle and switch assignments, and considered everyone's concerns but it nearly drove her crazy. She concluded there was nothing she could do to make everyone happy. She called another staff meeting and said, "I've tried to accommodate you, but it can't be done. Take the assignments I've given you and do your best."

The officers didn't take to this decision very well and started taking matters into their own hands. Earl said to Joe, "I know you hate the travelling presentations, so I'll do them if you'll take my assignment." Roz told Linda, "I'll give you my research work if you'll do the evidence cataloguing." When other staff heard about the trading, they joined right in also. With more people making more offers, this wheeling and dealing kept getting louder and louder. Donna came out of her office to see what the noise was all about.

When Donna learned the staff were trading assignments without her consent, she was upset. A few days later, while discussing other matters on the telephone with her immediate supervisor in the regional office, Donna mentioned the events. "Some officers seem happy with their trades, but the ones who didn't get the trade they wanted are unhappy and directing the blame at me. What did I do wrong? How should I have handled this? What am I going to do now?"

Discussion Questions

1. What leadership style did Donna use? Was it appropriate for the situation?

2. Analyze the environmental and employee factors in this case to determine which style she should have adopted.

3. Since her approach did not work, what style should Donna use now?

 TEAM EXERCISE 12.3

Leadership Diagnostic Analysis

Purpose   To help students learn about the different path-goal leadership styles and when to apply each style.

Instructions   • *Step 1:* Students individually write down two incidents in which someone had been an effective manager or leader over them. The leader and situation might be from work, a sports team, a student work group, or any other setting where leadership might emerge. For example, students might describe how their supervisor in a summer job pushed them to reach higher performance goals than they would have done otherwise. Each incident should state the actual behaviours that the leader used, not just general statements, e.g., "My boss sat down with me and we agreed on specific targets and deadlines, then he said several times over the next few weeks that I was capable of reaching those goals." Each incident only requires two or three sentences.

• *Step 2:* After everyone has written their two incidents, the instructor will form small groups (typically between four or five students). Each team will answer the following questions for each incident presented in that team:

1. Which path-goal theory leadership style(s)—directive, supportive, participative, or achievement-oriented—did the leader apply in this incident?

2. Ask the person who wrote the incident about the conditions that made this leadership style (or these styles, if more than one was used) appropriate in this situation? The team should list these contingency factors clearly and, where possible, connect them to the contingencies described in path-goal theory. (Note: the team might identify path-goal leadership contingencies that are not described in the book. These, too, should be noted and discussed.)

• *Step 3:* After the teams have diagnosed the incidents, each team will describe to the entire class the most interesting incidents as well as its diagnosis of that incident. Other teams will critique the diagnosis. Any leadership contingencies not mentioned in the textbook should also be presented and discussed.

www.mcgrawhill.ca/olc/mcshane

SELF-ASSESSMENT 12.4

What Type of Leader is Your Boss?

Purpose   This assessment is designed to help you understand two important dimensions of leadership and to identify which of these dimensions is more prominent in your supervisor, team leader, coach, or other person to whom you are accountable.

Instructions   Read each of the statements below and circle the response that you believe best describes your supervisor. You may substitute "supervisor" with anyone else to whom you are accountable, such as a team leader, CEO, course instructor, or sports coach. Then use the scoring key in Appendix B to calculate the results for each leadership dimensions. After completing this assessment, be prepared to discuss in class the distinctions between these leadership dimensions

Leadership Dimensions Instrument					
My supervisor...	Strongly Agree	Agree	Neutral	Disagree	Strongly Disagree
1. Focuses attention on irregularities, mistakes, exceptions, and deviations from what is expected of me.	5	4	3	2	1
2. Engages in words and deeds that enhance his/her image of competence.	5	4	3	2	1
3. Monitors performance for errors needing correction.	5	4	3	2	1
4. Serves as a role model for me.	5	4	3	2	1
5. Points out what I will receive if I do what is required.	5	4	3	2	1
6. Instills pride in being associated with him/her.	5	4	3	2	1
7. Keeps careful track of mistakes.	5	4	3	2	1
8. Can be trusted to help me overcome any obstacle.	5	4	3	2	1
9. Tells me what to do to be rewarded for my efforts.	5	4	3	2	1
10. Makes me aware of strongly held values, ideals, and aspirations which are shared in common.	5	4	3	2	1
11. Is alert for failure to meet standards.	5	4	3	2	1
12. Mobilizes a collective sense of mission.	5	4	3	2	1
13. Works out agreements with me on what I will receive if I do what needs to be done.	5	4	3	2	1
14. Articulates a vision of future opportunities.	5	4	3	2	1
15. Talks about special rewards for good work.	5	4	3	2	1
16. Talks optimistically about the future.	5	4	3	2	1

Source: Items and dimensions are adapted from D. N. Den Hartog, J. J. Van Muijen, and P. L. Koopman, "Transactional Versus Transformational Leadership: An Analysis of the MLQ," *Journal of Occupational & Organizational Psychology* 70 (March 1997), pp. 19–34. Den Hartog et al. label transactional leadership as "rational-objective leadership" and label transformational leadership as "inspirational leadership." Many of their items may have originated from B. M. Bass and B. J. Avolio, *Manual for the Multifactor Leadership Questionnaire* (Palo Alto, CA: Consulting Psychologists Press, 1989).

PART THREE VIDEO CASE STUDIES

Case 1   Boom (Drum Room Team Building)

CBC ◉

Over the years, employees have been put through many different forms of team build-ing, from board games to outdoor experiences. Now, some Canadian companies are putting a little more beat into team building by having their employees participate in drum circles and similar percussion activities. This CBC video takes the viewer to some of these events, from large assembly percussion orchestras to smaller group drum gatherings. In this program, you'll also hear what employees and executives who partici-pated in these sessions think about them.

Discussion Questions

1. In your opinion, how would these drum circle and percussion sessions improve team dynamics? Under what conditions might they not work effectively?

2. What other organizational behaviour topics seem to be related to the effects of drum circles?

Case 2   Celebrity CEO Charisma

Does the cult of CEO charisma really make a difference to company profits? This NBC program takes a brief look at chief executives who acted like super-heroes but failed to deliver, as well as a few low-key executives who really made a difference. The program hears from Harvard Business School professor Rakesh Khurana, author of *Searching for a Corporate Savior*, a book warning that charismatic leaders are not necessarily effective leaders.

Discussion Questions

1. Why do company boards tend to hire charismatic CEOs?

2. What can corporate boards do to minimize the charisma effect when filling chief executive officer and other senior executive positions?

Case 3   Southwest CEO: Get to Know Gary Kelly

Southwest Airlines remains one of the most successful airlines in the United States. Its secret to success? Treat customers as kings and queens, and treat employees even better. This video program shows how Southwest Airlines CEO Gary Kelly keeps in touch with day-to-day activities at the airline. It also describes some of the challenges that Kelly and his executive team have ahead of them.

Discussion Questions

1. Discuss the transactional and transformational leadership of Gary Kelly.

2. How does Gary Kelly's leadership reinforce Southwest Airlines' organizational culture?

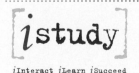

iStudy—Available 24/7 with instant feedback so you can study when you want, how you want, and where you want. Visit www.istudyob.ca to register—take practice quizzes, run interactive scenarios, practice concepts, and much more. Also visit the Student Online Learning Centre for additional study tools.

www.mcgrawhill.ca/olc/mcshane

CHAPTER 13

Organizational Structure

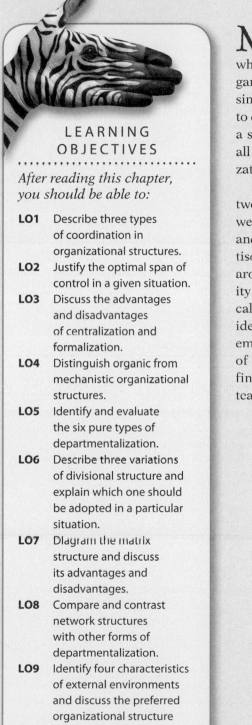

LEARNING OBJECTIVES

After reading this chapter, you should be able to:

LO1 Describe three types of coordination in organizational structures.

LO2 Justify the optimal span of control in a given situation.

LO3 Discuss the advantages and disadvantages of centralization and formalization.

LO4 Distinguish organic from mechanistic organizational structures.

LO5 Identify and evaluate the six pure types of departmentalization.

LO6 Describe three variations of divisional structure and explain which one should be adopted in a particular situation.

LO7 Diagram the matrix structure and discuss its advantages and disadvantages.

LO8 Compare and contrast network structures with other forms of departmentalization.

LO9 Identify four characteristics of external environments and discuss the preferred organizational structure for each environment.

LO10 Summarize the influence of organizational size, technology, and strategy on organizational structure.

Medical physicians Ray Muzyka and Greg Zeschuk didn't think much about organizational structure when they (along with a third partner who later returned to medical practice) launched Edmonton-based electronic games company BioWare Corp. in the mid-1990s. By default, they relied on a simple team structure in which a handful of talented people worked together to develop the company's first game, *Shattered Steel*. But when they launched a second project, *Baldur's Gate*, Muzyka and Zeschuk faced a question that all leaders need to ask themselves when their companies grow: What organizational structure would best support this company for the future?

BioWare's co-founders recognized that one option would be to simply have two (and eventually several) teams working independently. However, they were also concerned that a multi-team structure would duplicate resources, and might undermine resource sharing among people with the same expertise across teams. Alternatively, the game developer could create departments around the various specializations, including art, programming, audio, quality assurance, and design. This would allow employees with similar technical expertise to share information and create new ideas within their specialization. However, employees would not have the same level of teamwork or commitment to the final product as they would in a team-based project structure.[1]

BioWare Corp. co-founders Ray Muzyka (left) and Greg Zeschuk (right) had to choose which organizational structure would best serve the rapidly growing Edmonton-based electronic games company. © *Shaughn Butts/ Edmonton Journal*

organizational structure
The division of labour as
well as the patterns of coordination, communication,
workflow, and formal power
that direct organizational
activities.

What organizational structure will work best for BioWare? We'll find out in this chapter. **Organizational structure** refers to the division of labour as well as the patterns of coordination, communication, workflow, and formal power that direct organizational activities. The chapter begins by introducing the two fundamental processes in organizational structure: division of labour and coordination. This is followed by a detailed investigation of the four main elements of organizational structure: span of control, centralization, formalization, and departmentalization. The latter part of this chapter examines the contingencies of organizational design, including organizational size, technology, external environment, and strategy.

Throughout this chapter, we hope to show that an organization's structure is much more than an organizational chart diagramming which employees report to which managers. Organizational structure includes reporting relationships, but it also relates to job design, information flow, work standards and rules, reliance on teams, and power relationships. Organizational structure is also an important artifact of corporate culture and is often a critical tool for organizational change.[2] For example, when Charles Schwab Co. experienced financial trouble not long ago, founder Charles Schwab held a two-day marathon session in which the company's top executives were asked to redraw the organization chart in a way that would make the company simpler, more decentralized, and refocused on the customer. Every executive in the room, including those whose jobs would be erased from the new structure, were asked for their input.[3] The point we want to emphasize here is that organizational structure reconfigures power, communication patterns, and possibly the company's culture in the long term. As such, altering the organization's structure is an important component of the CEO's toolkit for organizational change.[4]

DIVISION OF LABOUR AND COORDINATION

All organizational structures include two fundamental requirements: the division of labour into distinct tasks and the coordination of that labour so that employees are able to accomplish common goals.[5] Organizations are groups of people who work interdependently toward some purpose. To efficiently accomplish their goals, these groups typically divide the work into manageable chunks, particularly when there are many different tasks to perform. They also introduce various coordinating mechanisms to ensure that everyone is working effectively toward the same objectives.

DIVISION OF LABOUR

Division of labour refers to the subdivision of work into separate jobs assigned to different people. Subdivided work leads to job specialization, because each job now includes a narrow subset of the tasks necessary to complete the product or service. To produce its first electronic game, BioWare's co-founders divided the work among a dozen or more employees. Some people were responsible for programming; others completed the artwork; still others developed the game's sound effects, and so forth. Today's computer games are so sophisticated that a project may require several dozen people with highly specialized expertise. As companies get larger, this horizontal division of labour is accompanied by vertical division of labour, where some people are assigned the task of managing employees.

Why do companies divide the work required to build a computer game into several jobs? As we learned earlier in this book, job specialization increases work efficiency.[6] Job incumbents can master their tasks quickly because work cycles are very short. Less time is wasted changing from one task to another. Training costs are reduced because employees require fewer physical and mental skills to accomplish the assigned work. Finally, job specialization makes it easier to match people with specific aptitudes or skills to the jobs for which they are best suited. Although one person might be able to design a computer game alone, it would take much longer than a game designed by a team of specialists. Also, an individual who produces superb animation might deliver only mediocre computer coding, whereas a highly skilled team of people would have higher quality across all areas of work.

LO1

COORDINATING WORK ACTIVITIES

As soon as people divide work among themselves, coordinating mechanisms are needed to ensure that everyone works in concert. Coordination is so closely connected to division of labour that the degree of specialization is limited by the feasibility of coordinating that work. Coordination tends to become more expensive and difficult as jobs become more specialized, so companies specialize jobs only to the point where it isn't too costly or challenging to coordinate people in those specialized jobs.[7]

Every organization—from the two-person corner convenience store to the largest corporate entity—uses one or more of the following coordinating mechanisms:[8] informal communication, formal hierarchy, and standardization (see Exhibit 13.1). These forms of coordination align the work of staff within the same department as well as across work units. Increasingly, they are also recognized as a critical feature of joint ventures, humanitarian aid programs, and other multi-organizational structures.[9]

Coordination through Informal Communication   Informal communication is a coordinating mechanism in all organizations. This includes sharing information on mutual tasks as well as forming common mental models so that employees synchronize work activities using the same mental road map.[10] Informal communication is vital in nonroutine and ambiguous situations because employees can exchange a large volume of information through face-to-face communication and other media-rich channels.

Coordination through informal communication is easiest in small firms such as when BioWare was a start-up firm, although information technologies have further leveraged this coordinating mechanism in large organizations.[11] Companies employing thousands of people also support informal communication by keeping each production site small. Magna International, the Aurora, Ontario-based global auto-parts manufacturer, is well known for keeping its plants to a maximum size of around 200 employees. Magna's leaders believe that employees have difficulty remembering each other's names in plants that are any larger, which makes informal communication more difficult as a coordinating mechanism.[12] Toyota, Fuji Xerox, and many other companies encourage informal communication as a coordinating mechanism during product development through concurrent engineering, in which specialists from design through to production are organized into a temporary cross-functional team, sometimes moving team members into one large room.[13]

EXHIBIT 13.1   Coordinating mechanisms in organizations

Form of coordination	Description	Sub-types
Informal communication	Sharing information on mutual tasks; forming common mental models to synchronize work activities	• Direct communication • Liaison roles • Integrator roles
Formal hierarchy	Assigning legitimate power to individuals, who then use this power to direct work processes and allocate resources	• Direct supervision • Corporate structure
Standardization	Creating routine patterns of behaviour or output	• Standardized skills • Standardized processes • Standardized output

Source: Based on information in J. Galbraith, *Designing Complex Organizations* (Reading, MA: Addison-Wesley, 1973), pp. 8–19; H. Mintzberg, *The Structuring of Organizations* (Englewood Cliffs, N.J.: Prentice Hall, 1979), Chapter 1; D. A. Nadler and M. L. Tushman, *Competing by Design: The Power of Organizational Architecture* (New York: Oxford University Press, 1997), Chapter 6.

Larger organizations also encourage coordination through informal communication by creating *integrator roles*. These people are responsible for coordinating a work process by encouraging employees in each work unit to share information and informally coordinate work activities. Integrators do not have authority over the people involved in that process, so they must rely on persuasion and commitment. Brand managers at Procter & Gamble coordinate work among marketing, production, and design groups.[14]

Coordination through Formal Hierarchy

Informal communication is the most flexible form of coordination, but it can be time-consuming. Consequently, as organizations grow, they develop a second coordinating mechanism: formal hierarchy.[15] Hierarchy assigns legitimate power to individuals, who then use this power to direct work processes and allocate resources. In other words, work is coordinated through direct supervision. Any organization with a formal structure coordinates work to some extent through the formal hierarchy. For instance, project leaders at BioWare are responsible for ensuring that employees on their computer game project remain on schedule and that their respective tasks are compatible with tasks completed by other team members.

The formal hierarchy also coordinates work among executives through the division of organizational activities. If the organization is divided into geographic areas, the structure gives those regional group leaders legitimate power over executives responsible for production, customer service, and other activities in those areas. If the organization is divided into product groups, then the heads of those groups have the right to coordinate work across regions. The formal hierarchy has traditionally been applauded as the optimal coordinating mechanism for large organizations. As we'll find out later in this chapter, however, formal hierarchy is not as agile as other forms of coordination.

Coordination through Standardization

Standardization, the third means of coordination, involves creating routine patterns of behaviour or output. This coordinating mechanism takes three distinct forms:

- *Standardized processes*—Quality and consistency of a product or service can often be improved by standardizing work activities through job descriptions and procedures.[16] This coordinating mechanism is feasible when the work is routine (such as mass production) or simple (such as making pizzas), but is less effective in nonroutine and complex work such as product design.

- *Standardized outputs*—This form of standardization involves ensuring that individuals and work units have clearly defined goals and output measures (e.g., customer satisfaction, production efficiency). For instance, to coordinate the work of salespeople, companies assign sales targets rather than specific behaviours.

- *Standardized skills*—When work activities are too complex to standardize through processes or goals, companies often coordinate work effort by extensively training employees or hiring people who have learned precise role behaviours from educational programs. This form of coordination is used in hospital operating rooms. Surgeons, nurses, and other operating room professionals coordinate their work more through training than goals or company rules.

Division of labour and coordination of work represent the two fundamental ingredients of all organizations. But how work is divided, which coordinating mechanisms are emphasized, who makes decisions, and other issues are related to the four elements of organizational structure.

ELEMENTS OF ORGANIZATIONAL STRUCTURE

Every company is configured in terms of four basic elements of organizational structure. This section introduces three of them: span of control, centralization, and formalization. The fourth element—departmentalization—is presented in the next section.

SPAN OF CONTROL

span of control
The number of people directly reporting to the next level in the hierarchy.

Span of control refers to the number of people directly reporting to the next level in the hierarchy. A narrow span of control exists when very few people report directly to a manager, whereas a wide span exists when a manager has many direct reports. A century ago, French engineer and management scholar Henri Fayol strongly recommended a relatively narrow span of control, typically no more than 20 employees per supervisor and six supervisors per manager. Fayol championed formal hierarchy as the primary coordinating mechanism, so he believed that supervisors should closely monitor and coach employees. His views were similar to those of Napoleon and other military leaders, who declared that somewhere between three and 10 subordinates is the optimal span of control. These prescriptions were based on the belief that managers simply cannot monitor and control any more subordinates closely enough.[17]

Today, we know better. The best performing manufacturing plants currently have an average of 38 production employees per supervisor.[18] What's the secret here? Did Fayol, Napoleon, and others miscalculate the optimal span of control? The answer is that those sympathetic to hierarchical control believed that employees should perform the physical tasks, whereas supervisors and other management personnel should make the decisions and monitor employees to make sure they performed their tasks. In contrast, the best performing manufacturing operations today rely on self-directed teams, so direct supervision (formal hierarchy) is supplemented with other coordinating mechanisms. Self-directed teams coordinate mainly through informal communication and specialized knowledge, so formal hierarchy plays a minor role. Similarly, hospital medical professionals coordinate their work mainly through standardized skills, so the chief physician and head of nursing are typically responsible for overseeing many professionals.

A second factor influencing the best span of control is whether employees perform routine tasks. A wider span of control is possible when employees perform routine jobs, because there is less need for direction or advice from supervisors. A narrow span of control is necessary when employees perform novel or complex tasks, because these employees tend to require more supervisory decisions and coaching. This principle is illustrated in a survey of North American property/casualty insurers. The average span of control in commercial policy processing departments is around 15 employees per supervisor, whereas the span of control is 6.1 in claims service and 5.5 in commercial underwriting. Staff members in the latter two departments perform more technical work, so they have more novel and complex tasks. Commercial policy processing, on the other hand, is production-like work where tasks are routine and have few exceptions.[19]

A third influence on span of control is the degree of interdependence among employees within the department or team.[20] Generally, a narrow span of control is necessary where employees perform highly interdependent work with others. More supervision is required for highly interdependent jobs because employees tend to experience more conflict with each other, which requires more of a manager's time to resolve. Also, employees are less clear on their personal work performance in highly interdependent tasks, so supervisors spend more time providing coaching and feedback.

Tall and Flat Structures   Span of control is interconnected with organizational size (number of employees) and the number of layers in the organizational hierarchy. Consider two companies with the same number of employees. If Company A has a wider span of control (more direct reports per manager) than Company B, then Company A must have fewer layers of management (i.e., a flatter structure) than does Company B. The reason for this relationship is that a company with a wider span of control necessarily has more employees per supervisor, more supervisors for each middle manager, and so on. This larger number of direct reports, compared to a company with a narrower span of control, is only possible by removing layers of management.

Also notice that as companies employ more people, they must widen the span of control, build a taller hierarchy, or both. Most companies end up building taller structures because they rely on direct supervision to some extent as a coordinating mechanism.

Unfortunately, increasing the size of the hierarchy creates problems. First, tall structures have higher overhead costs because most layers of hierarchy consist of managers rather than employees who actually make the product or supply the service. Second, senior managers in tall structures often receive lower quality and less timely information from the external environment because information from front-line employees is transmitted slowly or not at all up the hierarchy. Also, the more layers of management through which information must pass, the higher the probability that managers will filter out information that does not put them in a positive light. Finally, tall hierarchies tend to undermine employee empowerment and engagement because they focus power around managers rather than employees.[21]

These problems have prompted leaders to "delayer"—remove one or more levels in the organizational hierarchy.[22] Soon after Mark Hurd was hired as CEO of Hewlett-Packard, he stripped the high-technology company's 11 layers of hierarchy down to eight layers. He argued that this action reduced costs and would make HP more nimble. BASF's European Seal Sands plant went even further when it was dramatically restructured around self-directed teams. "Seven levels of management have been cut basically to two," says a BASF executive.[23] Although many companies enjoy reduced costs and more empowered employees when they reduce layers of hierarchy, some organizational experts warn that cutting out too much middle management may cause long-term problems. They point out that these managers serve a valuable function by controlling work activities and managing corporate growth. Furthermore, companies will always need managers to make quick decisions and represent a source of appeal over conflicts.[24] The conclusion here is that flatter structures offer several benefits, but cutting out too much management can offset these benefits.

LO3

CENTRALIZATION AND DECENTRALIZATION

centralization
The degree to which formal decision authority is held by a small group of people, typically those at the top of the organizational hierarchy.

Centralization and decentralization represents a second element of organizational design. **Centralization** means that formal decision-making authority is held by a small group of people, typically those at the top of the organizational hierarchy. Most organizations begin with centralized structures, as the founder makes most of the decisions and tries to direct the business toward his or her vision. But as organizations grow, they diversify and their environments become more complex. Senior executives aren't able to process all the decisions that significantly influence the business. Consequently, larger organizations typically *decentralize*, that is, they disperse decision authority and power throughout the organization.

The optimal level of centralization or decentralization depends on several contingencies that we will examine later in this chapter. However, we also need to keep in mind that different degrees of decentralization can occur simultaneously in different parts of

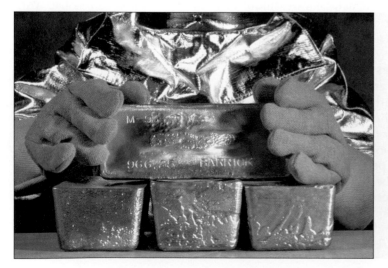

Barrick Finds Gold in a Decentralized Structure

For many years, Barrick Gold Corporation concentrated decision making at its Canadian headquarters even though it was becoming the world's largest gold producer with far flung operations around the world. "Barrick had always been run on this command-and-control model, a centrist approach that saw all the decision making made in Toronto," says CEO Greg Wilkins. "That worked while the company was small and operating only in North America. But all of a sudden we are in four continents and seven countries and it becomes pretty clear that you just can't do it any more." The solution that Wilkins and his senior leadership team implemented was a more decentralized structure in which Barrick's four regional business units are now responsible for their own operations and business growth. Headquarters provides the strategic guidance and oversight.[25] *Courtesy of Barrick Gold*

the organization.[26] Nestlé, the Swiss-based food company, has decentralized marketing decisions to remain responsive to local markets, but has centralized production, logistics, and supply chain management activities to improve cost efficiencies and avoid having too much complexity across the organization. "If you are too decentralized, you can become too complicated—you get too much complexity in your production system," explains a Nestlé executive.[27]

7-Eleven also relies on both centralization and decentralization in different parts of the organization. The convenience store chain leverages buying power and efficiencies by centralizing decisions about information technology and supplier purchasing. At the same time, it decentralizes local inventory decisions to store managers so they can adapt quickly to changing circumstances at the local level. Along with ongoing product training and guidance from regional consultants, store managers have the best information about their customers and can respond quickly to local market needs. "We could never predict a busload of football players on a Friday night, but the store manager can," explains a 7-Eleven executive.[28]

FORMALIZATION

formalization
The degree to which organizations standardize behaviour through rules, procedures, formal training, and related mechanisms.

Formalization is the degree to which organizations standardize behaviour through rules, procedures, formal training, and related mechanisms.[29] In other words, companies become more formalized as they increasingly coordinate work through standardization. McDonald's Restaurants and most other successful fast food chains typically have a high degree of formalization because they rely on standardization of work processes as a coordinating mechanism. Employees have precisely defined roles, right down to how much mustard should be dispensed, how many pickles should be applied, and how long each hamburger should be cooked.

Older companies tend to become more formalized because work activities become routinized, making them easier to document into standardized practices. Larger companies formalize as a coordinating mechanism, because direct supervision and informal communication among employees do not operate as easily. External influences, such as government safety legislation and strict accounting rules, also encourage formalization.

Formalization may increase efficiency and compliance, but it can also create problems. Rules and procedures reduce organizational flexibility, so employees follow prescribed behaviours even when the situation clearly calls for a customized response. High levels of formalization tend to undermine organizational learning and creativity. Some work rules become so convoluted that organizational efficiency would decline if they were actually followed as prescribed. Formalization is also a source of job dissatisfaction and work stress.[30]

LO4   MECHANISTIC VERSUS ORGANIC STRUCTURES

mechanistic structure
An organizational structure with a narrow span of control and a high degree of formalization and centralization.

organic structure
An organizational structure with a wide span of control, little formalization, and decentralized decision making.

We discussed span of control, centralization, and formalization together because they cluster around two broader organizational forms: mechanistic and organic structures.[31] A **mechanistic structure** is characterized by a narrow span of control and high degree of formalization and centralization. Mechanistic structures have many rules and procedures, limited decision making at lower levels, tall hierarchies of people in specialized roles, and vertical rather than horizontal communication flows. Tasks are rigidly defined, and are altered only when sanctioned by higher authorities. Companies with an **organic structure** have the opposite characteristics. They operate with a wide span of control, decentralized decision making, and little formalization. Tasks are fluid, adjusting to new situations and organizational needs.

As a general rule, mechanistic structures operate better in stable environments because they rely on efficiency and routine behaviours, whereas organic structures work better in rapidly changing (i.e., dynamic) environments because they are more flexible and responsive to these changes. Organic structures are also more compatible

with organizational learning, high-performance workplaces, and quality management because they emphasize information sharing and an empowered workforce rather than hierarchy and status.[33] However, the advantages of organic structures rather than mechanistic structures in dynamic environments occur only when employees have developed well-established roles and expertise.[34] Without these conditions, employees are unable to coordinate effectively with each other, resulting in errors and gross inefficiencies. Start-up companies often face this problem, known as the "liability of newness." Newness makes startup firms more organic, but their employees often lack industry experience and their teams have not developed sufficiently for peak performance. As a result, the organic structures of new companies cannot compensate for the poorer coordination and significantly lower efficiencies caused by this lack of structure from past experience and team mental models.

FORMS OF DEPARTMENTALIZATION

Span of control, centralization, and formalization are important elements of organizational structure, but most people think about organizational charts when the discussion of organizational structure arises. The organizational chart represents the fourth element in the structuring of organizations, called departmentalization. Departmentalization specifies how employees and their activities are grouped together. It is a fundamental strategy for coordinating organizational activities because it influences organizational behaviour in the following ways.[35]

- Departmentalization establishes the chain of command; that is, the system of common supervision among positions and units within the organization. It frames the membership of formal work teams and typically determines which positions and units must share resources. Thus, departmentalization establishes interdependencies among employees and subunits.

- Departmentalization focuses people around common mental models or ways of thinking, such as serving clients, developing products, or supporting a particular skill set. This focus is typically anchored around the common budgets and measures of performance assigned to employees within each departmental unit.

- Departmentalization encourages coordination through informal communication among people and subunits. With common supervision and resources, members within each configuration typically work near each other, so they can use frequent and informal interaction to get the work done.

There are almost as many organizational charts as there are businesses, but the six most common pure types of departmentalization are simple, functional, divisional, team-based, matrix, and network.

SIMPLE STRUCTURE

Most companies begin with a *simple structure*.[36] They employ only a few people and typically offer only one distinct product or service. There is minimal hierarchy—usually just employees reporting to the owners. Employees are grouped into broadly defined roles because there are insufficient economies of scale to assign them to specialized roles. The simple structure is highly flexible and minimizes the walls that form between employees in other structures. However, the simple structure usually depends on the owner's direct supervision to coordinate work activities, so it is very difficult to operate as the company grows and becomes more complex.

FUNCTIONAL STRUCTURE

functional structure
A type of departmentalization that organizes employees around specific knowledge or other resources.

Organizations that grow large enough use functional structures at some level of the hierarchy or at some time in their history. A **functional structure** organizes employees around specific knowledge or other resources. The opening vignette to this chapter described how the co-founders of BioWare contemplated the functional structure for the electronic games company. Specifically, they considered the possibility of creating departments around the various specializations, including art, programming, audio, quality assurance, and design.

Evaluating the Functional Structure   The functional structure creates specialized pools of talent that typically serve everyone in the organization. This provides more economies of scale than if functional specialists are spread over different parts of the organization. It increases employee identity with that specialization or profession. Direct supervision is easier in functional structures because managers oversee people with common issues and expertise.[37]

The functional structure also has limitations.[38] Grouping employees around their skills tends to focus attention on those skills and related professional needs rather than on the company's product/service or client needs. Unless people are transferred from one function to the next, they might not develop a broader understanding of the business. Compared with other structures, the functional structure usually produces higher dysfunctional conflict and poorer coordination in serving clients or developing products. These problems occur because employees need to work with co-workers in other departments to complete organizational tasks, yet they have different subgoals and mental models of ideal work. Together, these problems require substantial formal controls and coordination when people are organized around functions.

DIVISIONAL STRUCTURE

divisional structure
A type of departmentalization that groups employees around geographic areas, outputs (products/services), or clients.

The **divisional structure** (sometimes called the *multi-divisional* or *M-form* structure) groups employees around geographic areas, outputs (products/services), or clients. Exhibit 13.2 illustrates these three variations of divisional structure. The *geographic structure* organizes employees around distinct regions of the country or globe. Exhibit 13.2(*a*) illustrates a geographic divisional structure recently adopted by Toronto-based Barrick Gold Corporation, the world's largest gold mining company. The *product/service structure* organizes work around distinct outputs. Exhibit 13.2(*b*) illustrates this type of structure at Philips. The Dutch electronics company divides its workforce mainly into three divisions: healthcare products, lighting products, and consumer products. The

EXHIBIT 13.2   Three types of divisional structure

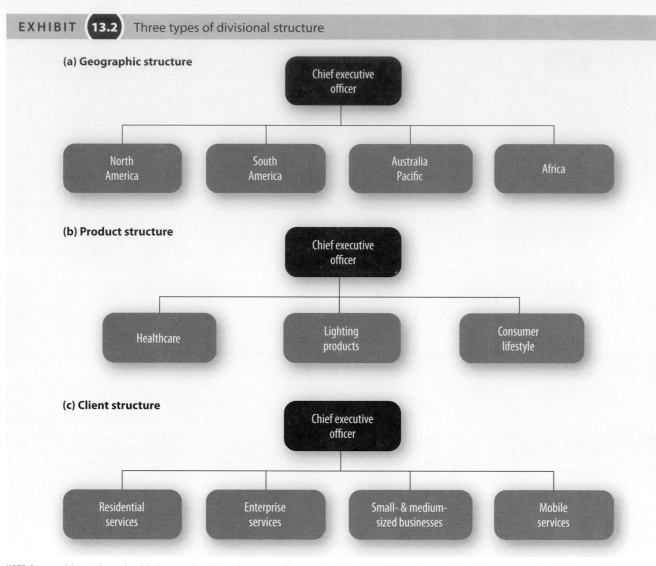

(a) Geographic structure

(b) Product structure

(c) Client structure

NOTE: Diagram (a) is similar to the global geographic divisional structure of Toronto-based Barrick Gold Corp.; diagram (b) is similar to the product divisions at Philips; diagram (c) is similar to the customer-focused structure at Bell Canada.

client structure represents the third form of divisional structure, in which employees are organized around specific customer groups. Exhibit 13.2(*c*) illustrates the customer-focused structure similar to one adopted by Bell Canada.[39]

Which form of divisional structure should large organizations adopt? The answer depends mainly on the primary source of environmental diversity or uncertainty.[40] Suppose an organization has one type of product sold to people across the country. If customer needs vary across regions, or if provincial governments impose different regulations on the product, then a geographic structure would be best to be more vigilant of this diversity. On the other hand, if the company sells several types of products across the country and customer preferences and government regulations are similar everywhere, then a product structure would likely work best.

Coca-Cola, Nestlé, and many other food and beverage companies are organized mainly around geographic regions because consumer tastes and preferred marketing strategies vary considerably around the world. Even though McDonald's makes the same Big Mac around the planet, it has more fish products in Hong Kong and more vegetarian products in India in line with traditional diets in those countries. Philips, on the other hand, is organized around products because consumer preferences around

A More Customer-Facing Caterpillar

For decades, Caterpillar, Inc., the world's largest manufacturer of construction and mining equipment, enjoyed a cozy dominance in the North American marketplace, resulting in an insular culture focused on fiefdoms of expertise rather than customers or cost efficiency. Reflecting this culture, Caterpillar operated with a functional structure, organizing employees around engineering, marketing, manufacturing, and other business processes with almost no communication across these units. The vice-presidents of these departments were so powerful that one CEO described them as "the kingpins of decisions." Several years ago, more agile competitors from Japan and elsewhere threatened Caterpillar's future. Fortunately, the company reacted quickly enough to remain in business. One of its first actions was to jettison the old corporate structure in favour of a divisional structure that paid more attention to customers and efficiency. The new structure essentially demoted the functional vice-presidents, so they now reported to the product and marketing people who previously reported to them![41] *The Canadian Press (Toby Talbot)*

the world are similar within each group. Hospitals from Geneva, Switzerland, to Santiago, Chile, purchase similar medical equipment from Philips, whereas manufacturing and marketing of these products are quite different from Philips' consumer electronics business.

Many divisional-structured companies are moving away from geographical structures.[42] One reason is that clients can purchase online and communicate with businesses from almost anywhere in the world, so local representation is less critical. Reduced geographic variation is another reason for the shift away from geographical structures; freer trade has reduced government intervention for many products, and consumer preferences for many products and services are becoming more similar (converging) around the world. The third reason is that large companies increasingly have global business customers who demand one global point of purchase, not one in every country or region.

Evaluating the Divisional Structure The divisional form is a building block structure; it accommodates growth relatively easily and focuses employee attention on products or customers rather than tasks. Different products, services, or clients can be accommodated by sprouting new divisions. These advantages are offset by a number of limitations. First, the divisional structure tends to duplicate resources, such as production equipment and engineering or information technology expertise. Also, unless the division is quite large, resources are not used as efficiently as in functional structures where resources are pooled across the entire organization. The divisional structure also creates silos of knowledge. Expertise is spread across several autonomous business units, which reduces the ability and perhaps motivation of these people to share their knowledge with counterparts in other divisions. In contrast, a functional structure groups experts together, which supports knowledge sharing.

Finally, as was explained above, the preferred divisional structure depends on the company's primary source of environmental diversity or uncertainty. This principle seems to be applied easily enough at Coca-Cola, McDonalds, and Philips. But the decision regarding whether to choose a geographic, product, or client structure is really quite difficult because global organizations experience diversity and uncertainties in many ways. The decision also affects political dynamics in the organization. If corporate leaders switch from a geographic to product structure, people who lead the geographical fiefdoms suddenly get demoted under the product chiefs. Consequently, global organizations revise their structures back and forth, with each transition usually resulting in one or more executives leaving the company.

TEAM-BASED STRUCTURE

The opening story to this chapter introduced the organizational structure dilemma that BioWare's co-founders faced when they decided to rapidly expand operations. One of the structural forms they considered was built entirely around teams. This **team-based structure** would have BioWare employees organized around several projects, each with its own autonomous team. Generally, a team-based organizational structure is built around self-directed teams that complete an entire piece of work, such as manufacturing a product or developing an electronic game. This type of structure is highly organic. There is a wide span of control because teams operate with minimal supervision. In extreme situations, there is no formal leader, just someone selected by other team members to help coordinate the work and liaise with top management. Team structures are highly decentralized because almost all day-to-day decisions are made by team members rather than someone further up the organizational hierarchy. Finally, many team-based structures have low formalization because teams are given relatively few rules about how to organize their work. Instead, executives assign quality and quantity output targets and often productivity improvement goals to each team. Teams are then encouraged to use available resources and their own initiative to achieve those objectives.

Team-based structures are usually found within the manufacturing operations of larger divisional structures. For example, automobile parts giant TRW Automotive has a team-based structure in many of its 200 plants, but these plants are organized together around the company's divisional structure. However, a small number of firms apply the team-based structure from top to bottom. Perhaps the most famous example of this is W. L. Gore & Associates, where almost all associates work in teams and no one is the boss.

Evaluating the Team-based Structure   The team-based organization represents an increasingly popular structure because it is usually more flexible and responsive to the environment.[43] It tends to reduce costs because teams have less reliance on formal hierarchy (direct supervision). A cross-functional team structure improves communication and cooperation across traditional boundaries. With greater autonomy, this structure also allows quicker and more informed decision making.[44] For this reason, some Canadian hospitals have shifted from functional departments to cross-functional teams. Teams composed of nurses, radiologists, anesthetists, a pharmacology representative, possibly social workers, a rehabilitation therapist, and other specialists communicate and coordinate more efficiently, thereby reducing delays and errors.[45]

W. L. Gore's Structural Fabric: Extreme Teams

W. L. Gore & Associates Inc. has an extreme team-based organizational structure that eliminates the traditional hierarchy. Most employees (or "associates" as they are known) at the global manufacturer of fabrics (Gore-Tex), electronics, industrial, and medical products work at four dozen self-sufficient manufacturing and sales offices around the world. Associates make day-to-day decisions within their expertise without approval from anyone higher up. Bigger issues, such as hiring and compensating staff, are decided by teams. Each facility is deliberately limited to about 200 people so they can coordinate more effectively through informal communication. Within those units, new projects are started through individual initiative and support from others.[46] © Bill Cramer

Against these benefits, the team-based structure can be costly to maintain due to the need for ongoing interpersonal skills training. Teamwork potentially takes more time to coordinate than formal hierarchy during the early stages of team development. Employees may experience more stress due to increased ambiguity in their roles. Team leaders also experience more stress due to increased conflict, loss of functional power, and unclear career progression ladders. In addition, team structures suffer from duplication of resources and potential competition (and lack of resource sharing) across teams.[47]

LO7

MATRIX STRUCTURE

Throughout this chapter we have referred back to the dilemma that Ray Muzyka and Greg Zeschuk faced regarding the best choice of an organizational structure for BioWare. The Edmonton-based computer game developer could adopt a functional structure, but this might not generate an optimal level of teamwork or commitment to the final product. Alternatively, Bioware's employees could be organized into a team-based structure. But having several teams would duplicate resources, and possibly undermine resource sharing among people with the same expertise across teams.

After carefully weighing the various organizational structure options, Muzyka and Zeschuk adopted a **matrix structure** to gain the benefits of both a functional structure and a project-based (team) structure. BioWare's matrix structure, which is similar to the diagram in Exhibit 13.3, is organized around both functions (art, audio, programming, etc.) and team-based game development projects. Employees are assigned to a cross-functional team responsible for a specific game project, yet they also belong to a permanent functional unit from which they are reassigned when their work is completed on a particular project.[48] Muzyka and Zeschuk say the matrix structure encourages employees to think in terms of the final product, yet keeps them organized around

> **matrix structure**
> A type of departmentalization that overlays two organizational forms in order to leverage the benefits of both.

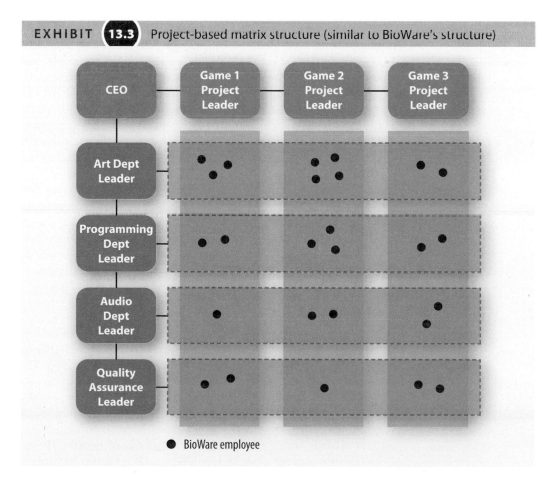

EXHIBIT 13.3 Project-based matrix structure (similar to BioWare's structure)

● BioWare employee

their expertise to encourage knowledge sharing. "The matrix structure also supports our overall company culture where BioWare is the team, and everyone is always willing to help each other whether they are on the same project or not," they add. BioWare's matrix structure has proven to be a good choice, particularly as the company (now as an independent division of Electronic Arts) has grown to almost 400 employees working on more than a half-dozen game projects in Edmonton, Alberta and Austin, Texas.

BioWare's structure, in which project teams overlap with functional departments, is just one form of matrix structure. Another variation, which is common in large global firms, is to have geography on one axis and products/services or client groups on the other. Procter & Gamble recently moved toward this type of global matrix structure with geographic divisions (called "market development organizations") on one axis and "global business units" representing global brands on the other axis. Previously, P&G had a geographic divisional structure, which gave too much power to country managers and not enough power or priority to globalizing its major brands (e.g., Pantene, Tide, Pringles). P&G's leaders believe that the new matrix structure will balance this power, thereby supporting its philosophy of thinking globally and acting locally.[49]

Evaluating the Matrix Structure   The matrix structure usually optimizes the use of resources and expertise, making it ideal for project-based organizations with fluctuating workloads. When properly managed, it improves communication efficiency, project flexibility, and innovation compared to purely functional or divisional designs. It focuses employees on serving clients or creating products, yet keeps people organized around their specialization so knowledge sharing improves and resources are used more efficiently. The matrix structure is also a logical choice when, as in the case of Procter & Gamble, two different dimensions (regions and products) are equally important. Structures determine executive power and what is important; the matrix structure works when two different dimensions deserve equal attention.

In spite of these advantages, the matrix structure has several well-known problems.[50] One concern is that it increases goal conflict and ambiguity. Employees working at the matrix level have two bosses and, consequently, two sets of priorities that aren't always aligned with each other. Project leaders might squabble over specific employees who are assigned to other projects. They may also disagree with employee decisions, but the employee's functional leader has more say than the project leader as to the individual's technical competence. Aware of these concerns, BioWare holds several "synchronization meetings" each year involving all department directors (art, design, audio, etc.), producers (i.e., game project leaders), and the human resources manager. These meetings sort out differences and ensure that staff members are properly assigned to each game project.

Another challenge is that the existence of two bosses can dilute accountability. In a functional or divisional structure, one manager is responsible for everything, even the most unexpected issues. But in a matrix structure, the unusual problems don't get resolved because neither manager takes ownership of them.[51] The result of conflict and ambiguity in matrix structures is that some employees experience more stress, and some managers are less satisfied with their work arrangements.

LO8

NETWORK STRUCTURE

A decade ago, Irwin Toy was a venerable Canadian toy company with more than 1,800 products and a few hundred employees. Family infighting, management problems, and globalization sent Irwin spiralling into receivership. George Irwin, whose family once owned Irwin, recently bought pieces of the company, including rights to the table hockey game that the former company invented in the 1930s. His new firm, iToys Inc., markets the highly popular electronic spinning top called i-Top and has many more contemporary products in the pipeline.

But while Irwin Toy employed hundreds of people, iToys counts only a dozen staff in Toronto and 30 more in Hong Kong. One reason for the small employment numbers is that iToys is the marketing hub of a network structure that spans the globe. "The i-Top was invented in Israel," Irwin explains. "The guy who sold it to us is in New York. We're in Toronto. It's manufactured in China. The package was designed in Boston. The design of the top itself was done in San Francisco. And the software developer was in Springfield, Massachusetts."[52]

network structure
An alliance of several organizations for the purpose of creating a product or serving a client.

iToys is a **network structure** because it is an alliance of several organizations for the purpose of creating a product or serving a client.[53] Exhibit 13.4 illustrates how this collaborative structure typically consists of several satellite organizations bee-hived around a "hub" or "core" firm. The core firm "orchestrates" the network process and provides one or two other core competencies, such as marketing or product development. In our example, iToys is the hub that provides marketing and management whereas other firms perform most other functions.

The core firm might be the main contact with customers, but most of the product or service delivery and support activities are farmed out to satellite organizations located anywhere in the world. Extranets (Web-based networks with partners) and other technologies ensure that information flows easily and openly between the core firm and its array of satellites. "The traditional idea of the unit of business has always been the company," explains an executive at the Alliance of Manufacturers and Exporters Canada. "Now, it's the network, going beyond one company and encompassing all its suppliers and many of its customers."[54]

One of the main forces pushing toward a network structure is the recognition that an organization has only a few *core competencies*. A core competency is a knowledge base that resides throughout the organization and provides a strategic advantage. As companies discover their core competency, they "unbundle" noncritical tasks to other organizations that have a core competency at performing those tasks. For instance, Mitel Networks decided that its core competency is designing Internet protocol based communications equipment, not manufacturing that equipment. Consequently, the

EXHIBIT 13.4   A network structure

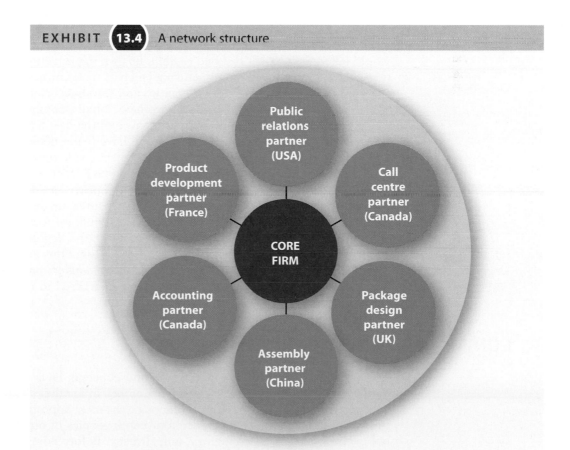

Ottawa-based high technology firm outsourced its manufacturing and repair business to BreconRidge Manufacturing Solutions, which has a contract to manufacture Mitel products.[55]

Companies are also more likely to form network structures when technology is changing quickly and production processes are complex or varied.[56] Many firms cannot keep up with the hyperfast changes in information technology, so they have outsourced their entire information systems departments to IBM, EDS, and other firms that specialize in information systems services. Similarly, many high-technology firms form networks with Toronto-based Celestica Inc. because Celestica has expertise in diverse production processes.

Virtual Corporations   The network structures that exist at iToys, Mitel Networks, Dell Computer, and other firms generally perform a patterned set of tasks for all clients. In contrast, some network structures—known as **virtual corporations**—represent several independent companies that form unique partnership teams to provide customized products or services, usually to specific clients, for a limited time.[57] Virtual corporations exist temporarily and reshape themselves quickly to fit immediate needs. When an opportunity emerges, a unique combination of partners in the alliance form a virtual corporation that works on the assignment until it is completed. Virtual corporations are self-organizing, meaning that they rearrange their own communication patterns and roles to fit the situation. The relationship among the partners is mutually determined rather than imposed by a core firm.

virtual corporations
Network structures representing several independent companies that form unique partnership teams to provide customized products or services, usually to specific clients, for a limited time.

Evaluating the Network Structure   For several years, organizational behaviour theorists have argued that organizational leaders must develop a metaphor of organizations as plasma-like organisms rather than rigid machines.[58] Network structures come close to the organism metaphor because they offer the flexibility to re-align their structure with changing environmental requirements. If customers demand a new product or service, the core firm forms new alliances with other firms offering the appropriate resources. For example, by finding partners with available plant facilities, Toronto-based iToys was able to launch i-Top soon after the company was formed, whereas product launch would take much longer if it had to build its own manufacturing facilities. When iToys needs a different type of manufacturing (such as metal rather than plastic fabrication), it isn't saddled with nonessential facilities and resources. Network structures also offer efficiencies because the core firm becomes globally competitive as it shops worldwide for subcontractors with the best people and the best technology at the best price. Indeed, the pressures of global competition have made network structures more vital, and computer-based information technology have made them possible.[59]

A potential disadvantage of network structures is that they expose the core firm to market forces. Other companies may bid up the price for subcontractors, whereas the short-term cost would be lower if the company hired its own employees to serve this function. Another problem is that although information technology makes worldwide communication much easier, it will never replace the degree of control organizations have when manufacturing, marketing, and other functions are in-house. The core firm can use arm's-length incentives and contract provisions to maintain the subcontractor's quality, but these actions are relatively crude compared to maintaining the quality of work performed by in-house employees.

CONTINGENCIES OF ORGANIZATIONAL DESIGN

Most organizational behaviour theories and concepts have contingencies—ideas that work well in one situation might not work as well in another situation. This contingency approach is certainly relevant when choosing the most appropriate organizational structure.[60] In this section, we introduce four contingencies of organizational design: external environment, size, technology, and strategy. Before doing so, however, we need to warn you that this discussion is necessarily simplified because of an unresolved debate among organizational structure experts.[61] The debate centres around the question of whether specific contingencies can be associated with specific elements of structure (centralization, formalization, etc.), or whether we need to examine *configurations* of contingencies with broad typologies of organizational structure (such as organic versus mechanistic). Some writers further suggest that more than two different structural typologies might work equally well in a particular situational configuration. With these caveats in mind, let's examine the four main contingencies of organizational structure.

LO9   EXTERNAL ENVIRONMENT

The best structure for an organization depends on its external environment. The external environment includes anything outside the organization, including most stakeholders (e.g., clients, suppliers, government), resources (e.g., raw materials, human resources, information, finances), and competitors. Four characteristics of external environments influence the type of organizational structure best suited to a particular situation: dynamism, complexity, diversity, and hostility.[62]

Dynamic versus Stable Environments   Dynamic environments have a high rate of change, leading to novel situations and a lack of identifiable patterns. Organic structures are better suited to this type of environment so that the organization can adapt more quickly to changes, but only if employees are experienced and coordinate well in teamwork.[63] In contrast, stable environments are characterized by regular cycles of activity and steady changes in supply and demand for inputs and outputs. Events are more predictable, enabling the firm to apply rules and procedures. Mechanistic structures are more efficient when the environment is predictable, so they tend to work better than organic structures.

Complex versus Simple Environments   Complex environments have many elements whereas simple environments have few things to monitor. As an example, a major university library operates in a more complex environment than a small town public library. The university library's clients require several types of services—book borrowing, online full-text databases, research centres, course reserve collections, and so on. A small town public library has fewer of these demands placed on it. The more complex the environment, the more decentralized the organization should become. Decentralization is a logical response to complexity because decisions are pushed down to people and subunits with the necessary information to make informed choices.

Diverse versus Integrated Environments   Organizations located in diverse environments have a greater variety of products or services, clients, and regions. In contrast, an integrated environment has only one client, product, and geographic area. The more diversified the environment, the more the firm needs to use a divisional structure aligned with that diversity. If it sells a single product around the world, a geographic divisional structure would align best with the firm's geographic diversity, for example.

Hostile versus Munificent Environments   Firms located in a hostile environment face resource scarcity and more competition in the marketplace. Hostile environments are typically dynamic ones because they reduce the predictability of access to resources and demand for outputs. Organic structures tend to be best in hostile environments. However, when the environment is extremely hostile—such as a severe shortage of supplies or lower market share—organizations tend to temporarily centralize so that decisions can be made more quickly and executives feel more comfortable being in control.[64] Ironically, centralization may result in lower-quality decisions during organizational crises, because top management has less information, particularly when the environment is complex.

The Nitro-daptive Ad Agency

How do you design an advertising agency that satisfies client demands for both a global footprint and local expertise? For Nitro Group, the answer is a structure that is mainly decentralized but is adaptive enough to bring in the company's top guns when needed. The upstart ad agency, which was founded in Shanghai in 2002, decentralizes decision making to account staff at its local satellite offices, so that clients have the benefit of creative people who know the local market. Yet, to solve tough advertising challenges, Nitro will parachute in a creative swat team from one of its three global hubs—Shanghai, New York, and London. This structure seems to work. Nitro has landed large regional accounts from Volvo, Mars, and other global companies, and is quickly gaining a reputation for innovation.[65] *Photo courtesy of Nitro Group*

  ORGANIZATIONAL SIZE

Larger organizations should have different structures from smaller organizations.[66] As the number of employees increases, job specialization increases due to a greater division of labour. This greater division of labour requires more elaborate coordinating mechanisms. Thus, larger firms make greater use of standardization (particularly work processes and outcomes) to coordinate work activities. These coordinating mechanisms create an administrative hierarchy and greater formalization. Historically, larger organizations make less use of informal communication as a coordinating mechanism. However, emerging information technologies and increased emphasis on empowerment have caused informal communication to regain its importance in large firms.[67]

Larger organizations also tend to be more decentralized. Executives have neither sufficient time nor expertise to process all the decisions that significantly influence the business as it grows. Therefore, decision-making authority is pushed down to lower levels, where incumbents are able to cope with the narrower range of issues under their control.

TECHNOLOGY

Technology is another factor to consider when designing the best organizational structure for the situation.[68] Technology refers to the mechanisms or processes by which an organization turns out its product or service. One technological contingency is its *variability*—the number of exceptions to standard procedure that tend to occur. In work processes with low variability, jobs are routine and follow standard operating procedures. Another contingency is *analyzability*—the predictability or difficulty of the required work. The less analyzable the work, the more it requires experts with sufficient discretion to address the work challenges. An organic rather than a mechanistic structure should be introduced where employees perform tasks with high variety and low analyzability, such as in a research setting. The reason is that employees face unique situations with little opportunity for repetition. In contrast, a mechanistic structure is preferred where the technology has low variability and high analyzability, such as an assembly line. The work is routine and highly predictable, an ideal situation for a mechanistic structure to operate efficiently.

ORGANIZATIONAL STRATEGY

organizational strategy
The way the organization positions itself in its setting in relation to its stakeholders, given the organization's resources, capabilities, and mission.

Organizational strategy refers to the way the organization positions itself in its setting in relation to its stakeholders, given the organization's resources, capabilities, and mission.[69] In other words, strategy represents the decisions and actions applied to achieve the organization's goals. Although size, technology, and environment influence the optimal organizational structure, these contingencies do not necessarily determine structure. Instead, corporate leaders formulate and implement strategies that shape both the characteristics of these contingencies as well as the organization's resulting structure.

This concept is summed up with the simple phrase: structure follows strategy.[70] Organizational leaders decide how large to grow and which technologies to use. They take steps to define and manipulate their environments, rather than let the organization's fate be entirely determined by external influences. Furthermore, organizational structures don't evolve as a natural response to these contingencies. Instead, they result from organizational decisions. Thus, organizational strategy influences both the contingencies of structure and the structure itself. If a company's strategy is to compete through innovation, then a more organic structure would be preferred because it is easier for employees to share knowledge and be creative. If a company chooses a low cost strategy, then a mechanistic structure is preferred because it maximizes production and service efficiency.[71] Overall, it is now apparent that organizational structure is influenced by size, technology, and environment, but the organization's strategy may reshape these elements and loosen their connection to organizational structure.

CHAPTER SUMMARY

Organizational structure refers to the division of labour as well as the patterns of coordination, communication, workflow, and formal power that direct organizational activities. All organizational structures divide labour into distinct tasks and coordinate that labour to accomplish common goals. The primary means of coordination are informal communication, formal hierarchy, and standardization.

The four basic elements of organizational structure include span of control, centralization, formalization, and departmentalization. The optimal span of control, which refers to the number of people directly reporting to the next level in the hierarchy, depends on the presence of coordinating mechanisms other than formal hierarchy, as well as whether employees perform routine tasks and the degree of interdependence among employees within the department.

Centralization occurs when formal decision authority is held by a small group of people, typically senior executives. Many companies decentralize as they become larger and more complex, but some sections of the company may remain centralized while other sections decentralize. Formalization is the degree to which organizations standardize behaviour through rules, procedures, formal training, and related mechanisms. Companies become more formalized as they get older and larger. Formalization tends

to reduce organizational flexibility, organizational learning, creativity, and job satisfaction.

Span of control, centralization, and formalization cluster into mechanistic and organic structures. Mechanistic structures are characterized by a narrow span of control and high degree of formalization and centralization. Companies with an organic structure have the opposite characteristics.

Departmentalization specifies how employees and their activities are grouped together. It establishes the chain of command, focuses people around common mental models, and encourages coordination through informal communication among people and subunits. A functional structure organizes employees around specific knowledge or other resources. This fosters greater specialization and improves direct supervision, but weakens the focus on serving clients or developing products.

A divisional structure groups employees around geographic areas, clients, or outputs. This structure accommodates growth and focuses employee attention on products or customers rather than tasks. However, this structure duplicates resources and creates silos of knowledge. Team-based structures are very flat with low formalization that organize self-directed teams around work processes rather than functional specialities. The matrix structure combines two structures to leverage the benefits of both types of structure. However, this approach requires more coordination than functional or pure divisional structures, may dilute accountability, and increases conflict. A network structure is an alliance of several organizations for the purpose of creating a product or serving a client. Virtual corporations are network structures that can quickly reorganize themselves to suit the client's requirements.

The best organizational structure depends on the firm's external environment, size, technology, and strategy. The optimal structure depends on whether the environment is dynamic or stable, complex or simple, diverse or integrated, and hostile or munificent. As organizations increase in size, they become more decentralized and more formalized. The work unit's technology—including variety of work and analyzability of problems—influences whether to adopt an organic or mechanistic structure. These contingencies influence but do not necessarily determine structure. Instead, corporate leaders formulate and implement strategies that shape both the characteristics of these contingencies as well as the organization's resulting structure.

KEY TERMS

centralization, p. 312

divisional structure, p. 315

formalization, p. 313

functional structure, p. 315

matrix structure, p. 319

mechanistic structure, p. 313

network structure, p. 321

organic structure, p. 313

organizational strategy, p. 325

organizational structure, p. 308

span of control, p. 311

team-based structure, p. 318

virtual corporations, p. 322

CRITICAL THINKING QUESTIONS

1. Nitro and TAXI, two creative advertising companies described in this chapter, have organic, team-based structures. What coordinating mechanism likely dominates in this type of organizational structure? Describe the extent and form in which the other two forms of coordination might be apparent at Nitro and TAXI.

2. Think about the business school or other organizational unit whose classes you are currently attending. What is the dominant coordinating mechanism used to guide or control the instructor? Why is this coordinating mechanism used the most here?

3. Administrative theorists concluded many decades ago that the most effective organizations have a narrow span of control. Yet, today's top-performing manufacturing firms have a wide span of control. Why is this possible? Under what circumstances, if any, should manufacturing firms have a narrow span of control?

4. If one could identify "trends" in organizational structure, one of them would be decentralization. Why is decentralization becoming more common in contemporary organizations? What should companies consider when determining the degree of decentralization?

5. Diversified Technologies Ltd. (DTL) makes four types of products, each type to be sold to different types of clients. For example, one product is sold exclusively to automobile repair shops, whereas another is used mainly in hospitals. Customer expectations and needs are surprisingly similar throughout the world. The company has separate marketing, product design, and manufacturing facilities in Asia, North America, Europe, and South America because, until recently, each jurisdiction had unique regulations governing the production and sales of these products. However, several governments have begun the process of deregulating the products that DTL designs and manufactures, and trade agreements have opened several markets to foreign-made products. Which form of departmentalization might be best for DTL if deregulation and trade agreements occur?

6. Why are many organizations moving away from the geographic divisional structures?

7. From an employee perspective, what are the advantages and disadvantages of working in a matrix structure?

8. Suppose that you have been hired as a consultant to diagnose the environmental characteristics of your college or university. How would you describe the school's external environment? Is the school's existing structure appropriate for this environment?

www.mcgrawhill.ca/olc/mcshane

CASE STUDY 13.1

FTCA—Regional and Headquarters Relations

By Swee C. Goh, University of Ottawa

The FTCA is a government agency that provides services to the public but also serves an enforcement role. It employs over 20,000 people, who are located at headquarters and in a large number of regional offices across the country. Most staff members are involved with direct counter-type services for both individuals and businesses. This includes collections, inquiries, payments, and audits. The agency also has large centres in various parts of the country to process forms and payments submitted by individuals and businesses.

FTCA is a typical federal government agency; many employees are unionized and have experienced numerous changes over the years. Because of the increasing complexity of regulations and the need to be more cost effective in the delivery of services, FTCA has evolved into an organization that uses technology to a great extent. The agency's leaders increasingly emphasize the need for easier and faster service and turnaround in dealing with clients. They also expect staff to depend more on electronic means of communication for interaction with the public.

As the population grew over the years, the regional offices of this government organization have expanded. Each regional office is headed by an Assistant Director (AD) who has a budget and an increasing number of staff for the various functional activities related to the region, such as a manager for information systems. Every region also has offices located in the major cities. The managers of these city centre offices report directly to the regional AD. The regional ADs report directly to the Director who is the overall head of the agency.

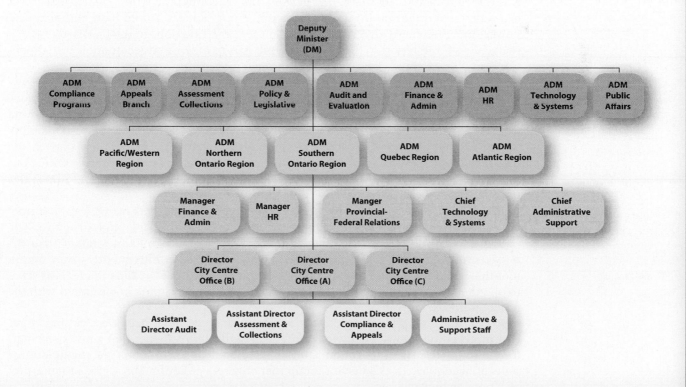

FTCA has a strong emphasis on centralized control, particularly in the functional units. This emphasis occurs because of legal requirements as well as the fact that the agency has extensive direct interaction with the public. For example, one functional unit at headquarters (HQ) is responsible for collections and enforcement. If a regional manager has the same functional activity, FTCA executives believe that person should be accountable to the HQ functional AD. However, as mentioned earlier, the regional manager also reports directly to the regional AD and the budget for the agency comes from the regional budget allocations and not from the HQ functional group.

This arrangement produces a dual reporting relationship for regional functional managers. Regional managers complain that this situation is very awkward. Who is the real boss under the circumstances: the regional AD or the functional HQ AD for these managers? Also, who should be responsible for evaluating the work performance of these dual-reporting regional managers? And if a regional manager makes a serious error, which of the two supervisors of that manager is ultimately accountable?

The potential for confusion about responsibility and accountability has made the roles and reporting relationships of the senior managers very vague. This also increased the occurrences of conflict between regional managers and HQ managers.

In order to deal with this growing problem, a consultant was brought in to do an independent evaluation of the current organizational structure of FTCA. The consultant asked for an organization chart of FTCA, which is shown below. The consultant became aware of the concerns described above by conducting interviews with various staff members throughout the agency. Other information such as budgets and financial allocations, some earlier organizational studies, and the mandate of the agency, etc. were also provided to the consultant.

The discussions with staff members were very interesting. Some viewed this issue as a people problem and not a structural one. They reasoned that if regional and HQ managers learned how to cooperate and work with each other this would not be an issue at all. That is, they should take a shared responsibility approach and try to work together. But the view of the HQ functional groups was very different. They argued that FTCA is a functional organization so these functional unit leaders should have authority and power over regional managers performing the same function. In effect, these regional managers should report to the functional unit ADs or at least be accountable to HQ policies and objectives.

To compound the problem, the regional managers saw this problem completely differently again. They argued that the functional HQ managers should have a policy development function. On an annual basis they should develop broad objectives and targets in consultation with regional managers. Once approved, it is the responsibility of the regional managers to carry them out in light of the environment and constraints they face. The functional unit ADs oppose the regional managers' position, pointing out that if the regional managers do not achieve their objectives, the functional ADs suffer the consequences.

After hearing these views, the consultant formed the opinion that this was an intractable and complex problem that could be related both to people and structure. The consultant also noted that the regional budgets were huge, sometimes larger than the budgets for functional groups at HQ. Regional ADs also met infrequently—only once a month—with the Director and functional ADs at HQ. Most of the time the regions seem to operate fairly autonomously, whereas the Director has ongoing involvement with the functional ADs.

An HQ staff member observed that over time the regional offices were getting larger and more autonomous, each with functional staff complements that mirror the staff functions at HQ. The implication is that the regional staff will soon view the functional units at headquarters as a distant group that only sets policy for the regions to interpret or ignore as they pleased.

A functional AD with several years of seniority at FTCA warned that the functional units must have some control over audit and other functional activities in the region. The AD explained that without clear roles, reporting relationships and accountabilities between the region and HQ, FTCA will not be able to provide citizens with transparent and fair treatment to the services under their mandate.

The regional ADs, however, saw their responsibilities as facilitating horizontal coordination within the region to ensure that actions and decisions are consistent and reflect the legislative responsibility of the agency.

After a month of study and discussions with staff at FTCA, the consultant realized that this was not going to be an easy problem to resolve. There were also rumblings as the project progressed that some regional ADs did not like the idea of restructuring FTCA to deal with this issue. They seem to have considerable clout and power in the organization as a group and would resist any change to the status quo.

As the consultant sat down to write the report, a number of critical questions became apparent: Was FTCA a purely functional organization? Can the accountability issues be resolved through an acceptable organizational process and people training without the need for restructuring? What about power, politics, and conflict in this situation? Finally, will resistance to change become a problem as well?

Discussion Questions

1. Describe the current organization structure of FTCA. What is it? What are the strengths and weaknesses of such a structure?

2. Can FTCA operate effectively as a pure functional structure?

3. In what way does power and politics play in the current situation?

4. What kind of conflict is FTCA experiencing between HQ and regional managers?

5. Suggest a practical and workable solution to the problem at FTCA. If a restructuring is part of your solution, describe what the structure would look like and justify from your knowledge of organization theory and design why it would work, i.e., improve the working relationship between headquarters and regional staff.

Materials in this case are based on factual and non-factual information of a government agency. This case is written for classroom discussion and not to demonstrate effective or ineffective management of an organization.

Copyright © 2005. Swee C. Goh.

TEAM EXERCISE 13.2

The Club Ed Exercise

By Cheryl Harvey and Kim Morouney, Wilfred Laurier University

Purpose   This exercise is designed to help you understand the issues to consider when designing organizations at various stages of growth.

Materials   Each student team should have enough overhead transparencies or flip chart sheets to display several organizational charts.

Instructions   Each team discusses the scenario presented. The first scenario is presented below. The instructor will facilitate discussion and notify teams when to begin the next step. The exercise and debriefing require approximately 90 minutes, although fewer scenarios can reduce the time somewhat.

- *Step 1*: Students are placed in teams (typically four or five people).

- *Step 2:* After reading Scenario #1 presented below, each team will design an organizational chart (departmentalization) that is most appropriate for this situation. Students should be able to describe the type of structure drawn and explain why it is appropriate. The structure should be drawn on an overhead transparency or flip chart for others to see during later class discussion. The instructor will set a fixed time (e.g., 15 minutes) to complete this task.

    > Scenario #1: Determined never to shovel snow again, you are establishing a new resort business on a small Caribbean island. The resort is under construction and is scheduled to open one year from now. You decide it is time to draw up an organizational chart for this new venture, called Club Ed.

- *Step 3*: At the end of the time allowed, the instructor will present Scenario #2 and each team will be asked to draw another organizational chart to suit that situation. Again, students should be able to describe the type of structure drawn and explain why it is appropriate.

- *Step 4*: At the end of the time allowed, the instructor will present Scenario #3 and each team will be asked to draw another organizational chart to suit that situation.

- *Step 5*: Depending on the time available, the instructor might present a fourth scenario. The class will gather to present their designs for each scenario. During each presentation, teams should describe the type of structure drawn and explain why it is appropriate.

Source: Adapted from C. Harvey and K. Morouney, *Journal of Management Education* 22 (June 1998), pp. 425–29. Used with permission of the authors.

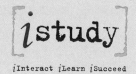 SELF-ASSESSMENT EXERCISE 13.3

What Organizational Structure Do You Prefer?

Purpose   This exercise is designed to help you understand how an organization's structure influences the personal needs and values of people working in that structure.

Instructions   Personal values influence how comfortable you are working in different organizational structures. You might prefer an organization with clearly defined rules or no rules at all. You might prefer a firm where almost any employee can make important decisions, or where important decisions are screened by senior executives. Read the statements below and indicate the extent to which you would like to work in an organization with that characteristic. When finished, use the scoring key in Appendix B to calculate your results. This self-assessment is completed alone so students will complete this self-assessment honestly without concerns of social comparison. However, class discussion will focus on the elements of organizational design and their relationship to personal needs and values.

Organizational Structure Preference Scale					
I would like to work in an organization where. . .	Not at all	A little	Somewhat	Very much	Score
1. A person's career ladder has several steps toward higher status and responsibility.	☐	☐	☐	☐	_____
2. Employees perform their work with few rules to limit their discretion.	☐	☐	☐	☐	_____
3. Responsibility is pushed down to employees who perform the work.	☐	☐	☐	☐	_____
4. Supervisors have few employees, so they work closely with each person.	☐	☐	☐	☐	_____
5. Senior executives make most decisions to ensure that the company is consistent in its actions.	☐	☐	☐	☐	_____
6. Jobs are clearly defined so there is no confusion over who is responsible for various tasks.	☐	☐	☐	☐	_____
7. Employees have their say on issues, but senior executives make most of the decisions.	☐	☐	☐	☐	_____
8. Job descriptions are broadly stated or nonexistent.	☐	☐	☐	☐	_____
9. Everyone's work is tightly synchronized around top management operating plans.	☐	☐	☐	☐	_____
10. Most work is performed in teams without close supervision.	☐	☐	☐	☐	_____
11. Work gets done through informal discussion with co-workers rather than through formal rules.	☐	☐	☐	☐	_____
12. Supervisors have so many employees that they can't watch anyone very closely.	☐	☐	☐	☐	_____
13. Everyone has clearly understood goals, expectations, and job duties.	☐	☐	☐	☐	_____
14. Senior executives assign overall goals, but leave daily decisions to front-line teams.	☐	☐	☐	☐	_____
15. Even in a large company, the CEO is only three or four levels above the lowest position	☐	☐	☐	☐	_____

iStudy—Available 24/7 with instant feedback so you can study when you want, how you want, and where you want. Visit www.istudyob.ca to register—take practice quizzes, run interactive scenarios, practice concepts, and much more. Also visit the Student Online Learning Centre for additional study tools.

*i*study

¡Interact ¡Learn ¡Succeed

www.mcgrawhill.ca/olc/mcshane

CHAPTER 14

Organizational Culture

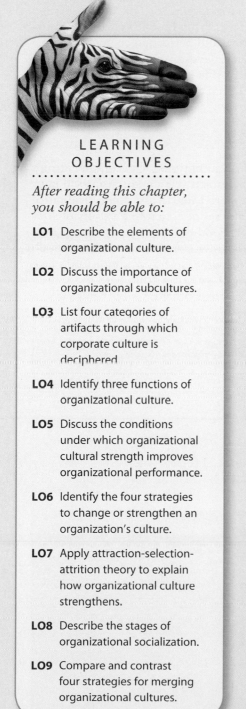

LEARNING OBJECTIVES

After reading this chapter, you should be able to:

LO1 Describe the elements of organizational culture.

LO2 Discuss the importance of organizational subcultures.

LO3 List four categories of artifacts through which corporate culture is deciphered.

LO4 Identify three functions of organizational culture.

LO5 Discuss the conditions under which organizational cultural strength improves organizational performance.

LO6 Identify the four strategies to change or strengthen an organization's culture.

LO7 Apply attraction-selection-attrition theory to explain how organizational culture strengthens.

LO8 Describe the stages of organizational socialization.

LO9 Compare and contrast four strategies for merging organizational cultures.

Propelled by a culture of cost efficiency and competitiveness, Dell, Inc. was the unstoppable leader in the computer industry for more than a decade. Experts praised its low-cost, responsive manufacturing and direct marketing sales model. Founder Michael Dell championed short-term objectives, while Kevin Rollins (until recently Dell CEO) was the architect of efficiency-oriented processes and measures. Dell culture emphasized "winning," meaning that it focused on beating the competition and staying on top through low prices. "There are some organizations where people think they're a hero if they invent a new thing," Rollins said a few years ago. "Being a hero at Dell means saving money."

Although still an efficient manufacturer of low-cost computers, Dell's spectacular success has stalled while HP and other competitors are moving ahead. The reason? Dell's strong culture blinded leaders and most staff to anything other than building low-cost computers, yet the market was shifting toward a preference for style and innovation. "Dell's culture is not inspirational or aspirational," suggests one industry expert. "[Its] culture only wants to talk about execution." These problems are also apparent in Canada. Dell Canada placed fifth on the list of Canada's most admired corporate cultures in 2006. A year later, the company's same culture was no longer admired.

A few staff warned that Dell's culture needed to change, but those who dared to criticize the company's deeply ingrained values and assumptions were quickly silenced. "A lot of red flags got waved—but only once," recalls a former Dell manager.

As Dell's fortunes continued to slide, Michael Dell took over again as CEO, replacing Kevin Rollins. Other senior executives have also left the company. "The company was too focused on the short term," Dell admits. He apparently also repeatedly emphasizes to staff that Dell's past culture "is not a religion." Dell is convinced that he can turn the company around, but others say that changing Dell's culture will be a mammoth task. "It's not an easy transition," warns a technology analyst. "You've got to change your mind-set and your culture."[1]

Dell's culture of killer competition and efficiency is now becoming a liability to the computer maker's future. The Canadian Press (Paul Sakuma)

organizational culture
The values and assumptions shared within an organization.

Dell's current challenges illustrate the perils of ignoring organizational culture. **Organizational culture** consists of the values and assumptions shared within an organization.[2] It defines what is important and unimportant in the company and, consequently, directs everyone in the organization toward the "right way" of doing things. You might think of organizational culture as the organization's DNA—invisible to the naked eye, yet a powerful template that shapes what happens in the workplace.[3]

This chapter begins by identifying the elements of organizational culture, then describing how culture is deciphered through artifacts. This is followed by a discussion of the relationship between organizational culture and performance, including the effects of cultural strength, fit, and adaptability. Then we examine ways to change or strengthen organizational culture. The final section of this chapter turns our attention to the challenges and solutions to merging organizational cultures.

ELEMENTS OF ORGANIZATIONAL CULTURE

LO1

Exhibit 14.1 illustrates how the shared values and assumptions of an organization's culture relate to each other and are associated with artifacts, which are discussed later in this chapter. *Values*, which were described in Chapters 1 and 2, are stable, evaluative beliefs that guide our preferences for outcomes or courses of action in a variety of situations.[4] They are conscious perceptions about what is good or bad, right or wrong. Values exist as a component of organizational culture in the form of *shared values*, which are values that people within the organization or work unit have in common and place near the top of their hierarchy of values.[5] At Dell, employees generally hold the shared values of efficiency and competitiveness (winning), whereas other possible values take a

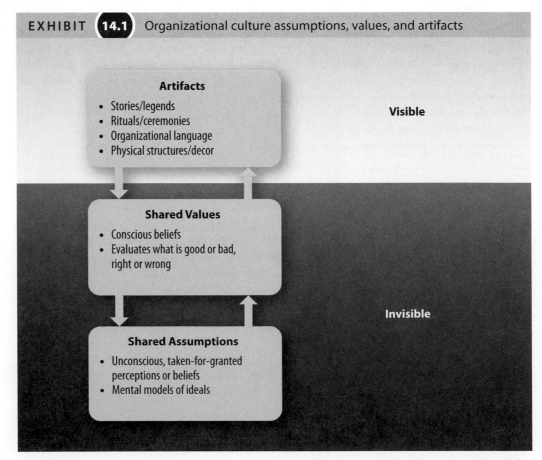

EXHIBIT 14.1   Organizational culture assumptions, values, and artifacts

Artifacts
- Stories/legends
- Rituals/ceremonies
- Organizational language
- Physical structures/decor

Visible

Shared Values
- Conscious beliefs
- Evaluates what is good or bad, right or wrong

Invisible

Shared Assumptions
- Unconscious, taken-for-granted perceptions or beliefs
- Mental models of ideals

Source: Based on information in E. H. Schein, *Organizational Culture and Leadership: A Dynamic View* (San Francisco: Jossey-Bass, 1985).

lower priority. Organizational culture also consists of *shared assumptions*—a deeper element that some experts believe is the essence of corporate culture. Shared assumptions are unconscious taken-for-granted perceptions or beliefs that are considered the correct way to think and act towards problems and opportunities. Shared assumptions are so deeply ingrained that you probably wouldn't discover them by surveying employees. Only by observing these employees, analyzing their decisions, and debriefing them on their actions would these assumptions rise to the surface.

It has become trendy for leaders to identify and publicly state their organization's culture or, more precisely, their shared values. Montreal-based engineering firm Teknika HBA identifies respect and development of the individual, teamwork, customer satisfaction, integrity, loyalty, and openness to change as its most important values. Information technology company RYCOM Inc., which operates out of Mississauga, Ontario and Dorval, Quebec, lists its top values as respect, fairness, integrity, teamwork, and service.[6] Do these values really represent the cultural content of Teknika-HBA and RYCOM? Possibly, to some extent. However, these values proclamations represent *espoused values*— the values that leaders say they and their staff rely on to guide their decisions and actions.[7] People construct a positive public image by claiming to believe in values that are socially desirable, even when they are not applied (see Chapter 2). These corporate values statements are also espoused because, although leaders might abide by them, lower level employees might not share these values. In contrast, organizational culture consists of shared *enacted values*—the values that leaders and employees truly rely on to guide their decisions and actions. These values-in-use are apparent by watching people in action.

CONTENT OF ORGANIZATIONAL CULTURE

Organizations differ in their cultural content; that is, the relative ordering of values. Dell's culture places efficiency and competitiveness far above innovation and aesthetics, whereas the culture at Apple, Inc. gives innovation and style equal or higher priority to cost efficiency. Many experts have tried to classify corporate culture into a few easy-to-remember categories. One of the most popular and respected models identifies seven corporate cultures (see Exhibit 14.2). Another popular model identifies four organizational cultures organized in a two-by-two table representing internal versus external focus and flexibility versus control. Other models organize cultures around a circle with eight or 12 categories. These circumplex models suggest that some cultures are opposite to others, such as an avoidance culture versus a self-actualization culture, or a power culture versus an affiliative culture.[8]

EXHIBIT 14.2 Organizational Culture Profile dimensions and characteristics

Organizational culture dimension	Characteristics of the dimension
Innovation	Experimenting, opportunity seeking, risk taking, few rules, low cautiousness
Stability	Predictability, security, rule-oriented
Respect for people	Fairness, tolerance
Outcome orientation	Action oriented, high expectations, results oriented
Attention to detail	Precise, analytic
Team orientation	Collaboration, people-oriented
Aggressiveness	Competitive, low emphasis on social responsibility

Source: Based on information in: C. A. O'Reilly III, J. Chatman, and D. F. Caldwell, "People and Organizational Culture: A Profile Comparison Approach to Assessing Person-Organization Fit," *Academy of Management Journal*, 34 (3), pp. 487–518.

These organizational culture models and surveys are popular with corporate leaders faced with the messy business of diagnosing their company's culture and identifying what kind of culture they want to develop. Unfortunately, they also present a distorted view of organizational culture. First, these models oversimplify the diversity of cultural values in organizations. The fact is, there are dozens of individual values, and many combinations of values, so there are likely many more organizational cultures than these models offer. Second, we must remember that organizational culture includes shared assumptions about the right way to do things, not just shared values. Few models take this more subterranean aspect of culture into account.

A third concern is that these organizational culture models and measures typically adopt an "integration" perspective; they assume that most organizations have a fairly clear, unified culture that is easily decipherable.[9] Indeed, they assert that an organization's culture is inherently measurable because any ambiguity is outside the domain of the culture. The integration perspective further assumes that when an organization's culture changes, it shifts from one unified condition to a new unified condition with only temporary ambiguity or weakness during the transition. These assumptions are probably incorrect or, at best, oversimplified. An organization's culture is usually quite blurry, so much so that it cannot be estimated through simple models and surveys. As we discuss next, organizations consist of diverse subcultures that stir up any potential consensus or consistency in values and assumptions across the organization. Indeed, even these subcultural clusters can be ill-defined because values and assumptions are ultimately unique to every individual. We are not suggesting here that organizational culture is nonexistent; some degree of shared values and assumptions do exist in many organizations. Instead, you should be aware that popular organizational culture models and measures oversimplify the variety of organizational cultures and falsely presume that organizations can easily be identified within these categories.

LO2   ORGANIZATIONAL SUBCULTURES

When discussing organizational culture, we are really referring to the *dominant culture*, that is, the values and assumptions shared most consistently and widely by the organization's members. The dominant culture usually includes senior management, but it sometimes exists in spite of senior management's desire for another culture. Furthermore, as was mentioned in the previous section, an organization's dominant culture is not as unified or clear as many consultants and business leaders assume. Instead, organizations are composed of *subcultures* located throughout its various divisions, geographic regions, and occupational groups.[10] Some subcultures enhance the dominant culture by espousing parallel assumptions and values; others differ from but do not oppose the dominant culture; still others are called *countercultures* because they embrace values or assumptions that directly oppose the organization's dominant culture. It is also possible that some organizations (including some universities, according to one study) operate with subcultures and no decipherable dominant culture at all.[11]

Subcultures, particularly countercultures, potentially create conflict and dissension among employees, but they also serve two important functions.[12] First, they maintain the organization's standards of performance and ethical behaviour. Employees who hold countercultural values are an important source of surveillance and critique over the dominant order. They encourage constructive conflict and more creative thinking about how the organization should interact with its environment. Subcultures potentially reduce unethical conduct, which can occur when people blindly follow a narrow set of values.

The second function of subcultures is that they are the spawning grounds for emerging values that keep the firm aligned with the needs of customers, suppliers, society, and other stakeholders. Companies eventually need to replace their dominant values with ones that are more appropriate for the changing environment. If subcultures are suppressed, the organization may take longer to discover and adopt values aligned with the emerging environment.

DECIPHERING ORGANIZATIONAL CULTURE THROUGH ARTIFACTS

artifacts
The observable symbols and signs of an organization's culture.

We can't directly see an organization's cultural assumptions and values. Instead, as Exhibit 14.1 illustrated earlier, we decipher organizational culture indirectly through artifacts. **Artifacts** are the observable symbols and signs of an organization's culture, such as the way visitors are greeted, the organization's physical layout, and how employees are rewarded.[13] A few experts suggest that these artifacts are the essence of organizational culture, whereas most others (including this book) view artifacts as symbols or indicators of culture. Either way, artifacts are important because they reinforce and potentially support changes to an organization's culture.

Artifacts are valuable as evidence about a company's culture.[14] As we mentioned earlier, an organization's culture is usually too blurry and its cultural assumptions too deeply ingrained to be measured through surveys. Instead, we need to observe workplace behaviour, listen to everyday conversations among staff and with customers, study written documents and emails, note physical structures and settings, and interview staff about corporate stories. In other words, we need to sample information from a range of organizational artifacts. For example, the Mayo Clinic conducted an assessment of its culture by hiring an anthropologist to decipher the medical organization's culture at its headquarters in Rochester, Minnesota, and to identify ways of transferring that culture to its two newer sites in Florida and Arizona. For six weeks, the anthropologist shadowed employees, posed as a patient in waiting rooms, did countless interviews, and accompanied physicians on patient visits. The final report outlined Mayo's dominant culture and how its satellite operations varied from that culture.[15]

In this section, we review the four broad categories of artifacts: organizational stories and legends, rituals and ceremonies, language, and physical structures and symbols.

Stories of Cirque du Soleil's Risky Culture

Cirque du Soleil, the Montreal-based troupe that combines circus with theatre, thrives on a culture of risk and creativity. This is apparent in stories about how the troupe was started. In 1980, Gilles Ste-Croix asked the Quebec government for funding to start up a street theatre group in Baie-Saint-Paul, northwest of Quebec City. When the government rejected the application, Ste-Croix walked 90 kilometres from Baie-Saint-Paul to Quebec City...on stilts! The gruelling 22-hour trip got the government's attention and financial support. Ste-Croix recalls a Quebec government representative saying, "If you're crazy enough to walk all this way on stilts, we'll give you some money to create jobs." Without that daring event, Cirque du Soleil probably wouldn't exist today, because Ste-Criox's band of 15 performers included Guy Laliberté who founded Cirque du Soleil in 1984 with Ste-Croix and others. In 1987, Cirque du Soleil was invited to perform at the Los Angeles Arts Festival, but the festival could not provide funds in advance to cover Cirque du Soleil's costs. Laliberté took a gamble by literally emptying the troupe's bank account to transport the performers and equipment to California. "I bet everything on that one night [at the Los Angeles Arts Festival]," Laliberté recalls. "If we failed, there was no cash for gas to come home." Fortunately, the gamble paid off. Cirque du Soleil was a huge success, which led to more opportunities and successes in the following years.[16] *Gorassini Giancarlo/The Canadian Press*

ORGANIZATIONAL STORIES AND LEGENDS

Stories permeate strong organizational cultures. Some tales recount heroic deeds, such as Michael Dell's determination to build his computer company, beginning from a dorm room at university. Other stories ridicule past events that deviated from the firm's core values. These stories and legends serve as powerful social prescriptions of the way things should (or should not) be done. They provide human realism to corporate expectations, individual performance standards, and the criteria for getting fired. Stories also produce emotions in listeners, which tend to improve their memory of the lesson within the story.[17] Stories have the greatest effect at communicating corporate culture when they describe real people, are assumed to be true, and are known by employees throughout the organization. Stories are also prescriptive—they advise people what to do or not to do.[18]

RITUALS AND CEREMONIES

rituals
The programmed routines of daily organizational life that dramatize the organization's culture.

ceremonies
Planned displays of organizational culture, conducted specifically for the benefit of an audience.

Rituals are the programmed routines of daily organizational life that dramatize the organization's culture. They include how visitors are greeted, how often senior executives visit subordinates, how people communicate with each other, how much time employees take for lunch, and so on. For instance, BMW's fast-paced culture is quite literally apparent in the way employees walk around the German carmaker's offices. "When you move through the corridors and hallways of other companies' buildings, people kind of crawl, they walk slowly," observes a BMW executive. "But BMW people tend to move faster."[19] **Ceremonies** are more formal artifacts than rituals. Ceremonies are planned activities conducted specifically for the benefit of an audience. This would include publicly rewarding (or punishing) employees, or celebrating the launch of a new product or newly won contract.

ORGANIZATIONAL LANGUAGE

The language of the workplace speaks volumes about the company's culture. How employees address co-workers, describe customers, express anger, and greet stakeholders are all verbal symbols of cultural values. Employees at The Container Store compliment each other about "being Gumby," meaning that they are being as flexible as the once-popular green toy to help a customer or another employee.[20] When Charles Schwab & Co. acquired U.S. Bank, executives at U.S. Bank winced when they heard Schwab executives use the word "customers"; U.S. Bank staff have "clients," a term that reflects more of a long term and deep relationship.[21] Language also highlights values held by organizational subcultures. For instance, consultants working at Whirlpool kept hearing employees talk about the appliance company's "PowerPoint culture." This phrase, which names Microsoft's presentation software, is a critique of Whirlpool's hierarchical culture in which communication is one-way (from executives to employees).[22]

PHYSICAL STRUCTURES AND SYMBOLS

Winston Churchill once said: "We shape our buildings; thereafter, they shape us."[23] The former British prime minister was reminding us that buildings both reflect and influence an organization's culture. The size, shape, location, and age of buildings might suggest the company's emphasis on teamwork, environmental friendliness, flexibility, or any other set of values. An extreme example is the "interplanetary headquarters" of Oakley, Inc. The eyewear and clothing company built a vault-like structure in Foothills Ranch, California, complete with towering metallic walls studded with oversized bolts, to represent its secretive and protective culture. "We've always had a fortress mentality," says an Oakley executive. "What we make is gold, and people will do anything to get it, so we protect it."[24] Even if the building doesn't make much of a statement, there is a treasure trove of physical artifacts inside. Desks, chairs, office space, and wall hangings (or lack of them) are just a few of the items that might convey cultural meaning.[25] Each artifact alone might not say much, but put enough of them together and the company's culture becomes easier to decipher.

IS ORGANIZATIONAL CULTURE IMPORTANT?

LO4

Does organizational culture affect corporate performance? Executives at WestJet, Dell, Mayo Clinic, Cirque du Soleil, and other companies think so. "Culture is one of the most precious things a company has, so you must work harder on it than anything else," says Herb Kelleher, founder of Southwest Airlines. Many writers of popular-press management books also assert that the most successful companies have strong cultures. In fact, one popular management book, *Built to Last*, suggests that successful companies are "cult-like" (although not actually "cults," the authors are careful to point out).[26]

The research evidence, however, is more ambivalent than the proclamations of popular-press management books. Specifically, companies with strong cultures tend to be more successful, but only under a particular set of conditions.[27] Before discussing these contingencies, let's examine organizational culture *strength* and its potential benefits. Corporate culture strength refers to how widely and deeply employees hold the company's dominant values and assumptions. In a strong organizational culture, most employees across all subunits understand and embrace the dominant values. These values and assumptions are also institutionalized through well-established artifacts, thereby making it difficult to change the culture. Furthermore, strong cultures tend to be long lasting; some can be traced back to the values and assumptions established by the company's founder. In contrast, companies have weak cultures when the dominant values are held mainly by a few people at the top of the organization, are barely discernible, and are in flux.

A strong corporate culture potentially increases the company's success by serving three important functions:

1. *Control system.* Organizational culture is a deeply embedded form of social control that influences employee decisions and behaviour.[28] Culture is pervasive and operates unconsciously. You might think of it as an automatic pilot, directing employees in ways that are consistent with organizational expectations.

2. *Social glue.* Organizational culture is the "social glue" that bonds people together and makes them feel part of the organizational experience.[29] Employees are motivated to internalize the organization's dominant culture because it fulfills their need for social identity. This social glue is increasingly important as a way to attract new staff and retain top performers.

WestJet's Cultural Formula for Success

When Canadian executives are asked to identify a company with a successful corporate culture, one organization stands out among the pack: WestJet Airlines Ltd. A strong culture of customer focus, fun, and empowerment have propelled the Calgary-based company from a small start-up to Canada's second largest and most profitable airline in just a dozen years. "We have deliberately built a culture of engagement and participation," says WestJet co-founder and executive chairman Clive Beddoe. WestJet CEO Sean Durfy believes that "culture is the most important element of what we do." He explains that WestJet's culture "is supported, promoted, and embraced at the top, but it really is in the 6,700 West-Jetters across our network. The culture is with each of them, encouraging them to provide the exceptional guest experience for which we are known."[30] © *Lonnie Ganz*

3. *Sense-making*. Organizational culture assists the sense-making process.[31] It helps employees understand what goes on and why things happen in the company. Corporate culture also makes it easier for them to understand what is expected of them and to interact with other employees who know the culture and believe in it. For instance, one recent study reported that employees have clearer role perceptions in organizations with strong cultures, which reduces their stress.[32]

CONTINGENCIES OF ORGANIZATIONAL CULTURE AND PERFORMANCE

LO5

Studies have found only a modestly positive relationship between culture strength and success because contingencies need to be considered. One contingency is whether the organization's culture content—its dominant values and assumptions—are aligned with the external environment. Consider the situation that Dell currently faces. As was described in the opening vignette to this chapter, Dell's culture gives the highest priority to cost efficiency and competitiveness, yet these values and assumptions are no longer ideal for the marketplace. Low cost computers are still popular, but consumers increasingly demand computers that are innovative and look "cool." Dell has a strong culture, but apparently no longer the best culture for the external environment.

Avoiding a Corporate Cult   A second contingency is the degree of culture strength. Various experts suggest that companies with very strong cultures (i.e., corporate "cults") may be less effective than companies with moderately strong cultures.[33] There are two reasons why corporate cults may undermine organizational effectiveness. First, very strong cultures lock decision makers into mental models that blind them to new opportunities and unique problems. They overlook or incorrectly define subtle misalignments between the organization's activities and the changing environment. Dell faced this problem. Kevin Rollins and Michael Dell sensed that the company's culture emphasized financial performance far too much (staff even had stock tickers on their computer screens) and tolerated people who didn't collaborate. Yet these leaders never thought about changing this culture. Instead, their solution (called "The Soul of Dell") merely supplemented the company's core values and assumptions. "It's not that we didn't have a culture with the qualities that drive business success," explained one Dell executive a few years ago. "We just aspired to do better."[34]

The other reason why very strong cultures may be dysfunctional is that they suppress dissenting subcultural values. At Dell, for instance, anyone who questioned the company's almost sacred values and assumptions were quickly silenced, even though these dissenting values could have provided Dell with a better aligned culture. The challenge for organizational leaders is to maintain a strong culture, but one that allows subcultural diversity. Subcultures encourage constructive conflict, which improves creative thinking and offers some level of ethical vigilance over the dominant culture. In the long run, the subculture's nascent values could become important dominant values as the environment changes. Corporate cults suppress subcultures, thereby undermining these benefits.

adaptive culture
An organizational culture in which employees focus on the changing needs of customers and other stakeholders, and support initiatives to keep pace with those changes.

Creating an Adaptive Culture   A third contingency between cultural strength and organizational effectiveness is whether the culture content includes an **adaptive culture**.[35] Adaptive cultures have an external focus. Employees hold a common mental model that the organization's success depends on continuous change to support stakeholders. For example, Nokia has shifted from toilet paper to rubber boots to cellphones to network services. It has maintained an adaptive culture because employees believe that change is both necessary and inevitable to keep pace with an evolving external environment.

Second, employees in adaptive cultures pay as much attention to organizational processes as they do to organizational goals. They engage in continuous improvement of internal processes (production, customer service, etc.) to serve external stakeholders. Third, employees in adaptive cultures have a strong sense of ownership. They assume responsibility for the organization's performance. In other words, they believe in "it's our job" rather than "it's not my job." Fourth, adaptive cultures are proactive and quick. Employees seek out opportunities, rather than wait for them to arrive. They act quickly to learn through discovery rather than engage in "paralysis by analysis."

ORGANIZATIONAL CULTURE AND BUSINESS ETHICS

An organization's culture influences more than just the bottom line; it can also affect the ethical conduct of its employees. This makes sense because good behaviour is driven by ethical values, and ethical values can become part of an organization's dominant culture. A few years ago, Michael Dell and former CEO Kevin Rollins saw this connection between culture and ethics when they launched the "Soul of Dell." Concerned about employee obsession with the company's stock price, the executives tried to shift the company's winning culture into one that emphasizes "winning with integrity."[36] For example, one of the computer maker's revised values was defined as "behaving ethically in every interaction and in every aspect of how we conduct business." Unfortunately, the Soul of Dell initiative probably didn't change the company's culture. Dell recently admitted that some executives had manipulated the company books to reach performance targets that would give them a larger bonus.[37] This earlier failure to change Dell's culture illustrates the challenges of changing organizational culture, which we discuss next.

CHANGING AND STRENGTHENING ORGANIZATIONAL CULTURE

LO6

As part of its strategy to develop a more engaged workforce, Bombardier Aerospace asked a representation of employees to select 10 phrases (out of a list of 40) that defined the Montreal-based company's current culture, and 10 phrases that would depict the company's ideal culture. Customer service topped both lists, but the two sets of phrases were otherwise quite different. Employees saw the current culture as competitive and bottom-line driven (results-oriented, demanding, quality emphasis, externally competitive, shareholder-oriented, etc.), whereas their ideal culture was more employee focused (stability, team-oriented, employment security, high pay for performance, professional growth, etc.). "It threw up some interesting issues," says Bombardier Aerospace director of internal communication, Lise St-Arnaud. "Things we perhaps knew instinctively, but having black-and-white evidence galvanized discussion among our senior leaders about where the company was headed culturally." St-Arnaud adds that changing an organization's culture is challenging: "Engagement for us is all about culture change, and that doesn't happen overnight."[38]

Bombardier Aerospace executives are correct in thinking that changing an organization's culture doesn't happen overnight. In fact, some writers argue that leaders shouldn't even bother to attempt such a transformation because organizational culture "cannot be managed."[39] This view is more extreme than most, but organizational culture experts generally agree that changing an organization's culture isn't easy, it rarely occurs quickly, and oftentimes the culture ends up changing (or replacing) corporate leaders. At the same time, under the right conditions, organizational culture can be a powerful influence on the company's success. So, how do leaders successfully change and strengthen organizational culture? Over the next few pages, we will highlight four strategies that have had some success. This list, outlined in Exhibit 14.3, is not exhaustive, but each activity seems to work well under the right circumstances.

ACTIONS OF FOUNDERS AND LEADERS

An organization's culture begins with its founders.[40] You can see this at Dell, Inc., where founder Michael Dell established a competitive and cost-focused culture. Founders are often visionaries who provide a powerful role model for others to follow. The company's culture sometimes reflects the founder's personality, and this cultural imprint can

EXHIBIT 14.3   Strategies to change and strengthen organizational culture

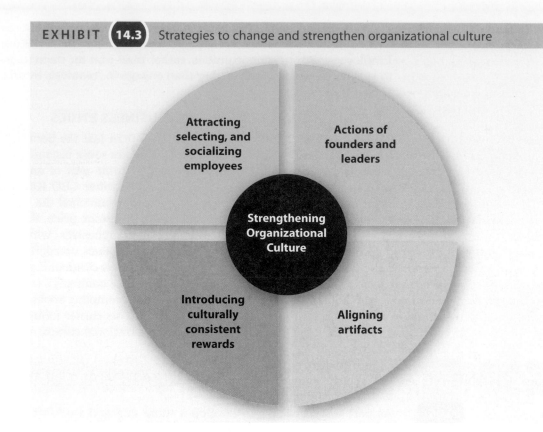

remain with the organization for decades. For example, some observers say that Dell's culture is so much part of Michael Dell's personal orientation to life that he might not be the best person to try to change Dell's culture.

Founders establish an organization's culture, but they and subsequent leaders are sometimes able to reshape that culture by applying transformational leadership and organizational change practices.[41] For instance, through his symbolic and substantive actions as a leader, Proctor & Gamble chief executive A. G. Lafley has transformed the consumer goods company's culture into one that is much more customer focused.

ALIGNING ARTIFACTS

Artifacts represent more than just the visible indicators of a company's culture. They are also mechanisms that keep the culture in place. By altering artifacts—or creating new ones—leaders can potentially adjust the organization's culture. A dramatic example is moving the company or business unit into new offices that reflect a different culture. National Australia Bank's (NAB) is a case in point. By moving into a low-rise campus-like building in Melbourne's docklands area, NAB executives hope to replace the company's hierarchical, bureaucratic culture with one that is more open, egalitarian, and creative. NAB's leaders knew that buildings can change the organization's culture because they observed this happen at MLC, a financial services firm that NAB had acquired a few years earlier. "There's no doubt that MLC has moved its culture over the last few years to a more open and transparent style which is a good example for the rest of the group to follow," admits a NAB executive.[42]

Corporate cultures are also altered and strengthened through the artifacts of stories and behaviours. According to Max De Pree, former CEO of furniture manufacturer Herman Miller Inc., every organization needs "tribal storytellers" to keep the organization's history and culture alive.[43] Leaders play a role by creating memorable events that symbolize the cultural values they want to develop or maintain. At Wall Street investment firm Goldman Sachs, this leadership function is so important that they are called "culture

carriers." Goldman's senior executives live and breathe the company's culture so much that they can effectively transmit and reinforce that culture.[45] Companies also strengthen culture in new operations by transferring current employees who abide by the culture.

INTRODUCING CULTURALLY CONSISTENT REWARDS

Reward systems are artifacts that often have a powerful effect on strengthening or reshaping an organization's culture.[46] When Robert Nardelli was hired to transform Home Depot's freewheeling culture, he introduced precise measures of corporate performance and drilled managers with weekly performance objectives around those metrics. A two-hour weekly conference call became a ritual in which Home Depot's top executives were held accountable for the previous week's goals. These actions reinforced a more disciplined (and centralized), performance-oriented culture.[47]

LO7

ATTRACTING, SELECTING, AND SOCIALIZING EMPLOYEES

Organizational culture is strengthened by attracting and hiring people who already embrace the cultural values, then socializing them to more clearly understand the company's culture. This process, along with weeding out people who don't fit the culture, is explained by **attraction selection attrition (ASA) theory**.[48] ASA theory states that organizations have a natural tendency to attract, select, and retain people with values and personality characteristics that are consistent with the organization's character, resulting in a more homogeneous organization and a stronger culture.

- *Attraction*—Job applicants engage in self-selection by avoiding employment in companies whose values seem incompatible with their own values.[49] Companies often encourage this self-selection by actively describing their culture, but applicants will look for evidence of the company's culture even when it is not advertised. Applicants also inspect organizational artifacts when visiting the company.

- *Selection*—How well the person "fits" in with the company's culture is often a factor in deciding which job applicants to hire. Companies with strong cultures routinely put applicants through several interviews and other selection tests, in part to better gauge the applicant's values and their congruence with the company's values.[50] This focus on values congruence is apparent at Apex Distribution Inc. The Calgary-based company opened its doors in 1999 and in less than a decade has become a leading distributor of oilfield equipment in Western Canada as well as one of Canada's

---

attraction-selection-attrition (ASA) theory
States that organizations have a natural tendency to attract, select, and retain people with values and personality characteristics that are consistent with the organization's character, resulting in a more homogeneous organization and a stronger culture.

50 best-managed companies. Executives quickly point to the company's employee ownership and strong culture as reasons for this success. "When the founders of Apex came together, they created a culture that is team focused and empowering," says Greg Abtosway, vice-president Business Development. Apex executives also emphasize that they intend to maintain that strong culture by hiring people who have compatible values. "We're an employee-owned company, so it's really important that people who join us are in line with that culture and can support the organizational objectives," says Apex vice-president of finance Linda Wyatt.[51]

- *Attrition*—People are motivated to seek out environments that are sufficiently congruent with their personal values, and to leave environments with a poor fit. This occurs because person-organization values congruence supports their social identity and minimizes internal role conflict. Consequently, if they are forced out, employees are more likely to quit if values incongruence is sufficiently high.[52]

Organizational Socialization   Toyota Canada recently opened its new assembly plant in Woodstock, Ontario, and is hiring dozens of people every few weeks. That hiring drive has kept Ray Tanguay busy. As president of Toyota Motor Manufacturing Canada, Tanguay makes a point of personally talking to new hires about "our culture" in orientation sessions. "As we hire the 2,000 new team members, the groups will be much bigger," says Tanguay.[53]

In addition to carefully recruiting and hiring people with compatible values, Toyota Canada and many other companies maintain strong cultures through **organizational socialization**. Organizational socialization is the process by which individuals learn the values, expected behaviours, and social knowledge necessary to assume their roles in the organization.[54] By communicating the company's dominant values, job candidates and new hires are more likely to internalize these values quickly and deeply. "The cultural aspects of our training programs are at least as important as the technical aspects," says an executive at JetBlue, the New York-based discount airline. "The People Department will find the right people and we will inculcate the culture into them and nurture that culture until we release them out into the operation."[55] When employees are effectively socialized into the organization, they tend to perform better and have higher job satisfaction.[56]

Organizational socialization is a process of both learning and adjustment. It is a learning process because newcomers try to make sense of the company's physical workplace, social dynamics, and strategic/cultural environment. They learn about the organization's performance expectations, power dynamics, corporate culture, company history, and jargon. Organizational socialization is also a process of adjustment, because individuals need to adapt to their new work environment. They develop new work roles that reconfigure their social identity, adopt new team norms, and practise new behaviours. Research reports that the adjustment process is fairly rapid for many people, usually within a few months. However, newcomers with diverse work experience seem to adjust better than those with limited previous experience, possibly because they have a larger toolkit of knowledge and skills to make the adjustment possible.[57]

Socialization is most intense when people move across organizational boundaries, such as when they first join a company, or get transferred to an international assignment. Exhibit 14.4 shows the three stages of socialization, which represent the individual's transition from outsider, to newcomer, and then to insider.[58] The pre-employment socialization stage encompasses all the learning and adjustment that occurs before the first day of work. In fact, a large part of the socialization adjustment process occurs during this stage.[59] As outsiders, however, people rely on indirect and often distorted information about what it is like to work in the organization. Job applicants might distort their resumes, while employers present overly positive images of organizational life.

The first day on the job typically marks the beginning of the encounter stage of organizational socialization. This is the stage in which newcomers test their prior expec-

organizational socialization

The process by which individuals learn the values, expected behaviours, and social knowledge necessary to assume their roles in the organization.

know ✳

EXHIBIT 14.4 Stages of organizational socialization

Pre-employment socialization (outsider)
- Learn about the organization and the job
- Form employment relationship expectations

Encounter (newcomer)
- Test expectations against perceived realities

Role management (insider)
- Strengthen work relationships
- Practise new role behaviours
- Resolve work–nonwork conflicts

Socialization outcomes
- Higher motivation
- Higher loyalty
- Higher satisfaction
- Lower stress
- Lower turnover

---

reality shock
The stress that results when employees perceive discrepancies between their pre-employment expectations and on-the-job reality.

tations with the perceived realities. Many companies fail the test, resulting in **reality shock**—the stress that results when employees perceive discrepancies between their pre-employment expectations and on-the-job reality.[60] Reality shock doesn't necessarily occur on the first day; it might develop over several weeks or even months as newcomers form a better understanding of their new work environment. Role management, the third stage of organizational socialization, actually begins during pre-employment socialization, but is most active as employees make the transition from newcomers to insiders. They strengthen relationships with co-workers and supervisors, practise new role behaviours, and adopt attitudes and values consistent with their new position and organization. Role management also involves resolving the conflicts between work and nonwork activities, including resolving discrepancies between their existing values and those emphasized by the organizational culture.

MERGING ORGANIZATIONAL CULTURES

LO9

4C Corporate Culture Clash and Chemistry is a company with an unusual name and mandate. The Dutch consulting firm helps clients to determine whether their culture is aligned ("chemistry") or incompatible with ("clash") a potential acquisition or merger partner. The firm also analyzes the company's culture with its strategy. There should be plenty of demand for 4C's expertise. According to various studies, most corporate mergers and acquisitions fail in terms of subsequent performance of the merged organization. Evidence suggests that these failures occur partly because corporate leaders are so focused on the financial or marketing logistics of a merger that they fail to conduct due-diligence audits on their respective corporate cultures.[61] Some forms of integration (which we discuss later in this section) may allow successful mergers between companies with different cultures. However, research concludes that mergers typically suffer when organizations with significantly divergent corporate cultures merge into a single entity with a high degree of integration.[62]

The marriage of AOL with Time Warner is one of the more spectacular culture clashes. In theory, the world's largest merger offered huge opportunities for converging AOL's dominance in Internet services with Time Warner's deep knowledge and assets in traditional media. Instead, the two corporate cultures mixed like oil and water. AOL's culture valued youthful, high-flying, quick deal-making. People were rewarded with stock options. Time Warner, on the other hand, had a button-down, hierarchical, and systematic culture. Executives were older and the reward was a decent retirement package (affectionately known as the "golden rubber band" because people who left invariably returned for the retirement benefit).[63]

Whole Foods Market Spreads its Culture like Yogurt

How do companies maintain their corporate culture when expanding operations? At Whole Foods Market, the solution is yogurt. "One of our secrets is what I refer to as our 'yogurt culture,'" explains Whole Foods Market co-founder John Mackey. This strategy involves transferring team members who carry Whole Foods Market's unique culture to new stores so recently hired team members learn and embrace that culture more quickly. "For example, in our Columbus Circle store in New York, about 25 percent of the team members transferred from existing stores," Mackey recalls. "They were the starting culture for the fermentation that turned Columbus Circle into a true Whole Foods Market store." Some team members even took lesser titles just to help Columbus Circle adopt Whole Foods Market's cultural values. For example, the store's two associate store team leaders previously operated their own stores in Georgetown, Maryland, and Albuquerque, New Mexico, before coming to New York.[64] © *Whole Foods Market*®

BICULTURAL AUDIT

bicultural audit
A process of diagnosing cultural relations between the companies and determining the extent to which cultural clashes will likely occur.

Organizational leaders can minimize these cultural collisions and fulfill their duty of due diligence by conducting a bicultural audit.[65] A **bicultural audit** diagnoses cultural relations between the companies and determines the extent to which cultural clashes will likely occur. The bicultural audit process begins by identifying cultural differences between the merging companies. Next, the bicultural audit data are analyzed to determine which differences between the two firms will result in conflict and which cultural values provide common ground on which to build a cultural foundation in the merged organization. The final stage involves identifying strategies and preparing action plans to bridge the two organizations' cultures.

A few years ago, Toronto-based pulp and paper conglomerate Abitibi-Price applied a bicultural audit before it agreed to merge with its Montreal rival, Stone Consolidated. Specifically, Abitibi developed the Merging Cultures Evaluation Index (MCEI), an evaluation system that helped Abitibi executives compare its culture with other companies in the industry. The MCEI analyzed several dimensions of corporate culture, such as concentration of power versus diffusion of power, innovation versus tradition, wide versus narrow flow of information, and consensus versus authoritative decision making. Abitibi and Stone executives completed the questionnaire to assess their own culture, then compared the results. The MCEI results, along with financial and infrastructural information, served as the basis for Abitibi-Price to merge with Stone Consolidated to become Montreal-based Abitibi-Consolidated (now Abitibi Bowater), the world's largest pulp-and-paper firm.[66]

STRATEGIES TO MERGE DIFFERENT ORGANIZATIONAL CULTURES

In some cases, the bicultural audit results in a decision to end merger talks because the two cultures are too different to merge effectively. However, even with substantially different cultures, two companies may form a workable union if they apply the appropriate merger strategy. The four main strategies for merging different corporate cultures are assimilation, deculturation, integration, and separation (see Exhibit 14.5).[67]

Assimilation Assimilation occurs when employees at the acquired company willingly embrace the cultural values of the acquiring organization. Typically, this strategy works best when the acquired company has a weak dysfunctional culture, whereas the acquiring company's culture is strong and aligned with the external environment. Culture clash is rare with assimilation because the acquired firm's culture is weak and employees are looking for better cultural alternatives. Research In Motion (RIM), the

EXHIBIT 14.5	Strategies for merging different organizational cultures	
Merger strategy	**Description**	**Works best when:**
Assimilation	Acquired company embraces acquiring firm's culture.	Acquired firm has a dysfunctional and weak culture.
Deculturation	Acquiring firm imposes its culture on unwilling acquired firm.	When acquired firm's employees cling to their culture even though it doesn't work. Difficult to implement well.
Integration	Combining the two or more cultures into a new composite culture.	Existing cultures overlap and require improvement.
Separation	Merging companies remain distinct entities with minimal exchange of culture or organizational practices.	Firms operate successfully in different businesses requiring different cultures.

Source: Based on ideas in A. R. Malekazedeh and A. Nahavandi, "Making Mergers Work by Managing Cultures," *Journal of Business Strategy*, May/June 1990, pp. 55–57; K. W. Smith, "A Brand-New Culture for the Merged Firm," *Mergers and Acquisitions*, 35 (June 2000), pp. 45–50.

Waterloo, Ontario, company that makes BlackBerry wireless devices, applies the assimilation strategy by deliberately acquiring only small start-up firms. "Small companies… don't have cultural issues," says RIM co-CEO Jim Balsillie, adding that they are typically absorbed into RIM's culture with little fuss or attention.[68]

Deculturation Assimilation is rare. Employees usually resist organizational change, particularly when they are asked to throw away personal and cultural values. Under these conditions, some acquiring companies apply a *deculturation* strategy by imposing their culture and business practices on the acquired organization. The acquiring firm strips away artifacts and reward systems that support the old culture. People who cannot adopt the acquiring company's culture are often terminated. Deculturation may be necessary when the acquired firm's culture doesn't work but employees aren't convinced of this. However, this strategy is difficult to apply effectively because the acquired firm's employees resist the cultural intrusions from the buying firm, thereby delaying or undermining the merger process.

Integration A third strategy is to combine the two or more cultures into a new composite culture that preserves the best features of the previous cultures. Integration is slow and potentially risky, because there are many forces preserving the existing cultures. Still, this strategy should be considered when the companies have relatively weak cultures, or when their cultures include several overlapping values. Integration

A Marriage of Cultural Separation

Cisco Systems, the California-based Internet equipment maker, has acquired approximately 90 companies over the past two decades, most of them small, privately held start-up firms with technical expertise in high growth niches compatible with Cisco's own products. For most acquisitions, Cisco assimilates the smaller firm into its own culture. Linksys, the home wireless network company founded by Janie and Victor Tsao, was an exception. Linksys employs 400 people and was just a few years younger than Cisco. Furthermore, unlike Cisco, Linksys had developed a low-cost business with mass-market retail channels. To avoid disrupting its success, Cisco made sure that Linksys kept its own culture. Cisco executives were so concerned about this that a "filtering team" was formed to prevent Cisco's culture or its leaders from taking over the smaller enterprise. So far, the strategy has worked. Linksys continues to thrive in a competitive low-cost market even though wholly owned by Cisco, which focuses on the high-end network business.[69] *The Canadian Press (Paul Sakuma)*

also works best when people realize that their existing cultures are ineffective and are, therefore, motivated to adopt a new set of dominant values.

(A) **Separation**   A separation strategy occurs where the merging companies agree to remain distinct entities with minimal exchange of culture or organizational practices. This strategy is most appropriate when the two merging companies are in unrelated industries or operate in different countries, because the most appropriate cultural values tend to differ by industry and national culture. Unfortunately, executives in the acquiring firm have difficulty keeping their hands off the acquired firm. It's not surprising, therefore, that only 15 percent of acquisitions leave the purchased organization as a stand-alone unit.[70]

CHAPTER SUMMARY

Organizational culture refers to the values and assumptions shared within an organization. Shared assumptions are unconscious taken-for-granted perceptions or beliefs that have worked so well in the past that they are considered the correct way to think and act towards problems and opportunities. Values are stable, evaluative beliefs that guide our preferences for outcomes or courses of action in a variety of situations.

Organizations differ in their cultural content; that is, the relative ordering of values. There are several classifications of organizational culture, but they tend to oversimplify the wide variety of cultures, and completely ignore the underlying assumptions of culture. Organizations have subcultures as well as the dominant culture. Subcultures maintain the organization's standards of performance and ethical behaviour. They are also the source of emerging values that replace aging core values.

Artifacts are the observable symbols and signs of an organization's culture. Four broad categories of artifacts include organizational stories and legends, rituals and ceremonies, language, physical structures and symbols. Understanding an organization's culture requires assessment of many artifacts because they are subtle and often ambiguous.

Organizational culture has three main functions. It is a deeply embedded form of social control. It is also the "social glue" that bonds people together and makes them feel part of the organizational experience. Third, corporate culture helps employees make sense of the workplace.

Companies with strong cultures generally perform better than those with weak cultures, but only when the cultural content is appropriate for the organization's environment. Also, the culture should not be so strong that it drives out dissenting values, which may form emerging values for the future. Organizations should have adaptive cultures so that employees focus on the need for change and support initiatives and leadership that keeps pace with these changes.

Organizational culture is very difficult to change, but it has been done and is sometimes necessary for the company's continued survival. Four strategies to change and strengthen an organization's culture are the actions of founders and leaders, aligning artifacts with the desired culture, introducing culturally consistent rewards, and attracting, selecting, and socializing employees.

Attraction-selection-attrition (ASA) theory states that organizations have a natural tendency to attract, select, and retain people with values and personality characteristics that are consistent with the organization's character, resulting in a more homogeneous organization and a stronger culture. Organizational socialization is the process by which individuals learn the values, expected behaviours, and social knowledge necessary to assume their roles in the organization. It is a process of both learning about the work context and adjusting to new work roles, team norms, and behaviours. Employees typically pass through three socialization stages: pre-employment, encounter, and role management.

Mergers should include a bicultural audit to diagnose the compatibility of the organizational cultures. The four main strategies for merging different corporate cultures are integration, deculturation, assimilation, and separation.

KEY TERMS

adaptive culture, p. 340

artifacts, p. 337

attraction-selection-attrition (ASA) theory, p. 343

bicultural audit, p. 346

ceremonies, p. 338

organizational culture, p. 334

organizational socialization, p. 344

reality shock, p. 345

rituals, p. 338

CRITICAL THINKING QUESTIONS

1. Superb Consultants have submitted a proposal to analyze the cultural values of your organization. The proposal states that Superb has developed a revolutionary new survey to tap the company's true culture. The survey takes just 10 minutes to complete and the consultants say results can be based on a small sample of employees. Discuss the merits and limitations of this proposal.

2. Some people suggest that the most effective organizations have the strongest cultures. What do we mean by the "strength" of organizational culture, and what possible problems are there with a strong organizational culture?

3. The CEO of a manufacturing firm wants everyone to support the organization's dominant culture of lean efficiency and hard work. The CEO has introduced a new reward system to reinforce this culture and personally interviews all professional and managerial applicants to ensure that they bring similar values to the organization. Some employees who criticized these values had their careers sidelined until they left. Two mid-level managers were fired for supporting contrary values, such as work/life balance. Based on your knowledge of organizational subcultures, what potential problems is the CEO creating?

4. Identify at least two artifacts you have observed in your department or faculty from each of the four broad cat-

egories: a) Organizational stories and legends b) Rituals and ceremonies c) Language d) Physical structures and symbols.

5. "Organizations are more likely to succeed when they have an adaptive culture." What can an organization do to foster an adaptive culture?

6. Suppose you are asked by senior officers of a city government to identify ways to reinforce a new culture of teamwork and collaboration. The senior executive group clearly supports these values, but it wants everyone in the organization to embrace them. Identify four types of activities that would strengthen these cultural values.

7. Socialization is most intense when people pass through organizational boundaries. One example is your entry into the college or university that you are now attending. What learning and adjustment occurred as you moved from outsider to newcomer to insider as a student here?

8. Acme Corp. is planning to acquire Beta Corp., which operates in a different industry. Acme's culture is entrepreneurial and fast paced, whereas Beta employees value slow, deliberate decision making by consensus. Which merger strategy would you recommend to minimize culture shock when Acme acquires Beta? Explain your answer.

CASE STUDY 14.1

Hillton's Transformation

Twenty years ago, the City of Hillton was a community of about 70,000 residents that was becoming an outer suburb of a large Canadian metropolitan city. Hillton's management treated employees like family and gave them a great deal of autonomy in their work. Everyone in the organization (including the two labour unions representing employees) implicitly agreed that the leaders and supervisors of the organization should rise through the ranks based on their experience. Few people were ever hired from the outside into middle or senior positions. The rule of employment at Hillton was to learn the job skills, maintain a reasonably good work record, and wait your turn for promotion.

Hillton has grown rapidly since the mid-1960s. As the population grew, so did the municipality's workforce to keep pace with the increasing demand for municipal services. This meant that employees were promoted fairly quickly and were almost assured guaranteed employment. In fact, until recently, Hillton had never laid off any employee. The organization's culture could be described as one of entitlement and comfort. Neither the elected city councilors nor city manager bothered the departmental managers about their work. There were few cost controls because the rapid growth placed more emphasis on keeping up with the population expansion. The public became somewhat more critical of the city's poor service, including road construction at inconvenient times and the apparent lack of respect some employees showed toward taxpayers.

www.mcgrawhill.ca/olc/mcshane

During these expansion years, Hillton put most of its money into "outside" (also called "hard") municipal services. These included road building, utility construction and maintenance, fire and police protection, recreational facilities, and land use control. This emphasis occurred because an expanding population demanded more of these services and most of Hillton's senior people came from the outside services group. For example, Hillton's city manager for many years was a road development engineer. The "inside" workers (taxation, community services, etc.) tended to have less seniority and their departments were given less priority.

As commuter and road systems developed, Hillton attracted more upwardly mobile professionals into the community. Some infrastructure demands continued, but now these suburban dwellers wanted more of the "soft" services, such as libraries, social activities, and community services. They also began complaining about the way the municipality was being run. The population had more than tripled between the 1960s and 1990s, and it was increasingly apparent that the organization needed more corporate planning, information systems, organization development, and cost control systems. In various ways, residents voiced their concerns that the municipality was not providing the quality of management that they would expect from a city of its size.

In 1996, a new mayor and council replaced most of the previous incumbents, mainly on the platform of improving the municipality's management structure. The new council gave the city manager, along with two other senior managers, an early retirement buyout package. Rather than promoting from the lower ranks, council decided to fill all three positions with qualified candidates from large municipal corporations in the region. The following year, several long-term managers left Hillton and at least half of those positions were filled by people from outside the organization.

In less than two years, Hillton had eight senior or departmental managers hired from other municipalities who played a key role in changing the organization's value system. These eight managers became known (often with negative connotations) as the "professionals." They worked closely with each other to change the way middle and lower level managers had operated for many years. They brought in a new computer system and emphasized cost controls where managers previously had complete autonomy. Promotions were increasingly determined by both performance and seniority.

These managers frequently announced in meetings and newsletters that municipal employees must provide superlative customer service, and that Hillton will become one of the most customer-friendly places for citizens and those who do business with the municipality. To this end, these managers were quick to support the public's increasing demand for more "soft" services, including expanded library services and recreational activities. And when population growth recently flattened out for a few years, the city manager and other professionals gained council support to lay off a few of the outside workers due to lack of demand for hard services.

One of the most significant changes was that the "outside" departments no longer held dominant positions in city management. Most of the "professional" managers had worked exclusively in administrative and related inside jobs. Two had Master of Business Administration degrees. This led to some tension between the professional managers and the older outside managers.

Even before the layoffs, managers of outside departments resisted the changes more than others. These managers complained that their employees with the highest seniority were turned down for promotions. They argued for more budget and warned that infrastructure problems would cause liability problems. Informally, these outside managers were supported by the labour union representing outside workers. The union leaders tried to bargain for more job guarantees whereas the union representing inside workers focused more on improving wages and benefits. Leaders of the outside union made several statements in the local media that the city had "lost its heart" and that the public would suffer from the actions of the new professionals.

Discussion Questions   **1.** Contrast Hillton's earlier corporate culture with the emerging set of cultural values.

2. Considering the difficulty in changing organizational culture, why does Hillton's management seem to be successful at this transformation?

3. Identify two other strategies that the city might consider to reinforce the new set of corporate values.

 WEB EXERCISE 14.2

Diagnosing Corporate Culture Proclamations

Purpose   To understand the importance and contents in which corporate culture is identified and discussed in organizations.

Instructions   This exercise is a take-home activity, although it can be completed in classes with computers and Internet connections. The instructor will divide the class into small teams (typically four or five people per team). Each team is assigned a specific industry, such as energy, biotechnology, computer hardware.

The team's task is to search websites of several companies in the selected industry for company statements about their corporate culture. Use the company website search engine (if it exists) to find documents with key phrases such as "corporate culture" or "company values."

In the next class, or at the end of the time allotted in the current class, students will report on their observations by answering the following three discussion questions:

Discussion Questions   **1.** What values seem to dominate the corporate culture of the companies you searched? Are these values similar or diverse across companies in the industry?

2. What was the broader content of the Web pages where these companies described or mentioned its corporate culture?

3. Do companies in this industry refer to their corporate culture on the websites more or less than companies in other industries searched by teams in this class?

www.mcgrawhill.ca/olc/mcshane

SELF-ASSESSMENT EXERCISE 14.3

What Are Your Corporate Culture Preferences?

Purpose   This self-assessment is designed to help you identify a corporate culture that fits most closely with your personal values and assumptions.

Instructions   Read each pair of statements in the Corporate Culture Preference Scale and circle the statement that describes the organization in which you would prefer to work. Then use the scoring key in Appendix B to calculate your results for each subscale. The scale does not attempt to measure your preference for every corporate culture, just a few of the more common varieties. Also, keep in mind none of these corporate cultures is inherently good or bad. The focus here is on how well you fit within each of them. This exercise is completed alone so students assess themselves honestly without concerns of social comparison. However, class discussion will focus on the importance of matching job applicants to the organization's dominant values.

Corporate Culture Preference Scale		
I would prefer to work in an organization:		
1a. Where employees work well together in teams.	**OR**	1b. That produces highly respected products or services.
2a. Where top management maintains a sense of order in the workplace.	**OR**	2b. Where the organization listens to customers and responds quickly to their needs.
3a. Where employees are treated fairly.	**OR**	3b. Where employees continuously search for ways to work more efficiently.
4a. Where employees adapt quickly to new work requirements.	**OR**	4b. Where corporate leaders work hard to keep employees happy.
5a. Where senior executives receive special benefits not available to other employees.	**OR**	5b. Where employees are proud when the organization achieves its performance goals.
6a. Where employees who perform the best get paid the most.	**OR**	6b. Where senior executives are respected.
7a. Where everyone gets their jobs done like clockwork.	**OR**	7b. That is on top of new innovations in the industry.
8a. Where employees receive assistance to overcome any personal problems.	**OR**	8b. Where employees abide by company rules.
9a. That is always experimenting with new ideas in the marketplace.	**OR**	9b. That expects everyone to put in 110 percent for peak performance.
10a. That quickly benefits from market opportunities.	**OR**	10b. Where employees are always kept informed of what's happening in the organization.
11a. That can quickly respond to competitive threats.	**OR**	11b. Where most decisions are made by the top executives.
12a. Where management keeps everything under control.	**OR**	12b. Where employees care for each other.

Copyright © 2000. Steven L. McShane.

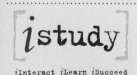

iStudy—Available 24/7 with instant feedback so you can study when you want, how you want, and where you want. Visit www.istudyob.ca to register—take practice quizzes, run interactive scenarios, practice concepts, and much more. Also visit the Student Online Learning Centre for additional study tools.

CHAPTER 15

Organizational Change

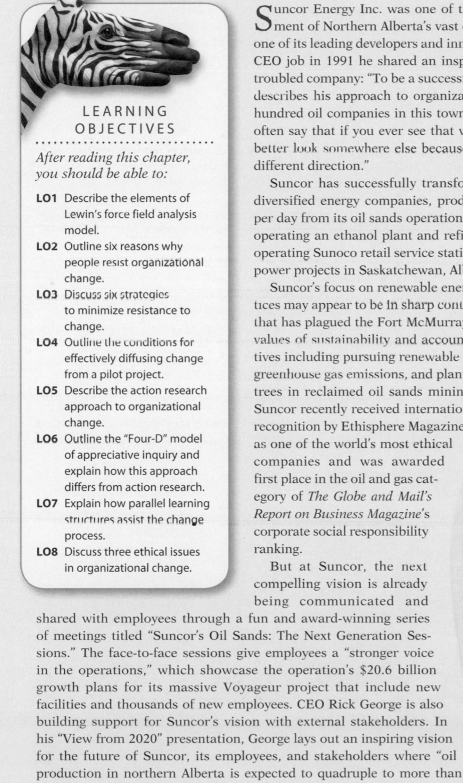

LEARNING OBJECTIVES

After reading this chapter, you should be able to:

LO1 Describe the elements of Lewin's force field analysis model.

LO2 Outline six reasons why people resist organizational change.

LO3 Discuss six strategies to minimize resistance to change.

LO4 Outline the conditions for effectively diffusing change from a pilot project.

LO5 Describe the action research approach to organizational change.

LO6 Outline the "Four-D" model of appreciative inquiry and explain how this approach differs from action research.

LO7 Explain how parallel learning structures assist the change process.

LO8 Discuss three ethical issues in organizational change.

Suncor Energy Inc. was one of the pioneers in the commercial development of Northern Alberta's vast oil sands. Today, Suncor continues to be one of its leading developers and innovators. When Rick George assumed the CEO job in 1991 he shared an inspiring strategic vision for the financially troubled company: "To be a successful sustainable energy company." George describes his approach to organizational change: "There are three or four hundred oil companies in this town and they tend to move in a herd. But I often say that if you ever see that whole herd move in one direction, you'd better look somewhere else because the money usually is being made in a different direction."

Suncor has successfully transformed itself into one of Canada's most diversified energy companies, producing more than 280,000 barrels of oil per day from its oil sands operations, developing and producing natural gas, operating an ethanol plant and refinery in Ontario, a refinery in Colorado, operating Sunoco retail service stations in Ontario, as well as operating wind power projects in Saskatchewan, Alberta, and Ontario.

Suncor's focus on renewable energy and environmentally conscious practices may appear to be in sharp contrast to the negative environmental image that has plagued the Fort McMurray megaproject over the years. At Suncor, values of sustainability and accountability are driving forces behind initiatives including pursuing renewable energy projects, aggressive reductions in greenhouse gas emissions, and planting millions of trees in reclaimed oil sands mining sites. Suncor recently received international recognition by Ethisphere Magazine as one of the world's most ethical companies and was awarded first place in the oil and gas category of *The Globe and Mail's Report on Business Magazine*'s corporate social responsibility ranking.

But at Suncor, the next compelling vision is already being communicated and shared with employees through a fun and award-winning series of meetings titled "Suncor's Oil Sands: The Next Generation Sessions." The face-to-face sessions give employees a "stronger voice in the operations," which showcase the operation's $20.6 billion growth plans for its massive Voyageur project that include new facilities and thousands of new employees. CEO Rick George is also building support for Suncor's vision with external stakeholders. In his "View from 2020" presentation, George lays out an inspiring vision for the future of Suncor, its employees, and stakeholders where "oil production in northern Alberta is expected to quadruple to more than 4 million barrels a day."[1]

Suncor has become one of Canada's most successful energy companies through an adaptive culture that supports continuous change.
The Canadian Press (Larry MacDougal)

Change is difficult enough in small firms. At Suncor and other large organizations, it requires monumental effort and persistence. Organizational change is also very messy. As we will describe throughout this chapter, the challenge of change is not so much in deciding which way to go; the challenge is in the execution of this strategy. Change agents need to bring employees on board, by developing their abilities, role perceptions, and motivation to act more consistently with the desired initiatives. This chapter begins by introducing Lewin's model of change and its component parts. This includes sources of resistance to change, ways to minimize this resistance, and stabilizing desired behaviours. Next, this chapter examines three approaches to organizational change—action research, appreciative inquiry, and parallel learning structures. The last section of this chapter considers both cross-cultural and ethical issues in organizational change.

LEWIN'S FORCE FIELD ANALYSIS MODEL

 LO1

force field analysis
Kurt Lewin's model of system-wide change that helps change agents diagnose the forces that drive and restrain proposed organizational change.

Social psychologist Kurt Lewin developed the force field analysis model to explain how the change process works (see Exhibit 15.1).[2] Although developed more than 50 years ago, recent reviews conclude that Lewin's **force field analysis** model remains one of the most widely respected ways of viewing this process.[3]

One side of the force field model represents the *driving forces* that push organizations toward a new state of affairs. These might include new competitors or technologies, evolving workforce expectations, or a host of other environmental changes. Corporate leaders also produce driving forces even when external forces for change aren't apparent. For instance, some experts call for "divine discontent" as a key feature of successful organizations, meaning that leaders continually urge employees to strive for higher standards or new innovations even when the company outshines the competition.

unfreezing
The first part of the change process whereby the change agent produces disequilibrium between the driving and restraining forces.

The other side of Lewin's model represents the *restraining forces* that maintain the status quo. These restraining forces are commonly called "resistance to change" because they appear as employee behaviours that block the change process. Stability occurs when the driving and restraining forces are roughly in equilibrium, that is, they are of approximately equal strength in opposite directions.

Lewin's force field model emphasizes that effective change occurs by **unfreezing** the current situation, moving to a desired condition, and then **refreezing** the system so that it remains in this desired state. Unfreezing involves producing disequilibrium between

refreezing
The latter part of the change process in which systems and conditions are introduced that reinforce and maintain the desired behaviours.

EXHIBIT 15.1   Lewin's force field analysis model

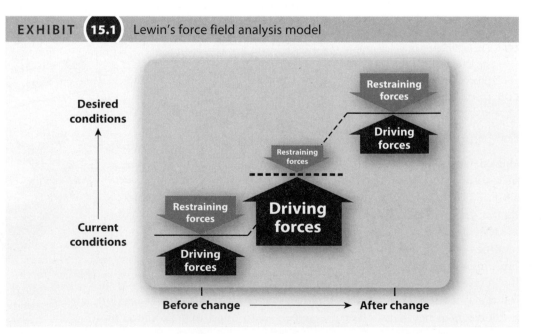

the driving and restraining forces. As we will describe later, this may occur by increasing the driving forces, reducing the restraining forces, or having a combination of both. Refreezing occurs when the organization's systems and structures are aligned with the desired behaviours. They must support and reinforce the new role patterns and prevent the organization from slipping back into the old way of doing things. Over the next few pages, we use Lewin's model to understand why change is blocked and how the process can evolve more smoothly.

RESTRAINING FORCES

Robert Nardelli pushed hard to transform Home Depot from a loose configuration of fiefdoms to a more performance-oriented operation with centralized buying power and customer experience consistency. Change did occur at the world's largest home improvement retailer, but at a price. A large number of talented managers and employees left the company and some of those remaining continued to resent Nardelli's transformation. Disenchanted staff referred to the company as "Home Despot" because the changes took away their autonomy. Others named it "Home GEpot," a cutting reference to the large number of former GE executives that Nardelli hired into top positions. After five years, the Home Depot board decided to replace Nardelli, partly because he made some unsuccessful strategic decisions and partly because of the after-effects of Nardelli's changes.[4]

Robert Nardelli, who is now CEO of Chrysler, experienced plenty of *resistance to change* when at Home Depot. Resistance to change takes many forms, ranging from overt work stoppages to subtle attempts to continue the "old ways." A recent study of employees at two Canadian banks reported that subtle resistance is much more common than overt resistance. Some bank staff avoided the desired changes by moving into different jobs. Others continued to perform tasks the old way as long as management didn't notice. Even when employees complied with the planned changes, they engaged in resistance by performing their work without corresponding cognitive or emotional support for the change.[5] In other words, they resisted by communicating nonverbally (and sometimes verbally!) to customers that they disliked the changes forced upon them. Some experts point out that these subtle forms of resistance create the greatest obstacles to change because they are not as visible. In the words of one manager: "[Change efforts] never die because of direct confrontation. Direct confrontation you can work with because it is known. Rather, they die a death of a thousand cuts. People and issues you never confront drain the life out of important [initiatives] and result in solutions that simply do not have the performance impact that they should have."[6]

John Thompson experienced this subtle resistance to change soon after he became CEO of Symantec Corporation. To reduce costs, Thompson suggested that the computer cable included in all Symantec software packages was an unnecessary expense because most customers already owned these cables. Everyone at the cost-cutting meeting agreed that the cables should no longer be shipped with the software, but would be provided free to customers who requested them. Yet several weeks later Thompson discovered that computer cables were still being shipped with the software, so he reminded the executive responsible that the team only makes these decisions once. "If you've got a disagreement or a point of view, bring it up when we're going through the discussion," Thompson advised the executive. "Don't hold back and give me this smiley kind of benign agreement. Go back and get it fixed. We're not shipping cables any more."[7]

Employee Resistance as a Resource for Change   Although Symantec's CEO was probably frustrated by the executive's passive resistance to change, change agents need to realize that resistance is a common and natural human response. As Canadian-born economist John Kenneth Galbraith once quipped: "In the choice between changing one's mind and proving there's no need to do so, most people get busy on the proof!"[8] Even when people do support change, they typically assume that it is others—not themselves—who need to change. The problem, however, isn't so much that resistance to change exists. The main problem is that change agents typically view resistance as an unreasonable, dysfunctional, and irrational response to a desirable initiative. They often form an "us versus them" perspective without considering that the causes of resistance may, in fact, be traced back to their own actions or inaction.[9]

The emerging view among change management experts is that resistance to change needs to be seen as a resource, rather than as an impediment to change. First, resistance incidents are symptoms of deeper problems in the change process. They are signals that the change agent has not sufficiently addressed the underlying conditions that support effective organizational change.[10] In some situations, employees may be worried about the *consequences* of change, such as how the new conditions will take away their power and status. In other situations, employees show resistance because of concerns about the *process* of change itself, such as the effort required to break old habits and learn new skills.

Second, resistance should be recognized as a form of constructive conflict. As we learned in Chapter 11, constructive conflict can potentially improve decision making, including identifying better ways to improve the organization's success. However, constructive conflict is typically accompanied by dysfunctional relationship conflict. This appears to be the case when change agents see resistance to change as an impediment rather than resource. They describe the people who resist as the problem, whereas their focus should be understanding the reasons why they resist. Thus, by viewing resistance as a form of constructive conflict, change agents may be able to improve the change strategy or change process.

Finally, resistance should be viewed in the context of justice and motivation. Resistance is a form of voice so, as was described in Chapter 5, it potentially improves procedural justice. By redirecting initial forms of resistance into constructive conversations, change agents can increase employee feelings of fairness. Furthermore, resistance is motivational; it potentially engages people to think about the change strategy and process. Change agents can harness that motivational force to ultimately strengthen commitment to the change initiative.

LO2   **Why Employees Resist Change**   Change management experts have developed a long list of reasons why people do not embrace change.[11] Many of these reasons relate to a lack of motivation, such as when employees estimate that the negative consequences that the change might impose on them outweigh the benefits. Another factor is the inability to change due to lack of inadequate skills and knowledge. Employees also resist change unwittingly because they lack a sufficiently clear understanding about what is expected of them (i.e., lack of role clarity). Six of the most commonly cited reasons why people resist change are summarized below.[12] GLOBAL Connections 15.1 describes how some of these sources of resistance existed at the FBI in spite of clear evidence that the U.S. law enforcement agency needed to develop a new mandate.

- *Direct costs*—People tend to block actions that result in higher direct costs or lower benefits than the existing situation. GLOBAL Connections 15.1 describes how some FBI managers likely resisted the bureau's new intelligence mandate because it would necessarily remove some of their resources, personal status, and career opportunities.

- *Saving face*—Some people resist change as a political strategy to "prove" that the decision is wrong or that the person encouraging change is incompetent. This not-invented-here syndrome is widespread, according to change experts. Says one consultant: "Unless they're scared enough to listen, they'll never forgive you for being right and for knowing something they don't."[13]

- *Fear of the unknown*—People resist change out of worry that they cannot adjust to the new work requirements. This fear of the unknown increases the *risk* of personal loss. For example, even if many FBI managers and professionals recognized that the agency should change its mandate, they likely were reluctant to push these changes forward because it is difficult to anticipate how this mandate would affect them personally.

global connections 15.1

The FBI Meets Its Own Resistance

In 1993, following the first terrorist attacks on the World Trade Center in New York City, the U.S. Federal Bureau of Investigation (FBI) was given a new mandate: refocus from a reactive law-enforcement agency (solving crimes) to a proactive domestic intelligence agency (preventing terrorism). Eight years later, the FBI was still mainly a crime investigation organization with limited intelligence gathering capabilities. This failure to change was identified as a factor in the FBI's inability to prevent terrorist attacks in 2001 on those buildings as well as the Pentagon and other planned sites. One government report even stated that the FBI (as well as the CIA) "seem to be working harder and harder just to maintain a status quo that is increasingly irrelevant to the new challenges."

One source of resistance, according to government reports, is that FBI employees and managers are unable or unwilling to change because solving crimes (rather than intelligence gathering) is burned into their mindset, routines, career paths, and decentralized structure. Most FBI field managers were trained in law enforcement, so they continue to give preferential treatment and resources to enforcement than terrorist prevention initiatives.

Even if FBI leaders were motivated to become more focused on intelligence gathering, the organization's systems and structures undermine these initiatives. The FBI has been a decentralized organization, where field agents operate without much orchestration from headquarters. Until recently, the FBI also lacked a secure centralized information system (in fact, most of its records were still paper-based), which is essential for intelligence work but less important for criminal investigations. Furthermore, information is so closely guarded further down the ranks (called "close holds") that an information access barrier called "the wall" isolates FBI intelligence officers from the mainstream criminal investigation

The FBI experienced many sources of resistance in its mandate of transforming from a reactive law enforcement agency into a proactive domestic intelligence agency. © *AP Images/Brennan Linsley*

staff. Overall, these structural characteristics effectively scuttled any attempt to transform the FBI into an intelligence agency.

Finally, resistance to change was likely due in part to an historical rivalry between the FBI and Central Intelligence Agency (CIA). Raising the profile and legitimacy of intelligence gathering at the FBI would have acknowledged that the CIA's work was valuable, so some FBI leaders and staff were reluctant to move in that direction.

The FBI is now making concerted steps to address these barriers to change. But John Miller, the FBI's assistant director of the office of public affairs, admits that the FBI continues to face challenges. "The FBI has no corner on the market of people being resistant to change," he says. "We don't recruit people from Planet Perfect; we recruit human beings."[14]

- *Breaking routines*—The organizational learning perspective introduced in Chapter 1 emphasizes the need to bring in new knowledge, but it also recognizes the need to *unlearn*. This means that employees need to abandon habits and routines that are no longer appropriate. Unfortunately, people like to stay within comfort zones, and typically resist initiatives that force them out of those comfort zones and require investing time and energy learning new role patterns. This is consistent with a recent survey in which most employees admitted they don't follow through with organizational changes because they "like to keep things the way they are" or the changes seem to be too complicated or time wasting.[15] For example, FBI agents were accustomed to working independently on investigations, so it would be a challenge for them to engage in more information sharing and collaboration across teams and departments.

- *Incongruent organizational systems*—Rewards, information systems, patterns of authority, career paths, selection criteria, and other systems and structures are both friends and foes of organizational change. When properly aligned, they reinforce desired behaviours. Unfortunately, the FBI and many other organizations fail to realign these systems to reinforce the change initiative. The result is that even enthusiastic employees lose momentum after failing to overcome the structural confines of the past.

- *Incongruent team dynamics*—Teams develop and enforce conformity to a set of norms that guide behaviour. However, conformity to existing team norms may discourage employees from accepting organizational change. Team norms that conflict with the desired changes need to be altered.

UNFREEZING, CHANGING, AND REFREEZING

According to Lewin's force field analysis model, effective change occurs by unfreezing the current situation, moving to a desired condition, and then refreezing the system so that it remains in this desired state. Unfreezing occurs when the driving forces are stronger than the restraining forces. This happens by making the driving forces stronger, weakening or removing the restraining forces, or a combination of both.

With respect to the first option, driving forces must increase enough to motivate change. Change rarely occurs by increasing driving forces alone, however, because the restraining forces often adjust to counterbalance the driving forces. It is rather like the coils of a mattress. The harder corporate leaders push for change, the stronger the restraining forces push back. This antagonism threatens the change effort by producing tension and conflict within the organization. The preferred option is to both increase the driving forces and reduce or remove the restraining forces. Increasing the driving forces creates an urgency for change, whereas reducing the restraining forces minimizes resistance to change.

CREATING AN URGENCY FOR CHANGE

Most organizations these days operate in a rapidly changing external environment. These environmental changes represent the driving forces that motivate people to face the risks that change creates. In many organizations, however, corporate leaders buffer employees from the external environment to such an extent that these driving forces are hardly felt below the top executive level. The result is that employees don't understand why they need to change, and leaders are surprised when their change initiatives do not have much effect.

Chrysler Plant Manager Communicates the Urgency for Change

Chrysler Corporation's initial attempt to create a team-based organizational structure at its Belvidere assembly plant met with stiff resistance. "There is a need to change," says plant manager Kurt Kavajecz. The problem, he explains, is that employees didn't see the need for change. They knew that "we build cars pretty well.... So why do we have to change?" To develop a stronger urgency for change, Kavajecz told employees about the challenges the company faces. "If you show them what's going on in the industry, if you give them the information, the data on why we are changing, at the end of the presentation, they get it. They see that plants are closing and jobs are going away. We talk very openly about those things, and they understand why we're changing." The Chrysler plant eventually introduced team-based work.[16] *The Canadian Press (Paul Beaty)*

Thus, the change process must begin by ensuring employees develop an urgency for change, and this typically occurs by informing them about competitors, changing consumer trends, impending government regulations, and other driving forces in the external environment.[17] "When a company is doing poorly, people are more likely to dig in together if they understand the situation," says Robert Meggy, CEO of Vancouver-based Great Little Box Co. "In every case of bankruptcy I've been aware of, the employees had no idea what was happening. If they'd known, I don't think they would have let it happen. I never see a downside to sharing information."[18]

Some companies fuel the urgency to change by putting employees in direct contact with customers. Dissatisfied customers represent a compelling driving force for change because of the adverse consequences for the organization's survival and success. Customers also provide a human element that further energizes employees to change current behaviour patterns.[19]

Executives at Shell Europe applied customer-driven change when they discovered that middle managers seemed blissfully unaware that Shell wasn't achieving either its financial goals or customer needs. So, to create an urgency for change, the European managers were loaded onto buses and taken out to talk with customers and employees who work with customers every day. "We called these 'bus rides.' The idea was to encourage people to think back from the customer's perspective rather than from the head office," explains Shell Europe's vice-president of retailing. "The bus rides were difficult for a lot of people who, in their work history, had hardly ever had to talk to a customer and find out what was good and not so good about Shell from the customer's standpoint."[20]

Creating an Urgency for Change without External Forces   Exposing employees to external forces can strengthen the urgency for change, but leaders often need to begin the change process before problems come knocking at the company's door. "You want to create a burning platform for change even when there isn't a need for one," says Steve Bennett, CEO of financial software company Intuit.[21] Creating an urgency for change when the organization is riding high requires a lot of persuasive influence that helps employees visualize future competitive threats and environmental shifts.

For instance, Apple Computer's iPod dominates the digital music market, but Steve Jobs wants the company to be its own toughest competitor. Just when sales of the iPod Mini were soaring, Jobs challenged a gathering of 100 top executives and engineers to develop a better product to replace it. "Playing it safe is the most dangerous thing we can do," Jobs warned. Nine months later, the company launched the iPod Nano, which replaced the still-popular iPod Mini before competitors could offer a better alternative.[22]

Experts warn, however, that employees may see this burning platform strategy as manipulative, which produces cynicism to change and undermines trust in the change agent.[23] Also, the urgency for change does not always need to be initiated from a problem-oriented perspective. Instead, as we will describe later in this chapter, effective change agents can adopt a positive orientation by championing a vision of a more appealing future state. By creating a future vision of a better organization, leaders effectively make the current situation less appealing. When the vision connects to employee values and needs, it can be a motivating force for change even when external "problems" are not strong.

LO3   ## REDUCING THE RESTRAINING FORCES

Employee resistance is a resource for change. Still, its underlying causes need to be addressed. As the mattress coils metaphor indicated earlier, it is not enough to increase the driving forces because employees may just push back. Exhibit 15.2 summarizes six strategies to address the sources of employee resistance. If feasible, communication, learning, employee involvement, and stress management should be attempted first.[24] However, negotiation and coercion are necessary for people who will clearly lose something from the change and when the speed of change is critical.

EXHIBIT 15.2   Strategies to minimize resistance to change

Strategy	Example	When Applied	Problems
Communication	Customer complaint letters shown to employees.	When employees don't feel an urgency for change, or don't know how the change will affect them.	Time-consuming and potentially costly.
Learning	Employees learn how to work in teams as company adopts a team-based structure.	When employees need to break old routines and adopt new role patterns.	Time-consuming and potentially costly.
Employee Involvement	Company forms task force to recommend new customer service practices.	When the change effort needs more employee commitment, some employees need to save face, and/or employee ideas would improve decisions about the change strategy.	Very time-consuming. Might also lead to conflict and poor decisions if employees' interests are incompatible with organizational needs.
Stress Management	Employees attend sessions to discuss their worries about the change.	When communication, training, and involvement do not sufficiently ease employee worries.	Time-consuming and potentially expensive. Some methods may not reduce stress for all employees.
Negotiation	Employees agree to replace strict job categories with multiskilling in return for increased job security.	When employees will clearly lose something of value from the change and would not otherwise support the new conditions. Also necessary when the company must change quickly.	May be expensive, particularly if other employees want to negotiate their support. Also tends to produce compliance but not commitment to the change.
Coercion	Company president tells managers to "get on board" the change or leave.	When other strategies are ineffective and the company needs to change quickly.	Can lead to more subtle forms of resistance, as well as long-term antagonism with the change agent.

Sources: Adapted from J. P. Kotter and L. A. Schlesinger, "Choosing Strategies for Change," *Harvard Business Review* 57 (1979), pp. 106–14; P. R. Lawrence, "How to Deal With Resistance to Change," *Harvard Business Review* (May–June 1954), pp. 49–57.

Communication   As GLOBAL Connections 15.1 described earlier, the FBI experienced a high level of resistance to changing into an intelligence gathering organization. One of the first strategies the FBI leaders are now applying to address that resistance is to communicate in every way possible and to as many audiences as possible that the FBI must change, why it must change, and what the new bureau will look like. "The word is out. Terrorism is the No. 1 priority, and intelligence is what the bureau is about," says former assistant attorney general Paul R. Corts, who has worked closely with the FBI during the change process. "You've got to say it, say it, and say it again."

Communication is the highest priority and first strategy required for any organizational change.[25] Communication improves the change process in at least two ways. First, as was mentioned earlier, leaders develop an urgency to change by candidly telling employees about the driving forces for change. Whether through town hall meetings with senior management or by directly meeting with disgruntled customers, employees become energized to change. Second, communication can potentially reduce fear of the unknown. The more corporate leaders communicate their images of the future, the more easily employees can visualize their own role in that future. This effort may also begin the process of adjusting team norms to be more consistent with the new reality.

Learning   Learning is an important process in most change initiatives because employees require new knowledge and skills to fit the organization's evolving requirements. The FBI is now addressing past resistance to change through heavy investment in training staff in counterterrorism and counter-intelligence. Hundreds of FBI executives have also been sent to week-long courses to learn how to coach employees during the change process. Coaching and other forms of learning are time consuming, but they help employees break routines by learning new role patterns.

Employee Involvement   Unless the change must occur quickly or employee interests are highly incompatible with the organization's needs, employee involvement is almost an essential part of the change process. Rather than viewing themselves as agents of someone else's decision, employees feel personally responsible for the success of the change effort.[27] Involvement also minimizes problems of saving face and fear of the unknown. Furthermore, the complexity of today's work environment demands that more people provide ideas regarding the best direction of the change effort.

Supporting the change process through employee involvement is also possible in large organizations. **Future search** conferences (and a similar process called *open space technology*) "put the entire system in the room," meaning that they try to involve as many employees and other stakeholders as possible associated with the organizational system.[28] These multi-day events ask participants to identify trends or issues and establish strategic solutions for those conditions. Every five years, Whole Foods Market gathers together several hundred employees, shoppers, and shareholders for a future search meeting to help identify new directions for the food retailer. Several Canadian school boards have conducted future search conferences, including the Ottawa-Carleton School Board, Toronto School Board, and Lester B. Pearson School Board. The Canadian Nature Federation also held a future search event to assist the change process.[29]

IKEA held a three-day future search event involving more than four dozen stakeholders, including the company president, product design staff, sales and distribution staff, information technology, retail managers, suppliers from three countries, and six customers. The Swedish furniture company, which was growing rapidly, wanted to "build a quicker, leaner, and simpler" pipeline for its product development and distribution. Focusing on a single product (the Ektorp sofa), participants overcame the immense complexity of the system, the language barriers (for most, English was a second language), and apprehension and suspicions about change to map out a new product development process. One year later, IKEA launched a new sofa line (the Fixhult) based on further iterations of the process designed in the future search workshop.[30]

Future search meetings and similar large-group change events potentially minimize resistance to change and assist the quality of the change process, but they also have limitations.[31] One problem is that involving so many people invariably limits the opportunity to contribute and increases the risk that a few people will dominate the process. Another concern is that these events focus on finding common ground, which may prevent the participants from discovering substantive differences that interfere with future

> **future search**
> System-wide group sessions, usually lasting a few days, in which participants identify trends and identify ways to adapt to those changes.

progress. A third issue is that these events generate high expectations about an ideal future state that are difficult to satisfy in practice. Employees become even more cynical and resistant to change if they do not see meaningful decisions and actions resulting from these meetings.

Stress Management   Organizational change is a stressful experience for many people because it threatens self-esteem and creates uncertainty about the future.[32] Communication, learning, and employee involvement can reduce some of these stressors. However, research indicates that companies also need to introduce stress management practices to help employees cope with the changes.[33] In particular, stress management minimizes resistance by removing some of the direct costs and fear of the unknown of the change process. Stress also saps energy, so minimizing stress potentially increases employee motivation to support the change process.

Negotiation   As long as people resist change, organizational change strategies will require some influence tactics. Negotiation is a form of influence that involves the promise of benefits or resources in exchange for the target person's compliance with influencer's request. This strategy potentially activates those who would otherwise lose out from the change. However, it merely gains compliance rather than commitment to the change effort, so it might not be effective in the long term.

Coercion   If all else fails, leaders rely on coercion to change organizations. Coercion can include persistently reminding people of their obligations, frequently monitoring behaviour to ensure compliance, confronting people who do not change, and using threats of sanctions to force compliance. Replacing people who will not support the change is an extreme step, but it is fairly common in senior management ranks.

For example, Baycrest Centre for Geriatric Care in Toronto recently began a major transformation to a more values-based caring and respectful (rather than just technically competent) workplace. Unfortunately, as with many deep change efforts, some people were unable or unwilling to support the change process. "We're turning over the rocks and a lot of worms are crawling out," says Joy Richards, Baycrest's vice-president of nursing and ambulatory and outreach services. "Some staff were not performing up to standard. Some of the clinical leadership was not interested in engaging with the nurses.... Half of my leadership group has turned over in the last year," admits Richards. "It's not easy and it's not fun. Things get ugly before they get better," she says of the change process.[34]

Replacing staff is a radical form of organizational unlearning because replacing executives removes knowledge of the organization's past routines. This potentially opens up opportunities for new practices to take hold.[35] At the same time, coercion is a risky strategy because survivors (employees who do not leave) may have less trust in corporate leaders and engage in more political tactics to protect their own job security.

REFREEZING THE DESIRED CONDITIONS

Unfreezing and changing behaviour patterns won't result in lasting change. People are creatures of habit, so they easily slip back into past patterns. Therefore, leaders need to refreeze the new behaviours by realigning organizational systems and team dynamics with the desired changes.[36] For instance, recall that the FBI experienced resistance to change because organizational structures interfered with the desired future of intelligence gathering. Now, change is not only occurring, it is being institutionalized through new systems and structures. New career paths have been established for intelligence officers rather than only for criminal investigation agents. The compensation system has been redesigned to reward staff who succeed in intelligence work rather than just criminal investigations. The FBI is also slowly developing information systems so agents can share knowledge quickly with each other and with other agencies.

CHANGE AGENTS, STRATEGIC VISIONS, AND DIFFUSING CHANGE

Kurt Lewin's force field analysis model is a useful template to explain the dynamics of organizational change. But it overlooks three other ingredients in effective change processes: change agents, strategic visions, and diffusing change.

CHANGE AGENTS AND STRATEGIC VISIONS

change agent
Anyone who possesses enough knowledge and power to guide and facilitate the change effort.

Every successful change requires a change agent who communicates an appealing vision of the desired future state.[37] A **change agent** is anyone who possesses enough knowledge and power to guide and facilitate the change effort. Change agents come in different forms, and more than one person is often required to serve these different roles.[38] Transformational leaders are the primary agents of change because they form a vision of the desired future state, communicate that vision in ways that are meaningful to others, behave in ways that are consistent with the vision, and build commitment to the vision.[39] A strategic vision is particularly important in the change process because it provides a sense of direction and establishes the critical success factors against which the real changes are evaluated. It also minimizes employee fear of the unknown and provides a better understanding about what behaviours employees must learn for the future state.

LO4

DIFFUSION OF CHANGE

Change agents often test the transformation process with a pilot project, and then diffuse what has been learned from this experience to other parts of the organization. Unlike centralized, system-wide changes, pilot projects are more flexible and less risky.[40] The pilot project approach also makes it easier to select organizational groups that are most ready for change, which increases the pilot project's success.

But how do we ensure that the change process started in the pilot project is adopted by other segments of the organization? The MARS model introduced in Chapter 2 offers a useful template to organize the answer to this question. First, employees are more likely to adopt the practices of a pilot project when they are motivated to do so.[41] This occurs when they see that the pilot project is successful and people in the pilot project receive recognition and rewards for changing their previous work practices. Diffusion

Leadership Missing from BC Ferries Safety Change

In 1997, BC Ferries adopted the International Maritime Organization's Safety Management System (SMS), a code of conduct that carefully assigns responsibility for safety and environmental issues across the organization. A decade later, an external evaluation concluded that although BC Ferries demonstrates high commitment to operational safety, the SMS code was not practised uniformly across the organization. Former British Columbia Auditor-General George Morfitt, who conducted the evaluation, concluded that the lack of change was partly due to poor leadership of the change process. "Some believe that not all senior operating staff [management] have 'bought into' the SMS," wrote Morfitt. Furthermore, he noted that "not all masters have embraced the SMS and are therefore not effectively promoting it." If some BC Ferries leaders and ship masters do not champion the safety management system, employees are less likely to follow the SMS guidelines. "BC Ferries staff have to see and believe that management stands behind the safety management system and is willing to commit the time and resources to ensuring that the system is operating efficiently and effectively across the organization," Morfitt explains.[42] *The Canadian Press (Chuck Stoody)*

also requires supervisor support and reinforcement of the desired behaviours. More generally, change agents need to minimize the sources of resistance to change that we discussed earlier in this chapter.

Second, employees must have the ability—the required skills and knowledge—to adopt the practices introduced in the pilot project. According to innovation diffusion studies, people adopt ideas more readily when they have an opportunity to interact and learn from others who have already applied the new practices.[43] Thus, pilot projects get diffused when employees in the original pilot are dispersed to other work units as role models and knowledge sources.

Third, pilot projects get diffused when employees have clear role perceptions; that is, they understand how the practices in a pilot project apply to them even though in a completely different functional area. For instance, accounting department employees won't easily recognize how they can adopt quality improvement practices developed by employees in the production department. The challenge here is for change agents to provide guidance that is neither too specific, because it might not seem relevant to other areas of the organization, nor too abstract, because this makes the instructions too vague. Finally, employees require supportive situational factors, including the resources and time necessary to adopt the practices demonstrated in the pilot project.

THREE APPROACHES TO ORGANIZATIONAL CHANGE

So far, this chapter has examined the dynamics of change that occur every day in organizations. However, organizational change agents and consultants also apply various approaches to organizational change. This section introduces three of the leading approaches to organizational change: action research, appreciative inquiry, and parallel learning structures.

LO5

ACTION RESEARCH APPROACH

action research
A problem-focused change process that combines action orientation (changing attitudes and behaviour) and research orientation (testing theory through data collection and analysis).

Along with introducing the force field model, Kurt Lewin recommended an **action research** approach to the change process. Action research takes the view that meaningful change is a combination of action-orientation (changing attitudes and behaviour) and research orientation (testing theory).[44] On the one hand, the change process needs to be action-oriented because the ultimate goal is to bring about change. An action orientation involves diagnosing current problems and applying interventions that resolve those problems. On the other hand, the change process is a research study because change agents apply a conceptual framework (such as team dynamics or organizational culture) to a real situation. As with any good research, the change process involves collecting data to diagnose problems more effectively and to systematically evaluate how well the theory works in practice.[45]

Within this dual framework of action and research, the action research approach adopts an open systems view. It recognizes that organizations have many interdependent parts, so change agents need to anticipate both the intended and unintended consequences of their interventions. Action research is also a highly participative process because open systems change requires both the knowledge and commitment of members within that system. Indeed, employees are essentially co-researchers as well as participants in the intervention. Overall, action research is a data-based, problem-oriented process that diagnoses the need for change, introduces the intervention, and then evaluates and stabilizes the desired changes. The main phases of action research are illustrated in Exhibit 15.3 and described below:[46]

1. *Form client-consultant relationship.*—Action research usually assumes that the change agent originates outside the system (such as a consultant), so the process begins by forming the client-consultant relationship. Consultants need to determine the client's readiness for change, including whether people are motivated to participate in the process, are open to meaningful change, and possess the abilities to complete the process.

The image shows handwritten text "Krow" or similar signature.

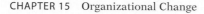

EXHIBIT 15.3   The action research process

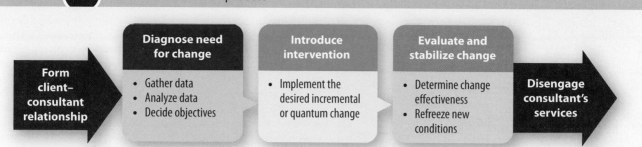

2. *Diagnose the need for change*—Action research is a problem-oriented activity that carefully diagnoses the problem through systematic analysis of the situation. Organizational diagnosis identifies the appropriate direction for the change effort by gathering and analyzing data about an ongoing system, such as through interviews and surveys of employees and other stakeholders. Organizational diagnosis also includes employee involvement in agreeing on the appropriate change method, the schedule for these actions, and the expected standards of successful change.

3. *Introduce intervention*—This stage in the action research model applies one or more actions to correct the problem. It may include any of the prescriptions mentioned in this textbook, such as building more effective teams, managing conflict, building a better organizational structure, or changing the corporate culture. An important issue is how quickly the changes should occur.[47] Some experts recommend *incremental change* in which the organization fine-tunes the system and takes small steps toward a desired state. Others claim that *quantum change* is often required, in which the system is overhauled decisively and quickly. Quantum change is usually traumatic to employees and offers little opportunity for correction. But incremental change is also risky when the organization is seriously misaligned with its environment, thereby threatening its survival.

4. *Evaluate and stabilize change*—Action research recommends evaluating the effectiveness of the intervention against the standards established in the diagnostic stage. Unfortunately, even when these standards are clearly stated, the effectiveness of an intervention might not be apparent for several years, or might be difficult to separate from other factors. If the activity has the desired effect, then the change agent and participants need to stabilize the new conditions. This refers to the refreezing process that was described earlier. Rewards, information systems, team norms, and other conditions are redesigned so that they support the new values and behaviours.

The action research approach has dominated organizational change thinking ever since it was introduced in the 1940s. However, some experts complain that the problem-oriented nature of action research—in which something is wrong that must be fixed—focuses on the negative dynamics of the group or system rather than its positive opportunities and potential. This concern with action research has led to the development of a more positive approach to organizational change, called appreciative inquiry.[48]

APPRECIATIVE INQUIRY APPROACH

appreciative inquiry
An organizational change strategy that directs the group's attention away from its own problems and focuses participants on the group's potential and positive elements.

Appreciative inquiry tries to break out of the problem-solving mentality of traditional change management practices by reframing relationships around the positive and the possible. It searches for organizational (or team) strengths and capabilities, then adapts or applies that knowledge for further success and well-being. Appreciative inquiry is therefore deeply grounded in the emerging philosophy of *positive organizational behaviour,*

Canadian Tire's Appreciative Journey

After effectively battling the American juggernauts Wal-Mart and Home Depot over the past decade, Canadian Tire's executive team wanted to hear from employees and store-owners about what makes the Canadian hardware and auto parts retailer so successful, then rebuild its core values around those positive experiences. Appreciative inquiry played an important role in this re-visioning process. Internal consultants conducted detailed interviews with 377 staff across the organization, asking each to describe occasions where they felt Canadian Tire was working at its best and what they value most about the company. Some people described the excitement of holiday season where products are flying out the door. Others recalled the teamwork of employees volunteering to work late to clean up a store after a major delivery. These appreciative incidents were organized around six team values (owners, driven, accountable, etc.), which the executive team discussed and affirmed. Canadian Tire then held a one-day conference in which middle and senior management developed a common understanding of these values. Next, store managers discussed the six team values with their staff and participated in an appreciative exercise in which employees visualized a good news story about Canadian Tire's success.[49] *Charlottetown Guardian/The Canadian Press (Brian McInnis)*

which suggests that focusing on the positive rather than negative aspects of life will improve organizational success and individual well-being. In other words, this approach emphasizes building on strengths rather than trying to directly correct problems.[50]

Appreciative inquiry typically directs its inquiry toward successful events and successful organizations or work units. This external focus becomes a form of behavioural modelling, but it also increases open dialogue by redirecting the group's attention away from its own problems. Appreciative inquiry is especially useful when participants are aware of their "problems" or already suffer from enough negativity in their relationships. The positive orientation of appreciative inquiry enables groups to overcome these negative tensions and build a more hopeful perspective of their future by focusing on what is possible.[51]

LO6

The "Four-D" model of appreciative inquiry (named after its four stages) shown in Exhibit 15.4 begins with *discovery*—identifying the positive elements of the observed events or organization.[52] This might involve documenting positive customer experiences elsewhere in the organization. Or it might include interviewing members of another organization to discover its fundamental strengths. As participants discuss their findings, they shift into the *dreaming* stage by envisioning what might be possible in an ideal organization. By directing their attention to a theoretically ideal organization or situation, participants feel safer revealing their hopes and aspirations than if they were discussing their own organization or predicament.

As participants make their private thoughts public to the group, the process shifts into the third stage, called *designing*. Designing involves the process of dialogue, in which participants listen with selfless receptivity to each other's models and assumptions and eventually form a collective model for thinking within the team. In effect, they create a common image of what should be. As this model takes shape, group members shift the focus back to their own situation. In the final stage of appreciative inquiry, called *delivering*, participants establish specific objectives and direction for their own organization based on their model of what will be.

Appreciative inquiry was developed 20 years ago, but it really only gained popularity within the past few years. Several success stories of organizational change from appreciative inquiry have emerged in a variety of organizational settings, including Castrol Marine, Canadian Tire, AVON Mexico, American Express, Green Mountain Coffee Roasters, and Hunter Douglas.[53] At the same time, appreciative inquiry has not always been successful and experts warn that it is not always the best approach to changing teams or organizations. Specifically, it requires participants to have a mindset where

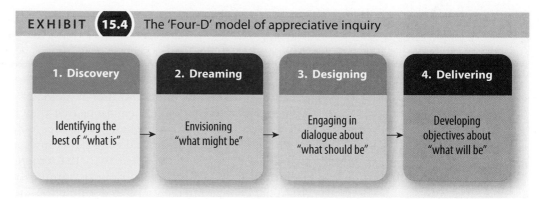

EXHIBIT 15.4   The 'Four-D' model of appreciative inquiry

1. Discovery	2. Dreaming	3. Designing	4. Delivering
Identifying the best of "what is"	Envisioning "what might be"	Engaging in dialogue about "what should be"	Developing objectives about "what will be"

Sources: Based on F. J. Barrett and D. L. Cooperrider, "Generative Metaphor Intervention: A New Approach for Working with Systems Divided by Conflict and Caught in Defensive Perception," *Journal of Applied Behavioural Science*, 26 (1990), p. 229; D. Whitney and C. Schau, "Appreciative Inquiry: An Innovative Process For Organization Change," *Employment Relations Today*, 25 (Spring 1998), pp. 11–21; J.M. Watkins and B.J. Mohr, *Appreciative Inquiry: Change at the Speed of Imagination* (San Francisco: Jossey-Bass, 2001), pp. 25, 42–45.

they are willing to let go of the problem-oriented approach, and where leaders are willing to accept appreciative inquiry's less structured process.[54] Another concern is that research has not yet examined the contingencies of this approach.[55] In other words, we don't yet know under what conditions appreciative inquiry is the best approach to organizational change, and under what conditions it is less effective. Overall, appreciative inquiry has much to offer the organizational change process, but we are just beginning to understand its potential and limitations.

LO7

PARALLEL LEARNING STRUCTURE APPROACH

parallel learning structure

Highly participative arrangements, composed of people from most levels of the organization who follow the action research model to produce meaningful organizational change.

Parallel learning structures are highly participative arrangements, composed of people from most levels of the organization who follow the action research model to produce meaningful organizational change. They are social structures developed alongside the formal hierarchy with the purpose of increasing the organization's learning.[56] Ideally, participants in parallel learning structures are sufficiently free from the constraints of the larger organization so they can more effectively solve organizational issues.

Royal Dutch/Shell relied on a parallel learning structure to introduce a more customer-focused organization.[57] Rather than try to change the entire organization at once, executives held week-long "retail boot camps" with six country teams of front-line people (e.g., gas station managers, truck drivers, marketing professionals). Participants learned about competitive trends in their regions and were taught powerful marketing tools to identify new opportunities. The teams then returned home to study their market and develop proposals for improvement. Four months later, boot camp teams returned for a second workshop where each proposal was critiqued by Royal/Dutch Shell executives. Each team had 60 days to put its ideas into action, then return for a third workshop to analyze what worked and what didn't. This parallel learning process did much more than introduce new marketing ideas. It created enthusiasm in participants that spread contagiously to their co-workers, including managers above them, when they returned to their home country.

CROSS-CULTURAL AND ETHICAL ISSUES IN ORGANIZATIONAL CHANGE

LO8

One significant concern with some organizational change interventions is that they originate in the United States and other Western countries and may conflict with cultural values in some other countries.[58] A few experts point out that this Western perspective of change is linear, such as in Lewin's force field model shown earlier. It also assumes that the change process is punctuated by tension and overt conflict. But these assumptions are incompatible with cultures that view change as a natural cyclical process with harmony and equilibrium as the objectives.[59] This dilemma suggests that we need to develop a more contingency-oriented perspective with respect to the cultural values of participants.

Some organizational change practices also face ethical issues.[60] One ethical concern is the risk of violating individual privacy rights. The action research model is built on the idea of collecting information from organizational members, yet this requires employees to provide personal information and emotions that they may not want to divulge.[61] A second ethical concern is that some change activities potentially increase management's power by inducing compliance and conformity in organizational members. For instance, action research is a system-wide activity that requires employee participation rather than allowing individuals to get involved voluntarily. A third concern is that some organizational change interventions undermine the individual's self-esteem. The unfreezing process requires participants to disconfirm their existing beliefs, sometimes including their own competence at certain tasks or interpersonal relations.

Organizational change is almost always more difficult than it initially seems. Yet, the dilemma is that most organizations operate in hyperfast environments that demand continuous and rapid adaptation. Organizations survive and gain competitive advantage by mastering the complex dynamics of moving people through the continuous process of change as quickly as the external environment is changing.

ORGANIZATIONAL BEHAVIOUR: THE JOURNEY CONTINUES

Nearly 100 years ago, American industrialist Andrew Carnegie said: "Take away my people, but leave my factories, and soon grass will grow on the factory floors. Take away my factories, but leave my people, and soon we will have a new and better factory." Carnegie's statement reflects the message woven throughout this textbook that organizations are not buildings, or machinery, or financial assets. Rather, they are the people in them. Organizations are human entities—full of life, sometimes fragile, always exciting.

CHAPTER SUMMARY

Lewin's force field analysis model states that all systems have driving and restraining forces. Change occurs through the process of unfreezing, changing, and refreezing. Unfreezing produces disequilibrium between the driving and restraining forces. Refreezing realigns the organization's systems and structures with the desired behaviours.

Restraining forces are manifested as employee resistance to change. Resistance to change should be viewed as a resource, not an inherent obstacle to change. The main reasons why people resist change are direct costs, saving face, fear of the unknown, breaking routines, incongruent organizational systems, and incongruent team dynamics. Resistance to change may be minimized by keeping employees informed about what to expect from the change effort (communicating); teach employees valuable skills for the desired future (learning); involve them in the change process; help employees cope with the stress of change; negotiate trade-offs with those who will clearly lose from the change effort; and use coercion (sparingly and as a last resort).

Organizational change also requires driving forces. This means that employees need to have an urgency for change by becoming aware of the environmental conditions that demand change in the organization. The change process also requires refreezing the new behaviours by realigning organizational systems and team dynamics with the desired changes. Every successful change also requires change agents with a clear, well-articulated vision of the desired future state. The change process also often applies a diffusion process in which change begins as a pilot project and eventually spreads to other areas of the organization.

Action research is a highly participative, open-systems approach to change management that combines an action-orientation (changing attitudes and behaviour) with research orientation (testing theory). It is a data-based, problem-oriented process that diagnoses the need for change, introduces the intervention, and then evaluates and stabilizes the desired changes.

Appreciative inquiry embraces the positive organizational behaviour philosophy by focusing participants on the positive and possible. It tries to break out of the problem-solving mentality that dominates organizational change through the action research model. The four stages of appreciative inquiry include discovery, dreaming, designing, and delivering. A third approach, called parallel learning structures, relies on social structures developed alongside the formal hierarchy with the purpose of increasing the organization's learning. They are highly participative arrangements, composed of people from most levels of the organization who follow the action research model to produce meaningful organizational change.

One significant concern is that organizational change theories developed with a Western cultural orientation potentially conflict with cultural values in some other countries. Also, organizational change practices can raise one or more ethical concerns, including increasing management's power over employees, threatening individual privacy rights, undermining individual self-esteem, and making clients dependent on the change consultant.

KEY TERMS

action research, p. 364

appreciative inquiry, p. 365

change agent, p. 363

force field analysis, p. 354

future search, p. 361

parallel learning structure, p. 367

refreezing, p. 354

unfreezing, p. 354

CRITICAL THINKING QUESTIONS

1. Chances are that the school you are attending is currently undergoing some sort of change to adapt more closely with its environment. Discuss the external forces that are driving these changes. What internal drivers for change also exist?

2. Use Lewin's force field analysis to describe the dynamics of organizational change at Suncor Energy Inc. (opening vignette to this chapter).

3. Employee resistance is a *symptom*, not a *problem*, in the change process. What are some of the real problems that may underlie employee resistance?

4. Senior management of a large multinational corporation is planning to restructure the organization. Currently, the organization is decentralized around geographical areas so that the executive responsible for each area has considerable autonomy over manufacturing and sales. The new structure will transfer power to the executives responsible for different product groups; the executives responsible for each geographic area will no longer be responsible for manufacturing in their area but will retain control over sales activities. Describe two types of resistance senior management might encounter from this organizational change.

5. Discuss the role of reward systems in organizational change. Specifically, identify where reward systems relate to Lewin's force field model and where they undermine the organizational change process.

6. Web Circuits is a Malaysian-based custom manufacturer for high-technology companies. Senior management wants to introduce lean management practices to reduce production costs and remain competitive. A consultant has recommended that the company start with a pilot project in one department and, when successful, diffuse these practices to other areas of the organization. Discuss the advantages of this recommendation and identify three ways (other than the pilot project's success) to make diffusion of the change effort more successful.

7. Suppose that you are vice-president of branch services at the Bank of Kelowna. You notice that several branches have consistently low customer service ratings even though there are no apparent differences in resources or staff characteristics. Describe an appreciative inquiry process in one of these branches that might help to overcome these problems.

8. This chapter suggests that some organizational change activities face ethical concerns. Yet, several consultants actively use these processes because they believe they benefit the organization and do less damage to employees than it seems on the surface. For example, some activities try to open up the employee's hidden area (such as the Johari Window described in Chapter 3) so that there is better mutual understanding with co-workers. Discuss this argument and identify where you think organizational change interventions should limit this process.

 CASE STUDY 15.1

The Excellent Employee

Mary Gander, Winona State University

Emily, who has the reputation of being an excellent worker, is a machine operator in a furniture manufacturing plant that has been growing at a rate of between 15 and 20 percent each year for the past decade. New additions have been built onto the plant, new plants opened in the region, workers hired, new product lines developed, lots of expansion, but with no significant change in overall approach to operations, plant layout, ways of managing workers, or in the design processes. Plant operations as well as organizational culture are rooted in traditional Western management practices and logic, based largely on the notion of mass production and economies of scale. Over the past four years, the company has been growing in number and variety of products produced and in market penetration, however, profitability has been flattening and showing signs of decline. As a result, management is beginning to focus on production operations (internal focus) rather than mainly focusing on new market strategies, new products, and new market segments (external focus), in developing their strategic plans. They hope to get manufacturing costs down, improve consistency of quality, and ability to meet delivery times better, while decreasing inventory and increasing flexibility.

One of several new programs initiated by management in this effort to improve flexibility and lower costs, was to get workers cross-trained. However, when a representative from Human Resources explained this program to Emily's supervisor, Jim, he reluctantly agreed to cross-train most of his workers, but NOT Emily.

Jim explained to the HR person that Emily works on a machine that is very complex and not easy to effectively operate. She has to "babysit" it much of the time. He has tried many workers on it, tried to train them, but Emily is the only one who can consistently get product through the machine that is within specification and still meet production schedules. When anyone else tries to operate the machine, which performs a key function in the manufacturing process, it either ends up being a big bottle neck or producing excessive waste, which creates a lot of trouble for Jim.

Jim goes on to explain that Emily knows this sophisticated and complicated machine inside and out, she has been running it for five years. She likes the challenge, she says it makes the day go by faster, too. She is meticulous in her work, a very skilled employee who really cares about the quality of her work. Jim told the HR person that he wished all of his workers were like Emily. In spite of the difficulty of running this machine, Emily can run it so well that product piles up at the next work station downstream in the production process, they can't keep up with her!

Jim was adamant about keeping Emily on this machine and not cross-training her. The HR person was frustrated. He could see Jim's point but he had to follow executive orders: "Get these people cross-trained."

Around the same period of time, a university student was doing a field study in the section of the plant where Emily worked and Emily was one of the workers he interviewed. Emily told the student that, in spite of the fact that the plant had some problems with employee morale and excessive employee turnover, she really liked working there. She liked the piece-rate pay system very much and hoped that she did not have to participate in the recent "Program of the Month," which was having operators learn each other's jobs. She told the student that it would just create more waste if they tried to have other employees run her machine. She told him that other employees had tried to learn how to operate her machine but couldn't do it as well as she could.

Emily seemed to take a special liking for the student and began to open up to him. She told him that her machine really didn't need to be so difficult and touchy to operate, with a couple of rather minor design changes in the machine and better maintenance, virtually anyone could run it. She had tried to explain this to her supervisor a couple of years ago but he just told her to "do her work and leave operations to the manufacturing engineers." She also said that, if workers up stream in the process would spend a little more time and care to keep the raw material in slightly tighter specifications, it would go through her machine much more easily and trouble-free, but that they were too focused on going fast and making more piece-rate pay. She expressed a lack of respect for the managers who couldn't see this and even joked about how "managers didn't know anything."

Discussion Questions

1. Identify the sources of resistance to change in this short case.

2. Discuss whether this resistance is justified or could be overcome.

3. Recommend ways to minimize resistance to change in this incident or in future incidents.

TEAM EXERCISE 15.2

Strategic Change Incidents

Purpose   This exercise is designed to help you identify strategies to facilitate organizational change in various situations.

Instructions
- *Step 1:* The instructor will place students into teams, and each team will be assigned one of the scenarios presented below.

- *Step 2:* Each team will diagnose its assigned scenario to determine the most appropriate set of change management practices. Where appropriate, these practices should (a) create an urgency to change, (b) minimize resistance to change, and (c) refreeze the situation to support the change initiative. Each of these scenarios is based on real events.

- *Step 3:* Each team will present and defend its change management strategy. Class discussion regarding the appropriateness and feasibility of each strategy will occur after all teams assigned the same scenario have presented. The instructor will then describe what the organizations actually did in these situations.

Scenario 1: Greener Telco

The board of directors at a large telephone company wants its executives to make the organization more environmentally friendly by encouraging employees to reduce waste in the workplace. There are also expectations by government and other stakeholders for the company to take this action and be publicly successful. Consequently, the managing director wants to significantly reduce the use of paper, refuse, and other waste throughout the company's many widespread offices. Unfortunately, a survey indicates that employees do not value environmental objectives and do not know how to "reduce, reuse, recycle." As the executive responsible for this change, you have been asked to develop a strategy that might bring about meaningful behavioural change toward these environmental goals. What would you do?

Scenario 2: Go Forward Airline

A major airline had experienced a decade of rough turbulence, including two bouts of bankruptcy protection, 10 managing directors, and morale so low that employees had ripped off company logos from their uniforms out of embarrassment. Service was terrible and the airplanes rarely arrived or left the terminal on time. This was costing the airline significant amounts of money in passenger layovers. Managers were paralyzed by anxiety and many had been with the firm so long that they didn't know how to set strategic goals that worked. One-fifth of all flights were losing money and the company overall was near financial collapse (just three months to defaulting on payroll obligations). The newly hired managing director and you must get employees to quickly improve operational efficiency and customer service. What actions would you take to bring about these changes in time?

SELF-ASSESSMENT EXERCISE 15.3

Are You Tolerant of Change?

Purpose   This exercise is designed to help you understand how people differ in their tolerance of change.

Instructions   Read each of the statements below and circle the response that best fits your personal belief. Then use the scoring key in Appendix B of this book to calculate your results. This self-assessment is completed alone so students rate themselves honestly without concerns of social comparison. However, class discussion will focus on the meaning of the concept measured by this scale and its implications for managing change in organizational settings.

Tolerance of Change Scale							
To what extent does each statement describe you? Indicate your level of agreement by marking the appropriate response on the right.	Strongly Agree	Moderately Agree	Slightly Agree	Neutral	Slightly Disagree	Moderately Disagree	Strongly Disagree
1. An expert who doesn't come up with a definite answer probably doesn't know too much.	☐	☐	☐	☐	☐	☐	☐
2. I would like to live in a foreign country for a while.	☐	☐	☐	☐	☐	☐	☐
3. There is really no such thing as a problem that can't be solved.	☐	☐	☐	☐	☐	☐	☐
4. People who fit their lives into a schedule probably miss most of the joy of living.	☐	☐	☐	☐	☐	☐	☐
5. A good job is one where it is always clear what is to be done and how it is to be done.	☐	☐	☐	☐	☐	☐	☐
6. It is more fun to tackle a complicated problem than to solve a simple one.	☐	☐	☐	☐	☐	☐	☐
7. In the long run, it is possible to get more done by tackling small, simple problems rather than large, complicated ones.	☐	☐	☐	☐	☐	☐	☐
8. Often the most interesting and stimulating people are those who don't mind being different and original.	☐	☐	☐	☐	☐	☐	☐
9. What we are used to is always preferable to what is unfamiliar.	☐	☐	☐	☐	☐	☐	☐
10. People who insist on a yes or no answer just don't know how complicated things really are.	☐	☐	☐	☐	☐	☐	☐
11. A person who leads an even, regular life in which few surprises or unexpected happenings arise really has a lot to be grateful for.	☐	☐	☐	☐	☐	☐	☐
12. Many of our most important decisions are based on insufficient information.	☐	☐	☐	☐	☐	☐	☐
13. I like parties where I know most of the people more than ones where all or most of the people are complete strangers.	☐	☐	☐	☐	☐	☐	☐
14. Teachers or supervisors who hand out vague assignments give one a chance to show initiative and originality.	☐	☐	☐	☐	☐	☐	☐
15. The sooner everyone acquires similar values and ideals, the better.	☐	☐	☐	☐	☐	☐	☐
16. A good teacher is one who makes you wonder about your way of looking at things.	☐	☐	☐	☐	☐	☐	☐

Source: Adapted from S. Budner, "Intolerance of Ambiguity as a Personality Variable," *Journal of Personality*, 30 (1962), pp. 29–50.

PART FOUR VIDEO CASE STUDIES

Case 1   Wendy's Restaurants of Canada

CBC Employees at Wendy's Restaurants of Canada are about to be swept up in a tide of extraordinary change. To boost profits, Wendy's wanted to break down the military style of management and, in its place, create a culture of vulnerability and trust. To launch this change process, Wendy's brought together 160 restaurant managers from across Canada to an Ontario resort where New Mexico-based Pecos River guided them to a new way of working with their employees. This classic CBC video program takes the viewer through the Pecos River program, and then transports us to Winnipeg where district manager Craig Stapon is responsible for getting his managers on-board the change process. Although this program was filmed in the early 1990s, it remains one of the best video clips to illustrate the trials and tribulations of introducing change in the workplace.

Discussion Questions

1. What changes did executives at Wendy's Restaurants of Canada expect to result from the Pecos River program? Did these changes occur in the Winnipeg restaurants?

2. Was there any resistance to change among the Winnipeg restaurant managers? If so, what form of resistance did it take?

3. What change management strategies did Craig Stapon use among the Winnipeg managers? Were these strategies effective? Why or why not?

iStudy—Available 24/7 with instant feedback so you can study when you want, how you want, and where you want. Visit www.istudyob.ca to register—take practice quizzes, run interactive scenarios, practice concepts, and much more. Also visit the Student Online Learning Centre for additional study tools.

www.mcgrawhill.ca/olc/mcshane

ADDITIONAL CASES

Case 1 A Mir Kiss?

By Steven L. McShane, The University of Western Australia

A team of psychologists at Moscow's Institute for Biomedical Problems (IBMP) wanted to learn more about the dynamics of long term isolation in space. This knowledge would be applied to the International Space Station, a joint project of several countries that would send people into space for more than six months. It would eventually include a trip to Mars taking up to three years.

IBMP set up a replica in Moscow of the Mir Space Station. They then arranged for three international researchers from Japan, Canada, and Austria to spend 110 days isolated in a chamber the size of a train car. This chamber joined a smaller chamber where four Russian cosmonauts had already completed half of their 240 days of isolation. This was the first time an international crew was involved in the studies. None of the participants spoke English as their first language, yet they communicated throughout their stay in English at varying levels of proficiency.

Judith Lapierre, a French-Canadian, was the only female in the experiment. Along with a PhD in public health and social medicine, Lapierre studied space sociology at the International Space University in France and conducted isolation research in the Antarctic. This was her fourth trip to Russia, where she had learned the language. The mission was supposed to have a second female participant from the Japanese space program, but she was not selected by IBMP.

The Japanese and Austrian participants viewed the participation of a woman as a favourable factor, says Lapierre. For example, to make the surroundings more comfortable, they rearranged the furniture, hung posters on the walls, and put a tablecloth on the kitchen table. "We adapted our environment, whereas the Russians just viewed it as something to be endured," she explains. "We decorated for Christmas, because I'm the kind of person who likes to host people."

New Year's Eve Turmoil

Ironically, it was at one of those social events, the New Year's Eve party, where events took a turn for the worse. After drinking vodka (allowed by the Russian space agency), two of the Russian cosmonauts got into a fistfight that left blood splattered on the chamber walls. At one point, a colleague hid the knives in the station's kitchen because of fears that the two Russians were about to stab each other. The two cosmonauts, who generally did not get along, had to be restrained by other men. Soon after that brawl, the Russian commander grabbed Lapierre, dragged her out of view of the television monitoring cameras, and kissed her aggressively—twice. Lapierre fought him off, but the message didn't register. He tried to kiss her again the next morning.

The next day, the international crew complained to IBMP about the behaviour of the Russian cosmonauts. The Russian institute apparently took no action against any of the aggressors. Instead, the institute's psychologists replied that the incidents were part of the experiment. They wanted crew members to solve their personal problems with mature discussion, without asking for outside help. "You have to understand that Mir is an autonomous object, far away from anything," Vadim Gushin, the IBMP psychologist in charge of the project, explained after the experiment had ended in March: "If the crew can't solve problems among themselves, they can't work together."

Following IBMP's response, the international crew wrote a scathing letter to the Russian institute and the space agencies involved in the experiment. "We had never expected such events to take place in a highly controlled scientific experiment where individuals go through a multistep selection process," they wrote. "If we had known . . . we would not have joined it as subjects." The letter also complained about IBMP's response to their concerns.

Informed of the New Year's Eve incident, the Japanese space program convened an emergency meeting on January 2 to address the incidents. Soon after, the Japanese team member quit, apparently shocked by IBMP's inaction. He was replaced with a Russian researcher on the international team. Ten days after the fight—a little over a month after the international team began the mission—the doors between the Russian and international crew's chambers were barred at the request of the international research team. Lapierre later emphasized that this action was taken because of concerns about violence, not the incident involving her.

A Stolen Kiss or Sexual Harassment

By the end of the experiment in March, news of the fistfight between the cosmonauts and the commander's attempts to kiss Lapierre had reached the public. Russian scientists attempted to play down the kissing incident by saying that it was one fleeting kiss, a clash of cultures, and a female participant who was too emotional.

"In the West, some kinds of kissing are regarded as sexual harassment. In our culture it's nothing," said Russian scientist Vadim Gushin in one interview. In another interview, he explained: "The problem of sexual harassment is given a lot of attention in North America but less in Europe. In Russia it is even less of an issue, not because we are more or less moral than the rest of the world; we just have different priorities."

Judith Lapierre says the kissing incident was tolerable compared to this reaction from the Russian scientists who conducted the experiment. "They don't get it at all," she complains. "They don't think anything is wrong. I'm more frustrated than ever. The worst thing is that they don't realize it was wrong."

Norbert Kraft, the Austrian scientist on the international team, also disagreed with the Russian interpretation of events. "They're trying to protect themselves," he says. "They're trying to put the fault on others. But this is not a cultural issue. If a woman doesn't want to be kissed, it is not acceptable."

Sources: G. Sinclair Jr., "If You Scream in Space, Does Anyone Hear?" *Winnipeg Free Press*, May 5, 2000, p. A4; S. Martin, "Reining in the Space Cowboys," *Globe & Mail*, April 19, 2000, p. R1; M. Gray, "A Space Dream Sours," *Maclean's*, April 17, 2000, p. 26; E. Niiler, "In Search of the Perfect Astronaut," *Boston Globe*, April 4, 2000, p. E4; J. Tracy, "110-Day Isolation Ends in Sullen . . . Isolation," *Moscow Times*, March 30, 2000, p. 1; M. Warren, "A Mir Kiss?" *Daily Telegraph (London)*, March 30, 2000, p. 22; G. York, "Canadian's Harassment Complaint Scorned," *Globe & Mail*, March 25, 2000, p. A2; and S. Nolen, "Lust in Space," *Globe & Mail*, March 24, 2000, p. A3.

Case 2 Arctic Mining Consultants

By Steven L. McShane, The University of Western Australia, and Tim Neale

Tom Parker enjoyed working outdoors. At various times in the past, he worked as a ranch hand, high steel rigger, headstone installer, prospector, and geological field technician. Now 43, Parker is a geological field technician and field coordinator with Arctic Mining Consultants. He has specialized knowledge and experience in all nontechnical aspects of mineral exploration, including claim staking, line cutting and grid installation, soil sampling, prospecting, and trenching. He is responsible for hiring, training, and supervising field assistants for all of Arctic Mining Consultants' programs. Field assistants are paid a fairly low daily wage (no matter how long they work, which may be up to 12 hours or more) and are provided meals and accommodation. Many of the programs are operated by a project manager who reports to Parker.

Parker sometimes acts as a project manager, as he did on a job that involved staking 15 claims near Eagle Lake, British Columbia. He selected John Talbot, Greg Boyce, and Brian Millar, all of whom had previously worked with Parker, as the field assistants. To stake a claim, the project team marks a line with flagging tape and blazes along the perimeter of the claim, cutting a claim post every 457 metres (500 yards) (called a "length"). The 15 claims would require almost 96 kilometres (60 miles) of line in total. Parker had budgeted seven days (plus mobilization and demobilization) to complete the job. This meant that each of the four stakers (Parker, Talbot, Boyce, and Millar) would have to complete a little over seven "lengths" each day. The following is a chronology of the project.

Day 1

The Arctic Mining Consultants crew assembled in the morning and drove to Eagle Lake, from where they were flown by helicopter to the claim site. On arrival, they set up tents at the edge of the area to be staked, and agreed on a schedule for cooking duties. After supper, they pulled out the maps and discussed the job—how long it would take, the order in which the areas were to be staked, possible helicopter landing spots, and areas that might be more difficult to stake.

Parker pointed out that with only a week to complete the job, everyone would have to average seven and a half lengths per day. "I know that is a lot," he said, "but you've all staked claims before and I'm confident that each of you is capable of it. And it's only for a week. If we get the job done in time, there's a $300 bonus for each man." Two hours later, Parker and his crew members had developed what seemed to be a workable plan.

Day 2

Millar completed six lengths, Boyce six lengths, Talbot eight, and Parker eight. Parker was not pleased with Millar's or Boyce's production. However, he didn't make an issue of it, thinking that they would develop their "rhythm" quickly.

Day 3

Millar completed five and a half lengths, Boyce four, and Talbot seven. Parker, who was nearly twice as old as the other three, completed eight lengths. He also had enough time remaining to walk over and check the quality of stakes that Millar and Boyce had completed, then walk back to his own area for helicopter pickup back to the tent site.

That night Parker exploded with anger. "I thought I told you that I wanted seven and a half lengths a day!" he shouted at Boyce and Millar. Boyce said that he was slowed down by unusually thick underbrush in his assigned area. Millar said that he had done his best and would try to pick up the pace. Parker did not mention that he had inspected their work. He explained that as far as he was concerned, the field assistants were supposed to finish their assigned area for the day, no matter what.

Talbot, who was sharing a tent with Parker, talked to him later. "I think that you're being a bit hard on them, you know. I know that it has been more by luck than anything else that I've been able to do my quota. Yesterday I only had five lengths done after the first seven hours and there was only an hour before I was supposed to be picked up. Then I hit a patch of really open bush, and was able to do three lengths in 70 minutes. Why don't I take Millar's area tomorrow and he can have mine? Maybe that will help."

"Conditions are the same in all of the areas," replied Parker, rejecting Talbot's suggestion. "Millar just has to try harder."

Day 4

Millar did seven lengths and Boyce completed six and a half. When they reported their production that evening, Parker grunted uncommunicatively. Parker and Talbot did eight lengths each.

Day 5

Millar completed six lengths, Boyce six, Talbot seven and a half, and Parker eight. Once again Parker blew up, but he concentrated his diatribe on Millar. "Why don't you do what you say you are going to do? You know that you have to do seven and a half lengths a day. We went over that when we first got here, so why don't you do it? If you aren't willing to do the job then you never should have taken it in the first place!"

Millar replied by saying that he was doing his best, that he hadn't even stopped for lunch, and that he didn't know how he could possibly do any better. Parker launched into him again: "You have got to work harder! If you put enough effort into it, you will get the area done!"

Later Millar commented to Boyce, "I hate getting dumped on all the time! I'd quit if it didn't mean that I'd have to walk 80 kilometres (50 miles) to the highway. And besides, I need the bonus money. Why doesn't he pick on you? You don't get any more done than me; in fact, you usually get less. Maybe if you did a bit more he wouldn't be so bothered about me."

"I only work as hard as I have to," Boyce replied.

Day 6

Millar raced through breakfast, was the first one to be dropped off by the helicopter, and arranged to be the last one picked up. That evening the production figures were Millar eight and a quarter lengths, Boyce seven, and Talbot and Parker eight each. Parker remained silent when the field assistants reported their performance for the day.

Day 7

Millar was again the first out and last in. That night, he collapsed in an exhausted heap at the table, too tired to eat. After a few moments, he announced in an abject tone, "Six lengths. I worked like a dog all day and I only got a lousy six lengths!" Boyce completed five lengths, Talbot seven, and Parker seven and a quarter.

Parker was furious. "That means we have to do a total of 34 lengths tomorrow if we are to finish this job on time!" With his eyes directed at Millar, he added: "Why is it that you never finish the job? Don't you realize that you are part of a team, and that you are letting the rest of the team down? I've been checking your lines and you're doing too much blazing and wasting too much time making picture-perfect claim posts! If you worked smarter, you'd get a lot more done!"

Day 8

Parker cooked breakfast in the dark. The helicopter dropoffs began as soon as morning light appeared on the horizon. Parker instructed each assistant to complete eight lengths and, if they finished early, to help the others. Parker said that he would finish the other 10 lengths. Helicopter pickups were arranged for one hour before dark.

By noon, after working as hard as he could, Millar had only completed three lengths. "Why bother," he thought to himself, "I'll never be able to do another five lengths before the helicopter comes, and I'll catch the same amount of abuse from Parker for doing six lengths as for seven and a half." So he sat down and had lunch and a rest. "Boyce won't finish his eight lengths either, so even if I did finish mine, I still wouldn't get the bonus. At least I'll get one more day's pay this way."

That night, Parker was livid when Millar reported that he had completed five and a half lengths. Parker had done ten and a quarter lengths, and Talbot had completed eight. Boyce proudly announced that he finished seven and a half lengths, but sheepishly added that Talbot had helped him with some of it. All that remained were the two and a half lengths that Millar had not completed.

The job was finished the next morning and the crew demobilized. Millar has never worked for Arctic Mining Consultants again, despite being offered work several times by Parker. Boyce sometimes does staking for Arctic, and Talbot works full time with the company.

Case 3   Big Screen's Big Failure

Fiona McQuarrie, University of the Fraser Valley

Bill Brosnan stared at the financial statements in front of him and shook his head. The losses from *Conquistadors*, the movie that was supposed to establish Big Screen Studios as a major Hollywood power, were worse than anyone had predicted. In fact, the losses were so huge that Brosnan's predecessor, Buck Knox, had been fired as a result of this colossal failure. Brosnan had wanted to be the head of a big movie production company for as long as he could remember, and was thrilled to have been chosen by the board of directors to be the new president. But he had never expected that the first task in his dream job would be to deal with the fallout from one of the most unsuccessful movies ever.

The driving force behind *Conquistadors* was its director, Mark Frazier. Frazier had made several profitable movies for other studios and had a reputation as being a maverick with a "vision." He was a director with clearly formulated ideas of what his movies should look like, and he also had no hesitations about being forceful with producers, studios, actors, and technical staff to ensure that his idea came to life as he had envisioned it. For several years, while Frazier had been busy on other projects, he had also been working on a script about two Spanish aristocrats in the 16ᵗʰ century who set out for America to find riches and gold, and encountered many amazing adventures on their travels. Frazier was something of an amateur historian, which led to his interest in the real-life stories of the Spanish conquistadors and bringing those stories to life for a 21ˢᵗ century audience. But he also felt that creating an epic tale like this would establish him as a serious writer and filmmaker in the eyes of Hollywood, some of whose major powers had dismissed his past work as unimaginative or clichéd.

At the time Big Screen Studios approached Frazier to see if he would be interested in working for them, the company was going through something of a rough spot. Through several years of hard work and mostly successful productions, Buck Knox, the president of Big Screen, had established Big Screen as a studio that produced cost-efficient and profitable films. The studio also had a good reputation for being supportive of the creative side of filmmaking; actors, writers, directors, and producers generally felt that Big Screen trusted them enough to give them autonomy in making decisions appropriate for their productions. (Other studios had reputations for keeping an overly tight rein on production budgets and for dictating choices based on cost rather than artistic considerations.) However, in the last two years Big Screen had invested in several major productions—a musical, a horror film, and the sequel to a wildly successful film adaptation of a comic book—that for various reasons had all performed well below expectations. Knox had also heard through the grapevine that several of the studio's board members were prepared to join together to force him out of the presidency if Big Screen did not come up with a hit soon.

Knox knew that Frazier was being wooed by several other studios for his next project, and decided to contact Frazier to see if he was interested in directing any of the productions Big Screen was considering in the next year or so. After hearing Knox's descriptions of the upcoming productions, Frazier said, "What I'd really be interested in doing is directing this script I've been writing." He described the plot of *Conquistadors* to Knox, and Knox was enchanted by the possibilities—two strong male lead characters, a beautiful woman the men encountered in South America whose affections they fought over, battles, sea journeys, and challenging journeys over mountains and through jungles. However, Knox could also see that this movie might be extremely expensive to produce. He expressed this concern to Frazier, and Frazier replied, "Yes, but it will be an investment that will pay off. I know this movie will work. And I've mentioned it to two other studios and they are interested in it. I would prefer to make it with Big Screen, but if I have to, I will go somewhere else to get it made. That is how strongly I believe in it. However, any studio I work with has to trust me. I won't make the film without adequate financial commitment from the studio, I want final approval over casting, and I won't make the film if I don't get final cut." ("Final cut" means the director, not the studio, edits the version of the movie that is released to theatres, and that the studio cannot release a version of the movie that the director does not approve.)

Knox told Frazier that he would get back to him later that week, and asked Frazier not to commit to any other project until then. He spent several days mulling over the possibilities. Like Frazier, he believed that *Conquistadors* could be a huge success. It certainly sounded like it had more potential than anything else Big Screen had in development. However, Knox was still concerned about the potential cost, and the amount of control over the project that Frazier was demanding. Frazier's reputation as a maverick meant that he likely would not compromise on his demands. Knox was also concerned about his own vulnerability if the movie failed. But on the other hand, Big Screen needed a big hit, and it needed one soon. Big Screen would look very bad if it turned down *Conquistadors* and the movie became a gigantic hit for some other studio. Frazier had a respectable track record of producing money-makers, so even if he might be difficult to work with, the end product usually was successful. At the end of the week, Knox phoned Frazier and told him that Big Screen was willing to produce *Conquistadors*. Frazier thanked Knox, and added, "This film is going to redeem me, and it's going to redeem Big Screen as well."

Pre-production on the film started almost immediately, after Frazier and the studio negotiated a budget of $50 million. This was slightly higher than Knox had anticipated, but he believed this was not an excessive amount to permit Frazier to realize the grand vision he had described. Knox further reassured himself by assigning John Connor, one of his trusted vice-presidents, to act as the studio's liaison with Frazier and to be executive producer on the film. Connor was a veteran of many years in the movie production industry and was experienced in working with directors and budgets. Knox trusted Connor to be able to make Frazier contain the costs of the production within the agreed-upon limits.

The first major problem the film encountered involved casting. The studio gave Frazier final approval over casting as he had requested. Frazier's first signing was Cole Rogan, a famous action star, to be one of the male leads. The studio did not object to this choice; in fact, Knox and Connor felt that Rogan was an asset because he had a reputation as a star that could "open" a film (in other words, audiences would come to a movie just because he was in it). However, Frazier then decided to cast Frank Monaco as the other male lead. Monaco had made only a few films to date, and those were fluffy romantic comedies. Frazier said that Monaco would bring important qualities of vulnerability and innocence to the role, which would be a strong contrast to Rogan's rugged machismo. However, Connor told Knox, he saw two major problems with Monaco's casting: Monaco had never proven himself in an epic adventure role, and he was an accomplished enough actor that he would make the rather wooden Rogan look bad. Knox told Connor to suggest to Frazier that Rogan's role be recast. Unfortunately, it turned out that Frazier had signed Rogan to a "pay or play" deal, meaning that if the studio released Rogan from the project, the studio would have to pay him a considerable sum of money. Knox was somewhat bothered that Frazier had made this deal with Rogan without consulting either him or Connor, but he told Connor to instruct Frazier to release Rogan and recast the role, and the studio would just accept the payment to Rogan as part of the production costs. Although Frazier complained, he did as the studio asked and chose as a replacement Marty Jones, an actor who had had some success in films but mostly in supporting roles. However, Jones was thrilled to be cast in a major role, and Connor felt that he would be capable of convincingly playing the part.

A few weeks after casting was completed, Connor called Knox and asked to see him immediately. "Buck," he told him once he arrived at Knox's office, "we have a really big problem." Connor said that Frazier was insisting the majority of the production be filmed in the jungles of South America, where most of the action took place, rather than on a studio soundstage or in a more accessible location that resembled the South American locale. Not only that, but Frazier was also insisting that he needed to bring along most of the crew that had worked on his previous films, rather than staffing the production locally. "Why does he want that? That's going to cost a hell of a lot," Knox said. "I know," Connor said, "but he says it's the only way that the film is going to work. He says it just won't be the same if the actors are in a studio or in some swamp in the southern U.S. According to him, the actors and the crew need to be in the real location to truly understand what the conquistadors went through, and audiences won't believe it's a real South American jungle if the film isn't made in one."

Knox told Connor that Frazier had to provide an amended budget to reflect the increased costs before he would approve the location filming. Connor took the request to Frazier, who complained that the studio was weakening on its promise to support the film adequately, and added that he might be tempted to take the film to another studio if he was not allowed to film on location in South America. After a few weeks, he produced an amended budget of $75 million. Knox was horrified that the budget for *Conquistadors* had nearly doubled by half in a few weeks. He told Connor that he would only accept the amended budget under two conditions: one, that Connor would go on the location shoot to ensure that costs stayed within the amended budget, and two, that if the costs exceeded Frazier's estimates, he would have to pay any excess himself. Frazier again complained that the studio was attempting to compromise his vision, but grudgingly accepted the modified terms.

Frazier, Connor, and the cast and crew then headed off to the South American jungles for a scheduled two-month shoot. Immediately it became apparent that there was more trouble. Connor, who reported daily to Knox, told him after two weeks had passed that Frazier was shooting scenes several times over—not because the actors or the crew were making mistakes, or because there was something wrong with the scene, but because the output just didn't meet his artistic standards. This attention to detail meant that the filming schedule was nearly a week behind after only the first week's work. Also, because the filming locations were so remote, the cast and crew were spending nearly four hours of a scheduled seven-hour work day travelling to and from location, leaving only three hours in which they could work at regular pay rates. Work beyond those hours meant they had to be paid overtime, and as Frazier's demanding vision required shooting 10 or 12 hours each day, the production was incurring huge overtime costs. As if that wasn't bad enough, the "rushes" (the finished film produced each day) showed that Monaco and Jones didn't have any chemistry as a pair, and Gia Norman, the European actress Frazier had cast as the love interest, had such a heavy accent that most of her lines couldn't be understood.

Knox told Connor that he was coming to the location right away to meet with Frazier. After several days of very arduous travel, Knox, Connor, and Frazier met in the canvas tent that served as the director's "office" in the middle of the jungle. Knox didn't waste any time with pleasantries. "Mark," he told Frazier, "there is no way you can bring this film in for the budget you have promised or within the deadline you agreed to. John has told me how this production is being managed, and it's just not acceptable. I've done some calculations, and at the rate you are going, this picture is going to cost $85 million and have a running time of four and a half hours. Big Screen is not prepared to support that. We need a film that's a commercially viable length, and we need it at a reasonable cost."

"It needs to be as long as it is," replied Frazier, "because the story has to be told. And if it has to cost this much, it has to cost this much. Otherwise it will look like crap and no one will buy a ticket to see it."

"Mark," replied Knox, "we are prepared to put $5 million more into this picture, and that is it. You have the choice of proceeding under those terms, and keeping John fully apprised of the costs so that he can help you stay within the budget. If you don't agree to that, you can leave the production, and we will hire another director and sue you for breach of contract."

Frazier looked as though he was ready to walk into the jungle and head back to California that very minute, but the thought of losing his dream project was too much for him. He muttered, "OK, I'll finish it."

Knox returned to California, nursing several nasty mosquito bites, and Connor stayed in the jungle and reported to him regularly. Unfortunately, it didn't seem like Frazier was paying much attention to the studio's demands. Connor estimated that the shoot would run three months rather than two, and that the total cost of the shoot would be $70 million. This only left $10 million of the budget for post-production, distribution, and marketing, which was almost nothing for an epic adventure. To add to Knox's problems, he got a phone call from Richard Garrison, the chairman of Big Screen's board of directors. Garrison had heard gossip about what was going on with *Conquistadors* in the jungles of South America, and wanted to know what Knox was going to do to curb Frazier's excesses. Knox told Garrison that Frazier was operating under clearly understood requirements, and that Connor was on the set to monitor the costs. Unfortunately, Knox thought, Connor was doing a good job of reporting, but he didn't seem to be doing much to correct the problems he was observing.

Frazier eventually came back to California after three and a half months of shooting, and started editing the several hundred hours of film he had produced. Knox requested that Frazier permit Connor or himself to participate in the editing, but Frazier retorted that permitting that would infringe on his right to "final cut," and refused to allow anyone associated with the studio to be in the editing room. Knox scheduled a release date for the film in six months' time, and asked the studio's publicity department to start working on an ad campaign for the film, but not much could be done on either of these tasks without at least a rough cut of the finished product.

Three weeks into the editing, Connor called Knox. "I heard from Mark today," he said. "He wants to do some reshoots." "Is that a problem?" Knox asked. "No," said Connor, "most of it is interior stuff that we can do here. But he wants to add a prologue. He says that the story doesn't make sense without more development of how the two lead characters sailed from Spain to South America. He wants to hire a ship."

"He wants to WHAT?" exclaimed Knox.

"He wants to hire a sailing ship, like the conquistadors travelled on. There's a couple of tall ships that would do, but the one he wants is in drydock in Mexico, and would cost at least a million to make seaworthy and sail up to southern California. And that's on top of the cost of bringing the actors and crew back for a minimum of a week. I suggested to him that we try some special effects or a computerized animation for the scenes of the ship on the ocean, and shoot the shipboard scenes in the studio, but he says that won't be the same and it needs to be authentic."

At this point, Knox was ready to drive over to the editing studios and take care of Frazier himself. Instead, he called Garrison and explained the situation. "I won't commit any more money to this without the board's approval. But we've already invested $80 million into this already, so is a few more million that much of a deal if it gets the damn thing finished and gets Frazier out of our hair? If we tell him no, we'll have to basically start all over again, or just dump the whole thing and kiss $80 million goodbye." At the other end of the line, Garrison sighed, and said, "Do whatever you have to do to get it done."

Knox told Connor to authorize the reshoots, with a schedule of two months and the expectation that Frazier would have a rough cut of the film ready for the studio executives to view in three months. However, because of the time Frazier had already spent in editing, Knox had to change the release date, which meant changing the publicity campaign as well—and releasing the film at the same time that one of Big Screen's major competitors was releasing another epic adventure that was considered a surefire hit. However, Knox felt he had no choice. If he didn't enforce some deadline, Frazier might sit in the editing room and tinker with his dream forever.

Connor supervised the reshoots, and reported that they went as well as could be expected. The major problem was that Gia Norman had had plastic surgery on her nose after the first shoot was completed, and looked considerably different than she had in the jungles of South America. However, creative lighting, makeup and costuming managed to minimize the change in her appearance. By all accounts, the (very expensive) sailing ship looked spectacular in the rushes, and Frazier was satisfied that his vision had been sufficiently dramatized.

Amazingly, Frazier delivered the rough cut of the film at the agreed-upon time. Knox, Connor, Garrison, and the rest of the studio's executives crowded into the screening room to view the realization of Frazier's dream. Five and a half hours later, they were in shock. No one could deny that the movie looked fantastic, and that it was an epic on a grand scale, but there was no way the studio could release a five-and-a-half-hour long film commercially, plus Frazier had agreed to produce a movie that was at most two-and-a-half-hours long. Knox was at his wits' end. He cornered Garrison in the hallway outside the screening room. "Will you talk to Mark? He won't listen to me, he won't listen to John. But we can't release this. It won't work." Garrison agreed, and contacted Frazier the next day. He reported back to Knox that Frazier, amazingly, had agreed to cut the film to two hours and fifteen minutes. Knox, heartened by this news, proceeded with the previously set release date, which by now was a month away, and got the publicity campaign going.

Two days before the scheduled release date, Frazier provided an advance copy of his shortened version of *Conquistadors* for a studio screening. Knox had asked him to provide a copy sooner, but Frazier said that he could not produce anything that quickly. As a consequence, the version of the film that the studio executives were seeing for the first time was the version that had already had thousands of copies duplicated for distribution to movie theatres all across North America. In fact, those copies were on their way by courier to the theatres as the screening started.

At the end of the screening, the studio executives were stunned. Yes, the movie was shorter, but now it made no sense. Characters appeared and disappeared randomly, the plot was impossible to follow, and the dialogue did not make sense at several key points in the small parts of plot that were discernible. The film was a disaster. Several of the executives present voiced the suspicion that Frazier had deliberately edited the movie this way to get revenge on the studio for not "respecting" his vision and forcing him to reduce the film's length. Others suggested that Frazier was simply a lunatic who never should have been given so much autonomy in the first place.

Knox, Garrison, and Connor held a hastily called meeting the next morning. What could the studio do? Recall the film and force Frazier to produce a more coherent shorter version? Recall the film and release the five-and-a-half-hour version? Or let the shorter version be released as scheduled and hope that it wouldn't be too badly received? Knox argued that the film should be recalled and Frazier should be forced to produce the product he agreed to produce. Connor said that he thought Frazier had been doing his best to do what the studio wanted, based on what Connor saw on the set, and that making Frazier cut the movie so short compromised the vision that Frazier wanted to achieve. He said the studio should release the long version and present it as a "special cinematic event." Garrison, as chairman of the board, listened to both sides, and after figuring out the costs of recalling and/or re-editing the film—not to mention the less tangible costs of further worsening the film's reputation—said, "Gentlemen, we really don't have any choice. *Conquistadors* will be released tomorrow."

Knox immediately cancelled the critics' screenings of *Conquistadors* scheduled for that afternoon, so that bad reviews would not appear on the day of the film's release. Despite that pre-emptive step and an extensive advertising campaign, *Conquistadors* was a complete and utter flop. On a total outlay of $90 million, the studio recouped less than $9 million. The reviews of the film were terrible, and audiences stayed away in droves. The only place *Conquistadors* was even close to successful was in some parts of Europe, where film critics called the edited version an example of American studios' crass obsession with making money by compromising the work of a genius. The studio attempted to capitalize on this note of hope by releasing the five-and-a-half-hour version of *Conquistadors* for screening at some overseas film festivals and cinema appreciation societies, but the revenues from these screenings were so small that they made no difference to the overall financial results.

Three months after *Conquistadors* was released, Garrison called Knox in and told him he was fired. Garrison told Knox the board appreciated what a difficult production *Conquistadors* had been to manage, but that the costs of the production had been unchecked to a degree that the board no longer had confidence in Knox's ability to operate Big Screen Studios efficiently. Connor was offered a very generous early retirement package, and accepted it. The board then hired Bill Brosnan, a vice-president at another studio, as Knox's replacement.

After reviewing *Conquistadors'* financial records and the notes that Knox had kept throughout the production, Brosnan was determined that a disaster like this would not undermine his career as it had Knox's. But what could he do to ensure this would not happen?

Case 4   Bridging the Two Worlds—The Organizational Dilemma

By William Todorovic, Indiana-Purdue University, Fort Wayne

I had been hired by Aluminum Elements Corp. (AEC), and it was my first day of work. I was 26 years old, and I was now the manager of AEC's customer service group, which looked after customers, logistics, and some of the raw material purchasing. My superior, George, was the vice-president of the company. AEC manufactured most of its products from aluminum, a majority of which were destined for the construction industry.

As I walked around the shop floor, the employees appeared to be concentrating on their jobs, barely noticing me. Management held daily meetings, in which various production issues were discussed. No one from the shop floor was invited to the meeting, unless there was a specific problem. Later I also learned that management had separate washrooms, separate lunchrooms, as well as other perks that floor employees did not have. Most of the floor employees felt that management, although polite on the surface, did not really feel they had anything to learn from the floor employees.

John, who worked on the aluminum slitter, a crucial operation required before any other operations could commence, had a number of unpleasant encounters with George. As a result, George usually sent written memos to the floor in order to avoid a direct confrontation with John. Because the directions in the memos were complex, these memos were often more than two pages in length.

One morning, as I was walking around, I noticed that John was very upset. Feeling that perhaps there was something I could do, I approached John and asked him if I could help. He indicated that everything was just fine. From the looks of the situation, and John's body language, I felt that he was willing to talk, but John knew that this was not the way things were done at AEC. Tony, who worked at the machine next to John's, then cursed and said that the office guys only cared about schedules, not about the people down on the floor. I just looked at him, and then said that I only began working here last week, and thought that I could address some of their issues. Tony gave me a strange look, shook his head, and went back to his machine. I could hear him still swearing as I left. Later I realized that most of the office staff were also offended by Tony's language.

On the way back to my office, Lesley, a recently hired engineer from Russia, approached me and pointed out that the employees were not accustomed to management talking to them. Management only issued orders and made demands. As we discussed the different perceptions between office and floor staff, we were interrupted by a very loud lunch bell, which startled me. I was happy to join Lesley for lunch, but she asked me why I was not eating in the office lunch room. I replied that if I was going to understand how AEC worked, I had to get to know all the people better. In addition, I realized that this was not how things were done, and wondered about the nature of this apparent division between the management and the floor. In the lunchroom, the other workers were amazed to see me there, commenting that I was just new and had not learned the ropes yet.

After lunch, when I asked George, my supervisor, about his recent confrontation with John, George was surprised that John got upset, and exclaimed, "I just wanted John to know that he did a great job, and as a result, we will be able to ship on time one large order to the West Coast. In fact, I thought I was complimenting him."

Earlier, Lesley had indicated that certain behaviour was expected from management, and therefore from me. I reasoned that I do not think that this behaviour works, and besides it is not what I believe or how I care to behave. For the next couple of months, I simply walked around the floor and took every opportunity to talk to the shop floor employees. Often, when the employees related specific information about their workplaces, I felt that it went over my head. Frequently, I had to write down the information and revisit it later. I made a point of listening to them, identifying where they were coming from, and trying to understand them. I needed to keep my mind open to new ideas. Because the shop employees expected me to make requests and demands, I made a point of not doing any of that. Soon enough, the employees became friendly, and started to accept me as one of their own, or at least as a different type of management person.

During my third month of work, the employees showed me how to improve the scheduling of jobs, especially those on the aluminum slitter. In fact, the greatest contribution was made by John who demonstrated better ways to combine the most common slitting sizes, and reduce waste by retaining some of the "common-sized" material for new orders. Seeing the opportunity, I programmed a spreadsheet to calculate and track inventory. This, in addition to better planning and forecasting, allowed us to reduce our new order turnarounds from four to five weeks to in by 10 a.m. out by 5 p.m. on the same day.

By the time I was employed for four months, I realized that members from other departments came to me and asked me to relay messages to the shop employees. When I asked why they were delegating this task to me, they stated that I spoke the same language as the shop employees. Increasingly, I became the messenger for the office to shop floor communication.

One morning, George called me into his office and complimented me on the levels of customer service and the improvements that have been achieved. As we talked, I mentioned that we could not have done it without John's help. "He really knows his stuff, and he is good," I said. I suggested that we consider him for some type of a promotion. Also, I hoped that this would be a positive gesture that would improve the communication between the office and shop floor.

George turned and pulled a flyer out of his desk; "Here is a management skills seminar. Do you think we should send John to it?"

"That is a great idea," I exclaimed, "Perhaps it would be good if he were to receive the news from you directly, George." George agreed, and after discussing some other issues, we parted company.

That afternoon, John came into my office, upset and ready to quit. "After all my effort and work, you guys are sending me for training seminars. So, am I not good enough for you?"

Case 5   Fran Hayden Joins Dairy Engineering

By Glyn Jones, University of Waikato, New Zealand

Background

Dairy Engineering (NZ) Ltd. has its headquarters in Hamilton, New Zealand with manufacturing plants in South Auckland and Christchurch. The company manufactures equipment for the dairy industry. In its early years it focused on the domestic market but in the last five years has expanded into the export market. The company employs 450 people, which makes it a large company by New Zealand standards.

The case focuses on events in the Accounting Department at head office which is organized into two sections, Cost Accounting and Management Information Services (MIS).

Fran, the New Graduate

Fran Hayden is in the final year of her Bachelor of Management Studies (BMS) degree at the University of Waikato where she has proved to be a high achiever. Fran was interested in a position with Dairy Engineering because of the opportunity to gain practical experience, the higher starting salary compared to the industry average, and that her boyfriend lived in that community.

Fran sent her curriculum vitae to the company and two weeks later she was invited to an interview with the Chief Accountant. She was surprised at the end of the interview to be offered the position of Assistant Cost Accountant. Fran said she would like to think it over. Two weeks later when she had still not replied she received a telephone call from Rob asking if she was going to take the position. Still not totally convinced, Fran decided nonetheless to accept the offer.

The First Day at Work

Like many of her peers, Fran was glad to be leaving university after four years of study. She was looking forward to having money to spend as well as reducing her student debt. In order to 'look the part' she had gone further into debt to buy new 'corporate clothing.' On reporting to the Accounting Department she got her first shock in the 'real world.' No one was expecting her! Even worse she discovered that there was no vacancy for her in Cost Accounting! Instead, she had been assigned to management information systems (MIS)!

Mike, a co-worker in MIS, accompanied Fran to the department, where she was introduced to two other colleagues, Tom and Adrian. They seemed to be a friendly bunch as apparently was her boss, Peter Bruton, who explained that her main duties were to assist with compiling information for the monthly Management Report known as 'Big Brother.'

After two weeks the time came for compiling 'Big Brother.' Fran found that her part was almost entirely clerical and consisted of photocopying, collating, binding, punching, and stamping the pages of the report. She then had to hand-deliver copies of the Report to the senior manager at headquarters. After 'Big Brother' was completed, Fran found again she had little to do. She began to wonder why MIS needed four people.

The Big Opportunity

One afternoon the Chief Accountant called Fran to his office to tell her about an upcoming management workshop in Auckland on Performance Measurement. Rob talked about the importance of staff development and that he would like to see one of his younger staff attending the workshop. He then asked Fran if she would be interested. She jumped at the opportunity. Unfortunately her boss was away on two weeks leave at the time but Rob said he would talk with Peter.

Fran enjoyed the workshop, particularly rubbing shoulders with experienced managers, living in an Auckland hotel, and generally acting the management part. Even before returning to Hamilton, she wrote a detailed report on the workshop for the Chief Accountant.

On her return to Hamilton however she found all was far from well.

On Sunday evening Fran was telephoned by her colleague Mike with some disturbing news. When Peter returned to work to find that Fran was in Auckland, he was furious, complaining that he had not been consulted and that his authority was being undermined. At one point in his tirade, Peter announced: "Fran is no longer employed in this section."

Fran returned to work full of trepidation only to find that the expected encounter with her boss did not take place because he was in Christchurch. She handed two copies of her report on the workshop to the Chief Accountant's secretary before taking the opportunity of her boss's absence to seek the advice of her colleagues:

Fran: I am really worried. What do you think I should do?

Adrian: Stop worrying about it. He's just letting off steam. I have seen this all before. He'll get over it.

Fran: Come on; get serious. He is my boss! He can make things very difficult for me.

Mike: I think you should talk with Rob. After all, he's the one who suggested you go. It's not like it was your idea. He has to stick up for you.

Next day Fran managed to get an appointment with the Chief Accountant. She started by saying that she found the workshop very useful. She then brought up her fears about Peter's displeasure with her attendance at the workshop to which the Chief Accountant responded:

Rob: Well yes, he was a bit upset but don't worry, I will sort it out. The report was really good. By the way, I think you should treat it as confidential. Don't show it to anyone or discuss it with anyone. Is that ok? Don't worry about this. I assure you that I will sort it out.

Fran left the meeting feeling reassured but also a bit puzzled, wondering how Rob could have read her report in such a short time.

On Thursday, Peter returned to work and just before lunch called Fran into his office where he proceeded to attack her verbally, saying that she had 'connived' behind his back to attend the workshop and that she had never asked for his permission. He said that he realized she was an intelligent 'girl' but that she was 'sneaky.' He went on:

Peter: You had better know which side your bread is buttered on—that for better or worse, you are in my section. No other section would want you.

He then called Mike in and told him:

Peter: I don't want Fran wasting any more time—she is not to make any private calls from work.

Later in 'confidence,' he also told Janet, one of the administration clerks:

Peter: Don't go talking with Fran—she has far too much work to catch up on.

Naturally Janet did tell Fran!

The following week, Vernon happened to pass Fran in the corridor and stopped to talk with her. Fran had met Vernon only briefly during her first week in the company and was surprised when he asked her why she looked so miserable. She explained and he said that they had better talk with the Chief Accountant and taking Fran with him, went to Rob's office. Vernon said that they needed a word and Fran listened as Vernon outlined the situation to Rob. Fran made it clear that if Peter continued to treat her this way, she would have to ask for a transfer. She also said that there was certainly not enough work in MIS to keep her occupied for more than a day or so each week.

The Chief Accountant listened and then asked her to give him a written report of what had happened since she had joined the company, including the latest incident with her boss. This, he said, would be brought up at the next senior management meeting. On the weekend Fran wrote the report that included a request for a transfer out of MIS on the basis of the lack of work and her boss's attitude towards her. On Monday morning she handed her report to the Chief Accountant's secretary.

Fran expected a reply but by early afternoon, had heard nothing. At the end of the day however, Peter called all his staff into his office. He was obviously in a good mood and told them that he had put his plan for revising 'Big Brother' to the management meeting and had received an enthusiastic response. As he spoke, Fran noticed the colour draining out of Mike's face. On the way out, he told her that what Peter was describing was his revision plans, not his own. Mike resolved never to give his boss another one of his ideas telling Fran:

Mike: He just uses other people's brains—but that's the last time he uses mine.

Fran drove home from work feeling despondent. She wished she had never joined the company. Her job was boring, almost entirely clerical and certainly did not require a degree. She was also taking the stresses home, resulting in quarrels with her boyfriend and flat mates.

Fran concluded that she had only two alternatives: a transfer or resignation. But to leave her job after less than five months would hardly impress any future employer. In desperation, she went to talk with Vernon who she thought would be sympathetic but received more unwelcome news. He told her about the outcome of the senior management meeting. Contrary to Fran's expectation, the Chief Accountant had not confronted Peter. In fact, it appeared he had been eclipsed by Peter's presentation for the revision of 'Big Brother' and the Chief Accountant had not attempted to raise the issue.

Vernon was frank—she must either transfer or resign. Then, to Fran's surprise, he suggested she apply for a position in his section that would become vacant in three weeks time. One of his assistant accountants was leaving to go overseas at short notice and he did not have a replacement. Vernon cautioned however that Fran's only chance was to apply directly to the Chief Accountant; that would force the issue. With a formal, written application before him, the Chief Accountant would have to make a decision. Just as certainly, Peter would resist the request. Later Fran drafted a letter to Rob requesting that she be transferred from MIS to the upcoming position in Cost Accounting.

The Confrontation

The next morning, Fran took her request to the Chief Accountant but after reading it he said:

Rob: You really needn't have done this, you know—I intended dealing with the situation.

Fran left Rob's office wondering what to believe. From her desk she watched as Peter made his way across to the Chief Accountant's office. The meeting was brief. Five minutes later, he left Rob's office and as he passed by, he said, in a loud voice;

Peter: Fran—you are finished in this company.

Fran saw her colleagues duck their heads down and pretend to be working. No one envied her position. She wondered how, in such a short time, she has ended up in such a situation.

Case 6 High Noon at Alpha Mills

....

By Arif Hassan and Thivagar Velayutham, International Islamic University Malaysia

Alpha Plantations Sdn. Bhd. is an oil palm plantation located in Malaysia. It consists of an oil palm estate and one palm oil mill. It is a wholly owned subsidiary of a British multinational company and was founded with the purpose of supplying crude palm oil for its parent company's detergent manufacturing business. Since its formation, most of the managers have been recruited from the U.K., with many British ex-soldiers and police officers joining up. Mr. Ang Siow Lee first joined Alpha mill in 1965 at the age of 15 as a labourer, and rose through the ranks to become the most senior non-managerial staff in Alpha. Mr. Ang is the senior production supervisor in Alpha's palm oil mill. His immediate superior is the mill manager and he has two junior supervisors to assist him. The mill operates on a three-shift cycle of 25 operators each and each supervisor (including Mr. Ang) is in charge of one shift.

Mr. Ang is responsible for the smooth daily palm oil processing operations. He coordinates the activities of all three shifts with the two supervisors, prepares the daily production reports, deals with short-term human resource planning issues and minor discipline issues, and sets and evaluates short-term performance targets for all the three shifts. In addition, he acts as the "gatekeeper," which means that any mill personnel who wish to see the mill manager must first see Mr. Ang, who tries to solve the problem first, which may be anything from house repairs to a request for an advance on wages. Only in rare cases when Mr. Ang cannot resolve the issue, is the matter brought up to the mill manager. Mr. Ang ran a tight ship, and never let anyone forget it. His superb technical competency helped him keep the mill in top shape. He was accustomed to receiving the highest appraisal ratings from the mill manager, who appreciated his firm, methodical, and almost militarily efficient way of running the mill. The palm oil industry in Malaysia faced many challenges in 1999. World oil prices plunged due to oversupply and with it, palm oil prices hit a 15-year low. This cut the profit margins of all palm oil producers and caused Alpha mill to post losses regularly.

Captain Chubb, the 54-year-old ex Royal Engineer and mill manager, was at a loss on how to improve performance. "We are doing nothing wrong, and have met all our efficiency targets. It's this market that is killing us!" he exasperatedly explained during the annual year-end visit of the directors from London. Very soon Captain Chubb was given his marching orders. In early 2000 a new mill manager was appointed who was very different from all his predecessors. Mr. Ian Davison, a 32-year-old who hailed from Edinburgh, Scotland, was not a career plantation engineer and had never managed an agricultural product-processing mill before. He was actually an electronics engineer with an Ivy-League MBA on the fast track to a top management position. His previous appointment was as factory manager of a detergent factory in Egypt where he managed to streamline and modernize operations and increase financial performance drastically. Headquarters in London had high hopes that he will be able to do the same with Alpha mill and return it to profitability. His first action was to analyze operations at Alpha mill and look for ways to reduce production costs and increase profits. He arrived at the following conclusions:

- Current performance standards allowed too much machine breakdown and change-over time. Better standards were achievable with the latest technology.

- Wastage could be reduced and yield improved drastically by installing machinery based on new technology.

- Personnel numbers were too high—they could be reduced with technology and multitasking and unleashing the full potential of workers.

- Personnel were just "cruising along"—they were not fully committed to achieving better performance.

- Hygiene needs were not being met.
- The old colonial and hierarchical company culture was not conducive to performance improvement.
- Information was not shared across the mill. Operators only knew about their own little area in the mill and almost nothing about the company as a whole.

He proposed to remedy the situation with the following initiatives:

- Empower operators by reorganizing the shifts into self-directed production teams where the supervisors would now play the role of "facilitators," and thereby gain commitment.
- Install new technology and automation.
- Adopt more stringent performance measures.

Mr. Davison implemented and executed these initiatives by first organizing an excursion to a local picnic spot for the entire factory. After the icebreakers, games, and lunch, he held a briefing session on the beach, where he explained the situation Alpha mill was in and the need to make changes. He then unveiled his plan for the first time. The response was enthusiastic, although some operators privately confessed to not understanding some of the terminology Mr. Davison used. At the end of the excursion, when there was some time allocated for feedback, Mr. Ang expressed his full support for Mr. Davison's plan. "We in Alpha mill have full confidence in you, our new leader and we assure you of our 110% support to make your plan a success!" he said at the end of his speech.

When the new machinery had been installed and each shift had been reorganized into self-directed work teams the plan was put into motion. Whenever the team faced a problem during processing and tried to find a solution using the techniques that had been taught, Mr. Ang would step in after some time, issue instructions, and take over the process. "This is a simple problem, no need to waste time over it. Just do it...." His instructions were always followed and the immediate problem was always solved. However, the production team reverted to the old ways of working, and none of the expected benefits of teaming were realized. Given the new tighter performance standards and reduced manpower, the team consistently underperformed. Team meetings were one-way affairs where Mr. Ang would tell everyone else what had gone wrong.

Mr. Ang's response to this was to push himself harder. He was always the first to arrive and the last to leave. He would spend a lot of time troubleshooting process problems. He pushed his operators even harder, but he felt that he had less of a "handle" on his operators now that they had direct access to the mill manager and most of their minor needs were seen to by him. Sometimes he became annoyed because of his operators' mistakes and would resort to shouting and cursing, which had the immediate effect of moving people in the direction he wanted. This was in contrast to the mere glare that would have sufficed previously.

The continued poor performance of Alpha mill affected Mr. Ang's mid-year appraisal rating, which fell down from "excellent" to merely "adequate." During the appraisal interview, an annoyed Mr. Davison bluntly told Mr. Ang that he needed to understand clearly what the initiatives were all about, and that he had to let the team take some responsibility, make mistakes, and learn from them. "With your knowledge of this mill, you should be able to provide them with all the technical input they need," he said. Mr. Davison also added. "It might help if you treated our people with a little more respect. We aren't living in the 1940s anymore you know." Mr. Ang was thunderstruck by the appraisal but did not raise any objections on the spot. He silently deferred to Mr. Davison's judgment and promised to do better. He also reiterated his utmost support for Mr. Davison and his plan.

After the mid-year appraisal, there was a noticeable change in Mr. Ang's demeanour. He became very quiet and began to take a less active role in the daily running of the mill. He was superficially polite to the operators and answered most requests for help with "Get the team together and discuss it amongst yourselves. Show the boss that you can solve it for yourselves." At first the teams were at a loss and mill performance suffered badly, but within two weeks the team had found its feet and performance began to improve. One of Mr. Ang's junior supervisors, Mr. Raman, was able to coordinate between production teams to ensure that the performance gains were maintained. The effect on Mr. Ang was devastating. He became withdrawn and began to drink more than usual. His presence at team meetings became a mere formality and he contributed next to nothing, taking a back seat to other team members. He spoke very little to mill personnel and became a mere shadow of his former self.

Mr. Davison was very aware of the changes taking place on the mill floor. He decided that it was time to have Mr. Ang removed from his position. He began to plan for a reshuffle of Alpha mill's organization chart where Mr. Ang would be promoted to the new position of mill executive, a staff position with a small pay raise. His responsibility would be to advise the mill manager on technical, quality, and efficiency problems faced by the mill. He would be assigned to carry out minor improvement projects and performance audits from time to time. Mr. Raman would be promoted as supervisor and report directly to the mill manager. Mr. Ang would no longer have any line authority over the production team. This reorganization was quickly approved by head office and Mr. Davison proceeded to lay the groundwork for the announcements and the necessary paperwork. Little did he foresee what was to follow.

Mr. Ang was in the head office one morning when the personnel executive's clerk congratulated him on his imminent promotion. A surprised Mr. Ang enquired further and learned of the plans that Mr. Davison had in store for him. It was the final straw. He rushed back to Alpha mill just as Mr. Davison was about to conduct his noon mill inspection. The confrontation was very loud, acrimonious, and in public. It ended with Mr. Ang being terminated for insubordination and gross misconduct.

After Mr. Ang had left, Mr. Davison felt that the obstacle to better commitment and morale was gone and that performance would improve greatly. He was very wrong. Team performance began to deteriorate and no amount of pep talks could improve it. He began to wonder what had gone wrong.

Case 7   Keeping Suzanne Chalmers

By Steven L. McShane, The University of Western Australia

Thomas Chan hung up the telephone and sighed. The vice-president of software engineering at Advanced Photonics Inc. (API) had just spoken to Suzanne Chalmers, who called to arrange a meeting with Chan later that day. She didn't say what the meeting was about, but Chan almost instinctively knew that Suzanne was going to quit after working at API for the past four years. Chalmers is a software engineer in Internet Protocol (IP), the software that directs fibre-optic light through API's routers. It is very specialized work, and Suzanne is one of API's top talents in that area.

Thomas Chan had been through this before. A valued employee would arrange a private meeting. The meeting would begin with a few pleasantries, then the employee announces that he or she wants to quit. Some employees say they are leaving because of the long hours and stressful deadlines. They say they need to decompress, get to know the kids again, or whatever. But that's not usually the real reason. Almost every organization in this industry is scrambling to keep up with technological advances and the competition. Employees would just leave one stressful job for another one.

Also, many of the people who leave API join a start-up company a few months later. These start-up firms can be pressure cookers where everyone works 16 hours each day and has to perform a variety of tasks. For example, engineers in these small firms might have to meet customers or work on venture capital proposals rather than focus on specialized tasks related to their knowledge. API now has over 6,000 employees, so it is easier to assign people to work that matches their technical competencies.

No, the problem isn't the stress or long hours, Chan thought. The problem is money—too much money. Most of the people who leave are millionaires. Suzanne Chalmers is one of them. Thanks to generous share options that have skyrocketed on the stock markets, many employees at API have more money than they can use. Most are under 40 years old, so it's too early for them to retire. But their financial independence gives them less reason to remain with API.

The Meeting

The meeting with Suzanne Chalmers took place a few hours after the telephone call. It began like the others, with the initial pleasantries and brief discussion about progress on the latest fibre-optic router project. Then, Suzanne made her well-rehearsed statement: "Thomas, I've really enjoyed working here, but I'm going to leave Advanced Photonics." Suzanne took a breath, then looked at Chan. When he didn't reply after a few seconds, she continued: "I need to take time off. You know, get away to recharge my batteries. The project's nearly done and the team can complete it without me. Well, anyway, I'm thinking of leaving."

Chan spoke in a calm voice. He suggested that Suzanne should take an unpaid leave for two or maybe three months, complete with paid benefits, then return refreshed. Suzanne politely rejected that offer, saying that she needs to get away from work for a while. Thomas then asked Suzanne whether she was unhappy with her work environment—whether she was getting the latest computer technology to do her work and whether there were problems with co-workers. The workplace was fine, Susanne replied. The job was getting a bit routine, but she had a comfortable workplace with excellent co-workers.

Chan then apologized for the cramped workspace, due mainly to the rapid increase in the number of people hired over the past year. He suggested that if Suzanne took a couple of months off, API would give her special treatment with a larger work space with a better view of the park behind the campus-like building when she returned. She politely thanked Chan for that offer, but it wasn't what she needed. Besides, it wouldn't be fair to have a large work space when other team members work in smaller quarters.

Chan was running out of tactics, so he tried his last hope: money. He asked whether Suzanne had higher offers. Suzanne replied that she regularly received calls from other companies, and some of them offered more money. Most were start-up firms that offered a lower salary but higher potential gains in share options. Chan knew from market surveys that Suzanne was already paid well in the industry. He also knew that API couldn't compete on share option potential. Employees working in start-up firms sometimes saw their shares increase by five or 10 times their initial value, whereas shares at API and other large firms increased more slowly. However, Chan promised Suzanne that he would recommend that she receive a significant raise—maybe 25 percent more—and more share options. Chan added that Chalmers was one of API's most valuable employees and that the company would suffer if she left the firm.

The meeting ended with Chalmers promising to consider Chan's offer of higher pay and share options. Two days later, Chan received her resignation in writing. Five months later, Chan learned that after a few months travelling with her husband, Chalmers joined a start-up software firm in the area.

Copyright © 2001. Steven L. McShane.

Case 8   Nirvana Art Gallery

By Christine Ho, University of Adelaide

It was an irony not lost on many of the employees of Nirvana Art Gallery. This gallery was far from being a place of harmony and joy. In fact, some of the employees preferred to refer to management using the acronym 'NAG' in a derogatory manner.

Nirvana was regarded as one of the leading museums of art in Australia. The collection of Australian art was one of the oldest and best known in the country. This museum also housed an enviable Aboriginal collection and an international collection of considerable breadth and depth.

Rod was the Assistant Curator for the Curatorial unit. Despite his job title, his time was divided between the Curatorial and Research units because there was not enough work in the former to keep him occupied from week to week. It was agreed between the managers of the two units that he work Monday to Wednesday at Curatorial and then the remaining days at Research. While Rod would have preferred to work solely for Curatorial because that was where his interests lay, he was in no position to argue with either manager. He hoped that when he finished his PhD in art history he would be employed full-time in Curatorial where he could fully utilize his specialized knowledge and meet his aspiration to be a curator.

Rod did not particularly enjoy coming to work on Thursdays. The research he was asked to do was okay. It was not that stimulating, but he convinced himself that it was useful to understand the functions of the different units in the gallery, and not restrict himself to purely curatorial issues. The Research unit was quite small and the staff were very serious. Because they were located within close proximity to each other, initially, he tried to be friendly to them while they worked.

When he kept getting frowns and annoyed looks from his colleagues, it became obvious that they did not like being disrupted. Further, they assumed he did not have enough work to do, so they kept giving him more tasks. Rod found himself falling behind and having to ask for permission to stay late to finish his work. Because the gallery housed expensive art works, security was tight. All staff were expected to leave by 5 p.m. and not return until the following morning after 8 a.m. Management were very strict about granting this special permission because Security had to be notified so that alarm systems could be adjusted and monitored accordingly. Because the Research manager, Nelly, often stayed late she did not mind granting Rod permission as well.

On Friday morning, Rod met with Nelly to give her the report he had written on business plans.

"Thanks Rod, it looks good," said Nelly, as she flipped through the document. "You're still working on that draft document on the current spending and budget allocation for this year, aren't you? Andrew can help you with this."

Rod hesitated. "Oh, I think I have all the necessary information, and I'm sure Andrew is busy anyway. If I stay late tonight, I might be able to give it to you before I leave work."

"What's wrong?" asked Nelly.

"It's nothing. I just always get the impression that I'm disturbing everyone in Research. They seem really busy all the time and don't seem to have time for anything else. I'm more of a sociable and friendly person, and like to talk with others while I work."

Nelly gave him a look, which Rod did not know how to decipher. I hope she does not think I am complaining about my job or my colleagues, Rod thought to himself as he walked out of her office. He liked the fact that no one was breathing down his neck all the time. And the last thing he needed was to create animosity between himself and the rest of Research. It was bad enough that they always would go out for lunch together and never invited him. But at least they could say 'hi' whenever he was there.

The following Thursday, when Nelly came into the Research area to talk to one of the researchers, she came by his desk to say that she had read both his reports that he finished last week, thanked him for his hard work, and asked how his work was going. He appreciated the attention. Over the following weeks when he was in Research, she would come by and talk to him. This sometimes included complimenting him on his appearance. How his shirt colour emphasized his eyes, or his new stylish haircut made him look more handsome. At least someone was talking to me, thought Rod. He did not think her comments were appropriate, but he accepted them graciously with a smile, but made sure he kept his comments professional. He also tried to minimize how often he had to stay late at work so as not to give the wrong impression. But usually that was not possible given his workload.

It was not long before the other researchers noticed the attention she gave him. He started noticing the surreptitious looks and frowns he received whenever she spoke to him. Rod thought he was being paranoid. A couple of times when he had walked into the Research area, some of the researchers were talking in low voices, but they would stop when they noticed him.

Rod wondered what was going on. It was not like he was not pulling his own weight around here. He got the projects done on time even though he only worked two days in Research and Nelly had told him numerous times that he was doing a good job. Rod put his thoughts aside and focused on his day's tasks. He went home that weekend pleased for once he did not have to work late.

He arrived to work on Monday in good spirits. He had studied all weekend and nearly completed his final draft of his PhD thesis. He always enjoyed working in the Curatorial unit. He found his work preparing upcoming exhibitions interesting. Further, he quite liked the Curatorial team. His manager, Sarah, was approachable and despite being the most junior member, his colleagues regularly asked for his input during the weekly Monday meetings. The team was friendly and he found he had a lot in common with many of them. Sometimes he would be invited to lunch when he was there on one of his Curatorial days. Working in Curatorial also meant that he was not in Research. He would not have to put up with Nelly's comments, which were beginning to really make him feel uncomfortable, and he did not have to put up with the whispers or silent stares he got from his Research colleagues. Rod was looking forward to working on a catalogue for an Aboriginal exhibition the gallery was to host next month when Nelly walked in.

"Rod, you're looking sexy today. Andrew is away sick. Can you come and work in Research today?" she asked.

"Um, I can't Nelly. I'm supposed to work in Curatorial today and it's really busy at the moment. We've got this exhibition coming up and we're behind. Claire is on maternity leave and two others in Curatorial are sick as well with that flu that's going around at the moment. Sorry, but I can't."

Nelly frowned and left without a backwards glance. I'll be at Research soon enough on Thursday anyway, thought Rod.

Later that day, Rod received an email from Nelly.

Rod,

There has been a change in your work arrangement to start this week. The Assistant Director and I have decided that instead of working in Curatorial three days and Research two days, you will now work in Curatorial only two days, and then on Wednesday switch over to Research for the rest of the week.

Nelly.

Rod began to feel panicky. The whole point of this job was to gain curatorial experience, which was why he had changed his PhD status to part-time. He went to see Sarah to see if she could get his work days changed back. Unfortunately, Sarah only confirmed the arrangement.

"There's nothing I can do about this, Rod. I wish I could, but Nelly helped me get this job. You're a valuable member of Curatorial and we both know everyone on the team is flat out with the others away sick or on leave. Nelly has more authority than me and is good friends with the Assistant Director."

When Rod arrived in Research on Wednesday, Nelly told him that the desk arrangements were to be changed around. His desk was now visible from her office at all times. Other things began to change in Research as well. Nelly rarely spoke to him except to pass on job assignments. And because he was there an extra day each week, he was able to complete his tasks without having to stay after hours. Rod was pleased about that. However, as the weeks passed, there were not even enough tasks to keep him occupied and he would be told to 'find something to do.' He felt like he was wasting his time, especially since Curatorial continued to be short staffed and Research was now brimming with staff and limited work. Rod hated that sometimes he had to pretend to be busy.

To make matters worse, when he would arrive at work Nelly had started to remark, "So *now* you've decided to turn up to work," or "getting your beauty sleep, were we?" His fellow researchers began to chime in with similar snide remarks, like "while you've been having your latte, we've been at work since 8 a.m."

It was getting unbearable in Research for Rod. Even though his colleagues were talking to him now, he much preferred it when they were not.

Rod was unhappy. He was at lunch with some of the Curatorial staff and told them about the email.

"You'll just have to do the time with Research, and hope that you get back on the good side of Nelly. She may eventually change things back so that you can work more in Curatorial. She's a NAG who likes to use her power over others. It's happened before."

Case 9   Northwest Canadian Forest Products Limited

By Peter Seidl, British Columbia Institute of Technology

Northwest Canadian Forest Products Limited owns and operates five sawmills in British Columbia and Alberta. These mills produce high-quality lumber for use in the manufacture of window frames, doors, and mouldings for markets in the United States and Japan in addition to lower-quality, commodity-type lumber used in the Canadian construction industry. Currently, the president of the company is thinking about the long-term prospects of each of the mills and is paying particular attention to the Jackson Sawmill located in the small town of Jackson, B.C.

This mill was originally built in 1950 and was last upgraded in 1986. The president knows she will soon (in 2008) have to decide whether or not to invest substantial sums of money ($50 million) in new plant and equipment at the Jackson Sawmill. New investment is required in order to keep the mill up-to-date and competitive with similar mills throughout North America. However, the mill has consistently been the poorest performer (in terms of productivity and product quality) in the company since 1986 even though its equipment is of similar age, type, and quality as that found in the other mills.

The president would like to invest the money needed because the alternative to reinvesting in Jackson would be to downsize the Jackson Sawmill by reducing production capacity and permanently laying off over half the 200-person workforce. The remaining part of the mill would serve the domestic market only. A new mill would then be built in Alberta in order to serve the more demanding, quality-conscious export markets. A new mill in Alberta would cost more than the $50-million investment required at the Jackson Sawmill. However, the president is willing to seriously consider implementing this alternative because she thinks that the labour relations climate in Alberta is much better than the one found at Jackson.

In fact, she attributes most, if not all, of the problems at Jackson to its poor labour-management relations. During the last round of collective bargaining, there was a strike at all four of the company's B.C. mills. The strike was, however, much more bitter at Jackson than elsewhere. Company buildings suffered minor damage during the strike at the hands of some striking employees. Since then, there were two separate occasions when the entire workforce walked off the job for a day to protest the firings of two employees who were dismissed for insubordination.

The Jackson Sawmill has the worst safety record of all the company's mills. There is a joint labour-management safety committee (as required by law) but it is viewed as a waste of time by both sides. One management member of the safety committee, Des, the production manager and the second highest manager at the mill, has said: "The union guys start each safety committee meeting by complaining about safety but they just can't wait to complain about everything else they can possibly think of. Their whining and complaining is so predictable that I go to every safety meeting ready for a fight on workload and production issues as well as for a fight on safety. Of course, safety is everyone's responsibility but production issues are none of their business. Production is a management responsibility. Plans, budgets, and other management concerns are very definitely not part of the committee's job. Most of what's said at these meetings isn't worth listening to."

The union is also dissatisfied with the functioning of the safety committee. Ivan, the chief union steward who also serves on the committee, observes: "If the safety committee wasn't mandatory by law, management wouldn't even pretend to listen to us. We put forward our safety concerns but management says that we are mixing safety in with workload and production issues. They only want to talk about what they think are safety issues—like serious accidents. Thankfully, we don't have too many of those! But safety is more than just avoiding major accidents. We get far too many 'little accidents' and 'near-accidents' here. At least that's what management calls them. They just want us to work faster and faster. We complain and complain at the meetings but they just say 'that's a production issue and this is a safety committee.' They accuse us of trying to run the company when we ask for better equipment. They say we don't understand things like costs and limited budgets. We don't care about their budgets, we've got work issues to talk about and we'll keep speaking out for the crew no matter what. That's what the union is for."

Big Bad John, one of the mill's toughest and most experienced supervisors, describes his job as follows: "The job of supervisor is to keep a close watch on every move the crew makes. If I look away for a second, some guy is going to be doing something wrong—either with the equipment or with the logs. They're always making mistakes. Lots of mistakes! Some of these guys are just plain dumb. And lazy, too! Any chance they can get to steal some company time, they take. They start work late, they take long lunch breaks, they talk too much during their shifts. A minute here, a minute there—it all adds up. The younger guys are the worst. They always want to talk back to me, they can't follow my orders like most of the older guys can. Lousy attitude, that's what they've got."

Vic, the youngest union steward, gives his view of labour-management relations: "The supervisors and the managers, they know it all. They think they're so smart. They treat the guys on the crew like children. Almost everyone on the crew has a high school education. Some even have college backgrounds. Most are raising families. We're not stupid! Sure, some guys come in late and miss a day of work now and then. Who can blame them? The pace of work is exhausting. How can you do a good job when you're tired and rushing all the time?" He adds: "Of course, we're not perfect. We make mistakes just like everyone else does. But nobody ever explains anything to the crew members. The supervisors just watch everyone like hawks and jump all over them, criticize them, and make them feel stupid when they use a piece of equipment the wrong way. We're always so rushed and busy here that the senior crew members don't have much time to explain things to the newer workers, the younger guys. Also, the equipment could be in better shape, that would help."

The production manager, Des, observes that "the union just doesn't understand—or even care about—the connection between the poor work ethic, the poor attitude on the part of the crew members here, and the mill's mediocre productivity and product quality. The union and the crew only take their very narrow 'employee-view' of how things are done around here. They don't understand the bigger picture. Well, it's very competitive out there. They don't understand what tight budgets, increasing costs, declining quality, missed production targets, and complaining customers mean to a business. They just sit back and complain about our management style. What they don't realize is that their attitude makes our management style necessary. Complaining is easy, no responsibility is needed. Managing, on the other hand, is challenging. And it's especially tough to control and manage this particular crew. We've currently got 30 unresolved grievances—that's a lot of formal complaints for a mill of our size. Some of the union stewards actually go out among the crew and look for grievances just because they're mad they can't run the mill the way they want to. Sometimes I think the stewards want to create grievances where no real problems exist. They want to give us in management headaches."

The president of the company has recently informed Digby, the mill's new general manager (he started at Jackson last month after a career in eastern Canada), of the decision she will soon have to make regarding the mill's future. She told Digby that significant improvements in mill productivity and product quality are required if the mill is to receive the $50-million investment in new plant and equipment. Without such improvements, the mill would be downsized and over half of the workforce would be permanently laid off. Half the supervisory and managerial personnel would also lose their jobs.

Digby has just telephoned Moe (the president of the local union who does not work at the mill but who is very familiar with developments at the mill) to tell him about the message from the company president. Upon hearing of the potential job losses, Moe was troubled and asked to meet with Digby to discuss the situation. However, Moe was also somewhat skeptical because the previous general manager once told him that some permanent layoffs would occur unless productivity was improved. No layoffs subsequently occurred. Therefore, Moe is uncertain if the company is serious about these potential future layoffs or merely bluffing in order to get the employees to work harder.

Case 10 Perfect Pizzeria

By J. E. Dittrich and R. A. Zawacki

Perfect Pizzeria in Southville, deep in southern Illinois, is the chain's second-largest franchise. The headquarters is located in Phoenix, Arizona. Although the business is prospering, it has employee and managerial problems.

Each operation has one manager, an assistant manager, and from two to five night managers. The managers of each pizzeria work under an area supervisor. There are no systematic criteria for being a manager or becoming a manager trainee. The franchise has no formalized training period for the manager. No college education is required. The managers for whom the case observer worked during a four-year period were relatively young (ages 24 to 27), and only one had completed college. They came from the ranks of night managers, assistant managers, or both. The night managers were chosen for their ability to perform the duties of the regular employees. The assistant managers worked a two-hour shift during the luncheon period five days a week to gain knowledge about bookkeeping and management. Those becoming managers remained at that level unless they expressed interest in investing in the business.

The employees were mostly college students, with a few high school students performing the less challenging jobs. Because Perfect Pizzeria was located in an area with few job opportunities, it was relatively easy for it to fill its employee quotas. All the employees, with the exception of the manager, were employed part-time. Consequently, they earned only the minimum wage.

The Perfect Pizzeria system is devised so that food and beverage costs and profits are set up according to a percentage. If the percentage of food unsold or damaged in any way is very low, the manager gets a bonus. If the percentage is high, the manager does not receive a bonus; rather, he or she receives only his or her normal salary.

There are many ways in which the percentage can fluctuate. Because the manager cannot be in the store 24 hours a day, some employees make up for their paycheques by helping themselves to the food. When a friend comes in to order a pizza, extra ingredients are put on the friend's pizza. Occasional nibbles by 18 to 20 employees throughout the day at the meal table also raise the percentage figure. An occasional bucket of sauce may be spilled or a pizza accidentally burned. Sometimes the wrong size of pizza may be made.

In the event of an employee mistake or a burned pizza by the oven person, the expense is supposed to come from the individual. Because of peer pressure, the night manager seldom writes up a bill for the erring employee. Instead, the establishment takes the loss and the error goes unnoticed until the end of the month when the inventory is taken. That's when the manager finds out that the percentage is high and that there will be no bonus.

In the present instance, the manager took retaliatory measures. Previously, each employee was entitled to a free pizza, salad, and all the soft drinks he or she could drink for every six hours of work. The manager raised this figure from six to 12 hours of work. However, the employees had received these six-hour benefits for a long time. Therefore, they simply took advantage of the situation whenever the manager or the assistant was not in the building. Although the night managers theoretically had complete control of the operation in the evenings, they did not command the respect that the manager or assistant manager did. That was because night managers received the same pay as the regular employees, could not reprimand other employees, and were basically the same age or sometimes even younger than the other employees.

Thus, apathy grew within the pizzeria. There seemed to be a further separation between the manager and his workers, who started out to be a closely knit group. The manager made no attempt to alleviate the problem, because he felt it would iron itself out. Either the employees who were dissatisfied would quit or they would be content to put up with the new regulations. As it turned out, there was a rash of employee dismissals. The manager had no problem in filling the vacancies with new workers, but the loss of key personnel was costly to the business.

With the large turnover, the manager found he had to spend more time in the building, supervising and sometimes taking the place of inexperienced workers. This was in direct violation of the franchise regulation, which stated that a manager would act as a supervisor and at no time take part in the actual food preparation. Employees were not placed under strict supervision with the manager working alongside them. The operation no longer worked smoothly because of differences between the remaining experienced workers and the manager concerning the way in which a particular function should be performed.

Within a two-month period, the manager was again free to go back to his office and leave his subordinates in charge of the entire operation. During this two-month period, in spite of the differences between experienced workers and the manager, the unsold/damaged food percentage had returned to the previous low level and the manager received a bonus each month. The manager felt that his problems had been resolved and that conditions would remain the same, since the new personnel had been properly trained.

It didn't take long for the new employees to become influenced by the other employees. Immediately after the manager had returned to his supervisory role, the unsold/damaged food percentage began to rise. This time the manager took a bolder step. He cut out *any* benefits that the employees had—no free pizzas, salads, or drinks. With the job market at an even lower ebb than usual, most employees were forced to stay. The appointment of a new area supervisor made it impossible for the manager to work behind the counter, because the supervisor was centrally located in Southville.

The manager tried still another approach to alleviate the rising unsold/damaged food percentage problem and maintain his bonus. He placed a notice on the bulletin board, stating that if the percentage remained at a high level, a lie detector test would be given to all employees. All those found guilty of taking or purposefully wasting food or drinks would be immediately terminated. This did not have the desired effect on the employees, because they knew if they were all subjected to the test, all would be found guilty and the manager would have to dismiss all of them. This would leave him in a worse situation than ever.

Even before the following month's unsold/damaged food percentage was calculated, the manager knew it would be high. He had evidently received information from one of the night managers about the employees' feelings toward the notice. What he did not expect was that the percentage would reach an all-time high. That is the state of affairs at the present time.

John E. Dittrich and Robert A. Zawacki, *People and Organizations* (Plano, TX: Business Publications, 1981), pp. 126–28. Used by permission of McGraw-Hill Ryerson.

Case 11   Rhonda Clark: Taking Charge at the Smith Foundation

By Joseph C. Santora, Essex County College & TST, Inc.

Dr. Rhonda Clark was ecstatic as she hung up the telephone. Bennett Mitchell, chairperson of KLS Executive Search firm, had just informed her that she landed the coveted position of chief executive officer (CEO) at the Smith Foundation, a nonprofit organization whose mission was to fund public awareness campaigns and research programs about eye care. Clark knew that she had just pulled off a major coup. Her appointment to this new, challenging position would indeed be *the* high point in a long arduous climb to the executive suite. As an organizational outsider—one with no work experience within the hiring organization—she assumed that her appointment as CEO signalled a strong desire by the board to shake up the organizational status quo. However, she heard from a very reliable inside source that the very board that hired her and charged her with the responsibility of transforming the foundation was extremely fragmented. The often-rambunctious board had forced the last five CEOs to resign after very short tenures. Clark's feeling of exhilaration was rapidly being replaced by cautious optimism. As a new CEO, she pondered the rather thorny question: how could she take charge of the board of directors to ensure the mission of the organization would be accomplished?

Background

Charlie Smith, an industrialist and philanthropist, founded the Smith Foundation 40 years ago with a multimillion-dollar endowment. Despite this generous financial start-up capital and additional income derived from several financial investments and major corporate donations, in recent years, the foundation's endowment has been slowly dwindling as a result of rather significant funding awards to academics, community organizations, and smaller, less well-funded foundations. Board members have held some preliminary discussions about developing new innovative strategies to strengthen the balance sheet of the organization. Currently, the foundation operates on an annual budget of slightly less than $1,500,000.

In the last five years, some foundation board members have begun to abandon many of their fiduciary responsibilities. Over the past few months, several board meetings have been cancelled because the meetings lacked a quorum. In general, this 13-member board seemed to drift aimlessly in one direction or another. The board has been operating at only 70-percent capacity for the past two years with nine active board members—five men and four women.

Challenges

Dr. Rhonda Clark believed she was the one who could lead the Smith Foundation. She had great academic credentials and management experience that would help her tackle her new position as the foundation head. In the last 30 years, the 54-year-old Clark, who holds a PhD in political science and policy analysis from a major U.S. west coast university, has gained an enviable amount of managerial experience in the nonprofit and public sectors. Past professional experiences included a graduate school professorship; a director of research for a major political office holder, the director of planning in a large metropolitan hospital, and the director of programs at a small foundation.

Immediately upon taking office, Clark was astounded to learn that a small, but active and influential faction on the board, had withdrawn its initial verbal promise to assist her in working closely with the corporate community. Essentially, she was informed that she was solely responsible for all external corporate relations. Clark thought to herself, "I wonder if they hired me because they thought they would get a 'do-nothing' female leader. These folks want me to either sink or swim on my own. Perhaps they set me up for failure by giving me a one-year appointment." She lamented: "I won't let this happen. I really need to learn about the key decision makers and stakeholders on the board and in the larger community, and fast."

At the last board meeting Clark detailed the major elements of her latest proposal. Yet, several board members seemed totally unfazed by it. Soon she began to encounter stiff resistance from some male board members. Jim Jackson, in particular, told Clark: "We are disappointed that you failed to win a city contract to conduct a feasibility study to determine if we can erect a facility in another section of town. We're not certain if you have the right stuff to run this foundation, and we certainly won't help you to gain financial support for the foundation by using our personal, corporate, or political contacts." Jackson thought to himself: "We've removed CEOs before, we can remove Clark, too."

After hearing Jackson's comments Clark decided to take another tack. She began to focus her attention on making external and internal inroads which she believed could result in some modest gains for the foundation. For example, she identified and developed a close relationship with a few well-connected city agency executives, persuaded some supporters to nominate her for membership on two very influential boards, and forged a relationship with two key foundation decision makers and political power brokers. She reconfigured the internal structure of the foundation to increase maximum productivity from the staff, and she tightened budgetary controls by changing some fiscal policies and procedures.

Clark also sought the support of Susan Frost, a board member who likely had been instrumental in Clark's appointment as CEO. Clark said to herself "If I can develop a strong symbiotic relationship with some female board members, like Sue, to support my plan, then maybe I get some traction." To do this Clark held a number of late evening meetings with Sue and another female board member. They indicated their willingness to help her, but only if she would consider implementing a few of their ideas for the foundation as well as recommending their close friend for a current staff vacancy. Clark knew they were trying to exercise their political influence; yet, she believed that everyone could benefit from this *quid quo pro* relationship. She said to herself "I guess it's a matter of you scratch my back, and I scratch yours." She eagerly agreed to move their agenda along. In a matter of a few weeks, as promised, they began working on a couple of relatively "sympathetic" board members. One day Clark got a very terse, but critical telephone call from Sue. "Several of us support you. Proceed!"

Once she heard this, Clark began to move at lightening speed. She formed a 15-member coalition of community, educational, and quasi-governmental agencies that would apply for a collaborative federal grant to create a public awareness eye campaign for children. Through the dissemination of various media, coalition members would help to inform the community-at-large about various eye diseases that afflict young school age children. Shortly afterwards, Clark received notification from a federal agency that this multi-agency project would be awarded a million-dollar grant. Clark would serve as the administrative and fiscal agent of the grant, and as a result, she would be able to earmark a considerable amount of the administrative oversight dollars for the foundation's budget. For her efforts at coordinating this project, Clark received high marks from coalition and community members alike.

Yet, despite this important initial accomplishment, Clark had the unpleasant task of notifying the full board that, due to some unforeseen problems and their lack of support on certain key initiatives, the foundation would still experience a financial deficit. She heard several rumours that her next employment contract would not be renewed by the executive committee of the board. At this point she thought about directly confronting the obstructionists on the board by telling them that they were unreasonable and in fact that they were why the foundation had not recovered during the past year...but she hesitated: she had signed on to do a job, and she was unsure if it was the wisest course of action to take at this time.

Despite this latest conflict between herself and certain board members, she paused to reflect on what she believed to have been a tumultuous year as CEO.

Note: *The names and some managerial actions in this case have been altered to preserve the integrity and anonymity of the organization. This case is intended to be used as a basis for class discussion rather than to illustrate either effective or ineffective handling of a management situation.*

Copyright © Joseph C. Santora, Essex County College & TST, Inc.

Case 12 Treetop Forest Products

Steven L. McShane, The University of Western Australia, and David Lebeter

Treetop Forest Products Ltd. is a sawmill operation in British Columbia, that is owned by a major forest products company, but operates independently of headquarters. It was built 30 years ago, and completely updated with new machinery five years ago. Treetop receives raw logs from the area for cutting and planing into building-grade lumber, mostly 2-by-4 and 2-by-6 pieces of standard lengths. Higher grade logs leave Treetop's sawmill department in finished form and are sent directly to the packaging department. The remaining 40 percent of sawmill output are cuts from lower grade logs, requiring further work by the planing department.

Treetop has one general manager, 16 supervisors and support staff, and 180 unionized employees. The unionized employees are paid an hourly rate specified in the collective agreement, whereas management and support staff are paid a monthly salary. The mill is divided into six operating departments: boom, sawmill, planer, packaging, shipping, and maintenance. The sawmill, boom, and packaging departments operate a morning shift starting at 6 a.m. and an afternoon shift starting at 2 p.m. Employees in these departments rotate shifts every two weeks. The planer and shipping departments operate only morning shifts. Maintenance employees work the night shift (starting at 10 p.m.).

Each department, except for packaging, has a supervisor on every work shift. The planer supervisor is responsible for the packaging department on the morning shift, and the sawmill supervisor is responsible for the packaging department on the afternoon shift. However, the packaging operation is housed in a separate building from the other departments, so supervisors seldom visit the packaging department. This is particularly true for the afternoon shift, because the sawmill supervisor is the furthest distance from the packaging building.

Packaging Quality

Ninety percent of Treetop's product is sold on the international market through Westboard Co., a large marketing agency. Westboard represents all forest products mills owned by Treetop's parent company as well as several other clients in the region. The market for building-grade lumber is very price competitive, because there are numerous mills selling a relatively undifferentiated product. However, some differentiation does occur in product packaging and presentation. Buyers will look closely at the packaging when deciding whether to buy from Treetop or another mill.

To encourage its clients to package their products better, Westboard sponsors a monthly package quality award. The marketing agency samples and rates its clients' packages daily, and the sawmill with the highest score at the end of the month is awarded a plaque. Package quality is a combination of how the lumber is piled (e.g., defects turned in), where the bands and dunnage are placed, how neatly the stencil and seal are applied, the stencil's accuracy, and how neatly and tightly the plastic wrap is attached.

Treetop Forest Products won Westboard's packaging quality award several times over the past five years, and received high ratings in the months that it didn't win. However, the mill's ratings have started to decline over the past year or two, and several clients have complained about the appearance of the finished product. A few large customers switched to competitors' lumber, saying that the decision was based on the substandard appearance of Treetop's packaging when it arrived in their lumber yard.

Bottleneck in Packaging

The planing and sawmilling departments have significantly increased productivity over the past couple of years. The sawmill operation recently set a new productivity record on a single day. The planer operation has increased productivity to the point where last year it reduced operations to just one (rather than two) shifts per day. These productivity improvements are due to better operator training, fewer machine breakdowns, and better selection of raw logs. (Sawmill cuts from high-quality logs usually do not require planing work.)

Productivity levels in the boom, shipping, and maintenance departments have remained constant. However, the packaging department has recorded decreasing productivity over the past couple of years, with the result that a large backlog of finished product is typically stockpiled outside the packaging building. The morning shift of the packaging department is unable to keep up with the combined production of the sawmill and planer departments, so the unpackaged output is left for the afternoon shift. Unfortunately, the afternoon shift packages even less product than the morning shift, so the backlog continues to build. The backlog adds to Treetop's inventory costs and increases the risk of damaged stock.

Treetop has added Saturday overtime shifts as well as extra hours before and after the regular shifts for the packaging department employees to process this backlog. Last month, the packaging department employed 10 percent of the work force but accounted for 85 percent of the overtime. This is frustrating to Treetop's management, because time and motion studies recently confirmed that the packaging department is capable of processing all of the daily sawmill and planer production without overtime. Moreover, with employees earning one and a half or two times their regular pay on overtime, Treetop's cost competitiveness suffers.

Employees and supervisors at Treetop are aware that people in the packaging department tend to extend lunch by 10 minutes and coffee breaks by 5 minutes. They also typically leave work a few minutes before the end of shift. This abuse has worsened recently, particularly on the afternoon shift. Employees who are temporarily assigned to the packaging department also seem to participate in this time loss pattern after a few days. Although they are punctual and productive in other departments, these temporary employees soon adopt the packaging crew's informal schedule when assigned to that department.

APPENDIX A

Theory Building and Systematic Research Methods

People need to make sense of their world, so they form theories about the way the world operates. A **theory** is a general set of propositions that describes interrelationships among several concepts. We form theories for the purpose of predicting and explaining the world around us.[1] What does a good theory look like? First, it should be stated clearly and simply as possible so that the concepts can be measured and there is no ambiguity regarding the theory's propositions. Second, the elements of the theory must be logically consistent with each other, because we cannot test anything that doesn't make sense. Finally, a good theory provides value to society; it helps people understand their world better than without the theory.[2]

Theory building is a continuous process that typically includes the inductive and deductive stages shown in Exhibit A.1.[3] The inductive stage draws on personal experience to form a preliminary theory, whereas the deductive stage uses the scientific method to test the theory.

The inductive stage of theory building involves observing the world around us, identifying a pattern of relationships, and then forming a theory from these personal observations. For example, you might casually notice that new employees want their supervisor to give direction, whereas this leadership style irritates long-service employees. From these observations, you form a theory about the effectiveness of directive leadership. (See Chapter 12 for a discussion of this leadership style.)

POSITIVISM VERSUS INTERPRETIVISM

Research requires an interpretation of reality, and researchers tend to perceive reality in one of two ways. A common view, called **positivism**, is that reality exists independent of people. It is "out there" to be discovered and tested. Positivism is the foundation for most quantitative research (statistical analysis). It assumes that we can measure

EXHIBIT A.1 Theory building and theory testing

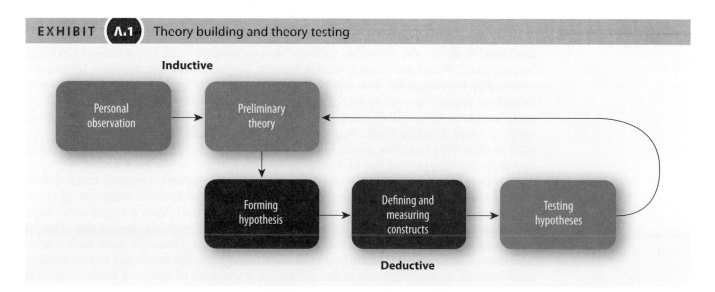

variables and those variables have fixed relationships with other variables. For example, the positivist perspective says that we could study whether a supportive style of leadership reduces stress. If we find evidence of this, then someone else studying leadership and stress would "discover" the same relationship.

Interpretivism takes a different view of reality. It suggests that reality comes from shared meaning among people in that environment. For example, supportive leadership is a personal interpretation of reality, not something that can be measured across time and people. Interpretivists rely mainly on qualitative data, such as observation and nondirective interviews. They particularly listen to the language people use to understand the common meaning that people have toward various events or phenomena. For example, they might argue that you need to experience and observe supportive leadership to effectively study it. Moreover, you can't really predict relationships because the specific situation shapes reality.[4]

Most OB scholars identify themselves somewhere between the extreme views of positivism and interpretivism. Many believe that inductive research should begin with an interpretivist angle. We should enter a new topic with an open mind and search for shared meaning of people in that situation. In other words, researchers should let the participants define reality rather than let the researcher's preconceived notions shape that reality. This process involves gathering qualitative information and letting this information shape their theory.[5] After the theory emerges, researchers shift to positivist perspective by quantitatively testing relationships in that theory.

THEORY TESTING: THE DEDUCTIVE PROCESS

Once a theory has been formed, we shift into the deductive stage of theory building. This process includes forming hypotheses, defining and measuring constructs, and testing hypotheses (see Exhibit A.1). **Hypotheses** make empirically testable declarations that certain variables and their corresponding measures are related in a specific way proposed by the theory. For instance, to find support for the directive leadership theory described earlier, we need to form and then test a specific hypothesis from that theory. One such hypothesis might be: "New employees are more satisfied with supervisors who exhibit a directive rather than nondirective leadership style." Hypotheses are indispensable tools of scientific research, because they provide the vital link between the theory and empirical verification.

DEFINING AND MEASURING CONSTRUCTS

Hypotheses are testable only if we can define and then form measurable indicators of the concepts stated in those hypotheses. Consider the hypothesis in the previous paragraph about new employees and directive leadership. To test this hypothesis, we first need to define the concepts, such as "new employees," "directive leadership," and "supervisor." These are known as **constructs**, because they are abstract ideas constructed by the researcher that can be linked to observable information. Organizational behaviour researchers developed the construct called *directive leadership* to help them understand the different effects that leaders have over followers. We can't directly see, taste, or smell directive leadership; instead, we rely on indirect indicators that it exists, such as observing someone giving directions, maintaining clear performance standards, and ensuring that procedures and practices are followed.

As you can see, defining constructs well is very important, because these definitions become the foundation for finding or developing acceptable measures of those constructs. We can't measure directive leadership if we only have a vague idea about what this concept means. The better the construct is defined, the better our chances of finding or developing a good measure of that construct. However, even with a good definition, constructs can be difficult to measure, because the empirical representation must capture several elements in the definition. A measure of directive leadership must be able to identify not only people who give directions, but also those who maintain performance standards and ensure that procedures are followed.

TESTING HYPOTHESES

The third step in the deductive process is to collect data for the empirical measures of the variables. Following our directive leadership example, we might conduct a formal survey in which new employees indicate the behaviour of their supervisors and their attitudes toward their supervisor. Alternatively, we might design an experiment in which people work with someone who applies either a directive or nondirective leadership style. When the data have been collected, we can use various procedures to statistically test our hypotheses.

A major concern in theory building is that some researchers might inadvertently find support for their theory simply because they use the same information used to form the theory during the inductive stage. Consequently, the deductive stage must collect new data that are completely independent of the data used during the inductive stage. For instance, you might decide to test your theory of directive leadership by studying employees in another organization. Moreover, the inductive process may have relied mainly on personal observation, whereas the deductive process might use survey questionnaires. By studying different samples and using different measurement tools, we minimize the risk of conducting circular research.

USING THE SCIENTIFIC METHOD

Earlier, we said that the deductive stage of theory building follows the scientific method. The **scientific method** is systematic, controlled, empirical, and critical investigation of hypothetical propositions about the presumed relationships among natural phenomena.[6] There are several elements to this definition, so let's look at each one. First, scientific research is systematic and controlled, because researchers want to rule out all but one explanation for a set of interrelated events. To rule out alternative explanations, we need to control them in some way, such as by keeping them constant or removing them entirely from the environment.

Second, we say that scientific research is empirical because researchers need to use objective reality—or as close as we can get to it—to test theory. They measure observable elements of the environment, such as what a person says or does, rather than rely on their own subjective opinion to draw conclusions. Moreover, scientific research analyses these data using acceptable principles of mathematics and logic.

Finally, scientific research involves critical investigation. This means that the study's hypotheses, data, methods, and results are openly described so that other experts in the field can properly evaluate this research. It also means that scholars are encouraged to critique and build on previous research. Eventually, the scientific method encourages the refinement and eventually the replacement of a particular theory with one that better suits our understanding of the world.

GROUNDED THEORY: AN ALTERNATIVE APPROACH

The scientific method dominates the quantitative approach to systematic research, but another approach, called **grounded theory**, dominates research using qualitative methods.[7] Grounded theory is a process of developing knowledge through the constant interplay of data collection, analysis, and theory development. It relies mainly on qualitative methods to form categories and variables, analyze relationships among these concepts, and form a model based on the observations and analysis. Grounded theory combines the inductive stages of theory development by cycling back and forth between data collection and analysis to converge on a robust explanatory model. This ongoing reciprocal process results in theory that is grounded in the data (thus, the name grounded theory).

Like the scientific method, grounded theory is a systematic and rigorous process of data collection and analysis. It requires specific steps and documentation, and adopts a positivist view by assuming that the results are generalizable to other settings. However, grounded theory also takes an interpretivist view by building categories and variables from the perceived realities of the subjects rather than from an assumed universal truth.[8] It also recognizes that personal biases are not easily removed from the research process.

SELECTED ISSUES IN ORGANIZATIONAL BEHAVIOUR RESEARCH

There are many issues to consider in theory building, particularly when we use the deductive process to test hypotheses. Some of the more important issues are sampling, causation, and ethical practices in organizational research.

SAMPLING IN ORGANIZATIONAL RESEARCH

When finding out why things happen in organizations, we typically gather information from a few sources and then draw conclusions about the larger population. If we survey several employees and determine that older employees are more loyal to their company, then we would like to generalize this statement to all older employees in our population, not just those whom we surveyed. Scientific inquiry generally requires researchers to engage in **representative sampling**—that is, sampling a population in such a way that we can extrapolate the results of that sample to the larger population.

One factor that influences representativeness is whether the sample is selected in an unbiased way from the larger population. Let's suppose that you want to study organizational commitment among employees in your organization. A casual procedure might result in sampling too few employees from the head office and too many located elsewhere in the country. If head office employees actually have higher loyalty than employees located elsewhere, then the biased sampling would cause the results to underestimate the true level of loyalty among employees in the company. If you repeat the process again next year but somehow overweight employees from the head office, the results might wrongly suggest that employees have increased their organizational commitment over the past year. In reality, the only change may be the direction of sampling bias.

How do we minimize sampling bias? The answer is to randomly select the sample. A randomly drawn sample gives each member of the population an equal probability of being chosen, so there is less likelihood that a subgroup within that population dominates the study's results.

The same principle applies to random assignment of subjects to groups in experimental designs. If we want to test the effects of a team development training program, we need to randomly place some employees in the training group and randomly place others in a group that does not receive training. Without this random selection, each group might have different types of employees, so we wouldn't know whether the training explains the differences between the two groups. Moreover, if employees respond differently to the training program, we couldn't be sure that the training program results are representative of the larger population. Of course, random sampling does not necessarily produce a perfectly representative sample, but we do know that this is the best approach to ensure unbiased selection.

The other factor that influences representativeness is sample size. Whenever we select a portion of the population, there will be some error in our estimate of the population values. The larger the sample, the less error will occur in our estimate. Let's suppose that you want to find out how employees in a 500-person firm feel about smoking in the workplace. If you asked 400 of those employees, the information would provide a very good estimate of how the entire work force in that organization feels. If you survey only

100 employees, the estimate might deviate more from the true population. If you ask only 10 people, the estimate could be quite different from what all 500 employees feel.

Notice that sample size goes hand in hand with random selection. You must have a sufficiently large sample size for the principle of randomization to work effectively. In our example of attitudes toward smoking, we would do a poor job of random selection if our sample consisted of only 10 employees from the 500-person organization. The reason is that these 10 people probably wouldn't capture the diversity of employees throughout the organization. In fact, the more diverse the population, the larger the sample size should be, to provide adequate representation through random selection.

CAUSATION IN ORGANIZATIONAL RESEARCH

Theories present notions about relationships among constructs. Often, these propositions suggest a causal relationship, namely, that one variable has an effect on another variable. When discussing causation, we refer to variables as being independent or dependent. Independent variables are the presumed causes of dependent variables, which are the presumed effects. In our earlier example of directive leadership, the main independent variable (there might be others) would be the supervisor's directive or nondirective leadership style, because we presume that it causes the dependent variable (satisfaction with supervision).

In laboratory experiments (described later), the independent variable is always manipulated by the experimenter. In our research on directive leadership, we might have subjects (new employees) work with supervisors who exhibit directive or nondirective leadership behaviours. If subjects are more satisfied under the directive leaders, then we would be able to infer an association between the independent and dependent variables.

Researchers must satisfy three conditions to provide sufficient evidence of causality between two variables.[9] The first condition of causality is that the variables are empirically associated with each other. An association exists whenever one measure of a variable changes systematically with a measure of another variable. This condition of causality is the easiest to satisfy, because there are several well-known statistical measures of association. A research study might find, for instance, that heterogeneous groups (in which members come from diverse backgrounds) produce more creative solutions to problems. This might be apparent because the measure of creativity (such as number of creative solutions produced within a fixed time) is higher for teams that have a high score on the measure of group heterogeneity. They are statistically associated or correlated with each other.

The second condition of causality is that the independent variable precedes the dependent variable in time. Sometimes, this condition is satisfied through simple logic. In our group heterogeneity example, it doesn't make sense to say that the number of creative solutions caused the group's heterogeneity, because the group's heterogeneity existed before it produced the creative solutions. In other situations, however, the temporal relationship among variables is less clear. One example is the ongoing debate about job satisfaction and organizational commitment. Do companies develop more loyal employees by increasing their job satisfaction, or do changes in organizational loyalty cause changes in job satisfaction? Simple logic does not answer these questions; instead, researchers must use sophisticated longitudinal studies to build up evidence of a temporal relationship between these two variables.

The third requirement for evidence of a causal relationship is that the statistical association between two variables cannot be explained by a third variable. There are many associations that we quickly dismiss as being causally related. For example, there is a statistical association between the number of storks in an area and the birth rate in that area. We know that storks don't bring babies, so something else must cause the association between these two variables. The real explanation is that both storks and birth rates have a higher incidence in rural areas.

In other studies, the third variable effect is less apparent. Many years ago, before polio vaccines were available, a study in the United States reported a surprisingly strong association between consumption of a certain soft drink and the incidence of polio. Was polio caused by drinking this pop, or did people with polio have an unusual craving for this beverage? Neither. Both polio and consumption of the pop drink were caused by a third variable: climate. There was a higher incidence of polio in the summer months and in warmer climates, and people drink more liquids in these climates.[10] As you can see from this example, researchers have a difficult time supporting causal inferences, because third variable effects are sometimes difficult to detect.

ETHICS IN ORGANIZATIONAL RESEARCH

Organizational behaviour researchers need to abide by the ethical standards of the society in which the research is conducted. One of the most important ethical considerations is the individual subject's freedom to participate in the study. For example, it is inappropriate to force employees to fill out a questionnaire or attend an experimental intervention for research purposes only. Moreover, researchers have an obligation to tell potential subjects about any potential risks inherent in the study so that participants can make an informed choice about whether or not to be involved.

Finally, researchers must be careful to protect the privacy of those who participate in the study. This usually includes letting people know when they are being studied as well as guaranteeing that their individual information will remain confidential (unless publication of identities is otherwise granted). Researchers maintain anonymity through careful security of data. The research results usually aggregate data in numbers large enough that they do not reveal the opinions or characteristics of any specific individual. For example, we would report the average absenteeism of employees in a department rather than state the absence rates of each person. When sharing data with other researchers, it is usually necessary to specially code each case so that individual identities are not known.

RESEARCH DESIGN STRATEGIES

So far, we have described how to build a theory, including the specific elements of empirically testing that theory within the standards of scientific inquiry. But what are the different ways to design a research study so that we get the data necessary to achieve our research objectives? There are many strategies, but they mainly fall under three headings: laboratory experiments, field surveys, and observational research.

LABORATORY EXPERIMENTS

A **laboratory experiment** is any research study in which independent variables and variables outside the researcher's main focus of inquiry can be controlled to some extent. Laboratory experiments are usually located outside the everyday work environment, such as a classroom, simulation lab, or any other artificial setting in which the researcher can manipulate the environment. Organizational behaviour researchers sometimes conduct experiments in the workplace (called *field experiments*) in which the independent variable is manipulated. However, the researcher has less control over the effects of extraneous factors in field experiments than in laboratory situations.

Advantages of Laboratory Experiments   There are many advantages of laboratory experiments. By definition, this research method offers a high degree of control over extraneous variables that would otherwise confound the relationships being studied. Suppose we wanted to test the effects of directive leadership on the satisfaction of new employees. One concern might be that employees are influenced by how much leadership is provided, not just the type of leadership style. An experimental design would allow us to control how often the supervisor exhibited this style so that this extraneous variable does not confound the results.

A second advantage of lab studies is that the independent and dependent variables can be developed more precisely than in a field setting. For example, the researcher can ensure that supervisors in a lab study apply specific directive or nondirective behaviours, whereas real-life supervisors would use a more complex mixture of leadership behaviours. By using more precise measures, we are more certain that we are measuring the intended construct. Thus, if new employees are more satisfied with supervisors in the directive leadership condition, we are more confident that the independent variable was directive leadership rather than some other leadership style.

A third benefit of laboratory experiments is that the independent variable can be distributed more evenly among participants. In our directive leadership study, we can ensure that approximately half of the subjects have a directive supervisor, whereas the other half have a nondirective supervisor. In natural settings, we might have trouble finding people who have worked with a nondirective leader and, consequently, we couldn't determine the effects of this condition.

Disadvantages of Laboratory Experiments   With these powerful advantages, you might wonder why laboratory experiments are the least appreciated form of organizational behaviour research.[11] One obvious limitation of this research method is that it lacks realism and, consequently, the results might be different in the real world. One argument is that laboratory experiment subjects are less involved than their counterparts in an actual work situation. This is sometimes true, although many lab studies have highly motivated participants. Another criticism is that the extraneous variables controlled in the lab setting might produce a different effect of the independent variable on the dependent variables. This might also be true, but remember that the experimental design controls variables in accordance with the theory and its hypotheses. Consequently, this concern is really a critique of the theory, not the lab study.

Finally, there is the well-known problem that participants are aware they are being studied and this causes them to act differently than they normally would. Some participants try to figure out how the researcher wants them to behave and then deliberately try to act that way. Other participants try to upset the experiment by doing just the opposite of what they believe the researcher expects. Still others might act unnaturally simply because they know they are being observed. Fortunately, experimenters are well aware of these potential problems and are usually (although not always) successful at disguising the study's true intent.

FIELD SURVEYS

Field surveys collect and analyze information in a natural environment—an office, factory, or other existing location. The researcher takes a snapshot of reality and tries to determine whether elements of that situation (including the attitudes and behaviours of people in that situation) are associated with each other as hypothesized. Everyone does some sort of field research. You might think that people from some provinces are better drivers than others, so you "test" your theory by looking at the way people with out-of-province licence plates drive. Although your methods of data collection might not satisfy scientific standards, this is a form of field research because it takes information from a naturally occurring situation.

Advantages and Disadvantages of Field Surveys   One advantage of field surveys is that the variables often have a more powerful effect than they would in a laboratory experiment. Consider the effect of peer pressure on the behaviour of members within the team. In a natural environment, team members would form very strong cohesive bonds over time, whereas a researcher would have difficulty replicating this level of cohesiveness and corresponding peer pressure in a lab setting.

Another advantage of field surveys is that the researcher can study many variables simultaneously, thereby permitting a fuller test of more complex theories. Ironically, this is also a disadvantage of field surveys, because it is difficult for the researcher to contain his or her scientific inquiry. There is a tendency to shift from deductive hypothesis testing to more inductive exploratory browsing through the data. If these two activities become mixed together, the researcher can lose sight of the strict covenants of scientific inquiry.

The main weakness with field surveys is that it is very difficult to satisfy the conditions for causal conclusions. One reason is that the data are usually collected at one point in time, so the researcher must rely on logic to decide whether the independent variable really preceded the dependent variable. Contrast this with the lab study in which the researcher can usually be confident that the independent variable was applied before the dependent variable occurred. Increasingly, organizational behaviour studies use longitudinal research to provide a better indicator of temporal relations among variables, but this is still not as precise as the lab setting. Another reason why causal analysis is difficult in field surveys is that extraneous variables are not controlled as they are in lab studies. Without this control, there is a higher chance that a third variable might explain the relationship between the hypothesized independent and dependent variables.

OBSERVATIONAL RESEARCH

In their study of brainstorming and creativity, Robert Sutton and Andrew Hargadon observed 24 brainstorming sessions at IDEO, a product design firm in Palo Alto, California. They also attended a dozen "Monday morning meetings," conducted 60 semi-structured interviews with IDEO executives and designers, held hundreds of informal discussions with these people, and read through several dozen magazine articles about the company.[12]

Sutton's and Hargadon's use of observational research and other qualitative methods was quite appropriate for their research objectives, which were to re-examine the effectiveness of brainstorming beyond the number of ideas generated. Observational research generates a wealth of descriptive accounts about the drama of human existence in organizations. It is a useful vehicle for learning about the complex dynamics of people and their activities, such as brainstorming. (The results of Sutton and Hargadon's study are discussed in Chapter 8.)

Participant observation takes the observation method one step further by having the observer take part in the organization's activities. This experience gives the researcher a fuller understanding of the activities compared to just watching others participate in those activities.

In spite of its intuitive appeal, observational research has a number of weaknesses. The main problem is that the observer is subject to the perceptual screening and organizing biases that we discuss in Chapter 3 of this textbook. There is a tendency to overlook the routine aspects of organizational life, even though they may prove to be the most important data for research purposes. Instead, observers tend to focus on unusual information, such as activities that deviate from what the observer expects. Because observational research usually records only what the observer notices, valuable information is often lost.

Another concern with the observation method is that the researcher's presence and involvement may influence the people whom he or she is studying. This can be a problem in short-term observations, but in the long term people tend to return to their usual behaviour patterns. With ongoing observations, such as Sutton and Hargadon's study of brainstorming sessions at IDEO, employees eventually forget that they are being studied.

Finally, observation is usually a qualitative process, so it is more difficult to empirically test hypotheses with the data. Instead, observational research provides rich information for the inductive stages of theory building. It helps us to form ideas about the way things work in organizations. We begin to see relationships that lay the foundation for new perspectives and theory. We must not confuse this inductive process of theory building with the deductive process of theory testing.

APPENDIX B

··

Scoring Keys for Self-Assessment Exercises

The following pages provide scoring keys for self-assessments that are fully presented in this textbook. These self-assessments, as well as the self-assessments that are only summarized in this book, can also be scored automatically on the student Online Learning Centre.

CHAPTER 2
SCORING KEY FOR "ARE YOU INTROVERTED OR EXTROVERTED?"

Scoring Instructions: Use the table below to assign numbers to each box you checked. For example, if you checked "Moderately Inaccurate" for statement #1 ("I feel comfortable around people."), you would assign a "1" to that statement. After assigning numbers for all 10 statements, add up the numbers to estimate your extroversion-introversion personality.

For statement items 1, 2, 6, 8, 9:	For statement items 3, 4, 5, 7, 10:
Very accurate description of me = 4	Very accurate description of me = 0
Moderately accurate — 3	Moderately accurate = 1
Neither accurate nor inaccurate — 2	Neither accurate nor inaccurate = 2
Moderately inaccurate = 1	Moderately inaccurate = 3
Very inaccurate description of me = 0	Very inaccurate description of me = 4

Interpreting Your Score: Extroversion characterizes people who are outgoing, talkative, sociable, and assertive. It includes several facets, including friendliness, gregariousness, assertiveness, activity level, excitement-seeking, and cheerfulness. The opposite of extroversion is introversion, which refers to the personality characteristics of being quiet, shy, and cautious. Extroverts get their energy from the outer world (people and things around them), whereas introverts get their energy from the internal world, such as personal reflection on concepts and ideas. Introverts are more inclined to direct their interests to ideas than to social events.

This is the short version of the IPIP Introversion-Extroversion Scale, so it estimates overall introversion-extroversion but not specific facets within the personality dimension. Scores range from 0 to 40. Low scores indicate introversion; high scores indicate extroversion. The norms in the following table are estimated from results of young adults (under 30 years old) in Scotland and undergraduate psychology students in the United States. However, introversion-extroversion norms vary from one group to the next; the best norms are likely based on the entire class you are attending or with past students in this course.

IPIP Introversion-Extroversion	Interpretation
35–40	High extroversion
28–34	Moderate extroversion
21–27	In-between extroversion and introversion
7–20	Moderate introversion
0–6	High introversion

CHAPTER 3
SCORING KEY FOR "HOW MUCH PERCEPTUAL STRUCTURE DO YOU NEED?"

Scoring Instructions: Use the table below to assign numbers to each box you checked. For example, if you checked "Moderately Disagree" for statement #3 ("I enjoy being spontaneous."), you would assign a "5" to that statement. After assigning numbers for all 12 statements, add up your scores to estimate your personal need for structure.

For statement items 1, 5, 6, 7, 8, 9, 10, 12:	For statement items 2, 3, 4, 11:
Strongly Agree = 6	Strongly Agree = 1
Moderately Agree = 5	Moderately Agree = 2
Slightly Agree = 4	Slightly Agree = 3
Slightly Disagree = 3	Slightly Disagree = 4
Moderately Disagree = 2	Moderately Disagree = 5
Strongly Disagree = 1	Strongly Disagree = 6

Interpreting Your Score: Some people need to "make sense" of things around them more quickly or completely than do other people. This personal need for perceptual structure relates to selective attention as well as perceptual organization and interpretation. For instance, people with a strong personal need for closure might form first impressions, fill in missing pieces, and rely on stereotyping more quickly than people who don't mind incomplete perceptual situations.

This scale, called the personal need for structure (PNS) scale, assesses the degree to which people are motivated to structure their world in a simple and unambiguous way. Scores range from 12 to 72 with higher scores indicating a high personal need for structure. PNS norms vary from one group to the next. For instance, a study of Finnish nurses reported a mean PNS score of 34 whereas a study of 236 male and 303 female undergraduate psychology students in the United States had a mean score of 42. The norms in the following table are based on scores from these undergraduate students.

Personal Need for Structure Scale	Interpretation
58–72	High need for personal structure
47–57	Above average need for personal structure
38–46	Average need for personal structure
27–37	Below average need for personal structure
12–26	Low need for personal structure

CHAPTER 4
SCORING KEY FOR "ARE YOU COMMITTED TO YOUR SCHOOL?"

Scoring Instructions: Use the table below to assign numbers to each box you checked. Insert the number for each statement on the appropriate line below the table. For example, if you checked "Moderately disagree" for statement #1 ("I would be very happy...."), you would write a "2" on the line with "(1)" underneath it. After assigning numbers for all 12 statements, add up your scores to estimate your affective and continuance school commitment.

For statement items 1, 2, 3, 4, 6, 8, 10, 11, 12:	For statement items 5, 7, 9:
Strongly Agree = 7	Strongly Agree = 1
Moderately Agree = 6	Moderately Agree = 2
Slightly Agree = 5	Slightly Agree = 3
Neutral = 4	Neutral = 4
Slightly Disagree = 3	Slightly Disagree = 5
Moderately Disagree = 2	Moderately Disagree = 6
Strongly Disagree = 1	Strongly Disagree = 7

Affective   ____ + ____ + ____ + ____ + ____ + ____ = _____
Commitment   (1)   (3)   (5)   (7)   (9)   (11)

Continuance   ____ + ____ + ____ + ____ + ____ + ____ = _____
Commitment   (2)   (4)   (6)   (8)   (10)   (12)

Interpreting Your Affective Commitment Score: This scale measures both affective commitment and continuance commitment. Affective commitment refers to a person's emotional attachment to, identification with, and involvement in a particular organization. In this scale, the organization is the school where you are attending as a student. How high or low is your affective commitment? The ideal would be to compare your score with the collective results of other students in your class. You can also compare your score with the following results, which are based on a sample of employees.

Affective Commitment	
Score	Interpretation
Above 37	High level of affective commitment
32–36	Above average level of affective commitment
28–31	Average level of affective commitment
20–27	Below average level of affective commitment
Below 20	Low level of affective commitment

Interpreting Your Continuance Commitment Score: Continuance commitment occurs when employees believe it is in their own personal interest to remain with the organization. People with a high continuance commitment have a strong calculative bond with the organization. In this scale, the organization is the school where you are attending as a student. How high or low is your continuance commitment? The ideal would be to compare your score with the collective results of other students in your class. You can also compare your score with the following results, which are based on a sample of employees.

Continuance Commitment	
Score	Interpretation
Above 32	High level of continuance commitment
26–31	Above average level of continuance commitment
21–25	Average level of continuance commitment
13–20	Below average level of continuance commitment
Below 12	Low level of continuance commitment

CHAPTER 5
SCORING KEY FOR "WHAT NEEDS ARE MOST IMPORTANT TO YOU?"

Scoring Instructions: Use the table below to assign numbers to each box you checked. Insert the number for each statement on the appropriate line below the table. For example, if you checked "Moderately inaccurate" for statement #1 ("I would rather be myself than be well thought of."), you would write a "3" on the line with "(1)" underneath it. After assigning numbers for all 15 statements, add up your scores to estimate your results for the two learned needs measured by this scale.

For statement items 2, 3, 4, 5, 6, 8, 9, 12, 14, 15:	For statement items 1, 7, 10, 11, 13:
Very accurate description of me = 4	Very accurate description of me = 0
Moderately accurate = 3	Moderately accurate = 1
Neither accurate nor inaccurate = 2	Neither accurate nor inaccurate = 2
Moderately inaccurate = 1	Moderately Inaccurate = 3
Very inaccurate description of me = 0	Very inaccurate description of me = 4

Need for Achievement   ____ + ____ + ____ + ____ + ____ + ____ + ____ = _____
                  (2)   (3)   (6)   (7)   (9) (12) (14)

Need for Social Approval   ____ + ____ + ____ + ____ + ____ + ____ + ____ + ____ = _____
                  (1)   (4)   (5)   (8) (10) (11) (13) (15)

Although everyone has the same innate drives, our secondary or learned needs vary based on our self-concept. This self-assessment provides an estimate of your need strength on two secondary needs: need for achievement and need for social approval.

Interpreting Your Need for Achievement Score: This scale, formally called "achievement striving," estimates the extent to which you are motivated to take on and achieve challenging personal goals. It includes a desire to perform better than others and to reach one's potential. This scale ranges from 0 to 28. How high or low is your need for achievement? The ideal would be to compare your score with the collective results of other students in your class. Otherwise, the following exhibit offers a rough set of norms for you to compare your score on this scale.

Need for Achievement	
Score	**Interpretation**
24–28	High level of need for achievement
18–23	Above average level of need for achievement
12–17	Average level of need for achievement
6–11	Below average level of need for achievement
0–5	Low level of need for achievement

Interpreting Your Need for Social Approval Score: The need for social approval scale estimates the extent to which you are motivated to seek favourable evaluation from others. Based on the drive to bond, the need for social approval is a secondary need in that people vary in this need based on their self-concept, values, personality, and possibly socialized social norms. This scale ranges from 0 to 32. How high or low is your need for social approval? The ideal would be to compare your score with the collective results of other students in your class. Otherwise, the following exhibit offers a rough set of norms for you to compare your score on this scale.

Need for Social Approval	
Score	**Interpretation**
28–32	High need for social approval
20–27	Above average need for social approval
12–19	Average need for social approval
6–11	Below average need for social approval
0–5	Low need for social approval

CHAPTER 6
SCORING KEY FOR "WHAT IS YOUR ATTITUDE TOWARD MONEY?"

Scoring Instructions: This instrument presents three dimensions with a smaller set of items from the original Money Attitude Scale. To calculate your score on each dimension, write the number that you circled in the scale to the corresponding item number in the scoring key below. For example, write the number you circled in the scale's first statement ("I sometimes purchase things….") on the line above "Item 1." Then add up the numbers for that dimension. The money attitude total score is calculated by adding up all scores and all dimensions.

Money as Power/Prestige	____ + ____ + ____ + ____ = _____ (1) (4) (7) (10) (P)
Retention Time	____ + ____ + ____ + ____ = _____ (2) (5) (8) (11) (R)
Money Anxiety	____ + ____ + ____ + ____ = _____ (3) (6) (9) (12) (M)
MONEY ATTITUDE TOTAL	____ + ____ + ____ = _____ (P) (R) (M)

Interpreting Your Score: The three Money Attitude Scale dimensions measured here, as well as the total score, are defined as follows:

Money as Power/Prestige: People with higher scores on this dimension tend to use money to influence and impress others.

Retention Time: People with higher scores on this dimension tend to be careful financial planners.

Money Anxiety: People with higher scores on this dimension tend to view money as a source of anxiety.

Money Attitude Total: This is a general estimate of how much respect and attention you give to money.

The following table shows how a sample of MBA students scored on the Money Attitude Scale. The table shows percentiles, that is, the percentage of people with the same or lower score. For example, the table indicates that a score of "12" on the retention scale is quite low because only 20 percent of students would have scored at this level or lower (80 percent scored higher). However, a score of "12" on the prestige scale is quite high because 80 percent of students score at or below this number (only 20 percent scored higher).

Percentile (% with scores at or below this number)	Prestige Score	Retention Score	Anxiety Score	Total Money Score
Average Score	9.89	14.98	12.78	37.64
Highest Score	17	20	18	53
90	13	18	16	44
80	12	17	15	42
70	11	17	14	40
60	10	16	14	39
50	10	15	13	38
40	9	14	12	36
30	8	14	11	34
20	7	12	10	32
10	7	11	8	29
Lowest Score	4	8	6	23

CHAPTER 7
SCORING KEY FOR "DO YOU HAVE A CREATIVE PERSONALITY?"

Scoring Instructions: Assign plus one (+1) point beside the following words if you put a checkmark beside them: Capable, Clever, Confident, Egotistical, Humorous, Individualistic, Informal, Insightful, Intelligent, Inventive, Original, Reflective, Resourceful, Self-confident, Sexy, Snobbish, Unconventional, Wide interests.

Assign negative one (–1) point beside the following words if you put a checkmark beside them: Affected, Cautious, Commonplace, Conservative, Conventional, Dissatisfied, Honest, Mannerly, Narrow interests, Sincere, Submissive, Suspicious. Words without a checkmark receive a zero. Add up the total score, which will range from –12 to +18.

Interpreting Your Score: This instrument estimates your creative potential as a personal characteristic. The scale recognizes that creative people are intelligent, persistent, and possess an inventive thinking style. Creative personality varies somewhat from one occupational group to the next. The exhibit below provides norms based on undergraduate and graduate university students.

Creative Disposition	
Score	Interpretation
Above +9	You have a high creative personality
+1 to +9	You have an average creative personality.
Below +1	You have a low creative personality.

CHAPTER 8
SCORING KEY FOR "WHAT TEAM ROLES DO YOU PREFER?"

Scoring Instructions: Write the scores circled for each item on the appropriate line below (statement numbers are in parentheses), and add up each scale.

Encourager   _____ + _____ + _____ = _____
            (6)   (9)   (11)

Gatekeeper   _____ + _____ + _____ = _____
            (4)   (10)   (13)

Harmonizer   _____ + _____ + _____ = _____
            (3)   (8)   (12)

Initiator   _____ + _____ + _____ = _____
            (1)   (5)   (14)

Summarizer   _____ + _____ + _____ = _____
            (2)   (7)   (15)

Interpreting Your Score: The five team roles measured here are based on one scholarly model regarding the roles that people adopt in teams. There are several models of team roles, but the roles measured here are similar to those described in other models. These five roles are defined as follows, along with the range of scores for high, medium, and low levels of each role. These norms are based on results from a sample of MBA students.

Team Role and Definition	Interpretation
Encourager: People who score high on this dimension have a strong tendency to praise and support the ideas of other team members, thereby showing warmth and solidarity to the group.	High: 12 and above Medium: 9 to 11 Low: 8 and below
Gatekeeper: People who score high on this dimension have a strong tendency to encourage all team members to participate in the discussion.	High: 12 and above Medium: 9 to 11 Low: 8 and below
Harmonizer: People who score high on this dimension have a strong tendency to mediate intragroup conflicts and reduce tension.	High: 11 and above Medium: 9 to 10 Low: 8 and below
Initiator: People who score high on this dimension have a strong tendency to identify goals for the meeting, including ways to work on those goals.	High: 12 and above Medium: 9 to 11 Low: 8 and below
Summarizer: People who score high on this dimension have a strong tendency to keep track of what was said in the meeting (i.e., act as the team's memory).	High: 10 and above Medium: 8 to 9 Low: 7 and below

CHAPTER 9
SCORING KEY FOR "ARE YOU AN ACTIVE LISTENER?"

Scoring Instructions: Use the table below to score the response you circled for each statement. Write the score for each item on the appropriate line below the table (statement numbers are in parentheses), and add up each subscale. For example, if you checked "A little" for statement #1 ("I keep an open mind...."), you would write a "1" on the line with "(1)" underneath it. Then calculate the overall Active Listening Skills Inventory score by summing all subscales.

For statement items 3, 4, 6, 7, 10, 13:	For statement items 1, 2, 5, 8, 9, 11, 12, 14, 15:
Not at all = 3	Not at all = 0
A little = 2	A little = 1
Somewhat = 1	Somewhat = 2
Very much = 0	Very much = 3

Avoiding Interruption (AI)   _____ + _____ + _____ = _____
                                      (3)   (7)   (15)

Maintaining Interest (MI)   _____ + _____ + _____ = _____
                                        (6)   (9)   (14)

Postponing Evaluation (PE)   _____ + _____ + _____ = _____
                                        (1)   (5)   (13)

Organizing Information (OI)   _____ + _____ + _____ = _____
                                        (2)   (10)   (12)

Showing Interest (SI)   _____ + _____ + _____ = _____
                                        (4)   (8)   (11)

Active Listening (total score):   _____

Interpreting Your Score: The five active listening dimensions and the overall active listening scale measured here are defined below, along with the range of scores for high, medium, and low levels of each dimension based on a sample of MBA students.

Active Listening Dimension and Definition	Score Interpretation
Avoiding Interruption: People with high scores on this dimension have a strong tendency to let the speaker finish his or her statements before responding.	High: 8 to 9 Medium: 5 to 7 Low: Below 5
Maintaining Interest: People with high scores on this dimension have a strong tendency to remain focused and concentrate on what the speaker is saying even when the conversation is boring or the information is well known.	High: 6 to 9 Medium: 3 to 5 Low: Below 3
Postponing Evaluation: People with high scores on this dimension have a strong tendency to keep an open mind and avoid evaluating what the speaker is saying until the speaker has finished.	High: 7 to 9 Medium: 4 to 6 Low: Below 4
Organizing Information: People with high scores on this dimension have a strong tendency to actively organize the speaker's ideas into meaningful categories.	High: 8 to 9 Medium: 5 to 7 Low: Below 5
Showing Interest: People with high scores on this dimension have a strong tendency to use nonverbal gestures or brief verbal acknowledgements to demonstrate that they are paying attention to the speaker.	High: 7 to 9 Medium: 5 to 6 Low: Below 5
Active Listening (total): People with high scores on this total active listening scale have a strong tendency to actively sense the sender's signals, evaluate them accurately, and respond appropriately.	High: Above 31 Medium: 26 to 31 Low: Below 26

NOTE: The Active Listening Skills Inventory does not explicitly measure two other dimensions of active listening, namely, empathizing and providing feedback. Empathizing is difficult to measure with behaviours; providing feedback involves similar behaviours as showing interest.

CHAPTER 10
SCORING KEY FOR "WHAT'S YOUR APPROACH TO UPWARD INFLUENCE?"

Scoring Instructions: To calculate your scores on the Upward Influence Scale, write the number circled for each statement on the appropriate line below (statement numbers are in parentheses), and add up each scale.

Assertiveness   _____ + _____ + _____ = _____
                  (8)   (15)   (16)

Exchange   _____ + _____ + _____ = _____
                  (2)   (5)   (13)

Coalition formation _____ + _____ + _____ = _____
                      (1)   (11)   (18)

Upward appeal   _____ + _____ + _____ = _____
                   (4)   (12)   (17)

Ingratiation   _____ + _____ + _____ = _____
                   (3)   (6)   (9)

Persuasion   _____ + _____ + _____ = _____
                   (7)   (10)   (14)

Interpreting Your Score: Influence refers to any behaviour that attempts to alter someone's attitudes or behaviour. There are several types of influence, including the following six measured by this instrument: assertiveness, exchange, coalition formation, upward appeal, ingratiation, and persuasion. This instrument assesses your preference for using each type of influence on your boss or other people at higher levels in the organization. Each scale has a potential score ranging from 3 to 15 points. Higher scores indicate that the person has a higher preference for that particular tactic. The six upward influence dimensions measured here are defined below, along with the range of scores for high, medium, and low levels of each tactic.

Influence Tactic and Definition	Score Interpretation
Assertiveness: Assertiveness involves actively applying legitimate and coercive power to influence others. This tactic includes persistently reminding others of their obligations, frequently checking their work, confronting them, and using threats of sanctions to force compliance.	High: 8 to 15 Medium: 5 to 7 Low: 3 to 4
Exchange: Exchange involves the promise of benefits or resources in exchange for the target person's compliance with your request. This tactic also includes reminding the target of past benefits or favours with the expectation that the target will now make up for that debt. Negotiation is also part of the exchange strategy.	High: 10 to 15 Medium: 6 to 9 Low: 3 to 5
Coalition Formation: Coalition formation occurs when a group of people with common interests band together to influence others. This tactic pools the power and resources of many people, so the coalition potentially has more influence than if each person operated alone.	High: 11 to 15 Medium: 7 to 10 Low: 3 to 6
Upward Appeal: Upward appeal occurs when you rely on support from a higher-level person to influence others. In effect, this is a form of coalition in which one or more members are someone with higher authority or expertise.	High: 9 to 15 Medium: 6 to 8 Low: 3 to 5
Ingratiation: Flattering your boss in front of others, helping your boss with his or her work, agreeing with your boss's ideas, and asking for your boss's advice are all examples of ingratiation. This tactic increases the perceived similarity of the source of ingratiation to the target person.	High: 13 to 15 Medium: 9 to 12 Low: 3 to 8
Persuasion: Persuasion refers to using logical and emotional appeals to change others' attitudes. According to several studies, it is also the most common upward influence strategy.	High: 13 to 15 Medium: 9 to 12 Low: 3 to 8

CHAPTER 11
SCORING KEY FOR "THE DUTCH TEST FOR CONFLICT HANDLING"

Scoring Instructions. To calculate your scores on the Dutch Test for Conflict Handling, write the number circled for each statement on the appropriate line below (statement numbers are in parentheses), and add up each scale.

Yielding   ____ + ____ + ____ + ____ = ____
                (1)   (6)   (11)   (16)

Compromising   ____ + ____ + ____ + ____ = ____
                (2)   (7)   (12)   (17)

Forcing   ____ + ____ + ____ + ____ = ____
                (3)   (8)   (13)   (18)

Problem Solving   ____ + ____ + ____ + ____ = ____
                (4)   (9)   (14)   (19)

Avoiding   ____ + ____ + ____ + ____ = ____
                (5)   (10)   (15)   (20)

Interpreting Your Score: The five conflict handling dimensions are defined below, along with the range of scores for high, medium, and low levels of each dimension:

Conflict Handling Dimension and Definition	Score Interpretation
Yielding: Yielding involves giving in completely to the other side's wishes, or at least cooperating with little or no attention to your own interests. This style involves making unilateral concessions, unconditional promises, and offering help with no expectation of reciprocal help.	High: 14 to 20 Medium: 9 to 13 Low: 4 to 8
Compromising: Compromising involves looking for a position in which your losses are offset by equally valued gains. It involves matching the other party's concessions, making conditional promises or threats, and actively searching for a middle ground between the interests of the two parties.	High: 17 to 20 Medium: 11 to 16 Low: 4 to 10
Forcing: Forcing involves trying to win the conflict at the other's expense. It includes "hard" influence tactics, particularly assertiveness, to get one's own way.	High: 15 to 20 Medium: 9 to 14 Low: 4 to 8
Problem Solving: Problem solving tries to find a mutually beneficial solution for both parties. Information sharing is an important feature of this style because both parties need to identify common ground and potential solutions that satisfy both (or all) of them.	High: 17 to 20 Medium: 11 to 16 Low: 4 to 10
Avoiding: Avoiding tries to smooth over or avoid conflict situations altogether. It represents a low concern for both self and the other party. In other words, avoiders try to suppress thinking about the conflict.	High: 13 to 20 Medium: 8 to 12 Low: 4 to 7

CHAPTER 12
SCORING KEY FOR "WHAT TYPE OF LEADER IS YOUR BOSS?"

Transactional Leadership

Scoring Instructions: Add up scores for the odd numbered items (i.e., 1, 3, 5, 7, 9, 11, 13, 15). The maximum score is 40.

Interpreting Your Score: Transactional leadership is "managing"—helping organizations to achieve their current objectives more efficiently, such as by linking job performance to valued rewards and ensuring that employees have the resources needed to get the job done. The following table shows the range of scores for high, medium, and low levels of transactional leadership.

Transactional Leadership	
Score	**Interpretation**
32–40	The person you evaluated seems to be a highly transactional leader.
25–31	The person you evaluated seems to be a moderately transactional leader.
Below 25	The person you evaluated seems to display few characteristics of a transactional leader.

Transformational Leadership

Scoring Instructions: Add up scores for the even numbered items (i.e., 2, 4, 6, 8, 10, 12, 14, 16). The maximum score is 40. Higher scores indicate that your supervisor has a strong inclination toward transformational leadership.

Interpreting Your Score: Transformational leadership involves changing teams or organizations by creating, communicating, and modelling a vision for the organization or work unit, and inspiring employees to strive for that vision. The following table shows the range of scores for high, medium, and low levels of transformational leadership.

Transformational Leadership	
Score	Interpretation
32 to 40	The person you evaluated seems to be a highly transformational leader.
25 to 31	The person you evaluated seems to be a moderately transformational leader.
Below 25	The person you evaluated seems to display few characteristics of a transformational leader.

CHAPTER 13
SCORING KEY FOR "WHAT ORGANIZATIONAL STRUCTURE DO YOU PREFER?"

Scoring Instructions: Use the table below to assign numbers to each response you circled. Insert the number for each statement on the appropriate line below the table. For example, if you checked "Not at all" for item #1 ("A person's career ladder...."), you would write a "0" on the line with "(1)" underneath it. After assigning numbers for all 15 statements, add up the scores to estimate your degree of preference for a tall hierarchy, formalization, and centralization. Then calculate the overall score by summing all scales.

For statement items 2, 3, 8, 10, 11, 12, 14, 15	For statement items 1, 4, 5, 6, 7, 9, 13
Not at all = 3	Not at all = 0
A little = 2	A little = 1
Somewhat = 1	Somewhat = 2
Very much = 0	Very much = 3

Tall Hierarchy (H)   _____ + _____ + _____ + _____ + _____ = _____
                       (1)   (4)   (10)   (12)   (15)   (H)

Formalization (F)   _____ + _____ + _____ + _____ + _____ = _____
                       (2)   (6)   (8)   (11)   (13)   (F)

Centralization (C)   _____ + _____ + _____ + _____ + _____ = _____
                       (3)   (5)   (7)   (9)   (14)   (C)

Total Score (Mechanistic)   _____ + _____ + _____ = _____
                             (H)   (F)   (C)   Total

Interpreting Your Score: The three organizational structure dimensions and the overall score are defined below, along with the range of scores for high, medium, and low levels of each dimension based on a sample of MBA students.

Organizational Structure Dimension and Definition	Interpretation
Tall hierarchy: People with high scores on this dimension prefer to work in organizations with several levels of hierarchy and a narrow span of control (few employees per supervisor).	High: 11 to 15 Medium: 6 to 10 Low: Below 6
Formalization: People with high scores on this dimension prefer to work in organizations where jobs are clearly defined with limited discretion.	High: 12 to 15 Medium: 9 to 11 Low: Below 9
Centralization: People with high scores on this dimension prefer to work in organizations where decision making occurs mainly among top management rather than spread out to lower level staff.	High: 10 to 15 Medium: 7 to 9 Low: Below 7
Total Score (Mechanistic): People with high scores on this dimension prefer to work in mechanistic organizations, whereas those with low scores prefer to work in organic organizational structures. Mechanistic structures are characterized by a narrow span of control and high degree of formalization and centralization. Organic structures have a wide span of control, little formalization, and decentralized decision making.	High: 30 to 45 Medium: 22 to 29 Low: Below 22

CHAPTER 14
SCORING KEY FOR "WHAT ARE YOUR CORPORATE CULTURE PREFERENCES?"

Scoring Instructions: In each space below, write in a "1" if you circled the statement and "0" if you did not. Then add up the scores for each subscale.

Control Culture ____ + ____ + ____ + ____ + ____ + ____ = _____
            (2a) (5a) (6b) (8b) (11b) (12a)

Performance Culture ____ + ____ + ____ + ____ + ____ + ____ = _____
            (1b) (3b) (5b) (6a) (7a) (9b)

Relationship Culture ____ + ____ + ____ + ____ + ____ + ____ = _____
            (1a) (3a) (4b) (8a) (10b) (12b)

Responsive Culture ____ + ____ + ____ + ____ + ____ + ____ = _____
            (2b) (4a) (7b) (9a) (10a) (11a)

Interpreting Your Score: These corporate cultures may be found in many organizations, but they represent only four of many possible organizational cultures. Also, keep in mind none of these cultures is inherently good or bad. Each is effective in different situations. The four corporate cultures are defined below, along with the range of scores for high, medium, and low levels of each dimension based on a sample of MBA students.

Corporate Culture Dimension and Definition	Interpretation
Control Culture: This culture values the role of senior executives to lead the organization. Its goal is to keep everyone aligned and under control.	High: 3 to 6 Medium: 1 to 2 Low: 0
Performance Culture: This culture values individual and organizational performance and strives for effectiveness and efficiency.	High: 5 to 6 Medium: 3 to 4 Low: 0 to 2
Relationship Culture: This culture values nurturing and well-being. It considers open communication, fairness, teamwork, and sharing a vital part of organizational life.	High: 6 Medium: 4 to 5 Low: 0 to 3
Responsive Culture: This culture values its ability to keep in tune with the external environment, including being competitive and realizing new opportunities.	High: 6 Medium: 4 to 5 Low: 0 to 3

CHAPTER 15
SCORING KEY FOR "ARE YOU TOLERANT OF CHANGE?"

Scoring Instructions: Use the table below to assign numbers to each box you checked. For example, if you checked "Moderately disagree" for statement #1 ("An expert who doesn't come up...."), you would write a "6" beside that statement. After assigning numbers for all 16 statements, add up your scores to estimate your tolerance for change.

For statement items 2, 4, 6, 8, 10, 12, 14, 16:	For statement items 1, 3, 5, 7, 9, 11, 13, 15:
Strongly Agree = 7	Strongly Agree = 1
Moderately Agree = 6	Moderately Agree = 2
Slightly Agree = 5	Slightly Agree = 3
Neutral = 4	Neutral = 4
Slightly Disagree = 3	Slightly Disagree = 5
Moderately Disagree = 2	Moderately Disagree = 6
Strongly Disagree = 1	Strongly Disagree = 7

Interpreting Your Score: This measurement instrument is formally known as the "tolerance of ambiguity" scale. Although it was developed 40 years ago, the instrument is still used today in research. People with a high tolerance of ambiguity are comfortable with uncertainty, sudden change, and new situations. These are characteristics of the hyperfast changes occurring in many organizations today. The exhibit below indicates the range of scores for high, medium, and low tolerance for change based on results for MBA students.

Tolerance for Change	
Score	Interpretation
81–112	You seem to have a high tolerance for change.
63–80	You seem to have a moderate level of tolerance for change.
Below 63	You seem to have a low degree of tolerance for change. Instead, you prefer stable work environments.

GLOSSARY

The number following each definition indicates the chapter in which the term receives the fullest description.

A

ability The natural aptitudes and learned capabilities required to successfully complete a task. (2)

achievement-nurturing orientation A cross-cultural value describing the degree to which people in a culture emphasize competitive versus cooperative relations with other people. (2)

action research A problem-focused change process that combines action orientation (changing attitudes and behaviour) and research orientation (testing theory through data collection and analysis). (15)

adaptive culture An organizational culture in which employees focus on the changing needs of customers and other stakeholders, and support initiatives to keep pace with those changes. (14)

appreciative inquiry An organizational change strategy that directs the group's attention away from its own problems and focuses participants on the group's potential and positive elements. (15)

artifacts The observable symbols and signs of an organization's culture. (14)

attitudes The cluster of beliefs, assessed feelings, and behavioural intentions toward a person, object, or event (called an *attitude object*). (4)

attraction-selection-attrition (ASA) theory States that organizations have a natural tendency to attract, select, and retain people with values and personality character istics that are consistent with the organization's charac ter, resulting in a more homogeneous organization and a stronger culture. (14)

attribution process The perceptual process of deciding whether an observed behaviour or event is caused largely by internal or external factors. (3)

autonomy The degree to which a job gives employees the freedom, independence, and discretion to schedule their work and determine the procedures used in completing it. (6)

B

balanced scorecard (BSC) A reward system that pays bonuses for improved results on a composite of financial, customer, internal process, and employee factors. (6)

behaviour modification A theory that explains learning in terms of the antecedents and consequences of behaviour. (3)

bicultural audit A process of diagnosing cultural relations between the companies and determining the extent to which cultural clashes will likely occur. (14)

bounded rationality Processing limited and imperfect information and satisficing rather than maximizing when choosing between alternatives. (7)

brainstorming A freewheeling, face-to-face meeting where team members aren't allowed to criticize, but are encouraged to speak freely, generate as many ideas as possible, and build on the ideas of others. (8)

Brooks's law Also called the "mythical man-month," this principle says that adding more people to a late software project only makes it later. (8)

C

categorical thinking Organizing people and objects into preconceived categories that are stored in our long-term memory. (3)

centrality A contingency of power referring to the degree and nature of interdependence between the powerholder and others. (10)

centralization The degree to which formal decision authority is held by a small group of people, typically those at the top of the organizational hierarchy. (13)

ceremonies Planned displays of organizational culture, conducted specifically for the benefit of an audience. (14)

change agent Anyone who possesses enough knowledge and power to guide and facilitate the change effort. (15)

coalition A group that attempts to influence people outside the group by pooling the resources and power of its members. (10)

cognitive dissonance Occurs when we perceive an inconsistency between our beliefs, feelings, and behaviour. (4)

collectivism A cross-cultural value describing the degree to which people in a culture emphasize duty to groups to which people belong, and to group harmony. (2)

communication The process by which information is transmitted and *understood* between two or more people. (9)

competencies Skills, knowledge, aptitudes, and other personal characteristics that lead to superior performance. (2)

conflict　A process in which one party perceives that its interests are being opposed or negatively affected by another party. (11)

conscientiousness　A personality dimension describing people who are careful, dependable, and self-disciplined. (2)

constructive conflict　Occurs when people focus their discussion on the issue while maintaining respectfulness for people having other points of view. (8)

constructive conflict (also known as *task or cognitive conflict*)　Occurs when people focus their discussion on the issue while maintaining respectfulness for people having other points of view. (11)

constructs　Abstract ideas constructed by researchers that can be linked to observable information. (Appendix A)

contact hypothesis　A theory stating that the more we interact with someone, the less we rely on stereotypes to understand that person. (3)

continuance commitment　An employee's calculative attachment to the organization, whereby an employee is motivated to stay only because leaving would be costly. (4)

corporate social responsibility (CSR)　Organizational activities intended to benefit society and the environment beyond the firm's immediate financial interests or legal obligations. (1)

counterproductive work behaviours (CWBs)　Voluntary behaviours that have the potential to directly or indirectly harm the organization. (1)

countervailing power　The capacity of a person, team, or organization to keep a more powerful person or group in the exchange relationship. (10)

creativity　The development of original ideas that make a socially recognized contribution. (7)

D

decision making　A conscious process of making choices among alternatives with the intention of moving toward some desired state of affairs. (7)

deep-level diversity　Differences in the psychological characteristics of employees, including personalities, beliefs, values, and attitudes. (1)

distributive justice　Perceived fairness in the outcomes we receive relative to our contributions and the outcomes and contributions of others. (5)

divergent thinking　Reframing the problem in a unique way and generating different approaches to the issue. (7)

divisional structure　A type of departmentalization that groups employees around geographic areas, outputs (products/services), or clients. (13)

drives　Neural states that energize individuals to correct deficiencies or maintain an internal equilibrium. (5)

E

electronic brainstorming　A recent form of brainstorming that relies on networked computers to submit and share creative ideas. (8)

emotional contagion　The automatic and nonconscious tendency to mimic and synchronize one's own nonverbal behaviours with those of other people. (9)

emotional dissonance　The conflict between required and true emotions. (4)

emotional intelligence (EI)　The ability to monitor our own and others' feelings and emotions, to discriminate between them and to use this information to guide our thinking and actions. (4)

emotional labour　The effort, planning, and control needed to express organizationally desired emotions during interpersonal transactions. (4)

emotions　Physiological, behavioural, and psychological episodes experienced toward an object, person, or event that create a state of readiness. (4)

empathy　A person's understanding of and sensitivity to the feelings, thoughts, and situation of others. (3)

employee engagement　The employee's emotional and cognitive motivation, self-efficacy to perform the job, a clear understanding of his or her role in the organization's vision, and a belief that he or she has the resources to perform their job. (5)

employee involvement　The degree to which employees influence how their work is organized and carried out. (7)

employee share ownership plans (ESOP)　A reward system that encourages employees to buy shares of the company. (6)

empowerment　A psychological concept in which people experience more self-determination, meaning, competence, and impact regarding their role in the organization. (6)

equity sensitivity　An individual's outcome/input preferences and reaction to various outcome/input ratios. (5)

equity theory　A theory that explains how people develop perceptions of fairness in the distribution and exchange of resources. (5)

ERG theory　A needs hierarchy theory consisting of three fundamental needs—existence, relatedness, and growth. (5)

escalation of commitment　The tendency to repeat an apparently bad decision or allocate more resources to a failing course of action. (7)

ethical sensitivity　A personal characteristic that enables people to recognize the presence and determine the relative importance of an ethical issue. (2)

ethics The study of moral principles or values that determine whether actions are right or wrong and outcomes are good or bad. (1)

evaluation apprehension Occurs when individuals are reluctant to mention ideas that seem silly because they believe (often correctly) that other team members are silently evaluating them. (8)

exit-voice-loyalty-neglect (EVLN) model The four ways, as indicated in the name, that employees respond to job dissatisfaction. (4)

expectancy theory A motivation theory based on the idea that work effort is directed towards behaviours that people believe will lead to desired outcomes. (5)

extroversion A personality dimension describing people who are outgoing, talkative, sociable, and assertive. (2)

F

false-consensus effect A perceptual error in which we overestimate the extent to which others have beliefs and characteristics similar to our own. (3)

Fiedler's contingency model Developed by Fred Fiedler, this early contingency leadership model suggests that leader effectiveness depends on whether the person's natural leadership style is appropriately matched to the situation. (12)

field surveys A research design strategy that involves collecting and analyzing information in a natural environment, such as an office, a factory, or other existing location. (Appendix A)

five-factor model (FFM) The five abstract dimensions representing most personality traits: conscientiousness, emotional stability, openness to experience, agreeableness, and extroversion. (2)

force field analysis Kurt Lewin's model of system-wide change that helps change agents diagnose the forces that drive and restrain proposed organizational change. (15)

formalization The degree to which organizations standardize behaviour through rules, procedures, formal training, and related mechanisms. (13)

four-drive theory A motivation theory based on the innate drives to acquire, bond, learn, and defend that incorporates both emotions and rationality. (5)

functional structure A type of departmentalization that organizes employees around specific knowledge or other resources. (13)

fundamental attribution error The tendency to see the person rather than the situation as the main cause of that person's behaviour. (3)

future search System-wide group sessions, usually lasting a few days, in which participants identify trends and identify ways to adapt to those changes. (15)

G

gainsharing plans Team-based rewards that calculate bonuses from the work unit's cost savings and productivity improvement (6)

general adaptation syndrome A model of the stress experience, consisting of three stages: alarm reaction, resistance, and exhaustion. (4)

globalization Economic, social, and cultural connectivity with people in other parts of the world. (1)

goal setting The process of motivating employees and clarifying their role perceptions by establishing performance objectives. (5)

grapevine An unstructured and informal network founded on social relationships rather than organizational charts or job descriptions. (9)

grounded theory A process of developing theory through the constant interplay between data gathering and the development of theoretical concepts. (Appendix A)

groupthink The tendency of highly cohesive groups to value consensus at the price of decision quality. (8)

H

halo effect A perceptual error whereby our general impression of a person, usually based on one prominent characteristic, colours our perception of other characteristics of that person. (3)

high performance work practices (HPWP) A perspective that effective organizations incorporate several workplace practices that leverage the potential of human capital. (1)

hypotheses Statements making empirically testable declarations that certain variables and their corresponding measures are related in a specific way proposed by the theory. (Appendix A)

I

implicit favourite A preferred alternative that the decision maker uses repeatedly as a comparison. (7)

implicit leadership theory A theory stating that people evaluate a leader's effectiveness in terms of how well that person fits preconceived beliefs about the features and behaviours of effective leaders (leadership prototypes), and that they tend to inflate the influence of leaders on organizational events. (12)

impression management The practice of actively shaping our public images. (10)

individualism A cross-cultural value describing the degree to which people in a culture emphasize independence and personal uniqueness. (2)

influence Any behaviour that attempts to alter someone's attitudes or behaviour. (10)

information overload Occurs when the volume of information received exceeds the person's capacity to get through it. (9)

ingratiation Any attempt to increase liking by, or perceived similarity to, some targeted person. (10)

inoculation effect A persuasive communication strategy of warning listeners that others will try to influence them in the future and that they should be wary about the opponent's arguments. (10)

intellectual capital Company's stock of knowledge, including human capital, structural capital, and relationship capital. (1)

interpretivism The view held in many qualitative studies that reality comes from shared meaning among people in that environment. (Appendix A)

intuition The ability to know when a problem or opportunity exists and to select the best course of action without conscious reasoning. (7)

J

job burnout The process of emotional exhaustion, depersonalization, and reduced personal accomplishment resulting from prolonged exposure to stress. (4)

job characteristics model A job design model that relates the motivational properties of jobs to specific personal and organizational consequences. (6)

job design The process of assigning tasks to a job, including the interdependency of those tasks with other jobs. (6)

job enlargement Increasing the number of tasks employees perform within their job. (6)

job enrichment Occurs when employees are given more responsibility for scheduling, coordinating, and planning their own work. (6)

job evaluation Systematically evaluating the worth of jobs within an organization by measuring their required skill, effort, responsibility, and working conditions. (6)

job rotation The practice of moving employees from one job to another. (6)

job satisfaction A person's evaluation of his or her job and work context. (4)

job specialization The result of division of labour in which each job includes a subset of the tasks required to complete the product or service. (6)

Johari Window A model of mutual understanding that encourages disclosure and feedback to increase our own open area and reduce the blind, hidden, and unknown areas. (3)

L

laboratory experiment Any research study in which independent variables and variables outside the researcher's main focus of inquiry can be controlled to some extent. (Appendix A)

leadership Influencing, motivating, and enabling others to contribute toward the effectiveness and success of the organizations of which they are members. (12)

leadership substitutes A theory identifying contingencies that either limit the leader's ability to influence subordinates or make that particular leadership style unnecessary. (12)

learning A relatively permanent change in behaviour (or behaviour tendency) that occurs as a result of a person's interaction with the environment. (3)

learning orientation A culture in which the organization rewards experimentation, accepts reasonable mistakes, and encourages employees to question long-held assumptions about past practices. (3)

legitimate power An agreement among organizational members that people in certain roles can request certain behaviours of others. (10)

locus of control A person's general belief about the amount of control he or she has over personal life events. (2)

M

Machiavellian values The belief that deceit is a natural and acceptable way to influence others. (10)

management by walking around (MBWA) A communication practice in which executives get out of their offices and learn from others in the organization through face-to-face dialogue. (9)

Maslow's needs hierarchy theory A motivation theory of needs arranged in a hierarchy, whereby people are motivated to fulfill a higher need as a lower one becomes gratified. (5)

matrix structure A type of departmentalization that overlays two organizational forms in order to leverage the benefits of both. (13)

mechanistic structure An organizational structure with a narrow span of control and a high degree of formalization and centralization. (13)

media richness The medium's data-carrying capacity, that is, the volume and variety of information that can be transmitted during a specific time. (9)

mental imagery Mentally practising a task and visualizing its successful completion. (6)

mental models Visual or relational images in our mind representing the external world. (3)

moral intensity The degree to which an issue demands the application of ethical principles. (2)

motivation The forces within a person that affect the direction, intensity, and persistence of voluntary behaviour. (2, 5)

motivator-hygiene theory   Herzberg's theory stating that employees are primarily motivated by growth and esteem needs, not by lower-level needs. (6)

multisource (360-degree) feedback   Information about an employee's performance collected from a full circle of people, including subordinates, peers, supervisors, and customers. (5)

Myers-Briggs Type Indicator (MBTI)   A personality test that measures each of the traits in Jung's model. (2)

N

needs   Goal-directed forces that people experience. (5)

negotiation   The process whereby two or more conflicting parties attempt to resolve their divergent goals by redefining the terms of their interdependence. (11)

network structure   An alliance of several organizations for the purpose of creating a product or serving a client. (13)

neuroticism   A personality dimension describing people with high levels of anxiety, hostility, depression, and self-consciousness. (2)

nominal group technique   A variation of traditional brainstorming that tries to combine the benefits of team decision making without the problems mentioned earlier. (8)

norms   The informal rules and shared expectations that groups establish to regulate the behaviour of their members. (8)

O

open systems   A perspective that organizations take their sustenance from the environment and, in turn, affect that environment through their output. (1)

organic structure   An organizational structure with a wide span of control, little formalization, and decentralized decision making. (13)

organizational (affective) commitment   The employee's emotional attachment to, identification with, and involvement in a particular organization. (4)

organizational behaviour (OB)   The study of what people think, feel, and do in and around organizations. (1)

organizational citizenship behaviours (OCBs)   Various forms of cooperation and helpfulness to others that support the organization's social and psychological context. (1)

organizational culture   The values and assumptions shared within an organization. (14)

organizational effectiveness   A broad concept represented by several perspectives, including the organization's fit with the external environment, internal subsystems configuration for high-performance, emphasis on organizational learning, and ability to satisfy the needs of key stakeholders. (1)

organizational efficiency   The amount of outputs relative to inputs in the organization's transformation process. (1)

organizational learning   A perspective that organizational effectiveness depends on the organization's capacity to acquire, share, use, and store valuable knowledge. (1)

organizational memory   The storage and preservation of intellectual capital. (1)

organizational politics   Behaviours that others perceive as self-serving tactics for personal gain at the expense of other people and possibly the organization. (10)

organizational socialization   The process by which individuals learn the values, expected behaviours, and social knowledge necessary to assume their roles in the organization. (14)

organizational strategy   The way the organization positions itself in its setting in relation to its stakeholders, given the organization's resources, capabilities, and mission. (13)

organizational structure   The division of labour as well as the patterns of coordination, communication, workflow, and formal power that direct organizational activities. (13)

organizations   Groups of people who work interdependently toward some purpose. (1)

P

parallel learning structure   Highly participative arrangements, composed of people from most levels of the organization who follow the action research model to produce meaningful organizational change. (15)

path-goal leadership theory   A contingency theory of leadership based on the expectancy theory of motivation that relates several leadership styles to specific employee and situational contingencies. (12)

perception   The process of receiving information about and making sense of the world around us. (3)

personality   The relatively enduring pattern of thoughts, emotions, and behaviours that characterize a person, along with the psychological processes behind those characteristics. (2)

persuasion   Presenting facts, logical arguments, and emotional appeals to change another person's attitudes and behaviour. (10)

positive organizational behaviour   A perspective of organizational behaviour that focuses on building positive qualities and traits within individuals or institutions as opposed to focusing on what is wrong with them. (5)

positivism   A view held in quantitative research in which reality exists independent of the perceptions and interpretations of people. (Appendix A)

postdecisional justification The tendency for people to support their selected alternative in a decision by forgetting or downplaying the negative features of the selected alternative, emphasizing its positive features, and doing the opposite for alternatives not selected. (7)

power The capacity of a person, team, or organization to influence others. (10)

power distance A cross-cultural value describing the degree to which people in a culture accept unequal distribution of power in a society. (2)

primacy effect A perceptual error in which we quickly form an opinion of people based on the first information we receive about them. (3)

procedural justice Perceived fairness of the procedures used to decide the distribution of resources. (5)

process losses Resources (including time and energy) expended toward team development and maintenance rather than the task. (8)

production blocking A time constraint in team decision making due to the procedural requirement that only one person may speak at a time. (8)

profit-sharing plans A reward system that pays bonuses to employees based on the previous year's level of corporate profits. (6)

prospect theory An effect in which losing a particular amount is more disliked than gaining the same amount. (7)

psychological harassment Repeated and hostile or unwanted conduct, verbal comments, actions, or gestures that affect an employee's dignity or psychological or physical integrity and that result in a harmful work environment for the employee. (4)

R

rational choice paradigm A deeply held perspective that people should or actually do make decisions based on pure logic or rationality. (7)

reality shock The stress that results when employees perceive discrepancies between their pre-employment expectations and on-the-job reality. (14)

recency effect A perceptual error in which the most recent information dominates our perception of others. (3)

referent power The capacity to influence others based on an identification with and respect for the powerholder. (10)

refreezing The latter part of the change process in which systems and conditions are introduced that reinforce and maintain the desired behaviours. (15)

relationship conflict Occurs when people view their differences as personal attacks rather than attempts to resolve an issue. (11)

representative sampling The process of sampling a population in such a way that one can extrapolate the results of that sample to the larger population. (Appendix A)

resilience The capability of individuals to cope successfully in the face of significant change, adversity, or risk. (4)

rituals The programmed routines of daily organizational life that dramatize the organization's culture. (14)

role A set of behaviours that people are expected to perform because they hold certain positions in a team and organization. (8)

role perceptions The accuracy of how people understand their job duties (roles) assigned to them or expected of them. (2)

S

satisficing Selecting a solution that is satisfactory or 'good enough,' rather than optimal or 'the best.' (7)

scenario planning A systematic process of thinking about alternative futures and what the organization should do to anticipate and react to those environments. (7)

scientific management Systematically partitioning work into its smallest elements and standardizing tasks to achieve maximum efficiency. (6)

scientific method A set of principles and procedures that help researchers to systematically understand previously unexplained events and conditions. (Appendix A)

selective attention The process of attending to some information received by our senses and ignoring other information. (3)

self-concept An individual's self-beliefs and self-evaluations. (2)

self-directed teams (SDTs) Cross-functional work groups organized around work processes, that complete an entire piece of work requiring several interdependent tasks, and that have substantial autonomy over the execution of those tasks. (8)

self-efficacy A person's belief that he or she has the ability, motivation, correct role perceptions, and favourable situation to complete a task successfully. (2)

self-fulfilling prophecy Occurs when our expectations about another person cause that person to act in a way that is consistent with those expectations. (3)

self-leadership The process of influencing oneself to establish the self-direction and self-motivation needed to perform a task. (6)

self-reinforcement Occurs whenever an employee has control over a reinforcer but doesn't "take" it until completing a self-set goal. (3)

self-serving bias The tendency to attribute our favourable outcomes to internal factors and our failures to external factors. (3)

self-talk Talking to ourselves about our own thoughts or actions for the purpose of increasing our self-confidence and navigating through decisions in a future event. (6)

servant leadership The view that leaders serve followers, rather than vice versa; they help employees fulfill their needs and are coaches, stewards, and facilitators of employee performance. (12)

sexual harassment Unwelcome conduct of a sexual nature that detrimentally affects the work environment or leads to adverse job-related consequences for its victims. (4)

share options A reward system that gives employees the right to purchase company shares at a future date at a predetermined price. (6)

shared leadership The view that leadership is broadly distributed rather than assigned to one person, such that people within the team and organization lead each other. (12)

situational leadership theory (SLT) A commercially popular but poorly supported leadership model, stating that effective leaders vary their style (telling, selling, participating, delegating) with the "readiness" of followers. (12)

skill variety The extent to which employees must use different skills and talents to perform tasks within their job. (6)

social capital The knowledge and other resources available to people or social units (teams, organizations) due to a durable network that connects them to others. (10)

social identity theory A theory that explains self-concept in terms of the person's unique characteristics (personal identity) and membership in various social groups (social identity). (2)

social learning theory A theory stating that much learning occurs by observing others and then modelling the behaviours that lead to favourable outcomes and avoiding behaviours that lead to punishing consequences. (3)

social loafing Occurs when people exert less effort (and usually perform at a lower level) when working in groups than when working alone. (8)

span of control The number of people directly reporting to the next level in the hierarchy. (13)

stakeholders Individuals, organizations, or other entities who affect, or are affected by, the organization's objectives and actions. (1)

stereotyping The process of assigning traits to people based on their membership in a social category. (3)

stress An adaptive response to a situation that is perceived as challenging or threatening to the person's well-being. (4)

stressors Any environmental conditions that place a physical or emotional demand on the person. (4)

subjective expected utility A rational choice calculation of the expected satisfaction or positive emotion experienced by choosing a specific alternative in a decision. (7)

substitutability A contingency of power referring to the availability of alternatives. (10)

superordinate goal Any goal that both conflicting parties value and whose attainment is beyond the resources and effort of either party alone. (11)

surface-level diversity Observable demographic and other overt differences in people, such as their race, ethnicity, gender, age, and physical capabilities. (1)

T

tacit knowledge Knowledge embedded in our actions and ways of thinking, and transmitted only through observation and experience. (3)

task identity The degree to which a job requires completion of a whole or an identifiable piece of work. (6)

task interdependence The extent that team members must share materials, information, or expertise in order to perform their jobs. (8)

task significance The degree to which the job has a substantial impact on the organization and/or larger society. (6)

team building Formal activities intended to improve the development and functioning of a work team. (8)

team cohesion The degree of attraction people feel toward the team and their motivation to remain members. (8)

team-based structure A type of departmentalization built around self-directed teams that complete an entire piece of work. (13)

teams Groups of two or more people who interact and influence each other, are mutually accountable for achieving common goals associated with organizational objectives, and perceive themselves as a social entity within an organization. (8)

theory A general set of propositions that describes interrelationships among several concepts. (Appendix A)

third-party conflict resolution Any attempt by a relatively neutral person to help the parties resolve their differences. (11)

transactional leadership Leadership that helps organizations achieve their current objectives more efficiently, such as linking job performance to valued rewards and ensuring that employees have the resources needed to get the job done. (12)

transformational leadership A leadership perspective that explains how leaders change teams or organizations by creating, communicating, and modelling a vision for the organization or work unit, and inspiring employees to strive for that vision. (12)

trust A psychological state comprising the intention to accept vulnerability based on positive expectations of the intent or behaviour of another person. (8)

trust Positive expectations one person has toward another person in situations involving risk. (4)

U

uncertainty avoidance A cross-cultural value describing the degree to which people in a culture tolerate ambiguity (low uncertainty avoidance) or feel threatened by ambiguity and uncertainty (high uncertainty avoidance). (2)

unfreezing The first part of the change process whereby the change agent produces disequilibrium between the driving and restraining forces. (15)

upward appeal A type of influence in which someone with higher authority or expertise is called upon in reality or symbolically to support the influencer's position. (10)

V

values Relatively stable, evaluative beliefs that guide a person's preferences for outcomes or courses of action in a variety of situations. (1)

values congruence The extent to which a person's values hierarchy is similar to the values hierarchy of another entity. (2)

virtual corporations Network structures representing several independent companies that form unique partnership teams to provide customized products or services, usually to specific clients, for a limited time. (13)

virtual teams Teams whose members operate across space, time, and organizational boundaries and are linked through information technologies to achieve organizational tasks. (8)

virtual work Work performed away from the traditional physical workplace using information technology. (1)

W

wikis Collaborative Web spaces in which anyone in a group can write, edit, or remove material from the website. (9)

win–lose orientation The belief that conflicting parties are drawing from a fixed pie, so the more one party receives, the less the other party will receive. (11)

win–win orientation The belief that the parties will find a mutually beneficial solution to their disagreement. (11)

work/life balance The degree to which a person minimizes conflict between work and nonwork demands. (1)

workaholic A person who is highly involved in work, feels compelled to work, and has a low enjoyment of work. (4)

NOTES

Chapter 1

1. D. Finlayson, "PCL Defies Critics with Employee Ownership," *Calgary Herald*, 2 March 2003, D8; V. Galt, "Keeping Employees in the Loop," *Globe & Mail*, 29 March 2006, B8; P. Marck, "Staff Are the Owners at Construction Giant PCL," *Regina Leader-Post*, 13 October 2007, D8. Information was also retrieved from PCL's website: www.pcl.com.

2. M. Warner, "Organizational Behavior Revisited," *Human Relations* 47 (October 1994): 1151-1166; R. Westwood and S. Clegg, "The Discourse of Organization Studies: Dissensus, Politics, and Paradigms," in *Debating Organization: Point-Counterpoint in Organization Studies*, ed. R. Westwood and S. Clegg (Malden, MA: Blackwood, 2003), 1-42.

3. D. Katz and R. L. Kahn, *The Social Psychology of Organizations* (New York: Wiley, 1966), Chap. 2; R. N. Stern and S. R. Barley, "Organizations as Social Systems: Organization Theory's Neglected Mandate," *Administrative Science Quarterly* 41 (1996): 146-162.

4. B. Schlender, "The Three Faces of Steve," *Fortune*, 9 November 1998, 96-101.

5. Some of the historical bases of OB mentioned in this paragraph are described in: T. R. Mitchell and W. G. Scott, "The Universal Barnard: His Micro Theories of Organizational Behavior," *Public Administration Quarterly* (Fall 1985): 239-259; J. A. Conger, "Max Weber's Conceptualization of Charismatic Authority: Its Influence on Organizational Research," *The Leadership Quarterly* 4, no. 3-4 (1993): 277-288; R. Kanigel, *The One Best Way: Frederick Winslow Taylor and the Enigma of Efficiency* (New York: Viking, 1997); J. H. Smith, "The Enduring Legacy of Elton Mayo," *Human Relations* 51, no. 3 (1998): 221-249; T. Takala, "Plato on Leadership," *Journal of Business Ethics* 17 (May 1998): 785-798; J. A. Fernandez, "The Gentleman's Code of Confucius: Leadership by Values," *Organizational Dynamics* 33, no. 1 (February 2004): 21-31.

6. S. L. Rynes *et al.*, "Behavioral Coursework in Business Education: Growing Evidence of a Legitimacy Crisis," *Academy of Management Learning & Education* 2, no. 3 (2003): 269-283; R. P. Singh and A. G. Schick, "Organizational Behavior: Where Does It Fit in Today's Management Curriculum?" *Journal of Education for Business* 82, no. 6 (July 2007): 349.

7. P. R. Lawrence and N. Nohria, *Driven: How Human Nature Shapes Our Choices* (San Francisco: Jossey-Bass, 2002), Chap. 6.

8. P. R. Lawrence "Historical Development of Organizational Behavior," in *Handbook of Organizational Behavior*, ed. L. W. Lorsch (Englewood Cliffs, N. J.: Prentice Hall, 1987), 1-9; S. A. Mohrman, C. B. Gibson, and A. M. Mohrman Jr., "Doing Research That Is Useful to Practice: A Model and Empirical Exploration," *Academy of Management Journal* 44 (April 2001): 357-375. For a contrary view, see: A. P. Brief and J. M. Dukerich, "Theory in Organizational Behavior: Can It Be Useful?" *Research in Organizational Behavior* 13 (1991): 327-352.

9. M. S. Myers, *Every Employee a Manager* (New York: McGraw Hill, 1970)

10. D. Yankelovich, "Got to Give to Get," *Mother Jones* 22 (July 1997): 60-63; D. MacDonald, "Good Managers Key to Buffett's Acquisitions," *Montreal Gazette*, 16 November 2001. The two studies on OB and financial performance are: B. N. Pfau and I. T. Kay, *The Human Capital Edge* (New York: McGraw-Hill, 2002); I. S. Fulmer, B. Gerhart, and K. S. Scott, "Are the 100 Best Better? An Empirical Investigation of the Relationship between Being a 'Great Place to Work' and Firm Performance," *Personnel Psychology* 56, no. 4 (Winter 2003): 965-993.

11. Mohrman, Gibson, and Mohrman Jr., "Doing Research That Is Useful to Practice: A Model and Empirical Exploration"; J. P. Walsh *et al.*, "On the Relationship between Research and Practice: Debate and Reflections," *Journal of Management Inquiry* 16, no. 2 (June 2007): 128-154. Similarly, in 1961, Harvard business professor Fritz Roethlisberger proposed that the field of OB is concerned with human behaviour "from the points of view of both (a) its determination...and (b) its improvement." See: P. B. Vaill, "F. J. Roethlisberger and the Elusive Phenomena of Organizational Behavior," *Journal of Management Education* 31, no. 3 (June 2007): 321-338.

12. R. H. Hall, "Effectiveness Theory and Organizational Effectiveness," *Journal of Applied Behavioral Science* 16, no. 4 (Oct. 1980): 536-545; K. Cameron, "Organizational Effectiveness: Its Demise and Re-Emergence through Positive Organizational Scholarship," in *Great Minds in Management*, ed. K. G. Smith and M. A. Hitt (New York: Oxford University Press, 2005), 304-330.

13. J. L. Price, "The Study of Organizational Effectiveness," *The Sociological Quarterly* 13 (1972): 3-15.

14. S. C. Selden and J. E. Sowa, "Testing a Multi-Dimensional Model of Organizational Performance: Prospects and Problems," *Journal of Public Administration Research and Theory* 14, no. 3 (July 2004): 395-416.

15. F. E. Kast and J. E. Rosenweig, "General Systems Theory: Applications for Organization and Management," *Academy of Management Journal* (1972): 447-465; P. M. Senge, *The Fifth Discipline: The Art and Practice of the Learning Organization* (New York: Doubleday Currency, 1990); A. De Geus, *The Living Company* (Boston: Harvard Business School Press, 1997); R. T. Pascale, M. Millemann, and L. Gioja, *Surfing on the Edge of Chaos* (London: Texere, 2000).

16. V. P. Rindova and S. Kotha, "Continuous 'Morphing': Competing through Dynamic Capabilities, Form, and Function," *Academy of Management Journal* 44 (2001): 1263-1280; J. McCann, "Organizational Effectiveness: Changing Concepts for Changing Environments," *Human Resource Planning* 27, no. 1 (2004): 42-50.

17. J. Arlidge, "McJobs That All the Family Can Share," *Daily Telegraph (London)*, 26 January 2006, 1.

18. C. Ostroff and N. Schmitt, "Configurations of Organizational Effectiveness and Efficiency," *Academy of Management Journal* 36, no. 6 (1993): 1345.

19. P. S. Adler *et al.*, "Performance Improvement Capability: Keys to Accelerating Performance Improvement in Hospitals," *California Management Review* 45, no. 2 (2003): 12-33; J. Jamrog, M. Vickers, and D. Bear, "Building and Sustaining a Culture That Supports Innovation," *Human Resource Planning* 29, no. 3 (2006): 9-19. Klaus Kleinfeld's quotation is from: "Siemens CEO Klaus Kleinfeld: 'Nobody's Perfect, but a Team Can Be'," *Knowledge@ Wharton*, 19 April 2006.

20. K. E. Weick, *The Social Psychology of Organizing* (Reading, MA: Addison-Wesley, 1979); S. Brusoni and A. Prencipe, "Managing Knowledge in Loosely Coupled Networks: Exploring the Links between Product and Knowledge Dynamics," *Journal of Management Studies* 38, no. 7 (Nov. 2001): 1019-1035; D. Pinelle and C. Gutwin, "Loose Coupling and Healthcare Organizations: Deployment Strategies for Groupware," *Computer supported cooperative work* 15, no. 5/6 (2006): 537-572.

21. G. Huber, "Organizational Learning: The Contributing Processes and Literature," *Organizational Science* 2 (1991): 88-115; D. A. Garvin, *Learning in Action: A Guide to Putting the Learning Organization to Work* (Boston: Harvard Business School Press, 2000); H. Shipton, "Cohesion or Confusion? Towards a Typology for Organizational Learning Research," *International Journal of Management Reviews* 8, no. 4 (2006): 233-252.

22. W. C. Bogner and P. Bansal, "Knowledge Management as the Basis of Sustained High Performance," *Journal of Management Studies* 44, no. 1 (2007): 165-188; D. Jiménez-Jiménez and J. G. Cegarra-Navarro, "The Performance Effect of Organizational Learning and Market Orientation," *Industrial Marketing Management* 36, no. 6 (2007): 694-708.

23. M. Liedtke, "Google vs. Yahoo: Heavyweights Attack from Different Angles," *Associated Press Newswires*, 18 December 2004; R. Basch, "Doing Well by Doing Good," *Searcher Magazine*, January 2005, 18-28; A. Ignatius and L. A. Locke, "In Search of the Real Google," *Time*, 20 February 2006, 36.

24. T. A. Stewart, *Intellectual Capital: The New Wealth of Organizations* (New York: Currency/ Doubleday, 1997); H. Saint-Onge and D. Wallace, *Leveraging Communities of Practice for Strategic Advantage* (Boston: Butterworth-Heinemann, 2003), pp. 9-10; J.-A. Johannessen, B. Olsen, and J. Olaisen, "Intellectual Capital as a Holistic Management Philosophy: A Theoretical Perspective," *International Journal of Information Management* 25, no. 2 (2005): 151-171.

25. M. N. Wexler, "Organizational Memory and Intellectual Capital," *Journal of Intellectual Capital* 3, no. 4 (2002): 393-414.

26. A. Wahl and L. Bogomolny, "Leaders Wanted," *Canadian Business*, 1-14 March 2004, 31-36.

27. P. Withers, "Few Rules Rule," *BC Business*, 1 January 2002, 24.

28. M. E. McGill and J. W. Slocum Jr., "Unlearn the Organization," *Organizational Dynamics* 22, no. 2 (1993): 67-79; A. E. Akgün, G. S. Lynn, and J. C. Byrne, "Antecedents and Consequences of Unlearning in New Product Development Teams," *Journal of Product Innovation Management* 23 (2006): 73-88.

29. J. Pfeffer, The Human Equation: Building Profits by Putting People First (Boston: Harvard University Press, 1998); E. Appelbaum et al., Manufacturing Advantage: Why High-Performance Work Systems Pay Off (Ithaca, N. Y.: Cornell University Press, 2000); G. S. Benson, S. M. Young, and E. E. Lawler III, "High-Involvement Work Practices and Analysts' Forecasts of Corporate Earnings," *Human Resource Management* 45, no. 4 (2006): 519-537; L. Sels et al., "Unravelling the HRM-Performance Link: Value-Creating and Cost-Increasing Effects of Small Business HRM," *Journal of Management Studies* 43, no. 2 (2006): 319-342.

30. M. A. Huselid, "The Impact of Human Resource Management Practices on Turnover, Productivity, and Corporate," *Academy of Management Journal* 38, no. 3 (1995): 635; B. E. Becker and M. A. Huselid, "Strategic Human Resources Management: Where Do We Go from Here?" *Journal of Management* 32, no. 6 (Dec. 2006): 898-925; J. Combs *et al.*, "How Much Do High-Performance Work Practices Matter? A Meta-Analysis of Their Effects on Organizational Performance," *Personnel Psychology* 59, no. 3 (2006): 501-528.

31. J. Barney, "Firm Resources and Sustained Competitive Advantage," *Journal of Management* 17, no. 1 (1991): 99-120.

32. E. E. Lawler III, S. A. Mohrman, and G. E. Ledford Jr., *Strategies for High Performance Organizations* (San Francisco: Jossey-Bass, 1998); S. H. Wagner, C. P. Parker, and D. Neil, "Employees That Think and Act Like Owners: Effects of Ownership Beliefs and Behaviors on Organizational Effectiveness," *Personnel Psychology* 56, no. 4 (Winter 2003): 847-871; P. J. Gollan, "High Involvement Management and Human Resource Sustainability: The Challenges and Opportunities," *Asia Pacific Journal of Human Resources* 43, no. 1 (April 2005): 18-33; Y. Liu *et al.*, "The Value of Human Resource Management for Organizational Performance," *Business Horizons* 50 (2007): 503-511; P. Tharenou, A. M. Saks, and C. Moore, "A Review and Critique of Research on Training and Organizational-Level Outcomes," *Human Resource Management Review* 17, no. 3 (2007): 251-273.

33. S. Fleetwood and A. Hesketh, "HRM-Performance Research: Under-Theorized and Lacking Explanatory Power," *International Journal of Human Resource Management* 17, no. 12 (Dec. 2006): 1977-1993.

34. J. Godard, "High Performance and the Transformation of Work? The Implications of Alternative Work Practices for the Experience and Outcomes of Work," *Industrial and Labor Relations Review* 54, no. 4 (July 2001): 776-805; G. Murray *et al.*, eds., *Work and Employment Relations in the High-Performance Workplace* (London: Continuum, 2002); B. Harley, "Hope or Hype? High Performance Work Systems," in *Participation and Democracy at Work: Essays in Honour of Harvie Ramsay*, ed. B. Harley, J. Hyman, and P. Thompson (Houndsmills, UK: Palgrave Macmillan, 2005), 38-54.

35. A. L. Friedman and S. Miles, *Stakeholders: Theory and Practice* (New York: Oxford University Press, 2006); M. L. Barnett, "Stakeholder Influence Capacity and the Variability of Financial Returns to Corporate Social Responsibility," *Academy of Management Review* 32, no. 3 (2007): 794-816; R. E. Freeman, J. S. Harrison, and A. C. Wicks, *Managing for Stakeholders: Survival, Reputation, and Success* (New Haven, CT: Yale University Press, 2007).

36. C. Eden and F. Ackerman, *Making Strategy: The Journey of Strategic Management* (London: Sage, 1998).

37. Three of the many recent sources on Wal-Mart's stakeholder dilemmas and failings are: T. A. Hemphill, "Rejuvenating Wal-Mart's Reputation," *Business Horizons* 48, no. 1 (2005): 11-21; A. Bianco, *The Bully of Bentonville: How the High Cost of Wal-Mart's Everyday Low Prices Is Hurting America* (New York: Random House, 2006); C. Fishman, *The Wal-Mart Effect* (New York: Penguin, 2006).

38. G. R. Salancik and J. Pfeffer, *The External Control of Organizations: A Resource Dependence Perspective* (New York: Harper & Row, 1978); T. Casciaro and M. J. Piskorski, "Power Imbalance, Mutual Dependence, and Constraint Absorption: A Closer Look at Dependence Theory," *Administrative Science Quarterly* 50 (2005): 167-199; N. Roome and F. Wijen, "Stakeholder Power and Organizational Learning in Corporate Environmental Management," *Organization Studies* 27, no. 2 (2005): 235-263.

39. R. E. Freeman, A. C. Wicks, and B. Parmar, "Stakeholder Theory and 'the Corporate Objective Revisited,'" *Organization Science* 15, no. 3 (May-June 2004): 364-369; D. Balser and J. McClusky, "Managing Stakeholder Relationships and Nonprofit Organization Effectiveness," *Nonprofit Management & Leadership* 15, no. 3 (Spring 2005): 295-315; Friedman and Miles, *Stakeholders: Theory and Practice*, Chap. 3.

40. B. M. Meglino and E. C. Ravlin, "Individual Values in Organizations: Concepts, Controversies, and Research," *Journal of Management* 24, no. 3 (1998): 351-389; B. R. Agle and C. B. Caldwell, "Understanding Research on Values in Business," *Business and Society* 38, no. 3 (September 1999): 326-387; A. Bardi and S. H. Schwartz, "Val-

ues and Behavior: Strength and Structure of Relations," *Personality and Social Psychology Bulletin* 29, no. 10 (October 2003): 1207-1220; S. Hitlin and J. A. Pilavin, "Values: Reviving a Dormant Concept," *Annual Review of Sociology* 30 (2004): 359-393.

41. K. Kernaghan, "Integrating Values into Public Service: The Values Statement as Centrepiece," *Public Administration Review* 63, no. 6 (November/December 2003): 711-719; Public Service of Canada, *Leadership in the Public Service of Canada: Leaders, the Leadership Environment and Canada's Public Service in the 21st Century*, (Ottawa: June 2007).

42. R. M. Patten, "From Implicit to Explicit: Putting Corporate Values and Personal Accountability Front and Centre," *Ivy Business Journal* (Sept-Oct 2004): H1-H4.

43. M. van Marrewijk, "Concepts and Definitions of CSR and Corporate Sustainability: Between Agency and Communion," *Journal of Business Ethics* 44 (May 2003): 95-105; Barnett, "Stakeholder Influence Capacity and the Variability of Financial Returns to Corporate Social Responsibility."

44. L. S. Paine, *Value Shift* (New York: McGraw-Hill, 2003); A. Mackey, T. B. Mackey, and J. B. Barney, "Corporate Social Responsibility and Firm Performance: Investor Preferences and Corporate Strategies," *Academy of Management Review* 32, no. 3 (2007): 817-835.

45. S. Hart and M. Milstein, "Creating Sustainable Value," *Academy of Management Executive* 17, no. 2 (2003): 56-69.

46. S. Zadek, *The Civil Corporation: The New Economy of Corporate Citizenship* (London: Earthscan, 2001), 50-51; "Canadians Inclined to Punish Companies Deemed Socially Irresponsible, Study Suggests," *Canadian Press*, 23 April 2005; M. Johne, "Show Us the Green, Workers Say," *Globe & Mail*, 10 October 2007, C1.

47. R. Martin, "The Virtue Matrix: Calculating the Return on Corporate Responsibility," *Harvard Business Review* 80 (March 2002): 68-85.

48. J. P. Campbell, "The Definition and Measurement of Performance in the New Age," in *The Changing Nature of Performance: Implications for Staffing, Motivation, and Development* ed. D. R. Ilgen and E. D. Pulakos (San Francisco: Jossey-Bass, 1999), 399-429; R. D. Hackett, "Understanding and Predicting Work Performance in the Canadian Military," *Canadian Journal of Behavioural Science* 34, no. 2 (2002): 131-140.

49. D. W. Organ, "Organizational Citizenship Behavior: It's Construct Clean-up Time," *Human Performance* 10 (1997): 85-97; S. J. Motowidlo, "Some Basic Issues Related to Contextual Performance and Organizational Citizenship Behavior in Human Resource Management," *Human Resource Management Review* 10, no. 1 (2000): 115-126; J. A. LePine, A. Erez, and D. E. Johnson, "The Nature and Dimensionality of Organizational Citizenship Behavior: A Critical Review and Meta-Analysis," *Journal of Applied Psychology* 87 (February 2002): 52-65.

50. K. Lee and N. J. Allen, "Organizational Citizenship Behavior and Workplace Deviance: The Role of Affect and Cognitions," *Journal of Applied Psychology* 87, no. 1 (2002): 131-142.

51. M. Rotundo and P. Sackett, "The Relative Importance of Task, Citizenship, and Counterproductive Performance to Global Ratings of Job Performance: A Policy-Capturing Approach," *Journal of Applied Psychology* 87 (February 2002): 66-80; P. D. Dunlop and K. Lee, "Workplace Deviance, Organizational Citizenship Behaviour, and Business Unit Performance: The Bad Apples Do Spoil the Whole Barrel," *Journal of Organizational Behavior* 25 (2004): 67-80. For discussion of various counterproductive workplace issues, see: J. Langan-Fox, C. L. Cooper, and R. J. Klimoski, eds., *Research Companion to the Dysfunctional Workplace* (Cheltenham, UK: Edward Elgar, 2007).

52. C. Sorensen, "Hotels Run out of Workers," *National Post*, 21 June 2006, FP1; J. Sinnema, "Nursing Shortages Push up Wait Times," *Edmonton Journal*, 27 October 2007, B1; L. Smyrlis, "A Growing Concern," *Canadian Transportation and Logistics*, October 2007, 18.

53. Watson Wyatt, "U.S. Workers City Hypocrisy and Favoritism—Rather Than Financial Misdeeds—as Biggest Ethical Lapses at Work," Watson Wyatt News release, (Washington, D.C.: 12 January 2005); Watson Wyatt, *WorkCanada 2004/2005—Pursuing Productive Engagement*, (Toronto: Watson Wyatt, January 2005).

54. E. B. Akyeampong, "Trends and Seasonality in Absenteeism," *Statistics Canada Perspectives* (June 2007).

55. D. A. Harrison and J. J. Martocchio, "Time for Absenteeism: A 20-Year Review of Origins, Offshoots, and Outcomes," *Journal of Management* 24 (Spring 1998): 305-350; C. M. Mason and M. A. Griffin, "Group Absenteeism and Positive Affective Tone: A Longitudinal Study," *Journal of Organizational Behavior* 24, no. 6 (2003): 667-687; A. Vaananen *et al.*, "Job Characteristics, Physical and Psychological Symptoms, and Social Support as Antecedents of Sickness Absence among Men and Women in the Private Industrial Sector," *Social Science & Medicine* 57, no. 5 (2003): 807-824.

56. "'Huge Responsibility' on Globalco to Perform," *New Zealand herald*, 18 June 2001; "A Major Player on the World Milk Stage," *Weekly Times (Sydney)*, 8 September 2004, 91; K. Newman, "Greener Pastures," *MIS New Zealand*, September 2004, 18; D. Blayney *et al.*, *U.S. Dairy at a Global Crossroads*, (Washington, D.C.: United States Department of Agriculture. Economic Research Service, Nov. 2006).

57. S. Fischer, "Globalization and Its Challenges," *American Economic Review* (May 2003): 1-29. For discussion of the diverse meanings of "globalization," see: M. F. Guillén, "Is Globalization Civilizing, Destructive or Feeble? A Critique of Five Key Debates in the Social Science Literature," *Annual Review of Sociology* 27 (2001): 235-260.

58. The ongoing debate regarding the advantages and disadvantages of globalization are discussed in: Guillén, "Is Globalization Civilizing, Destructive or Feeble?"; D. Doane, "Can Globalization Be Fixed?" *Business Strategy Review* 13, no. 2 (2002): 51-58; J. Bhagwati, *In Defense of Globalization* (New York: Oxford University Press, 2004); M. Wolf, *Why Globalization Works* (New Haven, CT: Yale University Press, 2004).

59. K. Ohmae, *The Next Global Stage* (Philadelphia: Wharton School Publishing, 2005).

60. R. House, M. Javidan, and P. Dorfman, "Project Globe: An Introduction," *Applied Psychology: An International Journal* 50 (2001): 489-505; M. M. Javidan *et al.*, "In the Eye of the Beholder: Cross Cultural Lessons in Leadership from Project Globe," *Academy of Management Perspectives* 20, no. 1 (February 2006): 67-90.

61. V. Galt, "Diversity at Work: 77 Employees, 27 Languages," *Globe & Mail*, 3 December 2007.

62. K. Kelly, *Visible Minorities: A Diverse Group*, Canadian Social Trends (Ottawa: Statistics Canada, 6 February 2004); A. Bélanger and E. C. Malenfant, *Population Projections of Visible Minority Groups, Canada, Provinces, and Regions: 2001-2017*, (Ottawa: Statistics Canada, March 2005).

63. D. A. Harrison *et al.*, "Time, Teams, and Task Performance: Changing Effects of Surface- and Deep-Level Diversity on Group Functioning," *Academy of Management Journal* 45, no. 5 (2002): 1029-1046.

64. R. Zemke, C. Raines, and B. Filipczak, *Generations at Work: Managing the Clash of Veterans, Boomers, Xers, and Nexters in Your Workplace* (New York: Amacom, 2000); M. R. Muetzel, *They're Not Aloof, Just Generation X* (Shreveport, LA: Steel Bay, 2003); S. H. Applebaum, M. Serena, and B. T. Shapiro, "Generation X and the Boomers: Organizational Myths and Lit-

erary Realities," *Management Research News* 27, no. 11/12 (2004): 1-28; N. Howe and W. Strauss, "The Next 20 Years: How Customer and Workforce Attitudes Will Evolve," *Harvard Business Review* (July-August 2007): 41-52.

65. O. C. Richard, "Racial Diversity, Business Strategy, and Firm Performance: A Resource-Based View," *Academy of Management Journal* 43 (2000): 164-177; D. D. Frink *et al.*, "Gender Demography and Organization Performance: A Two-Study Investigation with Convergence," *Group & Organization Management* 28 (March 2003): 127-147; T. Kochan *et al.*, "The Effects of Diversity on Business Performance: Report of the Diversity Research Network," *Human Resource Management* 42 (2003): 3-21; R. J. Burke and E. Ng, "The Changing Nature of Work and Organizations: Implications for Human Resource Management," *Human Resource Management Review* 16 (2006): 86-94.

66. C. Hymowitz, "The New Diversity," *Wall Street Journal*, 14 November 2005, R1.

67. R. J. Ely and D. A. Thomas, "Cultural Diversity at Work: The Effects of Diversity Perspectives on Work Group Processes and Outcomes," *Administrative Science Quarterly* 46 (June 2001): 229-273; T. Kochan *et al.*, "The Effects of Diversity on Business Performance: Report of the Diversity Research Network," *Human Resource Management* 42, no. 1 (2003): 3-21; D. van Knippenberg and S. A. Haslam, "Realizing the Diversity Dividend: Exploring the Subtle Interplay between Identity, Ideology and Reality," in *Social Identity at Work: Developing Theory for Organizational Practice*, ed. S. A. Haslam *et al.* (New York: Taylor and Francis, 2003), 61-80; D. van Knippenberg, C. K. W. De Dreu, and A. C. Homan, "Work Group Diversity and Group Performance: An Integrative Model and Research Agenda," *Journal of Applied Psychology* 89, no. 6 (2004): 1008-1022; E. Molleman, "Diversity in Demographic Characteristics, Abilities and Personality Traits: Do Faultlines Affect Team Functioning?" *Group Decision and Negotiation* 14, no. 3 (2005): 173-193.

68. W. G. Bennis and R. J. Thomas, *Geeks and Geezers* (Boston: Harvard Business School Press, 2002), 74-79; E. D. Y. Greenblatt, "Work/Life Balance: Wisdom or Whining," *Organizational Dynamics* 31, no. 2 (2002): 177-193.

69. Uyen Vu "A variety of options gives boost to remote work" *Canadian HR Reporter*, August 14, 2000.

70. "AT&T Telecommute Survey Indicates Productivity Is Up," AT&T News release, (New York: 6 August 2002); L. Duxbury and C. Higgins, "Telecommute: A Primer for the Millennium Introduction," in *The New World of Work: Challenges and Opportunities*, ed. C. L. Cooper and R. J. Burke (Oxford: Blackwell, 2002), 157-199; V. Illegems and A. Verbeke, "Telework: What Does It Mean for Management?" *Long Range Planning* 37 (2004): 319-334; S. Raghuram and B. Wiesenfeld, "Work-Nonwork Conflict and Job Stress among Virtual Workers," *Human Resource Management* 43, no. 2/3 (Summer/Fall 2004): 259-277.

71. TELUS 2006 Corporate Social Responsibility Report, pg. 12 Retrieved: September 20, 2007 http://about.telus.com/csr2006/csr/_pdf/en/TELUS_CSR_2006_commitment.pdf.

72. D. E. Bailey and N. B. Kurland, "A Review of Telework Research: Findings, New Directions, and Lessons for the Study of Modern Work," *Journal of Organizational Behavior* 23 (2002): 383-400; D. W. McCloskey and M. Igbaria, "Does 'Out of Sight' Mean 'out of Mind'?" An Empirical Investigation of the Career Advancement Prospects of Telecommuters," *Information Resources Management Journal* 16 (April-June 2003): 19-34; Sensis, *Sensis® Insights Report: Teleworking*, (Melbourne: Sensis, June 2005).

73. M. N. Zald, "More Fragmentation? Unfinished Business in Linking the Social Sciences and the Humanities," *Administrative Science Quarterly* 41 (1996): 251-261. Concerns about the "trade deficit" in OB are raised in: C. Heath and S. B. Sitkin, "Big-B Versus Big-O: What Is Organizational About Organizational Behavior?" *Journal of Organizational Behavior* 22 (2001): 43-58.

74. J. Pfeffer and R. I. Sutton, *Hard Facts, Dangerous Half-Truths, and Total Nonsense* (Boston: Harvard Business School Press, 2006); D. M. Rousseau and S. McCarthy, "Educating Managers from an Evidence-Based Perspective," *Academy of Management Learning & Education* 6, no. 1 (2007): 84-101.

75. C. M. Christensen and M. E. Raynor, "Why Hard-Nosed Executives Should Care About Management Theory," *Harvard Business Review* (September 2003): 66-74. For excellent critique of the "one best way" approach in early management scholarship, see: P. F. Drucker, "Management's New Paradigms," *Forbes* (October 5 1998): 152-177.

76. H. L. Tosi and J. W. Slocum Jr., "Contingency Theory: Some Suggested Directions," *Journal of Management* 10 (1984): 9-26.

77. D. M. H. Rousseau, R. J. , "Meso Organizational Behavior: Avoiding Three Fundamental Biases," in *Trends in Organizational Behavior*, ed. C. L. Cooper and D. M. Rousseau (Chichester, UK: John Wiley & Sons, 1994), 13-30.

Chapter 2

1. R. Langlois, "Fairmont Hotels: Business Strategy Starts with People," *Canadian HR Reporter*, 5 November 2001, 19; V. Galt, "A World of Opportunity for Those in Mid-Career," *Globe & Mail*, 7 June 2006, C1; M. T. Bitti, "Rewards of Hard Work," *National Post*, 17 October 2007, WK2.

2. L. L. Thurstone, "Ability, Motivation, and Speed," *Psychometrika* 2, no. 4 (1937): 249-254; N. R. F. Maier, *Psychology in Industry*, 2nd ed. (Boston: Houghton Mifflin Company, 1955); V. H. Vroom, *Work and Motivation* (New York: John Wiley & Sons, 1964); J. P. Campbell *et al.*, *Managerial Behavior, Performance, and Effectiveness* (New York: McGraw-Hill, 1970).

3. E. E. I. Lawler and L. W. Porter, "Antecedent Attitudes of Effective Managerial Performance," *Organizational Behavior and Human Performance* 2 (1967): 122-142; M. A. Griffin, A. Neal, and S. K. Parker, "A New Model of Work Role Performance: Positive Behavior in Uncertain and Interdependent Contexts," *Academy of Management Journal* 50, no. 2 (April 2007): 327-347.

4. Senior officers in the Singapore Armed Forces introduced the acronym "MARS". Chris Perryer at the University of Western Australia has pointed out that the full model should be called the "MARS BAR" because the outcomes might be labelled "behaviour and results"! Only a few literature reviews have included all four factors. These include: J. P. Campbell and R. D. Pritchard, "Motivation Theory in Industrial and Organizational Psychology," in *Handbook of Industrial and Organizational Psychology*, ed. M. D. Dunnette (Chicago: Rand McNally, 1976), 62-130; T. Mitchell, R., "Motivation: New Directions for Theory, Research, and Practice," *Academy of Management review* 7, no. 1 (Jan. 1982): 80-88; G. A. J. Churchill *et al.*, "The Determinants of Salesperson Performance: A Meta-Analysis," *Journal of Marketing Research (JMR)* 22, no. 2 (1985): 103-118; R. E. Plank and D. A. Reid, "The Mediating Role of Sales Behaviors: An Alternative Perspective of Sales Performance and Effectiveness," *Journal of Personal Selling & Sales Management* 14, no. 3 (Summer 1994): 43-56.

5. C. C. Pinder, *Work Motivation in Organizational Behavior* (Upper Saddle River, N. J.: Prentice-Hall, 1998); G. P. Latham and C. C. Pinder, "Work Motivation Theory and Research at the Dawn of the Twenty-First Century," *Annual Review of Psychology* 56 (2005): 485-516.

6. P. Tharenou, A. M. Saks, and C. Moore, "A Review and Critique of Research on Training and Organizational-Level Outcomes," *Human Resource Management Review* 17, no. 3 (2007): 251-273.

7. Canada Newswire, "Canadian Organizations Must Work Harder to Productively Engage Employees," News release, (25 January 2005).

8. "New Euro 16m Centre to Train 1,000 Toyota Staff a Year," *Just-Auto*, 24 March 2006; Y. Kageyama, "Toyota Workers Learn Knack of Auto Production in New Global Push," *Associated Press Newswires*, 17 April 2006.

9. K. F. Kane, "Special Issue: Situational Constraints and Work Performance," *Human Resource Management Review* 3 (Summer 1993): 83-175; S. B. Bacharach and P. Bamberger, "Beyond Situational Constraints: Job Resources Inadequacy and Individual Performance at Work," *Human Resource Management Review* 5, no. 2 (1995): 79-102; G. Johns, "Commentary: In Praise of Context," *Journal of Organizational Behavior* 22 (2001): 31-42.

10. W. Immen, "Prospective Hires Put to the Test," *Globe & Mail*, 26 January 2005, C1.

11. Personality researchers agree on one point about the definition of personality: it is difficult to pin down. A definition necessarily captures on perspective of the topic more than others, and the concept of personality is itself very broad. The definition presented here is based on: C. S. Carver and M. F. Scheier, *Perspectives on Personality*, 6th ed. (Boston: Allyn & Bacon, 2007); D. C. Funder, *The Personality Puzzle*, 4th ed. (New York: W. W. Norton & Company, 2007).

12. D. P. McAdams and J. L. Pals, "A New Big Five: Fundamental Principles for an Integrative Science of Personality," *American Psychologist* 61, no. 3 (2006): 204-217

13. B. Reynolds and K. Karraker, "A Big Five Model of Disposition and Situation Interaction: Why a 'Helpful' Person May Not Always Behave Helpfully," *New Ideas in Psychology* 21 (April 2003): 1-13; W. Mischel, "Toward an Integrative Science of the Person," *Annual Review of Psychology* 55 (2004): 1-22.

14. B. W. Roberts and A. Caspi, "Personality Development and the Person-Situation Debate: It's Déjà Vu All over Again," *Psychological Inquiry* 12, no. 2 (2001): 104-109.

15. K. L. Jang, W. J. Livesley, and P. A. Vernon, "Heritability of the Big Five Personality Dimensions and Their Facets: A Twin Study," *Journal of Personality* 64, no. 3 (1996): 577-591; N. L. Segal, *Entwined Lives: Twins and What They Tell Us About Human Behavior* (New York: Plume, 2000); T. Bouchard and J. Loehlin, "Genes, Evolution, and Personality," *Behavior Genetics* 31, no. 3 (May 2001): 243-273; G. Lensvelt-Mulders and J. Hettema, "Analysis of Genetic Influences on the Consistency and Variability of the Big Five across Differ-ent Stressful Situations," *European Journal of Personality* 15, no. 5 (2001): 355-371; P. Borkenau *et al.*, "Genetic and Environmental Influences on Person X Situation Profiles," *Journal of Personality* 74, no. 5 (2006): 1451-1480.

16. Segal, *Entwined Lives*, 116-118. For critiques of the genetics perspective of personality, see: J. Joseph, "Separated Twins and the Genetics of Personality Differences: A Critique," *American Journal of Psychology* 114, no. 1 (Spring 2001): 1-30; P. Ehrlich and M. W. Feldman, "Genes, Environments & Behaviors," *Daedalus* 136, no. 2 (Spring 2007): 5-12.

17. B. W. Roberts and W. F. DelVecchio, "The Rank-Order Consistency of Personality Traits from Childhood to Old Age: A Quantitative Review of Longitudinal Studies," *Psychological Bulletin* 126, no. 1 (2000): 3-25; A. Terracciano, P. T. Costa, and R. R. McCrae, "Personality Plasticity after Age 30," *Personality and Social Psychology Bulletin* 32, no. 8 (Aug. 2006): 999-1009.

18. M. Jurado and M. Rosselli, "The Elusive Nature of Executive Functions: A Review of Our Current Understanding," *Neuropsychology Review* 17, no. 3 (2007): 213-233.

19. B. W. Roberts and E. M. Pomerantz, "On Traits, Situations, and Their Integration: A Developmental Perspective," *Personality & Social Psychology Review* 8, no. 4 (2004): 402-416; W. Fleeson, "Situation-Based Contingencies Underlying Trait-Content Manifestation in Behavior," *Journal of Personality* 75, no. 4 (2007): 825-862.

20. J. M. Digman, "Personality Structure: Emergence of the Five-Factor Model," *Annual Review of Psychology* 41 (1990): 417-440; O. P. John and S. Srivastava, "The Big Five Trait Taxonomy: History, Measurement, and Theoretical Perspectives," in *Handbook of Personality: Theory and Research*, ed. L. A. Pervin and O. P. John, 2nd ed. (New York: Guildford Press, 1999), 102-138; A. Caspi, B. W. Roberts, and R. L. Shiner, "Personality Development: Stability and Change," *Annual Review of Psychology* 56, no. 1 (2005): 453-484.

21. J. Hogan and B. Holland, "Using Theory to Evaluate Personality and Job-Performance Relations: A Socioanalytic Perspective," *Journal of Applied Psychology* 88, no. 1 (2003): 100-112; D. S. Ones, C. Viswesvaran, and S. Dilchert, "Personality at Work: Raising Awareness and Correcting Misconceptions," *Human Performance* 18, no. 4 (2005): 389-404.

22. M. R. Barrick and M. K. Mount, "Yes, Personality Matters: Moving on to More Important Matters," *Human Performance* 18, no. 4 (2005): 359-372.

23. M. R. Barrick, M. K. Mount, and T. A. Judge, "Personality and Performance at the Beginning of the New Millennium: What Do We Know and Where Do We Go Next?" *International Journal of Selection and Assessment* 9, no. 1&2 (2001): 9-30; T. A. Judge and R. Ilies, "Relationship of Personality to Performance Motivation: A Meta-Analytic Review," *Journal of Applied Psychology* 87, no. 4 (2002): 797-807; A. Witt, L. A. Burke, and M. R. Barrick, "The Interactive Effects of Conscientiousness and Agreeableness on Job Performance," *Journal of Applied Psychology* 87 (February 2002): 164-169; J. Moutafi, A. Furnham, and J. Crump, "Is Managerial Level Related to Personality?" *British Journal of Management* 18, no. 3 (2007): 272-280.

24. K. M. DeNeve and H. Cooper, "The Happy Personality: A Meta-Analysis of 137 Personality Traits and Subjective Well-Being," *Psychological Bulletin* 124 (September 1998): 197-229; R. Ilies, M. W. Gerhardt, and H. Le, "Individual Differences in Leadership Emergence: Integrating Meta-Analytic Findings and Behavioral Genetics Estimates," *International Journal of Selection and Assessment* 12, no. 3 (September 2004): 207-219; B. Kozak, J. Strelau, and J. N. V. Miles, "Genetic Determinants of Individual Differences in Coping Styles," *Anxiety, Stress & Coping* 18, no. 1 (March 2005): 1-15.

25. C. G. Jung, *Psychological Types* trans. H. G. Baynes (Princeton, NJ: Princeton University Press, 1971); I. B. Myers, *The Myers-Briggs Type Indicator* (Palo Alto, CA: Consulting Psychologists Press, 1987).

26. M. Gladwell, "Personality Plus," *New Yorker*, 20 September 2004, 42-48; R. B. Kennedy and D. A. Kennedy, "Using the Myers-Briggs Type Indicator in Career Counseling," *Journal of Employment Counseling* 41, no. 1 (March 2004): 38-44. The Portsmouth City and Dell Computer examples are found in: E. Ross, "Enough Chiefs," *BRW*, 6 October 2005, 66, M. Hoyer, "The Quiet Man of Portsmouth: City Manager James Oliver," *Public Management*, April 2006, 28.

27. W. L. Johnson and e. al., "A Higher Order Analysis of the Factor Structure of the Myers-Briggs Type Indicator," *Measurement and Evaluation in Counseling and Development* 34 (July 2001): 96-108; R. M. Capraro and M. M. Capraro, "Myers-Briggs Type Indicator Score Reliability across Studies: A Meta-Analytic Reliability Generalization Study," *Educational and Psychological Measurement* 62 (August 2002): 590-602; J. Michael, "Using the Myers -Briggs Type Indicator as a Tool for Leadership Development? Apply with Caution," *Journal of Leadership & Organizational Studies* 10 (Summer 2003): 68-81.

28. R. R. McCrae and P. T. Costa, "Reinterpreting the Myers-Briggs Type Indicators Form the Perspective of the Five-Factor Model of Personality," *Journal of Personality* 57 (1989): 17-40; A. Furnham, "The Big Five Versus the Big Four: The Relationship between the Myers-Briggs Type Indicator (MBTI) and Neo-Pi Five Factor Model of Personality," *Personality and Individual Differences* 21, no. 2 (1996): 303-307.

29. J. D. Campbell, S. Assanand, and A. Di Paula, "The Structure of the Self-Concept and Its Relation to Psychological Adjustment," *Journal of Personality* 71, no. 1 (2003): 115-140; M. J. Constantino *et al.*, "The Direct and Stress-Buffering Effects of Self-Organization on Psychological Adjustment: The Direct and Stress-Buffering Effects of Self-Organization on Psychological Adjustment," *Journal of Social & Clinical Psychology* 25, no. 3 (2006): 333-360.

30. C. Sedikides and A. P. Gregg, "Portraits of the Self," in *The Sage Handbook of Social Psychology*, ed. M. A. Hogg and J. Cooper (London: Sage Publications, 2003), 110-138; M. R. Leary, "Motivational and Emotional Aspects of the Self," *Annual Review of Psychology* 58, no. 1 (2007): 317-344.

31. D. A. Moore, "Not So above Average after All: When People Believe They Are Worse Than Average and Its Implications for Theories of Bias in Social Comparison," *Organizational Behavior and Human Decision Processes* 102, no. 1 (2007): 42-58.

32. N. J. Hiller and D. C. Hambrick, "Conceptualizing Executive Hubris: The Role of (Hyper-)Core Self-Evaluations in Strategic Decision-Making," *Strategic Management Journal* 26, no. 4 (2005): 297-319; U. Malmendier and G. Tate, "CEO Overconfidence and Corporate Investment," *The Journal of Finance* 60, no. 6 (2005): 2661-2700; J. A. Doukas and D. Petmezas, "Acquisitions, Overconfident Managers and Self-Attribution Bias," *European Financial Management* 13, no. 3 (2007): 531-577.

33. W. B. Swann Jr, "To Be Adored or to Be Known? The Interplay of Self-Enhancement and Self-Verification," in *Foundations of Social Behavior*, ed. R. M. Sorrentino and E. T. Higgins (New York: Guildford, 1990), 408-448; W. B. Swann Jr, P. J. Rentfrow, and J. S. Guinn, "Self-Verification: The Search for Coherence," in *Handbook of Self and Identity*, ed. M. R. Leary and J. Tagney (New York: Guildford, 2002), 367-383.

34. Leary, "Motivational and Emotional Aspects of the Self."

35. T. A. Judge and J. E. Bono, "Relationship of Core Self-Evaluations Traits—Self-Esteem, Generalized Self-Efficacy, Locus of Control, and Emotional Stability—with Job Satisfaction and Job Performance: A Meta-Analysis," *Journal of Applied Psychol-ogy* 86, no. 1 (2001): 80-92; T. A. Judge and C. Hurst, "Capitalizing on One's Advantages: Role of Core Self-Evaluations," *Journal of Applied Psychology* 92, no. 5 (2007): 1212-1227.

36. W. B. Swann Jr., C. Chang-Schneider, and K. L. McClarty, "Do People's Self-Views Matter?: Self-Concept and Self-Esteem in Everyday Life," *American Psychologist* 62, no. 2 (2007): 84-94.

37. S. Lath, "Johnson & Johnson: Living by Its Credo," *Business Today (India)*, 5 November 2006, 126-129; R. Alsop, "How Boss's Deeds Buff a Firm's Reputation," *Wall Street Journal*, 21 January 2007, B1; F. Catteeuw, E. Flynn, and J. Vonderhorst, "Employee Engagement: Boosting Productivity in Turbulent Times," *Organization Development Journal* 25, no. 2 (Summer 2007): P151-P157; C. J. Corace, "Engagement—Enrolling the Quiet Majority," *Organization Development Journal* 25, no. 2 (Summer 2007): P171-P175; F. van de Ven, "Fulfilling the Promise of Career Development: Getting to the 'Heart' of the Matter," *Organization Development Journal* 25, no. 3 (Fall 2007): P45-P51.

38. A. Bandura, *Self-Efficacy: The Exercise of Control* (New York: W. H. Freeman, 1997).

39. G. Chen, S. M. Gully, and D. Eden, "Validation of a New General Self-Efficacy Scale," *Organizational Research Methods* 4, no. 1 (Jan. 2001): 62-83.

40. P. E. Spector, "Behavior in Organizations as a Function of Employee's Locus of Control," *Psychological Bulletin* 91 (1982): 482-497; K. Hattrup, M. S. O'Connell, and J. R. Labrador, "Incremental Validity of Locus of Control after Controlling for Cognitive Ability and Conscientiousness," *Journal of Business and Psychology* 19, no. 4 (2005): 461-481; T. W. H. Ng, K. L. Sorensen, and L. T. Eby, "Locus of Control at Work: A Meta-Analysis," *Journal of Organizational Behavior* 27 (2006): 1057-1087.

41. H. Tajfel, *Social Identity and Intergroup Relations* (Cambridge: Cambridge University Press, 1982); B. E. Ashforth and F. Mael, "Social Identity Theory and the Organization," *Academy of Management Review* 14 (1989): 20-39; M. A. Hogg and D. J. Terry, "Social Identity and Self-Categorization Processes in Organizational Contexts," *Academy of Management Review* 25 (January 2000): 121-140; S. A. Haslam, R. A. Eggins, and K. J. Reynolds, "The Aspire Model: Actualizing Social and Personal Identity Resources to Enhance Organizational Outcomes," *Journal of Occupational and Organizational Psychology* 76 (2003): 83-113.

42. Sedikides and Gregg, "Portraits of the Self." The history of the social self in human beings is described in: M. R. Leary and N. R. Buttermore, "The Evolution of the Human Self: Tracing the Natural History of Self-Awareness," *Journal for the Theory of Social Behaviour* 33, no. 4 (2003): 365-404.

43. M. R. Edwards, "Organizational Identification: A Conceptual and Operational Review," *International Journal of Management Reviews* 7, no. 4 (2005): 207-230; D. A. Whetten, "Albert and Whetten Revisited: Strengthening the Concept of Organizational Identity," *Journal of Management Inquiry* 15, no. 3 (Sept. 2006): 219-234.

44. B. M. Meglino and E. C. Ravlin, "Individual Values in Organizations: Concepts, Controversies, and Research," *Journal of Management* 24, no. 3 (1998): 351-389; B. R. Agle and C. B. Caldwell, "Understanding Research on Values in Business," *Business and Society* 38, no. 3 (September 1999): 326-387; S. Hitlin and J. A. Pilavin, "Values: Reviving a Dormant Concept," *Annual Review of Sociology* 30 (2004): 359-393.

45. D. Lubinski, D. B. Schmidt, and C. P. Benbow, "A 20-Year Stability Analysis of the Study of Values for Intellectually Gifted Individuals from Adolescence to Adulthood," *Journal of Applied Psychology* 81 (1996): 443-451.

46. Hitlin and Pilavin, "Values: Reviving a Dormant Concept"; A. Pakizeh, J. E. Gebauer, and G. R. Maio, "Basic Human Values: Inter-Value Structure in Memory," *Journal of Experimental Social Psychology* 43, no. 3 (2007): 458-465.

47. S. H. Schwartz, "Universals in the Content and Structure of Values: Theoretical Advances and Empirical Tests in 20 Countries," *Advances in Experimental Social Psychology* 25 (1992): 1-65; S. H. Schwartz, "Are There Universal Aspects in the Structure and Contents of Human Values?" *Journal of Social Issues* 50 (1994): 19-45; M. Schwartz, "The Nature of the Relationship between Corporate Codes of Ethics and Behaviour," *Journal of Business Ethics* 32, no. 3 (2001): 247; D. Spini, "Measurement Equivalence of 10 Value Types from the Schwartz Value Survey across 21 Countries," *Journal of Cross-Cultural Psychology* 34, no. 1 (January 2003): 3-23; S. H. Schwartz and K. Boehnke, "Evaluating the Structure of Human Values with Confirmatory Factor Analysis," *Journal of Research in Personality* 38, no. 3 (2004): 230-255.

48. G. R. Maio and J. M. Olson, "Values as Truisms: Evidence and Implications," *Journal of Personality and Social Psychology* 74, no. 2 (1998): 294-311; G. R. Maio *et al.*, "Addressing Discrepancies between Values and Behavior: The Motivating Effect of Reasons," *Journal of Experimental Social Psychology* 37, no. 2 (2001): 104-117; B. Verplanken and R. W. Holland, "Motivated Decision Making: Effects of Activation

and Self-Centrality of Values on Choices and Behavior," *Journal of Personality and Social Psychology* 82, no. 3 (2002): 434-447; A. Bardi and S. H. Schwartz, "Values and Behavior: Strength and Structure of Relations," *Personality and Social Psychology Bulletin* 29, no. 10 (October 2003): 1207-1220; M. M. Bernard and G. R. Maio, "Effects of Introspection About Reasons for Values: Extending Research on Values-as-Truisms," *Social Cognition* 21, no. 1 (2003): 1-25.

49. Aspen Institute, "Scandals, Economy Alter Attitudes of Next Generation Business Leaders, MBA Student Survey Shows,"News release, (20 May 2003); S. Klie, "Gap Exists between Worker, Employer Values," *Canadian HR Reporter*, 28 September 2007.

50. S. Whittaker, "Bringing Your Own Values to Work," *Ottawa Citizen*, 7 April 2001, J1. For research on values congruence, see: A. L. Kristof, "Person-Organization Fit: An Integrative Review of Its Conceptualizations, Measurement, and Implications," *Personnel Psychology* 49, no. 1 (Spring 1996): 1-49; M. L. Verquer, T. A. Beehr, and S. H. Wagner, "A Meta-Analysis of Relations between Person-Organization Fit and Work Attitudes," *Journal of Vocational Behavior* 63 (2003): 473-489; J. W. Westerman and L. A. Cyr, "An Integrative Analysis of Person-Organization Fit Theories," *International Journal of Selection and Assessment* 12, no. 3 (September 2004): 252-261; D. Bouckenooghe *et al.*, "The Prediction of Stress by Values and Value Conflict," *Journal of Psychology* 139, no. 4 (2005): 369-382.

51. M. Johne, "Show Us the Green, Workers Say," *Globe & Mail*, 10 October 2007, C1

52. T. Simons, "Behavioral Integrity: The Perceived Alignment between Managers' Words and Deeds as a Research Focus," *Organization Science* 13, no. 1 (Jan-Feb 2002): 18-35; Watson Wyatt, "Employee Ratings of Senior Management Dip, Watson Wyatt Survey Finds," Watson Wyatt News release, (New York: 4 January 2007).

53. T. A. Joiner, "The Influence of National Culture and Organizational Culture Alignment on Job Stress and Performance: Evidence from Greece," *Journal of Managerial Psychology* 16 (2001): 229-242 Z. Aycan, R. N. Kanungo, and J. B. P. Sinha, "Organizational Culture and Human Resource Management Practices: The Model of Culture Fit," *Journal Of Cross-Cultural Psychology* 30 (July 1999): 501-526.

54. D. Oyserman, H. M. Coon, and M. Kemmelmeier, "Rethinking Individualism and Collectivism: Evaluation of Theoretical Assumptions and Meta-Analyses," *Psychological Bulletin* 128 (2002): 3-72;C. P.

Earley and C. B. Gibson, "Taking Stock in Our Progress on Individualism-Collectivism: 100 Years of Solidarity and Community," *Journal of Management* 24 (May 1998): 265-304; F. S. Niles, "Individualism-Collectivism Revisited," *Cross-Cultural Research* 32 (November 1998): 315-341.

55. Oyserman, Coon, and Kemmelmeier, "Rethinking Individualism and Collectivism: Evaluation of Theoretical Assumptions and Meta-Analyses," Also see: F. Li and L. Aksoy, "Dimensionality of Individualism–Collectivism and Measurement Equivalence of Triandis and Gelfand's Scale," *Journal of Business and Psychology* 21, no. 3 (2007): 313-329. The relationship between individualism and collectivism is still being debated, but most experts now agree that individualism and collectivism have serious problems with conceptualization and measurement.

56. G. Hofstede, Culture's Consequences: Comparing Values, Behaviors, Institutions, and Organizations across Nations, 2nd ed. (Thousand Oaks, CA: Sage, 2001).

57. S. Klie, "Program Breaks Cultural Barriers," *Canadian HR Reporter*, 10 September 2007.

58. G. Hofstede, *Cultures and Organizations: Software of the Mind* (New York: McGraw-Hill, 1991). Hofstede used the terms "masculinity" and "femininity" for achievement and nurturing orientation, respectively. We have adopted the latter to minimize the sexist perspective of these concepts.

59. H. Trinca, "It's About Soul but Don't Get Too Soft," *Australian Financial Review*, 12 August 2005, 56.

60. J. S. Osland *et al.*, "Beyond Sophisticated Stereotyping: Cultural Sensemaking in Context," *Academy of Management Executive* 14 (February 2000): 65-79; S. S. Sarwono and R. W. Armstrong, "Microcultural Differences and Perceived Ethical Problems: An International Business Perspective," *Journal of Business Ethics* 30 (March 2001): 41-56; M. Voronov and J. A. Singer, "The Myth of Individualism-Collectivism: A Critical Review," *Journal of Social Psychology* 142 (August 2002): 461-480; N. Jacob, "Cross-Cultural Investigations: Emerging Concepts," *Journal of Organizational Change Management* 18, no. 5 (2005): 514-528.

61. M. Adams, "New Canadians, Old Values?" *Globe & Mail*, 2 March 2005, A17.

62. Z. Wu and D. Baer, "Attitudes toward Family and Gender Roles: A Comparison of English and French Canadian Women," *Journal of Comparative Family Studies* 27 (Autumn 1996): 437-452. The reference to "two solitudes" comes from: H. McLennan, *Two Solitudes* (Toronto: MacMillan of Canada, 1945).

63. M. Major *et al.*, "Meanings of Work and Personal Values of Canadian Anglophone and Francophone Middle Managers," *Canadian Journal of Administrative Sciences* 11 (September 1994): 251-263; M. Laroche *et al.*, "The Influence of Culture on Pro-Environmental Knowledge, Attitudes, and Behavior: A Canadian Perspective," *Advances in Consumer Research* 23 (1996): 196-202.

64. I. Chapman, D. McCaskill, and D. Newhouse, "Management in Contemporary Aboriginal Organizations," *Canadian Journal of Native Studies* 11, no. 2 (1991): 333-349; L. Redpath and M. O. Nielsen, "A Comparison of Native Culture, Non-Native Culture and New Management Ideology," *Canadian Journal of Administrative Sciences* 14, no. 3 (September 1997): 327-339.

65. M. Adams, *Fire and Ice: The United States, Canada, and the Myth of Converging Values* (Toronto: Penguin Canada, 2004), p. 142.

66. J. Laxer, *The Border: Canada, the U.S. And Dispatches from the 49th Parallel* (Toronto: Anchor Canada, 2004).

67. C. Cobb, "Canadians Want a Diverse Society: Poll," *Ottawa Citizen*, 18 February 2002, A5; K. May, "Canadian Nationalism Growing: Study," *Ottawa Citizen*, 5 June 2002, A8 C. Boucher, "Canada-Us Values: Distinct, Inevitably Carbon Copy, or Narcissism of Small Differences?" *Horizons: Policy Research Initiative* 7, no. 1 (June 2004): 42-49.

68. Adams, *Fire and Ice*. For earlier research, see: M. Adams, *Sex in the Snow* (Toronto: Penguin Canada, 1998); M. Adams, "What Makes Us Different," *Globe & Mail*, 4 July 2001, A11; M. Adams, *Better Happy Than Rich?* (Toronto: Viking, 2001).

69. D. Baer, E. Grabb, and W. Johnston, "National Character, Regional Culture, and the Values of Canadians and Americans," *Canadian Review of Sociology and anthropology* 30, no. 1 (1993): 13-36; E. Grabb and J. Curtis, *The Four Societies of Canada and the United States* (New York: Oxford University Press, 2005). Evidence of small differences in Canadian-American culture is also reported in: Boucher, "Canada-Us Values."

70. C. Savoye, "Workers Say Honesty Is Best Company Policy," *Christian Science Monitor*, June 15 2000; J. M. Kouzes and B. Z. Posner, *The Leadership Challenge*, 3rd ed. (San Francisco: Jossey-Bass, 2002); J. Schettler, "Leadership in Corporate America," *Training & Development*, September 2002, 66-73.

71. S. Pearlstein, "Hollinger Paid for Lord Black's Costly Hubris," *Washington Post*, 3 September 2004, E1; C. McLean, "Five Leave Nortel Board," *Globe & Mail*, 11

January 2005; R. Westhead, "Livent Preliminary Hearing Begins," *Toronto Star*, 11 January 2005, D1; D. A. Brown, *A Matter of Trust: Report of the Independent Investigator into Matters Relating to Rcmp Pension and Insurance Plans*, (Ottawa: Government of Canada, 15 June 2007).

72. P. L. Schumann, "A Moral Principles Framework for Human Resource Management Ethics," *Human Resource Management Review* 11 (Spring-Summer 2001): 93-111; J. Boss, *Analyzing Moral Issues*, 3rd ed. (New York: McGraw-Hill, 2005), Chap. 1; M. G. Velasquez, *Business Ethics: Concepts and Cases*, 6th ed. (Upper Saddle River, NJ: Prentice-Hall, 2006), Chap. 2.

73. T. J. Jones, "Ethical Decision Making by Individuals in Organizations: An Issue Contingent Model," *Academy of Management Review* 16 (1991): 366-395; B. H. Frey, "The Impact of Moral Intensity on Decision Making in a Business Context," *Journal of Business Ethics* 26 (August 2000): 181-195; D. R. May and K. P. Pauli, "The Role of Moral Intensity in Ethical Decision Making," *Business and Society* 41 (March 2002): 84-117.

74. J. R. Sparks and S. D. Hunt, "Marketing Researcher Ethical Sensitivity: Conceptualization, Measurement, and Exploratory Investigation," *Journal of Marketing* 62 (April 1998): 92-109.

75. K. F. Alam, "Business Ethics in New Zealand Organizations: Views from the Middle and Lower Level Managers," *Journal of Business Ethics* 22 (November 1999): 145-153; K. Blotnicky, "Is Business in Moral Decay?" *Chronicle-Herald (Halifax)*, 11 June 2000; B. Stoneman and K. K. Holliday, "Pressure Cooker," *Banking Strategies*, January-February 2001, 13.

76. B. Farrell, D. M. Cobbin, and H. M. Farrell, "Codes of Ethics: Their Evolution, Development and Other Controversies," *Journal of Management Development* 21, no. 2 (2002): 152-163; G. Wood and M. Rimmer, "Codes of Ethics: What Are They Really and What Should They Be?" *International Journal of Value-Based Management* 16, no. 2 (2003): 181.

77. J. Fortier, "Trust in the Workplace," *Ottawa Business Journal*, 4 January 2007

78. E. Aronson, "Integrating Leadership Styles and Ethical Perspectives," *Canadian Journal of Administrative Sciences* 18 (December 2001): 266-276; D. R. May et al., "Developing the Moral Component of Authentic Leadership," *Organizational Dynamics* 32 (2003): 247-260. The Vodafone director quotation is from: R. Van Lee, L. Fabish, and N. McGaw, "The Value of Corporate Values," *Strategy+Business* (Summer 2005): 1-13.

Chapter 3

1. S. Klie, "Canada Post CEO Walks in Employees' Shoes," *Canadian HR Reporter*, 23 October 2006, 12; K. Moore, "Canada Post Boss Sees Balanced Team as Crucial," *Globe & Mail*, 7 August 2006, B10; S. Silcoff, "Delivering a New Canada Post," *National Post*, 17 September 2007.

2. The effect of the target in selective attention is known as "bottom-up selection"; the effect of the perceiver's psychodynamics on this process is known as "top-down selection." See: C. E. Connor, H. E. Egeth, and S. Yantis, "Visual Attention: Bottom-up Versus Top-Down," *Current Biology* 14, no. 19 (2004): R850-R852; E. I. Knudsen, "Fundamental Components of Attention," *Annual Review of Neuroscience* 30, no. 1 (2007): 57-78.

3. A. Mack et al., "Perceptual Organization and Attention," *Cognitive Psychology* 24, no. 4 (1992): 475-501; A. R. Damasio, *Descartes' Error: Emotion, Reason, and the Human Brain* (New York: Putnam Sons, 1994); C. Frith, "A Framework for Studying the Neural Basis of Attention," *Neuropsychologia* 39, no. 12 (2001): 1367-1371; N. Lavie, "Distracted and Confused?: Selective Attention under Load," *Trends in Cognitive Sciences* 9, no. 2 (2005): 75-82; M. Shermer, "The Political Brain," *Scientific American* 295, no. 1 (July 2006): 36; D. Westen, *The Political Brain: The Role of Emotion in Deciding the Fate of the Nation* (Cambridge, MA: Public Affairs, 2007).

4. Confirmation bias is defined as "unwitting selectivity in the acquisition and use of evidence." R. S. Nickerson, "Confirmation Bias: A Ubiquitous Phenomenon in Many Guises," *Review of General Psychology* 2, no. 2 (1998): 175-220 This occurs in a variety of ways, including overweighting positive information, perceiving only positive information, and restricting cognitive attention to a favoured hypothesis. A recent study has found that confirmation bias is typically nonconscious and driven by emotions.

5. S. Lewandowsky et al., "Memory for Fact, Fiction, and Misinformation. The Iraq War 2003," *Psychological Science* 16, no. 3 (2005): 190-195.

6. E. Byron, "The Master the Art of Solving Crimes, Cops Study Vermeer," *Wall Street Journal*, 27 July 2005, A1; D. J. Hall, "The Justice System Isn't Always Just," *Capital Times & Wisconsin State Journal*, 27 November 2005, D1; I. Bailey, "Maintenance Man among Murder Victims," *Globe & Mail*, 22 October 2007, A1; Rossmo, 2006 #354.

7. C. N. Macrae and G. V. Bodenhausen, "Social Cognition: Thinking Categorically About Others," *Annual Review of Psychology* 51 (2000): 93-120. For literature on the automaticity of the perceptual organization and interpretation process, see: J. A. Bargh, "The Cognitive Monster: The Case against the Controllability of Automatic Stereotype Effects," in *Dual Process Theories in Social Psychology*, ed. S. Chaiken and Y. Trope (New York: Guilford, 1999), 361-382; J. A. Bargh and M. J. Ferguson, "Beyond Behaviourism: On the Automaticity of Higher Mental Processes," *Psychological Bulletin* 126, no. 6 (2000): 925-945; M. Gladwell, *Blink: The Power of Thinking without Thinking* (New York: Little, Brown, 2005).

8. E. M. Altmann and B. D. Burns, "Streak Biases in Decision Making: Data and a Memory Model," *Cognitive Systems Research* 6, no. 1 (2005): 5-16. For discussion of cognitive closure and perception, see: A. W. Kruglanski, *The Psychology of Closed Mindedness* (New York: Psychology Press, 2004).

9. N. Ambady and R. Rosenthal, "Half a Minute: Predicting Teacher Evaluations from Thin Slices of Nonverbal Behaviour and Physical Attractiveness," *Journal of Personality and Social Psychology* 64, no. 3 (March 1993): 431-441. For other research on thin slices, see: N. Ambady and R. Rosenthal, "Thin Slices of Expressive Behaviour as Predictors of Interpersonal Consequences: A Meta-Analysis," *Psychological Bulletin* 111, no. 2 (1992): 256-274; N. Ambady et al., "Surgeons' Tone of Voice: A Clue to Malpractice History," *Surgery* 132, no. 1 (July 2002): 5-9.

10. P. M. Senge, *The Fifth Discipline: The Art and Practice of the Learning Organization* (New York: Doubleday Currency, 1990), Chap. 10; P. N. Johnson-Laird, "Mental Models and Deduction," *Trends in Cognitive Sciences* 5, no. 10 (2001): 434-442; A. B. Markman and D. Gentner, "Thinking," *Annual Review of Psychology* 52 (2001): 223-247; T. J. Chermack, "Mental Models in Decision Making and Implications for Human Resource Development," *Advances in Developing Human Resources* 5, no. 4 (2003): 408-422.

11. M. A. Hogg et al., "The Social Identity Perspective: Intergroup Relations, Self-Conception, and Small Groups," *Small Group Research* 35, no. 3 (June 2004): 246-276; J. Jetten, R. Spears, and T. Postmes, "Intergroup Distinctiveness and Differentiation: A Meta-Analytic Integration," *Journal of Personality and Social Psychology* 86, no. 6 (2004): 862-879.

12. J. W. Jackson and E. R. Smith, "Conceptualizing Social Identity: A New Framework and Evidence for the Impact of Different Dimensions," *Personality & Social Psychology Bulletin* 25 (January 1999): 120-135.

13. L. Falkenberg, "Improving the Accuracy of Stereotypes within the Workplace,"

Journal of Management 16 (1990): 107-118; S. T. Fiske, "Stereotyping, Prejudice, and Discrimination," in *Handbook of Social Psychology*, ed. D. T. Gilbert, S. T. Fiske, and G. Lindzey, Fourth ed. (New York: McGraw-Hill, 1998), 357-411; Macrae and Bodenhausen, "Social Cognition: Thinking Categorically About Others."

14. C. N. Macrae, A. B. Milne, and G. V. Bodenhausen, "Stereotypes as Energy-Saving Devices: A Peek inside the Cognitive Toolbox," *Journal of Personality and Social Psychology* 66 (1994): 37-47; J. W. Sherman *et al.*, "Stereotype Efficiency Reconsidered: Encoding Flexibility under Cognitive Load," *Journal of Personality and Social Psychology* 75 (1998): 589-606; Macrae and Bodenhausen, "Social Cognition: Thinking Categorically About Others."

15. L. Sinclair and Z. Kunda, "Motivated Stereotyping of Women: She's Fine If She Praised Me but Incompetent If She Criticized Me," *Personality and Social Psychology Bulletin* 26 (November 2000): 1329-1342; J. C. Turner and S. A. Haslam, "Social Identity, Organizations, and Leadership," in *Groups at Work: Theory and Research*, ed. M. E. Turner (Mahwah, NJ: Lawrence Erlbaum Associates, 2001), 25-65.

16. A. L. Friedman and S. R. Lyne, "The Beancounter Stereotype: Towards a General Model of Stereotype Generation," *Critical Perspectives on Accounting* 12, no. 4 (2001): 423-451.

17. S. Hayward, "Discrimination Troubles," *Metro-Toronto*, 21 March 2005; "Workplace Discrimination the Biggest Hurdle for Older and Younger Canadians," Kelly Global Workforce Index News release, (Toronto: 17 October 2006).

18. "Employers Face New Danger: Accidental Age Bias," *Omaha World-Herald*, 10 October 2005, D1; "Tiptoeing through the Employment Minefield of Race, Sex, and Religion? Here's Another One," *North West Business Insider (Manchester, UK)*, February 2006.

19. S. O. Gaines and E. S. Reed, "Prejudice: From Allport to Dubois," *American Psychologist* 50 (February 1995): 96-103; Fiske, "Stereotyping, Prejudice, and Discrimination"; M. Hewstone, M. Rubin, and H. Willis, "Intergroup Bias," *Annual Review of Psychology* 53 (2002): 575-604.

20. M. Patriquin, "Quebec Farm Segregated Black Workers," *Globe & Mail*, 30 April 2005, A1.

21. J. A. Bargh and T. L. Chartrand, "The Unbearable Automaticity of Being," *American Psychologist* 54, no. 7 (July 1999): 462-479; S. T. Fiske, "What We Know Now About Bias and Intergroup Conflict, the Problem of the Century," *Current Directions in Psychological Science* 11, no. 4 (August 2002): 123-128. For recent evidence that shows that intensive training can minimize stereotype activation, see: K. Kawakami *et al.*, "Just Say No (to Stereotyping): Effects of Training in the Negation of Stereotypic Associations on Stereotype Activation," *Journal of Personality and Social Psychology* 78, no. 5 (2000): 871-888; E. A. Plant, B. M. Peruche, and D. A. Butz, "Eliminating Automatic Racial Bias: Making Race Non-Diagnostic for Responses to Criminal Suspects," *Journal of Experimental Social Psychology* 41, no. 2 (2005): 141.

22. H. H. Kelley, *Attribution in Social Interaction* (Morristown, N.J.: General Learning Press, 1971).

23. P. Ford, "Next French Revolution: A Less Colorblind Society," *Christian Science Monitor*, 14 November 2005, 1; J. W. Anderson, "French Firm Tests Colorblind Hiring," *Washington Post*, 29 January 2006, A20; P. Gumbel, "The French Exodus," *Time International*, 16 April 2007, 18; A. Sage, "L'oreal Accused of Discrimination in 'All-White Campaign,'" *The Times (London)*, 16 May 2007, 57; D. Vidal, "Affirmative Action Bypasses Those at the Bottom of the Pile," *Le Monde Diplomatique*, May 2007.

24. J. M. Feldman, "Beyond Attribution Theory: Cognitive Processes in Performance Appraisal," *Journal of Applied Psychology* 66 (1981): 127-148.

25. J. M. Crant and T. S. Bateman, "Assignment of Credit and Blame for Performance Outcomes," *Academy of Management Journal* 36 (1993): 7-27; B. Weiner, "Intrapersonal and Interpersonal Theories of Motivation from an Attributional Perspective," *Educational Psychology Review* 12 (2000): 1-14; N. Bacon and P. Blyton, "Worker Responses to Teamworking: Exploring Employee Attributions of Managerial Motives," *International Journal of Human Resource Management* 16, no. 2 (February 2005): 238-255.

26. Fundamental attribution error is part of a larger phenomenon known as correspondence bias. See: D. T. Gilbert and P. S. Malone, "The Correspondence Bias," *Psychological Bulletin* 117, no. 1 (1995): 21-38.

27. I. Choi, R. E. Nisbett, and A. Norenzayan, "Causal Attribution across Cultures: Variation and Universality," *Psychological Bulletin* 125, no. 1 (1999): 47-63; D. S. Krull *et al.*, "The Fundamental Fundamental Attribution Error: Correspondence Bias in Individualist and Collectivist Cultures," *Personality and Social Psychology Bulletin* 25, no. 10 (October 1999): 1208-1219; R. E. Nisbett, *The Geography of Thought: How Asians and Westerners Think Differently—and Why* (New York: Free Press, 2003), Chap. 5.

28. F. Lee and L. Z. Tiedens, "Who's Being Served? 'Self-Serving' Attributions in Social Hierarchies," *Organizational Behaviour and Human Decision Processes* 84, no. 2 (2001): 254-287; E. W. K. Tsang, "Self-Serving Attributions in Corporate Annual Reports: A Replicated Study," *Journal of Management Studies* 39, no. 1 (January 2002): 51-65; N. J. Roese and J. M. Olson, "Better, Stronger, Faster: Self-Serving Judgment, Affect Regulation, and the Optimal Vigilance Hypothesis," *Perspectives on Psychological Science* 2, no. 2 (2007): 124-141.

29. Similar models are presented in D. Eden, "Self-Fulfilling Prophecy as a Management Tool: Harnessing Pygmalion," *Academy of Management Review* 9 (1984): 64-73; R. H. G. Field and D. A. Van Seters, "Management by Expectations (MBE): The Power of Positive Prophecy," *Journal of General Management* 14 (Winter 1988): 19-33; D. O. Trouilloud *et al.*, "The Influence of Teacher Expectations on Student Achievement in Physical Education Classes: Pygmalion Revisited," *European Journal of Social Psychology* 32 (2002): 591-607.

30. D. Eden, "Interpersonal Expectations in Organizations," in *Interpersonal Expectations: Theory, Research, and Applications* (Cambridge, UK: Cambridge University Press, 1993), 154-178.

31. D. Eden, "Pygmalion Goes to Boot Camp: Expectancy, Leadership, and Trainee Performance," *Journal of Applied Psychology* 67 (1982): 194-199; R. P. Brown and E. C. Pinel, "Stigma on My Mind: Individual Differences in the Experience of Stereotype Threat," *Journal of Experimental Social Psychology* 39, no. 6 (2003): 626-633.

32. S. Madon, L. Jussim, and J. Eccles, "In Search of the Powerful Self-Fulfilling Prophecy," *Journal of Personality and Social Psychology* 72, no. 4 (April 1997): 791-809; A. E. Smith, L. Jussim, and J. Eccles, "Do Self-Fulfilling Prophecies Accumulate, Dissipate, or Remain Stable over Time?" *Journal of Personality and Social Psychology* 77, no. 3 (1999): 548-565; S. Madon *et al.*, "Self-Fulfilling Prophecies: The Synergistic Accumulative Effect of Parents' Beliefs on Children's Drinking Behaviour," *Psychological Science* 15, no. 12 (2005): 837-845.

33. W. H. Cooper, "Ubiquitous Halo," *Psychological Bulletin* 90 (1981): 218-244; K. R. Murphy, R. A. Jako, and R. L. Anhalt, "Nature and Consequences of Halo Error: A Critical Analysis," *Journal of Applied Psychology* 78 (1993): 218-225; T. H. Feeley, "Comment on Halo Effects in Rating and Evaluation Research," *Human Communication Research* 28, no. 4 (October 2002): 578-586. For a variation of the classic halo effect in business settings, see: P. Rosenzweig, *The Halo Effect...And the Eight Other*

Business Delusions That Deceive Managers (New York: Free Press, 2007).

34. C. L. Kleinke, *First Impressions: The Psychology of Encountering Others* (Englewood Cliffs, N.J.: Prentice Hall, 1975); E. A. Lind, L. Kray, and L. Thompson, "Primacy Effects in Justice Judgments: Testing Predictions from Fairness Heuristic Theory," *Organizational Behaviour and Human Decision Processes* 85 (July 2001): 189-210; O. Ybarra, "When First Impressions Don't Last: The Role of Isolation and Adaptation Processes in the Revision of Evaluative Impressions," *Social Cognition* 19 (October 2001): 491-520; S. D. Bond *et al.*, "Information Distortion in the Evaluation of a Single Option," *Organizational Behaviour and Human Decision Processes* 102, no. 2 (2007): 240-254.

35. D. D. Steiner and J. S. Rain, "Immediate and Delayed Primacy and Recency Effects in Performance Evaluation," *Journal of Applied Psychology* 74 (1989): 136-142; K. T. Trotman, "Order Effects and Recency: Where Do We Go from Here?" *Accounting & Finance* 40 (2000): 169-182; W. Green, "Impact of the Timing of an Inherited Explanation on Auditors' Analytical Procedures Judgements," *Accounting and Finance* 44 (2004): 369-392.

36. R. W. Clement and J. Krueger, "The Primacy of Self-Referent Information in Perceptions of Social Consensus," *British Journal of Social Psychology* 39 (2000): 279-299; R. L. Gross and S. E. Brodt, "How Assumptions of Consensus Undermine Decision Making," *Sloan Management Review* (January 2001): 86-94; J. Oliver *et al.*, "Projection of Own on Others' Job Characteristics: Evidence for the False Consensus Effect in Job Characteristics Information," *International Journal of Selection and Assessment* 13, no. 1 (2005): 63-74.

37. D. Eden *et al.*, "Implanting Pygmalion Leadership Style through Workshop Training: Seven Field Experiments," *Leadership Quarterly* 11 (2000): 171-210; S. S. White and E. A. Locke, "Problems with the Pygmalion Effect and Some Proposed Solutions," *Leadership Quarterly* 11 (Autumn 2000): 389-415; M. Bendick, M. L. Egan, and S. M. Lofhjelm, "Workforce Diversity Training: From Anti-Discrimination Compliance to Organizational Development HR," *Human Resource Planning* 24 (2001): 10-25; L. Roberson, C. T. Kulik, and M. B. Pepper, "Using Needs Assessment to Resolve Controversies in Diversity Training Design," *Group & Organization Management* 28, no. 1 (March 2003): 148-174; D. E. Hogan and M. Mallott, "Changing Racial Prejudice through Diversity Education," *Journal of College Student Development* 46, no. 2 (March/April 2005): 115-125.

38. For discussion of the Implicit Association Test, including critique, see: H. Blanton *et al.*, "Decoding the Implicit Association Test: Implications for Criterion Prediction," *Journal of Experimental Social Psychology* 42, no. 2 (2006): 192-212; A. G. Greenwald, B. A. Nosek, and N. Sriram, "Consequential Validity of the Implicit Association Test: Comment on Blanton and Jaccard (2006)," *American Psychologist* 61, no. 1 (2006): 56-61; W. Hofmann *et al.*, "Implicit and Explicit Attitudes and Interracial Interaction: The Moderating Role of Situationally Available Control Resources," *Group Processes Intergroup Relations* 11, no. 1 (Jan. 2008): 69-87.

39. P. Babcock, "Detecting Hidden Bias," *HRMagazine*, February 2006, 50.

40. T. W. Costello and S. S. Zalkind, *Psychology in Administration: A Research Orientation* (Englewood Cliffs, N.J.: Prentice Hall, 1963), pp. 45-46; J. M. Kouzes and B. Z. Posner, *The Leadership Challenge*, 4th ed. (San Francisco: Jossey-Bass, 2007), Chap. 3.

41. J. Luft, *Group Processes* (Palo Alto, Calif: Mayfield Publishing, 1984). For a variation of this model, see: J. Hall, "Communication Revisited," *California Management Review* 15 (Spring 1973): 56-67.

42. L. C. Miller and D. A. Kenny, "Reciprocity of Self-Disclosure at the Individual and Dyadic Levels: A Social Relations Analysis," *Journal of Personality and Social Psychology* 50 (1986): 713-719.

43. T. F. Pettigrew, "Intergroup Contact Theory," *Annual Review of Psychology* 49 (1998): 65-85; S. Brickson, "The Impact of Identity Orientation on Individual and Organizational Outcomes in Demographically Diverse Settings," *Academy of Management Review* 25 (January 2000): 82-101; J. Dixon and K. Durrheim, "Contact and the Ecology of Racial Division: Some Varieties of Informal Segregation," *British Journal of Social Psychology* 42 (March 2003): 1-23.

44. W. G. Stephen and K. A. Finlay, "The Role of Empathy in Improving Intergroup Relations," *Journal of Social Issues* 55 (Winter 1999): 729-743; S. K. Parker and C. M. Axtell, "Seeing Another Viewpoint: Antecedents and Outcomes of Employee Perspective Taking," *Academy of Management Journal* 44 (December 2001): 1085-1100; G. J. Vreeke and I. L. van der Mark, "Empathy, an Integrative Model," *New Ideas in Psychology* 21, no. 3 (2003): 177-207.

45. I. Nonaka and H. Takeuchi, *The Knowledge-Creating Company* (New York: Oxford University Press, 1995); P. Duguid, "'The Art of Knowing': Social and Tacit Dimensions of Knowledge and the Limits of the Community of Practice," *The Information Society* 21 (2005): 109-118.

46. B. F. Skinner, *About Behaviourism* (New York: Alfred A. Knopf, 1974); J. Komaki, T. Coombs, and S. Schepman, "Motivational Implications of Reinforcement Theory," in *Motivation and Leadership at Work*, ed. R. M. Steers, L. W. Porter, and G. A. Bigley (New York: McGraw-Hill, 1996), 34-52; R. G. Miltenberger, *Behaviour Modification: Principles and Procedures* (Pacific Grove, CA: Brooks/Cole, 1997).

47. T. K. Connellan, *How to Improve Human Performance* (New York: Harper & Row, 1978), pp. 48-57; F. Luthans and R. Kreitner, *Organizational Behaviour Modification and Beyond* (Glenview, Ill.: Scott, Foresman, 1985), pp. 85-88.

48. Miltenberger, *Behaviour Modification: Principles and Procedures*, Chap. 4-6.

49. Punishment can also include removing a pleasant consequence, such as when employees must switch from business to economy class flying when their sales fall below the threshold for top tier sales "stars."

50. T. R. Hinkin and C. A. Schriesheim, "'If You Don't Hear from Me You Know You Are Doing Fine,'" *Cornell Hotel & Restaurant Administration Quarterly* 45, no. 4 (November 2004): 362-372.

51. L. K. Trevino, "The Social Effects of Punishment in Organizations: A Justice Perspective," *Academy of Management Review* 17 (1992): 647-676; L. E. Atwater *et al.*, "Recipient and Observer Reactions to Discipline: Are Managers Experiencing Wishful Thinking?" *Journal of Organizational Behaviour* 22, no. 3 (May 2001): 249-270.

52. G. P. Latham and V. L. Huber, "Schedules of Reinforcement: Lessons from the Past and Issues for the Future," *Journal of Organizational Behaviour Management* 13 (1992): 125-149; B. A. Williams, "Challenges to Timing-Based Theories of Operant Behaviour," *Behavioural Processes* 62 (April 2003): 115-123.

53. S. Overman, "Many Offer Basic Wellness Initiatives, Few Track Results," *Employee Benefit News*, 15 April 2006; H. Wecsler, "Sick Day Incentive Plan Favored by NLR Board," *Arkansas Democrat Gazette*, 17 February 2006, 14.

54. ExxonMobil, *UK and Ireland Corporate Citizenship* (ExxonMobil, August 2004).

55. M. Colias, "Obese Police," *Crain's Chicago Business*, 26 February 2007, 1; D. Gibson, "Investing in Employees' Health," *Lane Report (Kentucky)*, December 2007, 28.

56. Bargh and Ferguson, "Beyond Behaviourism." Some writers argue that behaviourists long ago accepted the relevance of cognitive processes in behaviour modification. See: I. Kirsch *et al.*, "The Role of Cognition in Classical and Operant Condi-

tioning," *Journal of Clinical Psychology* 60, no. 4 (April 2004): 369-392.

57. A. Bandura, *Social Foundations of Thought and Action: A Social Cognitive Theory* (Englewood Cliffs, N.J: Prentice Hall, 1986).

58. A. Pescuric and W. C. Byham, "The New Look of Behaviour Modeling," *Training & Development* 50 (July 1996): 24-30.

59. M. E. Schnake, "Vicarious Punishment in a Work Setting," *Journal of Applied Psychology* 71 (1986): 343-345; Trevino, "The Social Effects of Punishment in Organizations: A Justice Perspective"; J. B. DeConinck, "The Effect of Punishment on Sales Managers' Outcome Expectancies and Responses to Unethical Sales Force Behaviour," *American Business Review* 21, no. 2 (June 2003): 135-140.

60. A. Bandura, "Self-Reinforcement: Theoretical and Methodological Considerations," *Behaviourism* 4 (1976): 135-155; C. A. Frayne and J. M. Geringer, "Self-Management Training for Improving Job Performance: A Field Experiment Involving Salespeople," *Journal of Applied Psychology* 85, no. 3 (June 2000): 361-372; J. B. Vancouver and D. V. Day, "Industrial and Organisation Research on Self-Regulation: From Constructs to Applications," *Applied Psychology* 54, no. 2 (April 2005): 155-185.

61. D. A. Kolb, *Experiential Learning* (Englewood Cliffs, NJ: Prentice-Hall, 1984); S. Gherardi, D. Nicolini, and F. Odella, "Toward a Social Understanding of How People Learn in Organizations," *Management Learning* 29 (September 1998): 273-297; D. A. Kolb, R. E. Boyatzis, and C. Mainemelis, "Experiential Learning Theory: Previous Research and New Directions," in *Perspectives on Thinking, Learning, and Cognitive Styles*, ed. R. J. Sternberg and L. F. Zhang (Mahwah, NJ: Lawrence Erlbaum, 2001), 227-248.

62. W. E. Baker and J. M. Sinkula, "The Synergistic Effect of Market Orientation and Learning Orientation on Organizational Performance," *Academy of Marketing Science Journal* 27, no. 4 (Fall 1999): 411-427; Z. Emden, A. Yaprak, and S. T. Cavusgil, "Learning from Experience in International Alliances: Antecedents and Firm Performance Implications," *Journal of Business Research* 58, no. 7 (2005): 883-892.

63. J. Jusko, "Always Lessons to Learn," *Industry Week* (February 15 1999): 23; R. Farson and R. Keyes, "The Failure-Tolerant Leader," *Harvard Business Review* 80 (August 2002): 64-71.

64. H. Shipton, "Cohesion or Confusion? Towards a Typology for Organizational Learning Research," *International Journal of Management Reviews* 8, no. 4 (2006): 233-252; D. Jiménez-Jiménez and J. G.

Cegarra-Navarro, "The Performance Effect of Organizational Learning and Market Orientation," *Industrial Marketing Management* 36, no. 6 (2007): 694-708.

65. R. Garud and A. Kumaraswamy, "Vicious and Virtuous Circles in the Management of Knowledge: The Case of Infosys Technologies," *MIS Quarterly* 29, no. 1 (March 2005): 9-33.

Chapter 4

1. S. Dobson, "Tri Fit in Good Shape Thanks to Creative Recognition Program," *Canadian HR Reporter*, 9 April 2007, 11-12; C. Foster, "Turning Ha-Ha into a-Ha!," *Employee Benefit News Canada*, December 2007; S. Osborne and E. Osborne, "Put Staff First, Clients Will Follow!," *The Practicing CPA*, July/August 2007, 1, 3; G. Teel, "WestJet Banks on Its Brand," *Calgary Herald*, 28 December 2007.

2. The centrality of emotions in marketing, economics, and sociology is discussed in: G. Loewenstein, "Emotions in Economic Theory and Economic Behavior," *American Economic Review* 90, no. 2 (May 2000): 426-432; D. S. Massey, "A Brief History of Human Society: The Origin and Role of Emotion in Social Life," *American Sociological Review* 67 (February 2002): 1-29; J. O'Shaughnessy and N. J. O'Shaughnessy, *The Marketing Power of Emotion* (New York: Oxford University Press, 2003).

3. The definition presented here is constructed from the following sources: N. M. Ashkanasy, W. J. Zerbe, and C. E. J. Hartel, "Introduction: Managing Emotions in a Changing Workplace," in *Managing Emotions in the Workplace* ed. N. M. Ashkanasy, W. J. Zerbe, and C. E. J. Hartel (Armonk, N. Y.: M. E. Sharpe, 2002), 3-18; H. M. Weiss, "Conceptual and Empirical Foundations for the Study of Affect at Work," in *Emotions in the Workplace* ed. R. G. Lord, R. J. Klimoski, and R. Kanfer (San Francisco: Jossey-Bass, 2002), 20-63. However, the meaning of emotions is still being debated. See, for example: M. Cabanac, "What Is Emotion?" *Behavioral Processes* 60 (2002): 69-83.

4. R. Kanfer and R. J. Klimoski, "Affect and Work: Looking Back to the Future," in *Emotions in the Workplace* ed. R. G. Lord, R. J. Klimoski, and R. Kanfer (San Francisco: Jossey-Bass, 2002), 473-490; J. A. Russell, "Core Affect and the Psychological Construction of Emotion," *Psychological Review* 110, no. 1 (2003): 145-172.

5. R. B. Zajonc, "Emotions," in *Handbook of Social Psychology*, ed. D. T. Gilbert, S. T. Fiske, and L. Gardner (New York: Oxford University Press, 1998), 591-634.

6. N. A. Remington, L. R. Fabrigar, and P. S. Visser, "Reexamining the Circumplex Model of Affect," *Journal of Personality*

and *Social Psychology* 79, no. 2 (2000): 286-300; R. J. Larson, E. Diener, and R. E. Lucas, "Emotion: Models, Measures, and Differences," in *Emotions in the Workplace* ed. R. G. Lord, R. J. Klimoski, and R. Kanfer (San Francisco: Jossey-Bass, 2002), 64-113; L. F. Barrett *et al.*, "The Experience of Emotion," *Annual Review of Psychology* 58, no. 1 (2007): 373-403.

7. A. H. Eagly and S. Chaiken, *The Psychology of Attitudes* (Orlando, FL: Harcourt Brace Jovanovich, 1993); A. P. Brief, *Attitudes in and around Organizations* (Thousand Oaks, CA: Sage, 1998). There is an amazing lack of consensus on the definition of attitudes. This book adopts the three-component model, whereas some experts define attitude as only the "feelings" component, with "beliefs" as a predictor and "intentions" as an outcome. Some writers specifically define attitudes as an "evaluation" of an attitude object, whereas others distinguish attitudes from evaluations of an attitude object. For some of these definitional variations, see: I. Ajzen, "Nature and Operation of Attitudes," *Annual Review of Psychology* 52 (2001): 27-58; D. Albarracín *et al.*, "Attitudes: Introduction and Scope," in *The Handbook of Attitudes*, ed. D. Albarracín, B. T. Johnson, and M. P. Zanna (Mahwah, NJ: Lawrence Erlbaum Associates, 2005), 3-20; W. A. Cunningham and P. D. Zelazo, "Attitudes and Evaluations: A Social Cognitive Neuroscience Perspective," *TRENDS in Cognitive Sciences* 11, no. 3 (2007): 97-104.

8. C. D. Fisher, "Mood and Emotions While Working: Missing Pieces of Job Satisfaction?" *Journal of Organizational Behavior* 21 (2000): 185-202; Cunningham and Zelazo, "Attitudes and Evaluations"; M. D. Lieberman, "Social Cognitive Neuroscience: A Review of Core Processes," *Annual Review of Psychology* 58, no. 1 (2007): 259-289.

9. S. Orbell, "Intention-Behavior Relations: A Self-Regulation Perspective," in *Contemporary Perspectives on the Psychology of Attitudes*, ed. G. Haddock and G. R. Maio (East Sussex, UK: Psychology Press, 2004), 145-168.

10. H. M. Weiss and R. Cropanzano, "Affective Events Theory: A Theoretical Discussion of the Structure, Causes, and Consequences of Affective Experiences at Work," *Research in Organizational Behavior* 18 (1996): 1-74; J. Wegge *et al.*, "A Test of Basic Assumptions of Affective Events Theory (Aet) in Call Centre Work," *British Journal of Management* 17 (2006): 237-254.

11. J. A. Bargh and M. J. Ferguson, "Beyond Behaviorism: On the Automaticity of Higher Mental Processes," *Psychological Bulletin* 126, no. 6 (2000): 925-945; R. H. Fazio, "On the Automatic Activation of Associated Evaluations: An Overview,"

Cognition and Emotion 15, no. 2 (2001): 115-141; M. Gladwell, *Blink: The Power of Thinking without Thinking* (New York: Little, Brown, 2005).

12. A. R. Damasio, *Descartes' Error: Emotion, Reason, and the Human Brain* (New York: Putnam Sons, 1994); A. Damasio, *The Feeling of What Happens* (New York: Harcourt Brace and Co., 1999); P. Ekman, "Basic Emotions," in *Handbook of Cognition and Emotion*, ed. T. Dalgleish and M. Power (San Francisco: Jossey-Bass, 1999), 45-60; J. E. LeDoux, "Emotion Circuits in the Brain," *Annual Review of Neuroscience* 23 (2000): 155-184; R. J. Dolan, "Emotion, Cognition, and Behavior," *Science* 298, no. 5596 (8 November 2002): 1191-1194.

13. N. Schwarz, "Emotion, Cognition, and Decision Making," *Cognition and Emotion* 14, no. 4 (2000): 433-440; M. T. Pham, "The Logic of Feeling," *Journal of Consumer Psychology* 14, no. 4 (2004): 360-369.

14. G. R. Maio, V. M. Esses, and D. W. Bell, "Examining Conflict between Components of Attitudes: Ambivalence and Inconsistency Are Distinct Constructs," *Canadian Journal of Behavioural Science* 32, no. 2 (2000): 71-83.

15. P. C. Nutt, *Why Decisions Fail* (San Francisco, CA: Berrett-Koehler, 2002); S. Finkelstein, *Why Smart Executives Fail* (New York: Viking, 2003); P. C. Nutt, "Search During Decision Making," *European Journal of Operational Research* 160 (2005): 851-876.

16. Weiss and Cropanzano, "Affective Events Theory."

17. L. Festinger, *A Theory of Cognitive Dissonance* (Evanston, Ill.: Row, Peterson, 1957); G. R. Salancik, "Commitment and the Control of Organizational Behavior and Belief," in *New Directions in Organizational Behavior*, ed. B. M. Staw and G. R. Salancik (Chicago: St. Clair, 1977), 1-54; A. D. Galinsky, J. Stone, and J. Cooper, "The Reinstatement of Dissonance and Psychological Discomfort Following Failed Affirmation," *European Journal of Social Psychology* 30, no. 1 (2000): 123-147.

18. T. A. Judge, E. A. Locke, and C. C. Durham, "The Dispositional Causes of Job Satisfaction: A Core Evaluations Approach," *Research in Organizational Behavior* 19 (1997): 151-188; Massey, "A Brief History of Human Society: The Origin and Role of Emotion in Social Life."

19. C. M. Brotheridge and A. A. Grandey, "Emotional Labor and Burnout: Comparing Two Perspectives of 'People Work,'" *Journal of Vocational Behavior* 60 (2002): 17-39; P. G. Irving, D. F. Coleman, and D. R. Bobocel, "The Moderating Effect of Negative Affectivity in the Procedural Justice-Job Satisfaction Relation," *Cana-*

dian Journal of Behavioural Science 37, no. 1 (January 2005): 20-32.

20. J. Schaubroeck, D. C. Ganster, and B. Kemmerer, "Does Trait Affect Promote Job Attitude Stability?" *Journal of Organizational Behavior* 17 (1996): 191-196; C. Dormann and D. Zapf, "Job Satisfaction: A Meta-Analysis of Stabilities," *Journal of Organizational Behavior* 22 (2001): 483-504.

21. R. Corelli, "Dishing out Rudeness," *Maclean's*, 11 January 1999, 44-47; D. Matheson, "A Vancouver Cafe Where Rudeness Is Welcomed," *Canada AM, CTV Television* (January 11 2000).

22. B. E. Ashforth and R. H. Humphrey, "Emotional Labor in Service Roles: The Influence of Identity," *Academy of Management Review* 18 (1993): 88-115. For a recent review of the emotional labour concept, see: T. M. Glomb and M. J. Tews, "Emotional Labor: A Conceptualization and Scale Development," *Journal of Vocational Behavior* 64, no. 1 (2004): 1-23.

23. P. Cowan, "Emergency Nurses 'a Very Special Breed,'" *Regina Leader-Post*, 10 October 2007, A6. for discussion of emotional labour in nursing, see: J. B. Davies, "They Never Told Me It Would Be Like This," *Accident and Emergency Nursing* 4 (1996): 165-166; M. Gunther and S. P. Thomas, "Nurses' Narratives of Unforgettable Patient Care Events," *Journal of Nursing Scholarship* 38, no. 4 (2006): 370-376; M. Secor-Turner and C. O'Boyle, "Nurses and Emergency Disasters: What Is Known," *American Journal of Infection Control* 34, no. 7 (Sept. 2006): 414-420; R. J. Erickson and W. J. C. Grove, "Emotional Labor and Health Care," *Sociology Compass* 2, no. 2 (March 2008): 704-733.

24. J. A. Morris and D. C. Feldman, "The Dimensions, Antecedents, and Consequences of Emotional Labor," *Academy of Management Review* 21 (1996): 986-1010; D. Zapf, "Emotion Work and Psychological Well-Being: A Review of the Literature and Some Conceptual Considerations," *Human Resource Management Review* 12 (2002): 237-268.

25. E. Forman, "'Diversity Concerns Grow as Companies Head Overseas,' Consultant Says," *Sun-Sentinel (Fort Lauderdale, FL)*, 26 June 1995. Cultural differences in emotional expression are discussed in: F. Trompenaars, "Resolving International Conflict: Culture and Business Strategy," *Business Strategy Review* 7, no. 3 (Autumn 1996): 51-68; F. Trompenaars and C. Hampden-Turner, *Riding the Waves of Culture*, 2nd ed. (New York: McGraw-Hill, 1998), Chap. 6; A. E. Raz and A. Rafaeli, "Emotion Management in Ross-Cultural Perspective: 'Smile Training' in Japanese and North American Service Organiza-

tions," *Research on Emotion in Organizations* 3 (2007): 199-220.

26. This relates to the automaticity of emotion, which is summarized in: P. Winkielman and K. C. Berridge, "Unconscious Emotion," *Current Directions in Psychological Science* 13, no. 3 (2004): 120-123; K. N. Ochsner and J. J. Gross, "The Cognitive Control of Emotions," *TRENDS in Cognitive Sciences* 9, no. 5 (May 2005): 242-249.

27. W. J. Zerbe, "Emotional Dissonance and Employee Well-Being," in *Managing Emotions in the Workplace* ed. N. M. Ashkanasy, W. J. Zerbe, and C. E. J. Hartel (Armonk, N.Y.: M. E. Sharpe, 2002), 189-214; R. Cropanzano, H. M. Weiss, and S. M. Elias, "The Impact of Display Rules and Emotional Labor on Psychological Well-Being at Work," *Research in Occupational Stress and Well Being* 3 (2003): 45-89.

28. J. Harding, "Help Wanted: Sign of Things to Come for All of Canada," *National Post*, 15 October 2007, P1; J. Verdon, "They Can Hardly Contain Themselves," *The Record (Bergen, NJ)*, 21 April 2007, A15.

29. Brotheridge and Grandey, "Emotional Labor and Burnout: Comparing Two Perspectives of 'People Work'"; Zapf, "Emotion Work and Psychological Well-Being"; J. M. Diefendorff, M. H. Croyle, and R. H. Gosserand, "The Dimensionality and Antecedents of Emotional Labor Strategies," *Journal of Vocational Behavior* 66, no. 2 (2005): 339-357.

30. D. McGinn, "The Emotional Workplace," *National Post*, 18 August 2007, FW3.

31. J. D. Mayer, P. Salovey, and D. R. Caruso, "Models of Emotional Intelligence," in *Handbook of Human Intelligence*, ed. R. J. Sternberg, 2nd ed. (New York: Cambridge University Press, 2000), 396-420. This definition is also recognized in: C. Cherniss, "Emotional Intelligence and Organizational Effectiveness," in *The Emotionally Intelligent Workplace* ed. C. Cherniss and D. Goleman (San Francisco: Jossey-Bass, 2001), 3-12; M. Zeidner, G. Matthews, and R. D. Roberts, "Emotional Intelligence in the Workplace: A Critical Review," *Applied Psychology: An International Review* 53, no. 3 (2004): 371-399.

32. These four dimensions of emotional intelligence are discussed in detail in: D. Goleman, R. Boyatzis, and A. McKee, *Primal Leadership* (Boston: Harvard Business School Press, 2002), Chap. 3. Slight variations of this model are presented in: R. Boyatzis, D. Goleman, and K. S. Rhee, "Clustering Competence in Emotional Intelligence," in *The Handbook of Emotional Intelligence* ed. R. Bar-On and J. D. A. Parker (San Francisco: Jossey-Bass, 2000), 343-362; D. Goleman, "An EI-Based

Theory of Performance," in *The Emotionally Intelligent Workplace* ed. C. Cherniss and D. Goleman (San Francisco: Jossey-Bass, 2001), 27-44.

33. Which model best represents EI and its abilities is debated in several sources, including several chapters in: K. R. Murphy, ed., *A Critique of Emotional Intelligence: What Are the Problems and How Can They Be Fixed?* (Mahwah, NJ: Lawrence Erlbaum Associates, 2006).

34. H. A. Elfenbein and N. Ambady, "Predicting Workplace Outcomes from the Ability to Eavesdrop on Feelings," *Journal of Applied Psychology* 87, no. 5 (2002): 963-971.

35. The hierarchical nature of the four EI dimensions is discussed by Goleman, but is more explicit in the Salovey and Mayer model. See: D. R. Caruso and P. Salovey, *The Emotionally Intelligent Manager* (San Francisco: Jossey-Bass, 2004).

36. P. N. Lopes *et al.*, "Emotional Intelligence and Social Interaction," *Personality and Social Psychology Bulletin* 30, no. 8 (August 2004): 1018-1034; C. S. Daus and N. M. Ashkanasy, "The Case for the Ability-Based Model of Emotional Intelligence in Organizational Behavior," *Journal of Organizational Behavior* 26 (2005): 453-466; J. E. Barbuto Jr and M. E. Burbach, "The Emotional Intelligence of Transformational Leaders: A Field Study of Elected Officials," *Journal of Social Psychology* 146, no. 1 (2006): 51-64; M. A. Brackett *et al.*, "Relating Emotional Abilities to Social Functioning: A Comparison of Self-Report and Performance Measures of Emotional Intelligence," *Journal of Personality and Social Psychology* 91, no. 4 (2006): 780-795; D. L. Reis *et al.*, "Emotional Intelligence Predicts Individual Differences in Social Exchange Reasoning," *NeuroImage* 35, no. 3 (2007): 1385-1391.

37. Some studies have reported situations where EI has a limited effect on individual performance. For example, see: A. L. Day and S. A. Carroll, "Using an Ability-Based Measure of Emotional Intelligence to Predict Individual Performance, Group Performance, and Group Citizenship Behaviours," *Personality and Individual Differences* 36 (2004): 1443-1458; Z. Ivcevic, M. A. Brackett, and J. D. Mayer, "Emotional Intelligence and Emotional Creativity," *Journal of Personality* 75, no. 2 (2007): 199-236; J. C. Rode *et al.*, "Emotional Intelligence and Individual Performance: Evidence of Direct and Moderated Effects," *Journal of Organizational Behavior* 28, no. 4 (2007): 399-421.

38. Lopes *et al.*, "Emotional Intelligence and Social Interaction"; C.-S. Wong *et al.*, "The Feasibility of Training and Development of EI: An Exploratory Study in Singapore, Hong Kong and Taiwan," *Intelligence* 35, no. 2 (2007): 141-150.

39. Goleman, Boyatzis, and McKee, *Primal Leadership*; S. C. Clark, R. Callister, and R. Wallace, "Undergraduate Management Skills Courses and Students' Emotional Intelligence," *Journal of Management Education* 27, no. 1 (February 2003): 3-23; H. A. Elfenbein, "Learning in Emotion Judgments: Training and the Cross-Cultural Understanding of Facial Expressions," *Journal of Nonverbal Behavior* 30, no. 1 (2006): 21-36.

40. C. Fox, "Shifting Gears," *Australian Financial Review*, 13 August 2004, 28; J. Thomson, "True Team Spirit," *Business Review Weekly*, 18 March 2004, 92.

41. Clark, Callister, and Wallace, "Undergraduate Management Skills Courses and Students' Emotional Intelligence"; R. Johnson, "Can You Feel It?" *People Management*, 23 August 2007, 34-37.

42. D. A. Harrison, D. A. Newman, and P. L. Roth, "How Important Are Job Attitudes? Meta-Analytic Comparisons of Integrative Behavioral Outcomes and Time Sequences," *Academy of Management Journal* 49, no. 2 (2006): 305-325.

43. E. A. Locke, "The Nature and Causes of Job Satisfaction," in *Handbook of Industrial and Organizational Psychology*, ed. M. Dunnette (Chicago: Rand McNally, 1976), 1297-1350; H. M. Weiss, "Deconstructing Job Satisfaction: Separating Evaluations, Beliefs and Affective Experiences," *Human Resource Management Review*, no. 12 (2002): 173-194. Some definitions still include emotion as an element of job satisfaction, whereas the definition presented in this book views emotion as a cause of job satisfaction. Also, this definition views job satisfaction as a "collection of attitudes," not several "facets" of job satisfaction.

44. Ipsos-Reid, "Ipsos-Reid Global Poll Finds Major Differences in Employee Satisfaction around the World," News release, (Toronto: 8 January 2001); International Survey Research, *Employee Satisfaction in the World's 10 Largest Economies: Globalization or Diversity?* (Chicago: International Survey Research, 2002); Watson Wyatt Worldwide, "Malaysian Workers More Satisfied with Their Jobs Than Their Companies' Leadership and Supervision Practices," Watson Wyatt Worldwide News release, (Kuala Lumpur: 30 November 2004); Kelly Global Workforce Index, *American Workers Are Happy with Their Jobs and Their Bosses*, (Troy, Michigan: Kelly Services, November 2006); D. Abma, "Canadian among World's Happiest Workers," *Vancouver Sun*, 6 September 2007, C4.

45. K. Macklem, "Vancity Confidential," *Maclean's*, 11-18 October 2004, 22; Watson Wyatt Worldwide, "Malaysian Workers More Satisfied with Their Jobs Than Their Companies' Leadership and Supervision Practices," News release; K. Keis, "HR Needs Happy Staff to Show Its Success," *Canadian HR Reporter*, 14 February 2005, 14.

46. M. Troy, "Motivating Your Workforce: A Home Depot Case Study," *DSN Retailing Today*, 10 June 2002, 29.

47. M. J. Withey and W. H. Cooper, "Predicting Exit, Voice, Loyalty, and Neglect," *Administrative Science Quarterly*, no. 34 (1989): 521-539; W. H. Turnley and D. C. Feldman, "The Impact of Psychological Contract Violations on Exit, Voice, Loyalty, and Neglect," *Human Relations*, no. 52 (July 1999): 895-922. Subdimensions of silence and voice also exist. See: L. van Dyne, S. Ang, and I. C. Botero, "Conceptualizing Employee Silence and Employee Voice as Multidimensional Constructs," *Journal of Management Studies* 40, no. 6 (Sept. 2003): 1359-1392.

48. T. R. Mitchell, B. C. Holtom, and T. W. Lee, "How to Keep Your Best Employees: Developing an Effective Retention Policy," *Academy of Management Executive* 15 (November 2001): 96-108; C. P. Maertz and M. A. Campion, "Profiles of Quitting: Integrating Process and Content Turnover Theory," *Academy of Management Journal* 47, no. 4 (2004): 566-582; K. Morrell, J. Loan-Clarke, and A. Wilkinson, "The Role of Shocks in Employee Turnover," *British Journal of Management* 15 (2004): 335-349; B. C. Holtom, T. R. Mitchell, and T. W. Lee, "Increasing Human and Social Capital by Applying Job Embeddedness Theory," *Organizational Dynamics* 35, no. 4 (2006): 316-331.

49. A. A. Luchak, "What Kind of Voice Do Loyal Employees Use?" *British Journal of Industrial Relations* 41 (March 2003): 115-134.

50. A. O. Hirschman, *Exit, Voice, and Loyalty: Responses to Decline in Firms, Organizations, and States* (Cambridge, Mass.: Harvard University Press, 1970); E. A. Hoffmann, "Exit and Voice: Organizational Loyalty and Dispute Resolution Strategies," *Social Forces* 84, no. 4 (June 2006): 2313-2330.

51. J. D. Hibbard, N. Kumar, and L. W. Stern, "Examining the Impact of Destructive Acts in Marketing Channel Relationships," *Journal of Marketing Research* 38 (February 2001): 45-61; J. Zhou and J. M. George, "When Job Dissatisfaction Leads to Creativity: Encouraging the Expression of Voice," *Academy of Management Journal* 44 (August 2001): 682-696.

52. M. J. Withey and I. R. Gellatly, "Situational and Dispositional Determinants of Exit, Voice, Loyalty and Neglect," *Proceed-*

ings of the Administrative Sciences Association of Canada, Organizational Behaviour Division (June 1998); D. C. Thomas and K. Au, "The Effect of Cultural Differences on Behavioral Responses to Low Job Satisfaction," *Journal of International Business Studies* 33, no. 2 (2002): 309-326; S. F. Premeaux and A. G. Bedeian, "Breaking the Silence: The Moderating Effects of Self-Monitoring in Predicting Speaking up in the Workplace," *Journal of Management Studies* 40, no. 6 (2003): 1537-1562.

53. T. A. Judge *et al.*, "The Job Satisfaction-Job Performance Relationship: A Qualitative and Quantitative Review," *Psychological Bulletin* 127 (2001): 376-407; L. Saari and T. A. Judge, "Employee Attitudes and Job Satisfaction," *Human Resource Management* 43, no. 4 (Winter 2004): 395-407. Other studies report stronger correlations with job performance when both the beliefs and feelings components of job satisfaction are consistent with each other, and when measuring overall job attitude (satisfaction and commitment combined). See: D. J. Schleicher, J. D. Watt, and G. J. Greguras, "Reexamining the Job Satisfaction-Performance Relationship: The Complexity of Attitudes," *Journal of Applied Psychology* 89, no. 1 (2004): 165-177; Harrison, Newman, and Roth, "How Important Are Job Attitudes?"

54. "The Greatest Briton in Management and Leadership," *Personnel Today* (18 February 2003): 20; J. Bonasia, "When Employees Occupy the Top Spot at Work," *Investor's Business Daily*, 5 November 2007; S. R. Ezzedeen, C. M. Hyde, and K. R. Laurin, "Is Strategic Human Resource Management Socially Responsible? The Case of Wegman's Food Markets, Inc.," *Employee rights and Responsibilities Journal* 18 (2007): 295-307.

55. J. I. Heskett, W. E. Sasser, and L. A. Schlesinger, *The Service Profit Chain* (New York: Free Press, 1997); D. J. Koys, "The Effects of Employee Satisfaction, Organizational Citizenship Behavior, and Turnover on Organizational Effectiveness: A Unit-Level, Longitudinal Study," *Personnel Psychology* 54 (April 2001): 101-114; W.-C. Tsai and Y.-M. Huang, "Mechanisms Linking Employee Affective Delivery and Customer Behavioral Intentions," *Journal of Applied Psychology* 87, no. 5 (2002): 1001-1008; T. DeCotiis *et al.*, "How Outback Steakhouse Created a Great Place to Work, Have Fun, and Make Money," *Journal of Organizational Excellence* 23, no. 4 (Autumn 2004): 23-33; G. A. Gelade and S. Young, "Test of a Service Profit Chain Model in the Retail Banking Sector," *Journal of Occupational & Organizational Psychology* 78 (2005): 1-22.

56. P. Guenzi and O. Pelloni, "The Impact of Interpersonal Realtionships on Cus-

tomer Satisfaction and Loyalty to the Service Provider," *International Journal Of Service Industry Management* 15, no. 3-4 (2004): 365-384; S. J. Bell, S. Auh, and K. Smalley, "Customer Relationship Dynamics: Service Quality and Customer Loyalty in the Context of Varying Levels of Customer Expertise and Switching Costs," *Journal of the Academy of Marketing Science* 33, no. 2 (Spring 2005): 169-183.

57. DeCotiis *et al.*, "How Outback Steakhouse Created a Great Place to Work, Have Fun, and Make Money."

58. S. Franklin, *The Heroes: A Saga of Canadian Inspiration* (Toronto: McClelland & Stewart, 1967), pp. 53-59.

59. R. T. Mowday, L. W. Porter, and R. M. Steers, Employee Organization Linkages: The Psychology of Commitment, Absenteeism, and Turnover (New York: Academic Press, 1982).

60. J. P. Meyer, "Organizational Commitment," *International Review of Industrial and Organizational Psychology* 12 (1997): 175-228. Along with affective and continuance commitment, Meyer identifies "normative commitment," which refers to employee feelings of obligation to remain with the organization. This commitment has been excluded so that students focus on the two most common perspectives of commitment.

61. R. D. Hackett, P. Bycio, and P. A. Hausdorf, "Further Assessments of Meyer and Allen's (1991) Three-Component Model of Organizational Commitment," *Journal of Applied Psychology* 79 (1994): 15-23.

62. J. P. Meyer *et al.*, "Affective, Continuance, and Normative Commitment to the Organization: A Meta-Analysis of Antecedents, Correlates, and Consequences," *Journal of Vocational Behavior* 61 (2002): 20-52; M. Riketta, "Attitudinal Organizational Commitment and Job Performance: A Meta-Analysis," *Journal of Organizational Behavior* 23 (2002): 257-266.

63. J. P. Meyer *et al.*, "Organizational Commitment and Job Performance: It's the Nature of the Commitment That Counts," *Journal of Applied Psychology* 74 (1989): 152-156; A. A. Luchak and I. R. Gellatly, "What Kind of Commitment Does a Final-Earnings Pension Plan Elicit?" *Relations Industrielles* 56 (Spring 2001): 394-417; Z. X. Chen and A. M. Francesco, "The Relationship between the Three Components of Commitment and Employee Performance in China," *Journal of Vocational Behavior* 62, no. 3 (2003): 490-510; D. M. Powell and J. P. Meyer, "Side-Bet Theory and the Three-Component Model of Organizational Commitment," *Journal of Vocational Behavior* 65, no. 1 (2004): 157-177.

64. E. W. Morrison and S. L. Robinson, "When Employees Feel Betrayed: A Model

of How Psychological Contract Violation Develops," *Academy of Management Review* 22 (1997): 226-256; J. E. Finegan, "The Impact of Person and Organizational Values on Organizational Commitment," *Journal of Occupational and Organizational Psychology* 73 (June 2000): 149-169.

65. D. M. Cable and T. A. Judge, "Person-Organization Fit, Job Choice Decisions, and Organizational Entry," *Organizational Behavior and Human Decision Processes* 67, no. 3 (1996): 294-311; T. J. Kalliath, A. C. Bluedorn, and M. J. Strube, "A Test of Value Congruence Effects," *Journal of Organizational Behavior* 20, no. 7 (1999): 1175-1198; J. W. Westerman and L. A. Cyr, "An Integrative Analysis of Person-Organization Fit Theories," *International Journal of Selection and Assessment* 12, no. 3 (September 2004): 252-261.

66. D. M. Rousseau *et al.*, "Not So Different after All: A Cross-Disicipline View of Trust," *Academy of Management Review* 23 (1998): 393-404.

67. S. Ashford, C. Lee, and P. Bobko, "Content, Causes, and Consequences of Job Insecurity: A Theory-Based Measure and Substantive Test," *Academy of Management Journal* 32 (1989): 803-829; C. Hendry, Chris, and R. Jenkins, "Psychological Contracts and New Deals," *Human Resource Management Journal* 7 (1997): 38-44.

68. T. S. Heffner and J. R. Rentsch, "Organizational Commitment and Social Interaction: A Multiple Constituencies Approach," *Journal of Vocational Behavior* 59 (2001): 471-490.

69. S. Semanak, "Work Eating into Family Time, Study Reveals," *The Gazette (Montreal)*, 14 February 2007.

70. There is some debate about whether stress can be classified within the realm of emotions. Stress is probably not a discrete emotion; it is more likely a cluster of emotions or the arousal component of emotion. Those who attempt to distinguish stress from emotion are challenged by the fact that both constructs are defined as physiological, psychological, and behavioural responses to the environment. For discussion of stress as emotion (or not), see: Weiss and Cropanzano, "Affective Events Theory"; A. L. Dougall and A. Baum, "Stress, Coping, and Immune Function," in *Handbook of Psychology*, ed. M. Gallagher and R. J. Nelson (Hoboken, N.J.: John Wiley & Sons, 2003), 441-455; S. Fineman, *Understanding Emotion at Work* (London: Sage, 2003).

71. J. C. Quick *et al.*, *Preventive Stress Management in Organizations* (Washington, D.C.: American Psychological Association, 1997), pp. 3-4; R. S. DeFrank and J. M. Ivancevich, "Stress on the Job: An Execu-

tive Update," *Academy of Management Executive* 12 (August 1998): 55-66.

72. M. Shields, "Stress and Depression in the Employed Population," *Health Reports (Statistics Canada)* 17, no. 4 (October 2006): 11-32; W. Lester, "A World of Stress," *Daily News (South Africa)*, 6 February 2007.

73. Quick *et al.*, *Preventive Stress Management in Organizations* pp. 5-6; B. L. Simmons and D. L. Nelson, "Eustress at Work: The Relationship between Hope and Health in Hospital Nurses," *Health Care Management Review* 26, no. 4 (October 2001): 7ff.

74. H. Selye, *Stress without Distress* (Philadelphia: J. B. Lippincott, 1974).

75. S. E. Taylor, R. L. Repetti, and T. Seeman, "Health Psychology: What Is an Unhealthy Environment and How Does It Get under the Skin?" *Annual Review of Psychology* 48 (1997): 411-447.

76. D. Ganster, M. Fox, and D. Dwyer, "Explaining Employees' Health Care Costs: A Prospective Examination of Stressful Job Demands, Personal Control, and Physiological Reactivity," *Journal of Applied Psychology* 86 (May 2001): 954-964; M. Kivimaki *et al.*, "Work Stress and Risk of Cardiovascular Mortality. Prospective Cohort Study of Industrial Employees," *British Medical Journal* 325 (19 October 2002): 857 860; A. Rosengren *et al.*, "Association of Psychosocial Risk Factors with Risk of Acute Myocardial Infarction in 11 119 Cases and 13 648 Controls from 52 Countries (the Interheart Study): Case-Control Study," *The Lancet* 364, no. 9438 (11 September 2004): 953-962.

77. R. C. Kessler, "The Effects of Stressful Life Events on Depression," *Annual Review of Psychology* 48 (1997): 191-214; L. Greenburg and J. Barling, "Predicting Employee Aggression against Coworkers, Subordinates and Supervisors: The Roles of Person Behaviors and Perceived Workplace Factors," *Journal of Organizational Behavior* 20 (1999): 897-913; M. Jamal and V. V. Baba, "Job Stress and Burnout among Canadian Managers and Nurses: An Empirical Examination," *Canadian Journal of Public Health* 91, no. 6 (Nov-Dec 2000): 454-458; L. Tourigny, V. V. Baba, and T. R. Lituchy, "Job Burnout among Airline Employees in Japan: A Study of the Buffering Effects of Absence and Supervisory Support," *International Journal of Cross Cultural Management* 5, no. 1 (April 2005): 67-85; M. S. Hershcovis *et al.*, "Predicting Workplace Aggression: A Meta-Analysis," *Journal of Applied Psychology* 92, no. 1 (2007): 228-238.

78. C. Maslach, W. B. Schaufeli, and M. P. Leiter, "Job Burnout," *Annual Review of Psychology* 52 (2001): 397-422; J. R. B. Halbesleben and M. R. Buckley, "Burnout in Organizational Life," *Journal of Management* 30, no. 6 (2004): 859-879.

79. K. Danna and R. W. Griffin, "Health and Well-Being in the Workplace: A Review and Synthesis of the Literature," *Journal of Management* (Spring 1999): 357-384.

80. A. Cresswell, "Bush Obstetrics 'Facing Collapse'," *The Australian*, 14 February 2005, 1.

81. This is a slight variation of the definition in the Quebec anti-harassment legislation. See www.cnt.gouv.qc.ca. For related definitions and discussion of workplace incivility, see: H. Cowiea and et al., "Measuring Workplace Bullying," *Aggression and Violent Behavior* 7 (2002): 33-51; C. M. Pearson and C. L. Porath, "On the Nature, Consequences and Remedies of Workplace Incivility: No Time for 'Nice'? Think Again," *Academy of Management Executive* 19, no. 1 (February 2005): 7-18.

82. "HR Bullied Just as Much as Anyone Else," *Personnel Today*, November 2005, 3; A. Marchand, A. Demers, and P. Durand, "Does Work Really Cause Stress? The Contribution of Occupational Structure and Work Organization to the Experience of Psychological Distress," *Social Science & Medicine* 61 (2005): 1-14; Pearson and Porath, "On the Nature, Consequences and Remedies of Workplace Incivility"; S. Toomey, "Bullying Alive and Kicking," *The Australian*, 16 July 2005, 9; J. Przybys, "How Rude!" *Las Vegas Review-Journal*, 25 April 2006, 1E.

83. Past predictions of future work hours are described in: B. K. Hunnicutt, *Kellogg's Six-Hour Day* (Philadelphia: Temple University Press, 1996).

84. C. Higgins and L. Duxbury, *The 2001 National Work–Life Conflict Study: Report One, Final Report* (Ottawa: Health Canada, March 2002); J. MacBride-King, *Wrestling with Workload: Organizational Strategies for Success* (Ottawa: Conference Board of Canada, 2005).

85. N. Chesley, "Blurring Boundaries? Linking Technology Use, Spillover, Individual Distress, and Family Satisfaction," *Journal of Marriage and Family* 67, no. 5 (2005): 1237-1248; T. Taylor, "Hard-Working Canadians Find It Tough to Disconnect," *Calgary Herald*, 18 May 2005, A10; R. Parloff, "Secrets of Greatness—How I Work: Amy W. Schulman," *Fortune*, 20 March 2006, 66; F. C. J. Morris, "Technology Addicted Employees," *New Jersey Law Journal* (2 March 2007).

86. R. Drago, D. Black, and M. Wooden, *The Persistence of Long Work Hours*, Melbourne Institute Working Paper Series (Melbourne: Melbourne Institute of Applied Economic and Social Research, University of Melbourne, August 2005).

87. C. B. Meek, "The Dark Side of Japanese Management in the 1990s: Karoshi and Ijime in the Japanese Workplace," *Journal of Managerial Psychology* 19, no. 3 (2004): 312-331; J. Shi, "Beijing's High Flyers Dying to Get Ahead," *South China Morning Post (Hong Kong)*, 8 October 2005, 8; N. You, "Mantra: Work for Life, Rather Than Live to Work," *China Daily*, 26 March 2005.

88. L. Wahyudi S, "'Traffic Congestion Makes Me Crazy," *Jakarta Post*, 18 March 2003 The effect of traffic congestion on stress is reported in: G. W. Evans, R. E. Wener, and D. Phillips, "The Morning Rush Hour: Predictability and Commuter Stress," *Environment and Behavior* 34 (July 2002): 521-530.

89. F. Kittell and et al., "Job Conditions and Fibrinogen in 14,226 Belgian Workers: The Belstress Study," *European Heart Journal* 23 (2002): 1841-1848; S. K. Parker, "Longitudinal Effects of Lean Production on Employee Outcomes and the Mediating Role of Work Characteristics," *Journal of Applied Psychology* 88, no. 4 (2003): 620-634.

90. S. J. Havlovic and J. P. Keenen, "Coping with Work Stress: The Influence of Individual Differences; Handbook on Job Stress [Special Issue]," *Journal of Social Behavior and Personality* 6 (1991): 199-212.

91. S. S. Luthar, D. Cicchetti, and B. Becker, "The Construct of Resilience: A Critical Evaluation and Guidelines for Future Work," *Child Development* 71, no. 3 (May-June 2000): 543-562; F. Luthans, "The Need for and Meaning of Positive Organizational Behavior," *Journal of Organizational Behavior* 23 (2002): 695-706; G. A. Bonanno, "Loss, Trauma, and Human Resilience: Have We Underestimated the Human Capacity to Thrive after Extremely Aversive Events?" *American Psychologist* 59, no. 1 (2004): 20-28.

92. M. Beasley, T. Thompson, and J. Davidson, "Resilience in Response to Life Stress: The Effects of Coping Style and Cognitive Hardiness," *Personality and Individual Differences* 34, no. 1 (2003): 77-95; M. M. Tugade, B. L. Fredrickson, and L. Feldman Barrett, "Psychological Resilience and Positive Emotional Granularity: Examining the Benefits of Positive Emotions on Coping and Health," *Journal of Personality* 72, no. 6 (2004): 1161-1190; I. Tsaousis and I. Nikolaou, "Exploring the Relationship of Emotional Intelligence with Physical and Psychological Health Functioning," *Stress and Health* 21, no. 2 (2005): 77-86; L. Campbell-Sills, S. L. Cohan, and M. B. Stein, "Relationship of Resilience to Personality, Coping, and Psychiatric Symptoms in Young Adults," *Behaviour Research and Therapy* 44, no. 4 (April 2006): 585-599.

93. J. T. Spence, A. S., and Robbins, "Workaholism: Definition, Measurement and Preliminary Results," *Journal of Personality Assessment* 58 (1992): 160-178; R. J. Burke, "Workaholism in Organizations: Psychological and Physical Well-Being Consequences," *Stress Medicine* 16, no. 1 (2000): 11-16; I. Harpaz and R. Snir, "Workaholism: Its Definition and Nature," *Human Relations* 56 (2003): 291-319; R. J. Burke, A. M. Richardson, and M. Martinussen, "Workaholism among Norwegian Senior Managers: New Research Directions," *International Journal of Management* 21, no. 4 (December 2004): 415-426.

94. R. J. Burke and G. MacDermid, "Are Workaholics Job Satisfied and Successful in Their Careers?" *Career Development International* 4 (1999): 277-282; R. J. Burke and S. Matthiesen, "Short Communication: Workaholism among Norwegian Journalists: Antecedents and Consequences," *Stress and Health* 20, no. 5 (2004): 301-308.

95. S.-A. Chia and E. Toh, "Give Employees a Break," *Straits Times (Singapore)*, 23 July 2005.

96. M. Siegall and L. L. Cummings, "Stress and Organizational Role Conflict," *Genetic, Social, and General Psychology Monographs* 12 (1995): 65-95.

97. "Employee Wellness," *Canadian HR Reporter*, 23 February 2004, 9-12; J. Bagnall, "Canada Post Puts Stamp on Mental Health Campaign," *Ottawa Citizen*, 4 October 2007, D1.

98. L. T. Eby *et al.*, "Work and Family Research in IO/OB: Content Analysis and Review of the Literature (1980-2002)," *Journal of Vocational Behavior* 66, no. 1 (2005): 124-197.

99. N. Davidson, "Vancouver Developer Looks to Make Video Games without Burning out Staff," *Canadian Press*, 21 February 2006. Some quotations are from Propaganda's website: www.propagandagames.go.com.

100. Y. Iwasaki *et al.*, "A Short-Term Longitudinal Analysis of Leisure Coping Used by Police and Emergency Response Service Workers," *Journal of Leisure Research* 34 (July 2002): 311-339.

101. F. Piccolo, "Brownie Points," *Atlantic Business*, Oct/Nov 2004, 22; L. Carter, "Teletech Is Wired Up," *Simcoe Business Magazine*, Spring 2005.

102. M. Waung, "The Effects of Self-Regulatory Coping Orientation on Newcomer Adjustment and Job Survival," *Personnel Psychology* 48 (1995): 633-650; A. M. Saks and B. E. Ashforth, "Proactive Socialization and Behavioral Self-Management," *Journal of Vocational Behavior* 48 (1996): 301-323.

103. V. A. Barnes, F. A. Treiber, and M. H. Johnson, "Impact of Transcendental Meditation on Ambulatory Blood Pressure in African-American Adolescents," *American Journal of Hypertension* 17, no. 4 (2004): 366-369; W. M. Ensel and N. Lin, "Physical Fitness and the Stress Process," *Journal of Community Psychology* 32, no. 1 (January 2004): 81-101.

104. K. MacQueen, "Dealing with the Stressed," *Maclean's*, 15 October 2007, 52-58.

105. S. E. Taylor *et al.*, "Biobehavioral Responses to Stress in Females: Tend-and-Befriend, Not Fight-or-Flight," *Psychological Review* 107, no. 3 (July 2000): 411-429; R. Eisler and D. S. Levine, "Nurture, Nature, and Caring: We Are Not Prisoners of Our Genes," *Brain and Mind* 3 (2002): 9-52.

Chapter 5

1. P. Brent, "Packaging Loyalty," National Post, 22 October 2005, WK2; M. Andrews, "Richmond Manufacturer Ties up Neat Package Deal," Vancouver Sun, 6 September 2007, C1; R. Colman, "Packing the Perfect HR Punch," CMA Management, March 2007, 40-43.

2. C. C. Pinder, *Work Motivation in Organizational Behavior* (Upper Saddle River, NJ: Prentice-Hall, 1998); R. M. Steers, R. T. Mowday, and D. L. Shapiro, "The Future of Work Motivation Theory," *Academy of Management Review* 29 (2004): 379-387.

3. For a selection of the more scholarly writing, see: N. P. Rothbard, "Enriching or Depleting? The Dynamics of Engagement in Work and Family Roles," *Administrative Science Quarterly* 46, no. 4 (December 2001): 655-684; R. Baumruk, "The Missing Link: The Role of Employee Engagement in Business Success," *Workspan*, November 2004, 48; F. D. Frank, R. P. Finnegan, and C. R. Taylor, "The Race for Talent: Retaining and Engaging Workers in the 21st Century," *Human Resource Planning* 27, no. 3 (January 2004): 12; D. R. May, R. L. Gilson, and L. M. Harter, "The Psychological Conditions of Meaningfulness, Safety and Availability and the Engagement of the Human Spirit at Work," *Journal of Occupational and Organizational Psychology* 77 (March 2004): 11-37; A. Saks, M., "Antecedents and Consequences of Employee Engagement," *Journal of Managerial Psychology* 21, no. 7 (2006): 600-619; F. Catteeuw, E. Flynn, and J. Vonderhorst, "Employee Engagement: Boosting Productivity in Turbulent Times," *Organization Development Journal* 25, no. 2 (Summer 2007): P151-P157.

4. "Towers Perrin Study Finds, Despite Layoffs and Slow Economy, a New, More Complex Power Game Is Emerging between Employers and Employees," Business Wire News release, (New York: 30 August 2001); "Few Workers Are 'Engaged' at Work and Most Want More from Execs," *Dow Jones Business News (San Francisco)*, 22 October 2007.

5. "Towers Perrin Study Finds, Despite Layoffs and Slow Economy, a New, More Complex Power Game Is Emerging between Employers and Employees," News release; K. V. Rondeau and T. H. Wagar, "Downsizing and Organizational Restructuring: What Is the Impact on Hospital Performance?" *International Journal of Public Administration* 26 (2003): 1647-1668.

6. C. Lachnit, "The Young and the Dispirited," *Workforce* 81 (August 2002): 18; S. H. Applebaum, M. Serena, and B. T. Shapiro, "Generation X and the Boomers: Organizational Myths and Literary Realities," *Management Research News* 27, no. 11/12 (2004): 1-28. Motivation and needs across generations is also discussed in: R. Zemke and B. Filipczak, *Generations at Work: Managing the Clash of Veterans, Boomers, Xers, and Nexters in Your Workplace* (N. Y.: AMACOM, 2000).

7. The confusing array of definitions about drives and needs has been the subject of criticism for a half century. See, for example: R. S. Peters, "Motives and Motivation," *Philosophy* 31 (1956): 117-130; H. Cantril, "Sentio, Ergo Sum: 'Motivation' Reconsidered," *Journal of Psychology* 65, no. 1 (Jan. 1967): 91-107; G. R. Salancik and J. Pfeffer, "An Examination of Need-Satisfaction Models of Job Attitudes," *Administrative Science Quarterly* 22, no. 3 (Sep. 1977): 427-456.

8. A. Blasi, "Emotions and Moral Motivation," *Journal for the Theory of Social Behaviour* 29, no. 1 (1999): 1-19; D. W. Pfaff, *Drive: Neurobiological and Molecular Mechanisms of Sexual Motivation* (Cambridge, MA: MIT Press, 1999); T. V. Sewards and M. A. Sewards, "Fear and Power-Dominance Drive Motivation: Neural Representations and Pathways Mediating Sensory and Mnemonic Inputs, and Outputs to Premotor Structures," *Neuroscience and Biobehavioral Reviews* 26 (2002): 553-579; K. C. Berridge, "Motivation Concepts in Behavioral Neuroscience," *Physiology & Behavior* 81, no. 2 (2004): 179-209. We distinguish drives from emotions, but future research may find that the two concepts are not so different as is stated here.

9. K. Passyn and M. Sujan, "Self-Accountability Emotions and Fear Appeals: Motivating Behavior," *Journal of Consumer Research* 32, no. 4 (2006): 583-589; S. G. Barsade and D. E. Gibson, "Why Does Affect Matter in Organizations?" *Academy of Management Perspectives* 21, no. 2 (Feb. 2007): 36-59.

10. G. Loewenstein, "The Psychology of Curiosity: A Review and Reinterpretation," *Psychological Bulletin* 116, no. 1 (1994): 75-98; R. E. Baumeister and M. R. Leary, "The Need to Belong: Desire for Interpersonal Attachments as a Fundamental Human Motivation," *Psychological Bulletin* 117 (1995): 497-529; A. E. Kelley, "Neurochemical Networks Encoding Emotion and Motivation: An Evolutionary Perspective," in *Who Needs Emotions? The Brain Meets the Robot*, ed. J.-M. Fellous and M. A. Arbib (New York: Oxford University Press, 2005), 29-78.

11. S. Hitlin, "Values as the Core of Personal Identity: Drawing Links between Two Theories of Self," *Social Psychology Quarterly* 66, no. 2 (2003): 118-137; D. D. Knoch and E. E. Fehr, "Resisting the Power of Temptations. The Right Prefrontal Cortex and Self-Control," *Annals of the New York Academy of Sciences* 1104, no. 1 (2007): 123; B. Monin, D. A. Pizarro, and J. S. Beer, "Deciding Versus Reacting: Conceptions of Moral Judgment and the Reason-Affect Debate," *Review of General Psychology* 11, no. 2 (2007): 99-111.

12. N. M. Ashkanasy, W. J. Zerbe, and C. E. J. Härtel, "A Bounded Emotionality Perspective on the Individual in the Organization," in *Emotions in Organizational Behavior*, ed. C. E. J. Härtel, W. J. Zerbe, and N. M. Ashkanasy (Mahwah, N. J.: Lawrence Erlbaum Associates, 2005), 113-117.

13. A. H. Maslow, "A Theory of Human Motivation," *Psychological Review* 50 (1943): 370-396; A. H. Maslow, *Motivation and Personality* (New York Harper & Row, 1954).

14. D. T. Hall and K. E. Nougaim, "An Examination of Maslow's Need Hierarchy in an Organizational Setting," *Organizational Behavior and Human Performance* 3, no. 1 (1968): 12; M. A. Wahba and L. G. Bridwell, "Maslow Reconsidered: A Review of Research on the Need Hierarchy Theory," *Organizational Behavior and Human Performance* 15 (1976): 212-240; E. L. Betz, "Two Tests of Maslow's Theory of Need Fulfillment," *Journal of Vocational Behavior* 24, no. 2 (1984): 204-220; P. A. Corning, "Biological Adaptation in Human Societies: A 'Basic Needs' Approach," *Journal of Bioeconomics* 2, no. 1 (2000): 41-86.

15. A. H. Maslow, "A Preface to Motivation Theory," *Psychsomatic Medicine* 5 (1943): 85-92; K. Dye, A.J. Mills, and T.G. Weatherbee, "Maslow: Man Interrupted— Reading management theory in context," *Management Decision* 43, no. 10 (2005): 1375-1395.

16. A. H. Maslow, *Maslow on Management* (New York: John Wiley & Sons, 1998).

17. W. L. Lee, "Net Value: That Loving Feeling," *The Edge Financial Daily (Malaysia)*, 25 April 2005; N. Mwaura, "Honour Staff for Good Work," *Daily Nation (Nairobi, Kenya)*, 27 September 2005; "Every Third German Worker Unhappy with Job, Poll Says," *Deutsche Welle (Bonn, Germany)*, 16 September 2007; "Rewards a Boost for Bank Employees," *National Post*, 18 April 2007, WK7; Bank of Nova Scotia, "Applause for Scotiabank Employee Recognition Program," Market News Publishing News release, (Toronto: 1 June 2007); "Firms Told to Buy Loyalty and Not Time," *The Kingdom (Killarney, Ireland)*, 10 January 2008.

18. F. F. Luthans, "Positive Organizational Behavior: Developing and Managing Psychological Strengths," *The Academy of Management Executive* 16, no. 1 (2002): 57-72; S. L. Gable and J. Haidt, "What (and Why) Is Positive Psychology?" *Review of General Psychology* 9, no. 2 (2005): 103-110; M. E. P. Seligman *et al.*, "Positive Psychology Progress: Empirical Validation of Interventions," *American Psychologist* 60, no. 5 (2005): 410-421.

19. C. P. Alderfer, *Existence, Relatedness, and Growth* (New York: Free Press, 1972).

20. J. Rauschenberger, N. Schmitt, and J. E. Hunter, "A Test of the Need Hierarchy Concept by a Markov Model of Change in Need Strength," *Administrative Science Quarterly* 25, no. 4 (December 1980): 654-670; J. P. Wanous and A. A. Zwany, "A Cross-Sectional Test of Need Hierarchy Theory," *Organizational Behavior and Human Performance* 18 (1977): 78-97.

21. B. A. Agle and C. B. Caldwell, "Understanding Research on Values in Business," *Business and Society* 38 (September 1999): 326-387; B. Verplanken and R. W. Holland, "Motivated Decision Making: Effects of Activation and Self-Centrality of Values on Choices and Behavior," *Journal of Personality and Social Psychology* 82, no. 3 (2002): 434-447; S. Hitlin and J. A. Pilavin, "Values: Reviving a Dormant Concept," *Annual Review of Sociology* 30 (2004): 359-393.

22. D. C. McClelland, *The Achieving Society* (New York: Van Nostrand Reinhold, 1961); D. C. McClelland and D. H. Burnham, "Power Is the Great Motivator," *Harvard Business Review* 73 (January-February 1995): 126-139; D. Vredenburgh and Y. Brender, "The Hierarchical Abuse of Power in Work Organizations," *Journal of Business Ethics* 17 (September 1998): 1337-1347; S. Shane, E. A. Locke, and C. J. Collins, "Entrepreneurial Motivation," *Human Resource Management Review* 13, no. 2 (2003): 257-279.

23. McClelland, The Achieving Society.

24. Shane, Locke, and Collins, "Entrepreneurial Motivation."

25. McClelland and Burnham, "Power Is the Great Motivator"; J. L. Thomas, M. W. Dickson, and P. D. Bliese, "Values Predicting Leader Performance in the U.S. Army Reserve Officer Training Corps Assessment Center: Evidence for a Personality-Mediated Model," *The Leadership Quarterly* 12, no. 2 (2001): 181-196.

26. Vredenburgh and Brender, "The Hierarchical Abuse of Power in Work Organizations."

27. D. Miron and D. C. McClelland, "The Impact of Achievement Motivation Training on Small Business," *California Management Review* 21 (1979): 13-28.

28. P. R. Lawrence and N. Nohria, *Driven: How Human Nature Shapes Our Choices* (San Francisco: Jossey-Bass, 2002).

29. L. Gaertner *et al.*, "The "I," The "We," And The "When": A Meta-Analysis of Motivational Primacy in Self-Definition," *Journal of Personality and Social Psychology* 83, no. 3 (2002): 574-591; M. R. Leary, "Motivational and Emotional Aspects of the Self," *Annual Review of Psychology* 58, no. 1 (2007): 317-344.

30. Baumeister and Leary, "The Need to Belong."

31. J. Litman, "Curiosity and the Pleasures of Learning: Wanting and Liking New Information," *Cognition and Emotion* 19, no. 6 (2005): 793 - 814; T. G. Reio Jr *et al.*, "The Measurement and Conceptualization of Curiosity," *Journal of Genetic Psychology* 167, no. 2 (2006): 117-135.

32. W. H. Bexton, W. Heron, and T. H. Scott, "Effects of Decreased Variation in the Sensory Environment," *Canadian Journal of Psychology* 8 (1954): 70-76; Loewenstein, "The Psychology of Curiosity: A Review and Reinterpretation."

33. A. R. Damasio, *Descartes' Error: Emotion, Reason, and the Human Brain* (New York: Putnam sons, 1994); J. E. LeDoux, "Emotion Circuits in the Brain," *Annual Review of Neuroscience* 23 (2000): 155-184; P. Winkielman and K. C. Berridge, "Unconscious Emotion," *Current Directions in Psychological Science* 13, no. 3 (2004): 120-123.

34. Lawrence and Nohria, Driven: How Human Nature Shapes Our Choices, pp. 145-147.

35. Lawrence and Nohria, Driven: How Human Nature Shapes Our Choices, Chap. 11.

36. T. Belford and K. Vermond, "Great Little Company Aims to Contain Great Little Products," *National Post*, 15 December 1999, E04.

37. Expectancy theory of motivation in work settings originated in V. H. Vroom, *Work and Motivation* (New York: Wiley, 1964). The version of expectancy theory presented here was developed by Edward Lawler. Lawler's model provides a clearer

presentation of the model's three components. P-to-O expectancy is similar to "instrumentality" in Vroom's original expectancy theory model. The difference is that instrumentality is a correlation whereas P-to-O expectancy is a probability. See: J. P. Campbell *et al.*, *Managerial Behavior, Performance, and Effectiveness* (New York: McGraw-Hill, 1970); E. E. Lawler III, *Motivation in Work Organizations* (Monterey, CA: Brooks-Cole, 1973); D. A. Nadler and E. E. Lawler, "Motivation: A Diagnostic Approach," in *Perspectives on Behavior in Organizations*, ed. J. R. Hackman, E. E. Lawler III, and L. W. Porter, second ed. (New York: McGraw-Hill, 1983), 67-78.

38. M. Zeelenberg *et al.*, "Emotional Reactions to the Outcomes of Decisions: The Role of Counterfactual Thought in the Experience of Regret and Disappointment," *Organizational Behavior and Human Decision Processes* 75, no. 2 (1998): 117-141; B. A. Mellers, "Choice and the Relative Pleasure of Consequences," *Psychological Bulletin* 126, no. 6 (November 2000): 910-924; R. P. Bagozzi, U. M. Dholakia, and S. Basuroy, "How Effortful Decisions Get Enacted: The Motivating Role of Decision Processes, Desires, and Anticipated Emotions," *Journal of Behavioral Decision Making* 16, no. 4 (October 2003): 273-295.

39. Nadler and Lawler, "Motivation: A Diagnostic Approach."

40. T. Matsui and T. Terai, "A Cross-Cultural Study of the Validity of the Expectancy Theory of Motivation," *Journal of Applied Psychology* 60 (1975): 263-265; D. H. B. Welsh, F. Luthans, and S. M. Sommer, "Managing Russion Factory Workers: The Impact of U.S.-Based Behavioral and Participative Techniques," *Academy of Management Journal* 36 (1993): 58-79.

41. This limitation was recently acknowledged by Victor Vroom, who had introduced expectancy theory in his 1964 book. See: G. P. Latham, *Work Motivation: History, Theory, Research, and Practice* (Thousand Oaks, CA: Sage, 2007), 47-48.

42. S. Zeller, "Good Calls," *Government Executive*, 15 May 2005; C. Bailor, "Checking the Pulse of the Contact Center," *Customer Relationship Management*, November 2007, 24-29.

43. A. Shin, "What Customers Say and How They Say It," *Washington Post*, 18 October 2006, D01; D. Ververidis and C. Kotropoulos, "Emotional Speech Recognition: Resources, Features, and Methods," *Speech Communication* 48, no. 9 (2006): 1162-1181.

44. G. P. Latham, "Goal Setting: A Five-Step Approach to Behavior Change," *Organizational Dynamics* 32, no. 3 (2003): 309-318; E. A. Locke and G. P. Latham,

A Theory of Goal Setting and Task Performance (Englewood Cliffs, N.J: Prentice Hall, 1990). The acronym "SMART" goals refer to goals that are specific, measurable, acceptable, relevant, and timely. However, this list duplicates some characteristics (e.g., specific goals *are* measurable and timely) and overlooks the characteristics of challenging and feedback-related.

45. Watson Wyatt, *WorkCanada 2004/2005 —Pursuing Productive Engagement*, (Toronto: Watson Wyatt, January 2005); Kelly Services, "Majority of Canada's Workers Happy, Bosses among Best in World," Kelly Services News release, (Toronto: 28 November 2006); Hudson, *Rising above the Average: 2007 Compensation & Benefits Report*, (New York: June 2007).

46. A. Li and A. B. Butler, "The Effects of Participation in Goal Setting and Goal Rationales on Goal Commitment: An Exploration of Justice Mediators," *Journal of Business and Psychology* 19, no. 1 (Fall 2004): 37-51.

47. Locke and Latham, *A Theory of Goal Setting and Task Performance* Chap. 6 and 7; J. Wegge, "Participation in Group Goal Setting: Some Novel Findings and a Comprehensive Model as a New Ending to an Old Story," *Applied Psychology: An International Review* 49 (2000): 498-516.

48. M. London, E. M. Mone, and J. C. Scott, "Performance Management and Assessment: Methods for Improved Rater Accuracy and Employee Goal Setting," *Human Resource Management* 43, no. 4 (Winter 2004): 319-336; G. P. Latham and C. C. Pinder, "Work Motivation Theory and Research at the Dawn of the Twenty-First Century," *Annual Review of Psychology* 56 (2005): 485-516.

49. E. White, "For Relevance, Firms Revamp Worker Reviews," *Wall Street Journal*, 17 July 2006, B1.

50. S. P. Brown, S. Ganesan, and G. Challagalla, "Self-Efficacy as a Moderator of Information-Seeking Effectiveness," *Journal of Applied Psychology* 86, no. 5 (2001): 1043-1051; P. A. Heslin and G. P. Latham, "The Effect of Upward Feedback on Managerial Behaviour," *Applied Psychology: An International Review* 53, no. 1 (2004): 23-37; D. Van-Dijk and A. N. Kluger, "Feedback Sign Effect on Motivation: Is It Moderated by Regulatory Focus?" *Applied Psychology: An International Review* 53, no. 1 (2004): 113-135; J. E. Bono and A. E. Colbert, "Understanding Responses to Multi-Source Feedback: The Role of Core Self-Evaluations," *Personnel Psychology* 58, no. 1 (Spring 2005): 171-203.

51. D. Hendry, "Game-Playing: The Latest Business Tool," *Globe & Mail*, 17 November 2006, C11.

52. L. Hollman, "Seeing the Writing on the Wall," *Call Center* (August 2002): 37; S. E. Ante, "Giving the Boss the Big Picture," *Business Week*, 13 February 2006, 48.

53. S. Bowness, "Full-Circle Feedback," *Profit*, May 2006, 77.

54. S. Brutus and M. Derayeh, "Multi-source Assessment Programs in Organizations: An Insider's Perspective," *Human Resource Development Quarterly* 13 (July 2002): 187-202.

55. F. P. Morgeson, T. V. Mumford, and M. A. Campion, "Coming Full Circle: Using Research and Practice to Address 27 Questions About 360-Degree Feedback Programs," *Consulting Psychology Journal* 57, no. 3 (2005): 196-209; J. W. Smither, M. London, and R. R. Reilly, "Does Performance Improve Following Multisource Feedback? A Theoretical Model, Meta-Analysis, and Review of Empirical Findings," *Personnel Psychology* 58, no. 1 (2005): 33-66; L. E. Atwater, J. F. Brett, and A. C. Charles, "Multisource Feedback: Lessons Learned and Implications for Practice," *Human Resource Management* 46, no. 2 (Summer 2007): 285-307.

56. A. S. DeNisi and A. N. Kluger, "Feedback Effectiveness: Can 360-Degree Appraisals Be Improved?" *Academy of Management Executive* 14 (February 2000): 129-139; M. A. Peiperl, "Getting 360 Degree Feedback Right," *Harvard Business Review* 79 (January 2001): 142-147; M.-G. Seo, L. F. Barrett, and J. M. Bartunek, "The Role of Affective Experience in Work Motivation," *Academy of Management Review* 29 (2004): 423-449.

57. S. J. Ashford and G. B. Northcraft, "Conveying More (or Less) Than We Realize: The Role of Impression Management in Feedback Seeking," *Organizational Behavior and Human Decision Processes* 53 (1992): 310-334; J. R. Williams *et al.*, "Increasing Feedback Seeking in Public Contexts: It Takes Two (or More) to Tango," *Journal of Applied Psychology* 84 (December 1999): 969-976.

58. J. B. Miner, "The Rated Importance, Scientific Validity, and Practical Usefulness of Organizational Behavior Theories: A Quantitative Review," *Academy of Management Learning and Education* 2, no. 3 (2003): 250-268. Also see: C. C. Pinder, *Work Motivation in Organizational Behavior* (Upper Saddle River, NJ: Prentice-Hall, 1997), p. 384.

59. P. M. Wright, "Goal Setting and Monetary Incentives: Motivational Tools That Can Work Too Well," *Compensation and Benefits Review* 26 (May- June 1994): 41-49; E. A. Locke and G. P. Latham, "Building a Practically Useful Theory of Goal Setting and Task Motivation: A 35-Year Odyssey,"

American Psychologist 57, no. 9 (2002): 705-717.

60. Latham, Work Motivation, 188.

61. Colman, "Packing the Perfect HR Punch."

62. J. Greenberg and E. A. Lind, "The Pursuit of Organizational Justice: From Conceptualization to Implication to Application," in *Industrial and Organizational Psychology: Linking Theory with Practice* ed. C. L. Cooper and E. A. Locke (London: Blackwell, 2000), 72-108; R. Cropanzano and M. Schminke, "Using Social Justice to Build Effective Work Groups," in *Groups at Work: Theory and Research* ed. M. E. Turner (Mahwah, N.J.: Lawrence Erlbaum Associates, 2001), 143-171; D. T. Miller, "Disrespect and the Experience of Injustice," *Annual Review of Psychology* 52 (2001): 527-553.

63. J. S. Adams, "Toward an Understanding of Inequity," *Journal of Abnormal and Social Psychology* 67 (1963): 422-436; R. T. Mowday, "Equity Theory Predictions of Behavior in Organizations," in *Motivation and Work Behavior*, ed. L. W. Porter and R. M. Steers, 5th ed. (New York: McGraw-Hill, 1991), 111-131; R. G. Cropanzano, J., "Progress in Organizational Justice: Tunneling through the Maze," in *International Review of Industrial and Organizational Psychology* ed. C. L. Cooper and I. T. Robertson (New York: Wiley, 1997), 317-372; L. A. Powell, "Justice Judgments as Complex Psychocultural Constructions: An Equity-Based Heuristic for Mapping Two and Three-Dimensional Fairness Representations in Perceptual Space," *Journal of Cross-Cultural Psychology* 36, no. 1 (January 2005): 48-73.

64. C. T. Kulik and M. L. Ambrose, "Personal and Situational Determinants of Referent Choice," *Academy of Management Review* 17 (1992): 212-237; G. Blau, "Testing the Effect of Level and Importance of Pay Referents on Pay Level Satisfaction," *Human Relations* 47 (1994): 1251-1268.

65. T. P. Summers and A. S. DeNisi, "In Search of Adams' Other: Reexamination of Referents Used in the Evaluation of Pay," *Human Relations* 43 (1990): 497-511.

66. Y. Cohen-Charash and P. E. Spector, "The Role of Justice in Organizations: A Meta-Analysis," *Organizational Behavior and Human Decision Processes* 86 (November 2001): 278-321.

67. Canadian Press, "Pierre Berton, Canadian Cultural Icon, Enjoyed Long and Colourful Career," *Times Colonist* (Victoria, B.C.), 30 November 2004.

68. K. S. Sauleya and A. G. Bedeian, "Equity Sensitivity: Construction of a Measure and Examination of Its Psychometric Properties," *Journal of Management* 26 (September 2000): 885-910; G. Blakely, M.

Andrews, and R. Moorman, "The Moderating Effects of Equity Sensitivity on the Relationship between Organizational Justice and Organizational Citizenship Behaviors," *Journal of Business and Psychology* 20, no. 2 (2005): 259-273.

69. M. Ezzamel and R. Watson, "Pay Comparability across and within UK Boards: An Empirical Analysis of the Cash Pay Awards to CEOs and Other Board Members," *Journal of Management Studies* 39, no. 2 (March 2002): 207-232; J. Fizel, A. C. Krautman, and L. Hadley, "Equity and Arbitration in Major League Baseball," *Managerial and Decision Economics* 23, no. 7 (Oct-Nov 2002): 427-435.

70. Greenberg and Lind, "The Pursuit of Organizational Justice: From Conceptualization to Implication to Application"; K. Roberts and K. S. Markel, "Claiming in the Name of Fairness: Organizational Justice and the Decision to File for Workplace Injury Compensation," *Journal of Occupational Health Psychology* 6 (October 2001): 332-347; J. B. Olson-Buchanan and W. R. Boswell, "The Role of Employee Loyalty and Formality in Voicing Discontent," *Journal of Applied Psychology* 87, no. 6 (2002): 1167-1174.

71. B. Murphy, "Rising Fortunes," *Milwaukee Journal Sentinel*, 10 October 2004, 1; S. Greenhouse, "How Costco Became the Anti-Wal-Mart," *New York Times*, 17 July 2005, BU1; "#19 James Dimon," *Forbes*, 3 May 2007.

72. R. Hagey *et al.*, "Immigrant Nurses' Experience of Racism," *Journal of Nursing Scholarship* 33 (Fourth Quarter 2001): 389-395; Roberts and Markel, "Claiming in the Name of Fairness: Organizational Justice and the Decision to File for Workplace Injury Compensation"; D. A. Jones and D. P. Skarlicki, "The Effects of Overhearing Peers Discuss an Authority's Fairness Reputation on Reactions to Subsequent Treatment," *Journal of Applied Psychology* 90, no. 2 (2005): 363-372.

73. Miller, "Disrespect and the Experience of Injustice."

74. M. L. Ambrose, M. A. Seabright, and M. Schminke, "Sabotage in the Workplace: The Role of Organizational Injustice," *Organizational Behavior and Human Decision Processes* 89, no. 1 (2002): 947-965.

Chapter 6

1. V. L. Parker, "Org Charts Turn around with Teams," *News & Observer* (Raleigh, N.C.), 21 July 2005, D1; N. Byrnes and M. Arndt, "The Art of Motivation," *BusinessWeek*, 1 May 2006, 56; P. Glader, "Nucor Bets on Growth in North America," *Wall Street Journal*, 3 January 2007, A3.

2. H. Das, "The Four Faces of Pay: An Investigation into How Canadian Managers View Pay," *International Journal of Commerce & Management* 12 (2002): 18-40. For recent ratings of the importance of pay and benefits, see: P. Babcock, "Find What Workers Want," *HRMagazine*, April 2005, 50-56.

3. S. L. Rynes, B. Gerhart, and K. A. Minette, "The Importance of Pay in Employee Motivation: Discrepancies between What People Say and What They Do," *Human Resource Management* 43, no. 4 (Winter 2004): 381-394; B. S. Frey, "Awards as Compensation," *European Management Journal* 4 (2007): 6-14.

4. R. Lynn, *The Secret of the Miracle Economy* (London: SAE, 1991), cited in A. Furnham and R. Okamura, "Your Money or Your Life: Behavioral and Emotional Predictors of Money Pathology," *Human Relations* 52 (September 1999): 1157-1177. The opinion polls are summarized in: J. O'Rourke, "Show Boys the Money and Tell Girls You Care," *Sydney Morning Herald*, 10 December 2000, 43; M. Steen, "Study Looks at What Good Employees Want from a Company," *San Jose Mercury* (19 December 2000).

5. A. Furnham, B. D. Kirkcaldy, and R. Lynn, "National Attitudes to Competitiveness, Money, and Work among Young People: First, Second, and Third World Differences," *Human Relations* 47 (January 1994): 119-132; V. K. G. Lim, "Money Matters: An Empirical Investigation of Money, Face and Confucian Work Ethic," *Personality and Individual Differences* 35 (2003): 953-970; T. L.-P. Tang, A. Furnham, and G. M.-T. Davis, "A Cross-Cultural Comparison of the Money Ethic, the Protestant Work Ethic, and Job Satisfaction: Taiwan, the USA, and the UK," *International Journal of Organization Theory and Behavior* 6, no. 2 (Summer 2003): 175-194.

6. "Seniority Pay System Seeing Revival," *Kyodo News (Tokyo)*, 29 March 2004; V. Kirsch, "Better Beef Workers Ok New Contract," *Guelph Mercury*, 8 February 2005, A3.

7. R. J. Long, "Job Evaluation in Canada: Has Its Demise Been Greatly Exaggerated?" in *Annual Conference of the Administrative Sciences Association of Canada, Human Resource Management Division*, ed. J. Carrière, (Winnipeg, May, 2002), 61-72; R. J. Long, *Strategic Compensation in Canada*, 2nd ed. (Toronto: Thomson Nelson, 2002), Chap. 9.

8. E. E. Lawler III, *Rewarding Excellence: Pay Strategies for the New Economy* (San Francisco: Jossey-Bass, 2000), pp. 30-35, 109-119; R. McNabb and K. Whitfield, "Job Evaluation and High Performance Work Practices: Compatible or Conflictual?"

Journal of Management Studies 38 (March 2001): 293-312.

9. N. Le Pan, Enhancing Integrated Market Enforcement Teams, Acheiving Results in Fighting Capital Markets, (Ottawa: RCMP, 25 October 2007).

10. P. K. Zingheim and J. R. Schuster, "Competencies and Rewards: Substance or Just Style?" *Compensation Benefits Review* 35, no. 5 (2003): 40-44; R. J. Long, "Paying for Knowledge: Does It Pay?" *Canadian HR Reporter*, 28 March 2005, 12-13; J. D. Shaw *et al.*, "Success and Survival of Skill-Based Pay Plans," *Journal of Management* 31, no. 1 (February 2005): 28-49; F. Giancola, "Skill-Based Pay—Issues for Consideration," *Benefits & Compensation Digest* 44, no. 5 (2007): 1-15.

11. S. Clarke, *Compensation Planning Outlook 2008*, (Ottawa: Conference Board of Canada, October 2007). The history of performance-based pay is described in: E. B. Peach and D. A. Wren, "Pay for Performance from Antiquity to the 1950s," *Journal of Organizational Behavior Management* (1992): 5-26.

12. L. Spiers, "Piece by Piecemeal," *Lawn & Landscape Magazine*, 5 August 2003; H.-H. Pai, "'Our Eyes Have Been Opened to the Abuse'," *The Guardian (London)*, 29 April 2006, 2.

13. D. Finlayson, "Top Employers—Premium Perks," *Edmonton Journal*, 22 October 2005, I1; "Keeping in Good Company" *Edmonton Journal*, 14 October 2006; P. Koven, "The Making of a Score Card for Job Seekers," *National Post*, 18 October 2006, WK1; L. Young, "Spruceland Millworks Benefits from Generosity," *Canadian HR Reporter*, 22 October 2007, 12.

14. K. Brady, W. Thomas, and J. Clipsham, *CSR Case Study: Syncrude Canada Ltd.*, (Ottawa: Government of Canada. Natural Resources Canada, November 2003); D. Jacobson, "Best-Kept Secrets of the World's Best Companies: Gainsharing," *Business 2.0*, April 2006, 82. For evaluations of gainsharing programs, see: L. R. Gomez-Mejia, T. M. Welbourne, and R. M. Wiseman, "The Role of Risk Sharing and Risk Taking under Gainsharing," *Academy of Management Review* 25 (July 2000): 492-507; K. M. Bartol and A. Srivastava, "Encouraging Knowledge Sharing: The Role of Organizational Reward System," *Journal of Leadership & Organizational Studies* 9 (Summer 2002): 64-76.

15. "Nucor Pays $200m in Bonuses to Employees," *Steel Business Briefing*, 16 December 2005.

16. "Cell-Loc Location Technologies Announces Grant of Incentive Stock Options to Directors, Officers and Employees," Marketwire News release, (Calgary: 7 March 2008).

17. T. Lester, "Performanca at Hugo Boss," *Executive Briefing (Economist Intelligence Unit)*, 4 May 2006, 1.

18. "KT Seeks New Growth Engines," *Korea Herald*, 2 March 2004. Some of the Canadian companies using balanced scorecard are described in: R. S. Kaplan and D. P. Norton, *The Strategy-Focused Organization* (Cambridge, MA: Harvard Business School Press, 2001); P. R. Niven, *Balanced Scorecard Step-by-Step* (New York: John Wiley & Sons, 2002); K. Hendricks, L. Menor, and C. Wiedman, "The Balanced Scorecard: To Adopt or Not to Adopt?" *Ivey Business Journal* (Nov/Dec 2004): 1-9.

19. J. Chelius and R. S. Smith, "Profit Sharing and Employment Stability," *Industrial and Labor Relations Review* 43 (1990): 256s-273s; S. H. Wagner, C. P. Parkers, and N. D. Christiansen, "Employees That Think and Act Like Owners: Effects of Ownership Beliefs and Behaviors on Organizational Effectiveness," *Personnel Psychology* 56, no. 4 (Winter 2003): 847-871; G. Ledford, M. Lucy, and P. Leblanc, "The Effects of Stock Ownership on Employee Attitudes and Behavior: Evidence from the Rewards at Work Studies," *Perspectives (Sibson)*, January 2004; P. Andon, J. Baxter, and H. Mahama, "The Balanced Scorecard: Slogans, Seduction, and State of Play," *Australian Accounting Review* 15, no. 1 (March 2005): 29-38.

20. A. J. Maggs, "Enron, Esops, and Fiduciary Duty," *Benefits Law Journal* 16, no. 3 (Autumn 2003): 42-52; C. Brodzinski, "Esop's Fables Can Make Coverage Risky," *National Underwriter. P & C*, 13 June 2005, 16-17.

21. J. Pfeffer, *The Human Equation* (Boston: Harvard Business School Press, 1998); B. N. Pfau and I. T. Kay, *The Human Capital Edge* (New York: McGraw-Hill, 2002); D. Guest, N. Conway, and P. Dewe, "Using Sequential Tree Analysis to Search for 'Bundles' of HR Practices," *Human Resource Management Journal* 14, no. 1 (2004): 79-96. The problems with performance-based pay are discussed in: W. C. Hammer, "How to Ruin Motivation with Pay," *Compensation Review* 7, no. 3 (1975): 17-27; A. Kohn, *Punished by Rewards* (Boston: Houghton Mifflin, 1993); M. O'Donnell and J. O' Brian, "Performance-Based Pay in the Australian Public Service," *Review of Public Personnel Administration* 20 (Spring 2000): 20-34; M. Beer and M. D. Cannon, "Promise and Peril of Implementing Pay-for-Performance," *Human Resource Management* 43, no. 1 (Spring 2004): 3-48.

22. M. Buckingham and D. O. Clifton, *Now, Discover Your Strengths* (New York: Free Press, 2001).

23. S. Kerr, "Organization Rewards: Practical, Cost-Neutral Alternatives That You May Know, but Don't Practice," *Organizational Dynamics* 28 (Summer 1999): 61-70.

24. J. S. DeMatteo, L. T. Eby, and E. Sundstrom, "Team-Based Rewards: Current Empirical Evidence and Directions for Future Research," *Research in Organizational Behavior* 20 (1998): 141-183; S. Rynes, B. Gerhart, and L. Parks, "Personnel Psychology: Performance Evaluation and Pay for Performance," *Annual Review of Psychology* 56 (2005): 571-600.

25. "Dream Teams," *Human Resources Professional* (November 1994): 17-19.

26. D. R. Spitzer, "Power Rewards: Rewards That Really Motivate," *Management Review* (May 1996): 45-50. For a classic discussion on the unintended consequences of pay, see: S. Kerr, "On the Folly of Rewarding A, While Hoping for B," *Academy of Management Journal* 18 (1975): 769-783.

27. F. F. Reichheld, *The Loyalty Effect* (Boston, MA: Harvard University Press, 1996), 236; D. R. Spitzer, "Power Rewards: Rewards That Really Motivate," *Management Review*, (May 1996): 45-50; J. A. Byrne, "How To Fix Corporate Governance," *Business Week*, May 6, 2002, p. 68; A. Holeck, "Griffith, Ind., Native Takes Over as Steel Plant Manager," *Northwest Indiana Times*, 25 May 2003; H. Connon, "Overhyped, Overpaid and Overextended," *The Observer (London)*, 20 March 2005, p. 5.

28. D. MacDonald, "Good Managers Key to Buffett's Acquisitions," *The Gazette (Montreal)*, 16 November 2001.

29. J. R. Edwards, J. A. Scully, and M. D. Brtek, "The Nature and Outcomes of Work: A Replication and Extension of Interdisciplinary Work-Design Research," *Journal of Applied Psychology* 85, no. 6 (2000): 860-868; F. P. Morgeson and M. A. Campion, "Minimizing Tradeoffs When Redesigning Work: Evidence from a Longitudinal Quasi-Experiment," *Personnel Psychology* 55, no. 3 (Autumn 2002): 589-612.

30. P. Siekman, "This Is Not a BMW Plant," *Fortune*, 18 April 2005, 208.

31. Accel-Team, "Scientific Management: Lessons from Ancient History through the Industrial Revolution," www.accel-team.com; A. Smith, *The Wealth of Nations* (London: Dent, 1910).

32. H. Fayol, *General and Industrial Management*, trans. C. Storrs (London: Pitman, 1949); E. E. Lawler III, *Motivation in Work Organizations* (Monterey, Calif.: Brooks/Cole, 1973), Chap. 7; M. A. Campion, "Ability Requirement Implications of Job Design: An Interdisciplinary Perspective," *Personnel Psychology* 42 (1989): 1-24.

33. F. W. Taylor, The Principles of Scientific Management (New York: Harper & Row, 1911); R. Kanigel, The One Best Way:

Frederick Winslow Taylor and the Enigma of Efficiency (NY: Viking, 1997).

34. C. R. Walker and R. H. Guest, *The Man on the Assembly Line* (Cambridge, MA: Harvard University Press, 1952); W. F. Dowling, "Job Redesign on the Assembly Line: Farewell to Blue-Collar Blues?" *Organizational Dynamics* (Autumn 1973): 51-67; E. E. Lawler III, *High-Involvement Management* (San Francisco: Jossey-Bass, 1986).

35. M. Keller, *Rude Awakening* (New York: Harper Perennial, 1989), p. 128.

36. F. Herzberg, B. Mausner, and B. B. Snyderman, *The Motivation to Work* (New York: Wiley, 1959).

37. S. K. Parker, T. D. Wall, and J. L. Cordery, "Future Work Design Research and Practice: Towards an Elaborated Model of Work Design," *Journal of Occupational and Organizational Psychology* 74 (November 2001): 413-440. For a decisive critique of motivator-hygiene theory, see: N. King, "Clarification and Evaluation of the Two Factor Theory of Job Satisfaction," *Psychological Bulletin* 74 (1970): 18-31.

38. J. R. Hackman and G. Oldham, *Work Redesign* (Reading, MA: Addison-Wesley, 1980).

39. D. Whitford, "A Human Place to Work," *Fortune*, 8 January 2001, 108-119.

40. J. E. Champoux, "A Multivariate Test of the Job Characteristics Theory of Work Motivation," *Journal of Organizational Behavior* 12, no. 5 (September 1991): 431-446; R. B. Tiegs, L. E. Tetrick, and Y. Fried, "Growth Need Strength and Context Satisfactions as Moderators of the Relations of the Job Characteristics Model," *Journal of Management* 18, no. 3 (September 1992): 575-593.

41. "Region Positioned among Dcx Leaders in Advanced Manufacturing," *Toledo Business Journal*, August 2004, 1; M. Connelly, "Chrysler Boosts Belvedere Flexibility," *Automotive News*, 13 February 2006, 44.

42. M. A. Campion and C. L. McClelland, "Follow-up and Extension of the Interdisciplinary Costs and Benefits of Enlarged Jobs," *Journal of Applied Psychology* 78 (1993): 339-351; N. G. Dodd and D. C. Ganster, "The Interactive Effects of Variety, Autonomy, and Feedback on Attitudes and Performance," *Journal of Organizational Behavior* 17 (1996): 329-347.

43. J. R. Hackman *et al.*, "A New Strategy for Job Enrichment," *California Management Review* 17, no. 4 (1975): 57-71; R. W. Griffin, *Task Design: An Integrative Approach* (Glenview, IL: Scott Foresman, 1982).

44. P. E. Spector and S. M. Jex, "Relations of Job Characteristics from Multiple Data Sources with Employee Affect, Absence, Turnover Intentions, and Health," *Journal*

of *Applied Psychology* 76 (1991): 46-53; P. Osterman, "How Common Is Workplace Transformation and Who Adopts It?" *Industrial and Labor Relations Review* 47 (1994): 173-188; R. Saavedra and S. K. Kwun, "Affective States in Job Characteristics Theory," *Journal of Organizational Behavior* 21 (2000): 131-146.

45. Hackman and Oldham, *Work Redesign* pp. 137-138.

46. A. Hertting *et al.*, "Personnel Reductions and Structural Changes in Health Care: Work-Life Experiences of Medical Secretaries," *Journal of Psychosomatic Research* 54 (February 2003): 161-170.

47. B. Lewis, "WestJet—A Crazy Idea That Took Off," *Vancouver Province*, 21 October 2001.

48. This definition is based mostly on G. M. Spreitzer and R. E. Quinn, *A Company of Leaders: Five Disciplines for Unleashing the Power in Your Workforce* (San Francisco: Jossey-Bass, 2001). However, most elements of this definition appear in other discussions of empowerment. See, for example: R. Forrester, "Empowerment: Rejuvenating a Potent Idea," *Academy of Management Executive* 14 (August 2000): 67-80; W. A. Randolph, "Re-Thinking Empowerment: Why Is It So Hard to Achieve?" *Organizational Dynamics* 29 (November 2000): 94-107; S. T. Menon, "Employee Empowerment: An Integrative Psychological Approach," *Applied Psychology: An International Review* 50 (2001): 153-180.

49. The positive relationship between these structural empowerment conditions and psychological empowerment is reported in: H. K. S. Laschinger *et al.*, "A Longitudinal Analysis of the Impact of Workplace Empowerment on Work Satisfaction," *Journal of Organizational Behavior* 25, no. 4 (June 2004): 527-545.

50. C. S. Koberg *et al.*, "Antecedents and Outcomes of Empowerment," *Group and Organization Management* 24 (1999): 71-91; Y. Melhem, "The Antecedents of Customer-Contact Employees' Empowerment," *Employee Relations* 26, no. 1/2 (2004): 72-93.

51. B. J. Niehoff *et al.*, "The Influence of Empowerment and Job Enrichment on Employee Loyalty in a Downsizing Environment," *Group and Organization Management* 26 (March 2001): 93-113; J. Yoon, "The Role of Structure and Motivation for Workplace Empowerment: The Case of Korean Employees," *Social Psychology Quarterly* 64 (June 2001): 195-206; T. D. Wall, J. L. Cordery, and C. W. Clegg, "Empowerment, Performance, and Operational Uncertainty: A Theoretical Integration," *Applied Psychology: An International Review* 51 (2002): 146-169.

52. D. Yedlin, "Service Soared with Beddoe at the Helm," *Calgary Herald*, 25 July 2007, F1. The organizational factors affecting empowerment are discussed in: G. M. Spreitzer, "Social Structural Characteristics of Psychological Empowerment," *Academy of Management Journal* 39 (April 1996): 483-504; J. Godard, "High Performance and the Transformation of Work? The Implications of Alternative Work Practices for the Experience and Outcomes of Work," *Industrial & Labor Relations Review* 54 (July 2001): 776-805; P. A. Miller, P. Goddard, and H. K. Spence Laschinger, "Evaluating Physical Therapists' Perception of Empowerment Using Kanter's Theory of Structural Power in Organizations," *Physical Therapy* 81 (December 2001): 1880-1888.

53. D. Furlonger, "Best Company to Work For," *Financial Mail* (South Africa), 30 September 2005, 20; A. Hogg, "John Gomersall: CEO, PPC," (South Africa, 26 October 2005), www.moneyweb.co.za/specials/corp_gov/509689.htm, (accessed 4 January 2006); Pretoria Portland Cement, "PPC Wins Best Company to Work for 2005," Meropa Communications News release, (Sandton, South Africa, 29 September 2005). Information was also collected from the 2003 to 2007 annual reports of Pretoria Portland Cement.

54. J-C. Chebat and P. Kollias, "The Impact of Empowerment on Customer Contact Employees' Role in Service Organizations," *Journal of Service Research* 3 (August 2000): 66-81; H. K. S. Laschinger, J. Finegan, and J. Shamian, "The Impact of Workplace Empowerment, Organizational Trust on Staff Nurses' Work Satisfaction and Organizational Commitment," *Health Care Management Review* 26 (Summer 2001): 7-23.

55. F. Piccolo, "freeTHINK Tank," *Atlantic Business Magazine*, Oct-Nov 2004; "Bosses Love Team Workers," *Lancashire Evening Post (U.K.)*, 25 May 2006.

56. C. P. Neck and C. C. Manz, "Thought Self-Leadership: The Impact of Mental Strategies Training on Employee Cognition, Behavior, and Affect," *Journal of Organizational Behavior* 17 (1996): 445-467.

57. C. C. Manz, "Self-Leadership: Toward an Expanded Theory of Self-Influence Processes in Organizations," *Academy of Management Review* 11 (1986): 585-600; C. C. Manz and C. Neck, *Mastering Self-Leadership*, 3rd ed. (Upper Saddle River, NJ: Prentice Hall, 2004); C. P. Neck and J. D. Houghton, "Two Decades of Self-Leadership Theory and Research," *Journal of Managerial Psychology* 21, no. 4 (2006): 270-295.

58. O. J. Strickland and M. Galimba, "Managing Time: The Effects of Personal Goal Setting on Resource Allocation Strat-

egy and Task Performance," *Journal of Psychology* 135 (July 2001): 357-367.

59. R. M. Duncan and J. A. Cheyne, "Incidence and Functions of Self-Reported Private Speech in Young Adults: A Self-Verbalization Questionnaire," *Canadian Journal of Behavioral Science* 31 (April 1999): 133-136.

60. J. E. Driscoll, C. Copper, and A. Moran, "Does Mental Practice Enhance Performance?" *Journal of Applied Psychology* 79 (1994): 481-492; C. P. Neck, G. L. Stewart, and C. C. Manz, "Thought Self-Leadership as a Framework for Enhancing the Performance of Performance Appraisers," *Journal of Applied Behavioral Science* 31 (September 1995): 278-302. Some research separates mental imagery from mental practice, whereas most studies combine both into one concept.

61. A. Joyce, "Office Parks: Re-Energize to Get through the Blahs," *Washington Post*, 28 August 2005, F05.

62. A. Wrzesniewski and J. E. Dutton, "Crafting a Job: Revisioning Employees as Active Crafters of Their Work," *Academy of Management Review* 26 (April 2001): 179-201.

63. M. I. Bopp, S. J. Glynn, and R. A. Henning, *Self-Management of Performance Feedback During Computer-Based Work by Individuals and Two-Person Work Teams*, Paper presented at the APA-NIOSH conference (March 1999).

64. A. W. Logue, *Self-Control: Waiting until Tomorrow for What You Want Today* (Englewood Cliffs, NJ: Prentice-Hall, 1995).

65. Neck and Manz, "Thought Self-Leadership: The Impact of Mental Strategies Training on Employee Cognition, Behavior, and Affect"; A. M. Saks and B. E. Ashforth, "Proactive Socialization and Behavioral Self-Management," *Journal of Vocational Behavior* 48 (1996): 301-323; L. Morin and G. Latham, "The Effect of Mental Practice and Goal Setting as a Transfer of Training Intervention on Supervisors' Self-Efficacy and Communication Skills: An Exploratory Study," *Applied Psychology: An International Review* 49 (July 2000): 566-578; J. S. Hickman and E. S. Geller, "A Safety Self-Management Intervention for Mining Operations," *Journal of Safety Research* 34 (2003): 299-308.

66. S. Ming and G. L. Martin, "Single-Subject Evaluation of a Self-Talk Package for Improving Figure Skating Performance," *Sport Psychologist* 10 (1996): 227-238; J. Bauman, "The Gold Medal Mind," *Psychology Today* 33 (May 2000): 62-69; L. J. Rogerson and D. W. Hrycaiko, "Enhancing Competitive Performance of Ice Hockey Goaltenders Using Centering and Self-Talk," *Journal of Applied Sport Psychology* 14, no. 1 (2002): 14-26; A. Papaioannou

et al., "Combined Effect of Goal Setting and Self-Talk in Performance of a Soccer-Shooting Task," *Perceptual and Motor Skills* 98, no. 1 (February 2004): 89-99; R. A. Hamilton, D. Scott, and M. P. MacDougall, "Assessing the Effectiveness of Self-Talk Interventions on Endurance Performance," *Journal of Applied Sport Psychology* 19, no. 2 (2007): 226-239. For a review of the self-talk research, including limitations of this self-leadership strategy, see: J. Hardy, "Speaking Clearly: A Critical Review of the Self-Talk Literature," *Psychology of Sport and Exercise* 7 (2006): 81-97.

67. S. Williams, "Personality and Self-Leadership," *Human Resource Management Review* 7, no. 2 (1997): 139-155; J. Houghton, D. *et al.*, "The Relationship between Self-Leadership and Personality: A Comparison of Hierarchical Factor Structures," *Journal of Managerial Psychology* 19, no. 4 (2004): 427-441; R. W. Renn *et al.*, "The Roles of Personality and Self-Defeating Behaviors in Self-Management Failure," *Journal of Management* 31, no. 5 (2005): 659-679.

68. J. D. Houghton and S. K. Yoho, "Toward a Contingency Model of Leadership and Psychological Empowerment: When Should Self-Leadership Be Encouraged?" *Journal of Leadership & Organizational Studies* 11, no. 4 (2005): 65-83; J. D. Houghton and D. L. Jinkerson, "Constructive Thought Strategies and Job Satisfaction: A Preliminary Examination," *Journal of Business and Psychology* 22 (2007): 45-53.

Chapter 7

1. D. Kloster, "High Tech Firms Take to the Track for Cancer Research," Times Colonist (Victoria) 2007; D. Meissner, "Hack Day Not a Slack Day," Globe & Mail, 19 July 2007; D. Kloster, "Personal Growth Is the Name of the Game," British Columbia Biolinks, 18 March 2008, www.lifesciencebc.ca.

2. F. A. Shull Jr., A. L. Delbecq, and L. L. Cummings, *Organizational Decision Making* (New York: McGraw-Hill, 1970), p. 31.

3. R. E. Nisbett, *The Geography of Thought: How Asians and Westerners Think Differently— and Why* (New York: Free Press, 2003); R. Hanna, "Kant's Theory of Judgment," (Stanford Encyclopedia of Philosophy, 2004), http://plato.stanford.edu/entries/kant-judgment/ (accessed March 31 2008); D. Baltzly, "Stoicism," (Stanford Encyclopedia of Philosophy, 2008), http://plato.stanford.edu/entries/stoicism/ (accessed March 30 2008).

4. This model is adapted from several sources, including: H. A. Simon, *The New Science of Management Decision* (New York: Harper & Row, 1960); H. Mintz-

berg, D. Raisinghani, and A. Théorét, "The Structure of 'Unstructured' Decision Processes," *Administrative Science Quarterly* 21 (1976): 246-275; W. C. Wedley and R. H. G. Field, "A Predecision Support System," *Academy of Management Review* 9 (1984): 696-703.

5. P. F. Drucker, *The Practice of Management* (New York: Harper & Brothers, 1954), 353-357; B. M. Bass, *Organizational Decision Making* (Homewood, Ill: Irwin, 1983), Chap. 3.

6. L. R. Beach and T. R. Mitchell, "A Contingency Model for the Selection of Decision Strategies," *Academy of Management Review* 3 (1978): 439-449; I. L. Janis, *Crucial Decisions* (New York: The Free Press, 1989), pp. 35-37; W. Zhongtuo, "Meta-Decision Making: Concepts and Paradigm," *Systematic Practice and Action Research* 13, no. 1 (February 2000): 111-115.

7. J. G. March and H. A. Simon, *Organizations* (New York: John Wiley & Sons, 1958).

8. N. Schwarz, "Social Judgment and Attitudes: Warmer, More Social, and Less Conscious," *European Journal of Social Psychology* 30 (2000): 149-176; N. M. Ashkanasy and C. E. J. Hartel, "Managing Emotions in Decision-Making," in *Managing Emotions in the Workplace*, ed. N. M. Ashkanasy, W. J. Zerbe, and C. E. J. Hartel (Armonk, N.Y: M. E. Sharpe, 2002); S. Maitlis and H. Ozcelik, "Toxic Decision Processes: A Study of Emotion and Organizational Decision Making," *Organization Science* 15, no. 4 (July-August 2004): 375-393.

9. A. Howard, "Opinion," *Computing* (8 July 1999): 18.

10. A. R. Damasio, *Descartes' Error: Emotion, Reason, and the Human Brain* (New York: Putnam Sons, 1994); P. Winkielman and K. C. Berridge, "Unconscious Emotion," *Current Directions in Psychological Science* 13, no. 3 (2004): 120-123; A. Bechara and A. R. Damasio, "The Somatic Marker Hypothesis: A Neural Theory of Economic Decision," *Games and Economic Behavior* 52, no. 2 (2005): 336-372.

11. T. K. Das and B. S. Teng, "Cognitive Biases and Strategic Decision Processes: An Integrative Perspective," *Journal Of Management Studies* 36, no. 6 (Nov 1999): 757-778; P. Bijttebier, H. Vertommen, and G. V. Steene, "Assessment of Cognitive Coping Styles: A Closer Look at Situation-Response Inventories," *Clinical Psychology Review* 21, no. 1 (2001): 85-104; P. C. Nutt, "Expanding the Search for Alternatives During Strategic Decision-Making," *Academy of Management Executive* 18, no. 4 (November 2004): 13-28.

12. J. Brandtstadter, A. Voss, and K. Rothermund, "Perception of Danger Signals: The

Role of Control," *Experimental Psychology* 51, no. 1 (2004): 24-32; M. Hock and H. W. Krohne, "Coping with Threat and Memory for Ambiguous Information: Testing the Repressive Discontinuity Hypothesis," *Emotion* 4, no. 1 (2004): 65-86.

13. P. Nason, "A Big Fat Hollywood Success Story," *United Press International*, 12 December 2002; G. MacDonald, "A Wedding Proposal for the Oscars," *Globe & Mail*, 12 February 2003, A2.

14. P. C. Nutt, *Why Decisions Fail* (San Francisco, CA: Berrett-Koehler, 2002); S. Finkelstein, *Why Smart Executives Fail* (New York: Viking, 2003).

15. "NASA Managers Differed over Shuttle Strike," *Reuters* (22 July 2003); Columbia Accident Investigation Board, *Report, Volume 1*, (Washington, DC: Government Printing Office, August 2003); C. Gibson, "Columbia: The Final Mission," *NineMSN* (13 July 2003); S. Jefferson, "NASA Let Arrogance on Board," *Palm Beach Post*, 30 August 2003; R. J. Smith, "NASA Culture, Columbia Probers Still Miles Apart," *Washington Post* (22 August 2003): A3.

16. E. Witte, "Field Research on Complex Decision-Making Processes—The Phase Theorum," *International Studies of Management and Organization* (1972): 156-182; J. A. Bargh and T. L. Chartrand, "The Unbearable Automaticity of Being," *American Psychologist* 54, no. 7 (July 1999): 462-479.

17. R. Rothenberg, "Ram Charan: The Thought Leader Interview," *strategy + business* (Fall 2004); C. Vander Doelen, "Toyota Hiring in Woodstock," *Windsor Star*, 30 November 2007.

18. H. A. Simon, *Administrative Behavior*, Second Ed. (New York: The Free Press, 1957); H. A. Simon, "Rational Decision Making in Business Organizations," *American Economic Review* 69, no. 4 (September 1979): 493-513.

19. D. Sandahl and C. Hewes, "Decision Making at Digital Speed," *Pharmaceutical Executive* 21 (August 2001): 62.

20. Simon, *Administrative Behavior*, pp. xxv, 80-84.

21. P. O. Soelberg, "Unprogrammed Decision Making," *Industrial Management Review* 8 (1967): 19-29; J. E. Russo, V. H. Medvec, and M. G. Meloy, "The Distortion of Information During Decisions," *Organizational Behavior & Human Decision Processes* 66 (1996): 102-110. This is consistent with the observations by Milton Rokeach, who famously stated that "Life is ipsative, because decisions in everyday life are inherently and phenomenoiogically ipsative decisions." M. Rokeach, "Inducing Changes and Stability in Belief Systems and Personality Structures," *Journal of Social Issues* 41, no. 1 (1985): 153-171.

22. A. L. Brownstein, "Biased Predecision Processing," *Psychological Bulletin* 129, no. 4 (2003): 545-568.

23. F. Phillips, "The Distortion of Criteria after Decision-Making," *Organizational Behavior and Human Decision Processes* 88 (2002): 769-784.

24. H. A. Simon, "Rational Choice and the Structure of Environments," *Psychological Review* 63 (1956): 129-138; H. Schwartz, "Herbert Simon and Behavioral Economics," *Journal of Socio-Economics* 31 (2002): 181-189.

25. P. C. Nutt, "Search During Decision Making," *European Journal of Operational Research* 160 (2005): 851-876.

26. J. P. Forgas, "Affective Intelligence: Towards Understanding the Role of Affect in Social Thinking and Behavior," in *Emotional Intelligence in Everyday Life*, ed. J. V. Ciarrochi, J. P. Forgas, and J. D. Mayer (New York: Psychology Press, 2001), 46-65; J. P. Forgas and J. M. George, "Affective Influences on Judgments and Behavior in Organizations: An Information Processing Perspective," *Organizational Behavior and Human Decision Processes* 86 (September 2001): 3-34; G. Loewenstein and J. S. Lerner, "The Role of Affect in Decision Making," in *Handbook of Affective Sciences*, ed. R. J. Davidson, K. R. Scherer, and H. H. Goldsmith (New York: Oxford University Press, 2003), 619-642; J. S. Lerner, D. A. Small, and G. Loewenstein, "Heart Strings and Purse Strings: Carryover Effects of Emotions on Economic Decisions," *Psychological Science* 15, no. 5 (2004): 337-341.

27. M. T. Pham, "The Logic of Feeling," *Journal of Consumer Psychology* 14 (September 2004): 360-369; N. Schwarz, "Metacognitive Experiences in Consumer Judgment and Decision Making," *Journal of Consumer Psychology* 14 (September 2004): 332-349.

28. L. Sjöberg, "Intuitive vs. Analytical Decision Making: Which Is Preferred?" *Scandinavian Journal of Management* 19 (2003): 17-29.

29. M. Lyons, "Cave-in Too Close for Comfort, Miner Says," *Saskatoon StarPhoenix*, 6 May 2002.

30. W. H. Agor, "The Logic of Intuition," *Organizational Dynamics* (Winter 1986): 5-18; H. A. Simon, "Making Management Decisions: The Role of Intuition and Emotion," *Academy of Management Executive* (February 1987): 57-64; O. Behling and N. L. Eckel, "Making Sense out of Intuition," *Academy of Management Executive* 5 (February 1991): 46-54.

31. M. D. Lieberman, "Intuition: A Social Cognitive Neuroscience Approach," *Psychological Bulletin* 126 (2000): 109-137; G. Klein, *Intuition at Work* (New York: Cur-

rency/Doubleday, 2003); E. Dane and M. G. Pratt, "Intuition: It's Boundaries and Role in Organizational Decision-Making" in *Academy of Management Best Papers Proceedings*, (New Orleans, 2004), A1-A6.

32. Klein, *Intuition at Work*, pp. 12-13, 16-17.

33. Y. Ganzach, A. H. Kluger, and N. Klayman, "Making Decisions from an Interview: Expert Measurement and Mechanical Combination," *Personnel Psychology* 53 (Spring 2000): 1-20; A. M. Hayashi, "When to Trust Your Gut," *Harvard Business Review* 79 (February 2001): 59-65. Evidence of high failure rates from quick decisions is reported in: Nutt, *Why Decisions Fail* ; Nutt, "Search During Decision Making"; P. C. Nutt, "Investigating the Success of Decision Making Processes," *Journal of Management Studies* 45, no. 2 (March 2008): 425-455.

34. P. Goodwin and G. Wright, "Enhancing Strategy Evaluation in Scenario Planning: A Role for Decision Analysis," *Journal of Management Studies* 38 (January 2001): 1-16; R. Bradfield *et al.*, "The Origins and Evolution of Scenario Techniques in Long Range Business Planning," *Futures* 37, no. 8 (2005): 795-812; G. Wright, G. Cairns, and P. Goodwin, "Teaching Scenario Planning: Lessons from Practice in Academe and Business," *European Journal of Operational Research* (in press 2008).

35. A. Papmehi, "Disciplined Vision," *CMA Magazine*, August-September 2005, 24-27.

36. J. Pfeffer and R. I. Sutton, "Knowing 'What' to Do Is Not Enough: Turning Knowledge into Action," *California Management Review* 42, no. 1 (Fall 1999): 83-108; R. Charan, C. Burke, and L. Bossidy, *Execution. The Discipline of Getting Things Done* (New York: Crown Business, 2002) The survey of managerial competencies is reported in: D. Nilsen, B. Kowske, and A. Kshanika, "Managing Globally," *HRMagazine*, August 2005, 111-115.

37. R. N. Taylor, *Behavioral Decision Making* (Glenview, Ill.: Scott, Foresman, 1984), pp. 163-166.

38. G. Whyte, "Escalating Commitment to a Course of Action: A Reinterpretation," *Academy of Management Review* 11 (1986): 311-321; J. Brockner, "The Escalation of Commitment to a Failing Course of Action: Toward Theoretical Progress," *Academy of Management Review* 17, no. 1 (January 1992): 39-61.

39. J. Lorinc, "Power Failure," *Canadian Business*, November 1992, 50-58; M. Fackler, "Tokyo's Newest Subway Line a Saga of Hubris, Humiliation," *Associated Press Newswires* (20 July 1999).

40. D. Collins, "Senior Officials Tried to Stop Spending," *Irish Examiner*, 5 October 2005; M. Sheehan, "Throwing Good Money

after Bad," *Sunday Independent (Dublin)*, 9 October 2005; "Computer System Was Budgeted at Eur9m...Its Cost Eur170m... Now Health Chiefs Want a New One," *Irish Mirror*, 7 July 2007, 16; E. Kennedy, "Health Boss Refuses to Ditch Ill-Fated PPARS System," *Irish Independent*, 5 February 2007.

41. F. D. Schoorman and P. J. Holahan, "Psychological Antecedents of Escalation Behavior: Effects of Choice, Responsibility, and Decision Consequences," *Journal of Applied Psychology* 81 (1996): 786-793.

42. G. Whyte, "Escalating Commitment in Individual and Group Decision Making: A Prospect Theory Approach," *Organizational Behavior and Human Decision Processes* 54 (1993): 430-455; D. J. Sharp and S. B. Salter, "Project Escalation and Sunk Costs: A Test of the International Generalizability of Agency and Prospect Theories," *Journal of International Business Studies* 28, no. 1 (1997): 101-121.

43. S. McKay, "When Good People Make Bad Decisions," *Canadian Business*, February 1994, 52-55.

44. J. D. Bragger *et al.*, "When Success Breeds Failure: History, Hysteresis, and Delayed Exit Decisions ", *Journal of Applied Psychology* 88, no. 1 (2003): 6-14. A second logical reason for escalation, called the martingale strategy, is described in: J. A. Aloysius, "Rational Escalation of Costs by Playing a Sequence of Unfavorable Gambles: The Martingale," *Journal of Economic Behavior & Organization* 51 (2003): 111-129.

45. I. Simonson and B. M. Staw, "De-Escalation Strategies: A Comparison of Techniques for Reducing Commitment to Losing Courses of Action," *Journal of Applied Psychology* 77 (1992): 419-426; W. Boulding, R. Morgan, and R. Staelin, "Pulling the Plug to Stop the New Product Drain," *Journal of Marketing Research*, no. 34 (1997): 164-176; B. M. Staw, K. W. Koput, and S. G. Barsade, "Escalation at the Credit Window: A Longitudinal Study of Bank Executives' Recognition and Write-Off of Problem Loans," *Journal of Applied Psychology*, no. 82 (1997): 130-142; M. Keil and D. Robey, "Turning around Troubled Software Projects: An Exploratory Study of the Deescalation of Commitment to Failing Courses of Action," *Journal of Management Information Systems* 15 (Spring 1999): 63-87.

46. D. Ghosh, "De-Escalation Strategies: Some Experimental Evidence," *Behavioral Research in Accounting*, no. 9 (1997): 88-112.

47. I. Macwhirter, "Let's Build a Parliament," *The Scotsman* (17 July 1997): 19; I. Swanson, "Holyrood Firms Face Grilling over Costs," *Evening News (Edinburgh)*, 6 June 2003, 2; Lord Fraser of Carmyllie QC, *The Holyrood Inquiry*, (Edinborough: Scottish Parliamentary Corporate Body, 15 September 2004).

48. M. Gardner, "Democratic Principles Making Businesses More Transparent," *Christian Science Monitor*, 19 March 2007, 13.

49. M. Fenton-O'Creevy, "Employee Involvement and the Middle Manager: Saboteur or Scapegoat?" *Human Resource Management Journal*, no. 11 (2001): 24-40. Also see: V. H. Vroom and A. G. Jago, *The New Leadership: Managing Participation in Organizations* (Englewood Cliffs, N.J.: Prentice Hill, 1988).

50. Some of the early OB writing on employee involvement includes: C. Argyris, *Personality and Organization* (New York: Harper & Row, 1957); D. McGregor, *The Human Side of Enterprise* (New York: McGraw-Hill, 1960); R. Likert, *New Patterns of Management* (New York: McGraw-Hill, 1961).

51. A. G. Robinson and D. M. Schroeder, *Ideas Are Free* (San Francisco: Berrett-Koehler, 2004).

52. S. W. Crispin, "Workers' Paradise," *Far Eastern Economic Review*, 17 April 2003, 40-41; "Thai Carbon Black: Worker-Driven Focus Key to Firm's Success," *The Nation (Thailand)*, 3 June 2004.

53. A. Kleingeld, H. Van Tuijl, and J. A. Algera, "Participation in the Design of Performance Management Systems: A Quasi-Experimental Field Study," *Journal of Organizational Behavior* 25, no. 7 (2004): 831-851.

54. K. T. Dirks, L. L. Cummings, and J. L. Pierce, "Psychological Ownership in Organizations: Conditions under Which Individuals Promote and Resist Change," *Research in Organizational Change and Development*, no. 9 (1996): 1-23; J. P. Walsh and S.-F. Tseng, "The Effects of Job Characteristics on Active Effort at Work," *Work & Occupations*, no. 25 (February 1998): 74-96; B. Scott-Ladd and V. Marshall, "Participation in Decision Making: A Matter of Context?" *Leadership & Organization Development Journal* 25, no. 8 (2004): 646-662. Brian Scudamore's quotation is from T. Fenton, "Inside the Worldblu List: 1-800-Got-Junk?'s CEO on Why "Being Democratic Is Extremely Important to Maintaining Our Competitive Advantage," (Atlanta: WorldBlu, 3 January 2008).

55. G. P. Latham, D. C. Winters, and E. A. Locke, "Cognitive and Motivational Effects of Participation: A Mediator Study," *Journal of Organizational Behavior*, no. 15 (1994): 49-63; J. A. Wagner III *et al.*, "Cognitive and Motivational Frameworks in U.S. Research on Participation: A Meta-Analysis of Primary Effects," *Journal of Organizational Behavior*, no. 18 (1997): 49-65.

56. J. Zhou and C. E. Shalley, "Research on Employee Creativity: A Critical Review and Directions for Future Research," *Research in Personnel and Human Resources Management* 22 (2003): 165-217; M. A. Runco, "Creativity," *Annual Review of Psychology* 55 (2004): 657-687.

57. G. Wallas, *The Art of Thought* (New York: Harcourt Brace Jovanovich, 1926). For recent applications of Wallas's classic model, see: T. Kristensen, "The Physical Context of Creativity," *Creativity and Innovation Management* 13, no. 2 (June 2004): 89-96; U.-E. Haner, "Spaces for Creativity and Innovation in Two Established Organizations," *Creativity and Innovation Management* 14, no. 3 (2005): 288-298.

58. R. S. Nickerson, "Enhancing Creativity," in *Handbook of Creativity* ed. R. J. Sternberg (New York: Cambridge University Press, 1999), 392-430.

59. R. I. Sutton, *Weird Ideas That Work* (New York: Free Press, 2002), p. 26.

60. For a thorough discussion of insight, see: R. J. Sternberg and J. E. Davidson, *The Nature of Insight* (Cambridge, MA: MIT Press, 1995).

61. R. J. Sternberg and L. A. O' Hara, "Creativity and Intelligence," in *Handbook of Creativity* ed. R. J. Sternberg (New York: Cambridge University Press, 1999), 251-272; S. Taggar, "Individual Creativity and Group Ability to Utilize Individual Creative Resources: A Multilevel Model," *Academy of Management Journal* 45 (April 2002): 315-330.

62. G. J. Feist, "The Influence of Personality on Artistic and Scientific Creativity," in *Handbook of Creativity*, ed. R. J. Sternberg (New York: Cambridge University Press, 1999), 273-296; Sutton, *Weird Ideas That Work*, pp. 8-9, Chap. 10; T. Åsterbro, S. A. Jeffrey, and G. K. Adomdza, "Inventor Perseverance after Being Tols to Quit: The Role of Cognitive Biases," *Journal of Behavioral Decision Making* 20 (2007): 253-272.

63. V. Laurie, "Gut Instinct," *The Australian Magazine*, 10 December 2005, 1; J. Robotham, "Of Guts and Glory," *Sydney Morning Herald*, 5 October 2005, 16; M. Irving, "Nobel Deeds, Words of Praise," *West Australian (Perth)*, 14 January 2006, 4. Some facts are also found in Robin Warren's 2005 Nobel lecture. See J. Robin Warren, "Nobel Lecture: The Ease and Difficulty of a New Discovery," RealVideo presentation at: http://nobelprize.org/medicine/laureates/2005/warren-lecture.html.

64. R. W. Weisberg, "Creativity and Knowledge: A Challenge to Theories," in *Handbook of Creativity*, ed. R. J. Sternberg (New

York: Cambridge University Press, 1999), 226-250.

65. Sutton, *Weird Ideas That Work*, pp. 121, 153-154; C. Andriopoulos, "Six Paradoxes in Managing Creativity: An Embracing Act," *Long Range Planning* 36 (2003): 375-388.

66. T. Koppell, *Powering the Future* (New York: Wiley, 1999), p. 15.

67. R. J. Sternberg and T. I. Lubart, *Defying the Crowd: Cultivating Creativity in a Culture of Conformity* (New York: Free Press, 1995); Feist, "The Influence of Personality on Artistic and Scientific Creativity"; S. J. Dollinger, K. K. Urban, and T. A. James, "Creativity and Openness to Experience: Validation of Two Creative Product Measures," *Creativity Research Journal* 16, no. 1 (2004): 35-47; C. E. Shalley, J. Zhou, and G. R. Oldham, "The Effects of Personal and Contextual Characteristics on Creativity: Where Should We Go from Here?" *Journal of Management* 30, no. 6 (2004): 933-958; T. S. Schweizer, "The Psychology of Novelty-Seeking, Creativity and Innovation: Neurocognitive Aspects within a Work-Psychological Perspective," *Creativity and Innovation Management* 15, no. 2 (2006): 164-172.

68. M. D. Mumford, "Managing Creative People: Strategies and Tactics for Innovation," *Human Resource Management Review* 10 (Autumn 2000): 313-351; T. M. Amabile *et al.*, "Leader Behaviors and the Work Environment for Creativity: Perceived Leader Support," *The Leadership Quarterly* 15, no. 1 (2004): 5-32; Shalley, Zhou, and Oldham, "The Effects of Personal and Contextual Characteristics on Creativity"; T. C. DiLiello and J. D. Houghton, "Creative Potential and Practised Creativity: Identifying Untapped Creativity in Organizations," *Creativity and Innovation Management* 17, no. 1 (2008): 37-46.

69. R. Westwood and D. R. Low, "The Multicultural Muse: Culture, Creativity and Innovation," *International Journal of Cross Cultural Management* 3, no. 2 (2003): 235-259.

70. T. M. Amabile, "Motivating Creativity in Organizations: On Doing What You Love and Loving What You Do," *California Management Review* 40 (Fall 1997): 39-58; A. Cummings and G. R. Oldham, "Enhancing Creativity: Managing Work Contexts for the High Potential Employee," *California Management Review*, no. 40 (Fall 1997): 22-38.

71. T. M. Amabile, "Changes in the Work Environment for Creativity During Downsizing," *Academy of Management Journal* 42 (December 1999): 630-640.

72. M. Strauss, "Retailers Tap into War-Room Creativity of Employees," *Globe & Mail*, 12 March 2007, B1.

73. L. Jen, "The Fun House," *Canadian Architect*, June 2007, 34-38.

74. J. M. Howell and K. Boies, "Champions of Technological Innovation: The Influence of Contextual Knowledge, Role Orientation, Idea Generation, and Idea Promotion on Champion Emergence," *The Leadership Quarterly* 15, no. 1 (2004): 123-143; Shalley, Zhou, and Oldham, "The Effects of Personal and Contextual Characteristics on Creativity."

75. A. Hiam, "Obstacles to Creativity—And How You Can Remove Them," *Futurist* 32 (October 1998): 30-34.

76. M. A. West, *Developing Creativity in Organizations* (Leicester, UK: BPS Books, 1997), pp. 33-35.

77. S. Hemsley, "Seeking the Source of Innovation," *Media Week*, 16 August 2005, 22.

78. J. Neff, "At Eureka Ranch, Execs Doff Wing Tips, Fire up Ideas," *Advertising Age*, 9 March 1998, 28-29.

79. A. Hargadon and R. I. Sutton, "Building an Innovation Factory," *Harvard Business Review* 78 (May-June 2000): 157-166; T. Kelley, *The Art of Innovation* (New York: Currency Doubleday, 2001), pp. 158-162.

80. K. S. Brown, "The Apple of Jonathan Ive's Eye," *Investor's Business Daily* (19 September 2003).

Chapter 8

1. C. Fishman, "The Anarchist's Cookbook," *Fast Company*, July 2004, 70; J. Mackey, "Open Book Company," *Newsweek*, 28 November 2005, 42; D. Jacobson, "Best-Kept Secrets of the World's Best Companies: Gainsharing," *Business 2.0*, April 2006, 82; A. Kimball-Stanley, "Bucking the Trend in Benefits," *Providence Journal (Rhode Island)*, 14 May 2006, H01; K. Zimbalist, "Green Giant," *Time*, 24 April 2006, 24.

2. J. S. McClenahen, "Prairie Home Champion," *Industry Week*, October 2005, 45-47; D. Hechler, "Teamwork Is Job One at Ford," *Fulton County Daily Report (Atlanta)*, 16 May 2006, 16; G. Macaluso, "Hotel Dieu Grace Gets New Critical Care Team," *Windsor Star*, 10 September 2007.

3. M. E. Shaw, *Group Dynamics*, 3 ed. (New York: McGraw-Hill, 1981), 8; S. A. Mohrman, S. G. Cohen, and A. M. Mohrman Jr., *Designing Team-Based Organizations: New Forms for Knowledge Work* (San Francisco: Jossey-Bass, 1995), 39-40; E. Sundstrom, "The Challenges of Supporting Work Team Effectiveness," in *Supporting Work Team Effectiveness* ed. E. Sundstrom and Associates (San Francisco, CA: Jossey-Bass, 1999), 6-9.

4. R. A. Guzzo and M. W. Dickson, "Teams in Organizations: Recent Research on Performance and Effectiveness," *Annual Review of Psychology* 47 (1996): 307-338; D. A. Nadler, "From Ritual to Real Work: The Board as a Team," *Directors and Boards* 22 (Summer 1998): 28-31; L. R. Offerman and R. K. Spiros, "The Science and Practice of Team Development: Improving the Link," *Academy of Management Journal* 44 (April 2001): 376-392.

5. B. D. Pierce and R. White, "The Evolution of Social Structure: Why Biology Matters," *Academy of Management Review* 24 (October 1999): 843-853; P. R. Lawrence and N. Nohria, *Driven: How Human Nature Shapes Our Choices* (San Francisco: Jossey-Bass, 2002); J. R. Spoor and J. R. Kelly, "The Evolutionary Significance of Affect in Groups: Communication and Group Bonding," *Group Processes & Intergroup Relations* 7, no. 4 (2004): 398-412.

6. M. A. Hogg *et al.*, "The Social Identity Perspective: Intergroup Relations, Self-Conception, and Small Groups," *Small Group Research* 35, no. 3 (June 2004): 246-276; N. Michinov, E. Michinov, and M.-C. Toczek-Capelle, "Social Identity, Group Processes, and Performance in Synchronous Computer-Mediated Communication," *Group Dynamics: Theory, Research, and Practice* 8, no. 1 (2004): 27-39; M. Van Vugt and C. M. Hart, "Social Identity as Social Glue: The Origins of Group Loyalty," *Journal of Personality and Social Psychology* 86, no. 4 (2004): 585-598.

7. S. Schacter, *The Psychology of Affiliation* (Stanford, CA: Stanford University Press, 1959), 12-19; R. Eisler and D. S. Levine, "Nurture, Nature, and Caring: We Are Not Prisoners of Our Genes," *Brain and Mind* 3 (2002): 9-52; A. C. DeVries, E. R. Glasper, and C. E. Detillion, "Social Modulation of Stress Responses," *Physiology & Behavior* 79, no. 3 (August 2003): 399-407.

8. "Teamwork and Collaboration Major Workplace Trends," *Ottawa Business Journal*, 18 April 2006; S. Wuchty, B. F. Jones, and B. Uzzi, "The Increasing Dominance of Teams in Production of Knowledge," *Science* 316 (18 May 2007): 1036-1039.

9. M. Moldaschl and W. Weber, "The 'Three Waves' of Industrial Group Work: Historical Reflections on Current Research on Group Work," *Human Relations* 51 (March 1998): 347-388. Several popular books in the 1980s encouraged team work, based on the Japanese economic miracle. These books included: W. Ouchi, *Theory Z: How American Management Can Meet the Japanese Challenge* (Reading, Mass.: Addison-Wesley, 1981); R. T. Pascale and A. G. Athos, *Art of Japanese Management* (New York: Simon and Schuster, 1982).

10. A. Doak, "New-Age Style, Old-Fashioned Grunt, but How Will It Look with Fluffy Dice?" *The Age (Melbourne)*, 16 October 1998, 4; W. Webster, "How a Star

Was Born," *Daily Telegraph (Sydney)*, 17 October 1998, 11; R. Edgar, "Designers Front up to World Stage," *The Age (Melbourne)*, 11 February 2004, 6; P. Gover, "The Camaro Commandos," *Herald-Sun (Melbourne)*, 7 April 2006, G07.

11. C. R. Emery and L. D. Fredenhall, "The Effect of Teams on Firm Profitability and Customer Satisfaction," *Journal of Service Research* 4 (February 2002): 217-229; G. S. Van der Vegt and O. Janssen, "Joint Impact of Interdependence and Group Diversity on Innovation," *Journal of Management* 29 (2003): 729-751.

12. R. E. Baumeister and M. R. Leary, "The Need to Belong: Desire for Interpersonal Attachments as a Fundamental Human Motivation," *Psychological Bulletin* 117 (1995): 497-529; S. Chen, H. C. Boucher, and M. P. Tapias, "The Relational Self Revealed: Integrative Conceptualization and Implications for Interpersonal Life," *Psychological Bulletin* 132, no. 2 (2006): 151-179; J. M. Feinberg and J. R. Aiello, "Social Facilitation: A Test of Competing Theories," *Journal of Applied Social Psychology* 36, no. 5 (2006): 1087-1109; A. M. Grant, "Relational Job Design and the Motivation to Make a Prosocial Difference," *Academy of Management Review* 32, no. 2 (2007): 393-417; N. L. Kerr *et al.*, "Psychological Mechanisms Underlying the Kohler Motivation Gain," *Personality & Social Psychology Bulletin* 33, no. 6 (2007): 828-841.

13. E. A. Locke et al, "The Importance of the Individual in an Age of Groupism," in *Groups at Work: Theory and Research* ed. M. E. Turner (Mahwah, N. J.: Lawrence Erbaum Associates, 2001), 501-528; N. J. Allen and T. D. Hecht, "The 'Romance of Teams': Toward an Understanding of Its Psychological Underpinnings and Implications," *Journal of Occupational and Organizational Psychology* 77 (2004): 439-461.

14. I. D. Steiner, *Group Process and Productivity* (New York: Academic Press, 1972); N. L. Kerr and S. R. Tindale, "Group Performance and Decision Making," *Annual Review of Psychology* 55 (2004): 623-655.

15. D. Dunphy and B. Bryant, "Teams: Panaceas or Prescriptions for Improved Performance?" *Human Relations* 49 (1996): 677-699. For discussion of Brooke's Law, see: F. P. Brooks, ed., *The Mythical Man-Month: Essays on Software Engineering*, Second ed. (Reading, Mass.: Addison-Wesley, 1995).

16. S. J. Karau and K. D. Williams, "Social Loafing: A Meta-Analytic Review and Theoretical Integration," *Journal of Personality and Social Psychology* 65 (1993): 681-706; R. C. Liden *et al.*, "Social Loafing: A Field Investigation," *Journal of Management* 30 (2004): 285-304; L. L. Chidambaram, "Is Out of Sight, Out of Mind? An Empirical Study of Social Loafing in Technology-Supported Groups," *Information Systems Research* 16, no. 2 (2005): 149-168; U.-C. Klehe and N. Anderson, "The Moderating Influence of Personality and Culture on Social Loafing in Typical Versus Maximum Performance Situations," *International Journal of Selection and Assessment* 15, no. 2 (2007): 250-262.

17. M. Erez and A. Somech, "Is Group Productivity Loss the Rule or the Exception? Effects of Culture and Group-Based Motivation," *Academy of Management Journal* 39 (1996): 1513-1537; Kerr and Tindale, "Group Performance and Decision Making."

18. G. P. Shea and R. A. Guzzo, "Group Effectiveness: What Really Matters?" *Sloan Management Review* 27 (1987): 33-46; J. R. Hackman *et al.*, "Team Effectiveness in Theory and in Practice," in *Industrial and Organizational Psychology: Linking Theory with Practice*, ed. C. L. Cooper and E. A. Locke (Oxford, UK: Blackwell, 2000), 109-129.

19. M. A. West, C. S. Borrill, and K. L. Unsworth, "Team Effectiveness in Organizations," *International Review of Industrial and Organizational Psychology* 13 (1998): 1-48; R. Forrester and A. B. Drexler, "A Model for Team-Based Organization Performance," *Academy of Management Executive* 13 (August 1999): 36-49; J. E. McGrath, H. Arrow, and J. L. Berdahl, "The Study of Groups: Past, Present, and Future," *Personality & Social Psychology Review* 4, no. 1 (2000): 95-105; M. A. Marks, J. E. Mathieu, and S. J. Zaccaro, "A Temporally Based Framework and Taxonomy of Team Processes," *Academy of Management Review* 26, no. 3 (July 2001): 356-376.

20. J. S. DeMatteo, L. T. Eby, and E. Sundstrom, "Team-Based Rewards: Current Empirical Evidence and Directions for Future Research," *Research in Organizational Behavior* 20 (1998): 141-183; E. E. Lawler III, *Rewarding Excellence: Pay Strategies for the New Economy* (San Francisco: Jossey-Bass, 2000), 207-214; G. Hertel, S. Geister, and U. Konradt, "Managing Virtual Teams: A Review of Current Empirical Research," *Human Resource Management Review* 15 (2005): 69-95.

21. These and other environmental conditions for effective teams are discussed in: R. Wageman, "Case Study: Critical Success Factors for Creating Superb Self-Managing Teams at Xerox," *Compensation and Benefits Review* 29 (September-October 1997): 31-41; Sundstrom, "The Challenges of Supporting Work Team Effectiveness"; J. N. Choi, "External Activities and Team Effectiveness: Review and Theoretical Development," *Small Group Research* 33 (April 2002): 181-208; T. L. Doolen, M. E. Hacker, and E. M. Van Aken, "The Impact of Organizational Context on Work Team Effectiveness: A Study of Production Team," *IEEE Transactions on Engineering Management* 50, no. 3 (August 2003): 285-296; S. D. Dionne *et al.*, "Transformational Leadership and Team Performance," *Journal Of Organizational Change Management* 17, no. 2 (2004): 177-193.

22. D. McCutcheon, "Chipping Away: Celestica's Toronto Plant Cuts Waste Blitz by Blitz," *Advanced Manufacturing*, Nov/Dec 2004, 23.

23. M. A. Campion, E. M. Papper, and G. J. Medsker, "Relations between Work Team Characteristics and Effectiveness: A Replication and Extension," *Personnel Psychology* 49 (1996): 429-452; D. C. Man and S. S. K. Lam, "The Effects of Job Complexity and Autonomy on Cohesiveness in Collectivistic and Individualistic Work Groups: A Cross-Cultural Analysis," *Journal of Organizational Behavior* 24 (2003): 979-1001.

24. G. S. Van der Vegt, J. M. Emans, and E. Van de Vliert, "Patterns of Interdependence in Work Teams: A Two-Level Investigation of the Relations with Job and Team Satisfaction," *Personnel Psychology* 54 (Spring 2001): 51-69; R. Wageman, "The Meaning of Interdependence," in *Groups at Work: Theory and Research* ed. M. E. Turner (Mahwah, N. J.: Lawrence Erlbaum Associates, 2001), 197-217; S. M. Gully *et al.*, "A Meta-Analysis of Team-Efficacy, Potency, and Performance: Interdependence and Level of Analysis as Moderators of Observed Relationships," *Journal of Applied Psychology* 87, no. 5 (Oct 2002): 819-832; M. R. Barrick *et al.*, "The Moderating Role of Top Management Team Interdependence: Implications for Real Teams and Working Groups," *Academy of Management Journal* 50, no. 3 (2007): 544-557.

25. L. Gratton and T. J. Erickson, "Ways to Build Collaborative Teams," *Harvard Business Review* (November 2007): 100-109.

26. G. Stasser, "Pooling of Unshared Information During Group Discussion," in *Group Process and Productivity*, ed. S. Worchel, W. Wood, and J. A. Simpson (Newbury Park, California: Sage, 1992); J. R. Katzenbach and D. K. Smith, *The Wisdom of Teams: Creating the High-Performance Organization* (Boston: Harvard University Press, 1993), 45-47.

27. J. O'Toole and D. Tessmann-Keys, "The Power of Many: Building a High-Performance Management Team," *ceoforum. com.au*, March 2003.

28. Fishman, "The Anarchist's Cookbook."

29. F. P. Morgenson, M. H. Reider, and M. A. Campion, "Selecting Individuals in Team Setting: The Importance of Social Skills, Personality Characteristics, and Teamwork Knowledge," *Personnel Psychology* 58, no. 3 (2005): 583-611; V. Rous-

seau, C. Aubé, and A. Savoie, "Teamwork Behaviors: A Review and an Integration of Frameworks," *Small Group Research* 37, no. 5 (2006): 540-570. For a detailed examination of the characteristics of effective team members, see: M. L. Loughry, M. W. Ohland, and D. D. Moore, "Development of a Theory-Based Assessment of Team Member Effectiveness," *Educational and Psychological Measurement* 67, no. 3 (June 2007): 505-524.

30. "Shell Oil Introduces Undergrads to Gourami Business Challenge," University of Texas at Austin News release, (Austin, TX: 15 August 2005); S. Ganesan, "Reality-Style Recruitment," *Malasia Star*, 9 October 2005; J. Ng, "Shell Uses 'the Apprentice' Contest to Recruit Staff," *Straits Times (Singapore)*, 3 October 2005; J. Lim, "Prize for Overcoming Challenges on 'Island'? A Job with Shell," *Straits Times (Singapore)*, 12 March 2007; J. Porretto, "Wanted: Engineers," *The Commercial Appeal*, 4 September 2007, B3.

31. C. O. L. H. Porter *et al.*, "Backing up Behaviors in Teams: The Role of Personality and Legitimacy of Need," *Journal of Applied Psychology* 88, no. 3 (2003): 391-403; C. E. Härtel and D. Panipucci, "How 'Bad Apples' Spoil the Bunch: Faultlines, Emotional Levers, and Exclusion in the Workplace," *Research on Emotion in Organizations* 3 (2007): 287-310.

32. D. van Knippenberg, C. K. W. De Dreu, and A. C. Homan, "Work Group Diversity and Group Performance: An Integrative Model and Research Agenda," *Journal of Applied Psychology* 89, no. 6 (2004): 1008-1022; D. C. Lau and J. K. Murnighan, "Interactions within Groups and Subgroups: The Effects of Demographic Faultlines," *Academy of Management Journal* 48, no. 4 (August 2005): 645-659; R. Rico *et al.*, "The Effects of Diversity Faultlines and Team Task Autonomy on Decision Quality and Social Integration," *Journal of Management* 33, no. 1 (Feb. 2007): 111-132.

33. The NTSB and NASA studies are summarized in: J. R. Hackman, "New Rules for Team Building," *Optimize* (July 2002): 50-62.

34. B. W. Tuckman and M. A. C. Jensen, "Stages of Small-Group Development Revisited," *Group and Organization Studies* 2 (1977): 419-442; B. W. Tuckman, "Developmental Sequence in Small Groups," *Group Facilitation* (Spring 2001): 66-81.

35. D. L. Miller, "The Stages of Group Development: A Retrospective Study of Dynamic Team Processes," *Canadian Journal of Administrative Sciences* 20, no. 2 (2003): 121-134.

36. G. R. Bushe and G. H. Coetzer, "Group Development and Team Effectiveness: Using Cognitive Representations to Measure Group Development and Predict Task Performance and Group Viability," *Journal of Applied Behavioral Science* 43, no. 2 (June 2007): 184-212.

37. J. E. Mathieu and G. F. Goodwin, "The Influence of Shared Mental Models on Team Process and Performance," *Journal of Applied Psychology* 85 (April 2000): 273-284; J. Langan-Fox and J. Anglim, "Mental Models, Team Mental Models, and Performance: Process, Development, and Future Directions," *Human Factors and Ergonomics in Manufacturing* 14, no. 4 (2004): 331-352; B.-C. Lim and K. J. Klein, "Team Mental Models and Team Performance: A Field Study of the Effects of Team Mental Model Similarity and Accuracy," *Journal of Organizational Behavior* 27 (2006): 403-418; R. Rico, M. Sánchez-Manzanares, and C. Gibson, "Team Implicit Coordination Processes: A Team Knowledge-Based Approach," *Academy of Management Review* in press (2008).

38. A. P. Hare, "Types of Roles in Small Groups: A Bit of History and a Current Perspective," *Small Group Research* 25 (1994): 443-448; A. Aritzeta, S. Swailes, and B. Senior, "Belbin's Team Role Model: Development, Validity and Applications for Team Building," *Journal of Management Studies* 44, no. 1 (Jan. 2007): 96-118.

39. S. H. N. Leung, J. W. K. Chan, and W. B. Lee, "The Dynamic Team Role Behavior: The Approaches of Investigation," *Team Performance Management* 9 (2003): 84-90; G. L. Stewart, I. S. Fulmer, and M. R. Barrick, "An Exploration of Member Roles as a Multilevel Linking Mechanism for Individual Traits and Team Outcomes," *Personnel Psychology* 58, no. 2 (2005): 343-365.

40. W. G. Dyer, *Team Building: Current Issues and New Alternatives*, 3rd ed. (Reading, MA: Addison-Wesley, 1995); C. A. Beatty and B. A. Barker, *Building Smart Teams: Roadmap to High Performance* (Thousand Oaks, CA: Sage Publications, 2004).

41. P. White, "Bonding to the Beat of the Drum," *Globe & Mail*, 1 October 2007, L3.

42. Langan-Fox and Anglim, "Mental Models, Team Mental Models, and Performance: Process, Development, and Future Directions"; J. E. Mathieu *et al.*, "Scaling the Quality of Teammates' Mental Models: Equifinality and Normative Comparisons," *Journal of Organizational Behavior* 26 (2005): 37-56.

43. "German Businesswoman Demands End to Fun at Work," *Reuters* (9 July 2003).

44. R. W. Woodman and J. J. Sherwood, "The Role of Team Development in Organizational Effectiveness: A Critical Review," *Psychological Bulletin* 88 (1980): 166-186.

45. L. Mealiea and R. Baltazar, "A Strategic Guide for Building Effective Teams," *Personnel Management* 34, no. 2 (Summer 2005): 141-160.

46. G. E. Huszczo, "Training for Team Building," *Training and Development Journal* 44 (February 1990): 37-43; P. McGraw, "Back from the Mountain: Outdoor Management Development Programs and How to Ensure the Transfer of Skills to the Workplace," *Asia Pacific Journal of Human Resources* 31 (Spring 1993): 52-61.

47. D. C. Feldman, "The Development and Enforcement of Group Norms," *Academy of Management Review* 9 (1984): 47-53; E. Fehr and U. Fischbacher, "Social Norms and Human Cooperation," *Trends in Cognitive Sciences* 8, no. 4 (2004): 185-190.

48. N. Ellemers and F. Rink, "Identity in Work Groups: The Beneficial and Detrimental Consequences of Multiple Identities and Group Norms for Collaboration and Group Performance," *Advances in Group Processes* 22 (2005): 1-41.

49. J. J. Dose and R. J. Klimoski, "The Diversity of Diversity: Work Values Effects on Formative Team Processes," *Human Resource Management Review* 9, no. 1 (Spring 1999): 83-108.

50. S. Taggar and R. Ellis, "The Role of Leaders in Shaping Formal Team Norms," *Leadership Quarterly* 18, no. 2 (2007): 105-120.

51. D. J. Beal *et al.*, "Cohesion and Performance in Groups: A Meta-Analytic Clarification of Construct Relations," *Journal of Applied Psychology* 88, no. 6 (2003): 989-1004; S. W. J. Kozlowski and D. R. Ilgen, "Enhancing the Effectiveness of Work Groups and Teams," *Psychological Science in the Public Interest* 7, no. 3 (2006): 77-124.

52. K. A. Jehn, G. B. Northcraft, and M. A. Neale, "Why Differences Make a Difference: A Field Study of Diversity, Conflict, and Performance in Workgroups," *Administrative Science Quarterly* 44, no. 4 (1999): 741-763; van Knippenberg, De Dreu, and Homan, "Work Group Diversity and Group Performance: An Integrative Model and Research Agenda." For evidence that diversity/similarity does not always influence cohesion, see: S. S. Webber and L. M. Donahue, "Impact of Highly and Less Job-Related Diversity on Work Group Cohesion and Performance: A Meta-Analysis," *Journal of Management* 27, no. 2 (2001): 141-162.

53. E. Aronson and J. Mills, "The Effects of Severity of Initiation on Liking for a Group," *Journal of Abnormal and Social Psychology* 59 (1959): 177-181; J. E. Hautaluoma and R. S. Enge, "Early Socialization into a Work Group: Severity of Initiations

Revisited," *Journal of Social Behavior & Personality* 6 (1991): 725-748.

54. B. Mullen and C. Copper, "The Relation between Group Cohesiveness and Performance: An Integration," *Psychological Bulletin* 115 (1994): 210-227.

55. M. Rempel and R. J. Fisher, "Perceived Threat, Cohesion, and Group Problem Solving in Intergroup Conflict," *International Journal of Conflict Management* 8 (1997): 216-234; M. E. Turner and T. Horvitz, "The Dilemma of Threat: Group Effectiveness and Ineffectiveness under Adversity," in *Groups at Work: Theory and Research* ed. M. E. Turner (Mahwah, N. J.: Lawrence Erlbaum Associates, 2001), 445-470.

56. F. Piccolo, "Brownie Points," *Atlantic Business*, Oct/Nov 2004, 22.

57. W. Piper *et al.*, "Cohesion as a Basic Bond in Groups," *Human Relations* 36 (1983): 93-108; C. A. O'Reilly, D. E. Caldwell, and W. P. Barnett, "Work Group Demography, Social Integration, and Turnover," *Administrative Science Quarterly* 34 (1989): 21-37.

58. Mullen and Copper, "The Relation between Group Cohesiveness and Performance"; A. V. Carron *et al.*, "Cohesion and Performance in Sport: A Meta-Analysis," *Journal of Sport and Exercise Psychology* 24 (2002): 168-188; Beal *et al.*, "Cohesion and Performance in Groups."

59. C. Langfred, "Is Group Cohesiveness a Double-Edged Sword? An Investigation of the Effects of Cohesiveness on Performance," *Small Group Research* 29 (1998): 124-143; K. L. Gammage, A. V. Carron, and P. A. Estabrooks, "Team Cohesion and Individual Productivity: The Influence of the Norm for Productivity and the Identifiablity of Individual Effort," *Small Group Research* 32 (February 2001): 3-18.

60. S. L. Robinson, "Trust and Breach of the Psychological Contract," *Administrative Science Quarterly* 41 (1996): 574-599; D. M. Rousseau *et al.*, "Not So Different after All: A Cross-Discipline View of Trust," *Academy of Management Review* 23 (1998): 393-404; D. L. Duarte and N. T. Snyder, *Mastering Virtual Teams: Strategies, Tools, and Techniques That Succeed*, 2nd ed. (San Francisco, CA: Jossey-Bass, 2000), 139-155.

61. D. J. McAllister, "Affect- and Cognition-Based Trust as Foundations for Interpersonal Cooperation in Organizations," *Academy of Management Journal* 38, no. 1 (February 1995): 24-59; M. Williams, "In Whom We Trust: Group Membership as an Affective Context for Trust Development," *Academy of Management Review* 26, no. 3 (July 2001): 377-396.

62. O. E. Williamson, "Calculativeness, Trust, and Economic Organization," *Journal of Law and Economics* 36, no. 1 (1993): 453-486.

63. E. M. Whitener *et al.*, "Managers as Initiators of Trust: An Exchange Relationship Framework for Understanding Managerial Trustworthy Behavior," *Academy of Management Review* 23 (July 1998): 513-530; J. M. Kouzes and B. Z. Posner, *The Leadership Challenge*, 3rd ed. (San Francisco: Jossey-Bass, 2002), Chap. 2; T. Simons, "Behavioral Integrity: The Perceived Alignment between Managers' Words and Deeds as a Research Focus," *Organization Science* 13, no. 1 (Jan-Feb 2002): 18-35.

64. S. L. Jarvenpaa and D. E. Leidner, "Communication and Trust in Global Virtual Teams," *Organization Science* 10 (1999): 791-815; M. M. Pillutla, D. Malhotra, and J. Keith Murnighan, "Attributions of Trust and the Calculus of Reciprocity," *Journal of Experimental Social Psychology* 39, no. 5 (2003): 448-455.

65. K. T. Dirks and D. L. Ferrin, "The Role of Trust in Organizations," *Organization Science* 12, no. 4 (July-August 2004): 450-467.

66. S. A. Mohrman, S. G. Cohen, and J. Mohrman, A. M., Designing Team-Based Organizations: New Forms for Knowledge Work (San Francisco: Jossey-Bass, 1995); D. E. Yeatts and C. Hyten, High-Performing Self-Managed Work Teams: A Comparison of Theory and Practice (Thousand Oaks, CA: Sage, 1998); E. E. Lawler, Organizing for High Performance (San Francisco: Jossey-Bass, 2001); R. J. Torraco, "Work Design Theory: A Review and Critique with Implications for Human Resource Development," Human Resource Development Quarterly 16, no. 1 (Spring 2005): 85-109.

67. M. Connelly, "Chrysler Wants to Put Team Assembly in All Plants," *Automotive News*, 30 May 2005, 53; J. Leute, "Union, Management Work in Lockstep at Belvidere, Ill., Plant," *Janesville Gazette (Janesville, Wisc.)*, 18 July 2005; J. Smith, "Building Cars, Building Teams," *Plant Engineering*, December 2005, 41-50; M. Connelly, "Chrysler Boost Belvidere Flexibility," *Automotive News*, 13 February 2006, 44; C. Vander Doelen, "Chrysler Boss Urges Workers, Managers to Espouse Change," *Winnipeg Free Press*, 13 January 2006, E11; B. Vavra, "Stick with the Game Plan," *Plant Engineering*, 15 December 2007, 26.

68. Mackey, "Open Book Company."

69. P. Panchak, "Production Workers Can Be Your Competitive Edge," *Industry Week*, October 2004, 11; S. K. Muthusamy, J. V. Wheeler, and B. L. Simmons, "Self-Managing Work Teams: Enhancing Organizational Innovativeness," *Organization Development Journal* 23, no. 3 (Fall 2005): 53-66.

70. C. R. Emery and L. D. Fredendall, "The Effect of Teams on Firm Profitability and Customer Satisfaction," *Journal of Service Research* 4 (February 2002): 217-229; A. Krause and H. Dunckel, "Work Design and Customer Satisfaction: Effects of the Implementation of Semi-Autonomous Group Work on Customer Satisfaction Considering Employee Satisfaction and Group Performance (Translated Abstract)," *Zeitschrift fur Arbeits-und Organisationspsychologie* 47, no. 4 (2003): 182-193; H. van Mierlo *et al.*, "Self-Managing Teamwork and Psychological Well-Being: Review of a Multilevel Research Domain," *Group & Organization Management* 30, no. 2 (April 2005): 211-235.

71. M. Moldaschl and W. G. Weber, "The 'Three Waves' of Industrial Group Work: Historical Reflections on Current Research on Group Work," *Human Relations* 51 (March 1998): 259-287; W. Niepce and E. Molleman, "Work Design Issues in Lean Production from Sociotechnical System Perspective: Neo-Taylorism or the Next Step in Sociotechnical Design?" *Human Relations* 51, no. 3 (March 1998): 259-287.

72. E. Ulich and W. G. Weber, "Dimensions, Criteria, and Evaluation of Work Group Autonomy," in *Handbook of Work Group Psychology* ed. M. A. West (Chichester, UK: John Wiley and Sons, 1996), 247-282.

73. K. P. Carson and G. L. Stewart, "Job Analysis and the Sociotechnical Approach to Quality: A Critical Examination," *Journal of Quality Management* 1 (1996): 49-65; C. C. Manz and G. L. Stewart, "Attaining Flexible Stability by Integrating Total Quality Management and Socio-Technical Systems Theory," *Organization Science* 8 (1997): 59-70.

74. K. Marron, "Close Encounters of the Faceless Kind," *Globe & Mail*, 9 February 2005, C1.

75. J. Lipnack and J. Stamps, *Virtual Teams: People Working across Boundaries with Technology* (New York: John Wiley and Sons, 2001); B. S. Bell and W. J. Kozlowski, "A Typology of Virtual Teams: Implications for Effective Leadership," *Group & Organization Management* 27 (March 2002): 14-49; Hertel, Geister, and Konradt, "Managing Virtual Teams: A Review of Current Empirical Research."

76. G. Gilder, *Telecosm: How Infinite Bandwidth Will Revolutionize Our World* (New York: Free Press, 2001); L. L. Martins, L. L. Gilson, and M. T. Maynard, "Virtual Teams: What Do We Know and Where Do We Go Form Here?" *Journal of Management* 30, no. 6 (2004): 805-835.

77. Martins, Gilson, and Maynard, "Virtual Teams"; G. Hertel, U. Konradt, and

K. Voss, "Competencies for Virtual Teamwork: Development and Validation of a Web-Based Selection Tool for Members of Distributed Teams," *European Journal of Work and Organizational Psychology* 15, no. 4 (2006): 477-504.

78. G. Buckler, "Staking One for the Team," *Computing Canada*, 22 October 2004, 16.

79. V. H. Vroom and A. G. Jago, *The New Leadership* (Englewood Cliffs, NJ: Prentice-Hall, 1988), 28-29.

80. M. Diehl and W. Stroebe, "Productivity Loss in Idea-Generating Groups: Tracking Down the Blocking Effects," *Journal of Personality and Social Psychology* 61 (1991): 392-403; R. B. Gallupe et al., "Blocking Electronic Brainstorms," *Journal of Applied Psychology* 79 (1994): 77-86; B. A. Nijstad, W. Stroebe, and H. F. M. Lodewijkx, "Production Blocking and Idea Generation: Does Blocking Interfere with Cognitive Processes?" *Journal of Experimental Social Psychology* 39, no. 6 (November 2003): 531-548; B. A. Nijstad and W. Stroebe, "How the Group Affects the Mind: A Cognitive Model of Idea Generation in Groups," *Personality & Social Psychology Review* 10, no. 3 (2006): 186-213.

81. B. E. Irmer, P. Bordia, and D. Abusah, "Evaluation Apprehension and Perceived Benefits in Interpersonal and Database Knowledge Sharing," *Academy of Management Proceedings* (2002): B1-B6.

82. I. L. Janis, *Groupthink: Psychological Studies of Policy Decisions and Fiascoes*, Second ed. (Boston: Houghton Mifflin, 1982); J. K. Esser, "Alive and Well after 25 Years: A Review of Groupthink Research," *Organizational Behavior and Human Decision Processes* 73, no. 2-3 (1998): 116-141.

83. J. N. Choi and M. U. Kim, "The Organizational Application of Groupthink and Its Limitations in Organizations," *Journal of Applied Psychology* 84, no. 2 (April 1999): 297-306; W. W. Park, "A Comprehensive Empirical Investigation of the Relationships among Variables of the Groupthink Model," *Journal of Organizational Behavior* 21, no. 8 (Dec 2000): 873-887; D. D. Henningsen et al., "Examining the Symptoms of Groupthink and Retrospective Sensemaking," *Small Group Research* 37, no. 1 (Feb. 2006): 36-64.

84. D. Miller, *The Icarus Paradox: How Exceptional Companies Bring About Their Own Downfall* (New York: HarperBusiness, 1990); S. Finkelstein, *Why Smart Executives Fail* (New York: Viking, 2003); K. Tasa and G. Whyte, "Collective Efficacy and Vigilant Problem Solving in Group Decision Making: A Non-Linear Model," *Organizational Behavior and Human Decision Processes* 96, no. 2 (March 2005): 119-129.

85. H. Collingwood, "Best-Kept Secrets of the World's Best Companies: Outside-in R&D," *Business 2.0*, April 2006, 82.

86. K. M. Eisenhardt, J. L. Kahwajy, and L. J. Bourgeois III, "Conflict and Strategic Choice: How Top Management Teams Disagree," *California Management Review* 39 (1997): 42-62; R. Sutton, *Weird Ideas That Work* (New York: Free Press, 2002); C. J. Nemeth et al., "The Liberating Role of Conflict in Group Creativity: A Study in Two Countries," *European Journal of Social Psychology* 34, no. 4 (2004): 365-374. For discussion on how all conflict is potentially detrimental to teams, see: C. K. W. De Dreu and L. R. Weingart, "Task Versus Relationship Conflict, Team Performance, and Team Member Satisfaction: A Meta-Analysis," *Journal of Applied Psychology* 88 (August 2003): 587-604; P. Hinds and D. E. Bailey, "Out of Sight, out of Sync: Understanding Conflict in Distributed Teams," *Organization Science* 14, no. 6 (2003): 615-632.

87. K. Darce, "Ground Control: NASA Attempts a Cultural Shift," *Seattle Times*, 24 April 2005, A3; R. Shelton, "NASA Attempts to Change Mindset in Wake of Columbia Tragedy," *Macon Telegraph (Macon, GA)*, 7 July 2005.

88. B. Mullen, C. Johnson, and E. Salas, "Productivity Loss in Brainstorming Groups: A Meta-Analytic Integration," *Basic and Applied Psychology* 12 (1991): 2-23. The original description of brainstorming appeared in: A. F. Osborn, *Applied Imagination* (New York: Scribner, 1957).

89. R. I. Sutton and A. Hargadon, "Brainstorming Groups in Context: Effectiveness in a Product Design Firm," *Administrative Science Quarterly* 41 (1996): 685-718; T. Kelley, *The Art of Innovation* (New York: Currency Doubleday, 2001); V. R. Brown and P. B. Paulus, "Making Group Brainstorming More Effective: Recommendations from an Associative Memory Perspective," *Current Directions in Psychological Science* 11, no. 6 (2002): 208-212; K. Leggett Dugosh and P. B. Paulus, "Cognitive and Social Comparison Processes in Brainstorming," *Journal of Experimental Social Psychology* 41, no. 3 (2005): 313-320.

90. R. B. Gallupe, L. M. Bastianutti, and W. H. Cooper, "Unblocking Brainstorms," *Journal of Applied Psychology* 76 (1991): 137-142; W. H. Cooper et al., "Some Liberating Effects of Anonymous Electronic Brainstorming," *Small Group Research* 29, no. 2 (April 1998): 147-178; A. R. Dennis, B. H. Wixom, and R. J. Vandenberg, "Understanding Fit and Appropriation Effects in Group Support Systems Via Meta-Analysis," *MIS Quarterly* 25, no. 2 (June 2001): 167-193; D. M. DeRosa, C. L. Smith, and D. A. Hantula, "The Medium Matters: Mining the Long-Promised Merit of Group Interaction in Creative Idea Generation Tasks in a Meta-Analysis of the Electronic Group Brainstorming Literature," *Computers in Human Behavior* 23, no. 3 (2007): 1549-1581.

91. A. L. Delbecq, A. H. Van de Ven, and D. H. Gustafson, *Group Techniques for Program Planning: A Guide to Nominal Group and Delphi Processes* (Middleton, Wis: Green Briar Press, 1986).

92. S. Frankel, "NGT + MDS: An Adaptation of the Nominal Group Technique for Ill-Structured Problems," *Journal of Applied Behavioral Science* 23 (1987): 543-551; H. Barki and A. Pinsonneault, "Small Group Brainstorming and Idea Quality: Is Electronic Brainstorming the Most Effective Approach?" *Small Group Research* 32, no. 2 (April 2001): 158-205.

Chapter 9

1. J. Bennett and M. Beith, "Alternate Universe," *Newsweek*, 30 July 2007; S. Hatch, "Virtual Worlds, Real Meetings," *Corporate Meetings & Incentives*, Feb 2007, 12-17; W. Leung, "Strike!* (*Banana Suit Optional)," *Globe & Mail*, 15 October 2007.

2. C. Barnard, *The Functions of the Executive* (Cambridge, MA: Harvard University Press, 1938).

3. M. T. Hansen, M. L. Mors, and B. Løvås, "Knowledge Sharing in Organizations: Multiple Networks, Multiple Phases," *Academy of Management Journal* 48, no. 5 (2005): 776-793; R. Du, S. Ai, and Y. Ren, "Relationship between Knowledge Sharing and Performance: A Survey in Xu'an, China," *Expert Systems with Applications* 32 (2007): 38-46; S. R. Murray and J. Peyrefitte, "Knowledge Type and Communication Media Choice in the Knowledge Transfer Process," *Journal of Managerial Issues* 19, no. 1 (Spring 2007): 111-133.

4. S. Hamm, "International Isn't Just IBM's First Name," *BusinessWeek*, 28 January 2008.

5. N. Ellemers, R. Spears, and B. Doosje, "Self and Social Identity," *Annual Review of Psychology* 53 (2002): 161-186; S. A. Haslam and S. Reicher, "Stressing the Group: Social Identity and the Unfolding Dynamics of Responses to Stress," *Journal of Applied Psychology* 91, no. 5 (2006): 1037-1052; M. T. Gailliot and R. F. Baumeister, "Self-Esteem, Belongingness, and Worldview Validation: Does Belongingness Exert a Unique Influence Upon Self-Esteem?" *Journal of Research in Personality* 41, no. 2 (2007): 327-345.

6. S. Cohen, "The Pittsburgh Common Cold Studies: Psychosocial Predictors of Susceptibility to Respiratory Infectious Illness," *International Journal of Behavioral Medicine* 12, no. 3 (2005): 123-131; B. N.

Uchino, "Social Support and Health: A Review of Physiological Processes Potentially Underlying Links to Disease Outcomes," *Journal of Behavioral Medicine* 29, no. 4 (2006): 377-387.

7. D. Kirkpatrick, "It's Not a Game," *Fortune*, 5 Feb 2007, 34-38.

8. C. E. Shannon and W. Weaver, *The Mathematical Theory of Communication* (Urbana, Il: University of Illinois Press, 1949); R. M. Krauss and S. R. Fussell, "Social Psychological Models of Interpersonal Communication," in *Social Psychology: Handbook of Basic Principles*, ed. E. T. Higgins and A. Kruglanski (New York: Guilford Press, 1996), 655-701.

9. J. R. Carlson and R. W. Zmud, "Channel Expansion Theory and the Experiential Nature of Media Richness Perceptions," *Academy of Management Journal* 42 (April 1999): 153-170.

10. P. Shachaf and N. Hara, "Behavioral Complexity Theory of Media Selection: A Proposed Theory for Global Virtual Teams," *Journal of Information Science* 33 (2007): 63-75.

11. N. B. Ducheneaut and L. A. Watts, "In Search of Coherence: A Review of E-Mail Research," *Human-Computer Interaction* 20, no. 1-2 (2005): 11-48.

12. W. Lucas, "Effects of E-Mail on the Organization," *European Management Journal* 16, no. 1 (February 1998): 18-30; D. A. Owens, M. A. Neale, and R. I. Sutton, "Technologies of Status Management Status Dynamics in E-Mail Communications," *Research on Managing Groups and Teams* 3 (2000): 205-230; N. B. Ducheneaut, "Ceci N'est Pas Un Objet? Talking About Objects in E-Mail," *Human-Computer Interaction* 18, no. 1-2 (2003): 85-110.

13. N. B. Ducheneaut, "The Social Impacts of Electronic Mail in Organizations: A Case Study of Electronic Power Games Using Communication Genres," *Information, Communication, & Society* 5, no. 2 (2002): 153-188; N. Panteli, "Richness, Power Cues and Email Text," *Information & Management* 40, no. 2 (2002): 75-86.

14. N. Epley and J. Kruger, "When What You Type Isn't What They Read: The Perseverance of Stereotypes and Expectancies over E-Mail," *Journal of Experimental Social Psychology* 41, no. 4 (2005): 414-422.

15. J. B. Walther, "Language and Communication Technology: Introduction to the Special Issue," *Journal of Language and Social Psychology* 23, no. 4 (December 2004): 384-396; J. B. Walther, T. Loh, and L. Granka, "Let Me Count the Ways: The Interchange of Verbal and Nonverbal Cues in Computer-Mediated and Face-to-Face Affinity," *Journal of Language and Social Psychology* 24, no. 1 (March 2005): 36-65; K. Byron, "Carrying Too Heavy a Load?

The Communication and Miscommunication of Emotion by Email," *Academy of Management Review* 33, no. 2 (2008): 309-327.

16. G. Hertel, S. Geister, and U. Konradt, "Managing Virtual Teams: A Review of Current Empirical Research," *Human Resource Management Review* 15 (2005): 69-95; H. Lee, "Behavioral Strategies for Dealing with Flaming in an Online Forum," *The Sociological Quarterly* 46, no. 2 (2005): 385-403.

17. S. Williams, "Apologies and Rows by Email Are a New Sin for Hi-Tech Cowards," *Western Mail (Cardiff, Wales)*, 1 April 2006, 11.

18. K. Cox, "Irving Oil Fuels Its Leaders," *Globe & Mail*, 21 April 2004, C1.

19. D. D. Dawley and W. P. Anthony, "User Perceptions of E-Mail at Work," *Journal of Business and Technical Communication* 17, no. 2 (April 2003): 170-200; "Email Brings Costs and Fatigue," *Western News (University of Western Ontario) (London, Ontario)*, 9 July 2004; G. F. Thomas and C. L. King, "Reconceptualizing E-Mail Overload," *Journal of Business and Technical Communication* 20, no. 3 (July 2006): 252-287; S. Carr, "Email Overload Menace Growing," *Silicon.com*, 12 July 2007.

20. R. Dube, "No E-Mails, Please. I'm Trying to Work," *Globe & Mail*, 18 February 2008.

21. W. M. Bulkeley, "Playing Well with Others: How IBM's Employees Have Taken Social Networking to an Unusual Level," *Wall Street Journal*, 18 June 2007, R10; M. Rauch, "Virtual Reality," *Sales & Marketing Management* 159, no. 1 (Jan 2007): 18-23.

22. A. F. Cameron and J. Webster, "Unintended Consequences of Emerging Communication Technologies: Instant Messaging in the Workplace," *Computers in Human Behavior* 21, no. 1 (2005): 85-103.

23. P. Lima, "Why Facebook Is a Good Thing," *Globe & Mail*, 27 November 2007.

24. Hamm, "International Isn't Just IBM's First Name"; K. Jepson, "Web-Based Social Networking Sites," *Credit Union Journal*, 21 January 2008.

25. L. Z. Tiedens and A. R. Fragale, "Power Moves: Complementarity in Dominant and Submissive Nonverbal Behavior," *Journal of Personality and Social Psychology* 84, no. 3 (2003): 558-568.

26. P. Ekman and E. Rosenberg, *What the Face Reveals: Basic and Applied Studies of Spontaneous Expression Using the Facial Action Coding System* (Oxford, England: Oxford University Press, 1997); P. Winkielman and K. C. Berridge, "Unconscious Emotion," *Current Directions in Psychological Science* 13, no. 3 (2004): 120-123.

27. E. Hatfield, J. T. Cacioppo, and R. L. Rapson, *Emotional Contagion* (Cambridge, UK: Cambridge University Press, 1993); S. G. Barsade, "The Ripple Effect: Emotional Contagion and Its Influence on Group Behavior," *Administrative Science Quarterly* 47 (December 2002): 644-675; M. Sonnby-Borgstrom, P. Jonsson, and O. Svensson, "Emotional Empathy as Related to Mimicry Reactions at Different Levels of Information Processing," *Journal of Nonverbal Behavior* 27 (Spring 2003): 3-23; S. K. Johnson, "I Second That Emotion: Effects of Emotional Contagion and Affect at Work on Leader and Follower Outcomes," *Leadership Quarterly* 19, no. 1 (2008): 1-19.

28. J. R. Kelly and S. G. Barsade, "Mood and Emotions in Small Groups and Work Teams," *Organizational Behavior and Human Decision Processes* 86 (September 2001): 99-130.

29. L. K. Treviño, J. Webster, and E. W. Stein, "Making Connections: Complementary Influences on Communication Media Choices, Attitudes, and Use," *Organization Science* 11, no. 2 (2000): 163-182; B. Barry and I. S. Fulmer, "The Medium Is the Message: The Adaptive Use of Communication Media in Dyadic Influence," *Academy of Management Review* 29, no. 2 (2004): 272-292; J. W. Turner *et al.*, "Exploring the Dominant Media: How Does Media Use Reflect Organizational Norms and Affect Performance?" *Journal of Business Communication* 43, no. 3 (July 2006): 220-250; M. B. Watson-Manheim and F. Bélanger, "Communication Media Repertoires: Dealing with the Multiplicity of Media Choices," *MIS Quarterly* 31, no. 2 (2007): 267-293.

30. R. C. King, "Media Appropriateness: Effects of Experience on Communication Media Choice," *Decision sciences* 28, no. 4 (1997): 877-910.

31. K. Griffiths, "KPMG Sacks 670 Employees by E-Mail," *The Independent (London)*, 5 November 2002, 19; "Shop Worker Sacked by Text Message," *The Post (Claremont/Nedlands, Western Australia)*, 28 July 2007, 1, 78.

32. R. L. Daft and R. H. Lengel, "Information Richness: A New Approach to Managerial Behavior and Organization Design," *Research in Organizational Behavior* 6 (1984): 191-233; R. H. Lengel and R. L. Daft, "The Selection of Communication Media as an Executive Skill," *Academy of Management Executive* 2 (1988): 225-232.

33. "Employer Snapshots: 2008," *Toronto Star*, 13 October 2007; H. Schachter, "Strange but True: Some Staff Meetings Are Actually Efficient," *Globe & Mail*, 23 July 2007.

34. R. E. Rice, "Task Analyzability, Use of New Media, and Effectiveness: A Multi-Site Exploration of Media Richness," *Organization Science 3* (1992): 475-500.

35. J. W. Turner and N. L. Reinsch Jr, "The Business Communicator as Presence Allocator," *Journal of Business Communication* 44, no. 1 (2007): 36-58; J. Reinsch, N. Lamar, J. W. Turner, and C. H. Tinsley, "Multicommunicating: A Practice Whose Time Has Come?" *Academy of Management Review* (in press).

36. Carlson and Zmud, "Channel Expansion Theory and the Experiential Nature of Media Richness Perceptions"; N. Kock, "Media Richness or Media Naturalness? The Evolution of Our Biological Communication Apparatus and Its Influence on Our Behavior toward E-Communication Tools," *IEEE Transactions on Professional Communication* 48, no. 2 (June 2005): 117-130.

37. D. Muller, T. Atzeni, and F. Butera, "Coaction and Upward Social Comparison Reduce the Illusory Conjunction Effect: Support for Distraction-Conflict Theory," *Journal of Experimental Social Psychology* 40, no. 5 (2004): 659-665; L. P. Robert and A. R. Dennis, "Paradox of Richness: A Cognitive Model of Media Choice," *IEEE Transactions on Professional Communication* 48, no. 1 (2005): 10-21.

38. J. Kruger *et al.*, "Egocentrism over E-Mail: Can We Communicate as Well as We Think?" *Journal of Personality and Social Psychology* 89, no. 6 (2005): 925-936.

39. D. Goleman, R. Boyatzis, and A. McKee, *Primal Leaders* (Boston: Harvard Business School Press, 2002), pp. 92-95.

40. D. Woodruff, "Crossing Culture Divide Early Clears Merger Paths," *Asian Wall Street Journal*, 28 May 2001, 9.

41. R. M. Krauss, "The Psychology of Verbal Communication," in *International Encyclopedia of the Social and Behavioral Sciences*, ed. N. Smelser and P. Baltes (London: Elsevier, 2002), 16161-16165.

42. L. L. Putnam, N. Phillips, and P. Chapman, "Metaphors of Communication and Organization," in *Handbook of Organization Studies* ed. S. R. Clegg, C. Hardy, and W. R. Nord (London: Sage, 1996), 373-408; G. Morgan, *Images of Organization*, Second ed. (Thousand Oaks, CA: Sage, 1997); M. Rubini and H. Sigall, "Taking the Edge Off of Disagreement: Linguistic Abstractness and Self-Presentation to a Heterogeneous Audience," *European Journal of Social Psychology* 32 (2002): 343-351.

43. T. Koski, "Reflections on Information Glut and Other Issues in Knowledge Productivity," *Futures* 33 (August 2001): 483-495.

44. A. G. Schick, L. A. Gordon, and S. Haka, "Information Overload: A Temporal Approach," *Accounting, Organizations & Society* 15 (1990): 199-220; A. Edmunds and A. Morris, "The Problem of Information Overload in Business Organisations: A Review of the Literature," *International Journal of Information Management* 20 (2000): 17-28; R. Pennington, "The Effects of Information Overload on Software Project Risk Assessment," *Decision Sciences* 38, no. 3 (August 2007): 489-526.

45. D. C. Thomas and K. Inkson, *Cultural Intelligence: People Skills for Global Business* (San Francisco: Berrett-Koehler, 2004), Chap. 6; D. Welch, L. Welch, and R. Piekkari, "Speaking in Tongues," *International Studies of Management & Organization* 35, no. 1 (Spring 2005): 10-27.

46. S. Ohtaki, T. Ohtaki, and M. D. Fetters, "Doctor-Patient Communication: A Comparison of the USA and Japan," *Family Practice* 20 (June 2003): 276-282; M. Fujio, "Silence During Intercultural Communication: A Case Study," *Corporate Communications* 9, no. 4 (2004): 331-339.

47. D. C. Barnlund, Communication Styles of Japanese and Americans: Images and Realities (Belmont, Calif.: Wadsworth, 1988); H. Yamada, American and Japanese Business Discourse: A Comparison of Interaction Styles (Norwood, NJ: Ablex, 1992), Chap. 2; H. Yamada, Different Games, Different Rules (New York: Oxford University Press, 1997), pp. 76-79.

48. M. Griffin, "The Office, Australian Style," *Sunday Age* (22 June 2003): 6.

49. P. Harris and R. Moran, *Managing Cultural Differences* (Houston: Gulf, 1987); H. Blagg, "A Just Measure of Shame?" *British Journal of Criminology* 37 (Autumn 1997): 481-501; R. E. Axtell, *Gestures: The Do's and Taboos of Body Language around the World*, Revised ed. (New York: Wiley, 1998).

50. D. Tannen, *You Just Don't Understand: Men and Women in Conversation* (New York: Ballentine Books, 1990); D. Tannen, *Talking from 9 to 5* (New York: Avon, 1994); M. Crawford, *Talking Difference: On Gender and Language* (Thousand Oaks, CA: Sage, 1995), pp. 41-44; L. L. Namy, L. C. Nygaard, and D. Sauerteig, "Gender Differences in Vocal Accommodation: The Role of Perception," *Journal of Language and Social Psychology* 21, no. 4 (December 2002): 422-432.

51. A. Mulac *et al.*, "Uh-Huh. What's That All About?' Differing Interpretations of Conversational Backchannels and Questions as Sources of Miscommunication across Gender Boundaries," *Communication Research* 25 (December 1998): 641-668; N. M. Sussman and D. H. Tyson, "Sex and Power: Gender Differences in Computer-Mediated Interactions," *Computers in Human Behavior* 16 (2000): 381-394; D. R. Caruso and P. Salovey, *The Emotionally Intelligent Manager* (San Francisco: Jossey-Bass, 2004), p. 23; D. Fallows, *How Women and Men Use the Internet* (Washington, D.C.: Pew Internet and American Life Project, 28 December 2005).

52. K. Davis, *Human Behavior at Work: Organizational Behavior* (New York: McGraw-Hill, 1981), p. 413.

53. The three components of listening discussed here are based on several recent studies in the field of marketing, including: S. B. Castleberry, C. D. Shepherd, and R. Ridnour, "Effective Interpersonal Listening in the Personal Selling Environment: Conceptualization, Measurement, and Nomological Validity," *Journal of Marketing Theory and Practice* 7 (Winter 1999): 30-38; L. B. Comer and T. Drollinger, "Active Empathetic Listening and Selling Success: A Conceptual Framework," *Journal of Personal Selling & Sales Management* 19 (Winter 1999): 15-29; K. de Ruyter and M. G. M. Wetzels, "The Impact of Perceived Listening Behavior in Voice-to-Voice Service Encounters," *Journal of Service Research* 2 (February 2000): 276-284.

54. A. Leaman and B. Bordass, "Productivity in Buildings: The Killer Variables," *Building Research & Information* 27, no. 1 (1999): 4-19; T. J. Allen, "Architecture and Communication among Product Development Engineers," *California Management Review* 49, no. 2 (Winter 2007): 23-41; F. Becker, "Organizational Ecology and Knowledge Networks," *California Management Review* 49, no. 2 (Winter 2007): 42-61.

55. S. P. Means, "Playing at Pixar," *Salt Lake Tribune (Utah)*, 30 May 2003, D1; G. Whipp, "Swimming against the Tide," *Daily News of Los Angeles*, 30 May 2003, U6.

56. D. Walsberg, "Quiet Please!...We're Working," *National Post*, 30 May 2007.

57. M. Gardner, "Democratic Principles Make Businesses More Transparent," *Christian Science Monitor*, 19 March 2007, 13.

58. G. Evans and D. Johnson, "Stress and Open-Office Noise," *Journal of Applied Psychology* 85 (2000): 779-783; F. Russo, "My Kingdom for a Door," *Time Magazine*, 23 October 2000, B1.

59. C. Wagner and A. Majchrzak, "Enabling Customer-Centricity Using Wikis and the Wiki Way," *Journal of Management Information Systems* 23, no. 3 (2006): 17-43; R. B. Ferguson, "Build a Web 2.0 Platform and Employees Will Use It," *eWeek*, 20 June 2007; C. Karena, "Working the Wiki Way," *Sydney Morning Herald*, 6 March 2007.

60. T. Fenton, "Inside the Worldblu List: 1-800-Got-Junk?'S CEO on Why "Being Democratic Is Extremely Important to Maintaining Our Competitive Advantage," (Atlanta: WorldBlu, 3 January 2008). The original term is "management by *wandering* around," but this has been replaced with "walking around" over the years. See: W. Ouchi, *Theory Z* (New York: Avon Books, 1981), pp. 176-177; T. Peters and R. Waterman, *In Search of Excellence* (New York: Harper and Row, 1982), p. 122.

61. R. Rodwell, "Regular Staff Meetings Help Build Morale," *South China Morning Post (Hong Kong)*, 27 August 2005, 4.

62. R. Rousos, "Trust in Leaders Lacking at Utility," *The Ledger (Lakeland, Fl)*, 29 July 2003, B1; B. Whitworth and B. Riccomini, "Management Communication: Unlocking Higher Employee Performance," *Communication World*, Mar-Apr 2005, 18-21.

63. K. Davis, "Management Communication and the Grapevine," *Harvard Business Review* 31 (September-October 1953): 43-49; W. L. Davis and J. R. O'Connor, "Serial Transmission of Information: A Study of the Grapevine," *Journal of Applied Communication Research* 5 (1977): 61-72.

64. H. Mintzberg, *The Structuring of Organizations* (Englewood Cliffs, N.J.: Prentice Hall, 1979), pp. 46-53; D. Krackhardt and J. R. Hanson, "Informal Networks: The Company Behind the Chart," *Harvard Business Review* 71 (July-August 1993): 104-111.

65. C. J. Walker and C. A. Beckerle, "The Effect of State Anxiety on Rumor Transmission," *Journal of Social Behaviour & Personality* 2 (August 1987): 353-360; R. L. Rosnow, "Inside Rumor: A Personal Journey," *American Psychologist* 46 (May 1991): 484-496; M. Noon and R. Delbridge, "News from Behind My Hand: Gossip in Organizations," *Organization Studies* 14 (1993): 23-36.

66. N. Nicholson, "Evolutionary Psychology: Toward a New View of Human Nature and Organizational Society," *Human Relations* 50 (September 1997): 1053-1078; R. F. Baumeister, L. Zhang, and K. D. Vohs, "Gossip as Cultural Learning," *Review of General Psychology* 8, no. 2 (2004): 111-121; E. K. Foster, "Research on Gossip: Taxonomy, Methods, and Future Directions," *Review of General Psychology* 8, no. 2 (2004): 78-99.

Chapter 10

1. D. A. Brown, *A Matter of Trust*, (Ottawa: Government of Canada, 15 June 2007); N. Greenaway, "Ex-Rcmp Boss Showed 'Lack of Leadership'," *Ottawa Citizen*, 11 December 2007; T. MacCharles, "High Cost of Whistleblowing," *Toronto Star*, 30 June 2007; K. May, "Budget Check Led to RCMP Slush Fund," *Ottawa Citizen*, 14 April 2007.

2. J. R. P. French and B. Raven, "The Bases of Social Power," in *Studies in Social Power*, ed. D. Cartwright (Ann Arbor, Mich: University of Michigan Press, 1959), 150-167; A. D. Galinsky *et al.*, "Power and Perspectives Not Taken," *Psychological Science* 17, no. 12 (2006): 1068-1074. Also see: H. Mintzberg, *Power in and around Organizations* (Englewood Cliffs, NJ: Prentice Hall, 1983), Chap. 1; J. Pfeffer, *Managing with Power* (Boston: Harvard Business University Press, 1992), pp. 17, 30.

3. R. A. Dahl, "The Concept of Power," *Behavioral Science* 2 (1957): 201-218; R. M. Emerson, "Power-Dependence Relations," *American Sociological Review* 27 (1962): 31-41; A. M. Pettigrew, *The Politics of Organizational Decision-Making* (London: Tavistock, 1973).

4. R. Gulati and M. Sytch, "Dependence Asymmetry and Joint Dependence in Interorganizational Relationships: Effects of Embeddedness on a Manufacturer's Performance in Procurement Relationships," *Administrative Science Quarterly* 52, no. 1 (2007): 32-69.

5. French and Raven, "The Bases of Social Power"; P. Podsakoff and C. Schreisheim, "Field Studies of French and Raven's Bases of Power: Critique, Analysis, and Suggestions for Future Research," *Psychological Bulletin* 97 (1985): 387-411; P. P. Carson and K. D. Carson, "Social Power Bases: A Meta-Analytic Examination of Interrelationships and Outcomes," *Journal of Applied Social Psychology* 23 (1993): 1150-1169.

6. C. Barnard, *The Function of the Executive* (Cambridge, MA: Harvard University Press, 1938); C. Hardy and S. R. Clegg, "Some Dare Call It Power," in *Handbook of Organization Studies* ed. S. R. Clegg, C. Hardy, and W. R. Nord (London: Sage, 1996), 622-641.

7. A. I. Shahin and P. L. Wright, "Leadership in the Context of Culture: An Egyptian Perspective," *Leadership & Organization Development Journal* 25, no. 5/6 (2004): 499-511; Y. J. Huo *et al.*, "Leadership and the Management of Conflicts in Diverse Groups: Why Acknowledging Versus Neglecting Subgroup Identity Matters," *European Journal of Social Psychology* 35, no. 2 (2005): 237-254.

8. L. S. Sya, "Flying to Greater Heights," *New Sunday Times (Kuala Lumpur)*, 31 July 2005, 14.

9. J. M. Peiro and J. L. Melia, "Formal and Informal Interpersonal Power in Organisations: Testing a Bifactorial Model of Power in Role-Sets," *Applied Psychology* 52, no. 1 (2003): 14-35.

10. R. B. Cialdini and N. J. Goldstein, "Social Influence: Compliance and Conformity," *Annual Review of Psychology* 55 (2004): 591-621.

11. C. Perkel, "It's Not Csi," *Canadian Press*, 10 November 2007. The doctor-nurse study is reported in: C. K. Hofling *et al.*, "An Experimental Study in Nurse-Physician Relationships," *Journal of Nervous and Mental Disease* 143, no. 2 (1966): 171-177.

12. K. Miyahara, "Charisma: From Weber to Contemporary Sociology," *Sociological Inquiry* 53, no. 4 (Fall 1983): 368-388; J. D. Kudisch and M. L. Poteet, "Expert Power, Referent Power, and Charisma: Toward the Resolution of a Theoretical Debate," *Journal of Business & Psychology* 10 (Winter 1995): 177-195; D. Ladkin, "The Enchantment of the Charismatic Leader: Charisma Reconsidered as Aesthetic Encounter," *Leadership* 2, no. 2 (May 2006): 165-179.

13. G. Yukl and C. M. Falbe, "Importance of Different Power Sources in Downward and Lateral Relations," *Journal of Applied Psychology* 76 (1991): 416-423; B. H. Raven, "Kurt Lewin Address: Influence, Power, Religion, and the Mechanisms of Social Control," *Journal of Social Issues* 55 (Spring 1999): 161-186.

14. P. L. Dawes, D. Y. Lee, and G. R. Dowling, "Information Control and Influence in Emergent Buying Centers," *Journal Of Marketing* 62, no. 3 (July 1998): 55-68; D. Willer, "Power-at-a-Distance," *Social Forces* 81, no. 4 (2003): 1295-1334; D. J. Brass *et al.*, "Taking Stock of Networks and Organizations: A Multilevel Perspective," *Academy of Management Journal* 47, no. 6 (December 2004): 795-817.

15. C. R. Hinings *et al.*, "Structural Conditions of Intraorganizational Power," *Administrative Science Quarterly* 19 (1974): 22-44. Also see: C. S. Saunders, "The Strategic Contingency Theory of Power: Multiple Perspectives," *The Journal of Management Studies* 27 (1990): 1-21.

16. D. J. Hickson *et al.*, "A Strategic Contingencies' Theory of Intraorganizational Power," *Administrative Science Quarterly* 16 (1971): 216-227; Hinings *et al.*, "Structural Conditions of Intraorganizational Power"; R. M. Kanter, "Power Failure in Management Circuits," *Harvard Business Review* (July-August 1979): 65-75.

17. C. Russo, "Dodge Charger Case Study," *iMediaConnection*, 17 January 2006; D. Brady, "The It Girl," *Canadian Business*, 5 November 2007, 43-46; A. McMains, "TBWA Confirms Decourcy Hire," *AdWeek*, 21 August 2007, www.adweek.com/aw/national/article_display.jsp?vnu_content_id=1003628468.

18. Hickson *et al.*, "A Strategic Contingencies' Theory of Intraorganizational Power";

J. D. Hackman, "Power and Centrality in the Allocation of Resources in Colleges and Universities," *Administrative Science Quarterly* 30 (1985): 61-77; D. J. Brass and M. E. Burkhardt, "Potential Power and Power Use: An Investigation of Structure and Behavior," *Academy of Management Journal* 36 (1993): 441-470.

19. Kanter, "Power Failure in Management Circuits"; B. E. Ashforth, "The Experience of Powerlessness in Organizations," *Organizational Behavior and Human Decision Processes* 43 (1989): 207-242; L. Holden, "European Managers: HRM and an Evolving Role," *European Business Review* 12 (2000).

20. D. Hambrick, C. and E. Abrahamson, "Assessing Managerial Discretion across Industries: A Multimethod Approach," *Academy of Management Journal* 38, no. 5 (1995): 1427-1441; M. A. Carpenter and B. R. Golden, "Perceived Managerial Discretion: A Study of Cause and Effect," *Strategic Management Journal* 18, no. 3 (1997): 187-206.

21. J. Voight, "When Credit Is Not Due," *Adweek*, 1 March 2004, 24.

22. R. Madell, "Ground Floor," *Pharmaceutical Executive (Women in Pharma Supplement)*, June 2000, 24-31.

23. D. Krackhardt and J. R. Hanson, "Informal Networks: The Company Behind the Chart," *Harvard Business Review* 71 (July-August 1993): 104-111; P. S. Adler and S.-W. Kwon, "Social Capital: Prospects for a New Concept," *Academy of Management Review* 27, no. 1 (2002): 17-40.

24. A. Mehra, M. Kilduff, and D. J. Brass, "The Social Networks of High and Low Self-Monitors: Implications for Workplace Performance," *Administrative Science Quarterly* 46 (March 2001): 121-146.

25. B. R. Ragins and E. Sundstrom, "Gender and Power in Organizations: A Longitudinal Perspective," *Psychological Bulletin* 105 (1989): 51-88; M. Linehan, "Barriers to Women's Participation in International Management," *European Business Review* 13 (2001).

26. D. M. McCracken, "Winning the Talent War for Women: Sometimes It Takes a Revolution," *Harvard Business Review* (November-December 2000): 159-167.

27. D. Keltner, D. H. Gruenfeld, and C. Anderson, "Power, Approach, and Inhibition," *Psychological Review* 110, no. 2 (2003): 265-284; B. Simpson and C. Borch, "Does Power Affect Perception in Social Networks? Two Arguments and an Experimental Test," *Social Psychology Quarterly* 68, no. 3 (2005): 278-287; Galinsky *et al.*, "Power and Perspectives Not Taken."

28. "Many Nails in Zaccardelli's Coffin," *Toronto Star*, 11 December 2006, A18; A. Mayeda, "Top Mountie Unhorsed," *Montreal Gazette*, 7 December 2006, A1; B. Laghi and O. Moore, "Mounties Say Top Ranks Covered up Mismanagement of Pension Fund," *Globe & Mail*, 29 March 2007, A1.

29. K. Atuahene-Gima and H. Li, "Marketing's Influence Tactics in New Product Development: A Study of High Technology Firms in China," *Journal of Product Innovation Management* 17 (2000): 451-470; A. Somech and A. Drach-Zahavy, "Relative Power and Influence Strategy: The Effects of Agent/Target Organizational Power on Superiors' Choices of Influence Strategies," *Journal of Organizational Behavior* 23 (2002): 167-179.

30. D. Kipnis, S. M. Schmidt, and I. Wilkinson, "Intraorganizational Influence Tactics: Explorations in Getting One's Way," *Journal of Applied Psychology* 65 (1980): 440-452; A. Rao and K. Hashimoto, "Universal and Culturally Specific Aspects of Managerial Influence: A Study of Japanese Managers," *Leadership Quarterly* 8 (1997): 295-312; L. A. McFarland, A. M. Ryan, and S. D. Kriska, "Field Study Investigation of Applicant Use of Influence Tactics in a Selection Interview," *Journal of Psychology* 136 (July 2002): 383-398.

31. Cialdini and Goldstein, "Social Influence: Compliance and Conformity."

32. Rao and Hashimoto, "Universal and Culturally Specific Aspects of Managerial Influence." Silent authority as an influence tactic in non-Western cultures is also discussed in: S. F. Pasa, "Leadership Influence in a High Power Distance and Collectivist Culture," *Leadership & Organization Development Journal* 21 (2000): 414-426.

33. Laghi and Moore, "Mounties Say Top Ranks Covered up Mismanagement of Pension Fund."

34. "Be Part of the Team If You Want to Catch the Eye," *Birmingham Post (UK)*, 31 August 2000, 14; S. Maitlis, "Taking It from the Top: How CEOs Influence (and Fail to Influence) Their Boards," *Organization Studies* 25, no. 8 (2004): 1275-1311.

35. A. T. Cobb, "Toward the Study of Organizational Coalitions: Participant Concerns and Activities in a Simulated Organizational Setting," *Human Relations* 44 (1991): 1057-1079; E. A. Mannix, "Organizations as Resource Dilemmas: The Effects of Power Balance on Coalition Formation in Small Groups," *Organizational Behavior and Human Decision Processes* 55 (1993): 1-22; D. J. Terry, M. A. Hogg, and K. M. White, "The Theory of Planned Behavior: Self-Identity, Social Identity and Group Norms," *British Journal of Social Psychology* 38 (September 1999): 225-244.

36. Brown, *A Matter of Trust*, pp. 11-12.

37. A. P. Brief, *Attitudes in and around Organizations* (Thousand Oaks, CA: Sage, 1998), pp. 69-84; D. J. O'Keefe, *Persuasion: Theory and Research* (Thousand Oaks, CA: Sage Publications, 2002).

38. M. Hiltzik, "Apple CEO's Visions Don't Guarantee Sustained Gains," *Los Angeles Times* (14 April 2003): C1; D. Gilmor, "Opinion: Apple Could Use S Polishing of Jobs-Led Arrogance with Press," *PR Week*, 14 January 2008, 11. The origin of "reality distortion field" is described at www.folklore.org.

39. These and other features of message content in persuasion are detailed in: R. Petty and J. Cacioppo, *Attitudes and Persuasion: Classic and Contemporary Approaches* (Dubuque, Iowa: W. C. Brown, 1981); M. Pfau, E. A. Szabo, and J. Anderson, "The Role and Impact of Affect in the Process of Resistance to Persuasion," *Human Communication Research* 27 (April 2001): 216-252; O'Keefe, *Persuasion: Theory and Research*, Chap. 9; R. Buck *et al.*, "Emotion and Reason in Persuasion: Applying the Ari Model and the Case Scale," *Journal of Business Research* 57, no. 6 (2004): 647-656; W. D. Crano and R. Prislin, "Attitudes and Persuasion," *Annual Review of Psychology* 57 (2006): 345-374.

40. N. Rhodes and W. Wood, "Self-Esteem and Intelligence Affect Influenceability: The Mediating Role of Message Reception," *Psychological Bulletin* 111, no. 1 (1992): 156-171.

41. D. Strutton and L. E. Pelton, "Effects of Ingratiation on Lateral Relationship Quality within Sales Team Settings," *Journal of Business Research* 43 (1998): 1-12; R. Vonk, "Self-Serving Interpretations of Flattery: Why Ingratiation Works," *Journal of Personality and Social Psychology* 82 (2002): 515-526.

42. C. A. Higgins, T. A. Judge, and G. R. Ferris, "Influence Tactics and Work Outcomes: A Meta-Analysis," *Journal of Organizational Behavior* 24 (2003): 90-106.

43. D. Strutton, L. E. Pelton, and J. Tanner, J. F., "Shall We Gather in the Garden: The Effect of Ingratiatory Behaviors on Buyer Trust in Salespeople," *Industrial Marketing Management* 25 (1996): 151-162; J. O' Neil, "An Investigation of the Sources of Influence of Corporate Public Relations Practitioners," *Public Relations Review* 29 (June 2003): 159-169.

44. M. C. Bolino and W. H. Tunley, "More Than One Way to Make an Impression: Exploring Profiles of Impression Management," *Journal of Management* 29 (2003): 141-160.

45. T. Peters, "The Brand Called You," *Fast Company*, August 1997, www.fastcompany.com/magazine/10/brandyou.html; J. Sills, "Becoming Your Own Brand," *Psychology Today* 41, no. 1 (February 2008): 62-63.

46. "Kendal Harazny Named 2007 Alberta Student Entrepreneur Competition Champion," Ace Canada News release, (Toronto: 21 February 2007); D. Finlayson, "Student Launched Ticketgold at the Right Time, in the Right Place," *Edmonton Journal*, 1 March 2007; "Canadian Students Converge for Edmonton Conference," University of Alberta News release, (Edmonton: 5 March 2008).

47. S. L. McShane, "Applicant Misrepresentations in Résumés and Interviews in Canada," *Labor Law Journal* (January 1994): 15-24; S. Romero and M. Richtel, "Second Chance," *New York Times*, 5 March 2001, C1; P. Sabatini, "Fibs on Résumés Commonplace," *Pittsburgh Post-Gazette*, 24 February 2006.

48. J. Laucius, "Internet Guru's Credentials a True Work of Fiction," *Ottawa Citizen*, 12 June 2001.

49. A. W. Gouldner, "The Norm of Reciprocity: A Preliminary Statement," *American Sociological Review* 25 (1960): 161-178.

50. Y. Fan, "Questioning Guanxi: Definition, Classification, and Implications," *International Business Review* 11 (2002): 543-561; D. Tan and R. S. Snell, "The Third Eye: Exploring Guanxi and Relational Morality in the Workplace," *Journal of Business Ethics* 41 (December 2002): 361-384; W. R. Vanhonacker, "When Good Guanxi Turns Bad," *Harvard Business Review* 82, no. 4 (April 2004): 18-19.

51. C. M. Falbe and G. Yukl, "Consequences for Managers of Using Single Influence Tactics and Combinations of Tactics," *Academy of Management Journal* 35 (1992): 638-652.

52. R. C. Ringer and R. W. Boss, "Hospital Professionals' Use of Upward Influence Tactics," *Journal of Managerial Issues* 12 (2000): 92-108.

53. G. Blickle, "Do Work Values Predict the Use of Intraorganizational Influence Strategies?" *Journal of Applied Social Psychology* 30, no. 1 (January 2000): 196-205; P. P. Fu *et al.*, "The Impact of Societal Cultural Values and Individual Social Beliefs on the Perceived Effectiveness of Managerial Influence Strategies: A Meso Approach," *Journal of International Business Studies* 35, no. 4 (July 2004): 284-305.

54. This definition of organizational politics has become the dominant perspective over the past 15 years. See: G. R. Ferris and K. M. Kacmar, "Perceptions of Organizational Politics," *Journal of Management* 18 (1992): 93-116; R. Cropanzano *et al.*, "The Relationship of Organizational Politics and Support to Work Behaviors, Attitudes, and Stress," *Journal of Organizational Behavior* 18 (1997): 159-180; E. Vigoda, "Stress-Related Aftermaths to Workplace Politics: The Relationships among Politics, Job Distress, and Aggressive Behavior in Organizations," *Journal of Organizational Behavior* 23 (2002): 571-591. However, organizational politics was previously viewed as influence tactics outside the formal role that could be either selfish or altruistic. This older definition is less common today, possibly because it is incongruent with popular views of politics and because it overlaps too much with the concept of influence. For the older perspective of organizational politics, see: J. Pfeffer, *Power in Organizations* (Boston: Pitman, 1981); Mintzberg, *Power in and around Organizations*.

55. K. M. Kacmar and R. A. Baron, "Organizational Politics: The State of the Field, Links to Related Processes, and an Agenda for Future Research," in *Research in Personnel and Human Resources Management*, ed. G. R. Ferris (Greenwich, CT: JAI Press, 1999), 1-39; L. A. Witt, T. F. Hilton, and W. A. Hochwarter, "Addressing Politics in Matrix Teams," *Group & Organization Management* 26 (June 2001): 230-247; Vigoda, "Stress-Related Aftermaths to Workplace Politics: The Relationships among Politics, Job Distress, and Aggressive Behavior in Organizations."

56. C. Hardy, *Strategies for Retrenchment and Turnaround: The Politics of Survival* (Berlin: Walter de Gruyter, 1990), Chap. 14; M. C. Andrews and K. M. Kacmar, "Discriminating among Organizational Politics, Justice, and Support," *Journal of Organizational Behavior* 22 (2001): 347-366.

57. R. Gluyas, "Fear and Loathing in NAB's Forex Fiasco," *The Australian*, 6 August 2005, 35; E. Johnston, "'Anything Goes,' Ex-Trader Says," *Australian Financial Review*, 2 August 2005, 3; E. Johnston, "Expletives and Stench in Hothouse of NAB Dealers," *Australian Financial Review*, 6 August 2005, 3; M. Moncrief and D. Miletic, "The End Is Nigh for NAB's Rogue Traders," *Sydney Morning Herald*, 3 July 2006, 19.

58. S. Blazejewski and W. Dorow, "Managing Organizational Politics for Radical Change: The Case of Beiersdorf-Lechia S.A., Poznan," *Journal of World Business* 38 (August 2003): 204-223.

59. L. W. Porter, R. W. Allen, and H. L. Angle, "The Politics of Upward Influence in Organizations," *Research in Organizational Behavior* 3 (1981): 120-122; R. J. House, "Power and Personality in Complex Organizations," *Research in Organizational Behavior* 10 (1988): 305-357.

60. R. Christie and F. Geis, *Studies in Machiavellianism* (New York: Academic Press, 1970); S. M. Farmer *et al.*, "Putting Upward Influence Strategies in Context," *Journal of Organizational Behavior* 18 (1997): 17-42; K. S. Sauleya and A. G. Bedeian, "Equity Sensitivity: Construction of a Measure and Examination of Its Psychometric Properties," *Journal of Management* 26 (September 2000): 885-910.

61. G. R. Ferris *et al.*, "Perceptions of Organizational Politics: Prediction, Stress-Related Implications, and Outcomes," *Human relations* 49 (1996): 233-263.

Chapter 11

1. L. Belkin, "When Herbert Met Matthew: The Generation Clash," *Globe & Mail*, 27 July 2007; C. Silverman, "Attack of the Fresh-Faced Go-Getters," *Globe & Mail*, 25 June 2007; T. E. Winchell Sr., "Ten Principles for Coalescing the Generations," *Public Manager* 36, no. 3 (Fall 2007): 87-88; M. Gabriel and P. Robitaille, "Sustaining High Performance with Generation-Y Employees," *Canadian HR Reporter* 14 January 2008, 13; L. S. Rikleen, "Office Politics: Solve Generational Conflict in the Workplace," *Nova Scotia Business Journal* 19 March 2008.

2. D. Tjosvold, *Working Together to Get Things Done* (Lexington, Mass.: Lexington, 1986), 114-115; J. A. Wall and R. R. Callister, "Conflict and Its Management," *Journal of Management*, 21 (1995): 515-558; M. A. Rahim, "Toward a Theory of Managing Organizational Conflict," *International Journal of Conflict Management* 13, no. 3 (2002): 206-235; D. Tjosvold, "Defining Conflict and Making Choices About Its Management," *International Journal of Conflict Management* 17, no. 2 (2006): 87-95.

3. For example, see: L. Urwick, *The Elements of Administration*, 2nd ed. (London: Pitman, 1947); C. Argyris, "The Individual and Organization: Some Problems of Mutual Adjustment," *Administrative Science Quarterly* 2, no. 1 (1957): 1-24; K. E. Boulding, "Organization and Conflict," *Conflict Resolution* 1, no. 2 (June 1957): 122-134; R. R. Blake, H. A. Shepard, and J. S. Mouton, *Managing Intergroup Conflict in Industry* (Houston: Gulf Publishing, 1964).

4. C. K. W. De Dreu and L. R. Weingart, "A Contingency Theory of Task Conflict and Performance in Groups and Organizational Teams," in *International Handbook of Organizational Teamwork and Cooperative Working*, ed. M. A. West, D. Tjosvold, and K. G. Smith (Chicester, UK: John Wiley & Sons, 2003), 151-166; K. A. Jehn and C. Bendersky, "Intragroup Conflict in Organizations: A Contingency Perspective on the Conflict-Outcome Relationship," *Research In Organizational Behaviour* 25 (2003): 187-242.

5. N. Oudeh, "Functional Harmony— Assessing the Impact of Conflict on Organizational Health," Paper presented at

Workplace Health in a Tight Labour Market, Toronto, 7 March 2007.

6. Rahim, "Toward a Theory of Managing Organizational Conflict"; M. Duarte and G. Davies, "Testing the Conflict-Performance Assumption in Business-to-Business Relationships," *Industrial Marketing Management* 32 (2003): 91-99. Although the 1970s marked a point when the benefits conflict became widely acknowledged, this view was expressed earlier by some writers. See: L. A. Coser, *The Functions of Social Conflict* (New York: Free Press, 1956); J. A. Litterer, "Conflict in Organization: A Re-Examination," *Academy of Management Journal* 9 (1966): 178-186; H. Assael, "Constructive Role of Interorganizational Conflict," *Administrative Science Quarterly* 14, no. 4 (1969): 573-582. A much earlier statement in support of conflict comes from American poet and journalist Walt Whitman, who wrote in 1860: "Have you learned lessons only of those who admired you, and were tender with you, and stood aside for you? Have you not learned great lessons from those who braced themselves against you, and disputed the passage with you?" Cited in: D. Taras and P. Steel, "We Provoked Business Students to Unionize: Using Deception to Prove an Ir Point," *British Journal of Industrial Relations* 45, no. 1 (March 2007): 179-198.

7. K. M. Eisenhardt, J. L. Kahwajy, and L. J. Bourgeois III, "How Management Teams Can Have a Good Fight," *Harvard Business Review* (July-August 1997): 77-85; K. M. Eisenhardt, J. L. Kahwajy, and L. J. Bourgeois III, "Conflict and Strategic Choice: How Top Management Teams Disagree," *California Management Review* 39 (Winter 1997): 42-62; T. Greitemeyer *et al.*, "Information Sampling and Group Decision Making: The Effects of an Advocacy Decision Procedure and Task Experience," *Journal of Experimental Psychology-Applied* 12, no. 1 (Mar 2006): 31-42; U. Klocke, "How to Improve Decision Making in Small Groups: Effects of Dissent and Training Interventions," *Small Group Research* 38, no. 3 (June 2007): 437-468.

8. H. Guetzkow and J. Gyr, "An Analysis of Conflict in Decision-Making Groups," *Human Relations* 7, no. 3 (Aug. 1954): 367-382; L. H. Pelled, K. M. Eisenhardt, and K. R. Xin, "Exploring the Black Box: An Analysis of Work Group Diversity, Conflict, and Performance," *Administrative Science Quarterly* 44 (March 1999): 1-28; Jehn and Bendersky, "Intragroup Conflict in Organizations." The notion of two types of conflict dates back to the 1950s (see first reference above), but became the dominant perspective in the 1990s. We have avoided using the "cognitive" and "affective" conflict labels because each type of conflict includes both cognitive and emotional elements.

9. C. K. W. De Dreu, "When Too Little or Too Much Hurts: Evidence for a Curvilinear Relationship between Task Conflict and Innovation in Teams," *Journal of Management* 32, no. 1 (Feb. 2006): 83-107.

10. A. Grove, "How to Make Confrontation Work for You," in *The Book of Management Wisdom*, ed. P. Krass (New York: John Wiley & Sons, 2000), 83-89; B. Schlender, "Inside Andy Grove's Latest Crusade," *Fortune*, 23 August 2004, 68 J. Detar, "Andy Grove, Intel's inside Man," *Investor's Business Daily*, 24 July 2007.

11. C. K. W. De Dreu and L. R. Weingart, "Task Versus Relationship Conflict, Team Performance, and Team Member Satisfaction: A Meta-Analysis," *Journal of Applied Psychology* 88 (August 2003): 587-604; A. C. Mooney, P. J. Holahan, and A. C. Amason, "Don't Take It Personally: Exploring Cognitive Conflict as a Mediator of Affective Conflict," *Journal of Management Studies* 44, no. 5 (2007): 733-758.

12. J. Yang and K. W. Mossholder, "Decoupling Task and Relationship Conflict: The Role of Intergroup Emotional Processing," *Journal of Organizational Behaviour* 25 (2004): 589-605.

13. A. C. Amason and H. J. Sapienza, "The Effects of Top Management Team Size and Interaction Norms on Cognitive and Affective Conflict," *Journal of Management* 23, no. 4 (1997): 495-516.

14. L. Pondy, "Organizational Conflict: Concepts and Models," *Administrative Science Quarterly* 2 (1967): 296-320; K. W. Thomas, "Conflict and Negotiation Processes in Organizations," in *Handbook of Industrial and Organizational Psychology*, ed. M. D. Dunnette and L. M. Hough, 2nd ed. (Palo Alto, CA: Consulting Psychologists Press, 1992), 651-718.

15. H. Barki and J. Hartwick, "Conceptualizing the Construct of Interpersonal Conflict," *International Journal of Conflict Management* 15, no. 3 (2004): 216-244.

16. M. A. Von Glinow, D. L. Shapiro, and J. M. Brett, "Can We Talk, and Should We? Managing Emotional Conflict in Multicultural Teams," *Academy of Management Review* 29, no. 4 (2004): 578-592.

17. G. E. Martin and T. J. Bergman, "The Dynamics of Behavioural Response to Conflict in the Workplace," *Journal of Occupational & Organizational Psychology* 69 (December 1996): 377-387; J. M. Brett, D. L. Shapiro, and A. L. Lytle, "Breaking the Bonds of Reciprocity in Negotiations," *Academy of Management Journal* 41 (August 1998): 410-424.

18. B. Dudley, "Bring Back the Dazzle," *Seattle Times*, 23 September 2005; J. Greene, "Troubling Exits at Microsoft," *BusinessWeek*, 26 September 2005, 98; A. Linn, "Microsoft Reorganizes to Compete Better with Google, Yahoo," *Associated Press Newswires*, 21 September 2005; V. Murphy, "Microsoft's Midlife Crisis," *Forbes*, 3 October 2005, 88; L. Vaas, "Microsoft Expands Bureaucracy, Crowns MSN King," *eWeek*, 20 September 2005; J. L. Yang, "Microsoft's New Brain," *Fortune*, 1 May 2006, 56.

19. R. E. Walton and J. M. Dutton, "The Management of Conflict: A Model and Review," *Administrative Science Quarterly* 14 (1969): 73-84; S. M. Schmidt and T. A. Kochan, "Conflict: Toward Conceptual Clarity," *Administrative Science Quarterly* 17, no. 3 (Sept. 1972): 359-370.

20. D. Decloet, "More Than One Way to Craft a Takeover," *Globe & Mail*, 30 August 2007; J. Chevreau, "Patrick Farmer Joins Cymbria," *National Post*, 22 April 2008.

21. "Four-Generation Workplace Not Always a Big Happy Family," *Canadian Press*, 26 May 2007. Cross-generational conflict is discussed in: R. Zemke and B. Filipczak, *Generations at Work: Managing the Clash of Veterans, Boomers, Xers, and Nexters in Your Workplace* (New York: Amacom, 1999); P. Harris, "Boomers vs. Echo Boomer: The Work War," *T+D* (May 2005): 44-49.

22. P. Hinds and D. E. Bailey, "Out of Sight, out of Sync: Understanding Conflict in Distributed Teams," *Organization Science* 14, no. 6 (2003): 615-632; P. Hinds and M. Mortensen, "Understanding Conflict in Geographically Distributed Teams: The Moderating Effects of Shared Identity, Shared Context, and Spontaneous Communication," *Organization Science* 16, no. 3 (May-June 2005): 290-307.

23. R. Wageman and G. Baker, "Incentives and Cooperation: The Joint Effects of Task and Reward Interdependence on Group Performance," *Journal of Organizational Behaviour* 18, no. 2 (1997): 139-158; G. S. van der Vegt, B. J. M. Emans, and E. van der Vliert, "Patterns of Interdependence in Work Teams: A Two-Level Investigation of the Relations with Job and Team Satisfaction," *Personnel Psychology* 54, no. 1 (2001): 51-69.

24. P. C. Earley and G. B. Northcraft, "Goal Setting, Resource Interdependence, and Conflict Management," in *Managing Conflict: An Interdisciplinary Approach*, ed. M. A. Rahim (New York: Praeger, 1989), 161-170; K. Jelin, "A Multimethod Examination of the Benefits and Detriments of Intragroup Conflict," *Administrative Science Quarterly* 40 (1995): 245-282.

25. A. Risberg, "Employee Experiences of Acquisition Processes," *Journal of World Business* 36 (March 2001): 58-84.

26. Jehn and Bendersky, "Intragroup Conflict in Organizations."

27. M. Hewstone, M. Rubin, and H. Willis, "Intergroup Bias," *Annual Review of Psychology* 53 (2002): 575-604; J. Jetten, R. Spears, and T. Postmes, "Intergroup Distinctiveness and Differentiation: A Meta-Analytic Integration," *Journal of Personality and Social Psychology* 86, no. 6 (2004): 862-879.

28. M. P. Follett, "Constructive Conflict," in *Dynamic Administration: The Collected Papers of Mary Parker Follett*, ed. H. C. Metcalf and L. Urwick (New York: Harper and Brothers, 1942), 30-37; Blake, Shepard, and Mouton, *Managing Intergroup Conflict in Industry* ; T. Ruble and K. Thomas, "Support for a Two-Dimensional Model of Conflict Behaviour," *Organizaiotnal Behaviour and Human Performance* 16 (1976): 143-155; C. K. W. De Dreu *et al.*, "A Theory-Based Measure of Conflict Management Strategies in the Workplace," *Journal of Organizational Behaviour* 22 (2001): 645-668; Rahim, "Toward a Theory of Managing Organizational Conflict."

29. Jelin, "A Multimethod Examination of the Benefits and Detriments of Intragroup Conflict."

30. D. A. Cai and E. L. Fink, "Conflict Style Differences between Individualists and Collectivists," *Communication Monographs* 69 (March 2002): 67-87; C. H. Tinsley and E. Weldon, "Responses to a Normative Conflict among American and Chinese Managers," *International Journal of Conflict Management* 3, no. 2 (2003): 183-194; F. P. Brew and D. R. Cairns, "Styles of Managing Interpersonal Workplace Conflict in Relation to Status and Face Concern: A Study with Anglos and Chinese," *International Journal of Conflict Management* 15, no. 1 (2004): 27-57.

31. N. Brewer, P. Mitchell, and N. Weber, "Gender Role, Organizational Status, and Conflict Management Styles," *International Journal of Conflict Management* 13 (2002): 78-95; N. B. Florea *et al.*, "Negotiating from Mars to Venus: Gender in Simulated International Negotiations," *Simulation & Gaming* 34 (June 2003): 226-248.

32. G. A. Callanan, C. D. Benzing, and D. F. Perri, "Chcoie of Conflict-Handling Strategy: A Matter of Context," *Journal of Psychology* 140, no. 3 (2006): 269-288.

33. D. W. Johnson *et al.*, "Effects of Cooperative, Competitive, and Individualistic Goal Structures on Achievement: A Meta-Analysis," *Psychological Bulletin* 89 (1981): 47-62; Rahim, "Toward a Theory of Managing Organizational Conflict."

34. R. A. Friedman *et al.*, "What Goes around Comes Around: The Impact of Personal Conflict Style on Work Conflict and Stress," *International Journal of Conflict Management* 11, no. 1 (2000): 32-55; X. M. Song, J. Xile, and B. Dyer, "Antecedents and Consequences of Marketing Managers' Conflict-Handling Behaviours," *Journal of Marketing* 64 (January 2000): 50-66; M. Song, B. Dyer, and R. J. Thieme, "Conflict Management and Innovation Performance: An Integrated Contingency Perspective," *Academy of Marketing Science* 34, no. 3 (2006): 341-356; L. A. DeChurch, K. L. Hamilton, and C. Haas, "Effects of Conflict Management Strategies on Perceptions of Intragroup Conflict," *Group Dynamics* 11, no. 1 (2007): 66-78.

35. C. K. W. De Dreu and A. E. M. Van Vianen, "Managing Relationship Conflict and the Effectiveness of Organizational Teams," *Journal of Organizational Behaviour* 22 (2001): 309-328; R. J. Lewicki *et al.*, *Negotiation*, 4th ed. (Burr Ridge, Ill.: McGraw-Hill/Irwin, 2003), pp. 35-36.

36. D. Cox, "Goodenow's Downfall," *Toronto Star*, 29 July 2005, A1; A. Maki, "NHLPA's New Leader Is a Peacemaker, Not Warrior," *Globe & Mail*, 29 July 2005, S1; M. Spector, "Players: He Is Your Father," *National Post*, 29 July 2005, B8; "Report: Saskin Had Friends at NHL Head Office," *CanWest Newes Service*, 13 October 2007; C. Masisak, "For Kelly, It's a Big Job," *Washington Times*, 4 December 2007; R. Westhead, "Report: 'Big Brother' Spied on NHL Players," *Toronto Star*, 30 May 2007; M. Spector, "Nhlpa Enjoys Breath of Fresh Air," *Globe & Mail*, 12 January 2008.

37. K. Lewin, *Resolving Social Conflicts* (New York: Harper, 1948).

38. J. D. Hunger and L. W. Stern, "An Assessment of the Functionality of the Superordinate Goal in Reducing Conflict," *Academy of Management Journal* 19, no. 4 (1976): 591-605 M. Sherif, "Superordinate Goals in the Reduction of Intergroup Conflict," *The American Journal of Sociology* 63, no. 4 (1958): 349-356.

39. M. Sherif, "Superordinate Goals in the Reduction of Intergroup Conflict," *American Journal of Sociology* 68 (1958): 349-358; Eisenhardt, Kahwajy, and Bourgeois III, "How Management Teams Can Have a Good Fight"; Song, Xile, and Dyer, "Antecedents and Consequences of Marketing Managers' Conflict-Handling Behaviours."

40. H. C. Triandis, "The Future of Workforce Diversity in International Organisations: A Commentary," *Applied Psychology: An International Journal* 52, no. 3 (2003): 486-495.

41. E. Elron, B. Shamir, and E. Bem-Ari, "Why Don't They Fight Each Other? Cultural Diversity and Operational Unity in Multinational Forces," *Armed Forces & Society* 26 (October 1999): 73-97; "Teamwork Polishes This Diamond," *Philippine Daily Inquirer*, 4 October 2000, 10.

42. T. F. Pettigrew, "Intergroup Contact Theory," *Annual Review of Psychology* 49 (1998): 65-85; S. Brickson, "The Impact of Identity Orientation on Individual and Organizational Outcomes in Demographically Diverse Settings," *Academy of Management Review* 25 (January 2000): 82-101; J. Dixon and K. Durrheim, "Contact and the Ecology of Racial Division: Some Varieties of Informal Segregation," *British Journal of Social Psychology* 42 (March 2003): 1-23.

43. Triandis, "The Future of Workforce Diversity in International Organisations."

44. Von Glinow, Shapiro, and Brett, "Can We Talk, and Should We?"

45. K. R. Lewis, "(Drum) Beatings Build Corporate Spirit," *Star Tribune (Minneapolis, Minn.)*, 3 June 2003, 3E; D. McMurdy, "Marching to a Different Drummer," *Vancouver Sun*, 26 April 2004, D4; S. Wintrob, "Drum Circles Encourage Rhythm in Companies," *National Post*, 30 July 2005, FW3.

46. E. Horwitt, "Knowledge, Knowledge, Who's Got the Knowledge," *Computerworld* (April 8 1996): 80, 81, 84.

47. For a critical view of the problem solving style in negotiation, see: J. M. Brett, "Managing Organizational Conflict," *Professional Psychology: Research and Practice* 15 (1984): 664-678.

48. R. E. Fells, "Developing Trust in Negotiation," *Employee Relations* 15 (1993): 33-45; R. E. Fells, "Overcoming the Dilemmas in Walton and Mckersie's Mixed Bargaining Strategy," *Industrial Relations (Laval)* 53 (March 1998): 300-325.

49. R. Stagner and H. Rosen, *Psychology of Union--Management Relations* (Belmont, Calif.: Wadsworth, 1965), pp. 95-96, 108-110; R. E. Walton and R. B. McKersie, *A Behavioural Theory of Labor Negotiations: An Analysis of a Social Interaction System* (New York: McGraw-Hill, 1965), pp. 41-46; L. Thompson, *The Mind and Heart of the Negotiator* (Upper Saddle River, NJ: Prentice-Hall, 1998), Chap. 2.

50. J. W. Salacuse and J. Z. Rubin, "Your Place or Mine? Site Location and Negotiation," *Negotiation Journal* 6 (January 1990): 5-10; J. Mayfield *et al.*, "How Location Impacts International Business Negotiations," *Review of Business* 19 (December 1998): 21-24.

51. J. Margo, "The Persuaders," *Boss Magazine*, 29 December 2000, 38. For a full discussion of the advantages and disadvantages of face-to-face and alternative negotiations situations, see: M. H. Bazerman et al., "Negotiation," *Annual Review of Psychology* 51 (2000): 279-314.

52. A. F. Stuhlmacher, T. L. Gillespie, and M. V. Champagne, "The Impact of Time Pressure in Negotiation: A Meta-Analysis," *International Journal of Conflict Manage-*

ment 9, no. 2 (April 1998): 97-116; C. K. W. De Dreu, "Time Pressure and Closing of the Mind in Negotiation," *Organizational Behaviour and Human Decision Processes* 91 (July 2003): 280-295. However, one recent study reported that speeding up these concessions leads to better negotiated outcomes. See: D. A. Moore, "Myopic Prediction, Self-Destructive Secrecy, and the Unexpected Benefits of Revealing Final Deadlines in Negotiation," *Organizational Behaviour and Human Decision Processes* 94, no. 2 (2004): 125-139.

53. Lewicki *et al.*, *Negotiation*, pp. 298-322.

54. S. Doctoroff, "Reengineering Negotiations," *Sloan Management Review* 39 (March 1998): 63-71; D. C. Zetik and A. F. Stuhlmacher, "Goal Setting and Negotiation Performance: A Meta-Analysis," *Group Processes & Intergroup Relations* 5 (January 2002): 35-52.

55. B. McRae, *The Seven Strategies of Master Negotiators* (Toronto: McGraw-Hill Ryerson, 2002), pp. 7-11.

56. L. L. Thompson, "Information Exchange in Negotiation," *Journal of Experimental Social Psychology* 27 (1991): 161-179.

57. L. Thompson, E. Peterson, and S. E. Brodt, "Team Negotiation: An Examinaton of Integrative and Distributive Bargaining," *Journal of Personality and Social Psychology* 70 (1996): 66-78; Y. Paik and R. L. Tung, "Negotiating with East Asians: How to Attain "Win-Win" Outcomes," *Management International Review* 39 (1999): 103-122.

58. D. J. O'Keefe, *Persuasion: Theory and Research* (Thousand Oaks, CA: Sage Publications, 2002).

59. Lewicki *et al.*, *Negotiation*, pp. 90-96; S. Kwon and L. R. Weingart, "Unilateral Concessions from the Other Party: Concession Behaviour, Attributions, and Negotiation Judgments," *Journal of Applied Psychology* 89, no. 2 (2004): 263-278.

60. J. J. Zhao, "The Chinese Approach to International Business Negotiation," *Journal of Business Communication* (July 2000): 209-237; N. Crundwell, "U.S.-Russian Negotiating Strategies," *BISNIS Bulletin*, October 2003, 5-6.

61. J. Z. Rubin and B. R. Brown, *The Social Psychology of Bargaining and Negotiation* (New York: Academic Press, 1976), Chap. 9.

62. L. L. Putnam, "Beyond Third Party Role: Disputes and Managerial Intervention," *Employee Responsibilities and Rights Journal* 7 (1994): 23-36; A. R. Elangovan, "The Manager as the Third Party: Deciding How to Intervene in Employee Disputes," in *Negotiation: Readings, Exercises, and Cases*, ed. R. J. Lewicki, J. A. Litterer,

and D. Saunders, Third ed. (New York: McGraw-Hill, 1999), 458-469. For a somewhat different taxonomy of managerial conflict intervention, see: P. G. Irving and J. P. Meyer, "A Multidimensional Scaling Analysis of Managerial Third-Party Conflict Intervention Strategies," *Canadian Journal of Behavioural Science* 29, no. 1 (January 1997): 7-18. A recent review describes 10 species of third-party intervention, but these consist of variations of the three types described here. See: D. E. Conlon *et al.*, "Third Party Interventions across Cultures: No 'One Best Choice,'" in *Research in Personnel and Human Resources Management* (JAI, 2007), 309-349.

63. B. H. Sheppard, "Managers as Inquisitors: Lessons from the Law," in *Bargaining inside Organizations*, ed. M. H. Bazerman and R. J. Lewicki (Beverly Hills, CA: Sage, 1983); N. H. Kim, D. W. Sohn, and J. A. Wall, "Korean Leaders' (and Subordinates') Conflict Management," *International Journal Of Conflict Management* 10, no. 2 (April 1999): 130-153.

64. R. Karambayya and J. M. Brett, "Managers Handling Disputes: Third Party Roles and Perceptions of Fairness," *Academy of Management Journal* 32 (1989): 687-704; R. Cropanzano *et al.*, "Disputant Reactions to Managerial Conflict Resolution Tactics," *Group & Organization Management* 24 (June 1999): 124-153.

65. This information is found at: RBC Corporate Responsibility: Workplace: Engagement (www.rbc.com/responsibility/workplace/engagement.html). Accessed 30 April 2008.

66. A. R. Elangovan, "Managerial Intervention in Organizational Disputes: Testing a Prescriptive Model of Strategy Selection," *International Journal of Conflict Management* 4 (1998): 301-335; P. S. Nugent, "Managing Conflict: Third-Party Interventions for Managers," *Academy Of Management Executive* 16, no. 1 (February 2002): 139-154.

67. J. P. Meyer, J. M. Gemmell, and P. G. Irving, "Evaluating the Management of Interpersonal Conflict in Organizations: A Factor-Analytic Study of Outcome Criteria," *Canadian Journal of Administrative Sciences* 14 (1997): 1-13; M. Hyde *et al.*, "Workplace Conflict Resolution and the Health of Employees in the Swedish and Finnish Units of an Industrial Company," *Social Science & Medicine* 63, no. 8 (2006): 2218-2227.

Chapter 12

1. "Circus Founder Is Canada's Entrepreneur of the Year," Ernst & Young News release, (Ottawa: 2 November 2006); "#664 Guy Laliberte," (New York: Forbes.com, 2007), www.forbes.com/lists/2007/10/07billionaires_Guy-Laliberte_SY4I.html, (accessed 5 May 2008); G. Pitts, "Leading in the Shadow of Genius," *Globe & Mail*, 27 August 2007; G. Pitts, "The Tension between Freedom and Direction," *Globe & Mail*, 26 April 2007; K. Yakabuski, "The Greatest Canadian Company on Earth," *Report on Business Magazine (Globe & Mail)*, 31 August 2007.

2. R. House, M. Javidan, and P. Dorfman, "Project Globe: An Introduction," *Applied Psychology: An International Review* 50 (2001): 489-505; R. House *et al.*, "Understanding Cultures and Implicit Leadership Theories across the Globe: An Introduction to Project Globe," *Journal of World Business* 37 (2002): 3-10.

3. R. G. Isaac, W. J. Zerbe, and D. C. Pitt, "Leadership and Motivation: The Effective Application of Expectancy Theory," *Journal of Managerial Issues* 13 (Summer 2001): 212-226; C. L. Pearce and J. A. Conger, eds., *Shared Leadership: Reframing the Hows and Whys of Leadership* (Thousand Oaks, Calif: Sage, 2003); J. S. Nielson, *The Myth of Leadership* (Palo Alto, Calif.: Davies-Black, 2004); J. A. Raelin, "We the Leaders: In Order to Form a Leaderful Organization," *Journal of Leadership & Organizational Studies* 12, no. 2 (2005): 18-30.

4. A. Deutschman, "The Fabric of Creativity," *Fast Company*, December 2004, 54-; P. J. Kiger, "Power to the Individual," *Workforce Management*, 27 Feb. 2006, 1-7; G. Hamel, *The Future of Management* (Boston: Harvard Business School Press, 2007), Chap. 5.

5. J. A. Raelin, *Creating Leadersful Organizations: How to Bring out Leadership in Everyone* (San Francisco: Berret-Koehler, 2003).

6. S. Whittaker, "Good Ideas Should Not Be Hidden Away," *Montreal Gazette*, 28 July 2007.

7. L. Gyulai, "It Takes Children to Raise a Village," *Montreal Gazette*, 30 July 2005, A14; Time Canada, "Time Magazine Celebrates Canada's Heroes with Third Annual List," CanadaNewsWire News release, (Toronto: 11 June 2006).

8. Many of these perspectives are summarized in R. N. Kanungo, "Leadership in Organizations: Looking Ahead to the 21st Century," *Canadian Psychology* 39 (Spring 1998): 71-82; G. A. Yukl, *Leadership in Organizations*, 6th ed. (Upper Saddle River, NJ: Pearson Education, 2006).

9. The history of the trait perspective of leadership, as well as currently research on this topic, is nicely summarized in: S. J. Zaccaro, C. Kemp, and P. Bader, "Leader Traits and Attributes," in *The Nature of Leadership*, ed. J. Antonakis, A. T. Cianci-

olo, and R. J. Sternberg (Thousand Oaks, CA: Sage, 2004), 101-124.

10. R. M. Stogdill, *Handbook of Leadership* (New York: The Free Press, 1974), Chap. 5.

11. J. Intagliata, D. Ulrich, and N. Smallwood, "Leveraging Leadership Competencies to Produce Leadership Brand: Creating Distinctiveness by Focusing on Strategy and Results," *Human Resources Planning* 23, no. 4 (2000): 12-23; J. A. Conger and D. A. Ready, "Rethinking Leadership Competencies," *Leader to Leader* (Spring 2004): 41-47; Zaccaro, Kemp, and Bader, "Leader Traits and Attributes."

12. This list is based on: S. A. Kirkpatrick and E. A. Locke, "Leadership: Do Traits Matter?" *Academy of Management Executive* 5 (May 1991): 48-60; R. M. Aditya, R. J. House, and S. Kerr, "Theory and Practice of Leadership: Into the New Millennium," in *Industrial and Organizational Psychology: Linking Theory with Practice*, ed. C. L. Cooper and E. A. Locke (Oxford, UK: Blackwell, 2000), 130-165; D. Goleman, R. Boyatzis, and A. McKee, *Primal Leaders* (Boston: Harvard Business School Press, 2002); T. A. Judge *et al.*, "Personality and Leadership: A Qualitative and Quantitative Review," *Journal Of Applied Psychology* 87, no. 4 (August 2002): 765-780; T. A. Judge, A. E. Colbert, and R. Ilies, "Intelligence and Leadership: A Quantitative Review and Test of Theoretical Propositions," *Journal Of Applied Psychology* 89, no. 3 (June 2004): 542-552; Zaccaro, Kemp, and Bader, "Leader Traits and Attributes."

13. M. Popper *et al.*, "The Capacity to Lead: Major Psychological Differences between Leaders and Nonleaders," *Military Psychology* 16, no. 4 (2004): 245-263.

14. B. George, *Authentic Leadership* (San Francisco: Jossey-Bass, 2004); W. L. Gardner *et al.*, "'Can You See the Real Me?' a Self-Based Model of Authentic Leader and Follower Development," *Leadership Quarterly* 16 (2005): 343-372; B. George, *True North* (San Francisco: Jossey-Bass, 2007), Chap. 4; M. E. Palanski and F. J. Yammarino, "Integrity and Leadership:: Clearing the Conceptual Confusion," *European Management Journal* 25, no. 3 (2007): 171-184.

15. R. Charan, C. Burke, and L. Bossidy, *Execution: The Discipline of Getting Things Done* (New York: Crown Business, 2002); D. Nilsen, B. Kowske, and A. Kshanika, "Managing Globally," *HRMagazine*, August 2005, 111-115.

16. The large-scale studies are reported in: C. Savoye, "Workers Say Honesty Is Best Company Policy," *Christian Science Monitor*, June 15 2000; J. M. Kouzes and B. Z. Posner, *The Leadership Challenge*, 3rd ed. (San Francisco: Jossey-Bass, 2002), Chap.

2; J. Schettler, "Leadership in Corporate America," *Training & Development*, September 2002, 66-73.

17. Watson Wyatt Worldwide, "Asia-Pacific Workers Satisfied with Jobs Despite Some Misgivings with Management and Pay," Watson Wyatt Worldwide News release, (Singapore: 16 November 2004); J. Cremer, "Asian Workers Give Low Marks to Leaders," *South China Morning Post (Hong Kong)*, 30 July 2005, 8; D. Jones, "Optimism Puts Rose-Colored Tint in Glasses of Top Execs," *USA Today*, 16 December 2005, B1; E. Pondel, "Friends & Bosses?," *Seattle Post-Intelligencer*, 10 April 2006, C1.

18. R. Davidovitz *et al.*, "Leaders as Attachment Figures: Leaders' Attachment Orientations Predict Leadership-Related Mental Representations and Followers' Performance and Mental Health," *Journal of Personality and Social Psychology* 93, no. 4 (2007): 632-650.

19. J. B. Miner, "Twenty Years of Research on Role Motivation Theory of Managerial Effectiveness," *Personnel Psychology* 31 (1978): 739-760; R. J. House and R. N. Aditya, "The Social Scientific Study of Leadership: Quo Vadis?" *Journal of Management* 23 (1997): 409-473.

20. J. Hedlund *et al.*, "Identifying and Assessing Tacit Knowledge: Understanding the Practical Intelligence of Military Leaders," *Leadership Quarterly* 14, no. 2 (2003): 117-140; R. J. Sternberg, "A Systems Model of Leadership: Wics," *American Psychologist* 62, no. 1 (2007): 34-42.

21. J. George, "Emotions and Leadership: The Role of Emotional Intelligence," *Human Relations* 53 (August 2000): 1027-1055; Goleman, Boyatzis, and McKee, *Primal Leaders*; R. G. Lord and R. J. Hall, "Identity, Deep Structure and the Development of Leadership Skill," *Leadership Quarterly* 16, no. 4 (August 2005): 591-615; C. Skinner and P. Spurgeon, "Valuing Empathy and Emotional Intelligence in Health Leadership: A Study of Empathy, Leadership Behaviour and Outcome Effectiveness," *Health Services Management Research* 18, no. 1 (February 2005): 1-12.

22. R. Jacobs, "Using Human Resource Functions to Enhance Emotional Intelligence," in *The Emotionally Intelligent Workplace* ed. C. Cherniss and D. Goleman (San Francisco: Jossey-Bass, 2001), 161-163; Conger and Ready, "Rethinking Leadership Competencies."

23. R. G. Lord and D. J. Brown, *Leadership Processes and Self-Identity: A Follower-Centered Approach to Leadership* (Mahwah, NJ: Lawrence Erlbaum Associates, 2004); R. Bolden and J. Gosling, "Leadership Competencies: Time to Change the Tune?" *Leadership* 2, no. 2 (May 2006): 147-163.

24. P. G. Northouse, *Leadership: Theory and Practice*, 3rd ed. (Thousand Oaks, CA: Sage, 2004), Chap. 4; Yukl, *Leadership in Organizations*, Chap. 3.

25. A. K. Korman, "Consideration, Initiating Structure, and Organizational Criteria—a Review," *Personnel Psychology* 19 (1966): 349-362; E. A. Fleishman, "Twenty Years of Consideration and Structure," in *Current Developments in the Study of Leadership*, ed. E. A. Fleishman and J. C. Hunt (Carbondale, Ill.: Southern Illinois University Press, 1973), 1-40; T. A. Judge, R. F. Piccolo, and R. Ilies, "The Forgotten Ones?: The Validity of Consideration and Initiating Structure in Leadership Research," *Journal of Applied Psychology* 89, no. 1 (2004): 36-51; Yukl, *Leadership in Organizations*, pp. 62-75.

26. V. V. Baba, "Serendipity in Leadership: Initiating Structure and Consideration in the Classroom," *Human Relations* 42 (1989): 509-525.

27. S. Kerr *et al.*, "Towards a Contingency Theory of Leadership Based upon the Consideration and Initiating Structure Literature," *Organizational Behavior and Human Performance* 12 (1974): 62-82; L. L. Larson, J. G. Hunt, and R. N. Osbom, "The Great Hi--Hi Leader Behavior Myth: A Lesson from Occam's Razor," *Academy of Management Journal* 19 (1976): 628-641.

28. R. Tannenbaum and W. H. Schmidt, "How to Choose a Leadership Pattern," *Harvard Business Review* (May-June 1973): 162-180.

29. For a thorough study of how expectancy theory of motivation relates to leadership, see: Isaac, Zerbe, and Pitt, "Leadership and Motivation: The Effective Application of Expectancy Theory."

30. R. J. House, "A Path-Goal Theory of Leader Effectiveness," *Administrative Science Quarterly* 16 (1971): 321-338; M. G. Evans, "Extensions of a Path-Goal Theory of Motivation," *Journal of Applied Psychology* 59 (1974): 172-178; R. J. House and T. R. Mitchell, "Path-Goal Theory of Leadership," *Journal of Contemporary Business* (Autumn 1974): 81-97; M. G. Evans, "Path Goal Theory of Leadership," in *Leadership*, ed. L. L. Neider and C. A. Schriesheim (Greenwich, CT: Information Age Publishing, 2002), 115-138.

31. Various thoughts on servant leadership are presented in: L. C. Spears and M. Lawrence, eds., *Focus on Leadership: Servant-Leadership* (New York: John Wiley & Sons, 2002).

32. D. Tarrant, "The Leading Edge," *The Bulletin*, 15 November 2005; "2006 Movers & Shakers," *Financial Planning*, January 2006, 1.

33. R. J. House, "Path-Goal Theory of Leadership: Lessons, Legacy, and a Refor-

mulated Theory," *Leadership Quarterly* 7 (1996): 323-352.

34. "Why Geotechnical Instruments Boss Draper Is One in a Million," *Birmingham Post (United Kingdom)*, 2 June 2006, 26; N. Whitten, "Best Boss Sets Examples to Staff," *Evening Chronicle (Newcastle, U.K.)*, 15 June 2006, 24.

35. J. Indvik, "Path-Goal Theory of Leadership: A Meta-Analysis," *Academy of Management Proceedings* (1986): 189-192; J. C. Wofford and L. Z. Liska, "Path-Goal Theories of Leadership: A Meta-Analysis," *Journal of Management* 19 (1993): 857-876.

36. J. D. Houghton and S. K. Yoho, "Toward a Contingency Model of Leadership and Psychological Empowerment: When Should Self-Leadership Be Encouraged?" *Journal of Leadership & Organizational Studies* 11, no. 4 (2005): 65-83.

37. R. T. Keller, "A Test of the Path-Goal Theory of Leadership with Need for Clarity as a Moderator in Research and Development Organizations," *Journal of Applied Psychology* 74 (1989): 208-212.

38. C. A. Schriesheim and L. L. Neider, "Path-Goal Leadership Theory: The Long and Winding Road," *Leadership Quarterly* 7 (1996): 317-321.

39. P. Hersey and K. H. Blanchard, *Management of Organizational Behavior: Utilizing Human Resources*, 5th ed. (Englewood Cliffs, N.J.: Prentice Hall, 1988).

40. R. P. Vecchio, "Situational Leadership Theory: An Examination of a Prescriptive Theory," *Journal of Applied Psychology* 72 (1987): 444-451; W. Blank, J. R. Weitzel, and S. G. Green, "A Test of the Situational Leadership Theory," *Personnel Psychology* 43 (1990): 579-597; C. L. Graeff, "Evolution of Situational Leadership Theory: A Critical Review," *Leadership Quarterly* 8 (1997): 153-170.

41. F. E. Fiedler, *A Theory of Leadership Effectiveness* (New York: McGraw-Hill, 1967); F. E. Fiedler and M. M. Chemers, *Leadership and Effective Management* (Glenview, Ill.: Scott, Foresman, 1974).

42. F. E. Fiedler, "Engineer the Job to Fit the Manager," *Harvard Business Review* 43, no. 5 (1965): 115-122.

43. For a summary of criticisms, see: Yukl, *Leadership in Organizations*, pp. 217-218.

44. N. Nicholson, *Executive Instinct* (New York: Crown, 2000).

45. This observation has also been made by C. A. Schriesheim, "Substitutes-for-Leadership Theory: Development and Basic Concepts," *Leadership Quarterly* 8 (1997): 103-108.

46. D. F. Elloy and A. Randolph, "The Effect of Superleader Behavior on Autonomous Work Groups in a Government Operated Railway Service," *Public Personnel Management* 26 (Summer 1997): 257-272; C. C. Manz and H. Sims Jr., *The New SuperLeadership: Leading Others to Lead Themselves* (San Francisco: Berrett-Koehler, 2001).

47. M. L. Loughry, "Coworkers Are Watching: Performance Implications of Peer Monitoring," *Academy of Management Proceedings* (2002): O1-O6.

48. C. C. Manz and C. Neck, *Mastering Self-Leadership*, 3rd ed. (Upper Saddle River, NJ: Prentice Hall, 2004).

49. P. M. Podsakoff and S. B. MacKenzie, "Kerr and Jermier's Substitutes for Leadership Model: Background, Empirical Assessment, and Suggestions for Future Research," *Leadership Quarterly* 8 (1997): 117-132; S. D. Dionne et al., "Neutralizing Substitutes for Leadership Theory: Leadership Effects and Common-Source Bias," *Journal Of Applied Psychology* 87, no. 3 (June 2002): 454-464; J. R. Villa et al., "Problems with Detecting Moderators in Leadership Research Using Moderated Multiple Regression," *Leadership Quarterly* 14, no. 1 (February 2003): 3-23; S. D. Dionne et al., "Substitutes for Leadership, or Not," *The Leadership Quarterly* 16, no. 1 (2005): 169-193.

50. D. Menzies, "From Beer to Eternity," *Profit*, October 2000, 58; "CEO Buys Control of Hamilton's Lakeport Brewing," *Kitchener-Waterloo Record*, 7 January 2005, A10; E. Kobayashi, "Brewing up Business," *National Post*, 1 April 2005, 78; S. Nagy, "Teresa Casciolli," *Globe & Mail*, 21 September 2005.

51. J. M. Burns, *Leadership* (New York: Harper & Row, 1978); B. M. Bass, *Transformational Leadership: Industrial, Military, and Educational Impact* (Hillsdale, NJ: Erlbaum, 1998); S. B. Proctor-Thomson and K. W. Parry, "What the Best Leaders Look Like," in *Leadership in the Antipodes: Findings, Implications and a Leader Profile*, ed. K. W. Parry (Wellington, N. Z.: Institute of Policy Studies and Centre for the Study of Leadership, 2001), 166-191; B. J. Avolio and F. J. Yammarino, eds., *Transformational and Charismatic Leadership: The Road Ahead* (Greenwich, CT: JAI Press, 2002).

52. V. L. Goodwin, J. C. Wofford, and J. L. Whittington "A Theoretical and Empirical Extension to the Transformational Leadership Construct," *Journal of Organizational Behavior*, 22 (November 2001), pp. 759-774.

53. A. Zaleznik, "Managers and Leaders: Are They Different?" *Harvard Business Review* 55, no. 5 (1977): 67-78; W. Bennis and B. Nanus, *Leaders: The Strategies for Taking Charge* (New York: Harper & Row, 1985). For a recent discussion regarding managing versus leading, see: G. Yukl and R. Lepsinger, "Why Integrating the Leading and Managing Roles Is Essential for Organizational Effectiveness," *Organizational Dynamics* 34, no. 4 (2005): 361-375.

54. Both transformational and transactional leadership improve work unit performance. See: B. M. Bass et al., "Predicting Unit Performance by Assessing Transformational and Transactional Leadership," *Journal of Applied Psychology* 88 (April 2003): 207-218. This point is also argued in: Yukl and Lepsinger, "Why Integrating the Leading and Managing Roles Is Essential for Organizational Effectiveness."

55. For discussion on the tendency to slide from transformational to transactional leadership, see: W. Bennis, *An Invented Life: Reflections on Leadership and Change* (Reading, MA: Addison-Wesley, 1993).

56. R. J. House, "A 1976 Theory of Charismatic Leadership," in *Leadership: The Cutting Edge*, ed. J. G. Hunt and L. L. Larson (Carbondale, IL.: Southern Illinois University Press, 1977), 189-207; J. A. Conger, "Charismatic and Transformational Leadership in Organizations: An Insider's Perspective on These Developing Streams of Research," *Leadership Quarterly* 10 (Summer 1999): 145-179.

57. J. Barbuto, J. E., "Taking the Charisma out of Transformational Leadership," *Journal of Social Behavior & Personality* 12 (September 1997): 689-697; Y. A. Nur, "Charisma and Managerial Leadership: The Gift That Never Was," *Business Horizons* 41 (July 1998): 19-26; M. D. Mumford and J. R. Van Doorn, "The Leadership of Pragmatism - Reconsidering Franklin in the Age of Charisma," *Leadership Quarterly* 12, no. 3 (Fall 2001): 279-309; A. Fanelli, "Bringing out Charisma: CEO Charisma and External Stakeholders," *The Academy of Management review* 31, no. 4 (2006): 1049-1061; M. J. Platow et al., "A Special Gift We Bestow on You for Being Representative of Us: Considering Leader Charisma from a Self-Categorization Perspective," *British Journal of Social Psychology* 45, no. 2 (2006): 303-320.

58. B. Shamir et al., "Correlates of Charismatic Leader Behavior in Military Units: Subordinates' Attitudes, Unit Characteristics, and Superiors' Appraisals of Leader Performance," *Academy of Management Journal* 41, no. 4 (1998): 387-409; R. E. De Vries, R. A. Roe, and T. C. B. Taillieu, "On Charisma and Need for Leadership," *European Journal of Work and Organizational Psychology* 8 (1999): 109-133; R. Khurana, *Searching for a Corporate Savior: The Irrational Quest for Charismatic CEOs* (Princeton, NJ: Princeton University Press, 2002).

59. K. Brooker and J. Schlosser, "The Un-CEO," *Fortune*, 16 September 2002, 88-93; B. Nussbaum, "The Power of Design," *BusinessWeek*, 17 May 2004, 86; N. Buckley, "The Calm Reinventor," *Financial Times*

(London), 29 January 2005, 11; S. Ellison, "Women's Touch Guides P&G Chief's Firm Hand in Company Turnaround," *Wall Street Journal Europe*, 1 June 2005, A1; S. Hill Jr., "P&G's Turnaround Proves Listening to Customer Pays," *Manufacturing Business Technology*, July 2005, 64; J. Tylee, "Procter's Creative Gamble," *Campaign*, 18 March 2005, 24-26.

60. D. Olive, "The 7 Deadly Chief Executive Sins," *Toronto Star*, 17 February 2004, D01.

61. Y. Berson et al., "The Relationship between Vision Strength, Leadership Style, and Context," *The Leadership Quarterly* 12, no. 1 (2001): 53-73.

62. N. Nilekani, "How Do I Develop Next Generation Leaders," *Economic Times (India)*, 25 November 2005.

63. Bennis and Nanus, *Leaders*, pp. 27-33, 89; I. M. Levin, "Vision Revisited," *Journal of Applied Behavioral Science* 36 (March 2000): 91-107; R. E. Quinn, *Building the Bridge as You Walk on It: A Guide for Leading Change* (San Francisco: Jossey-Bass, 2004), Chap. 11; J. M. Strange and M. D. Mumford, "The Origins of Vision: Effects of Reflection, Models, and Analysis," *Leadership Quarterly* 16, no. 1 (2005): 121-148.

64. J. R. Baum, E. A. Locke, and S. A. Kirkpatrick, "A Longitudinal Study of the Relation of Vision and Vision Communication to Venture Growth in Entrepreneurial Firms," *Journal of Applied Psychology* 83 (1998): 43-54; S. L. Hoe and S. L. McShane, "Leadership Antecedents of Informal Knowledge Acquisition and Dissemination," *International Journal of Organisational Behaviour* 5 (2002): 282-291.

65. P. Quinn, "Management Team a Swimming Success," *National Post*, 3 February 2006; P. Waldie, "Newfoundland: The 'Promised Land' of Fishing," *Globe & Mail*, 28 October 2006; "Cooke Aquaculture," *National Post*, 3 December 2007; Ernst & Young, "Glenn Cooke, Cooke Aquaculture Inc. CEO, Named Ernst & Young Entrepreneur of the Year® 2007 for the Atlantic Region," Ernst & Young News release, (Halifax: 19 September 2007).

66. L. Manfield, "Creating a Safety Culture from Top to Bottom," *WorkSafe Magazine*, February 2005, 8-9. The Canadian CEO survey is reported in: "Canadian CEOs Give Themselves Top Marks for Leadership!" *Canada NewsWire*, 9 September 1999.

67. J. A. Conger, "Inspiring Others: The Language of Leadership," *Academy of Management Executive* 5 (February 1991): 31-45; G. T. Fairhurst and R. A. Sarr, *The Art of Framing: Managing the Language of Leadership* (San Francisco, CA: Jossey-Bass, 1996); A. E. Rafferty and M. A. Griffin, "Dimensions of Transformational

Leadership: Conceptual and Empirical Extensions," *Leadership Quarterly* 15, no. 3 (2004): 329-354.

68. S. Franklin, *The Heroes: A Saga of Canadian Inspiration* (Toronto: McClelland and Stewart, 1967); L. Black, "Hamburger Diplomacy," *Report on Business Magazine* August 1988, 30-36.

69. D. E. Berlew, "Leadership and Organizational Excitement," *California Management Review* 17, no. 2 (Winter 1974): 21-30; Bennis and Nanus, *Leaders*, pp. 43-55; T. Simons, "Behavioral Integrity: The Perceived Alignment between Managers' Words and Deeds as a Research Focus," *Organization Science* 13, no. 1 (Jan-Feb 2002): 18-35.

70. S. Ewart, "Unique Suncor Boasts Unique CEO," *Calgary Herald*, 11 September 1999, 1. For discussion of trust in leadership, see: C. S. Burke et al., "Trust in Leadership: A Multi-Level Review and Integration," *Leadership Quarterly* 18, no. 6 (2007): 606-632.

71. J. Barling, T. Weber, and E. K. Kelloway, "Effects of Transformational Leadership Training on Attitudinal and Financial Outcomes: A Field Experiment," *Journal of Applied Psychology* 81 (1996): 827-832.

72. A. Bryman, "Leadership in Organizations," in *Handbook of Organization Studies*, ed. S. R. Clegg, C. Hardy, and W. R. Nord (Thousand Oaks, CA: Sage, 1996), 276-292.

73. B. S. Pawar and K. K. Eastman, "The Nature and Implications of Contextual Influences on Transformational Leadership: A Conceptual Examination," *Academy of Management Review* 22 (1997): 80-109; C. P. Egri and S. Herman, "Leadership in the North American Environmental Sector: Values, Leadership Styles, and Contexts of Environmental Leaders and Their Organizations," *Academy of Management Journal* 43, no. 4 (2000): 571-604.

74. J. R. Meindl, "On Leadership: An Alternative to the Conventional Wisdom," *Research in Organizational Behavior* 12 (1990): 159-203; L. R. Offermann, J. J. K. Kennedy, and P. W. Wirtz, "Implicit Leadership Theories: Content, Structure, and Generalizability," *Leadership Quarterly* 5, no. 1 (1994): 43-58; R. J. Hall and R. G. Lord, "Multi-Level Information Processing Explanations of Followers' Leadership Perceptions," *Leadership Quarterly* 6 (1995): 265-287; O. Epitropaki and R. Martin, "Implicit Leadership Theories in Applied Settings: Factor Structure, Generalizability, and Stability over Time," *Journal of Applied Psychology* 89, no. 2 (2004): 293-310.

75. R. G. Lord et al., "Contextual Constraints on Prototype Generation and Their Multilevel Consequences for Leader-

ship Perceptions," *Leadership Quarterly* 12, no. 3 (2001): 311-338; T. Keller, "Parental Images as a Guide to Leadership Sensemaking: An Attachment Perspective on Implicit Leadership Theories," *Leadership Quarterly* 14 (2003): 141-160; K. A. Scott and D. J. Brown, "Female First, Leader Second? Gender Bias in the Encoding of Leadership Behavior," *Organizational Behavior and Human Decision Processes* 101 (2006): 230-242.

76. R. Ilies, M. W. Gerhardt, and H. Le, "Individual Differences in Leadership Emergence: Integrating Meta-Analytic Findings and Behavioral Genetics Estimates," *International Journal of Selection and Assessment* 12, no. 3 (September 2004): 207-219.

77. S. F. Cronshaw and R. G. Lord, "Effects of Categorization, Attribution, and Encoding Processes on Leadership Perceptions," *Journal of Applied Psychology* 72 (1987): 97-106; J. L. Nye and D. R. Forsyth, "The Effects of Prototype-Based Biases on Leadership Appraisals: A Test of Leadership Categorization Theory," *Small Group Research* 22 (1991): 360-379.

78. Meindl, "On Leadership: An Alternative to the Conventional Wisdom"; J. Felfe and L.-E. Petersen, "Romance of Leadership and Management Decision Making," *European Journal of Work and Organizational Psychology* 16, no. 1 (2007): 1-24; B. Schyns, J. R. Meindl, and M. A. Croon, "The Romance of Leadership Scale: Cross-Cultural Testing and Refinement," *Leadership* 3, no. 1 (February 2007): 29-46.

79. J. Pfeffer, "The Ambiguity of Leadership," *Academy of Management Review* 2 (1977): 102-112.

80. R. Weber et al., "The Illusion of Leadership: Misattribution of Cause in Coordination Games," *Organization Science* 12, no. 5 (2001): 582-598; N. Ensari and S. E. Murphy, "Cross-Cultural Variations in Leadership Perceptions and Attribution of Charisma to the Leader," *Organizational Behavior and Human Decision Processes* 92 (2003): 52-66; M. L. A. Hayward, V. P. Rindova, and T. G. Pollock, "Believing One's Own Press: The Causes and Consequences of CEO Celebrity," *Strategic Management Journal* 25, no. 7 (July 2004): 637-653.

81. G. N. Powell, "One More Time: Do Female and Male Managers Differ?" *Academy of Management Executive* 4 (1990): 68-75; M. L. van Engen and T. M. Willemsen, "Sex and Leadership Styles: A Meta-Analysis of Research Published in the 1990s," *Psychological Reports* 94, no. 1 (February 2004): 3-18.

82. R. Sharpe, "As Leaders, Women Rule," *BusinessWeek*, 20 November 2000, 74; M. Sappenfield, "Women, It Seems, Are Better Bosses," *Christian Science Monitor*, 16

January 2001; A. H. Eagly and L. L. Carli, "The Female Leadership Advantage: An Evaluation of the Evidence," *The Leadership Quarterly* 14, no. 6 (December 2003): 807-834; A. H. Eagly, M. C. Johannesen-Schmidt, and M. L. van Engen, "Transformational, Transactional, and Laissez-Faire Leadership Styles: A Meta-Analysis Comparing Women and Men," *Psychological Bulletin* 129 (July 2003): 569-591.

83. A. H. Eagly, S. J. Karau, and M. G. Makhijani, "Gender and the Effectiveness of Leaders: A Meta-Analysis," *Psychological Bulletin* 117 (1995): 125-145; J. G. Oakley, "Gender-Based Barriers to Senior Management Positions: Understanding the Scarcity of Female CEOs," *Journal of Business Ethics* 27 (2000): 821-834; N. Z. Stelter, "Gender Differences in Leadership: Current Social Issues and Future Organizational Implications," *Journal of Leadership Studies* 8 (2002): 88-99; M. E. Heilman *et al.*, "Penalties for Success: Reactions to Women Who Succeed at Male Gender-Typed Tasks," *Journal of Applied Psychology* 89, no. 3 (2004): 416-427; A. H. Eagly, "Achieving Relational Authenticity in Leadership: Does Gender Matter?" *The Leadership Quarterly* 16, no. 3 (June 2005): 459-474.

Chapter 13

1. R. Muzyka and G. Zeschuk, "Managing Multiple Projects," *Game Developer*, March 2003, 34-42; M. Saltzman, "The Ex Doctors Are In," *National Post*, 24 March 2004, AL4; R. McConnell, "For Edmonton's Bioware, Today's the Big Day," *Edmonton Journal*, 14 April 2005, C1; D. Gladstone and S. Molloy, "Doctors & Dragons," *Computer Gaming World*, December 2006.

2. S. Ranson, R. Hinings, and R. Greenwood, "The Structuring of Organizational Structure," *Administrative Science Quarterly* 25 (1980): 1-14; K. Walsh, "Interpreting the Impact of Culture on Structure," *Journal of Applied Behavioral Science* 40, no. 3 (Sept. 2004): 302-322.

3. B. Morris, "Charles Schwab's Big Challenge," *Fortune*, 30 May 2005, 60-69.

4. J.-E. Johanson, "Intraorganizational Influence," *Management Communication Quarterly* 13 (February 2000): 393-435.

5. H. Mintzberg, *The Structuring of Organizations* (Englewood Cliffs, N.J.: Prentice Hall, 1979), 2-3.

6. E. E. Lawler III, *Motivation in Work Organizations* (Monterey, Calif.: Brooks/Cole, 1973); M. A. Campion, "Ability Requirement Implications of Job Design: An Interdisciplinary Perspective," *Personnel Psychology* 42 (1989): 1-24.

7. G. S. Becker and K. M. Murphy, "The Division-of-Labor, Coordination Costs and

Knowledge," *Quarterly Journal of Economics* 107, no. 4 (Nov 1992): 1137-1160; L. Borghans and B. Weel, "The Division of Labour, Worker Organisation, and Technological Change," *The Economic Journal* 116, no. 509 (2006): F45-F72.

8. Mintzberg, *The Structuring of Organizations* Chap. 1; D. A. Nadler and M. L. Tushman, *Competing by Design: The Power of Organizational Architecture* (N. Y.: Oxford University Press, 1997), Chap. 6; J. R. Galbraith, *Designing Organizations: An Executive Guide to Strategy, Structure, and Process* (San Francisco: Jossey-Bass, 2002), Chap. 4.

9. J. Stephenson, Jr., "Making Humanitarian Relief Networks More Effective: Operational Coordination, Trust and Sense Making," *Disasters* 29, no. 4 (2005): 337.

10. A. Willem, M. Buelens, and H. Scarbrough, "The Role of Inter-Unit Coordination Mechanisms in Knowledge Sharing: A Case Study of a British MNC," *Journal of Information Science* 32, no. 6 (2006): 539-561; R. R. Gulati, "Silo Busting," *Harvard Business Review* 85, no. 5 (2007): 98-108.

11. Borghans and Weel, "The Division of Labour, Worker Organisation, and Technological Change."

12. T. Van Alphen, "Magna in Overdrive," *Toronto Star*, 24 July 2006.

13. K. Umemoto, A. Endo, and M. Machado, "From Sashimi to Zen-In: The Evolution of Concurrent Engineering at Fuji Xerox," *Journal of Knowledge Management* 8, no. 4 (2004): 89-99; M. Hoque, M. Akter, and Y. Monden, "Concurrent Engineering: A Compromise Approach to Develop a Feasible and Customer-Pleasing Product," *International Journal of Production Research* 43, no. 8 (2005): 1607-1624.

14. For a discussion of the role of brand manager at Procter & Gamble, see C. Peale, "Branded for Success," *Cincinnati Enquirer* (20 May 2001): A1. Details about how to design integrator roles in organizational structures are presented in: Galbraith, *Designing Organizations*, 66-72.

15. A. H. Van De Ven, A. L. Delbecq, and R. J. Koenig Jr., "Determinants of Coordination Modes within Organizations," *American Sociological Review* 41, no. 2 (1976): 322-338.

16. Y.-M. Hsieh and A. Tien-Hsieh, "Enhancement of Service Quality with Job Standardisation," *Service Industries Journal* 21 (July 2001): 147-166.

17. H. Fayol, *General and Industrial Management*, trans. C. Storrs (London: Pitman, 1949); D. D. Van Fleet and A. G. Bedeian, "A History of the Span of Management," *Academy of Management Review* 2 (1977): 356-372; D. A. Wren, A. G. Bedeian, and J. D. Breeze, "The Foundations of Henri

Fayol's Administrative Theory ", *Management Decision* 40, no. 9 (2002): 906-918.

18. D. Drickhamer, "Lessons from the Leading Edge," *Industry Week*, 21 February 2000, 23-26.

19. J. Greenwald, "Ward Compares the Best with the Rest," *Business Insurance*, 26 August 2002, 16.

20. J. H. Gittell, "Supervisory Span, Relational Coordination and Flight Departure Performance: A Reassessment of Postbureaucracy Theory," *Organization Science* 12, no. 4 (July-August 2001): 468-483.

21. T. D. Wall, J. L. Cordery, and C. W. Clegg, "Empowerment, Performance, and Operational Uncertainty: A Theoretical Integration," *Applied Psychology: An International Review* 51 (2002): 146-169.

22. J. Morris, J. Hassard, and L. McCann, "New Organizational Forms, Human Resource Management and Structural Convergence? A Study of Japanese Organizations," *Organization Studies* 27, no. 10 (2006): 1485-1511.

23. "BASF Culling Saves (GBP) 4m," *Personnel Today* 19 February 2002, 3; A. Lashinsky, "The Hurt Way," *Fortune*, 17 April 2006, 92.

24. O. N. Huy, "In Praise of Middle Managers," *Harvard Business Review* 79 (September 2001): 72-79; H. J. Leavitt, *Top Down: Why Hierarchies Are Here to Stay and How to Manage Them More Effectively* (Cambridge: Harvard Business School Press, 2005).

25. W. Stueck, "Revamped Barrick Keeps Eyes on the Hunt for the Golden Prize," *Globe & Mail*, 17 September 2005, B4; Barrick Gold Corporation, *Annual Report 2007*, (Toronto: Barrick Gold Corporation, April 2008).

26. H. A. Richardson *et al.*, "Does Decentralization Make a Difference for the Organization? An Examination of the Boundary Conditions Circumscribing Decentralized Decision-Making and Organizational Financial Performance," *Journal of Management* 28, no. 2 (2002): 217-244; G. Masada, "To Centralize or Decentralize?" *Optimize*, May 2005, 58-61. Nestle's centralized-decentralized structure is discussed in: S. Wetlaufer, "The Business Case against Revolution: An Interview with Nestle's Peter Brabeck," *Harvard Business Review* 79, no. 2 (February 2001): 112-119; T. Demos, "Going Global," *Fortune*, 6 March 2006, 48.

27. Wetlaufer, "The Business Case against Revolution: An Interview with Nestle's Peter Brabeck"; Richardson *et al.*, "Does Decentralization Make a Difference for the Organization? An Examination of the Boundary Conditions Circumscribing Decentralized Decision-Making and Orga-

nizational Financial Performance"; Masada, "To Centralize or Decentralize?"

28. J. G. Kelley, "Slurpees and Sausages: 7-Eleven Holds School," *Richmond (Va.) Times-Dispatch*, 12 March 2004, C1; S. Marling, "The 24-Hour Supply Chain," *InformationWeek*, 26 January 2004, 43.

29. Mintzberg, *The Structuring of Organizations* Chap. 5.

30. W. Dessein and T. Santos, "Adaptive Organizations," *Journal of Political Economy* 114, no. 5 (2006): 956-995; A. A. M. Nasurdin *et al.*, "Organizational Structure and Organizational Climate as Potential Predictors of Job Stress: Evidence from Malaysia," *International Journal of Commerce and Management* 16, no. 2 (2006): 116-129; C.-J. Chen and J.-W. Huang, "How Organizational Climate and Structure Affect Knowledge Management--the Social Interaction Perspective," *International Journal of Information Management* 27, no. 2 (2007): 104-118.

31. T. Burns and G. Stalker, *The Management of Innovation* (London Tavistock: 1961).

32. P. Lavoie, "Taxi," *Campaign*, 12 October 2007, 15; L. Sylvain, "Taxi Deconstructed," *Strategy*, June 2007, 50.

33. J. Tata, S. Prasad, and R. Thom, "The Influence of Organizational Structure on the Effectiveness of TQM Programs," *Journal of Managerial Issues* 11, no. 4 (Winter 1999): 440-453; A. Lam, "Tacit Knowledge, Organizational Learning and Societal Institutions: An Integrated Framework," *Organization Studies* 21 (May 2000): 487-513.

34. W. D. Sine, H. Mitsuhashi, and D. A. Kirsch, "Revisiting Burns and Stalker: Formal Structure and New Venture Performance in Emerging Economic Sectors," *Academy of Management Journal* 49, no. 1 (2006): 121-132.

35. Mintzberg, *The Structuring of Organizations*, 106.

36. Mintzberg, *The Structuring of Organizations*, Chap. 17.

37. Galbraith, *Designing Organizations*, 23-25.

38. E. E. Lawler III, *Rewarding Excellence: Pay Strategies for the New Economy* (San Francisco: Jossey-Bass, 2000), 31-34.

39. These structures were identified from corporate websites and annual reports. These companies include a mixture of other structures, so the charts shown are adapted for learning purposes.

40. M. Goold and A. Campbell, "Do You Have a Well-Designed Organization," *Harvard Business Review* 80 (March 2002): 117-124.

41. G. L. Neilson and B. A. Pasternack, "The Cat That Came Back," *strategy+business*, no. 40 (17 August 2005): 1-14.

42. J. R. Galbraith, "Structuring Global Organizations," in *Tomorrow's Organization* ed. S. A. Mohrman *et al.* (San Francisco: Jossey-Bass, 1998), 103-129; C. Homburg, J. P. Workman Jr., and O. Jensen, "Fundamental Changes in Marketing Organization: The Movement toward a Coorganizational Structure," *Academy of Marketing Science. Journal* 28 (Fall 2000): 459-478; T. H. Davenport, J. G. Harris, and A. K. Kohli, "How Do They Know Their Customers So Well?" *Sloan Management Review* 42 (Winter 2001): 63-73; J. R. Galbraith, "Organizing to Deliver Solutions," *Organizational Dynamics* 31 (2002): 194-207.

43. J. R. Galbraith, E. E. Lawler III, and Associates, *Organizing for the Future: The New Logic for Managing Complex Organizations* (San Francisco, CA: Jossey-Bass, 1993); R. Bettis and M. Hitt, "The New Competitive Landscape," *Strategic Management Journal* 16 (1995): 7-19.

44. P. C. Ensign, "Interdependence, Coordination, and Structure in Complex Organizations: Implications for Organization Design," *Mid-Atlantic Journal of Business* 34 (March 1998): 5-22.

45. M. M. Fanning, "A Circular Organization Chart Promotes a Hospital-Wide Focus on Teams," *Hospital & Health Services Administration* 42 (June 1997): 243-254; L. Y. Chan and B. E. Lynn, "Operating in Turbulent Times: How Ontario's Hospitals Are Meeting the Current Funding Crisis," *Health Care Management Review* 23 (June 1998): 7-18.

46. "The Firm That Lets Staff Breathe," *Sunday Times (London)*, March 24 2002; M. Weinreb, "Power to the People," *Sales & Marketing Management*, April 2003, 30-35; A. Deutschman, "The Fabric of Creativity," *Fast Company*, December 2004, 54-; M. L. Diamond, "Change in Management for Medical Device Company," *Asbury Park Press (Asbury Park, N. J.)*, 6 Feb. 2006; P. J. Kiger, "Power to the Individual," *Workforce Management*, 27 Feb. 2006, 1-7; G. Hamel, *The Future of Management* (Boston: Harvard Business School Press, 2007), Chap. 5; A. McCall, "Unbeatable Gore Marches Fourth into Top Spot Again," *Sunday Times (London)*, 11 March 2007.

47. R. Cross, "Looking before You Leap: Assessing the Jump to Teams in Knowledge-Based Work," *Business Horizons* (September 2000); M. Fenton-O'Creevy, "Employee Involvement and the Middle Manager: Saboteur or Scapegoat?," *Human Resource Management Journal* 11 (2001): 24-40; G. Garda, K. Lindstrom, and M. Dallnera, "Towards a Learning Organization: The Introduction of a Client-Centered Team-Based Organization in Administrative Surveying Work," *Applied Ergonomics* 34 (2003): 97-105; C. Douglas and W. L.

Gardner, "Transition to Self-Directed Work Teams: Implications of Transition Time and Self-Monitoring for Managers' Use of Influence Tactics," *Journal of Organizational Behavior* 25 (2004): 47-65.

48. R. C. Ford and W. A. Randolph, "Cross-Functional Structures: A Review and Integration of Matrix Organization and Project Management," *Journal of Management* 18 (1992): 267-294.

49. N. Buckley, "P&G Shakes up Its Global Units," *Financial Times (London)*, 19 May 2004; "Merely Splitting Hairs," *Marketing Week*, 17 Feb 2005, 26. Procter & Gamble's structure is actually more complex than we have described here. Its "four pillars" also include global business services and corporate functions. See: P&G Corporate Info, Corporate Structure, Four Pillars, www.pg.com/jobs/corporate_structure/four_pillars.jhtml.

50. G. Calabrese, "Communication and Co-Operation in Product Development: A Case Study of a European Car Producer," *R & D Management* 27 (July 1997): 239-252; T. Sy and L. S. D'Annunzio, "Challenges and Strategies of Matrix Organizations: Top-Level and Mid-Level Managers' Perspectives," *Human Resource Planning* 28, no. 1 (2005): 39-48.

51. Nadler and Tushman, *Competing by Design*, Chap. 6; M. Goold and A. Campbell, "Structured Networks: Towards the Well-Designed Matrix," *Long Range Planning* 36, no. 5 (October 2003): 427-439.

52. C. Nuttall-Smith, "How to Make Mega Bucks," *Globe & Mail*, 24 March 2005, 56.

53. R. F. Miles and C. C. Snow, "The New Network Firm: A Spherical Structure Built on a Human Investment Philosophy," *Organizational Dynamics* 23, no. 4 (1995): 5-18; C. Baldwin and K. Clark, "Managing in an Age of Modularity," *Harvard Business Review* 75 (September-October 1997): 84-93.

54. G. Ip, "Outsourcing Becoming a Way of Life for Firms," *Globe & Mail*, 2 October 1996, B8; J. Hagel III and M. Singer, "Unbundling the Corporation," *Harvard Business Review* 77 (March-April 1999): 133-141; R. Hacki and J. Lighton, "The Future of the Networked Company," *McKinsey Quarterly* 3 (2001): 26-39.

55. J. Vardy, "Mitel Outsources Manufacturing to New Company," *National Post* (September 6, 2001).

56. M. A. Schilling and H. K. Steensma, "The Use of Modular Organizational Forms: An Industry-Level Analysis," *Academy of Management Journal* 44 (December 2001): 1149-1168.

57. W. H. Davidow and T. W. Malone, *The Virtual Corporation* (New York: Harper Business, 1992); L. Fried, *Managing Infor-*

mation Technology in Turbulent Times (New York: John Wiley and Sons, 1995).

58. G. Morgan, *Images of Organization*, Second ed. (Newbury Park: Sage, 1996); G. Morgan, *Imagin-I-Zation: New Mindsets for Seeing, Organizing and Managing* (Thousand Oaks, CA: Sage, 1997).

59. H. Chesbrough and D. J. Teece, "When Is Virtual Virtuous? Organizing for Innovation," *Harvard Business Review* (January-February 1996): 65-73; P. M. J. Christie and R. Levary, "Virtual Corporations: Recipe for Success," *Industrial Management* 40 (July 1998): 7-11.

60. L. Donaldson, *The Contingency Theory of Organizations* (Thousand Oaks, CA: Sage, 2001); J. Birkenshaw, R. Nobel, and J. Ridderstråle, "Knowledge as a Contingency Variable: Do the Characteristics of Knowledge Predict Organizational Structure?" *Organization Science* 13, no. 3 (May-June 2002): 274-289.

61. A. D. Meyer, A. S. Tsui, and C. R. Hinings, "Configurational Approaches to Organizational Analysis," *Academy of Management Journal* 36, no. 6 (Dec 1993): 1175-1195; K. K. Sinha and A. H. Van De Ven, "Designing Work within and between Organizations," *Organization Science* 16, no. 4 (July-Aug 2005): 389-408.

62. P. R. Lawrence and J. W. Lorsch, *Organization and Environment* (Homewood, Ill.: Irwin, 1967); Mintzberg, *The Structuring of Organizations* Chap. 15.

63. Burns and Stalker, *The Management of Innovation* ; Lawrence and Lorsch, *Organization and Environment*.

64. Mintzberg, *The Structuring of Organizations*, p. 282.

65. R. Gardner, "Charismatic Clarke Brings His Client Service Approach to UK," *Campaign*, 8 October 2004, 18; N. O'Leary, "Chris Clarke Is Coming for Your Business," *Adweek*, 9 April 2007, 8, 39; S. Russell, "Global Ambitions," *B&T*, 8 June 2007, 17.

66. D. S. Pugh and C. R. Hinings, *Organizational Structure: Extensions and Replications* (Farnborough, England: Lexington Books, 1976); Mintzberg, *The Structuring of Organizations* Chap. 13.

67. Galbraith, *Designing Organizations*, 52-55; G. Hertel, S. Geister, and U. Konradt, "Managing Virtual Teams: A Review of Current Empirical Research," *Human Resource Management Review* 15 (2005): 69-95.

68. C. Perrow, "A Framework for the Comparative Analysis of Organizations," *American Sociological Review* 32 (1967): 194-208; D. Gerwin, "The Comparative Analysis of Structure and Technology: A Critical Appraisal," *Academy of Management Review* 4, no. 1 (1979): 41-51; C. C. Miller *et al.*, "Understanding Technology-Structure Relationships: Theory Development and Meta-Analytic Theory Testing," *Academy of Management Journal* 34, no. 2 (1991): 370-399.

69. R. H. Kilmann, *Beyond the Quick Fix* (San Francisco: Jossey-Bass, 1984), p. 38.

70. A. D. Chandler, *Strategy and Structure* (Cambridge, Mass.: MIT Press, 1962).

71. D. Miller, "Configurations of Strategy and Structure," *Strategic Management Journal* 7 (1986): 233-249.

Chapter 14

1. L. M. Fisher, "How Dell Got Soul," *strategy+business* 2004, 1-14; N. Byrnes, P. Burrows, and L. Lee, "Dark Days at Dell," *BusinessWeek*, 4 September 2006, 26; M. Kessler, "Dell Reverses, Steps into Wal-Mart," *USA Today*, 25 May 2007, B1; S. Lohr, "Can Michael Dell Refocus His Namesake?," *New York Times*, 9 September 2007, 1; D. Zehr, "Dell Challenge: New Ideas and Less Red Tape," *Austin American-Statesman*, 4 February 2007, A1; Waterstone Human Capital and National Post, *Canada's 10 Most Admired Corporate Cultures, 2007*, (Toronto: Warerstone Human Capital and National Post, February 2008).

2. A. Williams, P. Dobson, and M. Walters, *Changing Culture: New Organizational Approaches* (London: Institute of Personnel Management, 1989); E. H. Schein, "What Is Culture?" in *Reframing Organizational Culture*, ed. P. J. Frost *et al.* (Newbury Park, CA: Sage, 1991), 243-253.

3. Williams, Dobson, and Walters, *Changing Culture*; Schein, "What Is Culture?".

4. B. M. Meglino and E. C. Ravlin, "Individual Values in Organizations: Concepts, Controversies, and Research," *Journal of Management* 24, no. 3 (1998): 351-389; B. R. Agle and C. B. Caldwell, "Understanding Research on Values in Business," *Business and Society* 38, no. 3 (September 1999): 326-387; S. Hitlin and J. A. Pilavin, "Values: Reviving a Dormant Concept," *Annual Review of Sociology* 30 (2004): 359-393.

5. N. M. Ashkanasy, "The Case for Culture," in *Debating Organization*, ed. R. Westwood and S. Clegg (Malden, MA: Blackwell, 2003), 300-310.

6. The corporate values for Teknika HBA and RYCOM are described on their websites. See "Teknika HBA: Mission, Values and Commitment," www.teknika-hba.com/eng/entreprise.html; "RYCOM Vision, Values and Principles," www.rycom.ca.

7. B. Kabanoff and J. Daly, "Espoused Values in Organisations," *Australian Journal of Management* 27, no. Special issue (2002): 89-104.

8. C. A. O'Reilly III, J. Chatman, and D. F. Caldwell, "People and Organizational Culture: A Profile Comparison Approach to Assessing Person—Organization Fit," *Academy of Management Journal* 34 (1991): 487-516; J. J. van Muijen, "Organizational Culture," in *A Handbook of Work and Organizational Psychology: Organizational Psychology*, ed. P. J. D. Drenth, H. Thierry, and C. J. de Wolff, 2nd ed. (East Sussex, UK: Psychology Press, 1998), 113-132; P. A. Balthazard, R. A. Cooke, and R. E. Potter, "Dysfunctional Culture, Dysfunctional Organization: Capturing the Behavioral Norms That Form Organizational Culture and Drive Performance," *Journal of Managerial Psychology* 21, no. 8 (2006): 709-732; C. Helfrich *et al.*, "Assessing an Organizational Culture Instrument Based on the Competing Values Framework: Exploratory and Confirmatory Factor Analyses," *Implementation Science* 2, no. 1 (2007): 13. For recent reviews of organizational culture survey instruments, see: T. Scott *et al.*, "The Quantitative Measurement of Organizational Culture in Health Care: A Review of the Available Instruments," *Health Services Research* 38, no. 3 (2003): 923-945; D. E. Leidner and T. Kayworth, "A Review of Culture in Information Systems Research: Toward a Theory of Information Technology Culture Conflict," *MIS Quarterly* 30, no. 2 (2006): 357-399; S. Scott Findlay and C. A. Estabrooks, "Mapping the Organizational Culture Research in Nursing: A Literature Review," *Journal of Advanced Nursing* 56, no. 5 (2006): 498-513.

9. J. Martin, P. J. Frost, and O. A. O'Neill, "Organizational Culture: Beyond Struggles for Intellectual Dominance," in *Handbook of Organization Studies*, ed. S. Clegg *et al.*, 2nd ed. (London: Sage, 2006), 725-753; N. E. Fenton and S. Inglis, "A Critical Perspective on Organizational Values," *Nonprofit Management and Leadership* 17, no. 3 (2007): 335-347; K. Haukelid, "Theories of (Safety) Culture Revisited—An Anthropological Approach," *Safety Science* 46, no. 3 (2008): 413-426.

10. J. Martin and C. Siehl, "Organizational Culture and Counterculture: An Uneasy Symbiosis," *Organizational Dynamics* (Autumn 1983): 52-64; G. Hofstede, "Identifying Organizational Subcultures: An Empirical Approach," *Journal of Management Studies* 35, no. 1 (1990): 1-12; E. Ogbonna and L. C. Harris, "Organisational Culture in the Age of the Internet: An Exploratory Study," *New Technology, Work and Employment* 21, no. 2 (2006): 162-175.

11. H. Silver, "Does a University Have a Culture?" *Studies in Higher Education* 28, no. 2 (2003): 157-169.

12. A. Sinclair, "Approaches to Organizational Culture and Ethics," *Journal of Business Ethics* 12 (1993); A. Boisnier and J. Chatman, "The Role of Subcultures in

Agile Organizations," in *Leading and Managing People in Dynamic Organizations*, ed. R. Petersen and E. Mannix (Mahwah, NJ: Lawrence Erlbaum Associates, 2003), 87-112; C. Morrill, M. N. Zald, and H. Rao, "Covert Political Conflict in Organizations: Challenges from Below," *Annual Review of Sociology* 29, no. 1 (2003): 391-415.

13. J. S. Ott, *The Organizational Culture Perspective* (Pacific Grove, CA: Brooks/Cole, 1989), Chap. 2; J. S. Pederson and J. S. Sorensen, *Organizational Cultures in Theory and Practice* (Aldershot, England: Gower, 1989), pp. 27-29; M. O. Jones, *Studying Organizational Symbolism: What, How, Why?* (Thousand Oaks, CA: Sage, 1996).

14. E. H. Schein, "Organizational Culture," *American Psychologist* (February 1990): 109-119; A. Furnham and B. Gunter, "Corporate Culture: Definition, Diagnosis, and Change," *International Review of Industrial and Organizational Psychology* 8 (1993): 233-261; E. H. Schein, *The Corporate Culture Survival Guide* (San Francisco: Jossey-Bass, 1999), Chap. 4.

15. M. Doehrman, "Anthropologists—Deep in the Corporate Bush," *Daily Record (Kansas City, MO)*, 19 July 2005, 1.

16. M. Miller, "The Acrobat," *Forbes*, 15 March 2004, 100-103; R. Ouzounian, "Cirque's Dream Factory," *Toronto Star*, 1 August 2004.

17. C. J. Boudens, "The Story of Work: A Narrative Analysis of Workplace Emotion," *Organization Studies* 26, no. 9 (2005): 1285-1306; S. Denning, *The Leader's Guide to Storytelling* (San Francisco: Jossey-Bass, 2005).

18. A. L. Wilkins, "Organizational Stories as Symbols Which Control the Organization," in *Organizational Symbolism*, ed. L. R. Pondy *et al.* (Greenwich, CT: JAI Press, 1984), 81-92; R. Zemke, "Storytelling: Back to a Basic," *Training* 27 (March 1990): 44-50; J. C. Meyer, "Tell Me a Story: Eliciting Organizational Values from Narratives," *Communication Quarterly* 43 (1995): 210-224; W. Swap *et al.*, "Using Mentoring and Storytelling to Transfer Knowledge in the Workplace," *Journal of Management Information Systems* 18 (Summer 2001): 95-114.

19. "The Ultimate Chairman," *Business Times Singapore*, 3 September 2005.

20. D. Roth, "My Job at the Container Store," *Fortune* (10 January 2000): 74-78.

21. R. Frank and S. Craig, "White-Shoe Shuffle," *Wall Street Journal*, 15 September 2004, A1.

22. R. E. Quinn and N. T. Snyder, "Advance Change Theory: Culture Change at Whirlpool Corporation," in *The Leader's Change Handbook* ed. J. A. Conger, G. M. Spre-

itzer, and E. E. Lawler III (San Francisco: Jossey-Bass, 1999), 162-193.

23. Churchill apparently made this statement on October 28, 1943 in the British House of Commons, when London, damaged by bombings in World War II, was about to be rebuilt.

24. P. Roberts, "The Empire Strikes Back," *Fast Company*, no. 22 (February-March 1999): 122-131; H. Nguyen, "Oakley Shades for Her Eyes Only," *Orange County Register (Santa Ana, CA)*, 11 May 2006. Details and photos are also found at: www.oakley.com; and americahurrah.com/Oakley/Entry.htm.

25. K. D. Elsbach and B. A. Bechky, "It's More Than a Desk: Working Smarter through Leveraged Office Design," *California Management Review* 49, no. 2 (Winter 2007): 80-101.

26. J. C. Collins and J. I. Porras, *Built to Last: Successful Habits of Visionary Companies* (London: Century, 1994); T. E. Deal and A. A. Kennedy, *The New Corporate Cultures* (Cambridge, MA: Perseus Books, 1999); R. Barrett, *Building a Values-Driven Organization: A Whole System Approach to Cultural Transformation* (Burlington, MA: Butterworth-Heinemann, 2006); J. M. Kouzes and B. Z. Posner, *The Leadership Challenge*, Fourth ed. (San Francisco: Jossey-Bass, 2007), Chap. 3.

27. C. Siehl and J. Martin, "Organizational Culture: A Key to Financial Performance?," in *Organizational Climate and Culture*, ed. B. Schneider (San Francisco, CA: Jossey-Bass, 1990), 241-281; G. G. Gordon and N. DiTomasco, "Predicting Corporate Performance from Organizational Culture," *Journal of Management Studies* 29 (1992): 783-798; J. P. Kotter and J. L. Heskett, *Corporate Culture and Performance* (New York: Free Press, 1992); C. P. M. Wilderom, U. Glunk, and R. Maslowski, "Organizational Culture as a Predictor of Organizational Performance," in *Handbook of Organizational Culture and Climate*, ed. N. M. Ashkanasy, C. P. M. Wilderom, and M. F. Peterson (Thousand Oaks, CA: Sage, 2000), 193-210; A. Carmeli and A. Tishler, "The Relationships between Intangible Organizational Elements and Organizational Performance," *Strategic Management Journal* 25 (2004): 1257-1278; S. Teerikangas and P. Very, "The Culture-Performance Relationship in MA: From Yes/No to How," *British Journal of Management* 17, no. s1 (2006): 31-48.

28. J. C. Helms Mills and A. J. Mills, "Rules, Sensemaking, Formative Contexts, and Discourse in the Gendering of Organizational Culture," in *International Handbook of Organizational Climate and Culture*, ed. N. Ashkanasy, C. Wilderom, and M. Peterson (Thousand Oaks, CA: Sage, 2000), 55-70; J. A. Chatman and S.

E. Cha, "Leading by Leveraging Culture," *California Management Review* 45 (Summer 2003): 20-34.

29. B. Ashforth and F. Mael, "Social Identity Theory and the Organization," *Academy of Management Review* 14 (1989): 20-39.

30. D. George, "WestJet Founder Named Distinguished Entrepreneur," *The Ring (University of Victoria) (Victoria, B.C.)*, April 2008; Waterstone Human Capital and National Post, *Canada's 10 Most Admired Corporate Cultures, 2007*.

31. M. R. Louis, "Surprise and Sensemaking: What Newcomers Experience in Entering Unfamiliar Organizational Settings," *Administrative Science Quarterly* 25 (1980): 226-251; S. G. Harris, "Organizational Culture and Individual Sensemaking: A Schema-Based Perspective," *Organization Science* 5 (1994): 309-321.

32. J. W. Barnes *et al.*, "The Role of Culture Strength in Shaping Sales Force Outcomes," *Journal of Personal Selling & Sales Management* 26, no. 3 (Summer 2006): 255-270.

33. C. A. O'Reilly III and J. A. Chatman, "Culture as Social Control: Corporations, Cults, and Commitment," *Research in Organizational Behavior* 18 (1996): 157-200; B. Spector and H. Lane, "Exploring the Distinctions between a High Performance Culture and a Cult," *Strategy & Leadership* 35, no. 3 (2007): 18-24.

34. Fisher, "How Dell Got Soul," p. 6.

35. Kotter and Heskett, *Corporate Culture and Performance*; J. P. Kotter, "Cultures and Coalitions," *Executive Excellence* 15 (March 1998): 14-15.

36. A. Maitland and K. Rollins, "The Two-in-a-Box World of Dell," *Financial Times (London)*, 20 March 2003, 14.

37. D. Ho, "Michael Dell Says He Had No Role in Accounting Scandal," *Cox News Service*, 6 September 2007.

38. L. St-Arnaud, "Engaging to Improve Results at Bombardier Aerospace," *Strategic Communication Management* 9, no. 3 (2005): 18-21.

39. J. Martin, "Can Organizational Culture Be Managed?" in *Organizational Culture*, ed. P. J. Frost *et al.* (Beverly Hills, CA: Sage, 1985), 95-98.

40. E. H. Schein, "The Role of the Founder in Creating Organizational Culture," *Organizational Dynamics* 12, no. 1 (Summer 1983): 13-28; R. House, M. Javidan, and P. Dorfman, "Project Globe: An Introduction," *Applied Psychology: An International Review* 50 (2001): 489-505; R. House *et al.*, "Understanding Cultures and Implicit Leadership Theories across the Globe: An Introduction to Project Globe," *Journal of World Business* 37 (2002): 3-10.

41. A. S. Tsui *et al.*, "Unpacking the Relationship between CEO Leadership Behavior

and Organizational Culture," *Leadership Quarterly* 17 (2006): 113-137; Y. Berson, S. Oreg, and T. Dvir, "CEO Values, Organizational Culture and Firm Outcomes," *Journal of Organizational Behavior* (in press).

42. J. Hewett, "Office Politics," *Australian Financial Review*, 27 September 2003, 29.

43. M. De Pree, *Leadership Is an Art* (East Lansing, MI: Michigan State University Press, 1987).

44. B. Bouw, "Zen and the Art of Retailing," *Globe & Mail*, 30 November 2007; D. Flavelle, "Yoga-Wear Icon Brews up New Top Executive," *Toronto Star*, 3 April 2008; J. Wells, "Now It's Her Chance to Stretch," *Globe & Mail*, 3 April 2008.

45. B. McLean, "Inside the Money Machine," *Fortune*, 6 September 2004, 84.

46. J. Kerr and J. W. Slocum Jr., "Managing Corporate Culture through Reward Systems," *Academy of Management Executive* 1 (May 1987): 99-107; J. M. Higgins *et al.*, "Using Cultural Artifacts to Change and Perpetuate Strategy," *Journal of Change Management* 6, no. 4 (2006): 397-415.

47. S. Brimble, "Apex Distribution Enters Next Level of Growth through Product Diversification," *On Stream*, Summer 2006, 12-16; R. Charan, "Home Depot's Blueprint for Culture Change," *Harvard Business Review* (April 2006): 61-70.

48. B. Schneider, "The People Make the Place," *Personnel Psychology* 40, no. 3 (1987): 437-453; B. Schneider *et al.*, "Personality and Organizations: A Test of the Homogeneity of Personality Hypothesis," *Journal of Applied Psychology* 83, no. 3 (Jun 1998): 462-470; T. R. Giberson, C. J. Resick, and M. W. Dickson, "Embedding Leader Characteristics: An Examination of Homogeneity of Personality and Values in Organizations," *Journal of Applied Psychology* 90, no. 5 (2005): 1002-1010.

49. T. A. Judge and D. M. Cable, "Applicant Personality, Organizational Culture, and Organization Attraction," *Personnel Psychology* 50, no. 2 (1997): 359-394; D. Chapman, S. *et al.*, "Applicant Attraction to Organizations and Job Choice: A Meta-Analytic Review of the Correlates of Recruiting Outcomes," *Journal of Applied Psychology* 90, no. 5 (2005): 928-944; A. L. Kristof-Brown, R. D. Zimmerman, and E. C. Johnson, "Consequences of Individuals' Fit at Work: A Meta-Analysis of Person-Job, Person-Organization, Person-Group, and Person-Supervisor Fit," *Personnel Psychology* 58, no. 2 (2005): 281-342; C. Hu, H.-C. Su, and C.-I. B. Chen, "The Effect of Person-Organization Fit Feedback Via Recruitment Web Sites on Applicant

Attraction," *Computers in Human Behavior* 23, no. 5 (2007): 2509-2523.

50. A. Kristof-Brown, "Perceived Applicant Fit: Distinguishing between Recruiters' Perceptions of Person-Job and Person-Organization Fit," *Personnel Psychology* 53, no. 3 (Autumn 2000): 643-671; A. E. M. Van Vianen, "Person-Organization Fit: The Match between Newcomers' and Recruiters' Preferences for Organizational Cultures," *Personnel Psychology* 53 (Spring 2000): 113-149.

51. Brimble, "Apex Distribution Enters Next Level of Growth through Product Diversification"; D. Sankey, "Avoiding a Culture Clash in New Job," *Calgary Herald*, 25 August 2007.

52. D. M. Cable and J. R. Edwards, "Complementary and Supplementary Fit: A Theoretical and Empirical Integration," *Journal of Applied Psychology* 89, no. 5 (2004): 822-834.

53. C. Vander Doelen, "Toyota Hiring in Woodstock," *Windsor Star*, 30 November 2007.

54. J. Van Maanen, "Breaking In: Socialization to Work," in *Handbook of Work, Organization, and Society*, ed. R. Dubin (Chicago: Rand McNally, 1976).

55. S. Huettel, "Soaring Ahead," *St. Petersburg Times*, 24 October 2005; E. P. Lima, "Winning Cultures," *Air Transport World*, February 2006, 54.

56. C. L. Adkins, "Previous Work Experience and Organizational Socialization: A Longitudinal Examination," *Academy of Management Journal* 38 (1995): 839-862; J. D. Kammeyer-Mueller and C. R. Wanberg, "Unwrapping the Organizational Entry Process: Disentangling Multiple Antecedents and Their Pathways to Adjustment," *Journal of Applied Psychology* 88, no. 5 (2003): 779-794.

57. J. M. Beyer and D. R. Hannah, "Building on the Past: Enacting Established Personal Identities in a New Work Setting," *Organization Science* 13 (November/December 2002): 636-652; H. D. C. Thomas and N. Anderson, "Newcomer Adjustment: The Relationship between Organizational Socialization Tactics, Information Acquisition and Attitudes," *Journal of Occupational and Organizational Psychology* 75 (December 2002): 423-437.

58. L. W. Porter, E. E. Lawler III, and J. R. Hackman, *Behavior in Organizations* (New York: McGraw-Hill, 1975), pp. 163-167; Van Maanen, "Breaking In: Socialization to Work"; D. C. Feldman, "The Multiple Socialization of Organization Members," *Academy of Management Review* 6 (1981): 309-318.

59. B. E. Ashforth and A. M. Saks, "Socialization Tactics: Longitudinal Effects on Newcomer Adjustment," *Academy of Man-*

agement Journal 39 (1996): 149-178; Kammeyer-Mueller and Wanberg, "Unwrapping the Organizational Entry Process."

60. Louis, "Surprise and Sensemaking: What Newcomers Experience in Entering Unfamiliar Organizational Settings."

61. M. L. Marks, "Adding Cultural Fit to Your Diligence Checklist," *Mergers & Acquisitions* 34, no. 3 (Nov-Dec 1999): 14-20; Schein, *The Corporate Culture Survival Guide* Chap. 8; M. L. Marks, "Mixed Signals," *Across the Board* (May 2000): 21-26; J. P. Daly, R. W. Pouder, and B. Kabanoff, "The Effects of Initial Differences in Firms' Espoused Values on Their Postmerger Performance," *Journal of Applied Behavioral Science* 40, no. 3 (September 2004): 323-343.

62. Teerikangas and Very, "The Culture-Performance Relationship in MA: From Yes/No to How"; G. K. Stahl and A. Voigt, "Do Cultural Differences Matter in Mergers and Acquisitions? A Tentative Model and Examination," *Organization Science* 19, no. 1 (January 2008): 160-176.

63. A. Klein, "A Merger Taken AO-Ill," *Washington Post*, 21 October 2002, E1; A. Klein, *Stealing Time: Steve Case, Jerry Levin, and the Collapse of AOL Time Warner* (New York: Simon & Shuster, 2003).

64. C. Fishman, "The Anarchist's Cookbook," *Fast Company*, July 2004, 70; "World's Finest Food Retailers. Whole Foods, Not Holy Food," *The Grocer*, 12 November 2005, 32.

65. C. A. Schorg, C. A. Raiborn, and M. F. Massoud, "Using a 'Cultural Audit' to Pick M&A Winners," *Journal of Corporate Accounting & Finance* (May/June 2004): 47-55; W. Locke, "Higher Education Mergers: Integrating Organisational Cultures and Developing Appropriate Management Styles," *Higher Education Quarterly* 61, no. 1 (2007): 83-102.

66. S. Greengard, "Due Diligence: The Devil in the Details," *Workforce* (October 1999): 68; Marks, "Adding Cultural Fit to Your Diligence Checklist."

67. A. R. Malekazedeh and A. Nahavandi, "Making Mergers Work by Managing Cultures," *Journal of Business Strategy* (May-June 1990): 55-57; K. W. Smith, "A Brand-New Culture for the Merged Firm," *Mergers and Acquisitions* 35 (June 2000): 45-50.

68. T. Hamilton, "RIM on a Roll," *Toronto Star*, 22 February 2004, C01.

69. I. Mount, "Be Fast Be Frugal Be Right," *Inc* 26, no. 1 (January 2004): 64-70; S. Anthony and C. Christensen, "Mind over Merger," *Optimize* (February 2005): 22-27.

70. Hewitt Associates, "Mergers and Acquisitions May Be Driven by Business Strategy—but Often Stumble over People

and Culture Issues," PR Newswire News release (Lincolnshire, IL: 3 August 1998).

Chapter 15

1. D. Ebner, "The Greening of the Oil Sands," *Globe & Mail*, 6 January 2007; S. Klie, "Dawning of a New Day at Suncor," *Canadian HR Reporter*, 22 October 2007, 21; G. Pitts, "How to Avoid Being Trampled by the Herd," *Globe & Mail*, 28 May 2007; "Suncor Output Slides, Cold Winter, Emission Limit Blamed for New Target," *Edmonton Journal*, 25 April 2008; "Pioneers Get All the Perks," *Canadian Business*, 3 March 2008, 18; N. Scott, "Suncor Takes Aim at Better Operations," *Globe & Mail*, 23 January 2008.

2. K. Lewin, *Field Theory in Social Science* (New York: Harper & Row, 1951).

3. D. Coghlan and T. Brannick, "Kurt Lewin: The 'Practical Theorist' for the 21st Century," *Irish Journal of Management* 24, no. 2 (2003): 31-37; B. Burnes, "Kurt Lewin and the Planned Approach to Change: A Re-Appraisal," *Journal of Management Studies* 41, no. 6 (Sept. 2004): 977-1002.

4. D. Howell, "Nardelli Nears Five-Year Mark with Riveting Record," *DSN Retailing Today*, 9 May 2005, 1, 38; R. Charan, "Home Depot's Blueprint for Culture Change," *Harvard Business Review* (April 2006): 61-70; R. DeGross, "Five Years of Change: Home Depot's Results Mixed under Nardelli," *Atlanta Journal-Constitution*, 1 January 2006, F1; B. Grow, D. Brady, and M. Arndt, "Renovating Home Depot," *BusinessWeek*, 6 March 2006, 50-57.

5. S. Chreim, "Postscript to Change: Survivors' Retrospective Views of Organizational Changes," *Personnel Review* 35, no. 3 (2006): 315-335.

6. M. Johnson-Cramer, S. Parise, and R. Cross, "Managing Change through Networks and Values," *California Management Review* 49, no. 3 (Spring 2007): 85-109.

7. G. L. Neilson, B. A. Pasternack, and K. E. Van Nuys, "The Passive-Aggressive Organization," *Harvard Business Review* 83, no. 10 (2005): 82-92.

8. Several variations of this famous quotation are found in several books, articles, and websites, but unfortunately none cite the original source. This quotation is from: D. R. Henderson, "The New Industrial Economist," *Wall Street Journal*, 2 May 2006.

9. B. J. Tepper *et al.*, "Subordinates' Resistance and Managers' Evaluations of Subordinates' Performance," *Journal of Management* 32, no. 2 (April 2006): 185-209; J. D. Ford, L. W. Ford, and A. D'Amelio, "Resistance to Change: The Rest

of the Story," *Academy of Management Review* 33, no. 2 (2008): 362-377.

10. E. B. Dent and S. G. Goldberg, "Challenging 'Resistance to Change'," *Journal of Applied Behavioral Science* 35 (March 1999): 25-41; D. B. Fedor, S. Caldwell, and D. M. Herold, "The Effects of Organizational Changes on Employee Commitment: A Multilevel Investigation," *Personnel Psychology* 59, no. 1 (2006): 1-29.

11. For an excellent review of the resistance to change literature, see: R. R. Sharma, *Change Management: Concepts and Applications* (New Delhi: Tata McGraw-Hill, 2007), Chap. 4.

12. D. A. Nadler, "The Effective Management of Organizational Change," in *Handbook of Organizational Behavior*, ed. J. W. Lorsch (Englewood Cliffs, N.J.: Prentice Hall, 1987), 358-369; R. Maurer, *Beyond the Wall of Resistance: Unconventional Strategies to Build Support for Change* (Austin, TX: Bard Books, 1996); P. Strebel, "Why Do Employees Resist Change?," *Harvard Business Review* (May-June 1996): 86-92; D. A. Nadler, *Champions of Change* (San Francisco, CA: Jossey-Bass, 1998).

13. V. Newman, "The Psychology of Managing for Innovation," *KM Review* 9, no. 6 (2007): 10-15.

14. D. Eggen, "FBI Fails to Transform Itself, Panel Says," *Washington Post*, 7 June 2005, A04; C. Ragavan and C. S. Hook, "Fixing the FBI," *U.S. News & World Report*, 28 March 2005, 18-24, 26, 29-30; The Commission on the Intelligence Capabilities of the United States Regarding Weapons of Mass Destruction, *Report to the President of the United States*, (Washington, D.C.: 31 March 2005); J. J. Brazil, "Mission: Impossible?" *Fast Company*, April 2007, 92-97, 108-109.

15. *Bosses Want Change but Workers Want More of the Same!*, (Sydney: Talent2, 29 June 2005).

16. J. Smith, "Building Cars, Building Teams," *Plant Engineering*, December 2005, 41-50.

17. T. G. Cummings, "The Role and Limits of Change Leadership," in *The Leader's Change Handbook*, ed. J. A. Conger, G. M. Spreitzer, and E. E. Lawler III (San Francisco: Jossey-Bass, 1999), 301-320; J. P. Kotter and D. S. Cohen, *The Heart of Change* (Boston: Harvard Business School Press, 2002), pp. 15-36.

18. R. Colman, "Packing the Perfect HR Punch," *CMA Management*, March 2007, 40-43.

19. L. D. Goodstein and H. R. Butz, "Customer Value: The Linchpin of Organizational Change," *Organizational Dynamics* 27 (June 1998): 21-35.

20. I. J. Bozon and P. N. Child, "Refining Shell's Position in Europe," *McKinsey Quarterly*, no. 2 (2003): 42-51.

21. D. Darlin, "Growing Tomorrow," *Business 2.0*, May 2005, 126.

22. L. Grossman and S. Song, "Stevie's Little Wonder," *Time*, 19 September 2005, 63; S. Levy, "Honey, I Shrunk the iPod. A Lot," *Newsweek*, 19 September 2005, 58.

23. T. F. Cawsey and G. Deszca, *Toolkit for Organizational Change* (Los Angeles: Sage, 2007), p. 104.

24. J. P. Kotter and L. A. Schlesinger, "Choosing Strategies for Change," *Harvard Business Review* (March-April 1979): 106-114.

25. B. Nanus and S. M. Dobbs, *Leaders Who Make a Difference* (San Francisco: Jossey-Bass, 1999); Kotter and Cohen, *The Heart of Change* pp. 83-98.

26. E. Greenspon, "On Monday, We Present to You the Next Generation of the Globe," *Globe & Mail*, 21 April 2007, A2.

27. K. T. Dirks, L. L. Cummings, and J. L. Pierce, "Psychological Ownership in Organizations: Conditions under Which Individuals Promote and Resist Change," *Research in Organizational Change and Development* 9 (1996): 1-23; A. Cox, S. Zagelmeyer, and M. Marchington, "Embedding Employee Involvement and Participation at Work," *Human Resource Management Journal* 16, no. 3 (2006): 250-267.

28. M. Weisbord and S. Janoff, *Future Search: An Action Guide to Finding Common Ground in Organizations and Communities* (San Francisco: Berrett-Koehler, 2000); R. M. Lent, M. T. McCormick, and D. S. Pearce, "Combining Future Search and Open Space to Address Special Situations," *Journal of Applied Behavioral Science* 41, no. 1 (March 1, 2005 2005): 61-69; S. Janoff and M. Weisbord, "Future Search as 'Real-Time' Action Research," *Futures* 38, no. 6 (2006): 716-722.

29. J. Pratt, "Naturalists Deserve More Credit," *St. John's Telegram*, 22 June 2002, B3; C. Chowaniec, R. Gordezky, and J. Grieve, "Supporting the Merger of Two School Boards in Ottawa, Ontario, Canada: The Ottawa-Carleton Community and Public Education to 2015," in *Future Search in School District Change*, ed. R. Schweitz, K. Martens, and N. Aronson (Lanham, Maryland: ScarecrowEducation, 2005), 56-70; P. Deans, K. Martens, and R. Gordezky, "Success and System Readiness: Lester B. Pearson School Board and Its Commitment to Educational Excellence, Montreal, Quebec," in *Future Search in School District Change*, ed. R. Schweitz, K. Martens, and N. Aronson (Lanham, Maryland: ScarecrowEducation, 2005), 192-208.

30. M. Weisbord and S. Janoff, "Faster, Shorter, Cheaper May Be Simple; It's

Never Easy," *Journal of Applied Behavioral Science* 41, no. 1 (March 1, 2005 2005): 70-82.

31. For a critique of future search conferences and similar whole-system events, see: A. Oels, "Investigating the Emotional Roller-Coaster Ride: A Case Study-Based Assessment of the Future Search Conference Design," *Systems Research and Behavioral Science* 19 (July-August 2002): 347-355; M. F. D. Polanyi, "Communicative Action in Practice: Future Search and the Pursuit of an Open, Critical and Non-Coercive Large-Group Process," *Systems Research and Behavioral Science* 19 (July 2002): 357-366; A. De Grassi, "Envisioning Futures of African Agriculture: Representation, Power, and Socially Constituted Time," *Progress in Development Studies* 7, no. 2 (2007): 79-98.

32. N. T. Tan, "Maximising Human Resource Potential in the Midst of Organisational Change," *Singapore Management Review* 27, no. 2 (2005): 25-35.

33. M. McHugh, "The Stress Factor: Another Item for the Change Management Agenda?" *Journal of Organizational Change Management* 10 (1997): 345-362; D. Buchanan, T. Claydon, and M. Doyle, "Organisation Development and Change: The Legacy of the Nineties," *Human Resource Management Journal* 9 (1999): 20-37.

34. J. Mawhinney, "Baycrest: Brave New World," *Toronto Star*, 19 November 2004, G05.

35. D. Nicolini and M. B. Meznar, "The Social Construction of Organizational Learning: Conceptual and Practical Issues in the Field," *Human Relations* 48 (1995): 727-746.

36. E. E. Lawler III, "Pay Can Be a Change Agent," *Compensation & Benefits Management* 16 (Summer 2000): 23-26; Kotter and Cohen, *The Heart of Change* pp. 161-177; M. A. Roberto and L. C. Levesque, "The Art of Making Change Initiatives Stick," *MIT Sloan Management Review* 46, no. 4 (Summer 2005): 53-60.

37. R. E. Quinn, *Building the Bridge as You Walk on It: A Guide for Leading Change* (San Francisco: Jossey-Bass, 2004), Chap. 11.

38. R. Caldwell, "Models of Change Agency: A Fourfold Classification," *British Journal of Management* 14 (June 2003): 131-142.

39. J. P. Kotter, "Leading Change: Why Transformation Efforts Fail," *Harvard Business Review* (March-April 1995): 59-67; J. P. Kotter, "Leading Change: The Eight Steps to Transformation," in *The Leader's Change Handbook* ed. J. A. Conger, G. M. Spreitzer, and E. E. Lawler III (San Francisco: Jossey-Bass, 1999), 221-267.

40. M. Beer, R. A. Eisenstat, and B. Spector, *The Critical Path to Corporate Renewal* (Boston, Mass.: Harvard Business School Press, 1990).

41. R. E. Walton, "Successful Strategies for Diffusing Work Innovations," *Journal of Contemporary Business* (Spring 1977): 1-22; R. E. Walton, *Innovating to Compete: Lessons for Diffusing and Managing Change in the Workplace* (San Francisco: Jossey-Bass, 1987); Beer, Eisenstat, and Spector, *The Critical Path to Corporate Renewal* Chap. 5.

42. G. L. Morfitt, *A Review of Operational Safety at British Columbia Ferry Services Inc.*, (Victoria, B.C.: British Columbia Ferry Services Inc., January 2007).

43. E. M. Rogers, *Diffusion of Innovations*, Fourth ed. (New York: Free Pree, 1995).

44. P. Reason and H. Bradbury, *Handbook of Action Research, London* (Sage: 2001); Coghlan and Brannick, "Kurt Lewin: The 'Practical Theorist' for the 21st Century"; C. Huxham and S. Vangen, "Researching Organizational Practice through Action Research: Case Studies and Design Choices," *Organizational Research Methods* 6 (July 2003): 383-403.

45. V. J. Marsick and M. A. Gephart, "Action Research: Building the Capacity for Learning and Change," *Human Resource Planning* 26 (2003): 14-18.

46. L. Dickens and K. Watkins, "Action Research: Rethinking Lewin," *Management Learning* 30 (June 1999): 127-140; J. Heron and P. Reason, "The Practice of Co-Operative Inquiry: Research 'with' Rather Than 'on' People," in *Handbook of Action Research*, ed. P. Reason and H. Bradbury (Thousand Oaks, CA: Sage, 2001), 179-188.

47. D. A. Nadler, "Organizational Frame Bending: Types of Change in the Complex Organization," in *Corporate Transformation: Revitalizing Organizations for a Competitive World*, ed. R. H. Kilmann, T. J. Covin, and a. Associates (San Francisco: Jossey-Bass, 1988), 66-83; K. E. Weick and R. E. Quinn, "Organizational Change and Development," *Annual Review of Psychology* (1999): 361-386.

48. T. M. Egan and C. M. Lancaster, "Comparing Appreciative Inquiry to Action Research: OD Practitioner Perspectives," *Organization Development Journal* 23, no. 2 (Summer 2005): 29-49.

49. Canadian Tire, *Team Values Development Process (Powerpoint File)*, (Toronto: Canadian Tire, 24 September 2001); Canadian Tire, *Leadership Guide*, (Toronto: Canadian Tire, 2002).

50. F. F. Luthans, "Positive Organizational Behavior: Developing and Managing Psychological Strengths," *The Academy of Management Executive* 16, no. 1 (2002): 57-72; N. Turner, J. Barling, and A. Zacharatos, "Positive Psychology at Work," in *Handbook of Positive Psychology*, ed. C. R. Snyder and S. Lopez (Oxford, UK: Oxford University Press, 2002), 715-730; K. Cameron, J. E. Dutton, and R. E. Quinn, eds., *Positive Organizational Scholarship: Foundation of a New Discipline* (San Francisco: Berrett Koehler Publishers, 2003); J. I. Krueger and D. C. Funder, "Towards a Balanced Social Psychology: Causes, Consequences, and Cures for the Problem-Seeking Approach to Social Behavior and Cognition," *Behavioral and Brain Sciences* 27, no. 3 (June 2004): 313-327; S. L. Gable and J. Haidt, "What (and Why) Is Positive Psychology?," *Review of General Psychology* 9, no. 2 (2005): 103-110; M. E. P. Seligman *et al.*, "Positive Psychology Progress: Empirical Validation of Interventions," *American Psychologist* 60, no. 5 (2005): 410-421.

51. D. Whitney and D. L. Cooperrider, "The Appreciative Inquiry Summit: Overview and Applications," *Employment Relations Today* 25 (Summer 1998): 17-28; J. M. Watkins and B. J. Mohr, *Appreciative Inquiry: Change at the Speed of Imagination* (San Francisco: Jossey-Bass, 2001).

52. F. J. Barrett and D. L. Cooperrider, "Generative Metaphor Intervention: A New Approach for Working with Systems Divided by Conflict and Caught in Defensive Perception," *Journal of Applied Behavioral Science* 26 (1990): 219-239; Whitney and Cooperrider, "The Appreciative Inquiry Summit: Overview and Applications"; Watkins and Mohr, *Appreciative Inquiry: Change at the Speed of Imagination*, pp. 15-21.

53. M. Schiller, "Case Study: Avon Mexico," in *Appreciative Inquiry: Change at the Speed of Imagination* ed. J. M. Watkins and B. J. Mohr (San Francisco: Jossey Bass, 2001), 123-126; D. Whitney and A. Trosten-Bloom, *The Power of Appreciative Inquiry: A Practical Guide to Positive Change* (San Francisco: Berrett-Koehler Publishers, 2003); P. Babcock, "Seeing a Brighter Future," *HRMagazine* 50, no. 9 (September 2005): 48; D. S. Bright, D. L. Cooperrider, and W. B. Galloway, "Appreciative Inquiry in the Office of Research and Development: Improving the Collaborative Capacity of Organization," *Public Performance & Management Review* 29, no. 3 (2006): 285; D. Gilmour and A. Radford, "Using OD to Enhance Shareholder Value: Delivering Business Results in BP Castrol Marine," *Organization Development Journal* 25, no. 3 (2007): P97-P102.

54. T. F. Yaeger, P. F. Sorensen, and U. Bengtsson, "Assessment of the State of Appreciative Inquiry: Past, Present, and Future," *Research in Organizational Change and Development* 15 (2004): 297-319; G. R. Bushe and A. F. Kassam, "When Is Appreciative Inquiry Transformational?

A Meta-Case Analysis," *Journal of Applied Behavioral Science* 41, no. 2 (June 2005): 161-181.

55. G. R. Bushe, "Five Theories of Change Embedded in Appreciative Inquiry" in *18th Annual World Congress of Organization Development*, (Dublin, Ireland, July 14-18, 1998).

56. G. R. Bushe and A. B. Shani, *Parallel Learning Structures* (Reading, Mass.: Addison-Wesley, 1991); E. M. Van Aken, D. J. Monetta, and S. D. S., "Affinity Groups: The Missing Link in Employee Involvement," *Organization Dynamics* 22 (Spring 1994): 38-54.

57. D. J. Knight, "Strategy in Practice: Making It Happen," *Strategy & Leadership* 26 (July-August 1998): 29-33; R. T. Pascale, "Grassroots Leadership–Royal Dutch/Shell," *Fast Company*, no. 14 (April-May 1998): 110-120; R. T. Pascale, "Leading from a Different Place," in *The Leader's Change Handbook* ed. J. A. Conger, G. M. Spreitzer, and E. E. Lawler III (San Francisco: Jossey-Bass, 1999), 301-320; R. Pascale, M. Millemann, and L. Gioja, *Surfing on the Edge of Chaos* (London: Texere, 2000).

58. C.-M. Lau, "A Culture-Based Perspective of Organization Development Implementation," *Research in Organizational Change and Development* 9 (1996): 49-79.

59. T. C. Head and P. F. Sorenson, "Cultural Values and Organizational Development: A Seven-Country Study," *Leadership and Organization Development Journal* 14 (1993): 3-7; R. J. Marshak, "Lewin Meets Confucius: A Review of the OD Model of Change," *Journal of Applied Behavioral Science* 29 (1993): 395-415; C. M. Lau and H. Y. Ngo, "Organization Development and Firm Performance: A Comparison of Multinational and Local Firms," *Journal Of International Business Studies* 32, no. 1 (2001): 95-114.

60. M. McKendall, "The Tyranny of Change: Organizational Development Revisited," *Journal of Business Ethics* 12 (February 1993): 93-104; C. M. D. Deaner, "A Model of Organization Development Ethics," *Public Administration Quarterly* 17 (1994): 435-446.

61. G. A. Walter, "Organization Development and Individual Rights," *Journal of Applied Behavioral Science* 20 (1984): 423-439.

Appendix A

1. Kerlinger, *Foundations of Behavioral Research* (New York: Holt, Rinehart, & Winston, 1964), p. 11.

2. J. B. Miner, *Theories of Organizational Behavior* (Hinsdale, Ill.: Dryden, 1980), pp. 7-9.

3. Ibid. pp. 6-7.

4. J. Mason, Qualitative Researching (London: Sage, 1996).

5. A. Strauss and J. Corbin (Eds.). *Grounded Theory in Practice*. (London: Sage Publications, 1997); B. G. Glaser and A. Strauss. *The Discovery of Grounded Theory: Strategies for Qualitative Research*. (Chicago, IL: Aldine Publishing Co, 1967).

6. Kerlinger, *Foundations of Behavioral Research*, p. 13.

7. A. Strauss and J. Corbin (Eds.). *Grounded Theory in Practice*. (London: Sage Publications, 1997); B. G. Glaser and A. Strauss. *The Discovery of Grounded Theory: Strategies for Qualitative Research*. (Chicago, IL: Aldine Publishing Co, 1967).

8. W. A. Hall and P. Callery, "Enhancing the Rigor of Grounded Theory: Incorporating Reflexivity and Relationality," *Qualitative Health Research*, 11 (March 2001), pp. 257-72.

9. P. Lazarsfeld, *Survey Design and Analysis* (New York: The Free Press, 1955).

10. This example is cited in D. W. Organ and T. S. Bateman, *Organizational Behavior*, 4th ed. (Homewood, Ill.: Irwin, 1991), p. 42.

11. Ibid. p. 45.

12. R. I. Sutton and A. Hargadon, "Brainstorming Groups in Context: Effectiveness in a Product Design Firm," *Administrative Science Quarterly*, 41 (1996), pp. 685-718.

NAME INDEX

ORGANIZATION INDEX

URL INDEX

SUBJECT INDEX